UCLA

The *First Century*

Marina Dundjerski

UCLA: THE FIRST CENTURY
© 2011 The Regents of the University of California

First published in 2011 by Third Millennium Publishing Limited,
a subsidiary of Third Millennium Information Limited
in conjunction with the UCLA History Project/UCLA Alumni Association.

Los Angeles · London

Third Millennium Publishing Limited
2–5 Benjamin Street, London
United Kingdom EC1M 5QL
www.tmiltd.com

UCLA History Project/UCLA Alumni Association
James West Alumni Center
Los Angeles, CA 90095-1347

ISBN: 978 1 906507 37 4

Library of Congress Control Number: 2011935351

Written by Marina Dundjerski
Designed by Matthew Wilson
Production by Bonnie Murray
Proofreading by Marie Loggia-Kee
Indexing by Connie Binder

Reprographics by Asia Graphic Printing Ltd, Hong Kong
Printed and bound in China by 1010 Printing International Limited
on acid free paper from sustainable forestry.

Set in Sabon on 95lb/140gsm matte art

Contents

Foreword

UCLA is, by any measure, one of the world's great universities. And yet, like many of California's most notable institutions, our campus has a relatively short history. Established in 1919 to serve the rapidly expanding population of Southern California, UCLA transformed the University of California into the nation's first multicampus system. Within the mere flash of a century, UCLA evolved from a small junior college on Vermont Avenue into what is today a dynamic institution that is enhancing lives in innumerable ways, throughout California and around the world.

UCLA: The First Century charts UCLA's extraordinary ascent into a premier research university, whose world-class faculty counts among its ranks Nobel laureates, MacArthur Fellows, Pulitzer Prize winners and members of every major academic society; and an engine of opportunity: One-third of our graduates are the first in their families to earn four-year degrees and hundreds of thousands of alumni are pioneers in public service, business, medicine, science and technology, the arts and nearly every other field.

The journey was not without its challenges—among them, the struggle to forge a separate identity for our rather distinctive campus while respecting the values and traditions of the University of California. And there were, of course, a few pleasant surprises: The campus's academic reputation had climbed so dramatically that, by the early 1980s, our own administrators were astonished when one survey placed UCLA near the top of its national rankings of faculty and graduate programs.

With our centennial on the horizon, this volume—the first comprehensive and scholarly history of the university—is a testament to the unheralded builders and celebrated leaders who shaped the Southern Branch into today's UCLA, an internationally renowned center for academic excellence, transformational research and meaningful service to our global society. We are delighted to celebrate these milestones, and we look forward to ever greater achievement during our next hundred years.

Gene D. Block
CHANCELLOR

Preface

I had the great privilege a decade ago to spend the day with several Pioneer Bruins. In one afternoon, through their stories, I was transported back to the 1920s and received my first real lesson in UCLA history: whether it was hearing about the independent spirit that carved out new student traditions, or work in a potato chip factory during the Great Depression to afford the $25 registration fee, or what it was like to pile your friends into a Model T to trek as new "owners" to the Westwood campus for the dedication of Founders' Rock. There was a profound love and loyalty there for UCLA that awoke my own spirit toward my alma mater.

I'll admit I walked this campus as a student and, even as a *Daily Bruin* reporter, not inquiring too much about the past. It was all about the present—and the future—for the most part. But what questions would I have asked Chancellor Charles Young, for example, had I known the stands he made on issues of academic freedom? What context from UCLA's resilience in the Great Depression could apply to coverage of the budget? Through what lens would we all view present-day issues if we only knew where we came from and on whose shoulders we stand?

The one central notion that carries throughout UCLA's history is that the institution was built on risk. It appears to define all else: whether it be fighting against an overwhelming opposition to its creation, pushing to establish graduate and professional education, standing up to the regents in defense of First Amendment rights, or leading the search to treat and cure HIV/AIDS.

UCLA's founders, and all of those who shaped its course over the ensuing decades, followed their vision and took advantage of every opportunity along the way. Growing up with the diverse city that is its home, UCLA has played a central role in the development of Los Angeles. But it would not have risen to such prominence in the span of less than a century without the determination of everyone from administrators to Nobel laureates, from students to alumni leaders.

As we approach UCLA's 100th anniversary, the institution, while still relatively young, has a rich legacy to share. And many, ranging from the University Archives to the *Daily Bruin* staff, fulfill the critical role of documenting the university's journey. Without them, it would have been an impossible task to create this book. As University Librarian Lawrence Clark Powell once said:

> It is good that UCLA was founded and built by bookmen, and that its history and traditions are being written down and printed as they are made, and that there are individuals and groups who are devoting themselves to programs of collecting and recording and transmitting. Books are memory itself; books are more lasting than the men and women who make them; books are the means by which a university's traditions are accumulated and carried forward through generations and centuries.

I dedicate this book to the keepers of the UCLA story and to Bruins everywhere—past, present and future.

Marina Dundjerski
CLASS OF 1994

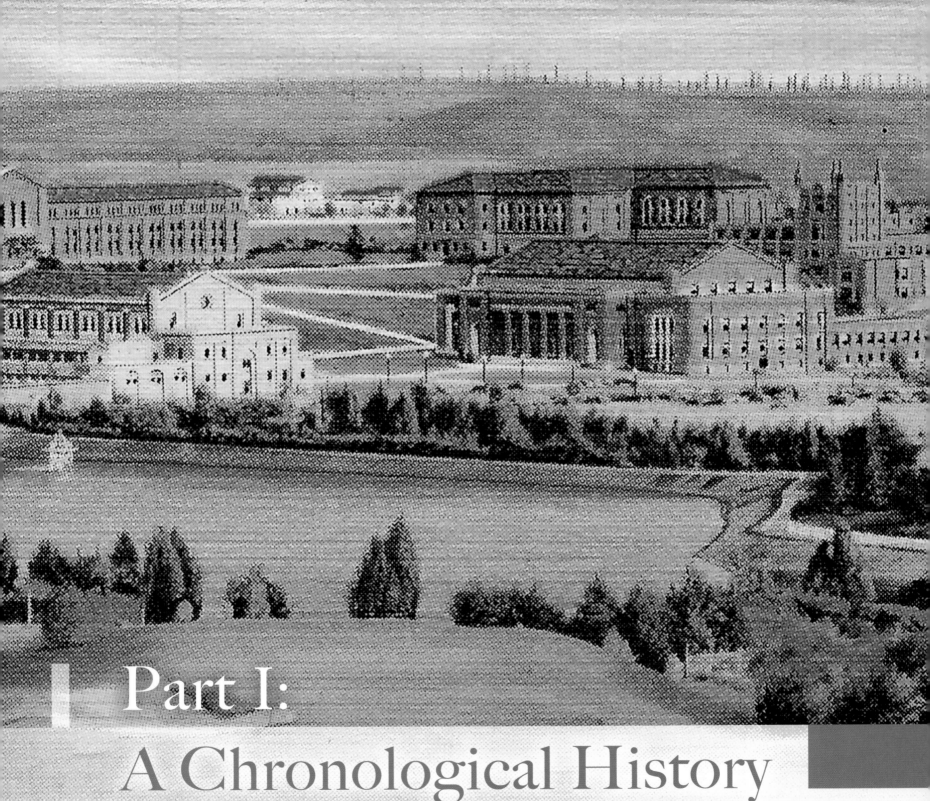

Part I:
A Chronological History

CHAPTER

01

Origins
1913–1919

Previous pages: Vintage postcard of the Westwood campus, 1930s.

Above: A young Edward A. Dickson.

Opposite: UCLA founders Edward A. Dickson (left) and Ernest Carroll Moore (center) with College of Letters and Science Dean Charles H. Rieber (right), 1925.

*I*n 1913, Edward A. Dickson, political editor of the Los Angeles Express, was offered a top government appointment: chairman of the California Railroad Commission. The progressive Republican co-founded the Lincoln-Roosevelt League that propelled Governor Hiram W. Johnson into office. The party had centered its campaign on better government and the condemnation of the entrenched power of the Southern Pacific Railroad. To the governor's astonishment, Dickson declined the highly visible and coveted post. "What do you want, Dick?" Johnson asked. A 1901 graduate of the University of California, Dickson was unfailingly dedicated to his alma mater: "The only appointment that interests me is that of regent."

So the 33-year-old crusader for government reform became one of the youngest individuals ever named to the university's governing board and, more significantly, one of only a handful to represent Southern California. It was an unheralded event that nonetheless would mark a turning point in the transformation of the University of California into the nation's first multicampus system. For Dickson, it was the beginning of a role he would hold for a record 43 years. During that time, Dickson not only successfully advocated for the creation of the institution that would eventually become UCLA, but also championed the campus's continued development during its critical formative years, earning him the moniker, "Godfather of UCLA."

Founding Dates of Notable Los Angeles Institutions

1867	Southern California Gas Company
1871	Farmers and Merchants Bank of Los Angeles
1873	Ralphs Grocery Company
1880	University of Southern California
1881	Los Angeles Times
1881	Los Angeles State Normal School
1887	Occidental College
1887	Pomona College
1887	Whittier College
1888	Los Angeles Area Chamber of Commerce
1891	California Institute of Technology
1891	University of La Verne
1900	Automobile Club of Southern California
1902	Los Angeles Department of Water and Power
1907	Port of Los Angeles
1907	Bullock's Inc.
1910	Los Angeles County Museum of Art
1915	Fox Film Corporation
1919	United Artists
1919	**UCLA**
1919	Los Angeles Philharmonic
1920	Occidental Petroleum
1922	Hollywood Bowl
1923	Los Angeles Memorial Coliseum
1923	The Walt Disney Company
1924	MGM
1927	Grauman's Chinese Theatre
1928	Los Angeles International Airport
1931	Village Theatre
1932	Hughes Aircraft Company
1935	Griffith Observatory
1938	California State Polytechnic University, Pomona
1939	Northrop Grumman
1942	Capitol Records
1947	California State University, Los Angeles
1961	California Institute of the Arts
1958	Los Angeles Dodgers
1964	Music Center

Top: *Los Angeles Times* at 1st Street and Broadway Avenue.

Above: Dedication of Mines Field, 1928 (later Los Angeles International Airport).

Left: More than 7,000 line up for *Hello Dolly!* tickets, Music Center, 1965.

THE PUBLIC INTEREST

Dickson's impassioned efforts leading to the establishment of the Southern Branch of the University of California—as UCLA was first called—started shortly after his appointment to the Board of Regents. A small, but determined, corps from Los Angeles sought him out as a sympathetic ally in its pursuit to establish a state-funded public university in the region.

When the University of California was created in 1868, the majority of Californians lived north of the Tehachapi Mountains. But that was steadily changing. While the Bay Area's economy and population had been adversely affected by the 1906 San Francisco earthquake and fire, the Southland's population near the turn of the century was booming.

An influx of residents migrating from other parts of the country, especially the Midwest, were settling in Southern California. New cities were cropping up around Los Angeles, including Pasadena, Santa Monica, Monrovia, Compton and Pomona. In 1913 alone, the cities of San Gabriel and San Marino were incorporated, with Beverly Hills just weeks behind. Also that year, William Mulholland's controversial Los Angeles Aqueduct began siphoning water from the Owens River in the Sierra Nevada into the San Fernando Valley and Los Angeles basin, bringing promise of new development once limited by water supply. The legendary chief engineer's edict: "Whoever brings water brings people."

Growth, it seemed, was unstoppable. While the City of Los Angeles was just beginning a series of territorial annexations that would include the vast San Fernando Valley, by the end of 1913 Los Angeles residents already numbered 412,000. Dickson argued that Southern Californian taxpayers were contributing two-thirds of the supporting funds to the state's only public university. Yet the University of California consisted of just one general campus and it was in Berkeley, some 400 miles to the north—too distant and, therefore, too impractical and costly for many Southland residents to pursue higher learning. (The University of California operated satellite units, including the University Farm in Davis, a medical school in San Francisco, the Citrus Experiment Station in Riverside, a marine program in La Jolla and the Lick Observatory on Mount Hamilton. It also ran a small medical college in downtown Los Angeles that had been transferred in 1909 from the University of Southern California. After offering undergraduate instruction for five years, the Los Angeles Medical Department limited instruction to medical graduates until it was disbanded by the regents in 1952.)

Below right: Downtown Los Angeles looking west on 7th Street, 1917.

Below: Territory annexed by the City of Los Angeles from 1859–1923.

The civic group leaders who called on Dickson brought the same message: A state-funded university in Los Angeles was not only sorely needed to educate an increasing number of high school graduates, but was Southern California's manifest right. And that destiny, they believed, would be fulfilled through indomitable will, one way or another.

Although ever-loyal to his Berkeley-based alma mater, as a Los Angeles resident Dickson understood that the southern region's emergent economic strength and growing political clout would soon change California's landscape.

"The rapid growth in population of this section, it was urged, was giving this end of the state a power and influence that could not long be ignored," Dickson wrote in his memoir. "A university was imperative, and if the Board of Regents should fail to initiate steps to extend educational advantages under its own auspices, means would be sought to secure a university in the south to operate under a separate board."

Dickson would face formidable obstacles and steadfast opposition, but he made it his mission to convince the board that it should embrace this inevitable change for the benefit of all Californians.

THREAT OF SEPARATISM

Unlike most public universities in the United States, the University of California is a constitutional entity afforded special protection from political control. California's first constitution in 1849 provided for the organization of a state university, which was established as the University of California under the Organic Act, signed by Governor Henry H. Haight on March 23, 1868. A decade later, California held a second constitutional convention. The resulting new state constitution, approved by the voters in 1879, listed the university as a "public trust" and gave the Board of Regents an unprecedented level of autonomy in managing its affairs. It called for the university to be "entirely independent of all political or sectarian influence" in the appointment of regents and its administration. A constitutional amendment ratified in 1918 further clarified this autonomy. While subject to normal legislative process regarding state budgets and fiduciary responsibilities, the board was given "full powers of organization and government." Any law passed by the Legislature in regard to the university's academic programs or operations would be nonbinding.

As the governing board for the institution with the sole right to grant degrees on behalf of the state, the regents ardently guarded their authority. They feared a second campus would erode their influence, decentralize the university and weaken the institution's prestige. They were not alone. Faculty members and alumni also voiced loud opposition to geographic expansion.

Sather Gate at the University of California, in Berkeley, c.1919.

The pervasive resistance mirrored broader tensions between Northern and Southern California as, along with population growth, political power was shifting southward. By 1915, there were more people living in Southern California (987,000) than the Bay Area (867,000). Forecasters were predicting that the 1920 census would create greater political representation for the Southland. Even the university's enrollment reflected the changing demographics. More students at the Berkeley-based institution were coming from Los Angeles than from San Francisco.

Because of the university's constitutional autonomy, the Legislature could not command the Board of Regents to create a southern campus of its university, but it could maneuver around it by approving legislation to create a new state institution under independent control.

Impatient for action, Southland citizens clamored for a bill that was introduced in the 1915 Legislature. The bill called for the establishment of a state university in Los Angeles, to be governed by an entirely separate board.

The notion of a separate state institution alarmed President Benjamin Ide Wheeler, the university's leader since 1899, as well as the majority of the regents, who voiced concern that a second campus would create a rivalry for tax dollars and reduce Berkeley's resources. In other states, where political pressure and ensuing legislation introduced two state-supported institutions to provide for an expanding population, academic mediocrity unfolded, Wheeler maintained.

President Wheeler elaborated on those concerns while testifying before the Legislature in opposition. The bill failed, but that did not quiet its proponents in Southern California. On the contrary, this threat of separatism gave Dickson a powerful negotiating platform, which he would gainfully use.

"The danger could not be averted by merely a resistance policy," Dickson advised Wheeler. "We ought to assume leadership, by gradually extending the facilities of our University to meet the pressing needs of the south."

At a subsequent regents meeting, Dickson added: "The University of California ought to lead, not follow, southern public sentiment on this vital issue."

Beginning to yield under the mounting pressure, Wheeler replied that he agreed in principle, but as a tempered measure, suggested "a step at a time."

STEP ONE: UNIVERSITY EXTENSION

Dickson was quick to spearhead that first step: creating a southern headquarters for University Extension, the adult education program.

The regents approved the move and President Wheeler appointed Nadine Crump as director for the southern Extension program. Dickson opened an office in the Union

League Building, at the corner of Hill and Second streets in downtown Los Angeles. On the door was boldly inscribed: "University of California—Extension Division." Class registration opened in 1917 with offerings ranging from commercial law to modern languages.

Wheeler personally opened a public lecture series on the university's service contributions in World War I to a full auditorium. Other visiting Berkeley scholars included: Charles Mills Gayley, English professor and lyricist of "The Golden Bear" and other university songs; Bernard Moses, who helped found the departments of history, economics, political science and jurisprudence at Berkeley; Carl C. Plehn, the first dean of the College of Commerce; the popular Henry Morse Stephens, chair of the history department and first director of University Extension; and A.O. Leuschner, dean of the Graduate Division and head of World War I naval training for the University of California.

E.G. Judah, head of the Merchants and Manufacturers Association, who presided over that first lecture, said he hoped the regents would soon start a branch of the university in the Southland.

It was a small, but firm step. As Dickson described it, "This was a very modest beginning, but it was the first visible appearance of the University of California in the southland."

STEP TWO: SUMMER SESSION

As efforts to start an Extension branch developed, Dickson was approached by local educators to endorse a proposal to turn over the old Los Angeles High School located above the Broadway Tunnel to the University of California. The plan was for a two-year college. If the regents rejected the proposal, its advocates emphasized they would turn to the Legislature to obtain an appropriation for a municipal university, under a separate governing board.

An article in the October 29, 1916, edition of the *Los Angeles Times*, "Municipal University Plan for Los Angeles," brought the proposal to the public's attention, adding that proponents hoped it would be "made a branch of the State University."

Dickson brought the development to the regents, who again resisted the idea. Its supporters threatened to move a bill creating an independent university through the Legislature. "While this bill met with the swift fate of the earlier measure, and was rejected by the legislators, it did serve to convince several of my colleagues on the Board of Regents of the danger to our University if we should fail to meet the challenge from the south, now becoming increasingly persistent and vocal," Dickson said.

About this time, the southern section of the California Teachers' Association called on Dickson with a petition urging the regents to implement an annual summer session in Los

Angeles. The teachers, led by Charles H. Covell of Redlands, stated they found it too costly to travel to Berkeley for summer courses. "We need such instruction right here in Los Angeles," Covell insisted.

Dickson pledged his support, but advised them to take the matter to Wheeler, who, when presenting it to the Board of Regents, was not as enthusiastic. After discussion, however, the board voted to direct the president to "investigate" the feasibility of such a plan on a self-supporting basis as an "experiment for one year."

In consulting Dickson afterward, Wheeler wrote: "We are not anxious to take the step."

To look into the matter, Wheeler sent Professor Leon J. Richardson (later director of University Extension), who reported back that there was no great demand for summer instruction in Los Angeles. Based on this finding, Wheeler submitted a report to the Board of Regents suggesting the Teachers' Association petition be rejected. "I was very much disappointed with the President's attitude, and at once requested that a further study be made," Dickson wrote in his memoir. "The Board supported my position, and President Wheeler was instructed to continue the investigation."

Dickson then found an unexpected ally in Walter M. Hart, dean of Summer Session at Berkeley, who had been sent by Wheeler to conduct another study. Unlike the first site visit, which occurred when Dickson was out of town, Dickson arranged a meeting for Hart with almost two dozen civic leaders, including the head of the Los Angeles State Normal School, principals of prominent local high schools, the county superintendent of schools and the president of the California Alumni Association. Hart returned to Berkeley with a positive report, stating he was convinced that "it is a distinct duty of the University to establish a summer session next year in the southern part of the state," and promised Dickson that he would engage in some "quiet campaigning" to help further its adoption.

Wheeler, still not convinced, placed the matter in the hands of a faculty committee, which ended up siding with the president and recommending against pursuing the Los Angeles summer session. One of his concerns was not encroaching on the successful summer program already in place at USC. "We would come into distinct rivalry with the University of Southern California, a thing we do not wish to do," Wheeler stated.

Dickson continued his agitation. More than a year later, in November 1917, after a meeting with Hart, two northern regents and Los Angeles delegates in favor of the plan, the reports finally persuaded Wheeler. The first Summer Session classes were held at Los Angeles High School in 1918. Twenty-two courses were offered, attracting a hefty enrollment of 630 students. "Step two" of Dickson's plan to create UCLA was in place.

Edward Augustus Dickson

Edward A. Dickson was born in Sheboygan, Wisconsin, on August 29, 1879. At the age of six, he lost his father and moved with his mother and older brother to Sacramento. As a boy, Dickson delivered newspapers to earn money for his family and developed the characteristic determination that would drive his unwavering efforts to secure the establishment of UCLA.

Dickson enrolled in the College of Social Sciences at the University of California, where he was elected junior class president, and became editor of the *Daily Californian* in his senior year. After graduating in May 1901, he left for a teaching job in Japan, and completed a thesis on education that he planned to submit for admission to the master's program. However, when he was boarding the steamship for his return to California, a mishap sent his trunk—and the manuscript—to the bottom of Yokohama harbor.

Dickson turned instead to journalism, his lifelong passion. He took an unpaid position as a reporter for the *Sacramento Union*. After six months, he was hired as a political reporter by the *San Francisco Chronicle*. In 1906, he moved to Southern California to become a political editor for the Los Angeles *Evening Express*, and a year later married Wilhelmina de Wolff. While still in his 20s, Dickson co-founded the progressive Lincoln-Roosevelt League, a powerful vehicle for political reform in California, which propelled Governor Hiram Johnson into office in 1911. He spent two years in Washington, D.C., as the political correspondent for the *Express*, before returning west and accepting Johnson's appointment to the Board of Regents of the University of California.

Shortly thereafter, Dickson began his campaign to create a branch of the university in Los Angeles. In 1919, he made arrangements to buy an interest in the *Express* and used the paper to advance his mission. "The fact that I was, in 1919, editor and publisher of a metropolitan newspaper—the Los Angeles *Evening Express*—was, I believe, an important factor in helping to influence public opinion in favor of the creation of a university in the southland," Dickson wrote in his memoir. "I dedicated my newspaper—editorially and through its news columns—to an intensive campaign, setting forth the educational needs of this section of the state."

Dickson, who held numerous civil positions, avoided the spotlight, preferring to work behind the scenes. He also focused his newspaper's agenda on developing other parts of Los Angeles, including the extension of Wilshire Boulevard toward the Pacific Ocean and building the Los Angeles Memorial Coliseum. But he never stopped watching over UCLA, earning the nickname, "Godfather of UCLA."

"Men of vision are not always men of action," wrote University Librarian Lawrence Clark Powell. "Edward A. Dickson is both a dreamer and a doer. The steps which had to be taken before his vision materialized of a university in southern California … often consisted of one backward and two forward, or two sideways and three forward, yet there was always a net gain in progress."

Dickson died February 22, 1956, having served as regent for an unprecedented 43 years—the final eight as the board's chairman. The Royce quad was dedicated Dickson Plaza in his honor, and the span of the Arroyo Bridge as well as the area between Schoenberg and Perloff halls was named Dickson Court.

Edward A. Dickson was editor and publisher of the Los Angeles *Evening Express*, which he purchased and used to advance UCLA.

Ernest Carroll Moore

Born on July 20, 1871, in Youngstown, Ohio, Ernest Carroll Moore grew up on a farm listening to his parents pray that he might have an education. "They kept repeating to us that it was the *sine qua non* of a full life," UCLA's founding chief executive remembered. "I had such implicit confidence in both of them that their conviction became mine."

Moore graduated from the Ohio Normal University in 1892, where he also earned a law degree. However, he decided he did not want to be a lawyer, instead following a conviction that "I should preach." He enrolled at Union Theological Seminary in New York while simultaneously attending Columbia University, earning an M.A. from the latter in 1896. He then taught for a year at Tugaloo University near Jackson, Mississippi—operated by the American Missionary Association of New York—before attending the University of Chicago, where he earned his doctorate in education in 1898. He was offered a position at Berkeley as an assistant professor of philosophy, and then, because of his ties with John Dewey at Columbia, was transferred to the education department. In 1905 he became dean of Summer Session.

After the San Francisco earthquake of 1906, Moore and his wife, Dorothea, who had lost their home in the resulting fire, moved to Los Angeles, where Moore served as superintendent of schools from 1906 to 1910. In the summer of 1910, Moore moved east, teaching at Yale University, and then Harvard University, over the next seven years. Offered the presidency of the Los Angeles State Normal School in 1917, he gladly accepted, even though some of his colleagues chided him for leaving the sanctity of the Ivy League. California was "an incurable disease," Moore said.

The trustees had given him the commission to convert the normal school into a teachers college. He sought out University of California Regent Edward A. Dickson, who had been one of his students at Berkeley, and who would become his premier collaborator in the establishment of UCLA in 1919. Moore was appointed its founding director, and eventually received the title of vice president and provost in 1931.

While running the university and fighting for its expansion, he also taught the introductory psychology course. Undergraduates such as student body President Thomas J. Cunningham recalled that Moore, who often wore high starched collars and a black felt or straw hat, "stressed time and time again that 'education is learning to use the tools the race has found indispensable'"—Moore's motto inscribed in the proscenium arch above the Royce Hall stage.

Moore retired from his administrative duties in 1936, returning to teaching as a professor of philosophy and education for five years before leaving the university. In 1943, a year after Dorothea's death, he married Kate Gordon, a former UCLA professor of psychology. Moore died on January 23, 1955, at the age of 83.

The education building, the fifth to be constructed on the campus, was renamed in Moore's honor. In tribute, University Librarian Lawrence Clark Powell wrote: "He was a pillar of a man—one of the toughest-minded, most stubbornly-determined, most eloquent, and most persuasive individuals ever to grace this earth."

Above: Ernest Carroll Moore dedicates Mira Hershey Hall in 1931.

Left: UCLA's first chief executive.

STEP THREE: A SOUTHERN BRANCH

The introduction of the university's Extension and Summer Session to Southern California coalesced sentiment that the beginnings of a permanent institution would be a natural progression.

A committee of local educators called on Dickson, urging his support to turn the old Los Angeles High School building into a "branch" of the University of California.

Just as Dickson was preparing to submit a report in favor of the proposition to the Board of Regents, a new idea surfaced.

In late 1917, Ernest Carroll Moore, the recently appointed director of the Los Angeles State Normal School—an elementary schoolteacher-training institution—wrote Dickson with a request to discuss mutual interests.

Moore—a former University of California professor who counted Dickson as one of his students, and who served as superintendent of schools in Los Angeles from 1906 to 1910—had recently resigned his post as professor of education at Harvard University to follow his dream of creating a four-year, degree-granting teachers college in Los Angeles. Moore's Normal School predecessor, Jesse F. Millspaugh, had spent years championing the idea of instituting the Bachelor of Education at the Normal School, but failed amid the university's staunch resistance. Illness

Above: Jesse F. Millspaugh, Los Angeles State Normal School president, 1906–1917.

Left: The Los Angeles State Normal School at 5th Street and Grand Avenue.

forced Millspaugh to resign as director in 1917. When Moore heard that Millspaugh was stepping down, Moore was only too glad to follow in his stead and revive the proposal, so much in line with his own thinking on education.

One of Moore's initial actions was to write to President Wheeler, whom he respected and had served under during his eight years as a philosophy and education instructor at the Berkeley campus. But, to Moore's disbelief, Wheeler responded negatively, citing the potential for competing interests. To succeed, Moore determined the proposal needed to be connected with a larger institution—as was the case with the teachers colleges affiliated with Columbia University and the University of Chicago.

On October 25, 1917, over lunch at the downtown Los Angeles Jonathan Club, Moore proposed to Dickson that the Normal School align itself with the University of California. The Normal School would relinquish its buildings and grounds on Vermont Avenue, in exchange for an agreement to have the University of California establish a four-year teachers college to create formal training leading to the Bachelor of Education for schoolteachers.

Dickson, familiar with the site, believed the Normal School offered facilities "superior" to those of the high school. The Normal School had recently moved from its downtown location on Fifth Street and Grand Avenue to a new campus on Vermont Avenue. The classrooms were modern and the campus, opened in 1914, was built to accommodate 3,000 students, but only about 700 were enrolled at the time.

Dickson grasped the significance of the offer: "I was not greatly interested in a teachers' college, but I did sense the possibility of utilizing the Normal School plant not only for a teachers' college, but for my own plan of expanding our work here by establishing the first two years of regular university work."

"My ultimate objective was a full-fledged university," Dickson added.

Moore agreed to the concept of the expanded university and on that day, the editor and educator forged a bond that would unite them in realizing both their goals.

CONVINCING THE REGENTS

At Dickson's suggestion, Moore wrote to President Wheeler, outlining their joint plan to be formally presented to the Board of Regents. Once again, when it came before the board, there "developed what seemed to be insurmountable objections," Dickson said.

Along with Wheeler, many board members continued to fear a competing institution—even the thought that it would be under their own control did little to dispel this apprehension.

"It was not easy to dislodge that fear from their minds," Dickson recalled. "They were strong men—men unselfishly devoted to their trust of protecting the interests of the University of California; and they were guided in the consideration of this important issue solely by what they considered to have a beneficial, or a harmful, effect on the University."

Regent Chester H. Rowell, newspaperman and co-founder of the Lincoln-Roosevelt League with Dickson, who might have been expected to support the plan, argued strongly against it. "The training of elementary teachers, especially those who teach the primary grades and kindergarten, is not the proper function of a university," Rowell told the regents. "The University's policy should continue to be restricted to the preparation of high school teachers, principals, superintendents, and college and university professors."

By 1918, some regents from Northern California were becoming sympathetic to the cause: lawyers Garret W. McEnerney and Guy C. Earl (brother of Edwin T. Earl, Dickson's boss at the Los Angeles *Express*), banker I.W. Hellman and Phoebe Apperson Hearst, mother of publishing magnate William Randolph Hearst. They began aiding Dickson, if just in secret by holding private conversations to persuade their fellow board members.

Dickson and Moore would not waver in their efforts. Occasionally, Moore confessed in his diary that the process was difficult and that he felt on the brink of defeat. In his memoir, he asked, "Is it not said in the Catholic Church that the stages of Purgatory become more terrible as you approach the Celestial Paradise? I had been through them all with this project."

But publicly, that sentiment was well hidden. As Dickson described him years later: "I found Dr. Moore to be an ideal teammate—persistent and resourceful. Not only was he a great scholar, but an indefatigable worker as well. An idealist, he nevertheless possessed a keen and practical mind. He knew how to get things done, and he carried on under the most discouraging circumstances."

By summer 1918, the regents were pressed into appointing a committee to analyze the proposal. It included regents Dickson, Rowell and Rudolph J. Taussig, a San Francisco businessman. Of the three, only Dickson was in favor of the plan.

The debate continued in committee and at board meetings throughout the winter. Projected U.S. census statistics again figured prominently. Earl, chairman of the board and Dickson ally, was instrumental in the discussion.

"The new Census will give the south a larger relative vote than they now have," Earl told the regents. "We realize that it is absolutely essential to the highest educational interests of the state that the university be maintained as a great unit, one first class institution of higher learning in the state. Yet something, if it can be done in the way of meeting the need in the south should be done without going the length of creating another institution." Rowell and the other regents were increasingly becoming convinced that in two years there would be an incontestable demand for another institution. Shifting political power was not the only influence. New enrollment projections were an added consideration.

Anticipating the end of World War I, educators who had experienced drops in enrollments when men went off to battle were now beginning to estimate the instructional needs for the return of veterans. And they were looking to the government to finance that education.

Los Angeles superintendent of schools Albert Shiels, who had been publicly advocating an "after-the-war step" to set aside a portion of Griffith Park (in the Santa Monica Mountains) to create a public university in Los Angeles, shifted his support in favor of creating a "branch" of the University of California.

"Los Angeles should contain a great center of education for the South Pacific Coast people; not a rival of, nor separate from, the State University, but complete for undergraduates," Shiels told the *Los Angeles Examiner* in November 1918.

Although many educators, like Shiels, came out in support of the plan, in the end it might have been opposition and professional rivalry that cemented the deal.

Governor William D. Stephens signed UCLA's enabling legislation in 1919.

The leaders of the other normal schools were envious of the proposed new status for the Los Angeles school. In a particularly heated meeting, led by President Edward L. Hardy of the State Normal School of San Diego, the normal school presidents voted unanimously to call all their institutions "teachers colleges," to offer instruction other than teacher training and to implement certification for junior high school teachers. Although skepticism remained, this action helped solidify the regents in favor of the Southern Branch plan.

THE LEGISLATION

Now it was time for Dickson and Moore to concentrate on the enabling legislation. Dickson had already discussed the matter with Governor William D. Stephens, who in 1917 succeeded Governor Johnson. Stephens—the former California lieutenant governor and U.S. congressman who as a fellow progressive had relied on

Dickson's advice for years—was supportive of the proposal. Assemblyman Alexander P. Fleming of Los Angeles, a friend of Governor Stephens, oversaw the legislation.

Assembly Bill 626, an act of the Legislature transferring the Los Angeles State Normal School to the Regents of the University of California, stalled because of a provision to which the regents took offense: that the Southern Branch would have degree-granting powers. Because of the constitutional protection, the regents felt this amounted to being legislated to, and they would not endorse it.

Moore, on the other hand, stood firm; he could not, on behalf of the Normal School trustees, accept less. "I saw our prized project beaten and lost a hundred times," Moore wrote of the intense discussions.

It was Moore who ultimately presented the solution: a gentlemen's agreement to grant the Southern Branch such authority. Moore believed the promise once made could not be broken, and Dickson reassured him that "the regents will deal fairly with the situation."

Assembly Bill 626, calling for the establishment of the Southern Branch and two years of instruction, passed both houses unanimously. Governor Stephens approved the legislation on May 23, 1919.

"The *Evening Express* says Governor Stephens has today signed the bill," Moore wrote in his diary. "No one can imagine what that means to the young people of this part of the world nor what this institution will one day become."

On the following Monday, Moore records that he gave students a reprieve from class so that they could enjoy the moment. "A few students were blowing horns about the campus & others were detonating anvils. Jubilation was in the air & I gave the word for an hour of it. They came from everywhere … with more shouting & cheering than they ever had in them before."

On July 23, 1919, the Los Angeles State Normal School property was officially transferred to the regents and became the Southern Branch of the University of California.

It took resourcefulness, determination and a great deal of politicking or "old-fashioned horse trading," but six years after Dickson's appointment as regent and his initial meeting with the Southern California constituency, Los Angeles had its own state campus. The road ahead would still prove arduous, but it was UCLA's beginning.

CHAPTER

02

A "Twig" Grows

1919–1925

Above: The "Dawn of Education" as depicted in an editorial cartoon from the *Cub Californian*, October 3, 1919.

Opposite: Millspaugh Hall, anchoring the main quadrangle of the Southern Branch of the University of California, on Vermont Avenue.

"*The Normal School is Dead! Long live the Branch University!*" *So cried the editorial page of the first issue of the* Cub Californian *on September 29, 1919.*

The hard-won and long-awaited opening of the Southern Branch of the University of California had arrived. Regent Edward A. Dickson and the campus's newly appointed founding Director Ernest Carroll Moore, along with the emerging Southern Californian constituency that demanded its creation, could feel a deep sense of accomplishment. Fittingly, however, no group was more pleased than the students who would directly benefit.

"We are all starting college life together, in a new institution, with, as yet, undeveloped possibilities," the student newspaper continued. "The future of the college depends, in a large measure, upon the attitude adopted by the present student body toward the various activities and enterprises of the school." These early students, dubbed "Pioneers" by Dickson and Moore—a name that was later extended to all students who spent time on the Vermont Avenue campus—included future choreographer Agnes de Mille, Lieutenant Governor Frederick F. Houser, and United Nations Under-Secretary-General and Nobel Peace Prize recipient Ralph J. Bunche.

The Great War had ended a year before the campus's founding and "normalcy" returned to the nation, as promoted by President Warren G. Harding. Some vestiges of war remained. Approximately 175 disabled veterans, known as the Federal Class, enrolled in courses at the Southern Branch through the Federal Board for Vocational Education.

During the 1920–21 academic year, having gained approval from the U.S. Secretary of War, Newton Diehl Baker, the Southern Branch welcomed its first ROTC unit to Vermont Avenue. First- and second-year male students

were required to take ROTC instruction. "The expressed object of the R.O.T.C. training is to create a reservoir of trained leaders classified as Reserve Officers, from which to draw in case of national emergency," Colonel Guy G. Palmer, instructor of military science, told the campus newspaper.

The Roaring '20s would bring a 50 percent increase in manufacturing, remarkable prosperity and the rise of consumerism promoted by new mass media. The government ban on radio stations, which had been ordered silent and reserved for military communications during the war, was lifted, making way for the formation of broadcast companies that aired music, news and other programming coast to coast. "Jazzy first-class dance music by wireless is the next step of endeavor to be taken by the Radio Club," the Cub Californian reported in 1921.

Southern Branch students enjoyed the Jazz Age by organizing myriad dances in the Women's Gymnasium ranging from the formal Military Ball to the plain-old Afternoon Dance. It was Prohibition, and like the nation, the campus was dry—but that didn't stop students from secretly sipping bootleg liquor in silver flasks or finding a local speakeasy.

All this prompted Moore to offer his sage counsel in the Frosh Bible: "The cards, the queens, the jazzy clothes— are not for you, Frosh." The Southern Branch still observed social mores and in loco parentis was in full force. Women, for example, could not complete class registration unless their living accommodations were first approved by Dean of Women Helen Matthewson Laughlin.

Amid the leisurely times of the early 1920s, the Pioneers took great pride in their university and recognized they carried a shared responsibility to develop the Southern Branch. Students did not lose sight of their educational ambition: to obtain a bachelor's degree. And they wanted to do so without transferring to Berkeley for third- and fourth-year instruction. Soon they would begin pushing to elevate the name of the university from under the shadows of Berkeley, and join Dickson, Moore and other campus leaders in their continued quest to make the campus a degree-awarding institution.

EARLY DAYS ON VERMONT AVENUE

In 1919, the Southern Branch—located at 855 North Vermont Avenue near the southern end of Hollywood—was considered out of the way, on the outskirts of downtown Los Angeles. But the lush 25-acre campus—bordered by Heliotrope Drive to the west and flanked by Willowbrook Avenue and Monroe Street to the north and south—was in a rapidly developing area of Los Angeles, and easily accessible by the red and yellow streetcars that were a ubiquitous part of the city's transportation system. Students could take the "V" (for Vermont) car to the campus at the end of the line. So many students took this transport that the university was labeled the "streetcar college."

Its 10 well-equipped buildings were designed to accommodate 3,000 students. The architectural style dated back to the 12th century, set in the Lombard Romanesque tradition by Allison & Allison. (David C. Allison would later use the same motif for the Westwood campus.)

The red brick buildings with clay tile roofs and stone trim were set against a backdrop of eucalyptus trees, acacias and palms. Ivy-covered Millspaugh Hall, named after

Top: The ROTC color guard, Vermont Avenue campus, 1927.

Above: Students board the "V" streetcar headed to the end of the line at the Vermont Avenue campus in the 1920s.

Left: The Federal Class, GIs of World War I, enrolled with an emphasis on vocational subjects such as automotive repair.

Right: Sophomore Grove, a gathering space reserved for upperclassmen.

Below: Millspaugh Hall was both the administration building and the hub for student life. Inset: The campus was designed with 10 well-equipped buildings.

and ducks, were native cohabitants. A grassy patch under a row of towering trees formed Sophomore Grove, strictly off-limits to freshman "peagreeners." There were separate gathering places for male and female students, as was the social norm of the day.

In 1918, the campus won the first annual award in its category from the Southern California Chapter of the American Institute of Architects, which cited the Vermont Avenue design for expressing "a sentiment sympathetic with the development of the American youth" with quiet façades "free from an institutional atmosphere or pedantry." (In 1929, the Los Angeles Board of Education acquired the site for the newly created Los Angeles Junior College, renamed Los Angeles City College in 1938. The original buildings were demolished in the 1960s because of seismic safety concerns.)

"The beautiful buildings and charming grounds surrounding assumed a new glamour which those who entered

longtime Los Angeles State Normal School President Jesse F. Millspaugh, served as the administration building and the center for student activities. The structure, with its octagonal dome, anchored the main quad. In front lay a flower-bordered fish pond, where hazing rituals were a way of life until banned in 1927. Other wildlife, including tortoises

after June, 1919, will never comprehend," wrote the editors of the 1920 *Southern Campus* yearbook. "They were enhanced and glorified to meet the new and welcome responsibilities which naturally followed."

The Southern Branch officially opened its doors on September 15, 1919, welcoming 260 undergraduates to the newly created Junior College and 1,078 students in the Teachers Training program. Women outnumbered men six to one—the ratio a reflection of the teaching profession's demographics coupled with the disparity in the spaces allocated for general undergraduates as proscribed by funding from the Legislature.

But there was little time for celebration. No sooner was the Southern Branch born than it started growing beyond the means provided for it. The waiting list for slots in the two-year general undergraduate college was crowded with names of students eager to enroll. In an effort to gain them admission, parents even more anxious than their children wrote warmly accepted—although futile—letters to Moore.

And so began a new struggle: transforming the Southern Branch from a modest two-year junior college into a four-year, degree-granting university.

THE FORMATIVE YEARS

As students and the public basked in the promise of unlimited possibility, behind the scenes pressures threatened to derail the new institution. All the while, the unified force of Dickson and Moore continued to labor in shaping the Southern Branch's future.

"We were off to a bad start," Moore wrote in his memoir. "We were embarked upon the perilous adventure of grading up a normal school to the standards of a state university when it seemed few folks greatly wanted the adventure to succeed." Not only were there the philosophical differences between providing a liberal education through the Junior College and vocational education through the Teachers Training program, but there were financial difficulties.

These issues were tackled head-on by the Advisory Administrative Board of the Southern Branch of the University of California, appointed by the regents. In addition to Moore, its members were Robert Gordon Sproul, the university's assistant comptroller, and Berkeley Professors Monroe E. Deutsch and Baldwin M. Woods—all of whom would go on to serve key leadership positions with the university: Sproul as president, Deutsch as Berkeley provost and Woods as head of University Extension.

Normal School employees tendered their resignations, and Moore was instructed by President Benjamin Ide Wheeler to make recommendations on continued appointments or dismissals. A total of 93 teaching staff were hired for the 1919–

20 academic year; 17 of those were in the Teachers Training program. The committee also determined what courses would be taught, staff classifications and associated salaries.

"In a normal school teachers are teachers," Moore explained in his memoir. "But in a university they are professors, associate professors, assistant professors, instructors, lecturers, and assistants."

James Sutton, the University of California's recorder, met with the committee in Los Angeles to review admissions records and the arrangements for registering students. While the regents restricted the number of students in the Junior College to 250, another 10 were accepted to account for "shrinkage," as Moore put it. The demand was great, a testament that "our kind of work was wanted," he reflected. Although no records were kept of the number of students initially declined admission for that first class, logs tracked those who inquired about attending once enrollment limits were met. More than 3,700 inquiries via letter, telephone or in-person delivery were received in those first few months.

Moore, who was expecting an immediate increase of funds to expand the Southern Branch commensurate with prospective student interest, was astonished when Sproul told him to expect the second year's budget to equal the first. "Mr. Sproul quite took my breath away," said Moore. The following academic year, 1920–21, Moore was obligated to work prudently in hiring professors and enrolling 567 additional students.

A more fundamental obstacle to expansion was the attitude exhibited by key professors, regents and the University of California's new president, David Prescott Barrows. The Berkeley political science professor, who had served as acting president during 1912–13, was chosen in December 1919 to succeed the retiring Wheeler. Barrows, a decorated lieutenant colonel in the Officers' Reserve Corps of the U.S. Army with a reputation as a brilliant military tactician, took a cautious approach toward development of the Southern Branch.

No sooner had Barrows assumed office than he presented the regents with the University of California's first-ever deficit budget— primarily due to the Southern Branch's swift growth. Barrows wanted to postpone expansion until 1928, stating the delay was required to create curriculum and hire faculty members able to teach junior and senior courses. Several regents supported him, including Regent Rudolph J.

David Prescott Barrows, University of California president, 1919–1923.

Vol. 1, No. 1: *Cub Californian*, September 29, 1919.

STUDENTS MOBILIZE

While Dickson and Moore tussled with continued resentment from the North, Southern Branch students faced their own, more local, challenge: belittlement. Sportswriters had started referring to the campus as "the Branch," and it didn't take long for enterprising University of Southern California students to grab hold with their own twist. Forming the beginnings of one of the most storied collegiate rivalries in the nation, USC students began calling the Southern Branch "the twig" and its students "twigs"—a blatantly disparaging reference to a diminutive "branch."

In addition, the Berkeley campus was often referred to by university insiders as the "mother" institution, watching over her infant. Even the Southern Branch's mascot, the Cub, was a younger version of Berkeley's Golden Bear.

Such sneering was coupled with more serious denigration. When the Southern Branch first opened, Moore had told the students that they needed to work harder than their Berkeley counterparts. "We must not only do as well as those up North but we must do at least 25 per cent better in order that they will recognize that we are even approaching their records," Moore said. This mantra was repeated on the *Cub Californian*'s editorial page and taken to heart by students, who had heard their university often tagged as, "the

Taussig, who went as far as stating that the Southern Branch "will never be anything but a junior college."

Dickson was concerned that the forceful objections could defer action indefinitely. "Six years was a long time to wait," Dickson wrote in his memoir. "So far as the southern section of the state was concerned, it was now or never."

Southern Campus

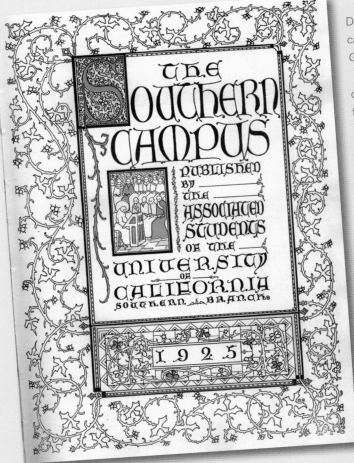

During the Southern Branch's first year, students were asked to suggest names for the campus yearbook. Among those submitted: *The Oski, Southern Bear, Blue and Gold Jr., The Golden Poppy, Utopian, Cali State, Cubangeles, Cubifornian* and *Southern Campus*.

After a student body vote, *The Oski,* named after Berkeley's "Oski wow-wow!" cheer (Oski, Berkeley's official mascot, was not introduced until 1941), was pronounced the victor.

The selection met with widespread disapproval. When it was revealed that the choice was made with fewer than 100 students voting, the matter was reopened. Other names were brought forth and three finalists emerged: *El Osito* (Spanish for Little Bear), *Copa de Oro* (Spanish for Gold Cup) and *Southern Campus*.

An election was held in Millspaugh Hall, and this time the winner, *Southern Campus,* would stick.

Just prior to the university's move from Vermont Avenue to Westwood in 1929, *Southern Campus* Editor J. Brewer Avery tried to rename the publication *Twin Towers,* in honor of Royce Hall. But that didn't take.

When Chancellor Franklin D. Murphy arrived in 1960, there was a drive to eliminate the "subservient to Berkeley" connotation. However, none of the names submitted was considered better than *Southern Campus*, so the name went unchanged.

Southern Campus it would remain for another two decades until, more than 60 years after it was first selected, another effort proved successful. In 1983, the yearbook debuted as *Bruin Life,* a name that seems destined to be long-lived.

normal school that thought it could be a university." All this spurred students to action.

Other names for the Southern Branch cropped up in the vernacular and in print. From the start, the Los Angeles campus yearbook was titled *Southern Campus*. And, moreover, "University of California at Los Angeles" began appearing in unofficial use—much to the dismay of university leaders in Berkeley.

A student editorial calling for both curricular expansion and a new name ran in November 1922. "It is an absolute surety that a complete University of California at Los Angeles will come," the *Cub Californian* pronounced. "When that time comes, and it will come, the students and faculty of this institution will not want it to be known as the 'Southern Branch,' a term which supposes inferiority, but will call it 'The University of California' and add—'at Los Angeles.'"

From that day forward, the student newspaper adopted an editorial policy that it acknowledged some would call "radical" and others "just the thing." It discontinued use of the "Southern Branch" name and instead adopted "The University of California at Los Angeles" and "The State University at Los Angeles."

The student body would soon begin rallying to push the regents to authorize the necessary steps for creating a Bachelor of Arts degree.

FIRST BACHELOR'S DEGREES

Once again Southland citizens would turn to the Legislature for action. Leading the public charge was the Los Angeles Chamber of Commerce, whose influential members drafted a resolution that touched off widespread reaction throughout Southern California in the form of petitions from other cities' chambers of commerce, as well as organizations such as the California Congress of Parents and Teachers and the Women's University Club.

President Barrows was unyielding in his opposition, saying that the venture would prove disastrous beyond the university. The *San Francisco Chronicle* (which newspaperman Dickson sardonically noted "as a rule editorially challenged the wisdom of the Board of Regents") ran an editorial on January 13, 1923, that cried, "Keep University Intact!" Barrows immediately wrote publisher M.H. de Young praising the newspaper's stand, and further stating that the issue affected the unity of the state.

"If something in the nature of an academic rival, laying siege to the State Treasury for the limited funds which are available for higher education, is to be established at Los Angeles," Barrows wrote in his letter, which the paper printed, "not only will higher education suffer in the

Above: *Southern Campus* sales, 1920s.

Left: Northern California newspapers, such as the *San Francisco Chronicle*, decried UCLA's push to implement baccalaureate instruction.

Above: Marvin L. Darsie, first dean of the Teachers College, 1922–1939.

Above right: William Wallace Campbell, University of California president, 1923–1930.

Below: The University of California Board of Regents approved the third year of undergraduate instruction on February 13, 1923.

Darsie was appointed the first dean of the Teachers College. Finally, Southern Branch students would be eligible to earn a Bachelor of Education without having to transfer to Berkeley.

On June 1, 1923, Moore conferred the first diplomas awarded by the Southern Branch. Twenty-eight students dressed in traditional black caps and gowns received Bachelor of Education degrees and listened to an address by Professor John Adams, formerly of the University of London.

THE THIRD YEAR

Even with limited funding, enrollment at the Southern Branch grew swiftly, as Moore tried to meet the growing demand for admission to the Junior College in particular. One year after opening, enrollment in the Junior College grew from 260 to 869; the following year it expanded to 1,298; and by 1922–23, there were 1,696 students enrolled in undergraduate general coursework. (Adding the Teachers College students, there were 3,535 students enrolled at the Southern Branch in 1922–23.)

The burgeoning enrollment, the difficulty experienced by some students transferring to Berkeley, and the success of the four-year Teachers College, all raised the critical issue of adding the third year of undergraduate coursework leading to the Bachelor of Arts.

"The 'third year issue' quickly took on an increasingly important aspect," wrote Dickson in his memoir. "Involved was the entire future of the University here. Many felt that a denial of the third year would be in effect a rejection of any hope of future expansion—a denial of our hopes of some day becoming a full-fledged university."

In his annual report for 1923, Moore referred to the continuing struggle over the development of the Southern Branch as a topic with national implications. "We are trying to discover whether or not a university can conduct its work in two localities," Moore wrote. "The experiment is significant, for, as the nation grows and the states increase in population, it is inevitable that the State University must either transform itself into a state-wide system of higher education, under a single Board of Regents, or become one of several competing state colleges."

State, but the prospects of our union as a people will be grievously hurt."

Barrows appeared not only to have the support of several regents, including chairman of the board Arthur W. Foster, but of his successor, President-elect William Wallace Campbell, and recently inaugurated Governor Friend Richardson. The new governor believed education was becoming too expensive and would during his term try unsuccessfully to close two colleges: California Polytechnic School and the Humboldt State Teachers College.

Yet, some progress was achieved. At the February 1922 meeting of the Board of Regents, a four-year curriculum for teacher training was approved, establishing the Teachers College at the Southern Branch. The courses would be available beginning with the 1922–23 academic year, and the expanded curriculum would cover the training of teachers at every level, from kindergarten through high school. Marvin L.

A crucial vote on the matter came at the February 13, 1923, meeting of the Board of Regents, held at Millspaugh Hall. Dickson made a motion for the third year, while Barrows led the opposition. By this time, three additional Southern Californians had been appointed to the Board of Regents: George I. Cochran, president of Pacific Mutual Life Insurance Company; Margaret R. Sartori, wife of noted banker Joseph F. Sartori; and John R. Haynes, philanthropist and civic leader. With Dickson, there were now four regents sympathetic to the Los Angeles cause.

The meeting lasted more than three hours, and meanwhile students outside Millspaugh Hall rallied, singing songs and cheering for—not against—the regents. Finally, after much contentious debate, the motion to add the third year of undergraduate studies passed by a single vote. Comptroller Sproul came through with a $1.5 million appropriation, approved by Governor Richardson.

Addition of Third Year Marks Greatest Forward Step In S. B. U. C. History

By ROBERT KERR

(Editor's Comment: The addition of third year work in the College of Letters and Science is the greatest forward step in the history of the University of California, Los Angeles, because it marks the beginning of the policy and genuine desire of the Board of Regents that the State University in the Southland shall be enlarged and developed as the needs are made evident. It shows the best kind of mind pace with the development of Southern California, and at present the Southern Branch can boast the third largest college in the state.

But the phenomenal development has not been in numbers alone. The Cubs have made a name for themselves in every collegiate activity that has been undertaken. In oratory, debating, dramatics, litera...

A FULL-FLEDGED UNIVERSITY

Once the third year of instruction was established, the fourth year followed without great impediment. Ten months later, on December 11, 1923, the Board of Regents, upon the recommendation of President Campbell, approved a senior year of curriculum to start the following September. Finally, students had the opportunity to obtain a Bachelor of Arts from the Southern Branch.

The decision arrived so quickly, students were amazed. "The welcome news came as a distinct surprise to the student body, as a Christmas gift of the fourth year was unexpected at this time," according to the *Cub Californian.* "Large numbers of high school students graduating this winter who might go elsewhere will enter this institution in February, because they will be able to graduate from the State University in Los Angeles."

The next day, students and faculty alike celebrated the decision with a Fourth Year Jubilee. The festivities began in Millspaugh Hall auditorium with requisite, yet sincere, speeches by administrators and student leaders, declaring their appreciation to all parties involved in the university's newest achievement.

"The regents have established an educational foundation which will last 10,000 years and will minister to millions of persons," Moore said.

Ultimately, it was biology Professor Loye Holmes Miller who expressed the sentiment of the whole gathering with his shocking exultation: "I'm drunk [despite Prohibition] and don't care who knows it." Such was the delirious spirit of the day.

"There was an intoxication in the prospect of the power and dignity to which we had thus arisen, which would have made any other description of our condition woefully inadequate," documented the 1924 *Southern Campus.* "We were drunk, and we wanted everybody to know why."

In that inspired state, students marched to the inner quad and spelled out in living formation "4 Years" enclosed

Above: *Cub Californian,* February 20, 1923.

Right: On December 12, 1923, students spell out "4 Years" within a giant "C" to celebrate the addition of a fourth year.

UCLA's first Bachelor of Arts degrees were conferred on June 12, 1925.

"The Great Divine Curiosity"

"What is research?" asked biology Professor Loye Holmes Miller at UCLA's inaugural Faculty Research Lecture in 1925. "It has been termed 'the great divine curiosity.'"

"The instructor needs the active mind … to discover, to weigh, to deduce, to discard," Miller continued. "No less does the university need this thing we call research. Human knowledge is not a static thing."

Miller—a renowned naturalist and ornithologist who as chairman helped build UCLA's biology department—delivered the first lecture in what has become a long-standing annual tradition. Among the first researchers to study the fossil remains of Rancho La Brea tar pits in 1906, and later considered California's founder of avian paleontology, Miller spoke on "The Fossil Birds of California."

One month before UCLA awarded its first Bachelor of Arts degrees, the Academic Senate created the Faculty Research Lecture to give the UCLA community, and the greater public, an opportunity to gain new perspective on the scholarly achievements and viewpoints of some of UCLA's most distinguished faculty members. The Faculty Research Lecture has been delivered every year since, with one exception: 1959, when the scheduled speaker, University of California President Emeritus Robert Gordon Sproul, fell ill.

A special committee composed of past lecturers has determined the annual selections since 1930. The program was expanded in 1986 to two lectures per year: one representing the natural sciences or engineering, and the other from the humanities, social disciplines or creative arts.

The series has included: neuropsychologist Shepherd Ivory Franz (1926) on "How the Brain Works;" Shakespearean authority Lily Bess Campbell (1935) with "History and Tragedy in the Mirror for Magistrates;" composer Arnold Schoenberg (1941) on "The Composition with Twelve Tones;" Arabist Gustave Edmund von Grunebaum (1964) regarding "Islam: The Experience of the Holy and the Concept of Man;" historian John S. Galbraith (1979) on "Anti-Imperialism in an Imperial Era: A Blunt Assessment of Victorian Britain;" chemist Paul D. Boyer (1982) addressing "How Living Cells Use Energy;" physiologist and evolutionary biologist Jared Diamond (1996) on "Why Did Human History Unfold Differently on Different Continents for the Last 13,000 Years?"; PET scan inventor Michael Phelps (2001) on "Imaging the Living Biology of Our Bodies in Health and Disease;" and astronomer Andrea M. Ghez (2003) on "Unveiling a Black Hole at the Center of the Milky Way."

In opening the lecture series, Miller said: "Research should be the great common ground of contact between peoples. It should overstep sectional lines. It should lead to a true internationalism."

Above: Shepherd Ivory Franz
Below: Jared Diamond.
Bottom: Andrea M. Ghez.

in a giant "C." There it stood, as described by the *Southern Campus*, "a symbol of a long task accomplished, a long period of probation ended, a new and freer road ahead."

With the addition of the fourth year of instruction, 13 departments were authorized as major fields of study in the newly created College of Letters and Science: chemistry, economics, English, French, history, Latin, mathematics, philosophy, physics, political science, psychology, Spanish and zoology. Charles H. Rieber, professor of philosophy, was named the first dean of the College of Letters and Science.

Moore would find that attracting notable faculty members from across the country was an easier task with the Southern Branch now a baccalaureate-granting university. Among those Moore recruited to form his academic nucleus: renowned neuropsychologist Shepherd Ivory Franz from Saint Elizabeths Hospital in Washington, D.C., who served as the first chair of the psychology department; political science Professor Charles Grove Haines from the University of Texas, an authority on the American judiciary; physicist and acoustical engineer Vern O. Knudsen from the University of Chicago, who would later serve as the university's fifth chief executive; and historian Waldemar Westergaard from Pomona College, who would play a key role in the development of graduate instruction. By 1923–24, there were 164 faculty members in the College of Letters and Science.

On June 12, 1925, the first Bachelor of Arts degrees in the College of Letters and Science were awarded to 98 women and 30 men.

The "twig" was at long last a full-fledged, four-year university. There was no going back.

Below: Charles H. Rieber, first dean of the College of Letters and Science, 1923–1936.

Below right: John Philip Sousa conducts the UCLA band on November 8, 1928. Drum major John Vaughn stands to his right.

Blue and Gold Forever

On November 8, 1928, renowned American composer John Philip Sousa was greeted by the UCLA band at the Southern Pacific railway station in downtown Los Angeles during what would be his final national tour.

The March King, then 74, led the Bruin band with its bombastic tubas and trilling piccolos in a rousing rendition of America's national march, his venerable "Stars and Stripes Forever." The band members, attired in newly commissioned uniforms featuring a reversible blue-and-gold cape, continued to play while following Sousa's car from Fifth Street and Central Avenue to the Biltmore Hotel.

Just one year prior, the band—originally formed in 1925 as a 50-member ROTC unit—was recognized by UCLA's student council as an official campus organization. Musician Ben Laietsky, who had performed with Sousa's band, was selected as the UCLA band's first director. Bugler John V. Vaughn was its first drum major.

Members of the Associated Students executive council were also on hand to celebrate the visit. President Kenneth M. Piper remarked that it was a great honor for the band and UCLA students to participate in what was being rumored as Sousa's last visit to Los Angeles before retiring from public life.

Sousa died four years later, but the memory of that magical musical day stayed with the Bruin band members for years to come.

CHAPTER

03

Westwood Bound
1925–1929

Above: The library rises, March 1, 1928.

Opposite: Aerial view, April 11, 1929. "The campus is so far out in the country that it's obvious only farmers will ever be the students' neighbors," a newspaper scoffed.

The Roaring '20s brought economic prosperity to the growing Southern California metropolis of Los Angeles, buoyed by oil, massive real estate development and the thriving film industry. The national census had shown that for the first time more people were living in cities rather than small-town America—and many were moving out West. Newly designated U.S. Route 66, which led from Chicago to Los Angeles, beckoned, and cars in the emergent Automobile Age would follow. The movement was hailed as the largest internal migration in American history, with 1.5 million new settlers in Southern California. Los Angeles was now the largest city in the state.

Nationwide, the postwar population was booming and the rush for higher learning was catching America's universities off guard as they stretched to meet the insatiable demand of students seeking a degree. With the ratification of women's suffrage came newfound independence, and more women were attending college than ever before. All of this sparked headlines in The New York Times *such as: "Eager Rush of Students Swamps Colleges" and "California Colleges Unequal to Demands."*

Indeed, the West led the way. In 1923, with its 14,061 students systemwide, the University of California had the world's largest enrollment. Admissions pressures mounted at Berkeley, where many students were being turned away. This vast growth confirmed that the Southern Branch was fulfilling a bona fide need for public higher education within the state, and particularly in the Southland, from where most of the students came.

No sooner had the Southern Branch conferred its first Bachelor of Arts degrees, than the institution began growing exponentially—and indications pointed to a continued increase in enrollment.

By the end of the 1925–26 academic year, the Southern Branch's College of Letters and Science, with its 3,178 students, was listed as the fifth largest liberal arts college in the nation by the Association of American Universities. (Berkeley held the top spot with 8,022 students, followed by Michigan's 4,757, Minnesota's 3,729 and Texas with 3,302.)

Including the students in the Teachers College, there were more than 6,000 students crowded into a campus designed to accommodate half that number. Also on campus were 250 teaching staff and 600 children—ages 3 to 14—who attended the training school. With the physical plant clearly inadequate, Ernest Carroll Moore and Edward A. Dickson began a new quest: securing a permanent home for the Southern Branch.

In 1927, after an assiduous search process and passage of several municipal bond measures to secure the site, a campus designed in the Italian Romanesque style began rising on the rolling hills of Westwood, some 13 miles west of downtown Los Angeles. Some scoffed at the location, with one local newspaper going so far as to say, "The campus is so far out in the country that it's obvious only farmers will ever be the students' neighbors." In 1929, the recently renamed University of California at Los Angeles welcomed students to its Westwood campus, ushering in a new era of higher education in Los Angeles.

SELECTING AN IDEAL SITE

Discussions for annexing property near Vermont Avenue, as well as moving to a new, larger site altogether, had commenced quickly after the establishment of the third year. Conversations with President William Wallace Campbell began in 1923 about buying land adjacent to the current campus, perhaps through legislative appropriation. Several regents and university supporters each issued $25,000 in personal notes, against which the university could borrow, for the potential property purchase.

Vice President and Comptroller Robert Gordon Sproul, who recognized early on the limitations of expanding the Vermont Avenue campus, advised that "the institution must almost immediately be moved to a more adequate site." Sproul added that the notion of a new site was "fairly widespread," even among legislators favoring appropriations for enlarging the existing campus. The concerns were that the nearby land was too expensive and that the annexation would be inadequate to provide for even greater enrollment growth. A proposal to merge with the California Institute of Technology in Pasadena (previously Throop University) near the rich resources of the Huntington Library was explored, but soon abandoned.

In November 1924, Campbell presented the need for a new site to the Board of Regents. The board agreed and a Citizens Committee of 17 members, chaired by prominent

attorney Henry W. O'Melveny, was assembled to work with the regents "to secure a satisfactory and permanent site for the Southern Branch." Other members included: *Los Angeles Times* Publisher Harry Chandler; investment banker and committee Secretary James R. Martin; Irwin J. Muma, former president of the Los Angeles Rotary Club; and Security Trust & Savings Bank President Joseph F. Sartori.

"A university location in the heart of a very large city is far from ideal," Campbell wrote to the committee members, describing some parameters for the future campus. "This is especially true of a state in which land is abundant and the people are given to outdoor life. In brief, the Regents favor a new campus for the Southern Branch, entirely outside of Los Angeles, but not too far away from the city."

Dickson—who all along had hoped for the day when the university would build a new campus—already had a specific property in mind: 200 acres near Beverly Hills called the Letts Tract (named for the late Arthur Letts, founder of the

Below: Brothers Harold Janss (left) and Edwin Janss (right) ran the Janss Investment Corporation, one of the largest real estate subdividers in Los Angeles, from their headquarters in Westwood (bottom left).

Bottom right: Sidewalks throughout Westwood bear the Janss seal.

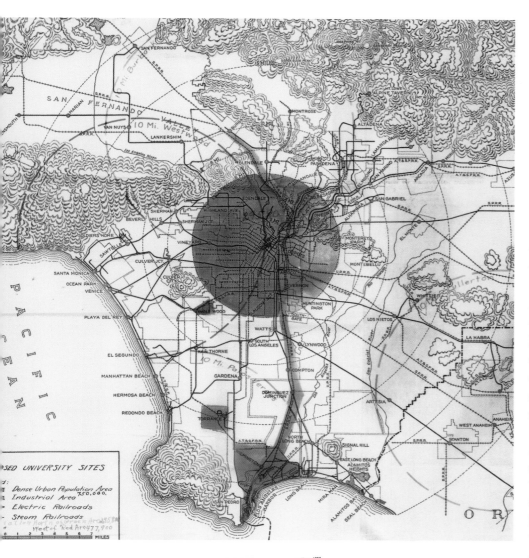

developed a plan to secure the site as the new home for the Southern Branch.

Dickson invited President Campbell, Sproul and other university officials to visit the property, arranging for a personal tour led by Harold Janss. Afterward, all agreed the setting was well-suited. In announcing the search for a new location for the Southern Branch, Campbell emphasized that the Letts Tract seemed "to possess superior advantages and to offer an ideal site" and that he doubted others would have the "stimulating climate of the Beverly Hills region."

Although sights were set on the Letts property, fiduciary responsibility required that other options be explored. Bids were invited from across Southern California. A public hearing was held January 15, 1925. The response was exceptional. "None of us was prepared for the widespread interest shown at that public hearing," Dickson wrote. "Representatives were present from areas extending from Santa Barbara to San Diego, all anxious to secure the 'Southern Branch' for their own locality." For months, Southern California newspapers covered the issue with major news articles, editorials favoring their local proposals and advertisements bought by representatives of the competing sites.

In total, 17 sites were presented for consideration. After the committee visited each of them, other frontrunners in addition to the Letts Tract emerged: Burbank, Fullerton, Palos Verdes and Pasadena. But the Letts (Beverly) location—by now taking on the name "Westwood"—was gaining favor. Its size had grown to 383 acres, after the Janss brothers added another 75 acres, and eight acres were offered by oilman and real estate developer Alphonzo Bell Sr., who founded Bel-Air.

However, Governor Friend Richardson and Ralph Palmer Merritt, former university comptroller and chairman of the regents committee on grounds and buildings, were strong champions of the Pasadena site. At a regents meeting March 14, 1925, a preliminary vote resulted in a tie of sorts: eight regents favored the Westwood site, eight the Pasadena option and eight were divided among the other locations.

University professors were enlisted to conduct rigorous land surveys and compile meticulous daily weather reports dating back a decade. It is also said that the Janss brothers hired salesmen to chauffeur site committee members to the disparate locations, shrewdly manipulating the itinerary to their advantage. First, they traveled to Palos Verdes in the morning and made sure to open the windows so that the members could feel how cool and foggy it could get on the peninsula. In the afternoon they were off to Burbank, where it was sweltering and the drivers kept the windows closed making it rather uncomfortable. By the time the tour finished at Westwood, it was late afternoon and an ocean breeze had rolled in just in time to make the site idyllic.

Broadway department store empire). Formerly part of the Wolfskill Ranch, it was owned by real estate developers and brothers Harold and Edwin Janss. In 1923, Dickson, along with friend and fellow Berkeley alumnus Muma, had been walking near the new Bel-Air development. After hiking to the top of a hill near Beverly Boulevard (later Sunset Boulevard), they stopped to take in their surroundings.

"We had a splendid view of the ocean," Dickson wrote in his memoir. "To the rear rose the green hills of Bel-Air. I remarked to Muma that the setting had much in common with our old U.C. campus on the sloping hills of Berkeley, with its breath-taking view of the Golden Gate and the Pacific Ocean." Muma shared Dickson's sentiment and, before leaving, the pair

Top: A map of potential campus sites shows the 10-mile radius surrounding Westwood with a population of 477,900.

Above: A 1925 telegram to President William Wallace Campbell from Regent Edward A. Dickson promotes Westwood's temperate climate.

A College Town

As early as 1922, brothers Harold and Edwin Janss began developing tracts of land for sale in an area of Los Angeles they named Westwood Hills. When it was announced that the University of California Board of Regents was considering the district as the new home for its Southern Branch, the brothers jumped at the opportunity to create a business and residential community around the university.

The pair, who ran the Janss Investment Corporation—one of the largest residential subdividers in Los Angeles—told the regents that they would work with them "in every way to promote the development of a University campus and any territory around it so that any and all objectionable features would be eliminated."

In this manner of cooperation, a college town grew up alongside the university. "In a few days, Westwood Hills is scheduled to take on a new meaning to thousands … students … and their families … for the University of California opens the Fall Semester in the new Campus!" read a Janss Investment Corporation advertisement. "Drive into Westwood Hills today! … Be prepared to share in the future returns which observers predict should make new Real Estate history for Los Angeles!"

Westwood was originally part of a larger tract of land called Westgate, which was annexed by the City of Los Angeles in 1916. Westwood Village, the commercial district immediately south of the campus, opened in August 1928. The *Los Angeles Times* marked the village's opening with the following description: "The corner store is occupied by the Westwood Pharmacy. … Next comes a beauty shop and barbershop adjoining … the Westwood Cleaners and a market." By 1976, the *Times* wrote: "The Village, with its charming Mediterranean architecture rigidly adhered to by all builders, became a unique business community. It grew by plan, not haphazardly, adjacent to a sprawling metropolis." By the end of 1929, soon after the Westwood campus opened, there were a reported 25 stores in Westwood Village and more than 2,000 homes, with approximately 10,000 residents, within a three-mile radius of the university.

Several of Westwood's major streets were named after distinguished Berkeley professors by University of California engineer Herbert B. Foster, who had been asked to work with the Janss company in surveying and preparing a map of the area surrounding the campus. When the map was completed, the roads were denoted with a letter, such as "A" or "B." Foster

Above: The Tropical Ice Gardens, later known as the Sonja Henie Ice Palace, opened in 1938 at the corner of Gayley and Weyburn avenues.

Left: A postcard of Westwood, 1950s.

Above: Westwood Village, 1936.

Right: The Fox Theater with its iconic tower, 1989.

thought the alphabetical scheme too dry, and took the liberty of writing in some names on his own. "I took my hydraulic course from 'Little Joe' Le Conte," he recounted. "So I put down 'Le Conte Avenue' on the map." He added: "Then I worked with Dean Eugene W. Hilgard on some of his books, so I put his name down. … I took the Great Books course from Gayley, so I added his name." The names would stick, much to the annoyance of those who would have preferred names not associated with Berkeley.

The Janss seal is still stamped on many of Westwood's original sidewalks. Near the center of Westwood Village, where Westwood Boulevard, and Broxton and Kinross avenues intersect, stands what was the Janss Investment headquarters building, with its original Moroccan-style dome. Over the years, the 1929 building has been home to a variety of tenants ranging from a bank to a grocery store to an Asian restaurant. Many businesses and favorite hangouts—like Bullock's department store and Tom Crumplar's Soda Shop—have come and gone. Campbell's Book Store and Desmond's clothing store, both of which relocated to Westwood from Vermont Avenue along with the university, had proprietors who were strong UCLA supporters and Bruins athletics fans. Joe Valentine, manager of Desmond's, helped organize UCLA's first homecoming parade in 1933. At the start of the 2010s, Oakley's Barber Shop was the longest continuous tenant, having opened its doors in 1929.

In keeping with the unifying theme, businesses in the village and homes in the surrounding area were built in a Mediterranean style. UCLA's recent additions on Weyburn Avenue for student graduate housing were designed to blend in with the neighboring architecture. It is said that one unusual characteristic of how the area immediately surrounding the campus was shaped can be traced back to Dean of Women Helen Matthewson Laughlin. She leaned on the Janss brothers to keep the sexes apart by building fraternity row along Gayley, bordering the western edge of the campus, and the sororities along the easternmost edge on Hilgard.

The popularity of Westwood Village has risen and fallen over the years. During Prohibition, a basement speakeasy catered to locals until it was raided. In the 1930s, Westwood became home to several movie theaters, including the landmark Fox Theater, and has since then continued to host numerous red-carpet movie premieres. As UCLA grew, residents and local business complained about increased traffic on the one hand, and competition on the other, as the Associated Students expanded its services to meet the growing needs of students living on campus. Westwood Village evolved from an intimate college town to a larger bustling enterprise, drawing in some national chain stores.

In its 1980s heyday, throngs of tourists and high school students flocked to the village. In 1988, however, a young woman—an innocent bystander—was killed in a gang-related drive-by shooting, and the area's popularity waned. Looting

episodes after a melee at the premiere of "New Jack City" in 1991, and then again during the Los Angeles riots in 1992, also took away some of its luster. Despite the negative publicity, the crime rate in the village—patrolled by Los Angeles and campus police—remains lower than in many parts of Los Angeles.

Westwood homes initially marketed by Janss as "the coming Park Avenue of the West" continue to be among the most coveted real estate in the city, and the village has revitalized itself many times over with new businesses popular with the UCLA community. Although both Westwood and UCLA have developed independent identities since their beginnings, they are destined to remain inextricably linked.

Said Chancellor Charles E. Young to the Westwood Village Rotary Club in 1980: "As UCLA and Westwood have gone through growing pains and reached full maturity together the relationship has always been a mutually beneficial one, each lending strength to the other."

THE EVENING EXPRESS — OFFICES 236 So. Mill St. ~PHONE~ METRO 7600

Evening Express

OLDEST LOS ANGELES NEWSPAPER · THE GREAT HOME JOURNAL

THE GREAT HOME PAPER

LOS ANGELES, CAL., MONDAY, FEBRUARY 15, 1926   13

New University Site Deed Will Be Accepted by Board of Regents

MAP SHOWING NEW LOCATION FOR UNIVERSITY IN WESTWOOD HILLS

SITE SELECTED FOR UNIVERSITY DECLARED IDEAL

Location in Westwood Hills Met Requirements of Committee

MOVE WAS URGENT

Crowded Condition at Present Place Made Another Site Necessary

PROPERTY TO BE FORMALLY TRANSFERRED

Ceremonies as Planned for Site Tomorrow Are Called Off

REGENTS TO MEET

Board to Formally Accept Deed to New Location Tuesday

UNIVERSITY HAD HUMBLE START

UNIVERSITY MET REAL NEED HERE

Heavy Enrollment Followed Establishment of First Two Years' Work

University of California, Fifty-Three Years Old, Is One of World's Largest

But there were more serious considerations than the weather. Proponents of the Westwood site argued that the university was already in the Los Angeles vicinity and to move it elsewhere would prompt strong opposition. "Being an established institution—one in which the people of Los Angeles have come to have a great pride—its removal by the Regents to some other locality would prove a just cause of resentment unless it could clearly be shown that such removal would prove a gain to the students," the selection committee reported. The city council adopted a resolution that stated: "We, the City Council of Los Angeles, unanimously protest against the removal of the Southern Branch of the University from the City of Los Angeles and urge upon the Regents of the University the great importance of securing at the present time, while land is available in sufficient quantities, a site within the city limits of Los Angeles."

Westwood, nestled in the path of urbanization leading from Los Angeles to the Pacific, appeared logical. (Other reports would inaccurately predict that Westwood "is protected on three sides from ever becoming the center of a congested area, to-wit: The Los Angeles Country Club on the east, the National Military home on the west and the hills of Beverly on the north.")

During the March 21, 1925, meeting to select the new location, Regent Guy C. Earl presented Westwood as "the golden site," while Merritt proposed the significantly larger, 700-acre Pasadena tract, criticizing Westwood for being too small, in particular for being unable to accommodate residential living for students and faculty. Governor Richardson, who was presiding over the meeting, turned to Merritt and said: "Ralph, I think you're absolutely right. You and I are going to vote for this site out in Pasadena, but it's a lost cause for we will be the only ones." And they were. The rest of the board chose the 383-acre Westwood tract as the new home for the Southern Branch.

"YES" ON PROPOSITION 2

The regents mandated that the Westwood campus property must come to the university without cost. Although the Janss brothers and Bell were offering to sell the land at a price greatly below market value, which was estimated between $3.5 million and $10 million, a sum of $1.1 million would still be needed to buy the land from the developers. In an effort to raise the money, Sproul suggested that the cities of Los Angeles, Santa

Top: The Los Angeles *Evening Express*, owned by Dickson, helped promote the Westwood site.

Above: Guy C. Earl, regent, 1902–1934.

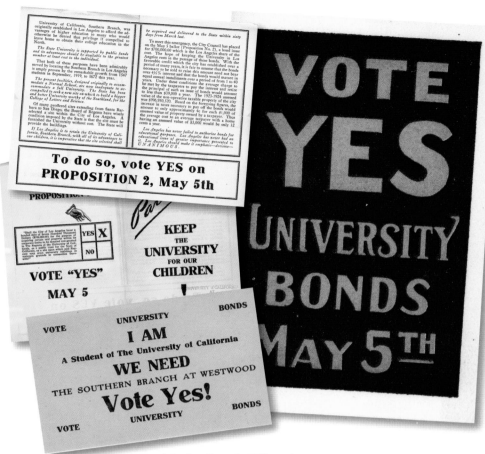

To do so, vote YES on PROPOSITION 2, May 5th

VOTE "YES" MAY 5

KEEP THE UNIVERSITY FOR OUR CHILDREN

VOTE UNIVERSITY BONDS

I AM
A Student of The University of California
WE NEED
THE SOUTHERN BRANCH AT WESTWOOD
Vote Yes!

VOTE UNIVERSITY BONDS

VOTE YES UNIVERSITY BONDS MAY 5TH

Some of the most effective campaigning came through the use of a medium fairly new to the political world: film. A few weeks prior to the election, through personal support from Hollywood entrepreneur William Fox, the Fox Film Company released a 10-minute film that was shown in theaters across Southern California. "College Days" opened with discussion between a father and son, and a mother and daughter as to where the prospective students would go for their college education, climaxed by an emotional farewell at the railroad station. The clear message: such sad partings would be unnecessary if an adequate local institution were available. The closing scene depicted a sample ballot with the exhortation to vote "YES" on Proposition 2.

To add even more emotional pull, Fox recommended that high school students be organized to speak in the theaters before the film showing, "for I am certain that no propaganda by mail, newspaper advertising, or any other kind could possibly compare to the personal appeal that these high school children would make to the voters." The advice was heeded and high school students guided by Southern Branch collegians made persuasive appeals before and after the showings.

Above: Leaflets promoted a "Yes" on Proposition 2, the city bond measure that raised $700,000 toward purchase of the Westwood property.

Right: The Janss brothers advertised Westwood Hills as an emerging area that would thrive with the growth of the university.

Monica, Beverly Hills and Venice (its own municipality until annexed by Los Angeles in November 1925) secure the money through the issuance of municipal bonds.

In Los Angeles, Proposition 2 was placed on the ballot. The city bond measure would raise $700,000 of the funds needed to purchase the Westwood property. Students and alumni worked together en masse to publicize and garner support for the proposition. They went door to door, distributing pamphlets, windshield stickers and posters citywide. The literature included slogans such as: "Parents! Keep the University for Our Children!" They addressed local improvement association gatherings, Parent Teacher Association meetings and high school assemblies.

With radio in its heyday and offering universal reach, students took to the airwaves on local stations KFI and KNX, among others. Student body leaders spoke each night during the week leading up to the election.

"The amount asked from the citizens of Los Angeles is a modest sum in comparison with the benefits which will be derived," broadcast student body President Fred Moyer Jordan over the air of KNX the evening of May 2. "There should not be a single vote against it, but to make sure that it shall carry, we, the students of the university who most need the facilities and who appreciate most what a splendid thing it will be for the boys and girls in the high schools and grammar schools who will come after us, we earnestly appeal to you to vote for this proposition without fail."

$3,000,000 University Buildings 6000 STUDENTS

Ready Soon

GIGANTIC "TALKIE" STUDIO announced by William Fox Now building!

Buy Today in Westwood Hills

NEARLY $3,000,000 already spent on the new University of California Buildings. More Millions, the Wm. Fox Film organization announces, are now going into their gigantic "Talkie" Studio at Westwood Hills, 25 buildings will be erected, the announcement said. The new University is expected to bring 6000 students — besides parents and families of many. The Studio is expected to regularly employ hundreds. What will people do for Homes, Flats, Apartments and other rentals in Westwood Hills a few months hence? Right now, with building permits higher than ever, homes are being sold as fast as they are built — flats rented before they are completed—and waiting lists being formed! Where will the surplus for the coming army of new residents be found? Westwood Hills economic surveys predict a population of 25,000 within a short time. Make sure of your home or your investment in Westwood Hills today! Buy ahead of the tremendous developments under way! Come out TODAY! Take advantage of EASY TERMS and WIDE SELECTION you now have!

Janss Investment Co.
PHONE MUtual 4221
SECOND FLOOR SUBWAY TERMINAL BLDG HILL ST.

Branch Offices
557 So. Western Avenue
W. Arlington 3181
6516 Hollywood Blvd.
GLadstone 9331
420 Canon Drive
Beverly Hills, OXford 1187
4115 Beverly Boulevard
OLympia 2310

27 years of responsibility behind each sale.

To
Californians
At Berkeley
FROM
Californians
At Los Angeles

No. 1536

I
OWN A
SOUTHERN
CAMPUS

All the campaigning culminated in a grand finale: the "pajamarino" and "bond fire" held at the site of the students' future alma mater. Students formed a huge automobile caravan, which, led by the band, yell leaders and members of the Rally Committee, wound its way to Westwood via the main streets of Hollywood. Newspapers reported that more than 40,000 people came from across Southern California to attend what the *Los Angeles Times* called the "greatest bonfire in the history of California."

"During the last two weeks the students have been piling ton upon ton of combustible material on the site so as to be in readiness for the big conflagration," the newspaper continued.

At Westwood, 1,500 pajama-clad students serpentined their way on the hillside. About 600 students holding up red torch lights crossed the gully, disappearing momentarily only to reappear on the other side of the hill and form a huge "C."

The next day, at 6 a.m., some 2,200 students were stationed across the city for the election, assigned in pairs to patrol each of the 1,100 precincts—the requisite 100 feet away from the polls—until they closed. On May 5, 1925, Proposition 2 passed with an almost 3–1 margin. Additional bond measures were later approved by the cities of Santa Monica ($120,000), Beverly Hills ($100,000) and Venice ($50,000). A final grant of $100,000 from the Los Angeles County Board of Supervisors allowed the Board of Regents to obtain UCLA's current Westwood location at no cost to the university.

Another bond measure, Proposition 10, was sent to the voters November 2, 1926, for $3 million to pay for new buildings. It passed by a greater than 2–1 majority.

"DIRT AND WEEDS AND FOUNDERS' ROCK"

The arrival of Founders' Rock in February 1926 marked the first step in converting the several hundred acres of untamed slopes into a university campus.

It took 10 days to haul the granite rock 85 miles from a hillside in Perris Valley to Westwood. One day, the crew moved the trailer carrying the 75-ton boulder a mere 10 feet because it was so heavily entrenched in mud. When the rock eventually arrived, it was placed to mark the spot where Dickson and Muma first stood to consider the property as the university's future home. (For years, Founders' Rock was a fixture in the middle of the roadway that led into campus—until it was

Top left: Students wore wristlets showcasing their proud ownership of the Southern Branch.

Above: In a day for "glowing hopes and glowing hopefuls," the Westwood campus was marked with Founders' Rock and dedicated on October 25, 1926.

Left: Ernest Carroll Moore surveys the new campus with his wife, Dorothea, 1929.

Opposite: The entrance to Westwood Village and the UCLA campus from the south.

cited as a traffic hazard and moved in 1942, its circular cutout remaining visible opposite the Administration Building's north façade. In 1965, it was moved again just northeast of the building, later renamed Murphy Hall.)

On October 25, 1926, Governor Richardson, regents and other university leaders, along with a crowd of students, joyfully amassed on the sprawling field to christen their new campus.

"The rock was the only thing there," recalled Sherman Grancell, who as a freshman piled classmates into his father's Model T Ford to bear witness. "There was dirt and weeds and Founders' Rock."

The day was for "glowing hopes and glowing hopefuls," wrote Professor Loye Holmes Miller. He added: "As the governor of the state and the president of the university stood together on a rude platform with other dignitaries behind them, we, standing below in the sun and dust, sensed a shadow pass swiftly overhead and looked up just in time to see a Prairie Falcon bowling across the newly consecrated brown

L.-17-20

mesa that by the magic of words just spoken had become a university campus."

At the end of the day, Moore logged in his diary: "Each person there tried to imagine what the open barley field would soon look like and no one succeeded."

Founders' Rock was intended to be an important gathering spot. *The Hollywood Citizen* wrote: "It is to be the scene of exercises every year on what will be known as Founder's Day." *The Los Angeles Herald* described the rock as a marker "around which student body jollifications will be staged in the future."

It was Dickson's idea to bring a "founders' rock" to the Los Angeles campus, emulating the landmark at his alma mater. The ritual never really caught on with students—perhaps, some suggest, precisely because the tradition was inspired by Berkeley. Nonetheless, for the pioneers, Grancell said, Founders' Rock would always represent the resolve to make Westwood's rolling hills the university's new home.

A NEW NAME AND MONIKER

As development of the Westwood campus continued, the Southern Branch's independent identity started to emerge. Much ill will was fermenting over the name "Southern Branch"—which with each passing day brought on greater indignation. One of the stories embedded into the university's early fabric is that of College of Letters and Science Dean Charles H. Rieber. As the account goes, Rieber had printed some stationery with the "UCLA" letters. Being soundly scolded for this by Berkeley officials, he rendered his opinion by printing more of it.

Simultaneously, the Southern Branch's athletic teams were attempting to enter the Pacific Coast Conference when an unexpected snag occurred. Originally, the Southern Branch students were dubbed Cubs, a nod to the school's fledgling status that didn't sit well for long. So in 1924, students adopted the more ferocious name Grizzlies. In 1926, however, as the Southern Branch sought to enter the PCC, the University of Montana Grizzlies—already a member—pressed its case for exclusive Grizzly ownership.

Once again, the Southern Branch students were in search of a moniker. After considering everything from Buccaneers to Gorillas, students remained in a quandary. At the time, Berkeley was using both Golden Bears and Bruins. Berkeley student leaders, in the spirit of university solidarity, decided to give up Bruins and offered it to their neighbor to the south. Finally, Los Angeles had its definite appellation. It took immediate effect with the student newspaper renaming itself *Daily Bruin* on October 22, 1926, after having debuted as *Cub Californian* with a subsequent stint as *California Grizzly*.

"We were extremely pleased, appreciative and set about changing our name," said *Daily Bruin* Editor William E. Forbes. "We did it on a Friday preceding a football game with Pomona. I went up to the print shop, and as copy came up, wherever there was the word Grizzly I just made it Bruin."

In acknowledgment of the growing dissatisfaction with the name Southern Branch, the regents appointed a committee to select a new name. Some names considered: Westwood University; California State, South; Golden State University; and Abraham Lincoln University of California. Dickson favored the name "University of California, Beverly," in honor of Bishop Beverley of England, "just as our parent institution in the north had taken its name from Bishop Berkeley." Not surprisingly, he had backing from Beverly Hills city leaders. But Los Angeles politicians would hold more sway.

On February 1, 1927, in the Southern Branch's eighth year of existence, the regents made it official and renamed the campus the University of California at Los Angeles. As the intrepid student journalists predicted on the editorial page of the 1922 *Cub Californian*, the name "University of California at Los Angeles" was adopted and the abbreviation "U.C.L.A." became a Bruin favorite. (The "at" was dropped in 1958 for a comma, emphasizing further independence, and "UCLA"—without periods—would become the preferred internal designation beginning with Franklin D. Murphy's tenure as chancellor in 1960.)

ORIGINAL CAMPUS STRUCTURES

On May 3, 1927, ground was broken at Westwood and the first order of business was the construction of a bridge to cross the deep arroyo that divided the east and west parts of the site. The bridge, modeled after the Roman aqueducts by University of California Supervising Architect George W. Kelham, was needed for transporting construction supplies over the chaparral-

Above: The lack of roads and heavy rains made it difficult to navigate supply trucks, so mules were used to transport materials to the heart of campus.

Right: Construction began on the main auditorium building (Royce Hall) and the library on September 21, 1927.

Below: Hidden underground when the northern end of the arroyo was filled in 1947, the Arroyo Bridge continues to function.

Above: For years, the Arroyo Bridge served as the formal entrance to the campus, from the east off Hilgard Avenue.

Right: Hailed as the "avenue to the future," the bridge was the first structure completed on campus and was dedicated on October 22, 1927, in a ceremony attended by Governor C.C. Young (with hand on ribbon).

covered ravine and was intended to be the campus's main entryway. Some materials were brought over the Arroyo Bridge by mule power from the east entrance on Hilgard Avenue.

The reinforced concrete walls of the bridge contained three huge arches, and Kelham's Romanesque design featured intricate rosette and diamond patterns of carved limestone and inlaid red brick, with decorative parapets, and a series of smaller arches running along the upper portion of the structure. The bridge stood approximately 300 feet long, 75 feet wide and 50 feet above the arroyo. (In the summer of 1947, hundreds of thousands of cubic yards of earth were dumped into the northern section of the arroyo to increase the amount of useable property on the campus. The bridge's arches remain hidden underground at Dickson Court.)

The $100,000 Arroyo Bridge, hailed as the "avenue to the future," was dedicated at a ceremony officiated by Associated Students President Thomas J. Cunningham and attended by Governor C.C. Young on October 22, 1927, marking the completion of the first structure on campus.

"In opening this bridge, we are opening the portals for a new era in the history of the university," Cunningham said.

Kelham, assisted by David C. Allison of the Los Angeles firm Allison & Allison, designed a master plan for the campus that respected the natural conditions and topography. A Spanish theme was considered, since "the traditions of

Southern California are basically of Spanish origin," Kelham wrote. However, that idea never matured. The Spanish style would have been less expensive since it did not rely on red brick, but it was so common throughout the region that it was feared pedestrian.

Influenced by the style Allison had used for the Vermont Avenue campus, the pair selected an Italian Romanesque motif for the Westwood site. The first four buildings—the Library and the Physics Building, both designed by Kelham, and the Chemistry Building and UCLA's iconic landmark, Royce Hall, designed by Allison—all were built in this style. For Royce, Allison was inspired by the asymmetry, towers and porticos of the Basilica di Sant'Ambrogio in Milan, the classic monument of Lombardy, Italy. (After the Great Depression, the Romanesque style would prove too costly, and future designs favored a more utilitarian approach until the 1990s when administrators made an effort to echo the original architectural theme in restorations and new construction.)

The Library (renamed in 1966 after longtime University Librarian Lawrence Clark Powell) was almost named after Josiah Royce, the native Californian philosopher who taught at Berkeley and then was lured to Harvard by pioneering American philosopher William James. One morning while heading toward the new campus, Dean Rieber suggested to Moore that the library be named for Royce. Moore appreciated the idea because he recalled James once saying, "Royce knows everything." However, Moore responded to Rieber: "His name will not be used if we attach it to the library. Let us ask the Regents instead to call our chief classroom building for him, then he will always be named whenever that building is referred to."

"INSTRUCTION OF THE WORLD"

As Royce Hall was nearing completion, Allison and noted muralist Julian Ellsworth Garnsey approached Moore for advice: The Lombards customarily painted frescoes on the porch ceilings of their churches—what subject would be most appropriate and grand for the hall's upper portico?

After some thought, Moore responded, "Why not paint the Instruction of the World?"

"Begin with Socrates," Moore explained, "for it all began with him. And opposite Socrates paint the figure of the Christ. And on their right hand and their left hand paint their two chief disciples, for they happen in fact to have been the same men, namely Plato and Aristotle. There you have your ancient world.

"Now fortunately for us, since we have three arches, human history has three parts—the Ancient, the Middle Age, and the Modern. For the medieval period

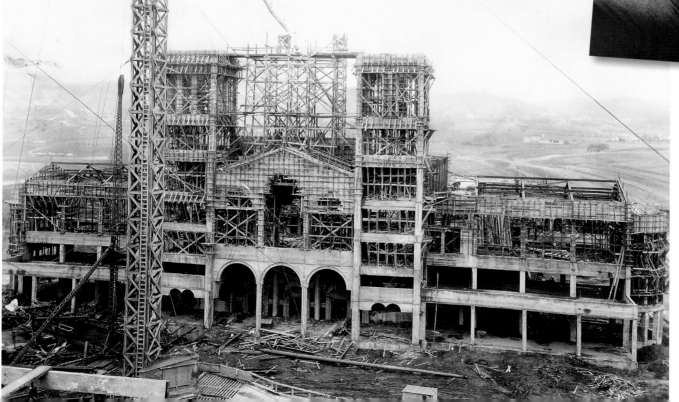

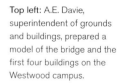

ᲖᕼᕮY SᕼOᕰᒪᕰ ᒪᕮᎪᖇᎥ ᗷᕮᖴOᖇᕮᕼᎪᕮᕰ ᖬᕼᕮY ᛕᎥOᗯᒪᕮᕰGᕮ ᗯᕼᎥᏟᕼ ᖬᕼᕮY ᗯᎥᒪᒪ ᖇᕮᕰᕰᎥᖇᕮ ᖴOᖇ ᖬᕼᕮᎥᖇ Ꭺᖇᖬ ᗴ ᕰᒪᎪᖬO

Above: Six stained glass depictions of academic subjects brighten corridors in Royce Hall, including chemistry (top) and the arts (bottom).

Top right: The grand rotunda of Powell Library.

Above right: Visitors to Royce are greeted by Plato's wisdom, inscribed over the southwest door.

start with Abelard, the father of universities; opposite him paint Petrarch, the prime mover of the Renaissance; and on their right hand and their left hand paint Melanchthon, the schoolmaster general of the Reformation, and Loyola, the director general of the Counter Reformation. There you have the organizing forces of the Middle Ages.

"Now, when you come to modern times it is harder going, there are so many more leaders. But … begin with Immanuel Kant; and there was a man in England named Charles Darwin. Paint him opposite Immanuel Kant. From our own country take that man who did the most to change the character of the universities and of teaching in general, both in our own country and beyond the United States, Charles W. Eliot. And lest the young people who come here may think that

these are just names of men who never lived at all, take one living man, the greatest of living scientists, Albert Einstein."

Another striking feature of Royce Hall is the inscription above the auditorium stage: "Education is learning to use the tools which the race has found indispensable." Many mistakenly believe that the quote is from Josiah Royce. Actually, it is a dictum by Moore, originally placed above the proscenium arch over the auditorium in Millspaugh Hall. Allison transferred the phrase to Royce Hall in an effort to symbolize the historic link between both campuses.

President Campbell was not pleased, informing Moore that only the university president is empowered to place inscriptions on its buildings. Moreover, Campbell told Moore that the saying was unsuitable.

Moore replied that he had not authorized the inscription. Nevertheless, he vigorously refuted the charge of its being inappropriate. "It states the only view of education that takes the learner into partnership with what his predecessors, the wise among mankind have learned," Moore explained, "and at the same time puts upon him the burden of improving the tools which they have wrought out to aid human beings in living."

The words would stay. However, Campbell issued a policy that all future university inscriptions had to be approved by the president and the regents Committee on Grounds and Buildings.

SEPARATION ANXIETY

The Royce inscription was not the only time that Moore and Campbell engaged in bitter disagreement about the Westwood campus. When Campbell announced the location for a new home for the Southern Branch, he began an effort to leave the Teachers College—and its director—behind at Vermont Avenue. The debate over vocational instruction versus liberal arts and science teaching became fervent once again. Campbell, several regents, and the Berkeley administration looked unfavorably at the Teachers College, regarding the training of elementary and kindergarten teachers to be beneath the university's purpose.

While enrollment in the College of Letters and Science continued to climb, registration in the Teachers College was declining. Campbell noted that there were approximately 7,000 students enrolled in the eight teachers colleges in California. One-third of those were enrolled at the Teachers

College in Los Angeles, governed by the regents, and two-thirds in the seven other teachers colleges under the charge of the California Department of Education.

"Here is an anomalous and unique condition in the history of American education," Campbell wrote to Regent Garret W. McEnerney. "The University of California, as represented by its Southern Branch on Vermont Avenue, is the only university in America charged with the duty of preparing

Above: Albert Einstein addressed an overflowing crowd in Royce Hall on February 15, 1932, elucidating his latest thinking on the theory of relativity.

Far left: Visionary educator Corinne A. Seeds was principal of the University Elementary School (UES) from 1925–1957. Founded in 1882 as part of the Los Angeles State Normal School, UES is part of the Graduate School of Education and Information Sciences. Renamed the University Lab School in 2009, it is an educational research center focusing on child development (left). The campus building, named in honor of Seeds, opened in 1950.

students to teach in the elementary schools, including the primary and kindergarten grades. The Teachers College in Los Angeles has this duty as its sole function. This is not a university function."

Since the College of Letters and Science and Teachers College had different functions, they should occupy different sites, Campbell argued.

In an executive session of the Board of Regents, on March 10, 1925, with Dickson absent, McEnerney presented the following: "Resolved, if and when a new site for the Southern Branch is selected, that the College of Letters and Science and other University courses, established from time to time, shall be conducted on the new site and that the Teachers' College shall be conducted at the present location." The regents approved the motion, 17–0.

A clash ensued between Moore and Campbell. Moore wrote a letter of resignation, but decided against submitting it, opting to fight instead. "I lived in a nightmare for four years and felt most of the time as if I had drunk kerosene," Moore recalled.

Dickson was stunned that his three southern colleagues had voted in favor of the matter and rallied to Moore's defense. He argued against separating the colleges on two grounds: first, that he regarded Moore as a qualified leader to head the university; and second, that the university needed the funds from the sale of the Vermont Avenue property to help pay for the buildings at Westwood. It was the second argument that resonated. Still, Campbell would not relent. "What I object to is that as President of the University of California I have to sign kindergarten credentials!" Moore recalled Campbell as replying in a terse exchange.

The battle ensued for years, culminating in a heated meeting on August 14, 1928, behind the closed doors of Governor Young's office. After three hours of debate, the regents approved, by narrow majority, Dickson's proposal to keep the two colleges together.

Dickson immediately sent a telegram to Moore, who hesitated for more than an hour before opening it. When he finally did, it read, "We Win."

MYSTERIOUS CHEMISTRY FIRE

In the early hours of January 3, 1929, two students living across the street from UCLA's Vermont Avenue campus were startled by an explosion and found California Hall, which housed the chemistry laboratories, on fire. By the time the fire department arrived, the blaze was out of control, fueled by highly combustible chemicals in the building. By dawn, California Hall was nothing more than charred embers.

The cause was not immediately clear to authorities. A chemical fire was one theory. But since a velvet curtain in Millspaugh Hall auditorium was found ablaze at

Top right: The charred ruins of California Hall after the mysterious chemistry fire.

approximately the same time, investigators decided arson was the likely cause of both incidents.

California Hall was a two-story wooden structure originally built during World War I as a barrack for the Student Army Training Corps. Chemistry instruction and labs had been relocated there after constant complaints about foul odors and corrosive fumes from other Science Building tenants.

Few seemed to mind the loss of the antiquated building. The *Southern Alumnus* ran a tongue-in-cheek story that began: " 'Cal' Hall—the bugaboo of the campus—the butt of many a college wise crack—no longer torments the U.C.L.A. campus."

"Everyone said that some day 'Cal' Hall would burn down," the article continued, "and [finally] 'California' Hall gave up the struggle and submitted to the universal opinion."

Some campus wits blamed USC pranksters. Others joshed that William Conger Morgan, head of the chemistry department, found a convenient way to get an emergency appropriation for new supplies and speed up the move to the larger, modernized building at Westwood. Even the characteristically stern chairman couldn't help but quip about the matter. "That old barracks should have burned down long ago," Morgan reportedly said the morning after the fire. "And wouldn't you know it—when it did, all the witnesses were looking the other way."

Director Moore telegraphed the news of the destruction to President Campbell, and measures were urgently adopted to replace the lost materials and push forward the construction of the Chemistry Building at the Westwood campus.

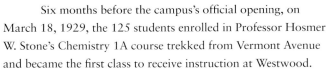

Six months before the campus's official opening, on March 18, 1929, the 125 students enrolled in Professor Hosmer W. Stone's Chemistry 1A course trekked from Vermont Avenue and became the first class to receive instruction at Westwood.

The mysterious fire that forced the early use of the new Chemistry Building (renamed in 1952 after political science Professor Charles Grove Haines) has remained one of UCLA's unsolved mysteries.

MOVING TO "HER NEW HOUSE"

Two months after the chemistry classes began at Westwood, Moore declared a half-day holiday for May 31, 1929, so that students, faculty and staff could join in "taking possession" of the new campus. Classes were dismissed in the early afternoon and everyone gathered at Heliotrope Drive for the 10-mile drive westward.

Police led the motorcade of more than 500 cars and trucks loaded with books, furniture and laboratory equipment. The Rally Committee had decorated cars with blue and gold streamers. Moore met the group as it entered campus, and the band played from the steps of the newly constructed Royce Hall.

"It was a thrilling sight to see 2,000 young people pour themselves among the buildings and into them," Moore said. While May 31 was known as "Moving Day," the move continued throughout the summer. The bulk was transferred during a three-day period, beginning in August, under the direction of Assistant Comptroller Robert M. Underhill and a staff of 300 students.

Above left: Students taking Chemistry 1A in March 1929 were the first to attend classes on the Westwood campus, six months before its official opening.

Above: May 31, 1929, was known as "Moving Day," beginning the summer-long process of relocating to Westwood.

Below: A police escorted "blue and gold" caravan made the 10-mile trek westward.

Bottom: Stocking the Associated Students' temporary bookstore.

Registration began on September 20, 1929, for the fall semester on the Westwood campus. The grounds were not yet graded, and lawns and shrubbery remained to be planted. Rain had fallen, turning dust to mud. Construction materials were piled nearby for the not-quite-yet-completed buildings and landscaping. Rieber suggested two new courses: one on whistling to keep up courage and another on nettle grasping. Classes officially commenced on September 23, 1929, with an enrollment of 5,500 students.

"Thus do long dreams come true," Moore said in a handwritten greeting published by the *California Daily Bruin*. "Your University welcomes you to her new house. It smells of plaster and new paint. It is not finished yet and there is much dust and confusion about it. No other class will ever enter here without finding grass between these buildings. But then no other class will be the first class."

That same day, the first assembly was held in Royce Hall. Robert Keith, student body president, had the honor of making the first speech ever given in the auditorium. "U.C.L.A. looks forward to a glorious future," said Keith, addressing the capacity crowd, "and it is our opportunity to convert the raw material we have here in these new buildings into a finished product that will rank with the best Universities in the country."

"IN THE NAME OF ALL THE PEOPLE OF CALIFORNIA"

The following spring, on March 27 and 28, 1930, an internationally distinguished group of scholars gathered to formally dedicate the Westwood campus and present it to the state. Delegates dressed in colorful academic regalia representing 161 American institutions and nine foreign universities in Europe, Asia and Latin America took part in the ceremony.

More than 5,000 people, including students and alumni, traveled to Westwood for the grand occasion, which included lectures from several renowned educators. Among them: Nobel laureate Arthur Holly Compton of the University of Chicago, who spoke on "The Relation of Physical Science to Philosophical Thought," and educational reformer John Dewey of Columbia University, who lectured on education as a cure for societal ills.

"It is well to remind ourselves from time to time ... that education is the most far-reaching and most fundamental way of correcting social evils," Dewey said. "When shall we realize that in every school building in the land a struggle is being waged against all that hems in and distorts human life?"

According to the *Los Angeles Times*, Dewey said that "California is more willing to start new things, to undertake educational experiments, than the East." The state's universities were free from traditional imperatives and "closer to the people and their needs" than the Eastern institutions.

Dewey, Compton, Scottish naturalist Sir John Arthur Thomson and Adam Blyth Webster, dean of the University of St. Andrews in Scotland, were awarded the campus's first honorary degrees. (Honorary degrees were awarded until 1972, when the Board of Regents placed a moratorium on the practice. In 1979, Chancellor Charles E. Young introduced the UCLA Medal to similarly recognize individuals for distinguished contributions to their profession or society.)

Mathematics Professor Earle R. Hedrick, chairman of the Faculty Committee on the Dedication, presided over the opening session. The ceremonies were held in Royce Hall, with overflow crowds seated in nearby buildings set up to hear the speeches broadcast over KNX radio.

Above left: (From left to right) Regent John R. Haynes, Governor William D. Stephens, Regent Edward A. Dickson, Regent Margaret R. Sartori and Director Ernest Carroll Moore at the formal dedication of the Westwood campus, March 27, 1930.

Left: The University of California Board of Regents awaiting the dedication of the campus.

Top: The first assembly on the Westwood campus, Royce Hall, September 23, 1929.

Above: Chairman of the Board of Regents, William H. Crocker (right), formally presents the campus to Lieutenant Governor Herschel L. Carnahan, accepting on behalf of the State of California.

Right: University of California President William Wallace Campbell (with top hat) and Moore after the dedication ceremony.

The following day, noted banker William H. Crocker, chairman of the Board of Regents, officiated at the dedication ceremony, presenting the campus to Lieutenant Governor Herschel L. Carnahan, representing the state. "We conceive of it as a home for those, and only those, who come and who remain with serious purpose; a home for those, and only those, whose aims are high, and who are ambitious to lead lives really worth living," Crocker said. "It is in this spirit and faith, your Excellency, that I ask you to accept this new campus and its new equipment in the name of all the people of California."

After two days of celebrations, Director Moore summed up the milestone: "This University, like every other university worthy of the name, exists to convert the raw material of untutored judgment into specific discerning of true from false, beauty from ugliness, and right from wrong."

"Boastfulness in California"
1929–1936

Opposite: More than 5,000 undergraduates gathered to dedicate Kerckhoff Hall (shown above in 2011), the new student union, on January 20, 1931, ushering in a new era of student life.

*S*carcely five weeks after UCLA students began the first fall classes in Westwood, the Wall Street crash of 1929 brought the Roaring '20s to an abrupt end, leading the country into the decade-long Great Depression.

While the economic downturn did not interfere with the stately dedication of the Westwood campus the following March, the ripples of financial hardship would soon reach UCLA, its students and faculty. However, under the leadership of newly selected University of California President Robert Gordon Sproul, UCLA would begin an unprecedented period of growth—despite increasing dominance by the charismatic and controlling president, who promulgated a "one university" philosophy often at odds with UCLA's emerging autonomy.

Dedicated UCLA alumni successfully challenged Berkeley's insistence on being the exclusive provider of graduate education, resulting in greater prestige for UCLA as the campus was finally able to award advanced degrees. For the first time, more men were enrolled than women, and UCLA shed its crosstown appellation of "Westwood School for Girls." UCLA would grow as enrollment hit record levels while students sought refuge from the bleak job market. President Franklin D. Roosevelt's New Deal brought federal funding for public works projects and jobs to the city and UCLA. Benefactors in a position to withstand the Depression also aided the campus's expansion at a time when state appropriations to the University of California were slashed 25 percent and the faltering economy could have brought growth to a halt.

Los Angeles had made good on its pledge to host the 1932 Olympics and built facilities for the summer games, which it held to great acclaim—contrary to expectations. "Los Angeles Rises Above

Depression," headlined The New York Times. *The Olympics focused international attention on Los Angeles, which, other than its Hollywood component, had been a relative unknown throughout the world. Sproul was in the limelight as the official California representative and gave the dedicatory address at the opening ceremony. UCLA's recently completed Women's Gymnasium was used by the defending gold medalist Indian men's field hockey team, which practiced on the campus drill field.*

But economic disparity and the onset of war in Europe would bring restlessness, particularly among young adults worldwide. Members of alleged Communist front groups organized rallies on or near the campus, and UCLA students espousing peace and those concerned about social conditions participated. UCLA was tagged the "little red schoolhouse," an unfortunate moniker that brought national notoriety and would resurface in future generations. The campus overcame the unwanted portrayal that implicated it as a home for radicals. UCLA chief executive Ernest Carroll Moore, whose unrestrained opposition to student activism caused him to inadvertently label the campus a "hotbed of communism," would not be as fortunate.

A PAL TOOK ME TO THE HOUSE-MOTHER. HE SAID I COULD WASH DISHES—SO I GOT MY FIRST JOB

Left: A *Los Angeles Times* illustration depicts a common means of earning money during the Great Depression: washing dishes at sorority houses.

THE GREAT DEPRESSION

Although the economy would steadily worsen, UCLA students felt the financial pinch just weeks after Black Thursday. Students did whatever was needed to get by, taking on odd jobs—if they were lucky enough to find one. Local businesses, keeping in mind their affinity to the university, tried to ease the hardship. The Janss Investment Corporation sales office in the heart of Westwood instructed its employees to give 25 cents to any hungry individual who came into the office looking for work. The Westwood Village Merchants Association hired 75 students to decorate the village for the Christmas season. Many withdrew from the semester to begin temporary holiday jobs at department stores. More than 300 female students were granted leaves of absence in December 1929 to find work. The practice was repeated in 1930.

Left: The Indian men's field hockey team practices on the campus drill field in preparation for the 1932 Los Angeles Olympic Summer Games.

Below: Fraternity Row along Gayley Avenue, 1930.

Above right: The Helen Matthewson Club, a cooperative founded by the longtime dean of women, provided affordable housing and a collegial atmosphere for the working female student.

"While it does not particularly approve of students absenting themselves from classes the week before vacation begins," reported the *California Daily Bruin*, "the Administration realizes that many students have counted on Christmas work as a means of recuperating their funds, and that this year many are in such straits that it is imperative."

Throughout the academic year, Dean of Women Helen Matthewson Laughlin helped female students find employment, as well as housing in co-ops, so they could continue their studies.

By winter 1931, the first full effects of the Depression hit California's economy. Students who could no longer afford public transport found themselves walking several miles to and from campus. Some scraped by to eat. Tales abounded of students getting together, each pitching in a nickel, to buy and split a hamburger; or of a male student who went without meals for days to give that money to his sweetheart.

An oft-repeated story was that of a student who was found living under the Arroyo Bridge on campus. "The girl under the bridge," as she became known, had reportedly hitchhiked from the Midwest after her father was ruined by the stock market. Determined to continue her education, she spent her days in class, evenings in the library, showered in the women's gym, and slept under the bridge on a pile of straw and planks—until she was discovered by a groundskeeper. Prytanean, an honorary female student-service organization established in 1922, raised money for the student, and Laughlin provided a loan from an emergency fund and found her a place to live. (The student graduated with honors and, without prompting, repaid the loan so "some other girl might be helped, as I have been.")

During the Depression, many students could not afford to be members of fraternities or sororities, which had dominated campus life the previous decade. As a result, the organizations had trouble paying the mortgages for their newly built homes along the campus border. To avoid multiple foreclosures, the Janss Investment Corporation, which originally financed the Greeks when the banks turned them down as risky investments, renegotiated the payments. In the end only one house failed.

Professors also struggled through difficult times. While none reportedly was let go because of the economy's tailspin, departmental budgets shrank and the faculty received an across-the-board 10 percent pay cut in 1933. Others on employment contracts, such as Associated Students Manager William C. Ackerman and football Coach William H. Spaulding, accepted voluntary pay reductions.

"This was really a very rough time, and people were extremely uneasy," recalled Bernice Woodson Park, wife of physical education Professor Donald K. Park, "because even though there was some assurance that individuals would remain, you never were exactly certain of it."

Despite the monetary challenges, optimism persisted. "Most of us in the student body were from lower-middle-class families, and I think we were pretty good at covering up how difficult a time our families were having," recalled Dean E. McHenry, UCLA's 1932 student body president, who would become founding chancellor of the University of California, Santa Cruz.

Many sought escapism as a way to lift spirits. In the fall of 1931, the seniors threw a "Depression Dance" at the Whitley Park Country Club near Hollywood. Any attire was declared "suitable"—except formal or hoboesque "patch garb" costume, which were taboo—and members of the Class of 1932 gave a modernistic interpretation of the economic situation, differentiating between "depression" and "hard times."

Some students looked beyond themselves to help others. The following year, the Associated Students sponsored a charity dance with proceeds aiding needy students.

In 1934, students organized a holiday food drive in the library's rotunda to benefit impoverished children and families living in the Sawtelle area of West Los Angeles. "Before we'd even done that, we'd begun to have second thoughts," said Adaline Guenther, assistant executive secretary of the University Religious Conference, who helped organize the students. "What's going to happen when a hungry family gets six cans of canned peaches and nothing else?"

Through the efforts of several students on the board of the University Religious Conference, on August 3, 1935, University Camp (shortened to UniCamp) welcomed its first campers. Under the guidance of their UCLA student counselors—among them, future Olympian James E. LuValle—54 children from disadvantaged backgrounds attended summer camp at Big Pines in the San Gabriel Mountains. The counselors worked with the children in hope that exposure to a new environment would inspire them to succeed. (UniCamp moved to the San Bernardino Mountains in 1941 and became UCLA's official student-run charity in 1948.)

EXPANSION DESPITE CRASH

In some ways, UCLA fared better than other universities around the country—at times benefiting directly from the Depression.

While the unemployment rate in the region continued to climb, so too did enrollment at UCLA, reaching record annual levels for much of the decade. UCLA had the distinct advantage of being new—brimming with promise. As a public university, it was considerably more affordable than most private institutions, which charged hundreds of dollars more. Students who would have attended private universities just months before chose UCLA instead. It cost about $25 to enroll for a semester at UCLA in 1930. In addition, as a commuter school, there was no costly room and board. UCLA proved a relatively inexpensive safe haven.

"With financial conditions at their lowest ebb, a sufficient number of old students have returned to complete the requirement for their degree," wrote the *California Daily Bruin* in September 1930. "The difficulty of securing jobs

Left: The first "woodseys" visit UniCamp at Big Pines in the San Bernardino Mountains in 1935.

Below left: The first UCLA professor elected to the National Academy of Sciences, William G. Young, accepted a postdoctoral fellowship at UCLA during the Great Depression.

Below: A view looking eastward over Janss Steps from the Goodyear Blimp, April 28, 1930.

elected to the National Academy of Sciences. The new chemistry building was named in his honor in 1970.)

By 1933, California's surplus funds had been spent as unemployment peaked with one in four American workers jobless. President Roosevelt established the Federal Emergency Relief Administration to supply matching federal dollars to states, and newly elected Governor Frank Merriam created the State Emergency Relief Administration, which began accepting work project proposals from municipalities. At UCLA, the botanical gardens and a Greek-style Open Air Theater—which could accommodate a capacity 18,000—were built in part with the use of state relief funds, providing more than 1,000 jobs to Californians. (The amphitheater, for years UCLA's largest venue, hosted events ranging from Greek plays to commencement exercises. However, concrete was never poured and in 1952 the project was abandoned to make way for the medical center.)

Above: The campus continued to grow during the 1930s despite tough economic times.

Below middle: An Open Air Theater was excavated by workers hired through New Deal-era state relief programs.

Below right: The Women's Gymnasium under construction, 1931.

of any kind has led many to return rather than continue an unavailing search for work. If such is the case, this group will be given a chance to find out that a man equipped with a University degree has an advantage in securing any position."

Faculty members also were drawn to UCLA. Unlike many universities experiencing financial trouble, UCLA was still able to hire. Professors who just a few years earlier might have been successfully recruited by the Ivy League or other universities were now joining UCLA's faculty. The campus was able to attract some of the brightest new talent, such as William G. Young, whose work would establish UCLA as an international research center in physical organic chemistry. Young accepted a postdoctoral fellowship at UCLA in summer 1930. (In 1951, Young was the first UCLA professor

Universities across the country were forced to scale back, but as a new university, UCLA had expectations—and appropriations—for growth. The building program slowed, but it did not stop.

"The air riveters are working hard on two new gymnasiums," Moore wrote to his friend John Graham Brooks at Harvard University in January 1932. "Even the depression, you see, does not stop this University, indeed, it enables us to build stronger, for the costs of construction are comparatively low now. When these two great gymnasiums are finished we shall have eleven buildings on this campus, all of them major buildings and most of them larger than your [Widener] Library. There is still, you see, boastfulness in California."

The University's Lifeblood

The UCLA Library contained more than 24,000 books when it opened in 1919. The collection, however, inherited in the property transfer of the Los Angeles State Normal School to the newly founded Southern Branch of the University of California, was deemed "inadequate to meet the needs of even a fledgling university."

The library contained, for example, 25 copies each of *Stepping Stones to Literature* and *Nature Stories for Young Readers*, while it lacked a single standard scholarly edition of Chaucer or Shakespeare. UCLA's founding chief executive Ernest Carroll Moore, an avid book collector, sought to significantly improve the library's holdings and encouraged everyone from students to outside donors to contribute to the effort.

Moore personally contributed eight Babylonian clay tablets with Cuneiform script that he had bought for $30. The Senior Class of 1922 raised $164 toward purchasing the Oxford Dictionary—a necessity for a college library. Berkeley donated the books purchased each year for the Los Angeles summer session held on the Vermont Avenue campus, and the regents raised the book acquisition budget to $10,000 in 1921–22. The library's holdings were growing, but still lacked consequence.

Then, through previous negotiations by Moore and Regent Edward A. Dickson, in 1934, arts patron William Andrews Clark Jr. bequeathed to UCLA his estate and library of more than 13,000 volumes—including the four Shakespeare folios, important editions of Chaucer and other priceless works, as well as two of the world's most complete collections of Oscar Wilde and John Dryden. The UCLA Library's status was instantly elevated. By 1946, the library reached 500,000 volumes, with the addition of a facsimile version of the Gutenberg Bible, the first printed book.

"The quality of the library is a measure of the quality—the intellectual quality—of the institution," said Chancellor Franklin D. Murphy, who helped the UCLA Library achieve greater growth in the 1960s by battling for equity with Berkeley's acquisition budget. "Curious scholars need books, and if the books are unavailable, you don't get the scholars. It's a deep interrelationship."

Long after retiring, Moore would take a daily stroll to campus, often stopping to visit Lawrence Clark Powell, university librarian from 1944–61. Powell would proudly show the former provost some of the newest arrivals. "Mr. Librarian," Moore would habitually say, "don't stop to read them. Leave that to others. Your job is to get them here. Don't let anything distract you. Books are the lifeblood of this University."

By 1984, the UCLA Library was ranked second among those at academic research institutions in the United States and Canada, and has remained one of the nation's top libraries. In 2010, its holdings reached nine million volumes. Each millionth acquisition has represented a celebrated milestone:

One Millionth, 1953
California in '41, Texas in '51: Memoirs
Nicholas Dawson (1819–1903)
One of only seven known copies, it contains the memoirs of a member of the Bidwell Party, the first group of emigrants to complete an overland journey to California.

Two Millionth, 1964
Omnia Platonis opera
Plato (c. 428-347 BC)
A two-volume publication of Plato's collected works, printed by Aldus Manutius, one of the greatest printers of the Italian Renaissance.

Three Millionth, 1971 (1)
Claudii Ptholemaei Alexandrini liber geographiae cum tabulis et universali figura et cum additione locorum quae a recentioribus reperta sunt diligenti cura emendatus et impressus
Ptolemy (c. 100–170 AD)
The first atlas to be printed in more than one color of ink.

Four Millionth, 1979
Opuscula
Jaime Pérez de Valencia (1408–90)
An incunable printed in Spain during the 15th century.

Five Millionth, 1983
Untitled
John Frederick Fitzgerald de Ros (1804–61)
Personal narrative of travels in the United States and Canada in 1826.

Six Millionth, 1989 (2)
A monograph of the Pittidae, or family of ant-thrushes
Daniel Giraud Elliot (1835–1915)
A richly illustrated book by one of the leading ornithologists of the 19th century.

Seven Millionth, 1996
Six Empty Bookcases
Sjoerd Hofstra
Contains dramatic pop-ups by the Dutch-born artist and master of paper construction. Number four in a limited edition of 12.

Eight Millionth, 2005
Some Dry Space
Michael Light
An oversized, handmade volume featuring black-and-white photography of both settled and unsettled areas of the American West from above.

Nine Millionth, 2010 (3)
Inamoramento de Rinaldo di Montealbano
Anonymous adaptation of a well-known Carolingian epic printed in Venice in 1533.

Below: The UCLA Library celebrates 500,000 volumes with its 1946 acquisition of a facsimile version of the Gutenberg Bible.

Left: The library's first volume: *The Twelfth Annual Report of the United States Geological and Geographical Survey of the Territories: A Report of Progress of the Exploration in Wyoming and Idaho for the Year 1878 in Two Parts.*

Right: On his deathbed, William G. Kerckhoff told his wife, Louise, to "build the building that Dr. Moore wants."

Below: Too overcome with emotion to speak at the dedication ceremony, Louise Kerckhoff (in hat) left words to others, silently presenting the key to the building to Governor James Rolph Jr.

Right: Stained glass images of a redwood tree and a dam, on the fourth floor of Kerckhoff Hall, represent the life of the German-American lumber and hydroelectric power pioneer.

Several individuals with enduring wealth made sizable donations that guided the expansion, even during the darkest times. From entire buildings to accoutrements, these donors provided critical gifts that would enhance the development of the campus. So much did these contributions alter the landscape that the Associated Students dedicated the 1931 yearbook to "Giving."

Kerckhoff Hall, with its Tudor Gothic spires reaching toward the heavens, symbolized limitless opportunity. The first building at Westwood named for a donor, the structure was the result of a $715,000 gift from Louise Kerckhoff, in memory of her late husband, William G. Kerckhoff, who on his deathbed asked his wife to provide funds for a student union.

The Gothic style was chosen to contrast with the rest of the campus's Romanesque architecture, emphasizing the unique significance of a student union in university life. Details embedded throughout the building, including the stained glass images of a redwood tree and a dam on the fourth floor, refer to Kerckhoff's successful career in the lumber business and his contributions to the development of hydroelectric power.

Louise Kerckhoff gave $100,000 to fully furnish the facility—making the $815,000 donation the largest single gift by an individual to UCLA up to that point. Operating costs were not covered, however, and an unforeseen problem resulted. After its dedication on January 20, 1931, the $1,000 monthly upkeep not provided for by the gift fell upon the Associated Students and this, adding to the economic stress of

the Depression, nearly bankrupted the organization until the regents supplied an emergency loan.

Nine months later, UCLA opened Mira Hershey Hall— its first residence hall—due to the generosity of philanthropist Almira "Mira" Hershey, who left $300,000 in her will to build a women's dormitory. Hershey, who owned the grand Hollywood Hotel (demolished in 1956) and founded Good Hope Hospital (later Hollywood Presbyterian Medical Center) for patients unable to afford medical care, was a distant cousin of chocolate entrepreneur Milton S. Hershey. She also left $100,000 to create a loan fund for UCLA students. (In fall 1969, Hershey Hall was turned into a graduate coed dormitory; in 1998, it was converted for academic uses.)

A bequest by arts patron William Andrews Clark Jr. greatly aided the development and expansion of the UCLA Library. Upon his death in 1934, the university acquired the William Andrews Clark Memorial Library, situated on five acres of land on Cimarron Street and West Adams Boulevard south of downtown Los Angeles. The 1926 building by Robert D. Farquhar (later a chief architect of the Pentagon) mixes Italian Baroque with French and English influences. The entrance hall ceiling is adorned with a mural of *Apollo and the Nine Muses* by Allyn Cox (who then spent more than 30 years painting murals in the U.S. Capitol). The gift was originally valued at $5 million.

Left: William Andrews Clark Jr.

Below left: Dedication of Mira Hershey Hall, the first dormitory on campus, October 13, 1931.

Below: Almira "Mira" Hershey.

Top: The main reading room of the William Andrews Clark Memorial Library.

Above: The Clark Library contains the world's most comprehensive collection of Oscar Wilde material, including this letter penned by the playwright in 1895.

Above: The first of the four Shakespeare folios in the Clark Library's collection.

Above right: More than 150 eucalyptus trees, donated by the Daughters of the American Revolution, line Westwood Boulevard, 1930s.

Clark, who founded the Los Angeles Philharmonic Orchestra, named the library after his father, the former U.S. senator from Montana who had amassed a copper mining fortune. The rare books library—consisting of 13,000 volumes mostly gathered by Clark during the heyday of American book collecting—significantly enhanced UCLA's holdings of English literature, history and scientific works of the 17th, 18th and 19th centuries. It contained one of the world's most complete collections of John Dryden and another of Oscar Wilde, as well as the four Shakespeare folios and important editions of Chaucer, Charles Dickens and Robert Louis Stevenson. Clark, who left a $1.5 million endowment for the library to ensure its vibrancy, stipulated that it was never to be moved, merged or consolidated with any other collection. (The library has grown to include more than 110,000 books and the building was designated a historic cultural monument by the City of Los Angeles in 1964.)

Several other donors made distinctive gifts during the Depression. The Daughters of the American Revolution presented UCLA with more than 150 eucalyptus trees to line Stone Canyon Road (later Westwood Boulevard) in honor of the presidents of the United States. (About half of the trees, which were planted beginning in 1930, succumbed to disease and pests over time. In 2001, the remaining trees were deemed a safety risk and were removed, replaced with Canary Island Pines.)

In 1930, brothers Harold and Edwin Janss contributed $50,000, which in part went toward the construction of Janss Steps—first known as "the 87" after the number of steps climbing up to Royce quad. Della Mullock Mudd donated $52,500 to commission the great pipe organ for Royce Hall. Installed in 1930, it was constructed by the Skinner Organ Co. in Boston and transported via the Panama Canal. Another UCLA landmark, the 100-foot steel flagpole at the eastern edge of the quad, was donated in 1937 by Jacob Gimbel, of the Gimbel department store family. On an impulse, he added a small brass plaque with a bas-relief of an electric fish—*Porotergus gimbeli*—which was discovered during a Gimbel-financed expedition on the Amazon River.

Above: Alexander Schreiner, UCLA's first organist, 1930–1938.

Right: Ernest Carroll Moore at the foot of Janss Steps, c.1930.

A NEW PRESIDENT

Overseeing all of this growth was Robert Gordon Sproul, who on July 1, 1930, assumed the presidency of the University of California. Regent Edward A. Dickson had nominated the comptroller, and Sproul's 28-year tenure would not only shape the University of California system, but directly influence the UCLA campus—which he would personally take charge of for several years during his administration.

A 1913 civil engineering graduate of Berkeley, Sproul was the first alumnus to become the university's president. He was also the first chief executive who did not hold an advanced degree. In searching for a new leader to replace the retiring William Wallace Campbell, the regents wanted an individual with strong business acumen, and someone not mired in the internal politics of academia, which had caused frustration between the Board of Regents and the university's previous two presidents.

Sproul had started out in the cashier's office at Berkeley in 1914 before being promoted to assistant comptroller and assistant secretary of the regents in 1918. In 1920, he was appointed comptroller and also became secretary of the regents and the university's land agent. In 1925, he was selected vice president in charge of business and financial affairs. By the time the regents were looking to appoint a successor to Campbell, Sproul had earned their respect after being intimately involved with the university's financial management for more than a decade. As comptroller, he understood the intricacies of state budgets and had developed key relationships in the Legislature. On June 11, 1929, the popular Sproul, 38, was chosen as the University of California's 11th president.

"Unlike his predecessor, President-Elect Sproul is no schoolman, no scholar, no holder of learned degrees," *Time* wrote in an article published shortly before Sproul began his term. "His business, which he entered the year he graduated from the institution, is the commerce of education."

Left: Jacob Gimbel, 1930.

Above: Dedication of the 100-foot flagpole on Royce quad, donated by Gimbel, 1937.

Robert Gordon Sproul

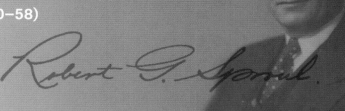

Born on May 22, 1891, San Francisco native son Robert Gordon Sproul would become the first alumnus of the University of California to head his alma mater—a distinction he held for an unprecedented 28 years.

As a Berkeley undergraduate, Sproul was heavily involved in student activities. He was president of his junior class, the band's drum major and a track star. Sproul earned a Bachelor of Science degree in engineering in 1913.

After graduation, Sproul went to work for the City of Oakland, where he met his future wife, Ida Wittschen. A year later, he accepted his first job at the University of California— as a cashier. In 1918, he was appointed assistant comptroller, as well as assistant secretary of the regents. Two years later, he was promoted to comptroller and secretary of the regents, and became the university's land agent. He was appointed vice president in charge of business and financial affairs in 1925.

Right: Robert Gordon Sproul, as the 1958 Tournament of Roses grand marshal, with his wife, Ida.

Below: Sproul in 1930.

The Board of Regents selected the 38-year-old Sproul as the University of California's 11th president in June 1929, and he assumed the presidency a year later. He was the first president not to have an advanced degree, but having served as the university's representative in Sacramento, he had developed key relationships in the Legislature and understood the intricacies of state budgets.

Sproul was a remarkable orator who took great care in crafting his speeches. He possessed a masterful memory with an instant recall of facts and statistics, which made it difficult to challenge him in debate. Of his characteristic booming voice, it was said: "If he leaned out of a window in Berkeley it was heard in Los Angeles."

Sproul took responsibility for directly overseeing UCLA during two key periods: after the retirement of Provost Ernest Carroll Moore, and during World War II following the retirement of Provost Earle R. Hedrick. Although he held firm to his "one university" philosophy, which many UCLA officials and alumni perceived as holding back UCLA's growth, Sproul spoke with pride of his role in developing UCLA. "My interest in U.C.L.A., I have always been proud to say, goes right back to the very beginning," Sproul told *The U.C.L.A. Magazine* in October 1939. "I sat in with the special committee which considered the possibility of taking over the Los Angeles Normal School, I was a member of the first Advisory Board, and mine was the first of the general offices of the University to have its chief and other members spend time on this campus—I have continued that policy ever since."

After his retirement, UCLA's second high-rise residence hall, completed in 1960, was named in his honor. Sproul died on September 10, 1975, at the age of 84.

"Bob Sproul was more than a president of the university," said University of California President David S. Saxon to the *Los Angeles Times*. "To many people—legislators, governors, and the man in the street—he was the university."

A distinguished orator who dedicated himself to being a scholar in his private life by devouring the classics, Sproul espoused his unique qualifications: "I realize I come to this office untainted by academic legitimacy." While he was president-elect, he took a six-month leave of absence to visit other universities, familiarizing himself with their administration, as well as the academic world from which he might recruit faculty members. Sproul understood that academe had the long-held view of "the greater the scholar, the better the president, because as a great scholar he could attract other scholars," said Cyril C. Nigg, a 1927 UCLA graduate, who later served as regent during Sproul's administration.

Although the faculty had initial misgivings about his lack of academic credentials, Sproul was embraced by the students. During his first address to UCLA students as president, he informed them that he had been a supporter of UCLA since its inception. "I am no carpet-bagger from the north," Sproul said. "I have been a part of this institution since the time it was a dream."

Afterward, the *California Daily Bruin* commented: "We doubt if there ever shall be a new president of the University who can leave the platform with as great a display of wholehearted support as did President Sproul yesterday."

PUSH FOR GRADUATE EDUCATION

In stark contrast to preceding university Presidents David Prescott Barrows and William Wallace Campbell, who resisted the development of UCLA in fear that it would weaken and divide the university, Sproul saw UCLA's expansion as a natural evolution in a rapidly growing state. He wanted

Commencement at the Hollywood Bowl, 1937.

The Big Snow

One of the most beautiful and rare mornings to ever befall UCLA occurred January 15, 1932, as the campus was unexpectedly covered in a wintry blanket of snow.

Bruins arriving to campus by 8 a.m. found an unforgettable panorama: red brick buildings frosted white, trees and shrubs made pillowy, and Royce quad coated with two inches of glistening snow.

It soon became clear that instead of the usual scholarly activities, the revised syllabus would feature snowman-building and a pandemonium of snowball fights.

"'Whizzzz-sock!' and another Bruin tasted the snow!" the *California Daily Bruin* cried. Some professors, joining in the diversion, officially dismissed classes. Those professors who tried to charge through the barrage to maintain a semblance of order found that "personalities were not respected," according to *The Bruin*.

The playful mayhem was met by a police officer. But as he reached Royce Hall, he was himself ambushed by snowballs from all sides, including those thrown from a balcony overhead.

The administration was understanding of the exuberant spirits. "Let them have their fun," *The Bruin* quoted UCLA leaders

UCLA to flourish. To achieve that, Sproul believed he needed to bolster morale at UCLA, where, for example, the long tradition of referring to Berkeley as "California" was considered a slight to the Los Angeles campus. (The "Cal" nickname still rankles many loyal Bruins.) Sproul undertook great effort to promote unity and accord among the campuses. His methods ranged from spending a half on each side of the field during the Berkeley-UCLA football games to dividing his time between Berkeley and Los Angeles. For years, Sproul commuted monthly, if not weekly, to UCLA via the night "owl" train.

In 1931, Moore was elevated to vice president and provost, a title in line with that held by Monroe E. Deutsch, his counterpart at Berkeley. In reality, both provosts' powers were limited on their respective campuses: Sproul retained authority in all budgetary matters, as well as academic appointments. (This control would become increasingly exasperating for Moore and succeeding chief executives as UCLA expanded and the level of administrative supervision overtaxed Sproul, who would not delegate his authority.)

One of Sproul's first actions as president was to explore the creation of graduate education at UCLA. On July 16, 1930, he appointed the Committee on the Organization of Graduate Work to evaluate departmental need and cost of implementation. The nine-member group, headed by Moore, also consisted of physics Professor Samuel J. Barnett, education Dean Marvin L. Darsie, psychology Professor Shepherd I. Franz, political science Professor Charles Grove Haines, mathematics Professor Earle R. Hedrick, history Professor Frank J. Klingberg, Berkeley Graduate Division Dean Charles B. Lipman, and A.O. Leuschner, Berkeley's former dean of graduate studies.

By summer's end, the committee advised that graduate degrees should be offered in biology, economics, education, English, geography, geology, history, mathematics, philosophy, physics, political science and psychology. It identified faculty members prepared to offer master's-level work. This was bolstered by the fact that at least 30 UCLA professors were among the nationwide group who rated graduate programs at top universities, including those at Harvard, Yale and Princeton, along with Berkeley.

Moving forward with the recommendation, Sproul included a request for $120,000 for UCLA graduate work in the preliminary budget for 1931. But Governor James Rolph Jr. stripped the request from the budget. Sproul included it again in an early version of the 1933–35 budget, but the regents withdrew the item when Rolph insisted upon strong cutbacks in state operations as the toll of the Depression wiped out state coffers.

as saying. This, even after rumors that Provost Ernest Carroll Moore was pelted by a snowball—a claim denied by his office. For three hours, "only the brave ventured out of buildings into the war zone," *The Bruin* wrote.

Then, as suddenly as it appeared, the snow vanished—melting by 11 a.m., under the bright sun. Even as UCLA returned to normal, evidence of the morning's events remained: a few black eyes and other minor injuries, a damaged lamppost, a broken chandelier and 14 shattered windows—some attributed to professors' inexpert aim. A good sport, Dean of Men Earl J. Miller offered to pay for damages, and all was forgiven.

Fortunately, student photographers Thelner B. Hoover and Durward "Bud" Graybill were on hand to document the historic happening. Hoover, alerted to the snow by the family milkman, got to campus by 6:15 a.m. and was able to capture the serene setting before the first snowball was thrown. Graybill, photographer for the *Southern Campus*, shot many of the action scenes on Royce quad.

Other snowfalls have been reported over the years, although none like the Big Snow of 1932. In January 1949, enough snow fell once again for students to build snowmen and engage in snowballing. More recently, in January 2007—75 years to the week of the 1932 snow—streets, rooftops and lawns in Westwood, Bel-Air and other surrounding areas were covered with a white dusting. While actual snow fell on Malibu's hills and other Southland locales, forecasters said the white stuff that accumulated in Westside neighborhoods was more likely to have been graupel—irregular hailstones that can be confused with snowflakes. Such semantics.

Above: Let the snowballing begin: "'Whizzzz-sock!' and another Bruin tasted the snow."

Opposite: A most unusual sight, snow on the Royce quad, January 1932.

The 17.5 percent reduction expected in the University of California's appropriations for 1933 did not deter the Citizens University Council of Organizations—a group of UCLA alumni, faculty members and local civic leaders led by Regent Dickson and Frederick F. Houser, head of the southern alumni and soon to be first president of the UCLA Alumni Association—from rallying for graduate instruction. Dickson argued that the depressed economy was actually a compelling reason for the establishment of graduate work at UCLA. They began lobbying the Legislature and in 1933 a bill appropriating $120,000 was introduced.

The action infuriated the regents, who believed that it was inappropriate to begin new programs when they were embattled to cut existing ones and that the Legislature was meddling in academic policy. The regents adopted a resolution stating that the action placed the university in an "impossible position" and rejected the funds—Dickson was the lone dissenter.

After debate in the Legislature, the bill passed, but the amount was reduced to $75,000. The regents argued the action was a direct violation of their constitutional autonomy regarding academic affairs. But proponents of graduate study pleaded their case to reverse the regents' decision.

"Probably no more important meeting of the Board of Regents was ever held—certainly none characterized by more tension—than the one held in San Francisco on August 8, 1933," Dickson said decades later. During the executive session, Regent John Francis Neylan called the appropriation "pork" and went so far as to suggest that UCLA should not be a part of the university. Asked Neylan: "Why do we abdicate our power as the governing body of this institution?"

Sproul issued a report recommending graduate studies at UCLA, and Regent Garret W. McEnerney offered a resolution that graduate instruction at UCLA could be implemented "if, when and as the financial condition of the people and the

The Graduate

Three years after the master's degree was authorized at UCLA, there were almost 300 graduate students on campus. But few of them knew each other because there was scarce opportunity for interaction outside of their respective departments.

James Ellis "Jimmy" LuValle, a charismatic student pursuing his master's in chemistry and physics, decided to take up the issue with Graduate Division Dean Vern O. Knudsen, who readily agreed.

"We thought we ought to have an organization of the graduate students so they could meet each other and get together, because they certainly weren't mixing in with the undergraduates very well," recalled LuValle.

A few months later, in 1936, LuValle was selected as the first president of the Associated Graduate Students. Knudsen hosted the organization's inaugural activity: a reception for all graduate students at his home. During the subsequent decade the organization was run by the Graduate Guild primarily as a social club. In 1949, it was renamed the Graduate Students Association and became an official student government branch, holding elections for a graduate student body president. It was brought into the fold of the Associated Students as an equal partner with the undergraduate Student Legislative Council in 1956.

"It was just trying to be an association where the graduate students would have a voice in what went on about them, and have a means of being heard," LuValle said of the organization he helped found.

LuValle had earned his bachelor's degree in chemistry in 1936 with a straight-A average while competing as a star athlete and captain of UCLA's track team. Nicknamed the "Westwood Whirlwind" by the press, he was one of the fastest quarter-milers in the world and won the bronze medal at the 1936 Summer Olympics in Berlin.

Almost 50 years later, the Associated Students dedicated the northeast campus student center in LuValle's honor. Completed in 1985, the James E. LuValle Commons was created particularly to meet the needs of graduate students, selling textbooks and reference books for the business and law schools. The coffeehouse in the upstairs food area was named "Jimmy's" as a reflection of LuValle's friendly "just call me Jimmy" informality.

At the dedication ceremony, Mayor Tom Bradley said that LuValle had been a personal inspiration to him and had encouraged his attending UCLA instead of pursuing a job straight out of high school. "Jimmy LuValle made it possible for me to come here and that changed my life," said Bradley, who also had been a Bruin track star. "He was my idol and hero from my days at Poly (Francis Polytechnic) High School."

Before his death at the age of 80 in 1993, LuValle sometimes visited the commons and socialized with the students there.

Below: Sprinter Jimmy LuValle, 1936.

Bottom: The former graduate student body president at the dedication of LuValle Commons, 1985.

government of the State and the University will allow." This left the decision in Sproul's hands, who after consultation with Dickson and UCLA leaders decided to forge ahead. However, to avoid setting a precedent, Sproul declined to utilize the $75,000 appropriation, and it eventually reverted to the state treasury.

In 1933, after the protracted battle, graduate study was finally authorized for the Master of Arts. Approximately 170 students were admitted. Programs were offered in 16 fields, and 42 master's degrees were awarded the following June. Helen Cecilia Bender, whose name was listed first alphabetically, was the first to receive a graduate diploma.

That same year the Academic Senate, the mechanism for faculty governance, was reorganized into two separate sections: a northern section, which included Berkeley, the medical center in San Francisco, the Davis branch of the College of Agriculture and the Lick Observatory atop Mount Hamilton; and a southern section, which included UCLA, the Citrus Experiment Station in Riverside and the Scripps Institution of Oceanography in La Jolla. The change, intended to give the faculty a more direct role in determining the university's academic policies, provided greater decision-making authority to UCLA's faculty, which previously had only advisory powers through a standing committee of the senate.

The Academic Senate established the Graduate Council in 1934 under Dean Vern O. Knudsen, a member of the physics department since 1922. In 1936, the mandate was expanded to include the doctorate in the departments of English, history, mathematics and political science. That same year, Knudsen sponsored the creation of the Graduate Students Association to cultivate closer relationships between graduate

students and the faculty. James LuValle was elected its first president.

Two years later, on June 11, 1938, history student Kenneth P. Bailey walked down the aisle at the Hollywood Bowl becoming UCLA's first graduating doctorate and triple degree holder. It was a triumph for all UCLA alumni. A headline in the *Los Angeles Examiner* proclaimed: "Bruin, Brain, Brawn." Bailey's dissertation, *The Ohio Company of Virginia and the Westward Movement*, was honored by the Pacific Coast Branch of the American Historical Society. On June 3, 1942, Marion Lucy Queal was the first woman to receive a doctorate, the previous 40 recipients being men. Queal specialized in zoology and had also earned her bachelor's and master's at UCLA.

On August 12, 1938, the regents established the Graduate Division-Southern Section, with overall responsibility for graduate

Kenneth P. Bailey (below) was the recipient of UCLA's first doctoral degree (above right) in 1938. Four years later, Marion Lucy Queal (below center) was the first woman to earn a doctorate.

MARION LUCY QUEAL, PhD.

FIRST WOMAN

First woman to receive the Doctor of Philosophy degree at U.C.L.A. is Miss Marion Lucy Queal '31. Miss Queal is one of a total of 41, all others being men, who have gained this honor. She received her award along with fourteen others at U.C. L.A.'s 1942 Commencement, held June 3 in the Outdoor Theatre on the Westwood campus.

Dr. Queal specialized in zoology and gained her master's degree as well as her doctorate under the instruction of Dr. Albert W. Bellamy, chairman of the department of zoology. She received her B.A. at U.C.L.A. in 1931, was a teaching assistant on the campus in 1934, obtained her master's degree in 1935.

activities at Los Angeles, Riverside and La Jolla. The organizational structure mirrored that of the northern campuses. This satisfied the UCLA faculty— some members believing that Provost Moore, hailing from a normal school, was not equipped to handle graduate education. "Our committees up to this time had been selected entirely by Dr. Moore sitting alone in his office," recalled history Professor Waldemar Westergaard. "Some of us felt that the committees looked sometimes as though he had picked the names out of a hat." The faculty looked forward to working directly with the university president.

"The most important step in the development of the graduate work here on this campus was the decision on the part of the regents, carried out by President Sproul, of course, and probably even initiated by him, that the Graduate Division would report directly to the president, not to the provost of the campus," said Gustave O. Arlt, who succeeded Knudsen as dean of the Graduate Division-Southern Section in 1958. "That put us into a position of practical equality with the Berkeley campus."

EMERGENCE OF PROFESSIONAL SCHOOLS

The development of graduate studies at UCLA led the way for the creation of new colleges and professional schools. The first professional school was the College of Commerce, established in 1935 under the leadership of Dean Howard S. Noble. The school (which changed names multiple times over the years and was renamed again in 1987 in recognition of a $15 million gift by John E. Anderson) admitted its first students in fall 1936, offering training in four disciplines: accounting, finance, marketing and general business.

"There has been a growing demand for a College of Commerce on the part of students, as well as of the business interests in the area served by the university," Noble told the *Los Angeles Times* in November 1935. "Of the more than 1000 students enrolled in the department of economics in the current year, three-fourths are primarily interested in professional courses in commerce."

In 1938, UCLA established a branch of the College of Agriculture under Assistant Dean William H. Chandler, who transferred from Berkeley. Agriculture instruction and experiments had begun at UCLA in 1932 when sections were moved from Berkeley, as well as from the College of Agriculture in Davis and the Citrus Experiment Station in

Riverside. (In 1965, the program was phased out and activities transferred back to the Davis and Riverside campuses, which had more open space than UCLA could dedicate to agricultural purposes in a rapidly growing, and increasingly expensive, metropolitan area.)

In 1939, the School of Education, under Dean Darsie, replaced the Teachers College, which moved its teacher training program into the new College of Applied Arts (discontinued in 1960 and replaced with the College of Fine Arts). Applied Arts Dean Frederick W. Cozens—who was UCLA's first basketball coach and athletic director—found the name of the college a bit difficult to explain because of its unique blend of offerings: Bachelor of Arts degrees for those in art and music; Bachelor of Science degrees for majors in home economics, mechanic arts and physical education—which included dance. The college also offered courses in public nursing.

"In its new College of Applied Arts the University of California is embarking upon an experimental college in every sense of the word, because there is not another college in the United States of a similar nature," Cozens said during his Academic Homecoming lecture that year. "I am not prepared as yet to say exactly what *an applied* art is." But he added, "We have something which may be a very intriguing thing, not only for the faculty engaged in promoting the interests of this college, but for the students who are to be engaged in curricula."

"DECLARATION OF INDEPENDENCE"

During the struggle to establish graduate studies at UCLA, the alumni faced their own battle for independence.

Southern Branch alumni had first organized themselves in 1925 at the Vermont Avenue campus. Five students gathered in Millspaugh Hall: Associated Students President Fred Moyer Jordan; Jerold E. Weil and Leslie Cummins, former student body presidents; and Elder Morgan and Thelma Gibson, former vice presidents. "We'll all be graduating soon," Gibson said. "We need some kind of an organization to bind us together. Why don't we petition to become a branch of Berkeley's alumni association?"

The plan was welcomed and Berkeley alumni living in Southern California pledged $6,000 to finance a local branch for the next two years. Jordan was selected "Southern Representative" and the Southern Office of the California Alumni Association was formed in the cafeteria on July 1,

Frederick W. Cozens, dean of the College of Applied Arts, 1939–1942.

1925. That first year, 200 Southern Branch alumni joined the association.

By 1933, the organization had grown considerably, but did not have commensurate representation up north. The membership of the Alumni Council included 20 Berkeley graduates and only six from UCLA. In addition, the Southern Representative was appointed by Berkeley, which maintained authority over the budget. "The [Berkeley] Alumni Association, when preparing their annual reports, would charge expenses against the UCLA dues that we had no control over," said John B. Jackson, named executive secretary of the UCLA Alumni Association in 1939. "They'd hold a banquet for Berkeley alumni down in Los Angeles and charge part of that banquet cost to us."

While UCLA members received Berkeley's *California Monthly* and the *Southern Alumnus*, a local magazine insert,

Above: Fred Moyer Jordan, Thelma Gibson and Leslie Cummins, UCLA Alumni Association founders, 1926.

Right: John B. Jackson, Alumni Association executive secretary, 1939–1955.

editorial control was under the auspices of the Berkeley alumni group and the issue reached a climax over support for establishing graduate education at UCLA.

UCLA alumni had raised $600 for an advertisement to run in the *California Monthly* in support of graduate education. "But the [Berkeley] alumni council said, 'Absolutely not. There will never be graduate work at UCLA,'" Jackson said. "They wouldn't allow us even to spend that $600. We couldn't speak in our magazine about it, they ruled. So we were pretty bitter."

It became clear there was one option for the Southern alumni: secession. On August 24, 1933, the Southern Alumni Board passed two resolutions that became known as UCLA's "Declaration of Independence." After seven months of deliberations, the California Alumni Association voted to sever all ties with the Southern alumni and recognize UCLA's complete autonomy. The UCLA Alumni Association was incorporated on July 1, 1934.

In the April 1934 *Southern Alumnus*, the UCLA Alumni Association's new publication, the achievement was summarized by associate editor George Elmendorf: "Independent control of finances will mean that no one not connected with the Los Angeles institution will be able to dictate how dues paid by U.C.L.A. graduates shall be spent. If the Los Angeles alumni association wishes to further a project in the interest of U.C.L.A., the necessary expenditures may be made, without first asking the approval of the General Council."

Said Jackson: "The Cal people in the alumni setup just sat back and waited for UCLA to starve to death, because we had no money, and we were in a bad financial position." He added, "Sproul tried to get us back together, but we declared our independence and somehow managed to survive."

"ONE UNIVERSITY"

The lingering resentment from the struggle to establish graduate work, the secession of the UCLA Alumni Association and UCLA's first football win over Berkeley in 1936, led to an altogether too-familiar movement. Divisive sounds reverberated once again. This time, however, it was the Berkeley alumni who were vocal in advocating splitting the north and south campuses of the university.

"When it was a lower division branch of the University there was no conflict," wrote Al E. Marsella, president of the Berkeley alumni in Fresno to California Alumni Association Executive Manager Robert Sibley. "But now that it has become a big college of its own, it should stand on its own feet. Our great state university, at Berkeley, is losing its [identity]. The Los Angeles branch has stolen our name, colors, traditions and reputation, and now even has taken our president."

The *California Daily Bruin* responded by reprinting Sproul's earlier remarks to UCLA students: "May I count upon you to raise your eyes beyond the narrow boundaries of provincialism and support me in a program built not alone for Los Angeles but for California? If not, we shall all go down together, for the dark clouds of unregulated educational expansion, now gathering on the horizon, presage a storm that no single part of the University can hope alone to ride to permanent safety."

Sproul, who viewed himself as the embodiment of unity for the campuses, began working for harmony. The independence of the UCLA Alumni Association went against his vision for a solidified university, and he kept an active interest in the situation, carefully tracking his futile efforts to reunite the two associations in his "special problem" files.

The president took other measures to promote cohesiveness, particularly among the students. With them, he would be more successful. In 1936, he formed the California Club, or "Cal Club," an organization for students from all campuses to bond, learn about the university and foster friendship and cooperation—and a way for Sproul to keep tabs on the inner workings of student agendas.

In 1937, as the calls for a separate institution intensified, Sproul presented his proposal for the future of the University of California to the Board of Regents.

Sproul outlined three options. The first was "a single University of California with a centralized administration, such as we have this year for the first time, with one president and such vice-presidents as are necessary." The second was "a single University of California with a decentralized administration such as we have had in the past (actually, though not on paper) with one president and such vice-presidents as are needed." And the third was "separation of the University of California into two independent universities, one comprising the departments, colleges, schools, etc. in Berkeley, Davis, San Francisco, Fresno [Kearney Vineyard Ranch], and Mt. Hamilton, the other the similar activities in Los Angeles, Riverside, Pomona [W.K. Kellogg Institute of Animal Husbandry] and San Diego."

While the third option of separating the two campuses had made headlines, Sproul knew that the regents would not accept it. That left the first two. Sproul criticized decentralization as bureaucratic and expensive, adding that the president "would have little or no authority" and would "be so divorced from the actual work of the University that he would inevitably become a politician rather than an educator."

The regents approved Sproul's first choice in February 1937. While educators and politicians in the state were wary of his "one university" vision, fearing it meant that the University of California would try to usurp all higher education in the state, internally, it calmed the call for decentralization until the early 1940s.

"HOTBED OF COMMUNISM"

The Great Depression was a catalyst for the emergence of Communist groups on campus, a generational unrest reflected by college students worldwide. Following the Red Scare that ensued after World War I and leading up to the anti-war sentiments of what would become World War II, UCLA students began regular protests on and off campus. The groups proliferated to include those with Communist, Socialist and isolationist tendencies. While originally started by the more left-leaning students on campus, the protests ultimately drew in many students who would not otherwise have been politically active.

One particularly volatile issue was compulsory military training, which the University of California required of its male students, based on the Morrill Land Grant Act of 1862. UCLA had made the training mandatory for men since 1920 and, with war looming abroad, students were increasingly averse to the requirement. Two students, Albert Hamilton and W. Alonzo Reynolds, refused to participate in ROTC drills citing religious objections, and were suspended by Moore. The students took their cause all the way to the U.S. Supreme Court, which on December 3, 1934, ruled unanimously in favor of the regents. (The issue of compulsory military training would remain an active student cause until 1962, when the Board of Regents rescinded the requirement.)

The public feared campus activism and the students' disdain for university protocol irritated the administration. Moore, described by *Time* as having "hypersensitivity against Red," led a personal campaign, spending great efforts soliciting universities, civic groups and government organizations for

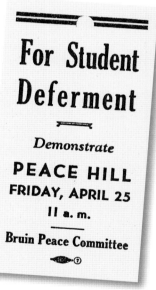

Top: Anti-war sentiments on the pages of the *California Daily Bruin*, April 21, 1937.

Above: Before World War II, the campus was awash with student activist groups that promoted an isolationist agenda.

Communist propaganda and anti-Communist literature—at times requesting several hundred copies of each document—amassing a sizable collection of such paraphernalia.

With his office in the Library overlooking Royce quad, Moore often overheard students talking outside. One day, a student mentioned the name Karl Marx and Moore dashed out of the building demanding: "Did I hear someone mention Karl Marx?" When the student admitted to it, Moore waved his arms shouting, "Disperse! Disperse!" It got to the point where Moore had a tendency to see Communists everywhere. Professor Westergaard later called it a "Communist psychosis."

The Social Problems Club, formed at UCLA in 1932 as a branch of the Berkeley organization of the same name, focused on poverty, job creation and housing—all conditions stemming from the Depression. With the escalating anti-war sentiments, groups such as the leftist National Student League changed the dynamics by pushing more militant and radical activism. To counter those efforts, about 150 students—primarily athletes and fraternity members—gathered by torchlight in the night rain to form the UCLA Americans, a vigilante faction that suggested it had Moore's support and pledged to rid the campus of radicals "by force if necessary." Such actions had the further effect of attracting the unwanted attention of outside organizations. The Ku Klux Klan burned 10-foot crosses on campus—at the top of Janss Steps, behind the library, and near Hilgard Avenue—"where they would be visible for miles," according to the *Los Angeles Times*, while "eerie figures swarmed about distributing dodgers which read: Communism will not be tolerated."

The University of California administration, not wanting to deal with such external influences, cited state proscription against partisan political activity and developed rules on the use of campus facilities, the beginnings of what would later become Regulation 17. Under this protocol, Moore enforced bans on political activity and related protests. So students began gathering across the Arroyo Bridge off campus in an area called "Peace Hill." There they held regular "peace strikes" and other rallies. (A greater percentage of UCLA students participated in the decade's activism than at any other time in history, including the 1970s.)

Right: Waldemar Westergaard, history professor, 1925–1949.

Below: The political fervor on campus during the mid-1930s drew unwanted outsiders.

Below right: A "peace strike" in 1940 on Peace Hill, located off campus just across the Arroyo Bridge.

Ku Klux Klan Rides on U.C.L.A. Campus

This fiery cross at the entrance to the grounds of the University of California at Los Angeles is one of three that blazed last night as a warning against Communistic activities and the threat of an anti-war strike on the campus. Leaflets distributed about the campus read, "Communism will not be tolerated—the Ku Klux Klan rides again."

FIERY CROSSES AT U.C.L.A. BLAZE WARNING TO REDS

(Continued from First Page) have something more important to think about than attending classes," was the way Miss Strack summed up the proposed walkout last night. And so intense is the feeling between Miss Strack's "anti-war" followers and other student leaders

hour mimeographed appeal for support yesterday indicated that the walkout will be felt outside Westwood.

"Many schools in California will either strike or in some way support the strike," was the assurance given in the handbill.

In October 1934, students requested permission to hold a forum regarding the upcoming gubernatorial election—long-time Socialist and novelist Upton Sinclair, who had called the University of California the "University of the Black Hand," was running on the Democratic ticket against Republican Frank Merriam. Student Celeste Strack filed for permission on behalf of the National Student League, but when Moore denied her request, she approached student body President John M. Burnside. Hearing of the plans, Moore prohibited Burnside to proceed.

However, Burnside opted to meet with Strack, and subsequently, on October 29, Moore suspended four student leaders, including Burnside, for "using their offices to assist the revolutionary activities of the National Student League, a Communist organization which has bedeviled the University for some months." The three others were: Tom Lambert,

Mendel Lieberman and Sidney Zsagri—all on student council. Strack, a member of the National Student League and admitted Communist, was also dismissed.

The campus became overrun with demonstrations. Fraternities and sororities lent their support to Moore by issuing a signed statement giving "100 per cent in any action taken in their drive to oust the radical element."

Petitioners show support for Provost Ernest Carroll Moore's stance against communists, 1934.

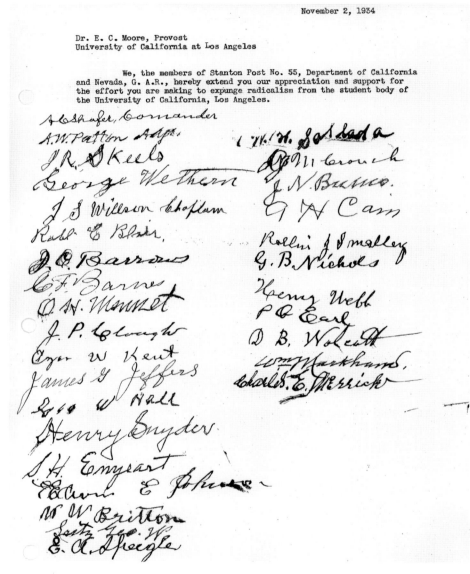

UPTON SINCLAIR
is no friend of the
UNIVERSITY OF CALIFORNIA

THE HARM that would come to the State University if Upton Sinclair were governor of California, can well be visualized from a reading of these excerpts from some of Mr. Sinclair's voluminous writings:

"The city, both the rich part and the poor, is completely dominated by a medieval fortress on the hill which I have called the University of the Black Hand and which is known officially as the University of California."

"Becoming aware of the Black Hand and its power in the institution, independent-minded men seek other occupations; the sycophants and sluggards remain, and as a result the quality of teaching goes down."

"Immorality is more common than scholarship; and conditions have become a scandal throughout the state . . . ."

This is the man who wants to be elected governor of the State of California, entitling him to sit as chairman of the Board of Regents of the State University.

Vote for Merriam
FOR GOVERNOR
at the November election

[This advertisement written by and paid for by a non-partisan group of Bruin alumni, who neither agree with Mr. Sinclair's description of our Alma Mater, nor do they agree with a lot of other things that this Democrat-Socialist-Communist advocates.]

Left: Five students, accused of subversive behavior after holding a forum to debate Socialist Upton Sinclair's bid for governor, were suspended in October 1934: (from left) John M. Burnside, Celeste Strack, Sidney Zsagri, Tom Lambert and Mendel Lieberman.

UCLA to investigate and reduce tensions. "I disapprove of Communists who use violence and I disapprove of vigilantes who use violence," Sproul declared. "They are both nuisances, and one breeds the other."

In an address earlier that year, Sproul explained his attitude toward the subject: "The University must tell its students about communism, socialism, bimetallism, even nudism, in order that they may balance different systems, one against the other, and determine where each has its elements of strength and weakness. This does not mean that the University in the slightest degree, teaches or espouses radical doctrines."

Both university counsel and independent attorney Henry W. O'Melveny each rendered opinions that the students were inappropriately suspended. All but Strack were reinstated on November 13, receiving a reprimand for insubordination, but otherwise exonerated of any charges of subversive activities. Strack remained dismissed pending further investigation, but was reinstated on December 10.

Sproul was hailed by moderates and liberals for his handling of the matter. The *Los Angeles Evening Post* said it was good fortune that the university president "happens to be a man who refuses to believe that anyone with an independent idea is a Communist." Moore, in turn, was praised by conservatives for his efforts against the alleged intrusion of communism.

But the regents and university administrators were displeased with Moore, some of it playing out in the press with reports of a faculty petition seeking his ouster. During a private meeting, Sproul asked UCLA professors what should be done. Westergaard suggested that Moore should not be fired, but instead removed to a teaching post and that a search for a new provost should commence straightaway.

Sproul wrote Moore alerting the provost that he was approaching the university's administrative officer mandatory retirement age of 65, and inquired as to his intentions. Moore responded that he wanted to continue serving as provost and submitted a letter to that effect. But the regents, who viewed Moore as a problem, voted to enforce the mandatory retirement, and Sproul declined to make an exception. Sproul requested a letter of resignation from Moore, who would return to teaching as a professor in philosophy and education until his academic retirement in 1941.

"It is 19 years since I began to build the university," Moore wrote in his diary on March 25, 1936. "It is built now and I can do no more for it."

Above: Hundreds of students on Royce quad protest the suspensions of five undergraduates, dismissed for alleged radical activity, November 1934.

Right: UCLA was tagged the "Little Red Schoolhouse" based on Provost Ernest Carroll Moore's remarks to the press that UCLA was one of the "worst hot beds of campus Communism in America."

Below right: A *California Daily Bruin* editorial cartoon shows appreciation for Berkeley students' solidarity with their UCLA brethren against accusations of improper political activities.

On the following day, an estimated 2,000 students held a rally to protest the suspensions. It got out of hand after Moore summoned police to break up the gathering. Injuries were reported and the incident attracted national media attention. Commenting on the protest, Moore called UCLA one of the "worst hot beds of campus Communism in America," a quote picked up by William Randolph Hearst's International News Service, and soon that phrase and "little red schoolhouse" were commonly used to refer to UCLA.

The affair became an embarrassment for the university. In November, more than 2,000 students at Berkeley protested the dismissals in a class walkout that resulted in egg and tomato throwing. Later that month, Sproul arrived at

CAL. U. CALLED 'RED' HOTBED

LOS ANGELES, Oct. 31.—(By International News Service.)—In the wake of rioting by students over suspension of five asserted radicals, the student body of the University of California today was termed one of the "worst hot beds of campus Communism in America," by Provost E. C. Moore.

Mr. Moore declared that the suspension order would stand until the student body "Purges itself of radical tendencies."

Rioting started after huge signs had been chalked on classroom blackboards calling a demonstration. Co-eds mixed freely in the rioting.

There were no serious injuries, although many students w   'earing black eyes and bruised   ıres to-day.

ALL PALS TOGETHER

"We are at War"
1936–1945

Above: Trainees in V-12 Navy College Training Program on their way to muster.

Opposite: Kerckhoff Hall was converted into a "mess" hall for Navy men, 1943.

As the 1930s drew to a close, national isolationist sentiment reached its pinnacle. With the Nazis advancing through Europe, President Franklin D. Roosevelt in 1940 implemented the first peacetime draft in American history, requiring men aged 21 through 30 to register for selective service. At UCLA, anti-war protests persisted and the students' collective voice grew stronger with shouts of "The Yanks are not coming!" and "Joe Bruin votes for a warless world."

After Japan's surprise attack on the U.S. Naval Base at Pearl Harbor in Hawaii on December 7, 1941, attitudes abruptly changed. Demonstrations at UCLA evaporated and Americans united behind the war mobilization.

The University of California, led by President Robert Gordon Sproul, had embraced defense efforts well before the United States officially entered the war. In March 1939, the U.S. War Department selected UCLA as the only experimental site for military acoustics education. Field artillery officers were sent to the campus for graduate study in military sound ranging, a method for pinpointing enemy gunfire, under renowned acoustics physicist Vern O. Knudsen. The Los Angeles division of University Extension began training air pilots in October 1939 under a program funded by the Civil Aeronautics Authority. In 1940, UCLA's fledgling meteorology department prepared students for jobs with the U.S. Army, U.S. Navy and the U.S. Weather Bureau.

In January 1941, Sproul formed the University Defense Council, which was transformed into the University War Council after war was declared. Among its recommendations, the War Council proposed a trimester system to move students more rapidly through the academic

machine. The Associated Students created its counterpart Student Defense Committee—later the Student War Board—to organize student activity.

Sproul, who had assumed control of UCLA after chief executive Ernest Carroll Moore retired, named UCLA mathematics Chairman Earle R. Hedrick as the campus's new provost in 1937. Hedrick was well respected in his field, but a relative unknown among non-mathematics scholars. Sproul kept a tight rein, and he—not Hedrick—lived in the University Residence. Hedrick, who complained that he was not given enough authority, was in turn criticized by the faculty for not showing enough independence from Sproul. Hedrick served five years before reaching mandatory retirement age in 1942, and an eager Sproul would not fill the position, opting to keep watch himself over UCLA until the war's end.

Enrollment at UCLA, which had hit a record 10,000 in 1940–41, dropped 10 percent in the semester immediately after Pearl Harbor as men left to join Uncle Sam. It would not bottom out until three years later, when civilian registrations fell to 4,400. With the university's approval, faculty members took leaves of absence to assist in the war effort, particularly in positions at federal research agencies.

The university itself would be tooled into the war apparatus of the United States. "War instead of peace must be the immediate goal of university training," Sproul said in February 1942. UCLA welcomed military stations and offered training for Navy and Army men and for civilians alike. In 1943, the College of Engineering was established to focus on aeronautics, in a city that had emerged as the capital of the aircraft industry.

Outwardly, UCLA was awash with military personnel in their navy, khaki and olive drab garb. Lingo such as "Gayley Gulch" and "Kerckhoff Mess" entered the campus vernacular. An Air Corps plane, for instructional purposes, was stationed on the athletic field, where ROTC cadets trained with their semiautomatic rifles— until federal demand required them for the armed forces, and wooden guns were substituted.

Covertly, the best scientific minds at the University of California were developing the world's first atomic bomb through the ultra-secret Manhattan Project. UCLA, with oversight from Robert M. Underhill, secretary and treasurer of the Board of Regents, was responsible for all purchasing and accounting for the project—although at the time, employees had no idea that they were aiding in the mission which would bring a swift, yet cataclysmic, conclusion to the war.

In 1944, UCLA celebrated a muted 25th anniversary of its founding, as war permeated every aspect of campus life. Little more than a year later, peace was heralded, and the university that early on had embraced defense efforts—and corresponding corporate and government partnerships—would be permanently altered into a research university, poised to flourish from the Atomic Age.

Top: From left, Ernest Carroll Moore, President Robert Gordon Sproul and Earle R. Hedrick, at Hedrick's investiture as provost, 1937.

Above: An ROTC cadet learns to operate a machine gun.

CALIFORNIA DAILY BRUIN
UNIVERSITY OF CALIFORNIA AT LOS ANGELES

JAPAN DECLARES WAR!

Sea Bases Bombed

Nation Hears Damage Toll

Nipponese Betray Peace Terms, Launch Attacks

Above: On December 8, 1941, the *California Daily Bruin* reports on the bombing of Pearl Harbor.

Below: A *Daily Bruin* editorial cartoon captures the end of normalcy and the advent of World War II.

Below right: Junior Peggy McQuilkin examines UCLA's air raid siren, which could be heard from as far away as the San Fernando Valley, 1942.

DAY OF INFAMY

On December 6, 1941, UCLA and USC played to a 7–7 tie in front of a raucous Coliseum crowd of 65,000. It wasn't a win against the crosstown gridiron rival (the Bruins had yet to achieve that), but it wasn't defeat either—spirits were high and uclans celebrated into the evening.

The next day thoughts of football were overshadowed as announcers broke into radio broadcasts with the news that Japan had attacked Pearl Harbor, killing 2,400 servicemen. The United States became embroiled in World War II and the years of Joe College were over. The anti-war tenor across the

United States and at UCLA dissipated. Bruins who played in the game on Saturday enlisted in the military on Monday.

Californians were panicked that a similar assault could reach their shores. Attacks by Japanese submarines on merchant ships off California only intensified these fears. Martial law was ordered on Terminal Island in the Los Angeles Harbor, one of the busiest ports in the nation. "The entire Los Angeles area which surrounds U.C.L.A. is a military objective of the first order," wrote the *California Daily Bruin*. "Located within the region are airplane factories, landing fields, docks, oil fields, refineries, and military and naval bases."

Blackouts were implemented and citizens were instructed to prepare for air raids. At UCLA, windows and skylights were painted black or boarded up. In case of an air raid, a series of signals would instruct those on campus through the classroom network: three 20-second buzzes, with a 10-second interval between them to announce the raid and a long one-minute buzzer that would indicate the "all-clear." Students were advised to go to identified floors of buildings including the Administration Building, the Library, the gyms, and the Kerckhoff Hall coffee shop and foyer. By February 1942, an air raid siren synched to a central control system in downtown Los Angeles was installed atop the Physics-Biology Building. Its shrill scream could be heard for up to 10 miles.

On December 8, 1941, students crowded into Royce Hall to hear the broadcast of President Roosevelt's "Day of Infamy" address to Congress requesting a declaration of war against Japan. The commander in chief's message was met

EVEN AS WE CHEERED, IT CAME

by Lester Buhai

with sober approval—applause was waived and tears were shed. Some Bruins had loved ones in the Pacific and were waiting for word. Classes were dismissed and the library was deserted, as students huddled over radios across campus for the latest updates.

The *California Daily Bruin* announced that it would hold its pages open for news flashes until 3 a.m. and would not devote as much attention to campus events in order to cover war-related reports. The paper fulfilled its duty, continuing to publish five days a week until July 1943, when staffing and budget shortfalls prompted a temporary reduction to three days and the consequent drop of "Daily" from its masthead. A poem by student Rosalee Tabor published in the paper in December 1941 captured perplexity as to the students' role on campus:

"We are at War"
And the phrase sounds deranged;
And our smug world seems changed;
And we don't give a damn
About an exam …
We're just wondering.

Provost Hedrick issued a statement to students and faculty advising them that the campus had been officially placed on a wartime basis. "The present emergency is novel and adjustment to it is not easy," Hedrick said. "Realization of war and the responsibilities that accompany it may not be immediate in all cases. Obedience to police and military instructions should be instantaneous and sincere." He further stated that Deming G. Maclise, University of California assistant comptroller and UCLA business manager, was put in charge of the campus's defense efforts. "Any order from his office should be obeyed at once," Hedrick instructed.

On the evening of December 10, 1941, Southern California was darkened for three hours and UCLA experienced its first blackout, catching those on campus off-guard despite earlier warnings. Bruins who had gathered to watch the Alumni Grid Show in Royce Hall emerged unknowingly onto the unlit campus, finding their way cautiously as searchlights swept the sky and distant anti-aircraft guns fired into the night. The Student Musicale in Kerckhoff Hall ended suddenly as lights were turned off and students exited "to look for enemy planes."

The Student Executive Council was in session at the nearby home of Dean of Undergraduates Earl J. Miller when the lights went out. "We went up to our upstairs windows," Miller said, "and there was quite a fireworks display of powerful flashlights lighting up the skies and anti-aircraft guns firing their rockets high into the air. It was really a most unusual sight."

Above: Deming G. Maclise, assistant comptroller and business manager, 1931–1942.

Left: Earl J. Miller, dean of men, 1925–1937, and dean of undergraduates 1937–1947.

Below: Volunteering for the American Red Cross, students sew a quilt for servicemen, 1944.

Continuing the meeting by candlelight, student body President Robert E. Alshuler and the council created the Student Defense Committee (later renamed Student War Board) to work as a unit of the Los Angeles Civilian Defense Council, coordinating student activities as part of the citizenry's national defense movement. Areas under its jurisdiction: an information bureau, air raid wardens, Red Cross and first aid assistance, auxiliary fire force, morale maintenance, a secretarial and clerical group, and a community service unit. The committee enlisted more than 5,500 student volunteers within weeks and it was not long before the majority of the work done by the Associated Students focused on assisting with the war.

Over the next several days, campus activities were rescheduled, modified or postponed indefinitely. The "Big C"

—a 40-by-100 foot cement letter painted blue with gold trim, prominent on the western hillside overlooking campus since 1939—was deemed an aerial landmark by the military science department and was dutifully buried with eight inches of soil in the interest of defense. In 1943, restrictions on the "Big C" were lifted, and the symbol was uncovered and freshly painted in time for homecoming. (The "Big C" would disappear again in 1958 to make way for Sproul Hall and "Big C Junior" was created on the hills below the dormitory. There it remained until razed permanently for the construction of the track stadium in 1967—and few clamored for a new one, since the "C" for California was by then considered passé.)

Right: In 1943, restrictions on the "Big C," which had been buried as a precaution since the start of the war, were lifted.

Far right: Pushing a Model T Ford to promote U.S. Treasury "T-Bills" during wartime homecoming.

UNIVERSITY WAR COUNCIL

For students returning from Christmas break in January 1942 the strangeness of war had begun to wear off, and they found themselves on an altered campus. Another Selective Service draft was called and more than 1,000 Bruin men aged 20 to 21 registered, along with an unknown number of faculty and staff members. They were among 2 million called nationwide. More conscription would follow.

Decisions were made to resume both the daytime and evening social functions of campus organizations to maintain "normalcy in as many phases of life as possible." But there was no escaping change as the university fully embraced the war effort. "A new University greeted students this morning," wrote the *California Daily Bruin* in January 1942. "It was a University stepping into high gear, ready to go all-out for war."

In late December 1941, President Sproul had convened his University War Council, consisting of 80 faculty members and administrators from the University of California, to survey its resources and revamp to meet defense needs. Sproul acted as chairman and Underhill as executive vice chairman. UCLA Business Manager Maclise; Frederick W. Cozens, dean of the College of Applied Arts; and G.E.F. Sherwood, mathematics professor and chair of the Academic Senate's Committee on Courses, formed the UCLA executive committee.

In March 1942, the Board of Regents approved the War Council's proposal to speed up the educational program by instituting a three-year curriculum, with three 16-week semesters per year instead of the usual two. Limits on class load were lifted. The changes were intended to enable most men to graduate before they reached draft age. Teaching staffs were placed on a six-day workweek and retired faculty members were recalled.

Students began graduating at record pace. The changes eliminated non-essential courses and instituted ones related to wartime activities. Added emphasis was placed on physical education and students were required to take at least one national service course. UCLA's departments of chemistry, history, mathematics, military science and physics added curricula, and new courses in conversational Japanese and celestial navigation were offered.

Students adapted to the hastened wartime rhythm of the swifter and more concentrated course, and in the process abandoned notions of "leisurely" study and discovery that were once taken for granted. Meanwhile, some academics pondered, while others defended, the future of liberal education.

"With all the changes introduced by the accelerated program, the new University is clearly also the old University," Sproul wrote in a column published in UCLA's *Alumni Monthly*. "Wartime tasks are performed at the expense of some of the enjoyments of yesterday, and also at the expense of some of the opportunities for explorations of new and strange fields, of no seeming immediate, practical importance, which have made California in the past such a varied, free, and democratic society of students, young and old. But the kernel of our University and of the high educational quality which has made its world-wide reputation will not be changed."

EXECUTIVE ORDER 9066

Within days of the attack at Pearl Harbor, amid the backdrop of FBI raids on Little Tokyo and the rounding up of Japanese fishermen on Terminal Island, a hub of numerous defense industries, the *California Daily Bruin* ran an editorial that cautioned students to "prepare ourselves to do battle with the rising tide of hatred."

"Intense, irrational feelings, emotions, hatreds, raging dislikes and tempers are all products of war eras— this one is no exception," *The Bruin* wrote. "Although *business as usual* is over, *feelings as usual* toward Americans of Japanese and German and Italian descent, must be maintained—this is the only democratic way of life, the way of life we now defend."

Many faculty members decried prejudice against those of Japanese heritage; and UCLA's Japanese-American students issued a loyalty statement in support of America's war effort.

"There are approximately 200 Americans of Japanese parentage on the U.C.L.A. campus," according to the statement. "None of us have known loyalty to any country other than America. We stand ready with all other Americans to act in whatever capacity we may be called upon to perform in order to carry out the resolution of our government." The declaration was signed by K. Kenneth Nakaoka, president of the Japanese Students Club; Toshi Ihara, president of the Japanese Bruin Club men's organization; Aki Hirashiki, president of Chi Alpha Delta sorority; and Lynn Takagaki, president of the UCLA Japanese Business Club.

"Since the Pearl Harbor incident, life as American citizens has been difficult for us," wrote student Jimmie Arima in a personal column to the *California Daily Bruin*. "We've willingly given up our radios and cameras. We've restricted our actions to the very necessities of getting along, in order to avoid unnecessary incidents which might affect public opinion against us Japanese-Americans as a whole." Arima noted that his concerns of being met with bigotry at UCLA, however, were not realized. "I haven't been more thankful for anything in all my life," Arima said. "And I know I voice the opinion of all the other Japanese students on campus when I say, 'Thanks and thanks again,' because I know all of them have met with the same wonderful treatment."

Still, some students stayed away out of fear and went home to their families immediately after December 7. Others

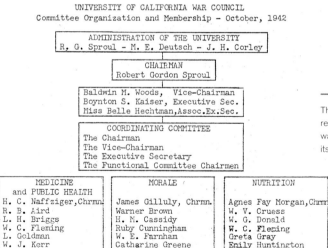

UNIVERSITY OF CALIFORNIA WAR COUNCIL
Committee Organization and Membership – October, 1942

ADMINISTRATION OF THE UNIVERSITY
R. G. Sproul – M. E. Deutsch – J. H. Corley

CHAIRMAN
Robert Gordon Sproul

Baldwin M. Woods, Vice-Chairman
Boynton S. Kaiser, Executive Sec.
Miss Belle Hechtman, Assoc. Ex. Sec.

COORDINATING COMMITTEE
The Chairman
The Vice-Chairman
The Executive Secretary
The Functional Committee Chairmen

The University of California reorganized itself to carry out wartime missives along with its academic mission.

AGRICULTURAL RESOURCES and PRODUCTION	MEDICINE and PUBLIC HEALTH	MORALE	NUTRITION	ADMINISTRATIVE ARRANGE-MENTS COMMITTEE
C. B. Hutchison, Chrmn.	H. C. Naffziger, Chrmn.	James Gilluly, Chrmn.	Agnes Fay Morgan, Chrmn.	H. M. Showman, Chrmn.
R. L. Adams	R. B. Aird	Warner Brown	W. V. Cruess	F. S. Durie
W. H. Chandler	L. H. Briggs	H. M. Cassidy	W. G. Donald	E. A. Hugill
B. H. Crocheron	W. C. Fleming	Ruby Cunningham	W. C. Fleming	G. D. Louderbach
G. H. Hart	L. Goldman	W. E. Farnham	Greta Gray	D. G. Maclise
B. A. Madson	W. J. Kerr	Catharine Greene	Emily Huntington	W. J. Norton
K. A. Ryerson	K. F. Meyer	E. H. Hughes	Max Kleiber	A. R. Robb
Harry S. Smith	J. F. Rinehart	E. L. Lazier	Marguerite G. Mallon	I. F. Smith
H. R. Wellman	C. L. A. Schmidt	G. E. F. Sherwood	H. C. Moffitt	J. H. Williams

SCIENTIFIC RESEARCH	SOCIAL SCIENCES	TECHNICAL TRAINING	WOMEN'S ACTIVITIES	INFORMATION
A. R. Olson, Chrmn.	G. S. Watkins, Chrmn.	E. A. Lee, Chrmn.	Alice G. Hoyt, Chrmn.	G. A. Pettitt, Chrmn.
B. M. Allen	D. K. Bjork	F. W. Cozens	Margaret Beattie	R. W. Desmond
A. W. Bellamy	Leonard Bloom	B. E. Mallary	Elinor Lee Beebe	Harold Ellis
Lee Bonar	H. S. Ellis	H. S. Noble	Helen Christianson	J. E. Jackson
L. F. Fuller	F. N. Freeman	M. P. O'Brien	Jessie Coles	E. J. Miller
J. H. Hildebrand	E. T. Grether	H. A. Spindt	Mildred Foreman	B. B. Rakestraw
Joseph Kaplan	R. J. Kerner	L. C. Uren	Maria de Lowther	Robert Sibley
E. O. Lawrence	H. L. Leupp	H. B. Walker	Emily Palmer	Ann Sumner
C. D. Shane	C. B. Lipman	T. A. Watson	Gladys T. Stevenson	J. E. Tippett

ADDRESS ALL COMMUNICATIONS TO:
President Robert G. Sproul, at Berkeley or Los Angles
IN AN EMERGENCY, telephone the Executive Secretary, or the Associate Executive Secretary

Earle Raymond Hedrick

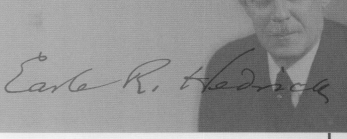

Above: Earl R. Hedrick, the father of nine children, became the leader of 7,000, 1937.

Right: After leading the campus for five years, Hedrick retired back to mathematics, 1942.

Earle R. Hedrick—renowned mathematician and UCLA's second chief executive—was born on September 27, 1876, in Union City, Indiana. By age 17, he had received a Bachelor of Arts from the University of Michigan, where he was known for having a keen mind that could grasp complex concepts almost instantly.

He then earned a master's at Harvard University, where he was awarded a fellowship to study at the University of Göttingen, Germany—a citadel of mathematics—receiving his doctoral degree at the age of 25. Hedrick did postdoctoral work and lectured at the École Normale Supérieure in Paris. From 1901–03, he taught at Yale University's Sheffield Scientific School, followed by 21 years as professor of mathematics at the University of Missouri. He joined the UCLA faculty in 1924, where under his leadership as chairman for 13 years, the mathematics department flourished. Hedrick was the first president of the Mathematical Association of America and was editor of the *American Mathematical Monthly* for 21 years. He wrote and edited many articles and textbooks on mathematics, which he called the "queen of the sciences." He spoke seven languages and could read in five more.

An inspiring lecturer who held students in rapt attention, Hedrick was known for his sharp wit and for solving problems with a characteristic chuckle. Once, in the middle of a particularly obscure presentation, Hedrick backed away from the blackboard toward the door which, left slightly ajar, flew open as he leaned on it. "Professor Hedrick stumbled clear across the hall, his lighted cigarette described a beautiful arc of a parabola as it flew from his hand but the good professor stayed on his feet," recalled 1929 alumnus A.L. Buckman. "He swept up the still lit cigarette, puffed heavily on a new one which he lighted from the first and asked, 'Would a volunteer please come to the board and write the general equation for the trajectory of my cigarette.'" Buckman added: "Only then did the class crack up."

In 1937, the Board of Regents named Hedrick to UCLA's top job. He assumed the post 10 days later at the Charter Day dinner, where he forecast war and suggested that, "America will be responsible for the educational and cultural work of the future, due to the break-down of Europe."

Hedrick and his wife, Helen, had nine children—four of whom graduated from UCLA—and they also raised a granddaughter after her mother's death. But the family did not reside in the University Residence, as University of California President Robert Gordon Sproul determined that he would continue to live there when business called him to Los Angeles. So the Hedricks lived in Westwood instead.

Hedrick retired in 1942 after leading UCLA for five years. He accepted a professorship at Brown University in Rhode Island, where he died one year later on February 3, 1943, at the age of 66. UCLA's fourth high-rise residence hall, completed in 1964, was named in his honor.

"Through his research, editorial work, and regular attendance at scientific meetings, he did much to focus attention on the Los Angeles campus as a growing center of research," wrote professors William M. Whyburn, Bennet M. Allen and Waldemar Westergaard, in a tribute on behalf of the Academic Senate. "The University of California lost a man of brilliant intellect, singular courage, and exceptional clear-sightedness."

Japanese Internees

In spring 1942, under Executive Order 9066, approximately 200 Japanese-American students at UCLA were forced to cut their education short and were sent to internment camps.

Below: Meriko Hoshiyama (in white sweater) was one of very few internees who returned to UCLA to complete their degree, after having spent much of the war in an internment camp.

Right: Hitoshi "Moe" Yonemura, an ROTC cadet, was sent to an internment camp in Wyoming before transferring to the 442nd Regimental Army, a highly decorated combat unit made up of Japanese-Americans, which suffered a 93 percent casualty rate. Yonemura wrote his friends often, reminiscing of days at UCLA. He was killed in Italy just before war's end.

Above: Iva G. Toguri, who graduated in 1941 with a degree in zoology, was stranded in Japan at the outbreak of World War II. Refusing to give up her American citizenship, the Japanese forced her to deliver anti-American radio broadcasts, and she became dubbed a so-called Tokyo Rose. "You forgot what they learned you at U.C.L.A.," blasted a popular postwar song. Convicted of treason in 1949, she was pardoned in 1977 by President Gerald Ford.

Left: In July 2009, the Board of Regents voted to waive their moratorium on honorary degrees, and in May 2010, 48 former UCLA students, or their family representative, were honored in a special commencement ceremony.

Edict Bans Japanese
from Westwood

Bruin Nisei
Exit Ruled

DeWitt Orders
Evacuation by
End of Month

The civilian evacuation program was brought home to U.C.L.A. students yesterday when an order of the Western Defense command posted in Westwood Village, all persons of Japanese ancestry in this area were ordered to remain in their present residences preparatory to being evacuated by the Army by noon next Wednesday, April 29.

The term of Civilian Exclusion Order No. 19, will affect many of the remaining Nisei students in school. Posters cave been placed in places throughout the Village as part of the program which under the leadership of General John L. DeWitt, is expected to affect 11,500 Japanese within the next few weeks.

GRADUATING SENIORS

Some graduating seniors of Japanese ancestry will be unable to complete their education by this June because of the orders, it was learned. The evacuation deadline will stop those Japanese who are English majors from taking the comprehensive examination next Wednesday and Thursday.

Special permits in unusual cases may be issued to a few Japanese living in this area to change residence, Army sources said. However, only in cases such as separation of families will exceptions be made.

ALIEN BOARDS

Boards have been set up to help the alien evacuees gain information and straighten out their affairs...

OFFICIAL NOTICE—Two Bruin students eye closely new government orders, posted yesterday in Westwood Village, banning aliens and Nisei from the local areas.

Popular yell king Hitoshi "Moe" Yonemura (top) was one of almost 200 Nisei students at UCLA who were ordered to internment camps in spring 1942, as the Pacific Coast was designated a military zone.

necessity." Ultimately, the government forced the mandatory internment of 120,000 individuals of Japanese ancestry on the West Coast and Arizona to 10 camps scattered in seven states, including two in California: Manzanar War Relocation Center in the Owens Valley and Tule Lake War Relocation Center in Northern California. The camps were under sentry watch and behind barbed wire. The majority sent to the internment camps were Nisei, second-generation Japanese Americans—although some individuals of Italian and German descent were also relocated.

On March 27, Japanese-Americans were placed under curfew, and prohibited from traveling more than five miles from their homes, except for employment or settling affairs through the Wartime Civil Control Administration. The five-mile limit was later lifted for students in a ruling by the U.S. Attorney General's office interpreting college as a place of "employment." But by April 1, 75 percent of the affected students had already withdrawn from UCLA, according to Registrar Harry M. Showman.

On April 22, fliers detailing "Instructions to All Persons of Japanese Ancestry," including reporting procedures and deadlines, were posted on utility poles and other public areas throughout Westwood. Individuals were ordered to report by the end of the month for evacuation.

Students who withdrew before midterms were refunded their $29 semester fee, and full or partial academic credit for the semester was granted to those who completed midterms. "All students who leave the University under government order, whether to join the armed forces or to comply with the enemy alien proclamation, will be treated alike," Hedrick said.

Dean of Undergraduates Miller and Dean of Women Helen Matthewson Laughlin counseled the students, while Sproul and Hedrick attempted to ease their transition to other institutions. Hedrick, as chairman of the Western College Association, assembled a Committee on Aliens. Its purpose was to find out which colleges and universities might accept transferred students, and whether individual institutions might ask for exceptions to the rules in regard to Nisei who were graduating in the current semester.

Hitoshi "Moe" Yonemura, an ROTC cadet and popular UCLA yell king who had led the crowd at the December 6, 1941, football game against the Trojans, was able to transfer from the Heart Mountain War Relocation Center in Wyoming to the 442nd Regimental Army combat unit. "Surprise! I am sitting here writing to you and hoping that this letter reaches you, as you probably noticed I have finally made the team and I am in my Uncle Sammy's service, thank God," Yonemura wrote to friend and fellow UCLA classmate Betty Jane Lissner.

returned to campus that week but decided not to come back following winter break. "I really don't know what made us quit," recalled Toshiko Nakamura Wilkerson decades later. Explained Meriko Hoshiyama Mori: "You felt like you were the only Japanese walking around." Added Naoyuki Takasugi: "To the general population we weren't considered Americans, but Japanese. We felt rather segregated."

Those who decided to stay at UCLA would soon find themselves being forced to leave. Amid the hysteria, on February 19, 1942, President Roosevelt issued Executive Order 9066, which authorized the secretary of war to "prescribe military areas." On March 2, a public proclamation was issued by Lieutenant General John L. DeWitt, head of the Army's Western Defense Command, who designated the region extending the length of the Pacific Coast an area from which those of Japanese descent would be excluded out of "military

By spring 1942, Sproul and Hedrick deferred requests to the War Relocation Authority, the U.S. civilian agency charged with the relocation and internment. Some of the Bruin Japanese-American students were able to transfer from the camps to other universities with the help of Quaker organizations. In the end, the university administration was not able to do as much as hoped and many of the students remained interned. Few would ever return to UCLA to complete their degrees.

Although they believed the relocation was unfair, the majority of the student body felt a level of resignation.

"Well, the government's done that, they must know what they're doing," said Frank Mankiewicz (future press secretary for Senator Robert F. Kennedy), recalling his reaction to the disappearance of the Nisei from campus during his freshman year. "And of course, as with most things governments do, they didn't know what they were doing. But the real criticism of it didn't begin to form until much later and even after the war."

RIVAL BOND BOWL

One year after the invasion of Pearl Harbor, USC-UCLA football organizers commemorated the event by turning the annual crosstown grudge match into a million-dollar war bond drive. Bruins received a letter from head football Coach Edwin C. "Babe" Horrell urging them to buy the war bonds at $18.75 apiece—a $5,000 contribution would entitle fans to "be our guests" on the team bench at the December 12, 1942, game.

The Student War Board bond and stamp savings committee, chaired by senior Tom Papich, marshaled celebrities and sponsored multiple fundraisers. In the week leading up to the big game, defense stamps were the currency of the day. They earned students the right to send a "message" to Japanese Emperor Hirohito by autographing a Douglas A-20 bomber on display between the men's and women's gyms, view a two-man Japanese submarine captured in Pearl Harbor, and dance the night away to the sounds of Rudy

Left: Coach Edwin C. "Babe" Horrell (center) led Bruin footballers during wartime.

Below left: Students sell war bonds from the Bruin Victory Cave, strategically located on Royce quad, 1944.

Below: During homecoming week, junior Alvira McCarthy signs the Douglas A-20 bomber on display between the men's and women's gyms, sending a "message" to Japanese Emperor Hirohito.

All-American Kenny Washington (above right) led the Bruins 14–7 in the first victory over USC, on December 12, 1942 (right). UCLA's No. 1 rooter, Joe E. Brown (above) gave away the game ball.

And Here's What You Can Do to Help Them!

Battleships cost money. Tanks don't grow on trees. And the storks don't bring anti-aircraft guns; so give them the planes, tanks, guns and ships they must have to win by putting 10% of every dollar you earn into the purchase of War Bonds and Stamps.

Follow the lead of the students, faculty, alumni and friends of U.C.L.A. and U.S.C. who have so magnificently supported their university's bond drive which undoubtedly will surpass the sales goal of $2,000,000.
Sales at present total U.S.C. $645,000; U.C.L.A. $607,000 —

TOTAL $1,252,000

Help to boost this figure over the $2,000,000 mark with your bond and stamp purchases at the game.

STAY BEHIND THE TEAM
But Above All Else
STAY BEHIND YOUR COUNTRY

Above: Students "buried" Hitler by covering him with salvaged metal, rubber and other scrap in an effort to collect materials for the defense industry.

Right: Senior Jean M. Bauer participates in the "bus your own dishes" campaign, in Kerckhoff Hall, September 1944.

Vallee and his Coast Guard ensemble. The seriousness of the times was felt even during periods of ostensible entertainment. The submarine, on loan from the Navy to the U.S. Treasury Department for war savings efforts, was under 24-hour watch at UCLA by a 12-man military guard.

The competing campuses quickly raised $1 million, so the goal was doubled. UCLA trailed by $250,000 early during the week of the big game, but caught up over the next several days, chalking up $610,000 to USC's $640,000 by Saturday. An ad in the *California Daily Bruin* the day before the game had encouraged fans to: "Stay behind the team but above all else stay behind your country."

The effort reached a climax on game day. During halftime, Army and Navy ROTC cadets along with female students worked the crowd of 90,000 to sell more bonds. All-Americans Kenny Washington of UCLA and Morley Drury of USC raffled the football used for kickoff, while comedian and Bruin booster Joe E. Brown gave away the game ball. Bruin and Trojan card stunts plugged sales, while the marching bands performed spellouts on the field and, according to *The Bruin*, "blew their horns right in 'Der Fuehrer's Face'" (a reference to the then-popular patriotic parody song by Spike Jones and his City Slickers).

The Bruins won, 14–7, beating the Trojans for the first time on their way to winning the Pacific Coast Championship and a first-ever season-ending Rose Bowl appearance. (The Bruins lost the New Year's Day game to Georgia, 9–0, but $50,000 of the game's proceeds were donated to the American Red Cross.)

The student newspaper didn't reveal which school won the war bond drive, but it did report that after all receipts were tallied, the rivals' united undertaking had resulted in almost $2.1 million for the war effort.

Throughout the war, students engaged in many civilian efforts, including blood drives, scrap collection and crop harvesting. One activity featured a "bury Hitler" motif, in which students collected pounds of salvaged metal and rubber—tires, hosiery and garters, old gas heaters, even bed frames—to aid ammunition makers and other defense industries, and in the process covered a large caricature of the Nazi dictator with the scrap.

Students turned to manual labor to bring in funds. In addition to picking fruit and vegetables in the San Fernando Valley or Culver City, Bruins tended to homegrown produce. Victory Gardens, a student plot north of the Women's Gymnasium, was planted to yield crops for the Associated Students, which promised to purchase the vegetables and contribute the proceeds to the students' war chest. North of the drill field, the faculty tended their own garden.

have given you your final grades in your courses and you have graduated. You now have a Bachelor of Science in Business Administration. Good luck." Hardwick, who returned to UCLA in 1959 as vice chairman of the chemistry department, said: "The university could hardly do less. We were taken away against our will, more or less, without notice, and the university had to do something. They couldn't just flunk us all out."

Enrollment declined as students joined the military or obtained jobs in the defense industry. Registrations continued to fall steadily for seven semesters with the number of male students decreasing precipitously. By the end of the war, the drop in men exceeded 50 percent.

"There was a constant attrition of students up and leaving," said Robert Alshuler, who entered the service after graduating in 1942 with his ROTC commission. "But there was a general feeling that you had to get in the war—for you to do your part. The attitude was that we had to get it done. It wasn't any choice. The country was in danger."

As students left for war assignments, the military arrived in large numbers and the campus began to provide specialty education for the service. In November 1942, as the draft age was lowered to 18, the armed forces found itself in need of programs to educate officers and proceeded to set them up at campuses across the nation.

At UCLA, V-12 Navy College Training Program cadets arrived in 1943. (One of the most illustrious alumni to complete this program at UCLA was Samuel L. Gravely Jr., who would become the first African-American to command a Navy warship and the first to advance to the rank of admiral.) The Navy continued to run its Naval Reserve Officer Training Corps, originally established at UCLA in 1938. The Army brought its troops to campus as well. The Army Specialized Training Program in engineering, medicine and languages, including Chinese, Italian and German, was accompanied by another Army contingent of meteorology cadets.

Fraternity houses—vacant from members having departed for war—were leased by the armed forces to provide

While soldiers prepared to take over the Kappa Sigma house, the fraternity men move out, May 1944 (above). As more and more military men moved into fraternity houses leased by the armed forces, such as Phi Gamma Delta at 611 Gayley Avenue (left), Fraternity Row became known as "Gayley Gulch."

living quarters for the Navy men stationed on campus, earning fraternity row the nickname "Gayley Gulch." The Kerckhoff cafeteria was converted into their mess hall.

By July 1943, one in three UCLA students was in uniform, shifting the dynamics of campus life. While athletic events continued, coaches were never certain which

Naval ROTC cadets parade at the foot of Janss Steps.

All-American Kenny Washington (above right) led the Bruins 14–7 in the first victory over USC, on December 12, 1942 (right). UCLA's No. 1 rooter, Joe E. Brown (above) gave away the game ball.

And Here's What You Can Do to Help Them!

Battleships cost money. Tanks don't grow on trees. And the storks don't bring anti-aircraft guns; so give them the planes, tanks, guns and ships they must have to win by putting 10% of every dollar you earn into the purchase of War Bonds and Stamps.

Follow the lead of the students, faculty, alumni and friends of U.C.L.A. and U.S.C. who have so magnificently supported their university's bond drive which undoubtedly will surpass the sales goal of $2,000,000. Sales at present total **U.S.C., $645,000; U.C.L.A., $607,000 —**

TOTAL **$1,252,000**

Help to boost this figure over the $2,000,000 mark with your bond and stamp purchases at the game

STAY BEHIND THE TEAM
But Above All Else
STAY BEHIND YOUR COUNTRY

Above: Students "buried" Hitler by covering him with salvaged metal, rubber and other scrap in an effort to collect materials for the defense industry.

Right: Senior Jean M. Bauer participates in the "bus your own dishes" campaign, in Kerckhoff Hall, September 1944.

Vallee and his Coast Guard ensemble. The seriousness of the times was felt even during periods of ostensible entertainment. The submarine, on loan from the Navy to the U.S. Treasury Department for war savings efforts, was under 24-hour watch at UCLA by a 12-man military guard.

The competing campuses quickly raised $1 million, so the goal was doubled. UCLA trailed by $250,000 early during the week of the big game, but caught up over the next several days, chalking up $610,000 to USC's $640,000 by Saturday. An ad in the *California Daily Bruin* the day before the game had encouraged fans to: "Stay behind the team but above all else stay behind your country."

The effort reached a climax on game day. During halftime, Army and Navy ROTC cadets along with female students worked the crowd of 90,000 to sell more bonds. All-Americans Kenny Washington of UCLA and Morley Drury of USC raffled the football used for kickoff, while comedian and Bruin booster Joe E. Brown gave away the game ball. Bruin and Trojan card stunts plugged sales, while the marching bands performed spellouts on the field and, according to *The Bruin*, "blew their horns right in 'Der Fuehrer's Face'" (a reference to the then-popular patriotic parody song by Spike Jones and his City Slickers).

The Bruins won, 14–7, beating the Trojans for the first time on their way to winning the Pacific Coast Championship and a first-ever season-ending Rose Bowl appearance. (The Bruins lost the New Year's Day game to Georgia, 9–0, but $50,000 of the game's proceeds were donated to the American Red Cross.)

The student newspaper didn't reveal which school won the war bond drive, but it did report that after all receipts were tallied, the rivals' united undertaking had resulted in almost $2.1 million for the war effort.

Throughout the war, students engaged in many civilian efforts, including blood drives, scrap collection and crop harvesting. One activity featured a "bury Hitler" motif, in which students collected pounds of salvaged metal and rubber—tires, hosiery and garters, old gas heaters, even bed frames—to aid ammunition makers and other defense industries, and in the process covered a large caricature of the Nazi dictator with the scrap.

Students turned to manual labor to bring in funds. In addition to picking fruit and vegetables in the San Fernando Valley or Culver City, Bruins tended to homegrown produce. Victory Gardens, a student plot north of the Women's Gymnasium, was planted to yield crops for the Associated Students, which promised to purchase the vegetables and contribute the proceeds to the students' war chest. North of the drill field, the faculty tended their own garden.

have given you your final grades in your courses and you have graduated. You now have a Bachelor of Science in Business Administration. Good luck." Hardwick, who returned to UCLA in 1959 as vice chairman of the chemistry department, said: "The university could hardly do less. We were taken away against our will, more or less, without notice, and the university had to do something. They couldn't just flunk us all out."

Enrollment declined as students joined the military or obtained jobs in the defense industry. Registrations continued to fall steadily for seven semesters with the number of male students decreasing precipitously. By the end of the war, the drop in men exceeded 50 percent.

"There was a constant attrition of students up and leaving," said Robert Alshuler, who entered the service after graduating in 1942 with his ROTC commission. "But there was a general feeling that you had to get in the war—for you to do your part. The attitude was that we had to get it done. It wasn't any choice. The country was in danger."

As students left for war assignments, the military arrived in large numbers and the campus began to provide specialty education for the service. In November 1942, as the draft age was lowered to 18, the armed forces found itself in need of programs to educate officers and proceeded to set them up at campuses across the nation.

At UCLA, V-12 Navy College Training Program cadets arrived in 1943. (One of the most illustrious alumni to complete this program at UCLA was Samuel L. Gravely Jr., who would become the first African-American to command a Navy warship and the first to advance to the rank of admiral.) The Navy continued to run its Naval Reserve Officer Training Corps, originally established at UCLA in 1938. The Army brought its troops to campus as well. The Army Specialized Training Program in engineering, medicine and languages, including Chinese, Italian and German, was accompanied by another Army contingent of meteorology cadets.

Fraternity houses—vacant from members having departed for war—were leased by the armed forces to provide

While soldiers prepared to take over the Kappa Sigma house, the fraternity men move out, May 1944 (above). As more and more military men moved into fraternity houses leased by the armed forces, such as Phi Gamma Delta at 611 Gayley Avenue (left), Fraternity Row became known as "Gayley Gulch."

living quarters for the Navy men stationed on campus, earning fraternity row the nickname "Gayley Gulch." The Kerckhoff cafeteria was converted into their mess hall.

By July 1943, one in three UCLA students was in uniform, shifting the dynamics of campus life. While athletic events continued, coaches were never certain which

Naval ROTC cadets parade at the foot of Janss Steps.

All-American Kenny Washington (above right) led the Bruins 14–7 in the first victory over USC, on December 12, 1942 (right). UCLA's No. 1 rooter, Joe E. Brown (above) gave away the game ball.

And Here's What You Can Do to Help Them!

Battleships cost money. Tanks don't grow on trees. And the storks don't bring anti-aircraft guns; so give them the planes, tanks, guns and ships they must have to win by putting 10% of every dollar you earn into the purchase of War Bonds and Stamps.

Follow the lead of the students, faculty, alumni and friends of U.C.L.A. and U.S.C. who have so magnificently supported their university's bond drive which undoubtedly will surpass the sales goal of $2,000,000.
Sales at present total U.S.C., $645,000; U.C.L.A., $607,000 —

TOTAL $1,252,000

Help to boost this figure over the $2,000,000 mark with your bond and stamp purchases at the game.

STAY BEHIND THE TEAM
But Above All Else
STAY BEHIND YOUR COUNTRY

Above: Students "buried" Hitler by covering him with salvaged metal, rubber and other scrap in an effort to collect materials for the defense industry.

Right: Senior Jean M. Bauer participates in the "bus your own dishes" campaign, in Kerckhoff Hall, September 1944.

Vallee and his Coast Guard ensemble. The seriousness of the times was felt even during periods of ostensible entertainment. The submarine, on loan from the Navy to the U.S. Treasury Department for war savings efforts, was under 24-hour watch at UCLA by a 12-man military guard.

The competing campuses quickly raised $1 million, so the goal was doubled. UCLA trailed by $250,000 early during the week of the big game, but caught up over the next several days, chalking up $610,000 to USC's $640,000 by Saturday. An ad in the *California Daily Bruin* the day before the game had encouraged fans to: "Stay behind the team but above all else stay behind your country."

The effort reached a climax on game day. During halftime, Army and Navy ROTC cadets along with female students worked the crowd of 90,000 to sell more bonds. All-Americans Kenny Washington of UCLA and Morley Drury of USC raffled the football used for kickoff, while comedian and Bruin booster Joe E. Brown gave away the game ball. Bruin and Trojan card stunts plugged sales, while the marching bands performed spellouts on the field and, according to *The Bruin*, "blew their horns right in 'Der Fuehrer's Face' " (a reference to the then-popular patriotic parody song by Spike Jones and his City Slickers).

The Bruins won, 14–7, beating the Trojans for the first time on their way to winning the Pacific Coast Championship and a first-ever season-ending Rose Bowl appearance. (The Bruins lost the New Year's Day game to Georgia, 9–0, but $50,000 of the game's proceeds were donated to the American Red Cross.)

The student newspaper didn't reveal which school won the war bond drive, but it did report that after all receipts were tallied, the rivals' united undertaking had resulted in almost $2.1 million for the war effort.

Throughout the war, students engaged in many civilian efforts, including blood drives, scrap collection and crop harvesting. One activity featured a "bury Hitler" motif, in which students collected pounds of salvaged metal and rubber—tires, hosiery and garters, old gas heaters, even bed frames—to aid ammunition makers and other defense industries, and in the process covered a large caricature of the Nazi dictator with the scrap.

Students turned to manual labor to bring in funds. In addition to picking fruit and vegetables in the San Fernando Valley or Culver City, Bruins tended to homegrown produce. Victory Gardens, a student plot north of the Women's Gymnasium, was planted to yield crops for the Associated Students, which promised to purchase the vegetables and contribute the proceeds to the students' war chest. North of the drill field, the faculty tended their own garden.

By July 1943, one out of every three Bruins was in uniform. Navy men (top) register for wartime classes, while soldiers outside Kerckhoff Hall (above) inspect their course books on specialized subjects such as engineering, medicine and meteorology.

Women participated in the annual Frosh-Soph Brawl for the first time in October 1944 (above right), while Junior Proms were kept on campus to keep costs low (right).

Rationing became a way of life. In the campus cafeteria, "Meatless Tuesdays" were adopted. Sugar was in scarce supply. Other luxuries such as nylons and matches were done without. Once more, transportation to UCLA became a challenge—this time because of gas and tire rationing and minimized public transportation. The U.S. Office of Price Administration provided an extra incentive for carpooling and through the Associated Students a program matching potential passengers was developed. A November 1942 *California Daily Bruin* editorial admonished: "If a single car drives through Janss Gate without a full load of students on the morning after gasoline rationing starts, the Associated Students has failed to fulfill its responsibility."

MILITARY PRESENCE

As Hedrick stepped down from his post upon reaching retirement age in July 1942, Sproul again assumed direct oversight responsibility for the UCLA campus—a role he would maintain until the end of the war. Sproul reasoned that wartime savings were necessary and that it was imperative to have a single individual overseeing the multicampus university in the service of the nation. "The immediate duty of the University," Sproul said, "is to prepare as many as possible of its students and of the public generally to take some competent part in the gigantic effort that the United Nations are putting forth, being consciously mindful at the same time of the ultimate long-range objectives, 'a just and durable peace.'"

Sproul traveled weekly to Los Angeles and lived in the University Residence, making UCLA the university's *de facto* headquarters. He appointed a three-member administrative committee to assist him: Acting Dean of the Graduate Division-Southern Section Bennet M. Allen; Dean of the College of Letters and Science Gordon S. Watkins; and Director of Summer Sessions J. Harold Williams.

The university administration took additional steps, such as adjusting credits and arranging for honorable withdrawals, to assist male students leaving UCLA to enter the armed forces.

Senior E. Russell Hardwick was one of many students whose entire ROTC class was forced to depart on short notice, just before final exams. "We were plucked up by the Army and sent away," Hardwick said. Six weeks later, in the middle of summer at Fort Benning, Georgia, Hardwick received a postcard from UCLA, which he remembers as saying: "We

The University House
University of California at Los Angeles

have given you your final grades in your courses and you have graduated. You now have a Bachelor of Science in Business Administration. Good luck." Hardwick, who returned to UCLA in 1959 as vice chairman of the chemistry department, said: "The university could hardly do less. We were taken away against our will, more or less, without notice, and the university had to do something. They couldn't just flunk us all out."

Enrollment declined as students joined the military or obtained jobs in the defense industry. Registrations continued to fall steadily for seven semesters with the number of male students decreasing precipitously. By the end of the war, the drop in men exceeded 50 percent.

"There was a constant attrition of students up and leaving," said Robert Alshuler, who entered the service after graduating in 1942 with his ROTC commission. "But there was a general feeling that you had to get in the war—for you to do your part. The attitude was that we had to get it done. It wasn't any choice. The country was in danger."

As students left for war assignments, the military arrived in large numbers and the campus began to provide specialty education for the service. In November 1942, as the draft age was lowered to 18, the armed forces found itself in need of programs to educate officers and proceeded to set them up at campuses across the nation.

At UCLA, V-12 Navy College Training Program cadets arrived in 1943. (One of the most illustrious alumni to complete this program at UCLA was Samuel L. Gravely Jr., who would become the first African-American to command a Navy warship and the first to advance to the rank of admiral.) The Navy continued to run its Naval Reserve Officer Training Corps, originally established at UCLA in 1938. The Army brought its troops to campus as well. The Army Specialized Training Program in engineering, medicine and languages, including Chinese, Italian and German, was accompanied by another Army contingent of meteorology cadets.

Fraternity houses—vacant from members having departed for war—were leased by the armed forces to provide

While soldiers prepared to take over the Kappa Sigma house, the fraternity men move out, May 1944 (above). As more and more military men moved into fraternity houses leased by the armed forces, such as Phi Gamma Delta at 611 Gayley Avenue (left), Fraternity Row became known as "Gayley Gulch."

living quarters for the Navy men stationed on campus, earning fraternity row the nickname "Gayley Gulch." The Kerckhoff cafeteria was converted into their mess hall.

By July 1943, one in three UCLA students was in uniform, shifting the dynamics of campus life. While athletic events continued, coaches were never certain which

Naval ROTC cadets parade at the foot of Janss Steps.

CIVILIAN DEFENSE TRAINING

It was not uncommon for female students to serve double duty. "Nowadays, practically every one of the girls has either a father, brother or boy friend in the war," Doris Burns, a senior who kept a full study load and worked as a glass inspector on the graveyard shift at Douglas Aircraft, told the *Los Angeles Times* in 1943. "They're proud to do all they can to help."

Growing demand for military airplanes fed into the expansion of the aeronautical industry. UCLA was surrounded by aircraft companies, including Douglas in Santa Monica, Hughes in Culver City, Lockheed in Burbank and Northrup (later Northrop) in Hawthorne. The University Extension division in Los Angeles expanded its offerings crucial to the war. A new course in aircraft engineering was given tuition-free to prepare women not regularly enrolled for work in engineering departments of aircraft industries.

UCLA was designated by the federal government to offer the Engineering, Science and Management War Training program geared toward those already employed in the defense industry who wanted to upgrade their professional skills in industrial science, production management, tool design, foundry metallurgy and radio communications. Approximately 50 percent of the courses were in the field of engineering, and the training was designed particularly for those in aircraft manufacturing or shipbuilding.

Among the occupations of those who signed up: a model, a soloist from a funeral parlor, a former member of the Belgian consulate, wallpaper saleswomen, real estate salesmen, housewives and teachers. "It goes to prove that Mr. and Mrs. America are going all-out to fit themselves for a vital role in helping Uncle Sam win this war," wrote Lucy Guild Quirk in *The U.C.L.A. Magazine* in February 1943.

Individuals were paid to take classes such as aircraft drafting, tool engineering and physical testing of petroleum products. Classes were offered up to six days a week, eight hours a day, and trainees were paid at least $100 per month with a $10 raise each month. Courses were taught by UCLA faculty, and while some were held on the UCLA campus, others were offered downtown at the Extension offices and still more at the aircraft training centers.

Many classes were taught at night and some in the wee hours of the morning, so as not to impede with daytime jobs—further adding to the university as a 'round-the-clock operation in fulfillment of war service. Welcoming these students was a boon for the university at a time when many seats may have otherwise remained empty.

Senior Molly Malcolmson (top) was one of many women who enrolled in the Engineering, Science and Management War Training Program. Instructor Clark Lay (middle) explains the slide rule, while students (above) gain experience in the first women's tool-designing class.

would be available. The Navy ruled that its men stationed on university campuses could play football; however, the Army decreed its men could not. To ease the crunch, the NCAA's long-held prohibition of freshmen participating in varsity sports was lifted as the emergency situation created a need for replacement players. (The freshman ban was reinstated in 1947.)

Women took on an expanded and more significant campus role. When Associated Students President William C. Farrer, an advanced ROTC member, ended his term early to depart for service, Vice President Jo Anne Hollister ascended into the office. In spring 1943, Josephine Rosenfield filled the job of editor of the *California Daily Bruin*, replacing Robert Weil, to become the newspaper's first female chief. It was a signal moment to have both influential positions held by women. As the war went on, such transitions became commonplace as the majority of Associated Students posts were filled by women.

As senior Flora Lewis, who later broke barriers as a female foreign correspondent for *The Washington Post*, astutely predicted on *The Bruin's* editorial page: "The day will surely come when women will be occupying positions previously stamped 'Reserved for Men' in factories, offices and perhaps even fields. When the work is done and the men come back, they will once again be chagrined to find their [indispensability] has been challenged."

ENGINEERING AN AERONAUTICAL FUTURE

Prominent UCLA alumni and government officials stressed that the campus could do more to contribute to the local and fast-rising aeronautical industry, especially since it was in extreme demand during wartime.

"What part has the University of California at Los Angeles played in building this great industry?" asked John B. Jackson, executive secretary of the UCLA Alumni Association, in the March 1943 issue of *The U.C.L.A. Magazine*. "A meager and indirect one. It has supplied manpower in executive, personnel, scientific and other lines; some of the highest ranking executives of the aircraft world are U.C.L.A. graduates. Its faculty has assisted in many basic fields through research, counsel, and experimentation. The lack of a college of engineering, however, has prevented U.C.L.A. from serving the industry directly in the training of engineering and technical personnel, or in the solving of engineering problems."

UCLA possessed a strong foundation upon which to build a college of engineering focused on aeronautical science. The campus boasted strong departments of chemistry, geology, mathematics, meteorology and physics. Undergraduates could also complete a two-year pre-engineering curriculum that included courses in elementary civil engineering and mechanical engineering.

A proposal for developing a UCLA engineering college relating to aeronautics emerged as early as 1933. During wartime, the need intensified. Proponents argued that creating a school immediately would provide valuable assistance to the war effort. Once the war ended, it was predicted there would be an increased demand for applying scientific engineering principles to air transportation and expanded aircraft

manufacturing. Both the aircraft industry and air transportation authorities threw their support behind the plan.

During an Alumni Association Executive Council meeting on January 21, 1943, the industry's need for aeronautical engineers and the advisability of establishing a school of engineering at UCLA coalesced as alumni leaders decided to take their cause directly to the Legislature. Political science Professor Dean E. McHenry, the faculty representative to the alumni council, drafted the initial proposal.

Lieutenant Governor Frederick F. Houser, a regent and former UCLA Alumni Association president, asked Assemblyman Jesse Randolph Kellems, who represented the Santa Monica–Westwood area, to sponsor the bill. On January 28, 1943, Kellems introduced Assembly Bill 1140, "An Act to provide for the establishment and maintenance of a School of Aeronautical Engineering and Sciences in the University of California at Los Angeles." He enlisted 33 other assemblymen to coauthor the bill, requesting an appropriation of $1 million. Regent Fred Moyer Jordan, a former UCLA student body president, led the discussion at the regents meeting, with support from Houser and Regent Edward A. Dickson. With Governor Earl Warren not voting because legislation was involved, the Board of Regents moved unanimously on March 26, 1943, to support the establishment of an engineering school at UCLA.

After approval by the Assembly, the Senate Finance Committee slashed the request to $650,000—eliminating the

Above: A rendering of the first unit of the College of Engineering, designed by Allison & Rible, and completed in 1950.

Below right: Llewellyn M.K. Boelter, dean of the engineering school, 1944–1965.

Below: Meteorology cadets in UCLA's pioneering program take an oath to protect their country.

funding for a building citing wartime material shortages. On June 8, 1943, Governor Warren reduced the appropriation further to $300,000 and then signed the bill creating the new College of Engineering, specializing in aeronautics.

"It is particularly appropriate and desirable that such a school should be established in an area that is contributing so much to the manufacture of aircraft," said Los Angeles Mayor Fletcher Bowron. Added Frank P. Doherty, president of the Los Angeles Chamber of Commerce: "Southern California is now and will continue to be the center of the aircraft industry. It is logical therefore that the principal educational activities in the field be centered here at U.C.L.A."

In November 1944, Llewellyn M.K. Boelter, associate dean of the College of Engineering at Berkeley, was recruited as founding dean. The college, initially housed in the Mechanic

Arts Building and other temporary facilities, received its first class of 379 students in fall 1945. One year later, the enrollment more than tripled to 1,443. (The first of a series of engineering buildings was completed in 1950, and the professional school was renamed in 1999 after a $30 million donation by alumnus and Broadcom Corporation co-founder Henry A. Samueli.)

"EXILED INTO PARADISE"

The so-called brain drain from Europe in the 1930s and early 1940s of hundreds of physicists, philosophers, writers, musicians and other creative individuals—including Albert Einstein in 1933—operated greatly to the benefit of America. The "hotbed of communism" epithet—which UCLA had to vigorously shake in the 1930s—produced the unexpected effect of portraying the campus as a liberal haven at a time when the world was being trampled by Fascist regimes. UCLA wound up attracting some of Europe's best scientific and artistic minds.

One of UCLA's pioneering programs during World War II was the meteorology division of the physics department, chaired by Professor Joseph Kaplan. The department was built with the arrival of several émigrés from Norway.

Jacob Bjerknes, an international authority on weather forecasting who helped develop the modern idea of cold and warm "fronts," was on a 1939–40 lecture tour in the United States when Norway was invaded by the Germans. Bjerknes, son of noted Norwegian physicist and meteorologist Vilhelm Bjerknes, was approached by Kaplan to start a meteorology program at UCLA for training military weather forecasters and assisting aviators in dealing with upper air masses.

Once settled in 1940, Bjerknes recruited fellow Norwegian meteorologist Jorgen Holmboe, who was also stranded in the United States. Later that summer, Bjerknes added Norwegian scientist Harald Sverdrup, noted oceanographer and director of the Scripps Institution of Oceanography in La Jolla, to the UCLA faculty. Sverdrup taught classes on the interaction between the sea and atmosphere. The trio educated some 1,200 meteorologists during the war. The graduating officers were credited for the weather forecasts and surf predictions instrumental to the Allied landings in Normandy, North Africa and the South Pacific.

In the spring of 1944, Bjerknes traveled to battle zones in Italy, England and the South Pacific to aid in weather forecasting operations. In early 1945, Bjerknes toured Air Force weather stations to assist meteorologists—some his former students—with solutions to problems encountered under actual combat conditions. (In 1966, Bjerknes, whose cyclone theory in the 1950s became the basis for the first accurate computer-assisted weather forecasts and who in the 1960s identified what was later termed the El Niño phenomenon, was awarded the National Medal of Science by President Lyndon B. Johnson.)

Graduate Division-Southern Section Dean Gustave O. Arlt, who helped strengthen UCLA's music, theater and arts programs, was influential in forging ties with many exiled German writers and musicians who had taken up residence in Los Angeles.

Theater director and producer William Melnitz was in the prime of his career when he was forced to flee his native Germany in 1939 for Austria, and then Switzerland. After a few years in New York, where he learned English, Melnitz arrived in Los Angeles in 1941 and a year later walked into Arlt's office unannounced.

"He arrived here with the intention of continuing a career here, [but] found that he did not like the motion picture business," Arlt said. "He told me who he was and said he would like to get a Ph.D. in Germanic languages. I told him he would have to complete an undergraduate major before he could get into grad school." Melnitz, already in his 40s, earned his bachelor's within two years and then continued into the Ph.D. program. "I came to this country, and the heading is Einstein's word, 'Exiled into Paradise,' " Melnitz said. "Luckily enough, on account of the war, many people were drafted, and I could fill in right at UCLA as a teaching assistant, I could study."

Added Arlt: "He was a spectacular example of a refugee from war-torn Europe who made a great success here." (Melnitz was named chair of theater arts in 1953 and pioneered the creation of The Theatre Group, UCLA's professional theater company which would become the resident company of the Los Angeles Music Center's theater

William Melnitz, dean of the College of Fine Arts, 1960–1967.

complex—later the Mark Taper Forum. He was appointed founding dean of the College of Fine Arts in 1960.)

The philosophy department was shaped by Hans Reichenbach, who had left Germany for Turkey in 1933 and then moved to Los Angeles to accept a professorship at UCLA in 1938. Called "the greatest empiricist of the 20th century," Reichenbach, a resident German alien, was obliged to follow the government-ordered curfew and confined to his home with the exception of traveling to UCLA or to the doctor until he obtained his American citizenship in 1943. During the war, Reichenbach was instrumental in helping his Frankfurt School colleagues—Theodor Adorno and Max Horkheimer—obtain positions at UCLA. They, along with poet and playwright Berthold Brecht and Nobel laureate in literature Thomas Mann, formed part of the eminent circle of German intellectuals in Los Angeles.

In the field of music, there were many more opportunities in Los Angeles at that time than there were in New York, according to Bohemian-born Jan Popper, who was invited by John Vincent, chairman of UCLA's music department, to establish the Opera Workshop on campus in 1949. "UCLA presented this greener pasture with more resources," Popper said, referring to his transfer from Stanford University.

That opportunity and intellectual freedom drew noted Viennese composer Arnold Schoenberg to Los Angeles via Boston. Schoenberg, who became a U.S. citizen in April 1941, had been driven out of Europe by anti-Semitism and had suffered

whole cities were agitated, and visitors and critics came from neighboring towns to attend these events, and while, besides the riots with the first two quartets, there were long articles in the papers—this time it was a perfectly commonplace affair," Schoenberg wrote in his introductory note to the recording. "There was no special excitement and, at least, the anticipation was in no way exaggerated. Nevertheless, I was very content with the attitude of the public. The whole audience listened with respect and sincerity to the strange sounds with which they were faced and it seems a number of them were really impressed."

BRUINS IN UNIFORM

With isolationist tendencies long forgotten, patriotism among the American public and on campus was in vogue. Every afternoon, meteorology cadets would take down the Stars and Stripes from the Gimbel Flagpole. Passers-by respectfully paused and waited until it lowered. "Certainly that is not too much time for any of us to devote to our flag and our country," wrote the *California Bruin*.

As "Americanism" gained popularity nationwide, UCLA's College of Letters and Science formed a curriculum titled "The History, Culture and Institutions of the United States" to "gain a wide background on things American." A student could enroll in "Great American Personalities," which replaced "Great English Personalities." University Extension followed suit with its own courses such as "Public Opinion and Propaganda" and the compendium "Government of European Dictatorships."

College of Letters and Science Dean Gordon Watkins, who was in charge of developing the courses, said, "Students usually know more about European history and European institutions than they do about their own American civilization."

Above: Army meteorology cadets stand at attention daily at the Gimbel Flagpole. They were also responsible for lowering the Stars and Stripes every afternoon.

Far right: Alpha Gamma Delta sorority sisters sew stars on the Service Flag, honoring those at war.

Below: Austrian émigré and composer Arnold Schoenberg began teaching music composition at UCLA in 1936.

criticism for his ultramodern atonal compositions, which during performances had on occasion incited violence in Austria. After lecturing at USC in 1935, Schoenberg accepted a professorship at UCLA in 1936, teaching composition. He became professor emeritus in 1944 and died in 1951. (The music building was named in his honor five years after his death.)

"I like the young people," Schoenberg told *The U.C.L.A. Magazine* in May 1940. "I always like young people, and I think my students like me—at least I want to be liked by them, and I hope to do something to help them."

During his tenure at UCLA, Schoenberg was commissioned by music patron Elizabeth Sprague Coolidge to compose the "Fourth String Quartet, op. 37," which premiered in Royce Hall during a festival given by Coolidge for UCLA students on January 8, 1937.

"While every one of my premieres had caused a great sensation and excitement, so that

In honor of loved ones who were on active duty, families would display blue stars in a window of their home. If a family member died while serving, the star was changed to a gold one. At UCLA, the Service Flag, donated by the Associated Students and the Alumni Association in 1942, flew for the duration of the war over the entrance of Kerckhoff Hall. In the center rested a gold star with the number representing Bruins who died in the war; below it was a blue star with the number of Bruins active in the war.

The U.C.L.A. Magazine
JUNE, 1943

The Alumni Association's contribution to the war effort was to maintain extensive records, including photos, news clippings, promotion and decoration details, and casualty notices. By February 1944, the association recorded several thousand Bruins involved in the war, including hundreds of women serving in the Navy's WAVES (Women Accepted for Voluntary Emergency Service), U.S. Marines, Army Nurse Corps, WACs (Women's Army Corps), or other duty. The final count included 5,702 servicemen and servicewomen, and 151 who had died in the war. The association acknowledged that records were incomplete and that the figures may in actuality be two or three times as high as the number represented on the Service Flag. (Over the years, these files were lost and no other comprehensive statistics of Bruin veterans of World War II is known to exist, however, the Department of Military Science continues to compile records of Bruins in service during that time.)

The U.C.L.A. Magazine frequently published letters from those in combat on its pages, and the Alumni Association sent the *Bruin Outpost* to servicemen all over the world. Salve H. Matheson, a paratrooper in the Normandy invasion, wrote: "I know that the one [bullet] with my name on it hasn't been made yet; but it's those labeled 'To Whom It May Concern' that worry the hell out of me."

CODENAME: PROJECT 36

UCLA scholars and scientists made myriad contributions to the war effort through research in their own disciplines. Allied pilots were aided by UCLA studies on plane de-icing and keeping military airplane cabins heated.

Several professors took extended leaves to assist with America's defense through positions in the federal government, research laboratories or the armed forces, while continuing their service to the university. Physics Professor Vern O. Knudsen and several colleagues left to perform classified acoustical research for application to submarine

detection at the U.S. Navy Radio and Sound Laboratory in San Diego. Paul A. Dodd, associate professor of economics, served as an adviser to the National Labor Relations Board in Washington, D.C. Verz R. Goddard, assistant professor of home economics, also left for the nation's capital, as a senior home economist with the Department of Agriculture.

Secret war activities were being conducted in laboratories on and off campus. Some faculty departed for "destinations unknown." The most significant of these was the atomic bomb project, codenamed the Manhattan Engineer District.

Charles D. Coryell, UCLA associate professor of chemistry, went on leave in May 1942 to the Metallurgical Laboratory at the University of Chicago, one of the centers of atomic energy development, headed by UCLA alumnus and Berkeley Professor Glenn T. Seaborg, who co-discovered plutonium in 1941. Coryell later moved to the project laboratory at Oak Ridge, Tennessee, where he oversaw the work establishing chemical proof of element 61, or promethium. As chief of the Fission Products Section, his work was so clandestine that even his wife and parents were unaware of its purpose. His first report to the university said only, "I am engaged in work of completely secret nature, not likely to be disclosed publicly for several years."

Left: Alumna Marjorie Hall, third officer of the Selfridge Field detachment of the Women's Army Corps, was one of hundreds of UCLA women who signed up for active military service.

Below: Paul A. Dodd, dean of the College of Letters and Science, 1946–1961.

Bottom: Physics Professor Vern O. Knudsen took a leave of absence to conduct classified military acoustics research in San Diego.

Coryell was one of hundreds of University of California scientists who worked on the Manhattan Project, which dwarfed the largest of American corporations and had unlimited resources to focus on a singular objective: developing the world's first atomic bomb before the Axis powers could do the same.

Berkeley physics Professor J. Robert Oppenheimer served as the scientific director of the Manhattan Project and ran its new laboratory, which was being set up in remote Los Alamos, New Mexico. The University of California operated the lab—covertly named Project Y—under government contract. Underhill, secretary and treasurer of the Board of Regents, handled all arrangements between the university and the government and is believed to be the only university administrator privy to the bomb work. The entire project was under the executive authority of Major General Leslie R. Groves.

In February 1943, Oppenheimer devised a plan with the U.S. Army Corps of Engineers and the University of California in which the university would be responsible for management of the Los Alamos laboratory. For security reasons, the purchasing office—codenamed Project 36—was established in Los Angeles, far enough away from the Berkeley Radiation Laboratory to avert a connection and close to direct railway lines to New Mexico. UCLA became involved in the purchasing, payroll, accounting and delivery of a wide variety of equipment and material for the Manhattan Project.

The Los Angeles purchasing office began operations on March 16, 1943. Located off-campus in the Extension offices at Hill Street and protected by 24-hour guard, it was first headed by David L. Wilt and then by Albert E. Dyhre after September 1943. Accounting was handled by Max Robinson and matters of general business procedure were under the direction of UCLA Business Manager George F. Taylor, who replaced Deming Maclise after his death.

Nothing was shipped directly. All mail and library books from Berkeley and Los Angeles were routed to the project by way of the office's off-site warehouses. Checks and travel advances could not be delivered directly to employees. Instead they were sent to Los Angeles and then rerouted to post office boxes and individual bank accounts in different states. "The trouble here was that if these names of the important scientists who were being gathered there all appeared on the roll as clients of a bank in Albuquerque or Santa Fe, somebody might begin to find out that this was not a rest home for pregnant WACs," said Underhill.

Except for emergencies and special items, the lab's procurement office in New Mexico would make all requisitions by mail or teletype through Los Angeles. Requests for items not available in the Los Angeles area were forwarded to New York and Chicago sub-purchasing offices. Supplies would flow first to Los Angeles or Chicago and then be redirected to New Mexico under fresh shipping labels—nothing could be linked back to the University of California. All wastepaper was burned in UCLA's incinerator, with a trusted employee in attendance.

During its operations, the purchasing office spent millions of dollars scouring a market depleted by war. Because of the secrecy of the project, purchasing agents were not allowed to reveal their connection with the Army when placing their orders. This often caused manufacturers and suppliers to question the unusual products bought in the name of the university. Within a few months after Los Alamos opened, the procurement and business offices had to equip an entire lab that initially had nothing but a cyclotron, generators and some other electronics. Purchase officers secured items such as: workers' clothes, 10-ton trucks, rats, meteorological balloons, sewing and washing machines, and jeweler's tools. In the interest of speed, items ranging from typewriters to microscopes were loaned, or rented, from the UCLA campus.

Time itself was a vital war material, but few knew the immediate urgency under which they were operating because so much was shrouded in mystery. Pitting expeditiousness against such veiled secrecy posed inevitable complications. Some scientists blamed the Los Angeles purchasing office for not being more efficient. Since purchasing officers were not given information on what the items were for, or what specifications were crucial, they could not inquire as to the most important characteristics of the items requested, such as chemical composition. Oppenheimer struggled with these inefficiencies, until a meeting was called with Underhill to improve procedures by expressing the urgency of the

From left, physicist J. Robert Oppenheimer, Major General Leslie R. Groves, President Robert Gordon Sproul and Commodore W.S. Parson at the ceremony honoring the University of California for its role in the Manhattan Project, October 16, 1945.

Production Award

The University of California
Los Alamos Scientific Laboratory
Santa Fe, New Mexico

situation, and Groves finally determined that Underhill needed to be filled in.

"Now I knew what we were getting into, and perhaps I encouraged some of my colleagues and myself to put a little more steam into the job," Underhill explained. "But I couldn't tell anyone else around here. I was never allowed to tell Sproul."

On July 16, 1945, the results of this massive effort produced Trinity, the first successful test explosion of the atomic bomb, in the desert 150 miles south of Los Alamos. President Harry S. Truman ordered a bomb dropped on the Japanese city of Hiroshima on August 6, killing 70,000 immediately, plus an estimated 130,000 over the next five years. It was followed by another bomb dispatched to the city of Nagasaki on August 9, killing an estimated 40,000 directly and injuring 60,000 more. Japan surrendered on August 14.

The university's giant purchasing role was revealed as it received the Army-Navy "E" Production Award on October 16, 1945, for "our fighting forces' joint recognition of exceptional performance on the production front, of the determined, persevering, unbeatable American spirit which can be satisfied only by achieving today what yesterday seemed impossible."

At the time, the university released an unofficial count of 20 UCLA alumni involved in various phases of the atomic bomb research. (More names would surface later.) Most of the UCLA alumni were affiliated with the Clinton Laboratories in Oak Ridge or with the Metallurgical Laboratory, with others stationed at the Pasco Naval Air Station in Washington, or the Los Alamos laboratory.

During the award ceremony, Oppenheimer spoke briefly. "The peoples of this world must unite, or they will perish," he said. "This war, that has ravaged so much of the earth, has written these words. The atomic bomb has spelled them out for all men to understand."

V-J DAY

To a campus that had grown accustomed to alarming news and air raid signals, the sound at 4:30 p.m. on August 14, 1945, was unforgettable. The "all-clear" issued from the siren atop the Physics-Biology Building was a message long awaited: Emperor Hirohito had declared Japan's surrender, officially ending World War II.

The announcement gave rise to spontaneous celebrations across campus. Associate Editor Anne Stern

described the scene for *California Daily Bruin* readers in the August 17 edition.

"Late campus [habitués] came pouring out of the library, labs, late classes. The crowds assembled around the radios in [Kerckhoff Hall] 200 and K.H. 212 grew, drinking in every word of President Truman's and Prime Minister [Clement] Attlee's messages announcing the unconditional surrender of Nippon," Stern wrote. "Outside, the cacophony of noise mounted in volume, with incessant honking of automobile horns echoing and augmenting the sound of sirens."

Upon hearing the news, the UCLA band cut short its practice and headed toward an impromptu concert near the campus gyms. Cars filled with revelers headed toward Westwood. But amid the joyful celebrations, there was reflection as well.

"Many tears were openly or unnoticedly wiped away during the first realization that peace was finally returning to a world that had been constantly threatened by totalitarian aggression," Stern continued, "and that men in the services were coming home, safe."

And yet, still flying patriotically in front of Kerckhoff Hall, the Service Flag with its gold star was a reminder that not all Bruins would return.

Right: The Service Flag, with its gold star representing the number of Bruin war dead, and blue star, for those on active duty, flies above the entrance to Kerckhoff Hall, June 1945.

Below: A view eastward, 1940s.

THE UCLA SERVICE FLAG FLIES FROM KERCKHOFF HALL (SEE PAGE 2)

The U.C.L.A. Magazine

JUNE, 1945

A Maturing Campus
1945–1959

Above: A typical afternoon on the Kerckhoff patio, mid-1940s.

Opposite: Overlooking the campus, with medical school barracks (center), c.1951.

*A*mid a newfound affluence not shared by war-torn Europe or Asia, a college education in the United States promised upward mobility: the quintessential American dream. Some 7.8 million veterans pursued higher learning or vocational training under the "GI Bill of Rights" in a monumental democratization of education in America.

At UCLA, enrollment swelled to 7,000, the university's largest since the United States entered World War II in 1941. "Manpower will still be on the scanty side," the California Daily Bruin reported in the October 26, 1945, registration issue, "for 4500 of the fall term's population will be of the weaker sex. Approximately 1000 of the 2500 expected males will be veterans, who will add maturity to the male element which for so long consisted mostly of seventeen year olds." By 1949, the continued influx of veterans caused enrollment to more than double, hitting an all-time high of 15,000.

Peacetime brought an unprecedented economic prosperity propelled by the advent of the military industrial complex. With it came a surge of tax revenues and an emphasis on building infrastructure ranging from the sprawling California freeways to the expansive public university system. The state Legislature had dedicated the first portion of accumulated wartime taxes for construction. Much of those funds went to the development of the University of California system, with UCLA's portion cited by the Los Angeles Times as "the largest single amount earmarked for any one campus in the history of American education."

The arroyo separating east and west campus posed a static barrier to expansion and was filled in to create some 24 additional centralized acres. Longtime UCLA architect David C. Allison, not inclined to

abandon the classic Romanesque architecture, was succeeded by the more client-pleasing Welton Becket, dubbed "L.A.'s invisible builder." Becket, who would become UCLA's most prolific supervising architect, transformed the campus with his practical, minimalistic style of steel and brick that cost less and could be more quickly constructed to keep up with demand.

After two years with University of California President Robert Gordon Sproul filling in as chief executive of UCLA, the Board of Regents appointed Clarence Addison Dykstra, the first head of the U.S. Selective Service and president of the University of Wisconsin, to lead UCLA through the flourishing postwar period. Dykstra, who had taught at UCLA in the 1920s, became the first UCLA chief executive who had previously led a major university. His higher education experience and skills earned through positions in civic service, including acting as city manager of Cincinnati and as a commissioner of water and power in Los Angeles, guided UCLA through the beginning of an ambitious $50 million building program and the creation of multiple academic departments, a law school, medical school and hospital.

Dykstra strengthened the faculty by drawing in well-known scholars with distinguished reputations, as well as hiring younger individuals with promising futures. More than 300 faculty positions were added during his administration. Dykstra, with his charismatic charm, was so successful in recruiting prominent individuals from prestigious institutions that he earned a reputation for being a "raider," as UCLA was raising its profile with a faculty that included noted Manhattan Project medical director Stafford Leak Warren, geophysicist Louis B. Slichter, revered Harvard Law School Dean Roscoe Pound and motion picture producer Kenneth Macgowan.

As the Atomic Age evolved into the Cold War, President Harry S. Truman in 1947 created the U.S. Department of Defense and the CIA, and ordered loyalty oaths and background checks for all federal employees. Dykstra would soon tangle with Sproul and the Board of Regents on issues pertaining to the First Amendment and a newly revised university loyalty oath that catapulted the University of California into an American legal fray, but he remained popular with the faculty and alumni and beloved by students. Dykstra's sudden death in 1950 cut short a tenure that nevertheless set UCLA on a course to becoming a nationally renowned university in the decades that followed.

With anti-Communist hysteria escalating across the country, fueled by Sen. Joseph R. McCarthy and his congressional hearings, the University of California Board of Regents sought a new leader for UCLA with a strong anti-Red stance. They found Raymond B. Allen, president of the University of Washington, who had the reputation as a "foe of Reds" for his political beliefs and specific recommendations

resulting in the firing of tenured faculty members accused of having Communist ties. Ironically, Allen was hired for holding the same political wariness that forced Provost Ernest Carroll Moore into retirement. Six years later, Allen would be brought down not by his politics, but by a scandal in athletics that followed the rise and fall of UCLA football.

GI BILL SPURS STUDENT INFLUX

Under the Servicemen's Readjustment Act of 1944, popularly known as the "GI Bill of Rights," World War II veterans inducted into the military when they were no older than 25 and had served at least 90 days in the armed forces were eligible for federal subsidy of tuition and fees, as well as books and supplies, up to $500 a year.

In December 1944, eight months before the war's end, 150 servicemen and women were already enrolled at UCLA under the GI Bill or other federal and state provisions. The number of veterans continued to climb until peaking at 6,255, or 43 percent of all students, by September 1947.

To ease the transition from combat to classroom, Sproul established the Office of Veterans Affairs at UCLA and appointed Robert W. Webb, an assistant geology professor who had led the Army Special Training Programs on campus, as its coordinator.

"The University realizes that each returning veteran has different problems, and therefore it proposes to treat each man as an individual," Webb said. "By recognizing these individual academic problems at the outset, we believe that it will be

A GI Bill veteran enjoys the makeshift patio of his two-story, one-bedroom home, in Gayleyville, a neighborhood of converted wartime housing units.

Above: Veterans and their families moved into Gayleyville, soon thereafter nicknamed Maternity Row.

Right: Two veterans are fitted for artificial limbs, as part of a special College of Engineering training program in limb-fitting that led to the development of new prosthetic technologies, 1947.

Below right: "Wheelchair scholars" register for classes, September 1949.

possible for veterans to assume their work in the University quickly and with no more difficulty than other students."

Great speculation—which time would prove unfounded—arose among educators nationwide as to the aptitude and seriousness of the veterans. Rather than creating experimental colleges and curricula, as many American universities opted to do, the University of California instead relaxed its requirements and created "acceleration programs" so that veterans could more rapidly complete their undergraduate work and embark on their chosen field of graduate study.

"They knew better what they wanted," recalled Paul A. Dodd, dean of the College of Letters and Science. "Their goals were fixed, and they plunged in, and they did better academic work from the start—partly because of their experiences, the loss of time, precious time, in war service or war-related services, and again partly because their incentives had been strengthened, and their goals were far more definite."

The administration realized it needed to provide housing to accommodate the more mature students, many of whom were married. In 1946, it transported 22 two-story wartime housing units from the Kaiser Shipyards in Vanport, Oregon, to Gayley Avenue and converted them into one-bedroom homes for 250 veteran families. Later, another 50 units were added. The new neighborhood, located across from Fraternity Row, was called Gayleyville, soon to be nicknamed Maternity Row.

One year after its creation, with an ever-growing waiting list, Gayleyville turned into a cooperative under the auspices of the Associated Students. The Gayleyville Association, the co-op's self-governing body, created its own employment bureau, health plan, volunteer fire and police departments, and nursery for preschool youngsters. Gayleyvillagers included more than 400 children. Gayleyville

thrived, continuing to provide housing for veteran families throughout the Korean War. (By 1961, veteran demand dissipated and non-veteran married students and faculty moved in. By 1968, the dilapidated units, never intended to be permanent, were dismantled and married students could reside in permanent facilities on Sawtelle and Sepulveda boulevards.)

In addition to accommodating married veterans, UCLA made modifications to assist students who returned from war with injuries. Twelve housing units were converted for use by paraplegics. UCLA instituted a rehabilitation program that included swimming, exercise and other therapy for paralyzed ex-GIs. The campus was outfitted with ramps to aid wheelchair-users. A call-buzzer system was installed in the library to provide easy assistance to the stacks. Buzzers also were available outside the Office of Veterans Affairs so students could request service without getting out of their cars. The student-run Cal-Vet organization recruited volunteers to assist quadriplegics from cars into wheelchairs and take them to and from classes.

In 1948, UCLA reportedly enrolled the largest number of "wheelchair scholars" of any university in the country. Colonel T.J. Cross, acting deputy administrator of the Veterans Regional Office in San Francisco, called the program the "finest of its kind in any university in America."

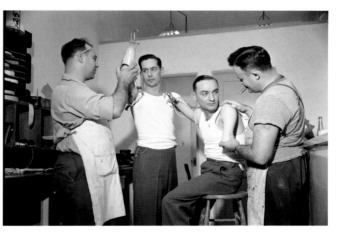

A BELOVED LEADER

As World War II wound down, UCLA alumni leaders began pressuring President Sproul and the regents for a new UCLA chief executive—and they had someone in mind: Clarence Addison Dykstra, who took a sabbatical as president of the University of Wisconsin to serve as President Franklin D. Roosevelt's first head of the U.S. Selective Service. Dykstra had previously taught at UCLA as a lecturer in municipal administration from 1923–27 and professor of political science from 1928–30, and alumni remembered him fondly and with great respect. Dykstra was familiar with the city of Los Angeles, having been director of personnel and efficiency for the Department of Water and Power while simultaneously teaching at UCLA.

The regents were looking for someone with university administrative experience and familiarity with veterans issues to lead the campus during a time of projected expansion and enrollment growth due to the GI Bill. But when Sproul first broached the subject with him, Dykstra declined, saying that while he felt sentimentally tied to UCLA, he could not leave Wisconsin. UCLA alumni, many of whom believed that

Sproul simply did not want to fill the position with a capable administrator because he preferred to continue running the campus himself, began pressuring not only Sproul and the regents, but Dykstra directly. Finally, in October 1944, the Board of Regents officially announced that Dykstra would be UCLA's new chief.

In a November 1944 letter to Wisconsin friend George I. Haight, Dykstra wrote: "Earlier in the year, I refused the position which I have now accepted. Those people out there would not take no for an answer and they did every possible thing to make me feel that I was essential in the new setup which they are inaugurating on the UCLA campus."

"In a sense it is home to me," Dykstra continued. "It is the fastest growing educational institution in the United States, I presume, and its future is quite unlimited. Furthermore it is young enough not to be so set that many things can be done easily and enthusiastically that are difficult to do in older institutions."

Dykstra, 61, held only the title of provost—the vice president title was not given to him until three years later—but was assured by Sproul that he would have final say on actions concerning the campus, subject to the president's approval, similar to the president's relationship to the regents. However, like the chief executives before him, Dykstra soon realized that he did not have as much authority as promised. He became increasingly frustrated, although he continued to champion the campus and push his goals forward.

Dykstra took office on February 8, 1945, and as soon as he settled into the University Residence, he and his wife, Lillian, held a series of open houses inviting the entire campus population to drop by. "We hope to get acquainted with as

Clarence Addison Dykstra

Clarence A. Dykstra—the first UCLA chief executive who had previously led a major university—was born in Cleveland on February 25, 1883.

Dykstra graduated from the University of Iowa in 1903, and pursued graduate work at the University of Chicago. From 1907–09, he taught history and government at Ohio State University. He then taught political science at the University of Kansas for nine years. A self-described bookworm, he decided to go "out into the world and see the things I am going to teach about."

Dykstra taught at UCLA from 1923–27 as a lecturer of municipal administration, and then from 1928–30 as a professor of political science. Also during that period, he served as commissioner of the Los Angeles Department of Water and Power, and as its director of personnel and efficiency.

In 1930, Dykstra was named Cincinnati's city manager and in 1937 became president of the University of Wisconsin. During World War II, he was called on by President Franklin D. Roosevelt to serve as the first head of the U.S. Selective Service and was also chairman of the National Defense Mediation Board.

Throughout his tenure, Clarence A. Dykstra championed on-campus housing for students.

After initial resistance, Dykstra accepted the provost position at UCLA in February 1945, stepping down from the presidency of Wisconsin. He was welcomed back to UCLA by an enthusiastic crowd on Royce quad. "We can do great things if we work together in harmonious cooperation," he said. "I have the greatest confidence in the future of this institution."

As he did at Wisconsin, Dykstra championed student housing, which he believed was an important part of the college experience. "Many of our larger universities are charged with being 'street car colleges,'" Dykstra said during his first weeks at UCLA. "Students live at home, commute to school via the subway, bus or private jalopy, eat lunch from a paper sack as they study, return home immediately after classes are over. This provides little time for enjoying the cultural and intellectual riches with which every college and university abounds."

Dykstra was beloved by the alumni, and the students adored him and his wife, Lillian. They would often serenade the couple outside the University Residence. "For he's a jolly good fellow!" wrote the 1949 *Southern Campus*. "We sang that refrain to him at the Christmas serenade and we sang his praises throughout the year. We boast of his school spirit, of his ability as our chief executive; but, above all, we're proud that UCLA's provost is Dr. Clarence Dykstra."

On May 6, 1950, a year before his scheduled retirement, Dykstra suffered a heart attack and died while tending to a fire adjacent to his summer home in Laguna Beach, California. He had had a stroke two years before, and was "taking it easy" under physician's orders. Nevertheless he continued to serve the university in vigorous fashion, "which was the only way he knew," wrote the May 1950 *UCLA Alumni Magazine*. "It was a difficult assignment but he loved UCLA too much to let go." Some faculty members speculated that the pressure Dykstra faced battling with University of California President Robert Gordon Sproul over the autonomy of UCLA was the reason for Dykstra's sudden death at the age of 67.

"Provost Dykstra will always be remembered by the students for his interest in student problems, for his inspirational wisdom, and for his personable character," said 1950 student body President Sherrill Luke at Dykstra's memorial service. "His imprint will remain as long as there stands a University of California at Los Angeles." In honor of the provost, UCLA's first high-rise residence hall, which opened in 1959, was named for him.

many of you as can come," Dykstra wrote in a *California Bruin* announcement addressed to students. His affable nature endeared him to professors, students and alumni alike. "Dyke," as he was affectionately called by friends and colleagues, or "Papa Dykstra" by his staff, kept an open-door policy and it was said that he was uniquely skilled in "being able to disagree without being disagreeable."

When it came to luring faculty from their posts at prestigious universities, Dykstra had no fear. "You've got to have fine teachers and brilliant scientists else you have no university at all," he said.

More than 300 educators from across the country joined UCLA's faculty during the early years of Dykstra's tenure. Academic circles were astonished when economist Neil H. Jacoby, widely thought to be next in line to lead the University of Chicago, resigned to head UCLA's College of Business Administration. Dykstra's charm, informality and premise of "it's your department, build it as you think it should be built" were credited in part for his success.

New hires came from all over the country, but one institution in particular—Vanderbilt University—was a fruitful conduit for three key hires that would profoundly shape UCLA: Lulu K. Wolf as dean of the new School of Nursing, Henry "Red" Sanders as head football coach, and L. Dale

Coffman as dean of the new School of Law. Sanders brought with him six members of his coaching staff, including future head football Coach James Thompson "Tommy" Prothro Jr., while two noted law professors, Rollin M. Perkins and Harold E. Verrall, followed Coffman.

One Vanderbilt jokester posted the following message on the Nashville-based university's bulletin boards: "Plane leaving for Los Angeles (U.C.L.A.) Saturday. Still room for two math professors and one soccer coach."

While the recruitment of professors from one university to another had long been standard competitive practice, Vanderbilt's administration was not laughing. "This series of losses, all to UCLA, we took at first in a joking manner," wrote Chancellor Harvie Branscomb in a letter to Dykstra asking him to stop or at the very least delay UCLA's recruiting from Vanderbilt. "In all seriousness, it seems to us that Vanderbilt University has made its contribution to UCLA and that we can fairly ask you to spare us further losses at this time, particularly since your institution is in position to draw from all of the country."

In addition to building the faculty, Dykstra had a vision of turning UCLA from a commuter school into a residential one, as he had done at the University of Wisconsin, where he doubled housing facilities. Dykstra

The Caps

Lulu Wolf Hassenplug, the founding dean of the School of Nursing credited with liberating the "handmaidens of medicine," encountered many challenges when she started at UCLA in 1948.

Hassenplug—recruited by Provost Clarence A. Dykstra from Vanderbilt University where she was a professor of nursing—helped create the first undergraduate nursing program in the western United States when the UCLA School of Nursing was founded in 1949. She followed that by implementing graduate programs. The nursing pioneer championed a movement to treat future nurses like students—not hospital employees—by moving nursing education to college campuses and away from the control of hospitals that often considered them free labor.

Lulu Wolf Hassenplug (right), founding dean of the School of Nursing, 1948–1968, and a pioneer in the modern education of nurses.

mentioned this during his first days as provost, when, according to the *California Bruin*, he told students that university housing was "purposeful as an important aspect of education" and that "residence halls would contribute to the intellectual life of the university." He championed this cause consistently throughout his tenure, but in the teeming postwar years, more urgent needs took precedence. Ultimately, his passionate crusading helped the university move toward an on-campus housing expansion that would accommodate the future baby boom generation. But he would not live to see his dream realized.

On May 6, 1950, Dykstra died after suffering a heart attack while tending to a small fire on a vacant lot adjoining his summer home in Laguna Beach. Shocked students called a three-day moratorium on campus elections, and classes were dismissed so that students could attend a public memorial held in Royce Hall or listen to it piped into classrooms over the public address system.

The 1950 *Southern Campus* was dedicated to Dykstra, and editors included the following to describe their esteemed provost: "Much to be said, little time in which to say it, no time to be wasted."

The day before he died, Dykstra had once again expressed his plans to student body leaders for a campus dormitory system. After his death, students took up his cause and a *California Bruin* editorial called for the first residence hall on campus to be named in Dykstra's memory. The Board of Regents approved a resolution to do so in June 1950, although Clarence A. Dykstra Hall would not be completed until November 1959.

"We are training nurses to think," Hassenplug told the *Los Angeles Times* in 1959. "This is the purpose of a liberal education. A well-trained mind can usually handle any difficulty. A well-trained mind is basic to giving individualized patient care."

Her goal was to accord nursing students the same status as other undergraduates and graduate students on campus. Nursing students were not expected to wear the traditional white hosiery, or to rise whenever a physician entered the classroom. She fought against the creation of a "nurses quarters" in the newly constructed UCLA Medical Center, where nursing students would have been required to live and provide their service to the hospital. She stood up to a physician chancellor, Franklin D. Murphy, who wanted to place the nursing school under the purview of the medical school.

And yet, no action caused more controversy than her elimination of the iconic nursing cap.

It all started at a faculty meeting, where Hassenplug acknowledged she was in a quandary about the cap. "I don't know what to do with that cap," Hassenplug said. "They certainly aren't going to wear it when they go into chemistry classes and English classes. We want them to be as inconspicuous as possible." In addition, the caps would get dirty but nurses did not wash them, and they became a sanitation concern.

"So we said, 'We won't need a cap, because we won't sit in an automobile holding a cap on our lap and then put it on when we go in the hospital,'" Hassenplug said. "We'll just become known as the UCLA nurses. They won't wear a cap.'"

After the change, a student's mother called Hassenplug and said that her daughter needed to wear a cap because otherwise she could not possibly be considered a nurse. Hassenplug said that was fine, "You can get your cap out of wherever you have stored it and give it to her, and she's perfectly right in wearing it if she wants to." The mother became upset, and asked, "How did you know I was a nurse?" Hassenplug's response: "No one but a nurse would call me and say that." The next morning the student went to the dean and said her mother had reconsidered about the cap.

"This was an interesting thing," Hassenplug recalled. "For a long time folks said, 'Oh, yes, I know what's going on at UCLA. That's where that woman won't allow the students to wear caps.'"

"A Dime Novel"

Many students have whiled away the hours immersed in the stacks of Powell Library—studying, writing or even dreaming. In the late 1940s, there among the library's thousands of books, author Ray Bradbury wrote *Fahrenheit 451*, his futuristic novel about censorship and defiance that would be hailed as a masterpiece.

Bradbury had just written a series of stories about book burning throughout history. He was influenced by photographs he had seen in his youth of the Nazis burning books on Berlin streets, and his knowledge of library purges and the killing of authors in the Soviet Union under Lenin and Stalin. He had an idea for a story, but at the time had a newborn at home and was in search of a quiet place to write.

"I had no money for an office, and while wandering around UCLA I heard typing from the basement of Powell Library," Bradbury wrote in the summer 2002 *UCLA Magazine*. "I went to investigate and found a room with 12 typewriters that could be rented for 10 cents a half hour. So, exhilarated, I got a bag of dimes and settled into the room, and in nine days I spent $9.80 and wrote my story; in other words, it was a dime novel.

"The wonderful thing about writing *Fahrenheit 451*, which I called *The Fireman* the first time out, was the fact that I could run up and down stairs in the library and seize books off the shelf, not knowing what I was going to find next, opening the books and discovering quotes to rush back down to the typing room to insert in my novel," Bradbury continued. "It was a passionate and exciting time for me. Imagine what it was like to be writing a book about book burning and doing it in a library where the passions of all those authors, living and dead, surrounded me."

MEDICAL CENTER FOR THE ATOMIC AGE

Echoing the impetus in the late 1930s and early 1940s for the founding of the UCLA schools of business and engineering, faculty and alumni in the postwar era set their sights on establishing a school of medicine at UCLA. They were joined by an influential lobbying force of doctors and medical professionals, which emphasized that a medical school in the Los Angeles area was urgently needed.

Although the University of California had long been operating the Los Angeles Medical Department on North Broadway Avenue, which it took over from the University of Southern California in 1909, the department provided instruction to medical graduates only.

In March 1945, Bennet M. Allen, a UCLA professor of zoology who oversaw the Los Angeles Medical Department, recommended to Dykstra that he consider creating a medical school at UCLA. Although Allen was not a medical doctor, he had devoted the previous nine years to improving the department's quality of care, as well as trying to foster scientific research in a unit that had been functioning primarily as a clinic assisting low-income patients. He argued that the University of California had never invested sufficient funding for it to develop as a proper medical school. However, when the regents originally assumed control of the department, it had been running as an undergraduate medical school and so, Allen maintained, they had a moral obligation to the people of Los Angeles to transform the department into a professional medical school.

Below left: Author Ray Bradbury wrote his dystopian novel *Fahrenheit 451* in the basement of Powell Library in the late 1940s.

Below: The Los Angeles Medical Department on North Broadway in downtown, transferred by USC to the University of California in 1909, existed a full decade before the founding of the Southern Branch.

Governor Earl Warren (left) and School of Medicine Dean Stafford Leak Warren inspect the future site of the medical school and hospital, 1949.

started developing a plan for establishing the school. The first issue was where to locate it. This led to months of dispute with individuals in the medical community aligning themselves into separate camps: those who believed the school should be on the Westwood campus and those who wanted it affiliated with an established hospital off campus. Specific proposals were made for affiliation with the Los Angeles County General Hospital (later Los Angeles County–USC Medical Center); and for the school to be built at Barnsdall Park, near Sunset Boulevard and Vermont Avenue—closer to nearby hospitals, including Children's Hospital Society of Los Angeles, Cedars of Lebanon, and Presbyterian Hospital, which submitted a joint report in support of the proposed site.

Those who favored the on-campus location argued it would stimulate scientific research through its proximity to other academic disciplines, including engineering, the physical sciences, psychology and the social sciences. Situated near Le Conte Avenue on the southern edge of campus, the school was to anchor the newly conceived Court of Sciences, promoting precisely such interaction. Opponents countered that the off-campus sites would provide more favorable clinical settings, presenting a wider array of ailments for observation. Still others worried that having a clinic on campus would, alarmingly, bring diseases better kept away from a university campus and its neighboring community.

Knudsen and committee members contacted universities with medical schools, as well as prominent medical scientists and other leaders in the field, to solicit advice. Almost unanimously the experts recommended that the UCLA medical school be built on campus—that going off site was an outmoded notion.

Among those surveyed was Stafford L. Warren, professor of radiology at the University of Rochester in upstate New York and former head of the Medical Division of the Manhattan Project. Warren, who had been asked by Sproul to serve as a consultant for the planning of the medical school, was appointed as the founding dean of the UCLA School of Medicine in 1947. Warren was a staunch proponent of tying the medical school to the university's research efforts and urged the construction of not only a medical school on campus, but also a full-scale hospital.

"It is vital that the medical school and hospital be built as a single physical plant so that the teaching can be integrated to best advantage and in keeping with modern trends," Warren wrote to University of California Comptroller James H. Corley in June 1947.

On February 19, 1946, Governor Earl Warren had signed Assembly Bill 35 and its $7 million provision for a medical school at UCLA, stating "there is no area in the United States comparable to southern California so devoid of medical training facilities."

Dykstra was in favor of creating a medical school and persuaded Sproul to appoint a faculty committee, which was headed by Graduate Division-Southern Section Dean Vern O. Knudsen, to look into the matter. Other members included Allen, Dodd and three faculty members from the University of California's San Francisco-based medical school. The committee's resulting study outlined the pressing need for additional medical facilities in Southern California, noting that two-thirds of Los Angeles' doctors had been educated at medical schools elsewhere. There were only two undergraduate medical schools in the region: the College of Medical Evangelists (later Loma Linda University), which admitted few non-Seventh-day Adventist students, and the USC School of Medicine, which admitted about 70 students per year.

On October 18, 1945, the study was presented to the Board of Regents, which approved the motion to create a medical school at UCLA—with only two dissenters from Northern California. Nine days later, the planning committee

OPENING DAY—Checking equipment for UCLA's School of Medicine, which began first sessions yesterday after several years of planning, are Helen Rohlfsen, left, Phyllis Johnson, Dr. W. H. Griffith, head of the new laboratory, and L. R. Stromberg. *Times photo.*

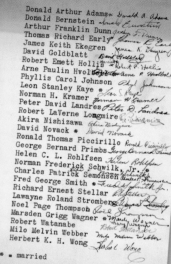

First Class Begins Study at UCLA Medical School

With the reading of the Hippocratic oath, Dr. Stafford L. Warren, dean of UCLA's school of medicine, began the session for the school's first group of students.

"This ancient creed provides a list of guiding principles in professional life," Dean Warren told the 26 men and two women who make up the school's enrollment.

284 Applicants

The students were selected from among 284 who sought admission to the school, which has been in the planning stage for several years. Selection was made on the basis of scholarship, examination and personal interview.

Classes are meeting in the old Religious Conference Building, but a six-floor unit of a planned UCLA medical center is in the second month of a two-year construction schedule.

Although the first class is small, it was noted that present building plans for the first unit are designed for 50 students a class, and provisions have been made for expanding it up to 100 students a class by adding three floors to the building.

Clinical study groups will be held at Veterans Administration Hospitals at Long Beach and at the Los Angeles Sawtelle and at the Los Angeles County Harbor Hospital in Torrance. These facilities will be used even after the UCLA center has been completed, it was announced.

But Dean Warren pushed forward his plans to have both a medical school and a hospital located on campus. He worked directly with University of California architect E. Vernon Barker and campus Supervising Architect Welton Becket. Strategically, the architectural plans called for integration of all units in one massive complex with more than 12 miles of corridors called Unit One. The building, designed in a double cross style known as the Cross of Lorraine, could be expanded in multiple directions with more floors added, but in the meantime, it would accommodate both school and hospital without sacrificing either.

After mobilization and strong support by alumni and local area doctors, including renowned urologist Elmer Belt, who had a direct connection with Governor Warren and was later characterized by Sproul as "The Life Belt of the UCLA Medical School," the budget was increased to $15.5 million.

While plans for the hospital were still far from complete, Dean Warren argued that given the doctor shortage UCLA need not hold back enrolling medical students. With regental approval, the first session of 28 students—26 men and two women, 11 of whom were veterans of World War II—selected from more than 500 applicants began classes in fall 1951, meeting at several temporary facilities, including relocated surplus Army barracks and the former University Religious Conference site on Tiverton and Le Conte avenues. Clinical study was conducted at the Veterans Administration hospitals in Sawtelle and Long Beach, as well as the Los Angeles County Harbor Hospital in Torrance (later Los Angeles County Harbor–UCLA Medical Center).

UCLA SCHOOL OF MEDICINE

Medical Students

Donald Arthur Adams*
Donald Bernstein
Arthur Franklin Dunn
Thomas Richard Early*
James Keith Ekegren
David Goldblatt
Robert Emett Hollis
Arne Paulin Hvolboll
Phyllis Carol Johnson
Leon Stanley Kaye*
Norman H. Kramer
Peter David Landres
Robert LaVerne Longmire
Akira Nishizawa
David Novack*
Ronald Thomas Piccirillo
George Bernard Primbs
Helen C. L. Rohlfsen
Norman Frederick Schwilk, Jr.
Charles Patrick Semonsen
Fred George Smith
Richard Ernest Stellar
Lawayne Roland Stromberg
Noel Page Thompson
Marsden Grigg Wagner*
Robert Watanabe
Milo Melvin Webber
Herbert K. H. Wong

* = married

DONALD A. ADAMS | DONALD BERNSTEIN | ARTHUR F. DUNN | THOMAS R. EARLY | ROBERT HANSEN | ROBERT E. HOLLIS | ARNE P. HVOLBOLL

KIRA NISHIZAWA | THEODORE E. MARSHBURN | ROBERT L. LONGMIRE | PETER D. LANDRES | NORMAN H. KRAMER | LEON S. KAYE | BYRON L. JOHNSON

RONALD T. PICCIRILLO | RENATE PLACZEK | GEORGE B. PRIMBS | HELEN R. SCHULZ | NORMAN F. SCHWILK | CHARLES P. SEMONSEN | FRED G. SMITH

RICHARD E. STELLAR | WAYNE STROMBERG | PHYLLIS G. TAYLOR | GIUSTINO TERRA | NOEL R. THOMPSON | MARSDEN G. WAGNER | ROBERT WATANABE

MILO M. WEBBER

CLASS OF 1955

HERBERT K. H. WONG

The founding five faculty members, including Warren, comprised William P. Longmire Jr. from Johns Hopkins University as chairman of the Department of Surgery, and three doctors from Rochester: John S. Lawrence as the first chairman of the Department of Medicine; Andrew H. Dowdy to lead the Department of Radiology; and Charles M. Carpenter as head of the Department of Infectious Diseases.

"Everyone expected me to appoint faculty eight feet tall, spellbinders, and so on," Warren said. "I wanted good workmen with high standards. These three had been my former associates in Rochester, and I knew they could do the job. They were not afraid of anything. With them, I had the nucleus of a pretty good organization." With regard to Longmire, Warren said that the 34-year-old was "the youngster with the most promise in the nation."

Warren's academic vision was unique: Each department was to have a chair, an assistant professor, an instructor, three residents, an intern and four medical students. "This means that you must have 16 beds as a minimum for this training hierarchy," Warren said. "Each one above trains in a pyramid fashion downward, so that the medical students get a great

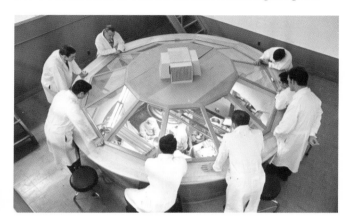

Below: The founding five faculty members (from left): Andrew H. Dowdy, chairman of the Department of Radiology; Stafford Leak Warren, dean of the School of Medicine; John S. Lawrence, chairman of the Department of Medicine; Charles M. Carpenter, chairman of the Department of Infectious Diseases; and William P. Longmire Jr., chairman of the Department of Surgery.

Early instruction included observing surgery through the dome above an operating room (top right), pathology class (above right), and learning about the negative pressure ventilator, also known as the iron lung (right).

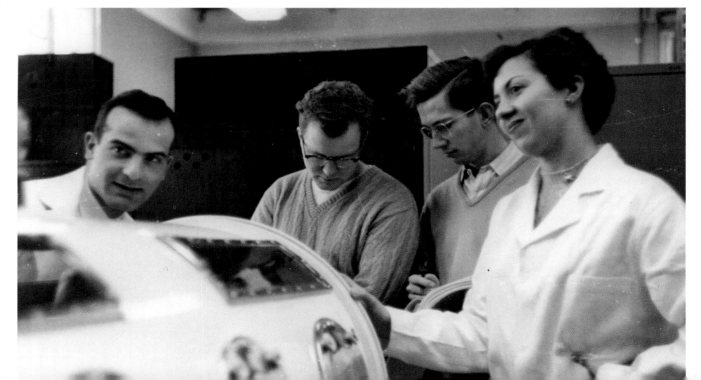

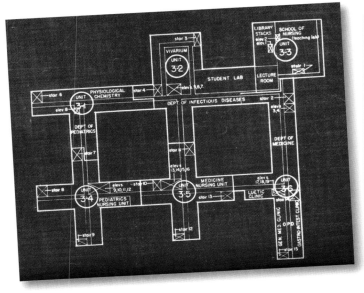

Far left: The massive edifice built to accommodate both the hospital and medical school was designed in a Cross of Lorraine style that could be expanded in multiple directions and with additional floors.

Left: The first steel beams for the hospital were set into place in February 1949 at a ceremony attended by (from left) President Robert Gordon Sproul, Governor Earl Warren, Regent Edward A. Dickson and Dean Stafford Leak Warren.

deal of education from their experience in each specialty. … Adding all of these elements together is how I came out with the space that's required."

Recalled Longmire: "What really gave this school such an appeal to me and others was the idea of participating in a complete medical school with sound academic principles behind it, with its own hospital, and designed around the number of students who were to be taught. It was a package that had never been put together before."

Excavation for the hospital began in 1949, and construction continued into the 1950s amid delays posed by the Korean War and a steel workers union strike. Costs

continued to increase and Sproul, while committed to the idea of a strong UCLA medical school and hospital, was ever vigilant about the widening scope and project budget. Warren pushed forward despite administrative obstacles.

The hospital was modeled after Rochester, which had opened just after World War I, and was then considered the future of medicine for including both medical school and hospital on the same site. Warren, who previously had been involved with the building of several hospitals, oversaw every phase of the

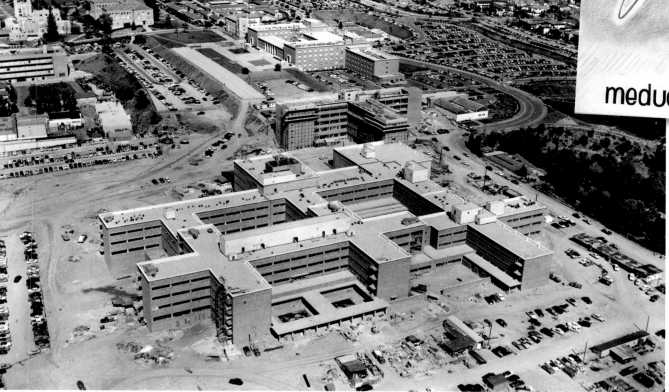

When it opened in 1955, the UCLA Medical Center was heralded as the first hospital of the Atomic Age.

or in other areas where natural light was abundant. Indicative of the developing Cold War, the underground rooms, which included the radiology department, were deemed to be safe in the event of aerial attack.

Occupying 35 acres and costing upward of $25 million, the comprehensive medical center would ultimately include not only the medical school and hospital, but the nursing and dental schools, a student health center and the Neuropsychiatric Institute—funded initially by the California State Department of Mental Hygiene.

To bring in additional dollars, Warren rallied Hollywood celebrities such as comedian Bob Hope in fundraising efforts. In 1952, screen star Marion Davies successfully petitioned the state to dissolve her philanthropic foundation and turned its assets valued at $1.5 million over to UCLA to build a wing to house the children's clinic she had created in 1926 and whose operation was assumed by the School of Medicine.

The UCLA Medical Center, containing the first medical school built in the United States in more than 20 years and heralded in the press as the first medical facility of the Atomic Age, opened to patients on July 7, 1955.

Above: Out of Cold War-era concerns, the hospital's radiology department was located underground.

Above right: Dean Stafford Leak Warren was also in charge of an Atomic Energy Commission group that was studying the consequences of radioactive exposure in the medical field.

UCLA Medical Center's development and incorporated designs innovative for the time.

"Because this is really going to be an entirely new kind of medical school and research center," Warren told the *Los Angeles Times*, "we have had to plan it for 50 years ahead of time—for A.D. 2000 instead of for 1953."

Operating rooms were placed in the basement in a vast system of underground rooms and corridors. Up until then, hospital operating rooms had routinely been built on top floors

Left: Alumnus J. Reginald Richardson (left), renowned accelerator physicist with UCLA faculty colleagues Byron Wright (center), Kenneth R. MacKenzie (right) and Steve H. Plunkett (kneeling), c.1962. Richardson led the design and construction of the physics department's 50 MeV Spiral-Ridge Cyclotron.

Above: Raymond B. Allen bids farewell to a UCLA group traveling to Bombay for Project India, July 2, 1953. Created long before the Peace Corps, and sponsored by the University Religious Conference, Project India sent undergraduates and faculty advisers overseas for a summer to work in local communities by helping build schools, harvest crops or engage in other humanitarian work, while intending to dispel Communist propaganda aimed at the United States.

The Highest Alumni Honor

From entertainers to Nobel laureates, politicians to athletes, those who have received the Edward A. Dickson Alumnus of the Year Award—UCLA's highest alumni honor—are among UCLA's most distinguished sons and daughters.

"Ever since the establishment of this great educational institution, our alumni—collectively and individually—have contributed mightily to the progress, power and prestige of our University," said Frank M. McKellar, president of the UCLA Alumni Association, during the presentation of the first award at the 1946 spring homecoming banquet. "Some have rendered unusual and conspicuous service and it has been felt that there ought to be some way by which the University's gratitude might be formally expressed."

The idea arose in an informal conversation between McKellar and University of California Regent Edward A. Dickson. A few days later, Dickson donated $3,000 to create a perpetual fund to endow the award, and also directed that a standing committee of the Alumni Council be created to select the recipient each year. The award was officially designated the Edward A. Dickson Achievement Award, but became popularly known as "Alumnus of the Year." It recognizes an alumnus or alumna who "has rendered a special and outstanding service to the University" or who, by personal achievement, "has brought honor and distinction to the University."

The inaugural award was bestowed upon Assemblyman M. Phillip Davis, a past president of the Alumni Association who authored the bill creating the UCLA School of Medicine. In 1947, William C. Ackerman, UCLA's first tennis coach and longtime director of the Associated Students, was honored, followed by Lieutenant Governor Frederick F. Houser in 1948.

Ralph J. Bunche, future under-secretary-general of the United Nations, received the award in 1949, a year before he earned the Nobel Peace Prize. "UCLA was where it all began for me," Bunche said. "I came from the ghetto of east Los Angeles. Very quickly, I gained a sense of purpose and direction, a feeling of belonging, of confidence, self-respect, and personal dignity. Nothing could have been more indispensable to me at that critical stage of my life."

Other Nobel laureates named Alumnus of the Year include scientist Glenn T. Seaborg in 1952 and biochemist Bruce Merrifield in 1997. Several artists and entertainers have received the honor, including choreographer Agnes de Mille (1953), opera singer Jerome Hine (1965), film director Francis Ford Coppola (1975), and comedienne Carol Burnett (1968). "It was during my years at UCLA that I decided to become a professional performer," Burnett said. "The initial experience of response from an audience in a student production was one of the turning points of my life. I value my years at UCLA more than I can express."

Track and field Olympian Jackie Joyner-Kersee (2001), basketball great Kareem Abdul-Jabbar (1990), Olympian decathlete Rafer Johnson (1986) and baseball legend Jackie Robinson (1962) are some of the distinguished athletes who have been honored. Tennis champion Arthur Ashe was selected to receive the award in 1993, but died before the ceremony, becoming the only individual to receive the recognition posthumously. Basketball Coach John R. Wooden was accorded special honorary alumnus status and received the award in 1973—the only non-alumnus so honored.

The awardees also include the infamous, such as Nixon White House aide H.R. Haldeman, who was honored in 1970, five years before he was convicted of conspiracy to obstruct justice and perjury in the Watergate scandal.

The recipient selections have not been without controversy. In 2003, Tim Robbins was chosen for his work in film, as well as his support of the School of Theater, Film and Television. Robbins, who also was known for his liberal activism, came under criticism for having expressed his views against the Iraq War and his selection was questioned by political conservatives.

As UCLA briefly caught the media glare, Alumni Association Executive Director Keith E. Brant appeared on the Fox News Channel's *O'Reilly Factor* to explain the Association's position.

Politics, Brant told host Bill O'Reilly, were "irrelevant to the process." He added: "If you look at the list of people we've honored in the last 60 years, they run the political spectrum." Indeed, the following year, the alumni committee chose Alaska Senator Ted Stevens, a Republican.

In 1946, Association President McKellar summed up the new tradition by calling inaugural recipient Davis "the forerunner of a long line of alumni who in future years will be the recipients of this token of our appreciation, our esteem and our affection."

William C. Ackerman (left) is bestowed Alumnus of the Year honors by the award's namesake, Edward A. Dickson, 1947.

L. Dale Coffman, founding dean of the School of Law, sits in the tractor's cab, while Regent Edward A. Dickson (left) and Professor Roscoe Pound inspect plans for the school's building.

A LAW SCHOOL OF INDEPENDENT RESOLVE

Along with an increasing emphasis in medicine and the sciences, veterans—determined to embark on professional careers—demonstrated an escalating interest in jurisprudence. During the war, enrollment in the nation's law schools fell by more than 80 percent, forcing several schools to temporarily cease operations. However, by 1947, there were more than 50,000 law students—almost twice as many as had been enrolled before the war. In California, law schools were packed and many prospective students were being turned away.

UCLA supporters, among them officers of the Los Angeles Bar Association and prominent members of the judiciary, had expressed their desire for the establishment of a law school on campus in the early 1930s, but the notion was rejected by Sproul, who stated that expansion of legal education in California was unwarranted.

"A law school will be established if, as, and when it becomes clear that there is an under supply of lawyers for the needs of the State of California or that the present law schools are not serving adequately and properly the population of the State," Sproul wrote in response to an inquiry from California Supreme Court Chief Justice William H. Waste, who had matriculated from Los Angeles High School before receiving degrees from Berkeley and the Hastings College of Law. "A limiting factor in any case, of course, will be the financial ability of the State to pay for such service as may prove to be desirable."

A review conducted by University of California Registrar William C. Pomeroy at Sproul's request in 1934 concluded that California's 20 law schools were already producing more lawyers than the state needed.

"In terms of numbers the profession of law is decidedly over crowded," Pomeroy wrote in his report, noting that California had one lawyer per every 562 inhabitants, compared with one for every 764 in the United States. "Pennsylvania has one lawyer for every 1190 inhabitants and yet the bar of that state is generally considered to be crowded. … It is evident that some reduction rather than increase in the bar membership is to be desired."

UCLA alumni would not formally push the issue, instead setting sights on successfully moving forward a postwar building agenda that included the creation of the schools of engineering and medicine. But in 1945, the idea would resurface from an unexpected supporter. Assemblyman William H. Rosenthal, who represented the community of Boyle Heights across town in East Los Angeles, introduced a bill to create a law school at UCLA. "I felt the need for boys and girls who didn't have enough money to go to 'SC or some of the other colleges at the time," Rosenthal explained, "so I decided it was time to have a law school in Los Angeles County near the major part of the population."

Rosenthal enlisted UCLA friend and Hollywood comedian Joe E. Brown to speak on behalf of the bill, but it died in committee and Rosenthal was told by a University of California legislative representative that Los Angeles was "too provincial and that we had no right to ask for a law school in Los Angeles County."

Recalled Rosenthal: "Being a novice, I didn't know just how difficult it would be. I didn't realize that California was the place where the law schools were maintained. California at Berkeley had all the money and dispersed it in their own way. I didn't realize, of course, that I was bucking a large organization."

Determined, in 1947 Rosenthal again sponsored the bill, this time with nine additional cosigners, including UCLA alumnus and future federal judge Laughlin E. Waters. To gain Northern legislator approval—Los Angeles had only one state senatorial district at the time—he amended an existing bill in support of an appropriation for the Hastings School of Law into the UCLA law school bill.

Sproul, increasingly frustrated in his effort to maintain control of the university's agenda, said he did not believe the university should submit to political pressure. The regents, too, opposed the bill, concerned that it might jeopardize

appropriations for other priority University of California projects, including additional funding for UCLA's medical center and engineering school, which were still not adequately financed. While the bill passed in both the Assembly and Senate, Governor Warren sent it back, asking Rosenthal to separate the Hastings and UCLA appropriations.

In a deft political move, Rosenthal drafted a new bill solely for the UCLA law school and shepherded it first through committee to the Assembly. When asked about the Hastings bill, Rosenthal responded, "As soon as my bill passes here, I assure you that the Hastings bill will come out of the committee." He repeated the same tactic in the Senate.

Surprisingly, the bill providing $1 million to establish a law school at UCLA met no resistance in the closing rush of the Legislature. In the meantime, support for a UCLA law school was mounting. The State Bar of California passed a resolution endorsing the bill and urged the regents and the governor to support the legislation. UCLA Alumni Association President Frank M. McKellar sent a telegram to Edward A. Dickson, chairman of the Board of Regents, stating that UCLA alumni had always been interested in creating a law school and requested that the regents actively support the bill.

The regents found themselves in the discomfited public position of endorsing something they had ardently opposed, or turning down funds. The *California Bruin* reported that the "unasked and unsponsored by the University" bill was

facing possible veto by the governor "if he receives word from the Board of Regents advocating postponement of the undertaking."

At the June 27, 1947, Board of Regents meeting, Dickson said he had been willing to oppose the bill when it was believed to put other funding in jeopardy, but since the bill had passed both houses of the Legislature, he believed the regents were in no position to refuse the money. The board voted 10–1 to recommend approval of the bill, with Sproul abstaining, noting that it would be embarrassing for him to vote in favor of a bill he had so vigorously opposed. Assembly Bill 1361 was signed by Governor Warren on July 18, 1947.

The search for a dean would prove difficult, exacerbated by the simultaneous deanship vacancy at Berkeley's law school and by the conservative political views of the regents. At one point, the search committee, led by Dykstra, Dodd and Social Sciences Division Dean A.C. Grant, wanted Harry Shulman of Yale, but were told the regents would not approve the well-respected labor-management dispute arbitrator because he was born in Russia. Without a dean at the helm, the opening of UCLA's new law school had to be delayed a year.

Finally, in January 1949, L. Dale Coffman, who had spent the previous two years rebuilding Vanderbilt's law school after its postwar reopening, was selected to head the school. Coffman impressed Dickson and other regents and was appointed over the search committee's objections. "His view concerning infiltration of 'Red' or 'Pink' elements in our university, and particularly our law school, coincides with the view of the Southern Regents," wrote Regent Victor R. Hansen to Sproul.

Coffman would become a vocal supporter of the regents during the emergent loyalty oath controversy that pitted faculty and academic freedom versus the regents and anti-Communist political beliefs at a time of growing nationwide fervor. In his first address as dean, Coffman said: "There are no Communists on this law faculty, and there will be no Communists on this faculty."

Coffman sought greater independence for the law school from the campus, specifically the Academic Senate. During the accreditation process, he enlisted the support of the Association of American Law Schools, and with support of his powerful allies within the regents, successfully

engineered the removal of the law school from the Academic Senate—a body he and the pro-oath regents viewed as comprising left-leaning liberals.

The result gave Coffman greater flexibility with faculty appointments, salaries, budgets and course selection, all of which were no longer subject to the senate committee process. (Coffman's autocratic style—particularly with regard to vetoing certain professorial hires promoted by the law faculty—would cost him, and he was removed from the deanship after a faculty revolt in 1956. In 1962, University of California President Clark Kerr persuaded the regents to put UCLA's law school—and Berkeley's, which had followed suit— back under the Academic Senate, with the exception of course review, which remained the jurisdiction of each law school.)

In trying to shape the nascent law school, Coffman made efforts to emulate the traditions of Harvard and other esteemed private law schools. He recruited Roscoe Pound, retired longtime dean of the Harvard School of Law, as a visiting professor. Pound, considered by many to be the father of modern American jurisprudence, had recently returned from two years in China, advising Chiang Kai-shek on codifying Chinese law. Pound, 78, was the pillar of the original law faculty, which also included: Brainerd Currie, conflicts-of-law innovator; Rollin M. Perkins, criminal law expert; and Harold E. Verrall, property law pioneer.

"Harvard was always ahead of its time, and Roscoe Pound brought that spirit with him," recalled Dorothy Wright Nelson, a member of the second law school class who became the first female law faculty member and later dean of USC's law school before becoming a federal judge. "Until I went into teaching myself, I didn't fully appreciate how far ahead some of our faculty were of many of their colleagues at other good law schools."

In temporary barracks behind Royce Hall and with provisional accreditation from the California Bar Association, the UCLA School of Law enrolled its first class in September 1949. The permanent building, constructed on the periphery of campus across from the administration building, was completed in 1951 and the law school's initial class of 44 graduated in 1952. The school's early students fashioned a strong, independent resolve that would leave its own imprint.

"Our first several classes included many returning war veterans who had command experience and were used to responsibility," recalled Frances McQuade, who was appointed secretary to Coffman in 1949 and rose to assistant dean of administration 31 years later. "These students rebelled against doing things just because that's how other law schools did them. With no tradition hanging over the school, they felt very free to make suggestions, and we had faculty who were quite open to hearing them. That set the tone."

DIVISIVE LOYALTY OATH

Just as the law school was getting underway, the university was embroiling itself in a constitutional conflict that would become "the greatest contaminant ever to enter the body politic of the University of California," in the words of future university President Clark Kerr, and the "greatest single confrontation between a university faculty and its board of trustees in American history."

In the world backdrop, communism was gaining a stronghold. The Soviet Union's influence spread into Eastern Europe, expanding the Soviet Bloc. In East Asia, the North Korean People's Army—which would receive support from the Soviets and the newly formed government of the People's Republic of China—invaded South Korea, bringing about U.S. involvement in the three-year Korean War. The Cold War was in full force.

While Communist sympathies and presence in the United States were minimal, concern was rampant over subversives infiltrating American hallmarks such as Hollywood's motion picture industry and institutions of higher learning whose research missions were increasingly supported by state and federal dollars. The University of California, with its nuclear laboratories and secret government work, was considered, if not particularly vulnerable, a highly visible target.

Politicians—the most notable being U.S. Senator Joseph McCarthy—used the hysteria to advance their political agendas with smear tactics and blacklisting: a strategy—and era—soon defined as "McCarthyism." In their zeal, they often overlooked civil liberties. Loyalties were in constant question and political tests were instituted, starting at the very highest levels. In 1947, President Truman had instituted mandatory background checks and loyalty oaths for all federal employees. By 1951, all 50 states had legislation dealing with subversive activities; 42 of them required loyalty oaths. California had a mandatory loyalty oath for state government employees dating back to 1849, just prior to its statehood. For 100 years, it required affirmers to uphold the constitutions of both California and the United States.

Like many states, California created its own legislative subcommittee to investigate "un-American" activities. In 1949, state Senator Jack Tenney, who represented Los Angeles and was chairman of the Legislature's Joint Fact-Finding Committee on Un-American Activities, introduced 13 bills seeking to "isolate, expose and remove from positions of power and influence persons who are a dangerous menace to our freedom and security." One bill directly affected the University of California's autonomy. It sought a constitutional amendment to give the Legislature power over ensuring the loyalty of all university employees.

At the suggestion of James H. Corley, the university's comptroller and representative to Sacramento, Sproul recommended that the regents preempt legislative intrusion by creating a new oath for the University of California, which in 1940 had already adopted a policy banning employment to Communists. Several regents made persuasive efforts to assure legislators that they would handle the matter effectively. Tenney's bill died in committee, but the regents, influenced by two publicly scrutinized events at UCLA, continued to move forward.

On February 1, 1949, the University of Washington dismissed two self-admitted Communists and tenured faculty members on the recommendation of Washington President Raymond B. Allen. Several weeks after his removal, one of the professors, Herbert J. Phillips, participated in a debate at UCLA over whether a Communist could be an impartial teacher and scholar. The Graduate Student Association received permission from Dykstra to hold the event. Dykstra, confident that having the other side represented by University of Washington Professor Merritt Benson made it a fair debate, gave his blessing with an additional caveat: that only graduate students and faculty members attend. This restriction drew criticism from some professors and 2,210 students signed a petition urging that the debate be opened. When Dykstra declined to change the forum, the petitioners turned to the local press and the

Alumnus Thelner Hoover (right) taking student identification photos, 1947.

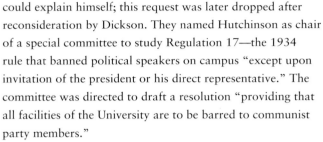

Right: The *Daily Californian* captures the loyalty oath controversy, July 7, 1949.

Below: Robert Gordon Sproul (below) addresses the Board of Regents, during its meeting on August 25, 1949, where 31 non-signers of the loyalty oath, four from UCLA, were fired. Members of the public (below right) crowded outside to await the board's vote.

publicity caught the regents' attention. Chairman Dickson, in particular, was not pleased that a known Communist was invited by the provost to speak at UCLA.

Paul Revere Hutchinson, the first UCLA Alumni Association president to serve as representative to the Board of Regents, defended Dykstra. He argued that it was Allen himself who gave the provost the name of one of the debate participants and that it was not a failure of Dykstra's decision making, but a result of unclear rules. Rather than taking any immediate action to censure the provost, the regents decided to summon Dykstra to their next meeting so that he

could explain himself; this request was later dropped after reconsideration by Dickson. They named Hutchinson as chair of a special committee to study Regulation 17—the 1934 rule that banned political speakers on campus "except upon invitation of the president or his direct representative." The committee was directed to draft a resolution "providing that all facilities of the University are to be barred to communist party members."

A few weeks later, there was concern over another UCLA event. Controversial British Socialist Harold J. Laski from the London School of Economics had reportedly been invited to speak on campus by the UCLA Institute of Industrial Relations. Dykstra said he had approved the invitation based on information that Laski would also be speaking at Berkeley, only to learn later that this was not the case. After further consultation, Dykstra withdrew the invitation. While Laski did not hold an elected office, the regents began to question whether left-leaning individuals should ever be allowed to speak on university grounds.

Dykstra had already come under scrutiny during his first year as provost for upholding students' rights to protest off campus outside Warner Bros. during a demonstration against movie-studio strike violence. "I have never separated students from other citizens in their rights to freedom of speech and religions," Dykstra told members of an Assembly investigating committee gathered in Kerckhoff Hall in November 1945, which had subpoenaed and interrogated student protesters. "Students have a right to express themselves as citizens as long as it does not violate civil laws, but they have no right to represent the whole University unless authorized." Dykstra stated that students would not be expelled as they had not violated university regulations.

Influenced by the UCLA incidents, on March 25, 1949, the regents in an unpublicized open session action made a unanimous decision to further strengthen the employment prohibition of Communists and their use of university facilities for speaking engagements and any other activities.

In executive session on June 12, 1949, the following oath was adopted: "I do not believe in, and I am not a member of, nor do I support any party or organization that believes in, advocates or teaches the overthrow of the United States Government, by force or by any illegal or unconstitutional methods." On June 24, the oath was amended to more specifically include: "I am not a member of the Communist Party or under any oath or a party to any agreement or under any commitment that is in conflict with my obligations under this oath." The new oath would have to be signed or the employee, whether faculty or staff, would be discharged from the university.

All of this was instituted without consulting the Academic Senate and most professors first learned of the new

The Royce quad, mid-1940s.

oath from a vague reference in the faculty bulletin. Both the Northern and Southern sections of the Senate passed resolutions protesting the oath on the grounds that it was an ineffective way to detect Communists and that it challenged the principle of tenure and, moreover, was unconstitutional. The faculty's indignation caught Sproul off guard. It had not been his intention to affect the senate's integrity of self-government, or infringe upon its academic freedom and the privilege of tenure.

The issue became divisive, was debated in academic circles and made headlines in newspapers across the country. In California, the *Los Angeles Times* and the Hearst newspapers supported the oath requirement, while the *Los Angeles Daily News* and the *San Francisco Chronicle* opposed it.

"The University of California, over a span of 90 years, has become one of the great universities of the world," began an editorial in the February 28, 1950, edition of the *San Francisco*

Chronicle. "Now a majority action by the Board of Regents has threatened to eclipse its prestige and undermine its effectiveness as a seat of culture and a builder of character. That was not the purpose of the non-Communist oath but that will be its effect. You can't catch a Communist by making him swear that he isn't one. But you can ruin a university by destroying the atmosphere of intellectual freedom in which it has thrived."

Sproul, who initially recommended the oath, reversed his position and fought to keep the non-signers employed. The regents' opposition to the oath was led by Governor Warren, who publicly lambasted the oath to the *San Francisco Chronicle* because it "singled out" the university faculty and because it was not "an oath required by law," and as such he said no Communist taking it could be punished for perjury. Regent John Francis Neylan, who initially opposed the oath, ardently led the pro-oath regents, who included Edwin W.

Pauley and John E. Canaday, president of the UCLA Alumni Association. While most faculty members signed the oath, internal surveys and petitions conducted by the Senate revealed that the majority were against it.

The issue progressed from concern over Communists to control of the university by the regents. At the August 25, 1950 regents meeting, while discussing the dismissal of non-signers, Warren asked: "Do I understand that we are firing these people merely because they are recalcitrant?" Regent Arthur J. McFadden responded, "It is not a question of Communism, but one of discipline."

During the meeting, 31 non-signers were fired, four of them from UCLA: John Caughey, history professor; Stephen Enke, lecturer in business administration; Charles L. Mowat, assistant professor of history; and David S. Saxon, assistant professor of physics, who two decades later would become the first University of California president from UCLA. Nationwide, 69 professors were dismissed from their university posts for their political views—including the 31 from the University of California. Within days, 20 of the faculty non-signers—none from UCLA—took the University of California to court for their jobs, although two later dropped out of the suit. The California appellate court ruled on April 6, 1951, that the university's oath was unconstitutional. The regents, however, were not ready to give up.

Two years later, on October 17, 1952, the California State Supreme Court, in a unanimous decision in *Tolman v. Underhill*, voided the university's loyalty oath requirement with the opinion that "university personnel cannot properly be required to execute any other oath or declaration relating to loyalty than that prescribed for all state employees." The court further ordered that the non-signers who were dismissed be reinstated with back pay. The same day the court upheld the Levering Act, emergency legislation signed by Governor Warren on October 3, 1950, which made all state employees "civil defense workers" and required them to uphold the state and U.S. constitutions and disavow membership in any party or organization that advocated overthrowing the government. (In 1967, following U.S. Supreme Court decisions on cases across the country, the California Supreme Court held that the Levering Act's clause on subversive organizations and advocacy was unconstitutional. California's constitution still includes a loyalty oath for state employees, but it does not contain any political conditions.)

In November 1952, while still waiting for the appeal decision, the regents dropped the loyalty oath requirement by a vote of 12–5. Some of the damage, however, could not be undone.

"The cost was not as great as those with an apocalyptic view of these events thought it would be, that the university

was not destroyed obviously, manifestly not destroyed," Saxon recounted years later. "It remained a great institution and it is still a great institution. But there is nonetheless an exception to it. I do believe that there were costs to the university which are hard to measure. They have to do with people who didn't come, who were offered jobs and chose not to come, and people who were here and who quietly left without making any fuss."

TRANSITION OF POWER

After Dykstra's sudden death in 1950, Sproul appointed an administrative committee consisting of Graduate Division Dean Knudsen, School of Medicine Dean Warren and College of Letters and Sciences Dean Dodd. The committee, selected to represent a broad cross-section of campus, had even less authority than Dykstra in running affairs at UCLA. By now, however, Sproul's relationship with the faculty and the regents had been singed by his handling of the loyalty oath matter— something he would never fully restore.

On March 10, 1954, the regents approved a plan to reorganize the university and give UCLA greater autonomy. A decentralization plan had been recommended by the Academic Senate as early as 1943, and in October 1948, the regents had received similar recommendations from the Public Administration Service, which it had commissioned to study the university's governance structure. In light of the war, and with deference to Sproul's continued strong leadership, those past recommendations had gone unheeded by the regents.

After the loyalty oath mess, however, Sproul was weakened and had less unified support from the regents, particularly the pro-oath, conservative regents from the south, who were restless for UCLA to have more power. UCLA deans and the increasingly powerful Alumni Association were clamoring for change and greater control. These groups noted that the explosive growth of the University of California, and UCLA in particular, had made it impossible for one person to oversee the university without implementing clear delegations of authority.

The southern regents committee, headed by Canaday, charged bluntly that the problems emanated from the Office of the President under what they termed the "evils of centralized administrative authority." Further, the committee outlined that the president's office was too encumbered by administrative details; that the president was responsible for directly supervising too many individuals to be effective; that the congestion has resulted in delay and uncertainty down through administrative channels; and that the solution was in officially delegating more authority to the campus heads. The committee reported that these problems needed to be corrected before a new chief executive for UCLA was appointed, but that the appointment of a new campus leader was urgent and should be made as soon as possible.

Sproul fought with strong conviction to stave off changes that would diminish his authority and "one-university" vision. The university needed a "single head not on paper, but in fact," he argued, and he cautioned against the development of a provost-regents relationship instead of a president-regents one because it could "set the stage for conversion of the University of California from a strong, statewide institution, under unified administration to a loosely knit federation of institutions without strong leadership." Sproul successfully prevented the southern regents' recommendation that the university's headquarters be moved away from Berkeley. The regents also wanted to change the provost title to "president" and the president's title to "chancellor and president."

Card catalog, Powell Library, 1950s.

Raymond Bernard Allen

UCLA's first chief executive to hold the title "chancellor," Raymond B. Allen was born in Cathay, North Dakota, on August 7, 1902. The son of a Methodist minister, he would become one of academia's most outspoken anti-Communists.

Allen earned his bachelor's degree in 1924 and his medical degree in 1928, both at the University of Minnesota. He practiced as a family doctor in North Dakota for a few years, before heading to the Mayo Clinic as a fellow in 1930. He then went into medical administration, becoming an associate dean at Columbia University's College of Physicians and Surgeons, as well as associate director of the New York Post-Graduate Medical School and Hospital.

In 1936, Allen was named dean of the Wayne State University College of Medicine in Detroit, and three years later was appointed executive dean of the University of Illinois and its College of Medicine. In February 1946, he was chosen as president of the University of Washington. President Harry Truman appointed Allen as director of the Psychological Strategy Board in November 1951. "He has threaded his diplomatic way through a succession of high posts," wrote *Time*.

Allen's views on medical care were conservative and pro-establishment. And at the University of Washington, he became known as an "outstanding foe of Reds" for his recommendations to fire two professors, and place three others on probation, for allegedly being Communists, maintaining "a Communist is incompetent to teach the truth."

On December 14, 1951, the University of California Board of Regents announced that Allen would be UCLA's new chief executive. "His appointment at UCLA was viewed at the time as an effort to mollify many in the community who found the growing university too liberal for their McCarthy Era tastes," wrote the *Los Angeles Times*, years later.

Allen, his wife, Dorothy, and their four children, moved on campus in fall 1952, marking the first time that a chief executive with a young family occupied the University Residence. Alumni and campus leaders were hoping that Allen would bring a zeal for advancing UCLA and the fortitude to stand up to President Robert Gordon Sproul. But it was clear from the start that he would continue his diplomatic ways. In fact, Allen was widely believed to be Sproul's successor-in-waiting.

"I feel that I have adequate authority to match my responsibilities," Allen told *UCLA Alumni Magazine* in December 1952, one month after taking office. "I am an organization man. I do not intend to be at odds with President Sproul or the Board of Regents, and I do intend to work vigorously to get what UCLA should have."

After the Pacific Coast Conference booster scandal, and UCLA's departure from the conference, Allen's reputation with alumni and campus leaders was significantly damaged. He began to travel more and more on university and government business, until finally announcing his resignation on June 12, 1959, stating, "I feel that I have completed my job."

Three months later, Allen was sworn in as the new chief of the U.S. Foreign Aid Mission to Indonesia. He moved to Virginia in 1967, holding a number of government positions before his death in 1986 at the age of 83.

Right: Raymond B. Allen, UCLA's first chancellor.

Far right: Allen with Hollywood film producer Samuel Goldwyn.

Realizing changes were inevitable, Sproul took the lead and suggested that the provost title be changed to "chancellor" and that the president title not be altered. He put forward a reorganization plan that he said was "designed to do three things: 1) to streamline the administrative machinery of the enlarged University of California; 2) to define clearly the duties of the various university offices; and 3) to give each of the eight campuses within the statewide university the maximum degree of autonomy consistent with unity."

The regents approved the restructuring and elevated the title of both UCLA's and Berkeley's chief executives to "chancellor." Rather than "provost," which was traditionally considered an academic title, the new term would portend a greater administrative role, such as attending all Board of Regents meetings, presiding over formal campus functions, and being responsible for nominating faculty and administrative personnel.

Clark Kerr, who was appointed Berkeley's first chancellor in 1952, quipped that the term "chancellor" had been ill-defined and when asked early in his tenure about what a chancellor did, he responded that "the position was totally new within the university but was an ancient title in Great Britain." The Oxford English Dictionary, he noted, defined it as "honorary," the "Keeper of His Majesty's conscience," and "guardian of infants, lunatics, and idiots."

In his memoir, Kerr wrote that he did not realize until later that Sproul had not really accepted the regents' decision to decentralize. "Sproul's opposition, it turned out, was just taking a different form at a different level: quiet opposition in practice at the level of relations between president and the chancellors instead of open confrontation over a policy of decentralization with the deans and some of the regents," explained Kerr.

"FOE OF REDS"

On December 14, 1951, the regents, seeking to rebuild the erosion of public confidence in the university, selected former University of Washington President Raymond B. Allen as UCLA's first chancellor. Allen, who was appointed by President Truman to temporarily head the U.S. Psychological Strategy Board in coordinating U.S. propaganda during the Korean War, had the well-known distinction of bucking the tenet of academic freedom and tenure in the firing of the two Communist faculty members. It was the first formal challenge to the American Association of University Professors' position that "there is, then, nothing in the nature of the teaching profession which requires the automatic exclusion of Communists, and the attempt to exclude them would threaten our educational system."

After his action made national news, Allen became an outspoken voice in keeping universities free from subversive individuals and was dubbed in the press as a "foe of Reds." His view, often repeated and quoted across the country, became

known as the "Allen formula." In his words: "Academic freedom consists of something more than merely an absence of restraints placed upon the teacher by the institution that employs him. It demands as well an absence of restraints placed upon him by his political affiliations, by dogmas that may stand in the way of a free search for truth or by rigid adherence to a 'party line' that sacrifices dignity, honor and integrity to … political ends."

About Allen's selection, Lieutenant Governor Goodwin J. Knight told the *Los Angeles Times*: "His fight to oust the Communists at the University of Washington was fearless and inspiring. UCLA is such an important educational institution that it must have a big man as its chief administrator."

Added Regent Fred Moyer Jordan, the former president of both the UCLA student body and the Alumni Association: "We have looked at many men and he has passed muster 100% with all of us. In his new post as chancellor he will have more autonomy and responsibility than Provost Dykstra had."

Starting his tenure after the bitter battle over the loyalty oath, of which Allen had a precipitating role, he would have many hurdles to overcome to earn the respect and trust of UCLA's faculty—something he would not achieve. But that may not have been at the forefront of his mind. Allen, who had never stayed more than six years at any one job, held the trust of the regents—and Sproul—and there was talk of his replacing the university president when the time came. Several university leaders and faculty later speculated that this may have accounted for Allen's deference to the president and regents over championing greater UCLA interests.

Subpoenaed UCLA professors wait to testify at the California Legislature's Committee on Un-American Activities in January 1946. From left, Dean E. McHenry, Franklin Fearing, Ralph Beals, Leonard Bloom, David Appleman and Harry Hoijer.

Whatever the reason, Allen's administration did not achieve the independence from Berkeley and the Office of the President that faculty and alumni leaders expected.

As the effects of McCarthyism continued nationwide, in November 1952, Allen was made the campus "contact man" between UCLA and the State Senate Fact-Finding Committee on Un-American Activities as a "cooperative effort to assist colleges and universities in their continuing fight against the highly developed techniques by the Communist Party to insinuate its members into key positions of our college campuses." The *Daily Bruin* charged that the university had "committed itself to setting up an 'espionage system' to ferret out Communism on all campuses." Sproul, who, along with several other university presidents, agreed to the plan, responded that "it involved no espionage." But, indeed there were Communist checks on faculty, and in the law school, for example, it was standard practice to turn over student files to the FBI whenever requested.

"It's hard for anyone who has not lived through that period to really understand that this was not then a reprehensible activity—very respectable people were engaged in it," said Dean of Students Byron H. "Barney" Atkinson. "Very highly placed people, especially university presidents who were rooting out Reds on their campuses, were applauded for this by nearly everyone. There were very few student groups who opposed this process. Faculty groups were utterly silent on the matter, or practically so, unless such things as the loyalty oath got in, which cut across their own specific interests."

PCC SCANDAL

The 1950s ended with yet another controversy that would alter the course of UCLA's future, but this one did not result from political beliefs; instead, it spilled over from the hallowed gridiron.

In football, UCLA had long been overshadowed by USC and other members of the Pacific Coast Conference (PCC)—until the arrival of Red Sanders in 1949. During Sanders' first five seasons at UCLA, the Bruins beat USC three times, greater success than UCLA had against the Trojans in all of the 20 years prior.

Then, on November 20, 1954, UCLA's undefeated football team battled it out with USC in front of 102,548 fans at a sold-out Los Angeles Memorial Coliseum and beat the Trojans 34–0, earning a perfect season and a second consecutive PCC crown. Because

of a "no repeat" rule, the Bruins were denied the opportunity to play in the Rose Bowl. But the 1954 team was voted national champions by United Press International and No. 2 by The Associated Press (Ohio State was No. 1).

Such success often brings scrutiny and the Pacific Coast Conference was already rife with diverging philosophies. Some regents thought that the Pacific Northwest universities in Oregon and Washington were of a lesser caliber academically, and that the University of California teams should not play them. "The Oregon schools, they just took anybody," said Regent Cyril C. Nigg. For its part, UCLA continued to view Berkeley as receiving preferential treatment and maintained an intense rivalry with its northern sibling.

In 1951, the conference began an investigation into alleged athletics "booster" support provided to athletes at the University of Oregon. After Head Coach Jim Aiken resigned amid code violations regarding financial aid and athletic subsidies, Oregon officials reportedly suggested the PCC take a look at other schools' practices, specifically UCLA's. For the next five years, the conference conducted a quiet probe of its

Henry R. "Red" Sanders (right) coached the Bruins to the 1954 national football title.

member schools. During this time, Chancellor Allen declined to allow PCC officials to conduct an investigation at UCLA, instead opting to look into the matter internally, the results of which he provided to the conference commissioner.

In March 1956, the investigation and accusations surfaced publicly, including that of an ex-Bruin football player who had transferred to Berkeley and alleged that UCLA assistant coaches made "secret deals with athletes."

On May 19, the PCC fined UCLA $93,000 and placed the campus on a three-year probation, making it ineligible for conference titles and excluding it from Rose Bowl and NCAA championship competition. The PCC cited that Bruin athletes were receiving $40 above the $75 NCAA limit, and it removed the Bruin Bench and Young Men's Club of Westwood from good standing for making the unsanctioned payments. Some athletes, including All-American football player Donn Moomaw, were named for receiving the improper payments. Two weeks earlier, the University of Washington was also fined, although to a lesser degree; later sanctions would be imposed on Berkeley and USC, but not others.

Allen made a statement to the press that the PCC's action came as "no surprise," since UCLA had made full disclosure and provided the booster club information upon which the suspension was based. However, he urged investigators to look into other schools and to develop reasonable regulations. Allen added that several years earlier a group of booster club officials from multiple PCC institutions wanted to discuss how to help student athletes meet cost of living issues with conference executives, but no meeting ever took place.

"If out of the investigations at UCLA and the University of Washington a straightforward approach to the problems of the Pacific Coast Conference is begun, the investigation will have been worthwhile," Allen said. "But if no constructive steps are taken toward development of a realistic athletic code, then the investigation and the penalties assessed against the two institutions can only be considered discriminatory."

Bruins, however, were shocked and angry at the sanctions slapped on UCLA, which had swept conference championships in football, basketball and track that year. On May 23, an effigy of PCC Commissioner Victor O. Schmidt hung from a lamppost in Westwood Village—a prank attributed to UCLA fans.

Goodwin Knight, a Stanford alumnus who had attended high school in Los Angeles and became governor in 1953 after Warren became Chief Justice of the United States, publicly called upon the Board of Regents to take an official look at the PCC's sanctions against UCLA after receiving numerous telegrams from protesting Southern Californians that claimed "injustice" and "discriminatory treatment." Knight told the *Los Angeles Times*: "It is hard for me to believe that UCLA is so different from other members of the conference."

The sanctions were perceived as inequitable both internally and externally. UCLA Alumni Association Executive Secretary Harry J. Longway wrote in an editorial in the summer issue of *The UCLA Alumni Magazine*: "The reaction has been, 'Everyone is guilty, why pick on a few?' These reactions are the result of an athletic code that is both hypocritical and unrealistic."

Meetings of the Alumni Association executive council were contentious. The alumni pushed Allen, whose general response of "I'll get it done the next time," did not satisfy them. They accused him of inattention and inaction. Telegram exchanges between Allen and Sproul depict Allen's deferment to Sproul.

For the first time since before the war, tensions led to a call for UCLA's secession. There was a movement to get a proposition on the state ballot to make UCLA separate from the University of California. Assemblyman Joseph C. Shell of Los Angeles was spearheading a similar effort to introduce a bill in the 1957 Legislature.

"It is regrettable that well-meaning U.C.L.A. supporters have attacked the unity of the University of California," Allen said in a statement released May 22, 1956. "Nothing, in the long run, could do the Los Angeles campus more harm. I especially deplore the fact that unhappiness over recent PCC penalties against U.C.L.A. has been directed against

Carol Burnett, 21, took her final campus bow in a Royce Hall performance of "Love Thy Coach," the 1954 Varsity Show.

President Robert Gordon Sproul." At a speech before the Commonwealth Club in San Francisco the following month, Allen said: "I shall fight with every resource at my command to prevent any such preposterous and divisive move."

In a four-page letter to Sproul on July 13, 1956, UCLA's public information manager, Andrew Hamilton, summed up the reaction. "What it all boils down to is this: people in the Los Angeles area consider that both UCLA and USC have been unjustly dealt with by the rest of the conference. Here are some of the opinions frequently expressed: The PCC code is unrealistic—it's been broken by all institutions and their booster clubs, so why pick on UCLA and USC? Why penalize student athletes when educators have for years winked at subsidization? Why were the entire Trojan and Bruin squads declared ineligible when 29 football players at California were given the right to 'buy back' their eligibility? Why were Washington, UCLA and USC banned from the Rose Bowl and their receipts confiscated—and not California? Furthermore, who gets the shares of the banned schools, those who voted for the heavy financial penalties? ... What has the Commissioner's office been doing all this time? Seems like only those who were honest with the PCC are the ones that were penalized."

Hamilton noted that questions had been pouring into his office regarding comparative Berkeley and UCLA figures for budgets, number of buildings, student-faculty ratio, among others. "Their thought processes run something like this," Hamilton wrote, "If Berkeley can grind UCLA under its heel in athletics, what about such things as budgets, buildings, staff, future growth?"

On July 13, in advance of the PCC meeting of university and college presidents, Knight proposed that California schools pull out of the PCC and form an athletic conference of their own. The Los Angeles City Council recommended that UCLA and USC both seriously consider withdrawing from the PCC, suggesting it could gross higher receipts if it played better teams in nearby venues. Stanford President Wallace Sterling broke his silence on the controversy and said that his university had no intention of withdrawing from the PCC. A Los Angeles Times article wryly noted, "His coach, Chuck Taylor, whose football team can't possibly fail getting to the Rose Bowl if present sanctions against SC, UCLA and Washington persist, put in his two cents worth by echoing his president's comments."

At the PCC meeting of university and college presidents on July 18, the chief executives suggested they might restore eligibility to seniors so that they could play in the fall if certain measures were taken against coaches and their staffs. Allen and USC President Fred D. Fagg Jr. both firmly said they had no intention of firing their football coaches or athletic staff.

Heated discussions continued. In November, the UCLA faculty voted in support of leaving the PCC, and the UCLA

Alumni Association's executive council announced at a press conference that it had unanimously recommended that Allen take "immediate steps" to remove UCLA from the PCC. In December, at the PCC presidents winter meeting at the Beverly Hilton Hotel, Allen was prepared to announce UCLA's withdrawal, but at the last minute caved to pressure from Sproul and Pauley.

"Telephone switchboards at Southern Cal and Westwood were lit up like Times Square on Saturday night as irate supporters of the two local schools expressed vociferous disapproval," the Los Angeles Times reported. "They had been led to believe that President Fred D. Fagg Jr. of SC and Chancellor Raymond B. Allen of UCLA would go into the presidents meeting swinging big sticks."

In May 1957, after a year of probation, the PCC by a tally of 5–4 voted confidence in UCLA's athletic program, with Stanford, Oregon, Washington State and Idaho—four non-sanctioned schools—voting to expel UCLA. This led to particular animosity between Stanford and UCLA that would last for years. Later that month, a UCLA Alumni Association delegation of past presidents led by Regent Nigg appeared before the regents urging withdrawal. On December 13, the regents announced that both UCLA and Berkeley would sever their ties with the PCC after fulfilling existing membership obligations extending through June 30, 1959.

After a three-year ordeal, the conference dissolved and on July 1, 1959, was replaced with the newly formed Athletic Association of Western Universities (AAWU). Its charter members were UCLA, USC, Berkeley, Washington and Stanford, which thanks in part to diplomatic efforts by

Kerr, joined two weeks after the conference officially began operations—despite derision from Stanford alumni. (The conference was renamed Pacific-8 in 1968, and then Pacific-10 in 1978 after two Arizona universities joined. In 2010, the conference announced it would expand to include the University of Colorado at Boulder and the University of Utah.)

In 1960, in an effort for greater oversight, Kerr removed the athletics departments from student control at UCLA and Berkeley and put them under the chancellors.

"In the end, we proved that you could have a better sports program while playing within the rules," Kerr wrote. "The prior road led to disintegration of good relationships and of good sportsmanship. Along the way, we regretfully had to take away ownership and control of intercollegiate athletics from the Associated Students at both Berkeley and UCLA so that the university could directly guarantee compliance with the new rules. The regents gave their total support. They were appalled at what had become highly publicized scandals."

POISED FOR CHANGE

After a record 28 years as president of the University of California, Sproul was approaching the institution's mandatory retirement age of 67 and regretfully announced he would step down in 1958. All told, he had served the university for 44 years, starting as a cashier in the comptroller's office and overseeing its growth into a multicampus system to serve the needs of the state while preserving his "one university" vision.

While for years it had been assumed that Allen would succeed Sproul, anger lingered over his handling of the PCC situation, and the regents instead selected Kerr as the university's 12th president.

Consequently, Allen began spending more time off campus. In December 1958, Kerr appointed Allen as the University of California's representative in the National Defense Education Act, which was created in the rush to fund American science development after the Russians launched Sputnik, the world's first satellite. Allen spent time in Washington, D.C., representing the university's interests. Next, he would leave on a months-long U.S. mission to Indonesia to survey higher education facilities.

One week after returning from Indonesia, on June 12, 1959, confirming rumors that had been circulating for weeks, Allen announced that he would be stepping down from the chancellorship at UCLA. The *Los Angeles Times* reported that there had been "long-simmering differences about policy between Dr. Allen and higher levels in the university administration." Years later, in a personal letter to Sproul, Allen wrote, "Perhaps I was wrong in not putting up a fight to stay at UCLA, but the thought of having to depend on Clark Kerr was the deciding factor."

Bruin fans play cards while camping out (above), and thousands wait in line (left), for a chance to cheer on the first undefeated, untied team in UCLA's gridiron history at the 1947 Rose Bowl.

Allen was appointed director of the State Department's International Cooperation Administration in Indonesia. In his public statement, Allen wrote, "These are interesting and challenging times and each of us must do what lies within him to resolve the problems that divide men and nations."

Kerr started the search for a new chancellor by talking with some of the southern regents. To his surprise, Kerr learned that they did not want to consider any potential internal candidates because it could result in "factional fighting" on campus. "In particular, their wishes ruled out Dean Paul Dodd, who would have been my first choice," Kerr wrote in his memoir.

On Kerr's nomination, Knudsen, who had been appointed vice chancellor of UCLA and served as acting chancellor in Allen's absence, was appointed by the regents as UCLA's chancellor in July for a one-year term only. Knudsen, although approaching mandatory retirement age, expressed interest in staying on for a longer period.

The regents and UCLA's alumni leaders, however, were eager to find a new chief executive to move UCLA into the 1960s. With Sproul's retirement after almost three decades at the helm; the death in 1956 of UCLA champion Dickson, who served on the board of regents for an unprecedented 43 years; and an opening for a new campus chancellor, the possibilities were boundless.

Vern Oliver Knudsen

Born in Provo, Utah, on December 27, 1893, Vern O. Knudsen "may or may not have started his research in acoustics at birth." UCLA's fifth chief executive—chosen to fill a one-year transition period—was a renowned acoustical physicist whose love of music began at the tender age of six when he attended his first concert in the Mormon Tabernacle.

Below: Vern O. Knudsen, the acoustical engineer.

Bottom: President Clark Kerr (right) appointed Knudsen to fill a one-year transition period.

After earning his bachelor's degree from Brigham Young University in 1915, Knudsen served as a Mormon missionary and as acting head of the Northern States Mission in Chicago. It was there he met his wife, Florence, whom he married in 1919.

In 1918, Knudsen joined Western Electric where he helped develop vacuum-tube technology, which he used during World War I to study parasitic currents. After the war, he earned his doctorate at the University of Chicago, focusing his dissertation on the application of acoustics to hearing loss. He would later develop instruments to measure and improve hearing.

Knudsen was said to have confounded colleagues by turning down job offers from both Bell Telephone Laboratories and the University of Chicago in favor of a teaching position at the nascent UCLA. He served as the physics department chairman from 1932–38. During World War II, Knudsen took a brief sabbatical to conduct top-secret acoustical work for the federal government concerning anti-submarine radar technology. He was the first director of what would become the Naval Undersea Research and Development Center in San Diego.

In 1933, Knudsen was appointed as the first dean of the Graduate Division, a position he held for 24 years, until he was named vice chancellor in 1956. Three years later, and one year shy of the mandatory retirement age, he was appointed by the Board of Regents to serve as chancellor until a successor for Raymond B. Allen was found.

In his 1960 commencement address, Knudsen encouraged graduates to "keep on thinking and doing as befits the highest standards of your alma mater." He added: "As either graduate student or employee, you are entering the life of reality, where knowledge without action is barren."

After stepping down as chancellor in 1960, Knudsen returned to his physics laboratory, where he focused his research on architectural acoustics. His contributions to the field over the span of his career were profound. When motion-picture "talkies" were introduced, he designed sound stages for the studio lots. He advised the architects of Royce Hall concerning acoustical treatments for its auditorium. In all, he served as a consultant on the construction of more than 500 auditoriums and concert halls, and was president of the Hollywood Bowl. In recognition of his many accomplishments, the physics building was named in his honor on May 16, 1964.

The acoustical engineer also waged a lifelong campaign in support of urban noise reduction. "Over the past 30 years the general noise level of our civilization has increased one decibel per year, and is now approaching the danger level," he said.

"Most men would be content with success and fame in one career," declared a *Los Angeles Times* editorial on the occasion of Knudsen's retirement in 1960. "Vern Knudsen has achieved them in three—as teacher, administrator and scientist."

Knudsen died at the UCLA Medical Center on May 13, 1974, at the age of 80.

CHAPTER 7

Fighting for Identity

1959–1968

Above: Crossing the quad, early 1960s.

Opposite: The new student union ballroom, shortly after its opening on April 3, 1961, offered Bruins a stylish lounge by day, and space for 1,000 couples to dance by night.

*A*s the campus anxiously awaited the selection of a new chief executive to succeed short-term Chancellor Vern O. Knudsen, UCLA *was poised for transformation.*

By 1960, California's population had expanded by 48 percent over the previous decade to almost 16 million, and the first "tidal wave" of baby boomers was approaching college age. With an eye toward building its economic future, the state sought to create an educated workforce. As legislators wrangled to create new public university campuses for their constituents, and competition among the state university systems peaked, politicians and educators alike acknowledged that reform was necessary. With the support of Governor Edmund G. "Pat" Brown, recently appointed University of California President Clark Kerr and his academic staff, including former UCLA political science Professor Dean E. McHenry and 29-year-old aide and UCLA alumnus Charles E. Young, started to work on a solution.

Completed in 1960, the Master Plan for Higher Education in California made the Golden State the first to guarantee in-state qualified high school students access—"tuition free"—to higher education. This would be done within a three-tiered system of the junior colleges (later the California Community Colleges), the State College System (renamed the California State University) and the University of California, which would accept the top 12.5 percent of high school graduates and prepare to double its enrollment by the end of the decade to 106,000.

UCLA already enrolled more than 17,000 students in 1959–60, while Berkeley had almost 22,000 students. Under the Master Plan, each would grow to 27,500 over a 15-year period. (By 1959, the university's

satellites at Davis, Riverside, Santa Barbara and San Diego had been officially designated as general campuses offering both undergraduate and graduate instruction; by fall 1965, new campuses would be opened in Irvine and Santa Cruz.)

Along with enrollment growth, UCLA's academic profile was also steadily rising. In 1957—24 years after the campus instituted graduate programs—UCLA was ranked No. 14 by a respected survey conducted by Hayward Keniston of the University of Pennsylvania. The study analyzed the top departments in 24 graduate disciplines, and UCLA surpassed Northwestern, Johns Hopkins and Ohio State universities overall. Despite not having a permanent campus chief executive for many of those years, UCLA possessed strong deans whose contributions helped elevate its academic stature. Then, in 1960, an internationally heralded moment for the faculty: Willard F. Libby became the first UCLA professor to be awarded a Nobel Prize. Libby, who joined the UCLA chemistry department in 1959, was honored for his prior work in the development of radiocarbon dating, which revolutionized archaeology.

After a months-long search, University of Kansas Chancellor Franklin D. Murphy was finally chosen in March 1960 as UCLA's sixth chief executive. Murphy's determination and boldness would guide UCLA into a flourishing period that forever changed the campus.

He oversaw a massive physical expansion that included building an indoor sporting arena and student union, while paying special attention to incorporating both infrastructure and beautification. His ever-growing network of influential friends, ranging from southern regents to members of the Los Angeles business and cultural communities, tied UCLA closer to the city than it ever had been before and made the university a dominant force in the region.

"'Independence' seems to be in the mind of all Bruins in this year of change," the Daily Bruin wrote on March 20, 1961. "With the arrival of Chancellor Franklin D. Murphy as the new campus chief officer comes a quest for a distinguished University without the formal ties, but with necessary association, with the statewide university system."

While Kerr prioritized long-range physical and academic planning and the elevation of the University of California and its campuses on the national landscape, Murphy pushed for UCLA to develop its own identity within Kerr's "multiversity." The two educational titans would engage in a continuous struggle over authority, but by the end of the decade—as UCLA neared its 50th anniversary—the campus emerged stronger for it.

Murphy managed to raise UCLA's profile nationally and internationally despite the discord of an American era that included civil rights clashes, political assassinations and mass protest. He supported civil rights and espoused progress—

underscored by his intense drive, and willingness to delegate responsibility, to achieve it.

"We must be in the library, but we must also be in Watts," Murphy told graduates at the 1966 commencement. "We must be in the laboratory, but we must also be on the moon. We will be in the lecture rooms, but we will also be in the operating rooms. Without apology, indeed with undisturbed and I hope growing commitment, we will serve the world of pure scholarship and the world of man and his problems, and both with distinction." The university, he added, was "a free marketplace of ideas."

The 1960s evolved into the decade of counterculture, and the birth in 1964 of the Free Speech Movement at the Berkeley campus was a harbinger of rebellion that would define a generation of college students. Such fervent activism, which spread across the country in the mid-1960s, seemed to bypass UCLA for much of the decade. There was a variety of protests on campus, but none hit the fever pitch of Berkeley or other universities.

Ronald Reagan took advantage of the social times and campaigned for governor with a platform that attacked the University of California for its "filthy speech" demonstrators. While UCLA's stability raised Murphy's esteem among the regents, Berkeley's tumult would lead to Kerr's dismissal. However, amid the heightening of the Vietnam War, as UCLA's own protest era was emerging, Murphy decided it was time that he move on—but not before he helped transform UCLA from a well-regarded state institution to a preeminent educational center woven into the fabric of greater Los Angeles and beyond.

"FIGHTING IRISHMAN"

As the search commenced in June 1959 to find a UCLA chancellor, familiar names cropped up in the press. College of Letters and Science Dean Paul A. Dodd and "favorite son"

Franklin D. Murphy addresses more than 5,000 members of the UCLA community at his inauguration, held outdoors on the courtyard east of Haines Hall, September 23, 1960.

Franklin David Murphy

Born in Kansas City, Missouri, on January 29, 1916, Franklin D. Murphy was the son of a physician father and musician mother, both of whom helped shape his love of medicine and of the arts from an early age.

Murphy, an avid Bruin football and basketball fan, was the quarterback on his high school championship team. He was a Phi Beta Kappa graduate of the University of Kansas in 1936, and earned his medical degree from the University of Pennsylvania School of Medicine in 1941.

He married Judith Harris in 1940, before serving with the U.S. Army conducting malaria research during World War II. After the war, he returned to Kansas City where he practiced cardiology while teaching at the University of Kansas' medical school, which his father had helped found. Two years into his professorship, Murphy was asked to serve as the school's dean, and in 1951, at the age of 35, he was appointed chancellor of the University of Kansas. He served for nine years, engaging in highly publicized battles with Kansas Governor George Docking over state support for the

university. In 1960, Murphy announced that he had had enough, and accepted the chancellorship at UCLA. More than 600 students burned Docking in effigy on the eve of Murphy's resignation, and 4,000 gathered the following day to protest his departure.

Murphy came to UCLA even though he had been warned it would be "an impossible job." He was drawn to the fast-rising university and saw possibilities in bridging it with a growing metropolis. He stood up to the Office of the President with a constant demand for equal terms with Berkeley in regard to funding and status. Murphy preferred to work in the press of argument, rather than via pensive thought. He propelled UCLA to a higher plane among American research universities through vocal debate and indomitable will.

Known for his intensity and dynamism, Murphy would not read from prepared speeches. His administrative assistant, Hansena Frederickson, said he was the only person who "could enter a room through two doors at the same time." His frequently uttered phrases, dubbed "Murphyisms," included: "free marketplace of ideas," "intellectual ferment" and "exponential explosion."

With the election of Governor Ronald Reagan, and amid growing student unrest during the turbulent anti-war movement, Murphy grew increasingly frustrated in fighting for the university. After eight years, he decided to move on.

Murphy resigned as chancellor to accept the position of chairman and chief executive officer of the Times Mirror Company. He held the post from 1968–80, and remained a director of the company's board until 1986. After retirement, Murphy turned his attention to philanthropy and raising money for the arts and the institutions he loved. He served on the board of the Los Angeles County Museum of Art, and as chairman of the National Gallery of Art. He was also a longtime trustee of the Ahmanson Foundation and the J. Paul Getty Trust.

The sculpture garden, one of his enduring legacies, and the administration building were both named in his honor in 1968. "Often such a designation might be *pro forma*," wrote Robert Vosper, who was hired by Murphy as head librarian both at Kansas and UCLA, of the naming of Murphy Hall. "But in this case it correctly recalls that Franklin Murphy gave meaning and power to the office of chancellor at UCLA, and thus the campus administration, in a unique and enduring way."

Murphy died at the UCLA Medical Center on June 16, 1994, at the age of 78.

Franklin D. Murphy, a strong advocate of civil rights, tours campus with Martin Luther King Jr., April 27, 1965.

Faculty Nobel Laureates

Willard Frank Libby (1908–1980)
Chemistry (1960)

Willard F. Libby, who joined the UCLA chemistry department in 1959, was the first UCLA professor to be awarded a Nobel Prize.

Libby was recognized for developing carbon dating, which revolutionized many fields. The method uses carbon-14 (an isotope of carbon with an atomic weight of 14 found in carbon dioxide) for age determination in archaeology, geology, geophysics and other branches of science.

"The future of the world, dependent as it is upon atomic energy, requires more understanding and knowledge about the atom," Libby said. "I hope that in some small way our efforts have helped people to learn about the atom and the way in which it works and may have helped them to see that isotopes are real and that they may hold much promise for the future—that in them lies a principal hope for the betterment of human life on earth and for the preservation and improvement of our standard of living."

In 1962, Libby became the director of UCLA's Institute of Geophysics and Planetary Physics.

Julian Seymour Schwinger (1918–1994)
Physics (1965)

Julian S. Schwinger was awarded the Nobel Prize in physics, an award he shared with American physicist Richard Feynman and Japanese physicist Sin-Itiro Tomonaga, for their independent contributions to quantum electrodynamics—how light interacts with matter.

"The theoretical achievements of Schwinger and Feynman in the late 1940s and early 1950s ignited a revolution in quantum field theory and laid the foundations for much of the spectacular progress that has been made during the ensuing four decades in understanding the fundamental forces of nature," noted his University of California memorial tribute.

Schwinger, a professor at Harvard University when he received the award, joined UCLA's department of physics in 1972, where he continued his research for 22 years.

Donald James Cram (1919–2001)
Chemistry (1987)

Chemistry Professor Donald J. Cram was awarded the Nobel Prize, along with French scholar Jean-Marie Lehn and American scientist Charles J. Pedersen, "for their development and use of molecules with structure-specific interactions of high selectivity."

Cram, a pioneer of host-guest chemistry, focused his work on creating molecular "cages," which act like natural proteins, attaching themselves only to certain complex molecules. These models help scientists synthesize molecules that can mimic important biological processes.

"I have always felt I couldn't understand things I couldn't visualize," Cram said. "I'm a very simple person who does basic research. I didn't aim at solving practical problems, just at answering fun questions."

Cram joined the UCLA faculty in 1947, and taught organic chemistry to about 12,000 undergraduate students over the course of his almost 50-year tenure.

Paul Delos Boyer (1918–)
Chemistry (1997)

Biochemist Paul D. Boyer was awarded the Nobel Prize for his breakthrough work in investigating how ATP (adenosine triphosphate)—the carrier for cellular energy—is formed. He shared half of the prize with John E. Walker, of the Medical Research Council Laboratory of Molecular Biology of Cambridge, England, for their work on how the enzyme ATP synthase catalyzes the formation of ATP. (Danish scholar Jens C. Skou was awarded the other half of the prize.)

Boyer, who called ATP the "currency of cells," helped illuminate the process of how the various subunits of the ATP enzyme work together like gears, levers and ratchets to generate cellular energy. Every cell function relies on ATP.

Boyer joined the UCLA faculty in 1963 and served as founding director of the Molecular Biology Institute from 1965–83. The building that houses the institute was renamed in his honor in 1999.

Louis Joseph Ignarro (1941–)
Physiology or Medicine (1998)

Professor Louis J. Ignarro, together with fellow American pharmacologists Robert F. Furchgott and Ferid Murad, received the 1998 Nobel Prize for discoveries related to the role of nitric oxide as a signaling molecule in the cardiovascular system.

Ignarro's research helped show that the chemical compound nitric oxide—also an air pollutant created by car exhaust fumes—occurs naturally in the body. He also found that the molecule is an important factor in helping the body regulate key functions such as blood pressure, and in preventing blood clots that can cause strokes. The research established the scientific foundation for development of the anti-impotence drug Viagra, a drug to treat shock, and a treatment for newborns with dangerously high blood pressure.

"The Nobel Prize is not given out when the research is over, but in a field where there's still a lot more work to do," Ignarro said. "I want to increase the productivity of my lab to answer many more important questions."

Ignarro joined the faculty of the UCLA School of Medicine in 1985. A professor in molecular and medical pharmacology, he is the winner of multiple Golden Apple awards presented by medical students to the year's best teacher.

Louis J. Ignarro receives the Nobel Prize from Carl XVI Gustaf, king of Sweden, at the Stockholm Concert Hall, December 10, 1998.

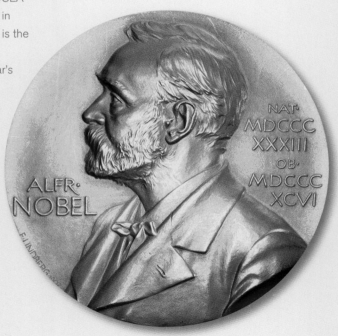

Alumni Nobel Laureates

Ralph Johnson Bunche (1904–1971)
Peace Prize (1950)

Ralph J. Bunche, a 1927 alumnus and valedictorian, was awarded the Nobel Peace Prize in 1950 for his mediation in the first Arab-Israeli War.

Bunche began working for the United Nations in 1946. After the 1948 assassination of the United Nations mediator in Palestine, Count Folke Bernadotte, Bunche was appointed by the Security Council as the new acting mediator. In this capacity, he directed the negotiations held at Rhodes and elsewhere from January to July 1949, which resulted in the four Armistice Agreements between the new state of Israel and four of its Arab neighbors: Egypt, Jordan, Lebanon and Syria.

"May there be, in our time, at long last, a world at peace in which we, the people, may for once begin to make full use of the great good that is in us," Bunche said.

In 1969, the Social Sciences Building was renamed in his honor.

Glenn Theodore Seaborg (1912–1999)
Chemistry (1951)

In 1951, Glenn T. Seaborg was awarded the Nobel Prize in chemistry jointly with Edwin Mattison McMillan "for their discoveries in the chemistry of the transuranium elements."

Seaborg took a leave of absence from the University of California from 1942–46 to head the plutonium work of the Manhattan Project. He was co-discoverer of plutonium and all further transuranium elements through Nobelium—element 102.

Seaborg earned his bachelor's degree at UCLA in 1934. "UCLA was my only chance, and I resolved to do whatever it took to succeed there," said Seaborg, who worked his way through school with odd jobs such as apricot picker and stevedore. He was influenced by John Mead Adams, who taught a class in atomic physics. "After that course, I knew that I wanted to get into nuclear research," Seaborg said.

Later he attended Berkeley and served as the campus's chancellor from 1958–61, but Seaborg always kept close ties with UCLA's chemistry department.

Robert Bruce Merrifield (1921–2006)
Chemistry (1984)

Bruce Merrifield was awarded the Nobel Prize in chemistry for inventing a "simple and ingenious" method of synthesizing proteins and peptides that stimulated great advances in the fields of biochemistry, molecular biology, pharmacology and medicine.

In the early 1950s, synthesizing peptides was a nearly impossible task, sometimes taking years to complete. Then, Merrifield discovered a method to bind amino acids—the building blocks of proteins—to a solid structure rather than in a liquid solution. His biochemist colleagues heralded this as the "Merrifield Breakthrough," for they could now assemble biological molecules in mere weeks.

Merrifield came to UCLA as a transfer student from Pasadena Junior College. After earning his bachelor's degree in chemistry in 1943, he worked for a year before returning to UCLA for graduate school. He earned UCLA's first doctorate in biochemistry in 1949. He affectionately credited his alma mater with inspiring his work: "I received *all* my training in chemistry and biochemistry at UCLA."

William Forsyth Sharpe (1934–)
Economics (1990)

William F. Sharpe was awarded the Nobel Memorial Prize in Economic Sciences for pioneering work in the theory of financial economics. Sharpe, who shared the prize with former RAND colleague Harry M. Markowitz and American scholar Merton H. Miller, helped develop the Capital Asset Pricing Model, a theory for pricing financial assets.

Sharpe took accounting and economics courses, both required for the business degree, during his first semester at UCLA. "Both had a major influence on my career," he said. "The accounting course dealt primarily with bookkeeping, while the economics course focused on microeconomic theory. I found bookkeeping tedious and light on intellectual content. But I was greatly attracted to the rigor and relevance of microeconomic theory. Hence, I changed my major to Economics."

Sharpe earned three degrees in economics from UCLA: a bachelor's in 1955, master's in 1956 and doctorate in 1961. He became a professor emeritus at Stanford University's business school.

Elinor Ostrom (1933–)
Economics (2009)

Elinor Ostrom was awarded the Nobel Memorial Prize in Economic Sciences for her "analysis of economic governance, especially the commons." She shared the prize with Berkeley economist Oliver E. Williamson.

Ostrom, the first female recipient of the Nobel Prize in economics and UCLA's first female laureate, challenged conventional wisdom by demonstrating how local property can be successfully user-managed without any regulation by central authorities or privatization.

A triple UCLA degree holder in political science, Ostrom earned her bachelor's in 1954, master's in 1962 and doctorate in 1965. Ostrom's dissertation is titled *Public entrepreneurship: a case study in ground water basin management.*

"I was assigned to study the West Basin, which underlay multiple cities along the coast of the Pacific Ocean," Ostrom said. "The city of Los Angeles partially overlapped the basin as well as a good portion of Los Angeles County. Without knowing I was studying a common-pool resource problem."

Ostrom has been on the faculty of Indiana University since 1965.

Richard Fred Heck (1931–)
Chemistry (2010)

In 2010, the Nobel Prize in chemistry was awarded jointly to alumnus Richard F. Heck, Purdue University scholar Ei-ichi Negishi and Japanese scholar Akira Suzuki "for palladium-catalyzed cross couplings in organic synthesis." Heck's research vastly improved the possibilities for chemists to create sophisticated chemicals, for example carbon-based molecules as complex as those found in nature.

Heck earned two chemistry degrees from UCLA: a bachelor's in 1952 and doctorate in 1954. He did his graduate work at UCLA under future National Medal of Science winner Saul Winstein. Heck's dissertation was titled *Methoxyl and aryl groups in substitution and rearrangement.* He went on to discover the Heck reaction, a method where carbon atoms meet on a palladium atom and their proximity to one another kick-starts a chemical reaction.

Heck worked in industry for Hercules Incorporated before joining the University of Delaware in 1971. He retired in 1989.

Dean McHenry—UCLA's 1932 student body president and Kerr's top academic assistant before becoming founding chancellor in 1961 of the University of California, Santa Cruz—were featured as leading candidates on the pages of the *Daily Bruin*. The southern regents, however, had made clear to Kerr that they did not want a UCLA insider for the post. They also held to the previous edict that the ideal candidate "must definitely not be a controversial figure in any respect."

Kerr gave consideration to Berkeley alumnus and University of Oregon President O. Meredith Wilson, but alumni leaders were opposed, stating that Wilson had been "anti-UCLA" in the Pacific Coast Conference debacle.

Kerr also proposed a UCLA alumnus he knew as a trustee from the Rockefeller Foundation: Ralph J. Bunche. A star athlete and 1927 valedictorian, Bunche was a Pioneer Bruin who had gone on to serve the country and the world by helping to found the United Nations, where he would become under-secretary-

general. He was awarded the Nobel Peace Prize in 1950, becoming the first African-American—indeed, the first person of color of any origin—to be so honored, as well as UCLA's first-ever Nobel recipient. Bunche expressed interest in leading his alma mater, but Kerr met with internal resistance yet again.

"Dominant regents and alumni leaders," Kerr wrote in his memoir, "believed that his appointment was too advanced an action for that time and place—to my great regret. UCLA was, after all, the campus of Jackie Robinson, who broke the racial barriers in professional sports, and later of Arthur Ashe."

The nationwide pursuit then focused on a strong contender whose name had been on a university shortlist once before—during the search that resulted in Kerr's selection as president.

University of Kansas Chancellor Franklin D. Murphy, a physician and the institution's former medical dean, was known to University of California Regent Edwin W. Pauley,

Vern O. Knudsen and Franklin D. Murphy at a press conference, shortly after the transition of power on July 1, 1960.

as well as to a close Pauley friend, former President Harry S. Truman. Kerr, too, knew Murphy from their respective memberships in the Association of American Universities and the Council on Higher Education in the American Republics. Murphy had a reputation for being full of energy and ideas, as well as being "brash" and "pushy" in order to attain his goals. Kerr believed that Murphy was "perfect for UCLA" in part because he had the "charismatic and self-confident personality to make his way in both the business and cultural communities of the greater Los Angeles area."

During nine years as Kansas chancellor, Murphy had elevated that university's national academic reputation, in part by increasing funding for research, distinguished professorships, faculty salaries and student scholarships from public and private sources. His efforts were not without political ramifications as they brought him into constant contention with Kansas Governor George Docking, who considered funding items other than the direct cost of educating students as luxuries. Murphy was dubbed by the press as the "fighting Irishman," an outgrowth of his bitter feud with Docking over, among other things, state appropriations for the University of Kansas that had often manifested in gubernatorial vetoes and subsequent political maneuvering for legislative overrides.

Several of Murphy's friends and colleagues warned him that the UCLA post was an "impossible job" that "would destroy a man." But Murphy was satisfied that the regents and Kerr were determined in their policy of operational decentralization and that he would "have the necessary local administrative authority and flexibility to do a strong and sound administrative job," as he wrote to Pauley shortly after accepting the position.

On March 18, 1960, 44-year-old Murphy was officially named UCLA's new chief executive, and he took the helm on July 1, 1960. "The man from the Midwest" quickly won the respect and admiration of the UCLA faculty and students.

UCLA needs to find its own destiny, Murphy told the *Daily Bruin* at the start of the school year in 1960, and "we must have the means and tools to do it."

Soon, he would find himself in familiar territory: brazenly championing the best interests of the campus he led while surmounting ingrained obstacles.

THE INNER CIRCLE

One of Murphy's earliest actions was to form his executive team. Dodd was Murphy's original choice for handling academic affairs; however, Kerr cautioned Murphy that Dodd would not be approved by the regents because of his previous stand on the loyalty oath and academic freedom. "You have no idea of the depth of feeling in these people related to that time," Murphy recounted Kerr as saying. Murphy confirmed this independently by broaching the idea with a couple of regents and determining "that was the best possible way to get off on a bad start."

After canvassing the faculty, Murphy selected political scientist Foster H. Sherwood as his vice chancellor for

Onlookers from the top of Janss Steps take in one of the worst fires in Los Angeles history, which broke out in the canyons of the Santa Monica Mountains on November 6, 1961. The Bel-Air–Brentwood blaze displaced 3,500 individuals on its first day, although the fire raged unchecked for a day, ultimately consuming more than 450 homes. Among those lost were the homes of Professor Willard F. Libby and UCLA booster Joe E. Brown. UCLA provided emergency loans for faculty members who were left homeless. "Everything went—just as quick as that …" Brown told the *Los Angeles Times*.

academic affairs. "A man of integrity, he was a man who knew the university well," Murphy said. "He knew the operations of the senate; he could keep me out of the sand traps and the quicksand." In addition, Murphy appreciated that Kerr thought highly of Sherwood and, since he was not on the regents' radar, "didn't have any scars."

Next, Murphy wanted an administrative assistant or "troubleshooter" and decided on Charles Young, whom he had met in McHenry's office in Berkeley. Young was strongly recommended by Kerr, on whose staff he had served.

The appointment was "the most effective working relationship I've ever had with another human being in any situation," Murphy later said. "After a little while I could communicate what I was interested in in less than a sentence—almost with a look or a gesture." Young, who found a mentor in Murphy and would succeed him as UCLA chancellor in 1968, took on much of the day-to-day administration of the campus.

All this suited Murphy's preference for delegating authority—a management style that had not been practiced by previous UCLA chief executives, symptomatic of what little power they had. "I like to preoccupy myself with what I conceive to be the big problem and not have to worry about a lot of other things," Murphy said. "The more I began delegating to Chuck, the more I realized that he would just eat it right up. You could just visibly see him grow with authority and responsibility. So pretty soon I said, 'Look, he's no more an assistant to the chancellor. He's assistant chancellor.'" A year-and-a-half later, in October 1963, Young was promoted to vice chancellor for administration.

The third individual in Murphy's senior management group was noted chemist William G. Young, who was already vice chancellor for planning. "Bill is a very deceiving person," Murphy said. "He's not very articulate, and he's not a great orator, and he seems to be sort of floating around. You just wonder whether anything will get done, and I discovered that remarkable things were getting done." Young supervised the doubling in size of UCLA's physical plant and oversaw the creation of UCLA's first formal long-range development plan in 1963, implemented under the direction of campus planner George Vajna and consulting architect Welton Becket. The ambitious plan included everything from landscaping to transportation infrastructure such as roads and parking. (In 1967, Murphy added two more vice chancellors to his trusted team: Rosemary Park, former president of both Barnard College and Connecticut College for Women, to steer educational planning and programs; and James W. Hobson, from Oakland Community College in Michigan, to oversee business and finance. Park was the first female vice chancellor appointed in the University of California system.)

"So I had the team, Foster, Bill and ultimately Chuck," Murphy said. "I conceived of myself as a coordinator of that

Below left: William G. Young, vice chancellor for planning, was a key member of Franklin D. Murphy's inner circle.

Below: Charles E. Young was Murphy's "troubleshooter" and handled much of the day-to-day administration of the campus.

University of California at Los Angeles

Above: A postcard shows a northwesterly view of the campus in the mid-1960s.

Right: The UCLA inaugural ceremony for President Clark Kerr, September 26, 1958.

team. I also conceived of myself as someone who really had to project the image of UCLA—in the community, within the regents—and to carry the UCLA message right directly head-on to the Berkeley administration. I also … had to convince the UCLA community that they were as good as I knew they were. They had so long been Berkeley's little brother."

KERR'S DECENTRALIZATION

The University of California's decentralization policy had been passed by the regents in 1951, but the first major overhaul to strengthen the chancellors as "executive heads" was driven by Kerr, starting just after his selection as president in October 1957. Kerr, as Berkeley's first chancellor, had served under President Robert Gordon Sproul and experienced firsthand the difficulties of working with a controlled, centralized structure. He described his previous role as "in charge of whatever nobody else wanted. I was slated to be a garbage can."

While historically advocated by UCLA supporters, Kerr's "equal opportunities" policy would eventually be applied to all of the system's campuses—moving greater power from the regents to the president and from the president to the chief executives at the campus level. In December 1957, at President-elect Kerr's recommendation, the regents created a committee on administrative reorganization whose members included: Pauley as chair, Edward W. Carter, Donald H. McLaughlin and Jesse H. Steinhart. President Sproul also was a member and attended every meeting, but did not actively engage. "He must have suffered internally as he sat there silent and, I am sure, sad, witnessing the destruction of his system of governance," Kerr reflected in his memoir.

Kerr transferred 750 of 1,025 president's office staff to the campuses. This covered accounting, purchasing, business affairs, admissions, architects and engineers, the nonacademic personnel office, public relations, public ceremonies and the police force. The chief executives on the general campuses all were elevated to chancellor status and assumed the responsibility of preparing academic, fiscal and physical plans for their respective campuses.

In July 1958, Kerr appointed Harry R. Wellman as vice president of the university, a position long left unfilled by Sproul. Wellman, who had been vice president for agricultural sciences, assumed responsibility for academic matters and budget preparation, so Kerr could focus on large-scale planning and external relations.

One of the most significant personnel changes came in January 1959 when Kerr made James H. Corley vice president for governmental relations, removing him from business affairs. Previously, Corley reported directly to the regents and had in essence acted as each campus's chief officer with regard to all business matters. Elmo R. Morgan was appointed vice president for physical planning and construction and oversaw the building

programs at UCLA and the emerging general campuses, but he "fully accepted the chancellor's control of business affairs on each campus," Kerr wrote, calling this the "end of the Corley empire"—one that had often exasperated former UCLA chief executives, in particular Clarence A. Dykstra.

In addition, Kerr created several advisory groups to bridge the campuses: a council of chancellors, a cabinet of universitywide officers and a council of Associated Students presidents.

Decentralization also meant empowering the president to act on matters previously handled by the Board of Regents, focusing the board more on policy and review than detailed administration. One change, intended to strengthen the authority of the president as the main conduit to the regents, ended a long-standing practice that had served UCLA and the southern campuses since 1920: the elimination of the regental Committee on Southern California Schools, Colleges and Institutions. This closed a formal channel for UCLA administrators and faculty members to go directly to the regents, bypassing the president. It was this committee—which had from its inception included the "Godfather of UCLA," the late Regent Edward A. Dickson—that had so often been a forum for staff and alumni leaders to present their case

for UCLA's advancement. Kerr described the change as "an unspoken vote of confidence by the southern regents that I would treat UCLA fairly."

More decentralization was achieved from 1957–59 than in the 90 years prior. But these changes were enacted before Murphy was installed as UCLA chancellor, and Murphy acknowledged that perhaps he did not see Kerr's move toward decentralization as clearly as he might have, but that any new chief executive is always going to see room for more delegation of authority. "I came in later and didn't know this history," Murphy told the *Los Angeles Times* in 1966. "I saw a lot of things that were still centralized that should not be, so I complained. A chancellor who comes into the system now sees still other areas where he thinks he should have more say."

MURPHY'S BATTLE

Once Murphy took the helm, he found that Kerr's changes were simply not enough and he argued to the president and the regents that while he believed in the strength of "one university," the institution was "no stronger than its weakest link." He began to implement small but symbolic changes that rattled the president's office.

One of the first such moves came early in his tenure, when Murphy was appalled to hear campus operators answer the phone with "University of California" and straightaway ordered them to say "UCLA" instead. Two months later, Vice President Wellman called Murphy to inquire about who

approved the change. With characteristic intensity, Murphy responded: "Harry, I authorized it. And make it quite clear to everybody up there that if I can't authorize the telephone operators to identify the institution, I sure as hell shouldn't stay at UCLA or in the University of California because it would be my belief that my authority is zero."

Murphy also had stationery changed, and in a move reminiscent of UCLA's first chief executive, Ernest Carroll Moore, who pressed for "Southern Branch" signage to be added to streetcars near the Vermont Avenue campus, Murphy had "UCLA" emblazoned on street signs and local buses.

"Berkeley had preempted, out of history, the title of the University of California, as a practical matter," Murphy recalled. "So I said, OK, let's not fight that battle. Let's just give that to Berkeley, as it were ... *de facto*."

"We will make those four letters just as visible and indelible as MIT," Murphy added. "In order to get the kind of loyalty and the kind of commitment, the old school-tie commitment, you had to have something visible and something specific and precise, and the concept of the University of California was simply much too fuzzy for this particular point of view."

Students and alumni had been organizing for a new song to sing as their unique alma mater, objecting to a reference to UCLA as the "California of the South" in the current piece, "Hail Blue and Gold," which was generic enough to be used by other campuses like Riverside. With Murphy's approval, in February 1961 the students adopted the more campus-specific "Hail to the Hills of Westwood," written by 1929 graduate Jeane M. Emerson.

When Murphy learned that his executive secretary, Hansena Frederickson, concurrently acted as Kerr's assistant, he was astounded. Frederickson, a 1929 alumna, had been hired by Sproul as his UCLA assistant when he oversaw the campus after Moore's retirement. Ever since then, Frederickson worked in a dual capacity, serving both UCLA's chief executive and the university's president. Murphy phoned Wellman demanding a change: Frederickson could either be his secretary or Kerr's, but her loyalty could not be divided. Begrudgingly, Wellman agreed.

"There were hundreds of these things," Murphy said. "I began to realize this whole symbolism of control, and the subconscious—or even deliberate—desire up there to keep this little brother from getting too big and keep it from gaining its own strength and visibility and self-confidence."

Then Murphy started to tackle large-scale issues of equality, asking for parity with Berkeley with regard to library acquisitions, overall budget appropriations and faculty-student ratio. It was a seemingly unending struggle, but Murphy made strides where no UCLA chief executive had succeeded in the past. He set out by asking direct questions and seeking comparative budgetary information for UCLA and Berkeley. Murphy found that the information was not forthcoming; further, he was told it was none of his concern.

"Any time you ask me for something solely because Berkeley has it, I will say no," Kerr recalled telling Murphy. "Any time you ask me because Columbia or Michigan has it, I will take a careful look. Any time you say this proposal specially fits UCLA, I will say yes."

While advocating for UCLA, Murphy did not notice—or perhaps mind—that he was doing so by essentially "tearing down Clark Kerr's Berkeley," explained Charles Young, who noted that sometimes the tensions that ensued were the result of Murphy's style over necessity. "Whether it was the governor of Kansas, Clark Kerr or somebody in the Los Angeles community, Franklin deliberately said, 'OK, who's the villain—who's the person I can make into a villain to use to produce the result I want to produce?' He prospered in that kind of cockfight environment."

After a while, Murphy realized he was not making enough progress and decided to pursue a different course.

"The Berkeley people were already beginning to get a little leery of me—that they were beginning to sense that they had gotten a fox into the chicken pen," Murphy said. "I also began to realize that I would never get anywhere in getting equity, in getting authority, without working directly with the regents, because I was convinced that the regents would never be told. There would never be a transference of my concerns."

"I knew this was a dangerous game to play; and in retrospect, it was a disloyal game, because I do believe in a system—I believe in channels," he added. "I would never have gone the regents route had Kerr and Wellman been full and open with me."

Murphy turned to his powerful and influential friends, a network that since his arrival in Los Angeles had grown steadily, and now included alumni leaders and several regents from Southern California with whom he socialized regularly. Among them: Regents Pauley, Carter, Dorothy Buffum Chandler, John E. Canaday and William E. Forbes. "I finally concluded that either I ought to get out of this job or win this battle," Murphy said. "And since I had no troops except the regents, I had to get it done through the regents."

Believing that a strong library attracts superior scholars, Murphy made the UCLA Library a priority. He drew on his supporters among the regents to help reach an agreement with Kerr in April 1961 that ramped up UCLA Library acquisitions at a rate greater than Berkeley, so that the two libraries would be of equal caliber. Working first with University Librarian Lawrence Clark Powell and then with his successor, Robert Vosper—who returned to UCLA from the University of Kansas—library volumes doubled to 3 million

by 1971. (By 1984, the UCLA Library was ranked No. 2 in the nation, behind Harvard; Berkeley was No. 3.) The new University Research Library, completed in 1964 in North Campus, housed books for graduate students and the faculty. The original library building on Royce quad, renamed for Powell, was converted to an undergraduate library.

While Murphy initially worked behind the scenes with alumni leaders and the regents, he later gained support from several of his fellow chancellors, including Emil M. Mrak at Davis, who were becoming increasingly frustrated. Together they succeeded in obtaining from the regents direct chancellorial approval over faculty appointments.

Another issue that Murphy affected: the reallocation of university "incidental fees." For years, these fees for non-instructional student services were collected from students at UCLA and sent to Berkeley for redistribution. However, fewer dollars than collected were being returned to UCLA, as Berkeley benefited from greater funds than those generated from its students. Murphy argued that UCLA's needs were in effect greater than Berkeley's because UCLA was younger and had fewer endowments and other sources of ongoing support. Three years after Murphy first forced the issue, fees were collected and dispensed on each campus.

Throughout his tenure, Murphy continued to push for greater executive power and budget equity with Berkeley.

"Without Clark Kerr up there, it wouldn't have happened," said Adrian Harris, assistant to the vice chancellor for administration from 1963–67 before being appointed director of planning in 1967 and vice chancellor for planning in 1984. "But it wouldn't have happened anywhere near as fast if it hadn't been for Franklin Murphy."

Below: University Librarian Robert Vosper (center) announces the library's three millionth acquisition in January 1971, culminating a 10-year program intended to double its holdings.

Excavation for a new student union gets underway in summer 1959 and progresses over the next 18 months. Several generations of Bruins repaid a $500,000 construction bond through student fees collected over a period of 40 years. The union, which officially opened on April 3, 1961, was renamed for longtime Associated Students executive director William C. Ackerman upon his retirement in 1967.

ARTFUL TRANSFORMATION

While the university system was undergoing its administrative reorganization, the UCLA campus was experiencing an extensive physical transformation. Voters passed three successive state bond measures in 1962, 1964 and 1966, providing UCLA with $95 million for campus building expansion. With another $55 million obtained through matching federal funds, gifts and self-amortizing projects, UCLA designed a long-range development plan that was its most ambitious building program to date.

More than 50 building projects were completed during this period. They included: a second student union building, named for William C. Ackerman, longtime Associated Students executive director, after his retirement in 1967; the Social Sciences Building, later renamed Bunche Hall; Slichter (named for geophysicist Louis B. Slichter) and Knudsen halls; and the Engineering Nuclear Reactor Building, near the Court of Sciences; the Neuropsychiatric Institute and Brain Research Institute; the School of Public Health and School of Dentistry buildings; the Jules Stein Eye Institute; and a doubling in size of the medical center, which was renamed the Center for the Health Sciences.

Jules Stein, ophthalmologist and founder of the Music Corporation of America, donated the $1.3 million initial pledge to create the Jules Stein Eye Institute, which opened in 1966.

Due largely to the efforts of Regent Carter, who requested parity with Berkeley, two new high-rise residence halls—Rieber completed in 1963 and Hedrick in 1964—joined Dykstra (1959) and Sproul (1960) halls, already in use. A track-and-field stadium to be named after longtime coach and athletic trainer Elvin C. "Ducky" Drake, and a basketball and general-use indoor arena, temporarily named the Memorial Activities Center, were underway. Although the Legislature prohibited the use of state funds to build parking structures, something had to be done to relieve traffic and parking congestion. Murphy's administration came up with a self-supporting plan creating six multilevel parking lots that could accommodate 16,000 cars. An interior road that looped around the campus—University Circle Drive (soon shortened to Circle Drive)—was constructed to connect them.

Murphy cared not only about the quality of the buildings—to enable the activity that went on inside them—but he also stressed the importance of UCLA's physical setting and landscape beautification. There was an unwritten rule on campus that a tree could not be cut down without consulting the chancellor.

An arts aficionado, Murphy made sure there were places of artistic respite. He was behind every element, from the commissioning of the Inverted Fountain anointing the Grand Axis of the campus, to the acquisition of a Japanese garden in nearby Bel-Air using funds donated by Regent Carter. The one-acre garden, with its authentic tea house and Hokura shrine originally built in Japan and reassembled locally, was commissioned by oil executive Gordon Guiberson. It was later named the UCLA Hannah Carter Japanese Garden in honor of the board chairman's wife.

One of Murphy's enduring legacies was the development of North Campus as a hub for the arts that featured the Dickson Art Center—which included the UCLA Art Galleries and the Grunwald Graphic Arts Foundation—and the theater arts complex of Macgowan and Melnitz halls. But the crown jewel of North Campus as envisioned by Murphy was the five-acre sculpture garden named after him in 1968.

"All my life in academia, I've believed that a university campus ought to be a good deal more than just efficient and functional, that it ought to have beauty in it," Murphy said. "Young people should be encouraged to grow up in the presence of beauty, to think of art as something you live with rather than something you just look at."

"BONNE FÊTE" MONSIEUR PICASSO
25 OCTOBER - 12 NOVEMBER 1961

PICASSO
SELECTED FROM SOUTHERN CALIFORNIA COLLECTIONS
PRESENTED BY
THE UCLA ART COUNCIL
AT THE
UCLA ART GALLERIES
LOS ANGELES, CALIFORNIA

Above: In 1961, Picasso created "Flowers for UCLA," a lithograph that he donated to the UCLA Art Council in appreciation of an on-campus exhibition of his work. A limited-edition, signed lithograph was sold to raise scholarship money for art students so they could travel abroad.

Circle inset: Students in newly constructed high-rise dorms, c.1960.

Opposite: Murphy had long wanted to acquire a Japanese garden in neighboring Bel-Air, and in 1965 it was donated to UCLA by Regent Edward W. Carter and his wife, Hannah. The one-acre garden features a koi pond, tea house and Hokura shrine.

Left: Rodin's *Walking Man*, a gift from the UCLA Alumni Association and an anonymous donor, is a central fixture in the sculpture garden created by Franklin D. Murphy as a place of campus respite.

UCLA Residence Halls

Above left: After decades without significant on-campus housing, four high-rise dormitories opened between 1959–1964, including Sproul and Dykstra halls, located on the hill just above the "Big C."

Left: A 12,000-seat track-and-field stadium was completed by 1969, and infrastructure roads had been built to ease traffic around campus.

arking at UCLA…

fresh fancies
by Dick Goldstone

Though you get here at dawning,
At daylight or dark,
Be it ever so humble,
There's no place to park.
No corner or crevice,
No cranny or crack,
No niche for bestowing
The travel-worn hack.
Though you search every alley,
Each field freshly plowed,
You are met with the notice—
"No parking allowed."
So arrive with the sunbeam
That heralds the day—
And park out on Wilshire,
Miles away.
Bring blankets and breakfast
And boots, if you like,
A compass and sextant
Prepared for a hike—
But no matter how early
You get here, alas
You can ne'er park in time
For an eight o'clock class!

Left: A poem penned in the *Daily Bruin* captures early Bruins' parking frustrations, while a determined Chandler Harris finds a convenient spot on the steps of Royce Hall in 1932.

001940

UCLA PARKING $1.00

Good only on date sold. One entry only. Not transferable. Ticket to be visibly displayed on windshield or dashboard.

THIS SIDE UP
LOCK YOUR CAR

DILLINGHAM TICKET CO. L.A.

ENTRANCE PERMIT
EXPOSITION PARK

ENTER STATE DRIVE FROM FIGUEROA OR MENLO.
PARK BEHIND STATE EXPOSITION BUILDING

ISSUED TO ___ Mr. C. A. Dykstra

VALID FOR ___ Season 1948 - 49

NO. 4   APPROVED

NOT TRANSFERABLE   M G R.

DIDN'T MAKE IT.

Above: Some Bruins had to travel a bit too far from their parking space in the 1950s.

Right: "It takes four years to get through UCLA, or five if you park in Lot 32," Bob Hope once quipped.

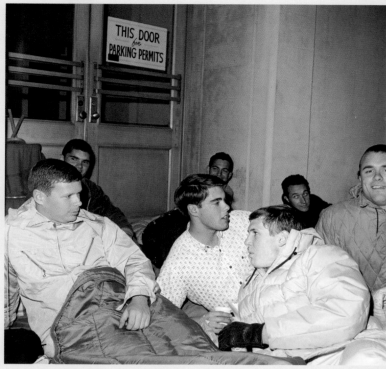

Right: Campers wait out the night for the privilege of buying a semester parking pass, 1964.

Below: A commuter campus, 1956.

Murphy asked landscape architect Ralph D. Cornell to begin designing and constructing the garden before UCLA had a single piece of sculpture for it—a trivial matter Murphy would worry about later.

"In his way of thinking, his way of managing, his way of doing things, you'd move, move, move," explained Charles Young. "Keep things going. Don't sit around [saying], 'Oh! Somebody wants something done—better think about that.'"

It didn't take long for the sculpture to arrive. During a Jacques Lipchitz exhibit on campus in 1963, the artist's *Song of the Vowels* was on view in front of the Dickson Art Center. The UCLA Art Council, with assistance from regent and arts patron Norton Simon, raised $75,000 to buy the piece.

Then, a fortuitous donation and some savvy negotiation brought an entire collection of sculpture. UCLA donor David Bright had left a quarter of his collection of modern paintings to UCLA and the rest to the Los Angeles County Museum of Art, along with a recently acquired collection of outdoor sculpture to his wife, Dolly. After Bright's death, Murphy, a member of the museum's board, met with Dolly Bright and suggested a trade: the sculpture for UCLA's portion of the paintings, which would be donated to the museum. After seeing the landscaped garden, Dolly Bright was so enthusiastic that she not only agreed, but contributed several additional pieces that she bought with her own funds. The garden soon became one of the most distinguished outdoor sculpture collections in the country.

Murphy's interest in ethnic art led to the creation in 1963 of the Museum and Laboratories of Ethnic Arts and Technology, an independent research unit, which acquired artifacts from donations and archaeological digs. In 1966, UCLA received the Sir Henry Wellcome Collection of primitive and ethnic art, a collection of 15,000 masks, ceremonial robes, religious items and other artifacts from around the world. Subsequently, this gift generated many others. In 1971, the name was changed to the Museum of Cultural History, and by 1975 its collections ranked it among the top four university museums in the country, in numbers and in quality. (Located in the basement of Haines Hall, the collection was not easily accessible until 1992, when the Fowler Museum of Cultural History opened its doors near the base of Janss Steps.)

One of the qualities that most attracted Murphy to UCLA was that the university was located within a growing and dynamic cosmopolitan city. Until his arrival, UCLA had not been truly embraced by the community or its influential leaders, but Murphy pressed to make UCLA a part of Los Angeles' cultural fabric.

"He had ties to every element of the establishment in local, regional, national and international realms," Young said. "He realized that one of the things he could do best for UCLA was to tie UCLA to the power structure of Los Angeles."

Murphy reorganized the performing arts program at UCLA (renamed UCLA Live in 2000), removing it from

Top left: The sculpture garden takes shape on North Campus, 1965.

Top: Blending art with every day life was one of Franklin D. Murphy's aims in creating the garden.

Above: Murphy with Dolly Bright, who donated several pieces to the garden, including Barbara Hepworth's *Oval Form*, 1967.

LBJ at UCLA

On February 21, 1964, U.S. military helicopters bearing President Lyndon B. Johnson and Mexican President Adolfo López Mateos landed on the athletic field, while an audience of 34,000, sitting in a temporary stadium constructed nearby, eagerly awaited them.

In honor of the occasion, students had painted the "Big C," normally blue in color, to a more patriotic red, white and blue. They also managed some precarious moves to drape Sproul Hall in American flag colors on one side and the green, white and red colors of the Mexican flag on the other. In the center hung a giant greeting: "UCLA Welcomes Presidents."

The event occurred barely three months after the assassination of President John F. Kennedy and security was heightened, with snipers visibly stationed on campus rooftops overlooking the field, as well as on roofs and balconies of nearby homes along Sunset Boulevard. Students in Sproul Hall were allowed to watch the proceedings from the dormitory—but all windows were required closed, and doors leading into the halls were ordered open so that the rooms could be observed by security patrols.

Johnson and López Mateos, in Southern California to discuss a wide array of policy issues, stopped at UCLA to be keynote speakers at the 96th Charter Day observance. (Charter Day, an anniversary celebration of the University of California's founding on March 23, 1868, was celebrated annually on each campus until 1967, when the tradition at UCLA ended, and an emphasis was placed on marking the campus's own founding of May 23, 1919 with Anniversary Day.) At the end of the ceremony, both heads of state were awarded honorary doctorates of law by University of California President Clark Kerr.

The first American president to speak at UCLA while in office, Johnson reaffirmed the solidarity between the United States and Mexico, but spoke primarily of the "dangers of today"—confirming foreign-policy aims in Vietnam, Cuba, Panama and Cyprus.

Johnson concluded his remarks by saying: "Let us, with brave hearts and with cool heads, advance with the task of building the citadels of peace, in a world set free from fear." The speech, billed by the White House as a major foreign-policy address, aired on national television and received international press coverage.

López Mateos, whose Spanish message was translated, emphasized the role of the university and its people in the world at large. "Knowledge and freedom cannot be kept apart," the Mexican president said.

University students have the power to make a difference in society, López Mateos continued, noting that "from these classrooms will go forward many young people with talent and dedication, who will apply their best efforts to contribute to the study of human relations and, especially, to the operation of law as the basis for order, peace, progress and fraternity."

Right: Residents of Sproul Hall, led by juniors Don Korn and Stan Benson, organized an elaborate display to welcome the presidents, under the watchful eye of the Secret Service.

Below: Mexican President Adolfo López Mateos shakes hands with President Lyndon B. Johnson during Charter Day, 1964. Johnson's visit was the first by a sitting U.S. president.

Bottom right: An audience of 34,000 cram into a stadium—built just for the day—to hear the presidents speak.

the auspices of Extension and bringing it into the fold of the university. The Committee on Fine Arts Productions began offering a rich variety of music, events, dance and movies, attracting 350,000 people a year to campus.

Conversely, in 1966, Extension's highly acclaimed UCLA Theatre Group (later the Mark Taper Forum), moved to the Los Angeles Music Center. And in 1969, UCLA's Design for Sharing, a community outreach program for the performing arts, was created. These moves bridged UCLA with the flourishing cultural life of Los Angeles.

On campus, Murphy enhanced the place of the arts in the academic curriculum. In 1968, the Graduate School of Architecture and Urban Planning was created under the direction of Dean Harvey S. Perloff. The school contained three separate programs: architecture, urban design and urban planning.

Murphy continued the transformation begun under Chancellor Knudsen to turn the College of Applied Arts into the College of Fine Arts. Headed by theater arts Professor William W. Melnitz, the new college combined the core departments of art, music and the theater arts. Physical education and home economics were transferred briefly to the College of Letters and Science until they were phased out. Dance classes, previously part of the physical education curriculum, became a new department in the College of Fine Arts—the first department of its kind in the nation—under the direction of innovative modern dance educator Alma Hawkins.

The Institute of Ethnomusicology, founded by UCLA alumnus Mantle Hood, a recognized authority in the field, was moved to the music department. The program's mission was to foster research and dissemination of information about traditional, folk and popular music from around the world. (In 1989, ethnomusicology became its own department—another national first.)

"Franklin Murphy was the greatest supporter of the arts," Melnitz said. "He was interested in everything."

Above: The groundbreaking Institute of Ethnomusicology was founded by alumnus Mantle Hood in 1960.

Above left: Alma Hawkins, pioneer in modern dance education, transformed what was once part of the physical education curriculum into the nation's first department of dance in 1962.

Notable speakers delivered Charter Day addresses during the 1960s, including Ethiopian Emperor Haile Selassie (above) in 1967 and former President Dwight D. Eisenhower (right) in 1963.

"I WANT A PAVILION"

One of the largest projects undertaken during Murphy's tenure as chancellor was the creation of a 13,000-seat indoor sporting and multipurpose arena. Alumni leaders and students had wanted such a venue dating back to 1946, and later organized petitions, but funding was the primary obstacle. During Chancellor Raymond B. Allen's administration, a surplus World War II hangar was considered briefly. Athletes had to settle for the Men's Gymnasium, nicknamed the "B.O. Barn."

In the 1960s, most major American universities already had a large sports venue, or were in the process of building one. UCLA was glaringly behind the times, and it was particularly noticeable with the rising acclaim of Coach John R. Wooden and his championship-winning men's basketball teams. As Wooden recalled, "being on the third floor [of the Men's Gymnasium], and with heating rising and everything—not the best ventilation in the world, you know."

Not only was the men's gym woefully inadequate as a practice facility, but there weren't enough seats for those who wanted to attend the games. It originally accommodated 2,200 fans but, due to overcrowding, the fire marshal cut the seating in half. As a result, home games were moved to larger venues, including Santa Monica City College, Venice High School, Long Beach City College, the Long Beach Auditorium, the Shrine Auditorium, the Pan Pacific Auditorium, and later, the Los Angeles Memorial Sports Arena. "We were down there playing double headers with USC," Wooden said, "and I felt like we were going to USC's campus and playing [an away] game."

It was clear that building an on-campus arena could be put off no longer. Funding was an issue, but Murphy would do something that had not been done before: He set in motion UCLA's first formal large-scale fund-raising effort.

Murphy enlisted the support of Pauley, an oil magnate, for a lead gift. It was a matter of matching the individual with an interest, Murphy said, and Pauley was a die-hard Bruin sports fan. One account of the story has Murphy asking Pauley for $500,000. After a pause, Pauley responded that he thought

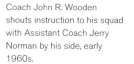

Coach John R. Wooden shouts instruction to his squad with Assistant Coach Jerry Norman by his side, early 1960s.

$1 million was more appropriate—especially, he suggested, if the arena was to have his name on it. The $1 million donation was made as a challenge to invigorate alumni to raise a 2:1 match, which they met. The state added $2 million and students provided another $1 million through fees.

"I Want a Pavilion" buttons sprouted across campus. All proceeds from the specifically themed "Sing for a Pavilion" Spring Sing were donated to the cause. Future Alumni Association President H.R. Haldeman chaired the campaign and 1,000 volunteers organized by the Association contacted alumni to secure gifts ranging from $1 to $50,000.

Architect Welton Becket designed a structure that cost $7 million, but only $5 million was raised, so the scope of the project was modified. Among other changes, planned

Above: The 1964 men's basketball team with Coach John R. Wooden in the glow of victory after winning the first of Wooden's 10 national titles.

Left: Alumnus H.R. Haldeman, at the Pauley Pavilion excavation site in 1964, led the effort to raise money for the all-purpose indoor arena.

escalators were eliminated and the concourse steps were adjusted to reduce costs on architectural demands. (In 2010, ground was broken for a multimillion-dollar expansion and renovation of the pavilion.)

The Edwin W. Pauley Pavilion was dedicated during commencement in 1965. Over the years, it has hosted numerous graduation ceremonies, a U.S. presidential debate, rock concerts, political speakers ranging from Eldridge Cleaver to Ronald Reagan, and the 1984 Summer Olympics gymnastics events. It is best known, however, as the iconic home court for UCLA's nationally decorated volleyball and gymnastic teams, and most notably, the celebrated basketball program.

The first game played in Pauley Pavilion—later dubbed "the house that Wooden built" because of his 149–2 record in

the arena—was the freshman-varsity men's basketball contest on November 27, 1965. In the 1960s, NCAA rules prohibited freshmen from playing on varsity teams, and a tradition under Wooden was to have the freshmen play the varsity. Excitement had been building. Not only was UCLA coming off two national championships and ranked No. 1 in the preseason, but it was the college debut for Lew Alcindor (later Kareem Abdul-Jabbar), who had been one of the most coveted high school players ever.

Wooden credited the arena for making a "night and day" difference in recruiting. "The best thing that ever happened to me when I came to UCLA was getting Pauley Pavilion," Wooden said. "Alcindor would never have come if we hadn't this place. When he made his visit during his senior year, I showed him Pauley Pavilion [and said], 'You're going to break it in. … With you coming there'll be as many in there for the freshman game as there will be for the rest of the games.'"

Indeed, the 1965 freshman-varsity game sold out and aired on local television. The resulting score of 75–60 was not a surprise—but, shockingly, it was the freshmen who were victorious.

"We broke their famed full-court press and won the game so easily that Coach Gary Cunningham took the regulars out with a couple minutes left in the game," recalled Lynn

Shackelford, who followed that season as a starting forward on three consecutive NCAA championship teams, 1966-69. "Poor Gary. It was his first game as a UCLA freshman coach and he didn't know how to react in the locker room. But we were yelling and having a good time."

At the other end of the hall, the varsity locker room was quiet and the players could hear the freshmen chanting, "We're No. 1!" Wooden, dumbfounded, was pacing and didn't visit the freshmen. Finally, he broke his silence: "Well … looks like we're going to be pretty good next year."

The 1965 team was one of only two that did not win national championships in a 12-year run. "We used to

joke that varsity was ranked the No. 1 team in the country," Shackelford said, "but they were only the second-best team on campus."

JOINING THE MOVEMENT

Although the 1960s started off with a placid period, it belied a fractured American society that broke along the color line and included a segregated South, despite the U.S. Supreme Court's landmark 1954 decision in *Brown v. Board of Education* that ruled all school segregation was unconstitutional. In California, the Unruh Civil Rights Act—named after its author, Assemblyman Jesse M. Unruh—was passed in July

"Segregation Must Die"

More than 4,500 gathered near Janss Steps on April 27, 1965 to hear the Reverend Martin Luther King Jr. speak about racial injustice and the evils of segregation.

Under heavy guard and the gaze of television cameras, the 1964 Nobel Peace Prize recipient addressed the UCLA community and society on the need for racial integration, increased educational opportunity and guaranteed voting rights.

The hour-long speech came one month after his successful march from Selma to the Alabama capital of Montgomery, and outlined both the accomplishments and setbacks of the civil rights movement. King also appealed to students, specifically recruiting them for a summer program that would work to double the number of blacks registered to vote in the South.

The civil rights leader was invited to campus as part of the Associated Students Speakers Program, which hosted notable social activists and political figures of the time. King was offered $2,500 for his appearance, and students later presented him with $700 they had collected for his work on voter registration efforts in the South.

The crowd, which filled the quad between the men's and women's gyms, remained intent as King spoke, interrupting only with an occasional thundering ovation.

"It may be true that you can't legislate integration, but you can legislate desegregation," King said. "It may be true that morality cannot be legislated, but behavior can be regulated. It may be true that the law cannot change the heart, but it can restrain the heartless. It may be true that the law can't make a man love me, but it can restrain him from lynching me."

King warned that while progress had been made, there was no time for complacency.

"Old Man Segregation is on his deathbed," King said. "But history has proven that social systems have a great last-minute breathing power, and the guardians of the status quo are always on hand with their oxygen tents to keep the old order alive."

He continued: "If democracy is to live, segregation must die."

Below: The Reverend Martin Luther King Jr. addresses the campus as part of the Associated Students Speakers Program at the foot of Janss Steps, April 27, 1965.

Bottom left: A silent vigil for the slain civil rights leader along Election Walk on April 5, 1968.

Right: Bruin CORE members picket against discriminatory rental practices in Westwood, c.1960.

Below right: Stevens House, which opened in 1948, provided nearby housing for two dozen minority female UCLA students each year. The co-operative, which closed in 1992, was a shelter for many students who could not find housing in Westwood due to discrimination.

1959 and prohibited discrimination by businesses that offer services to the public. Simultaneously, the regents adopted a nondiscrimination policy for all campus organizations, including fraternities and sororities.

Under the leadership of the Reverend Martin Luther King Jr. and his promotion of nonviolent resistance, the civil rights movement was gaining momentum. Many college students nationwide joined in protest efforts that helped pave the way for the Civil Rights Act of 1964 and the Voting Rights Act of 1965.

UCLA students affiliated with local-area chapters of several civil rights organizations, including the National Association for the Advancement of Colored People (NAACP), the Student Nonviolent Coordinating Committee and the Congress of Racial Equality (CORE), began demonstrating off campus in promotion of social change.

First they picketed Westwood barbershops, which were refusing to cut black customers' hair. Many of the barbershops—held to the Unruh Civil Rights Act—ended the practice. But some refused. The protests coincided with Murphy's arrival as chancellor. "[Murphy] immediately threatened the barbers in Westwood that if they would not cut everybody's hair, he was going to open up barbershops on campus," recalled Robert Singleton, a senior who was president of UCLA's NAACP chapter in 1960. "Because there were a few holdouts ... he did it." A barbershop was set up in the basement of Kerckhoff Hall, and incorporated into the plans for the new student union.

Next students turned their focus to discrimination in Westwood apartments. They obtained a list from UCLA's housing office of all landlords offering rentals. "We would go to their places and do what we called a CORE test," explained Singleton, who was appointed to the Chancellor's Committee on Discrimination. "We'd send them a white group and a black group and ask them the same question. If the black group was rejected and the white group was not, then we'd all come out and we'd confront them." The students would then give the names of the discriminating landlords to the UCLA housing office, which, under Murphy's directive, removed them permanently from the listings.

In the summer of 1961, after CORE founder James L. Farmer Jr. spoke on campus, more than a dozen UCLA students—black and white—traveled on interstate buses in the segregated South on "freedom rides," challenging local Jim Crow laws that perpetuated racial discrimination in public areas such as bus depots.

"One of the things [Farmer] said was, 'The freedom rides are going into a different phase: We're not gonna run around trying to get desegregation of all sorts of places; we're gonna fill the jails in this one place, which we think is the worst place in the world, and that is Jackson, Mississippi,"

said Singleton, who was pursuing his master's at the time. "I volunteered at that, like a nut."

On July 30, 1961, a group of 15 freedom riders were arrested while sitting in the "whites only" waiting room at the Jackson railway station. Nine, including Singleton, were UCLA students. Most of the riders spent 40 days at Mississippi State Penitentiary, a maximum security prison known as Parchman Farm, until released on bond pending trial. Another group of riders, including UCLA student Steven McNichols, departed for Jackson in August, but were arrested en route at the railway

Recalling the days of the loyalty oath and McCarthyism, soon after Kerr became president he sought to ease some restrictions stipulated under Regulation 17, which banned political speakers and imposed other limits on free speech and campus activism.

The regents-supported Kerr Directives, implemented in phases from 1958 to 1963, included the following actions: no restriction would be imposed on political candidates who spoke on campus and no longer would there be a requirement to balance candidates against each other on the same platform; students would not be punished for their off-campus activism; distribution of noncommercial literature would not be restricted; the ban on Communist speakers was lifted; and all chancellors were encouraged to create a "Hyde Park," or free speech area, on campus.

Left: Robert Singleton (left) and Steven McNichols (right) were among those arrested in 1961 during their participation in Freedom Rides in the South, protesting Jim Crow segregation laws. McNichols (below left) receives emergency treatment after he was badly beaten in his holding cell.

Below left: Senator John F. Kennedy, on the stump before formally announcing his presidential campaign, speaks in Royce Hall, November 2, 1959.

station in Houston. Overnight, McNichols and three other white, male riders were badly beaten in their holding cell.

After the students were found guilty, they were required to pay an additional $1,000 to remain out on bail as their cases were appealed to the U.S. Supreme Court. To help five of the students continue with their UCLA studies while their cases were pending, the Student Legislative Council presented a special referendum to determine whether the student body favored a $5,000 loan from the Associated Students.

The *Daily Bruin* endorsed the ballot measure, approved by 60 percent of the 3,532 votes cast on February 14 and 15, 1962. But on March 8, the Board of Control voted 5–3 to reject the loan. The *Daily Bruin* called the controversial vote "a sham," and several protests were held to force the issue. However, Murphy declined to reverse the decision stating that doing so would "create a precedent without limit or bounds" and that the students could apply for funds through the Student Loan Office. After his announcement, Murphy made a personal contribution of an undisclosed sum to increase the funds available when the riders submitted their applications. (In 1965, the Supreme Court reversed the riders' convictions citing its previous 1960 ruling in *Boynton v. Virginia*, which declared such segregation unconstitutional.)

Just before his death, Meyerhoff had represented Vietnam War opposition speakers, delivering his speech to more than 2,000 students who had congregated to hear opposing views on the conflict that included the president of the conservative John Birch Society. In January 1966, the Board of Regents formally approved the naming of Hans Meyerhoff Park in his memory.

Murphy encouraged another highly successful program that promoted the free exchange of ideas: the Speakers Program run by the Associated Students. Thanks in part to Murphy's connections, and UCLA's rising prominence, dozens of political leaders, social activists and other influential figures accepted invitations to address the UCLA community during the 1960s. The impressive array of speakers covered the broad political spectrum, ranging from Nobel Peace Prize recipient Martin Luther King Jr. to Alabama Governor George C. Wallace, who tried to bar desegregation

TEACH - IN

DORTHY GUYOT
MASAMORI KOJIMA
SIMON CASADY
SUDDI CHAWLA
GEORGE E. BROWN JR.
HANS MEYERHOFF
RICHARD N. ROSECRANCE
ROBERT SCHEER
PHIL KIRBY

WILLIAM STANTON
AMROM KATZ
PAUL SWEEZY
STANLEY SHEINBAUM
DAVID WILKINSON
DAVID MCREYNOLDS
MARK MANCALL
STANLEY MILLET
Marshall WINDMILLER

**UCLA STUDENT UNION
GRAND BALLROOM
NOV. 12   NOON - MIDNITE**
UNIVERSITY COMMITTEE ON VIET NAM

At UCLA, Hyde Park—a reference to the London park famous for an area devoted to public displays of free speech—was established near Janss Steps. It was inaugurated on October 24, 1962, two days after President John F. Kennedy revealed the Cuban Missile Crisis to Americans. Shouts of "American imperialism" and "Communist domination" shared the platform atop the green soapbox as a crowd of 500 gathered to debate the issue. "We firmly believe that any college age person should have the same rights under the Constitution of the United States as anyone else, and this includes the right of free speech," Murphy told the *Examiner*.

In March 1964, Hyde Park moved to the grassy knoll nestled between Kerckhoff Hall and Bruin Walk, where it has long served as a platform for everything from shouting matches and student protests to impromptu celebrations and performances. On December 1, 1965, it was renamed by the Student Legislative Council in memory of alumnus and beloved philosophy Professor Hans Meyerhoff. Known for using his philosophy teachings to explain the societal concerns of the time, Meyerhoff had died one month earlier in a car accident.

The popular Associated Students Speakers Program brought myriad speakers to the campus during its 20 years of existence, including boxer Muhammad Ali (below), actress Jane Fonda (bottom left) and Southern Californian Communist Party leader Dorothy Healey (bottom right).

Above: Remnants of preparations for the 1963 homecoming parade, canceled in the wake of President John F. Kennedy's assassination, line the streets of Westwood.

at universities and schools. Others included: Communist Party leader Dorothy Healey; National Farm Workers Association founder César Chávez; actress and anti-Vietnam War protester Jane Fonda; beatnik poet Ralph Ginzburg; science fiction author Ray Bradbury; cultural anthropologist Margaret Mead; conservative South Carolina Senator Strom Thurmond; and Israel's first prime minister, David Ben-Gurion. For the first time since the Regulation 17 speaker ban was instituted in 1937, UCLA was awash with political debate.

Not all restrictions on freedom of expression had been lifted, however. Students were still subject to a strict ban on using university facilities to recruit or raise funds for off-campus political or religious causes, and could not exploit the name of the university in their activism. And some rules were actually tightened. Under the new "open forum" policy, access was limited to "*bona fide* students, faculty members, and employees of the University" and students needed to obtain the

signature of a faculty member, senior university administrator or someone approved by the dean of students to serve as an adviser to the organization. This incensed students at UCLA and Berkeley, who decried the university's *in loco parentis* role. "Far from fostering 'aroused social conscience,'" wrote *Daily Bruin* editorial editor (and future actor and comedian) Harry Shearer, "the Directives are in fact an ideological filter tip to screen out harsh dissenting ideas and irritating thoughts and to make the University milder, much milder."

On November 22, 1963, the nation was left reeling as President Kennedy was assassinated, marking what would become known as "the end of Camelot." UCLA students had stayed up late the night before decorating floats for the homecoming parade, which was canceled as the nation mourned.

"It was like the world was coming apart," recalled Andrea L. Rich, a junior at the time, who would become UCLA's first female executive vice chancellor in 1991. "Everything that you thought was stable—that you believed in—it was all coming unglued."

A year later an unfortunate series of missteps at Berkeley led to an unprecedented student revolt and the birth of what would be hailed as the Free Speech Movement. Due to a technicality, the Berkeley administration informed students that they were banned from an off-campus free-speech area that they were using to garner support for political and social causes. The tradition dated back to Sproul, who in 1933 supported the creation of an area outside Sather Gate. As the campus expanded, the area was moved in September 1959 one block south to the new site. Beyond the loyalty oath scandal, Kerr would deem the Berkeley administration's decision—which occurred while he was abroad—the "second greatest administrative

Right: Students surround Charles E. Young, vice chancellor for administration, during a Free Speech Movement protest on campus in 1964.

Below: Mario Savio (center) inspired the Free Speech Movement from Sproul Plaza at Berkeley on October 1, 1964, but the agenda did not spur as much direct action at UCLA.

blunder" in the university's history and regretted not taking immediate action.

Creating the United Front, 18 diverse student groups banded together, and openly defied the ban by setting up their tables anyway, and added a new location: in front of the administration building's steps, in Sproul Plaza. There, Berkeley alumnus Jack Weinberg was distributing CORE materials on October 1, 1964, when he was arrested by campus police. A group of 3,000 students swarmed the police car for 32 hours. Weinberg and philosophy student Mario Savio climbed on top of the car and addressed the crowd. The United Front turned into the Free Speech Movement and Savio became its chief spokesman.

On November 25, 1964, Savio spoke at UCLA, explaining the movement's policy and trying to admonish students to join the movement. "Your fellow students at Cal are risking their careers by freeing themselves and you," Savio told students gathered in Ackerman Grand Ballroom.

The following week in Berkeley's Sproul Plaza, with his speech decrying the university's "autocracy," Savio would galvanize a generation—who adopted the movement's direct-action tactics in anti-war, anti-draft and other protests throughout the 1960s and 1970s. "There's a time when the operation of the machine becomes so odious—makes you so sick at heart—that you can't take part," Savio proclaimed from the top of the Berkeley administration building's steps before leading a mass sit-in that lasted for almost 36 hours and led to some 800 arrests. "You can't even passively take part. And you've got to put your bodies upon the gears and upon the wheels, upon the levers, upon all the apparatus, and you've got to make it stop. And you've got to indicate to the people who run it, to the people who own it that unless you're free, the machine will be prevented from working at all."

But the Free Speech Movement never caught on with any comparable intensity at UCLA. Several rallies took place at Hyde Park and UCLA students asked the administration for a "me-too clause"—seeking the implementation of any changes adopted at Berkeley. The crowds numbered in the hundreds, compared to the thousands at Berkeley. In opposition, some 500 UCLA students formed the "Responsible Free Speech Movement" and gathered 3,000 signatures on a petition supporting the administration.

UCLA's Jeff Donfeld was the only student body president in the University of California to speak out against the movement. Donfeld said he was concerned that there would be political backlash. "I didn't want the Free Speech Movement to adversely affect the fiscal well-being of the University of California," reflected Donfeld, who served as President Richard M. Nixon's head of drug-abuse policy from 1969–71. "My view was, go step off the campus—one block,

10 steps—and advocate as much as you want, but don't bring the university into a situation where you would give political conservatives an opportunity to say, 'Look at what those damn kids are doing. Why are we funding that place?' "

The UCLA Alumni Association sought to quell anxiety among alumni. Executive Director Douglas K. Kinsey wrote a letter to alumni in January 1965, reassuring them that "individual rights of free speech and political freedom have never been questioned by the University." He also conveyed that there was not as much interest in the movement at UCLA as there had been at Berkeley. "Even though Mario Savio, the leader of the so-called 'Free Speech Movement' at Berkeley, came to establish a chapter at UCLA," Kinsey wrote, "he found little support among our students."

In a waggish *Daily Bruin* column, senior (and future film critic) Joel Siegel described what he thought was the key difference between UCLA and Berkeley with regard to student activism: UCLA was still largely a commuter campus, so many students lived at home with their parents.

"The Free Speech Movement has begun here in earnest, but it will never be as successful at fomenting student dissent as was the similar group at Berkeley," wrote Siegel, also an editor of the campus humor magazine *Satyr*. "The reason is deceptively simple—my mother. … Berkeley students have mothers they write, not mothers they talk to. And there is an infinite difference between a mother you write and a mother you talk to. … Yes our administration can rest easy. For as long as there are mothers, there will be peace at UCLA."

While regents and government officials were critical of Kerr and Berkeley Chancellor Edward W. Strong (who resigned in March 1965 amid the upheaval), they lauded Murphy for the relative stability at UCLA. Murphy was repeatedly asked about the dichotomy.

"Considering the fact that Berkeley and U.C.L.A. are part of the same university, why did the Free Speech riots not spread south to Westwood?" asked *Time* in October 1966. "One reason, answers Murphy, is that Berkeley has traditionally had a bigger share of student activists than U.C.L.A., and thus far more troublemaking 'nonstudent hangers-on in the periphery.' " Murphy was also publicly critical of Berkeley's administration, adding, "You can't substitute memos and bulletins for the courtesy of a dialogue and an explanation."

TWO CONSEQUENTIAL EXITS

Seizing political opportunity—in addition to criticizing the growing cost of welfare and high taxes—Governor Reagan had campaigned for office by attacking the University of California and accused a "vacillating administration" of

Below: Chancellor Franklin D. Murphy addresses students incensed about the firing of President Clark Kerr, January 24, 1967.

Far left: Before becoming the "Lizard King," Jim Morrison, the iconic lead singer of the 1960s counterculture rock band The Doors, graduated in 1965 with a bachelor's degree in theater arts and a B-plus average.

Left: Student body President Robert S. Michaels promises to fight the implementation of "tuition" as advocated by Governor Ronald Reagan, 1967.

Right: Governor Ronald Reagan holds a press conference August 31, 1967, following a regents meeting in the UCLA Faculty Center, where a proposal to implement "tuition" was hotly debated.

allowing a "fractional minority of beatniks, filthy-speech advocates, and malcontents" to derail and bring "shame" to the university. Reagan found that concern over student rebels and the free speech demonstrations was an energizing issue among voters. He repeatedly vowed "to clean up the mess at Berkeley" and declared that students should "observe the rules or get out." He also appealed to parents who believed that the university—since admissions were tightened under Master Plan guidelines—had become elitist.

Bowing to political pressure, on January 20, 1967—at Reagan's first meeting as an *ex-officio* member of the Board of Regents and just two weeks into his governorship—the regents dismissed Kerr as president by a vote of 14–8. The action ignited a national outcry. The lead editorial headline in *The New York Times* cried, "Twilight of a Great University." Protests ensued at several University of California campuses.

"There was a lot of strong, hostile feeling toward Reagan," said Andrea Rich, who, in 1967, was working toward her doctorate. "He appeared to be genuinely anti-intellectual, anti-university, and I think we all felt that the glowing place had lost favor, at least in the eyes of the state government."

The day following Kerr's dismissal, more than 8,000 poured into Pauley Pavilion in an organized protest against his firing, budget cuts and "tuition." On January 24, more than 6,000 animated UCLA students held a demonstration in support of Kerr on Royce quad.

Robert S. Michaels, 1967 student body president, told the cheering crowd that a newly formed coalition of students from across the state would fight against the implementation of "tuition" and state budget cuts to the university—both sought by Reagan—and push for a student voice in the search for Kerr's successor as well as on university governing boards. Michaels suggested that "if they want tuition, it should be retroactive, so that all the students who have ever gone here would have to pay back tuition." After the rally ended, 1,000 students went to the Administration Building, where Murphy promised a "free and open discussion on the difficult problems confronting us."

Several weeks after being let go, Kerr remarked that he had ended his job just as he had started it: "fired with enthusiasm." Almost four decades later, it would be revealed that other factors affected his ouster, including efforts by Regent Pauley and FBI Director Edgar J. Hoover

to discredit Kerr by alleging he was a Communist. After a 17-year legal battle brought by the *San Francisco Chronicle* under the Freedom of Information Act, the Ninth Circuit Court of Appeals ordered the release of 200,000 pages of FBI documents spanning from the 1940s through the 1970s. The *Chronicle* reported in June 2002 that the FBI had "engaged in sprawling covert intelligence operations that involved thousands of [University of California] students and faculty involved in legitimate debate about public policy."

According to Kerr, one handwritten comment summed up Hoover's reaction: "Kerr is no good." Kerr noted, "I look on this as the equivalent of an honorary degree."

Years later, Murphy called Kerr's dismissal a "tragedy." Despite their constant disagreement over decentralization, the chancellor lost a key ally in preserving the university's quality and in protecting it from budget cuts pushed by Reagan.

"In spite of everything, my job was to build UCLA, and I wasn't about to let anybody prevent that from happening," Murphy said. "I had no problem in wanting to fight him." Murphy became an outspoken critic of Reagan's budget reductions to the University of California. In anticipation of cuts, the regents held an emergency meeting at UCLA on January 9, 1967. "I do not intend to preside at the liquidation or substantial erosion of the quality which [50 years] of effort have created at UCLA," Murphy blasted to the board.

The university asked the state for $278 million for 1967–68, an increase over the $240 million it had received the prior year to accommodate increasing enrollments. However, Reagan's initial budget proposal cut the university's support by 20 percent from 1966–67, to $192 million.

Top left: Editorial cartoonist Paul Conrad's vision of the University of California under Governor Ronald Reagan, 1971.

Above: Mayor Sam Yorty is heckled by anti-war protesters in Meyerhoff Park, c.1968.

Left: Protesters outside the Student and Alumni Placement Center picket Dow Chemical Company recruiting efforts at UCLA, c.1967.

In addition, Reagan advocated the implementation of "tuition." The majority of the regents, including Pauley, were against the notion of the dreaded word—the Master Plan, after all, ensured Californians a "tuition-free" education. In 1967, annual student non-education fees were already about $250, and Reagan proposed adding $400, but then dropped that amount to $250. The issue was at the forefront of the August 31, 1967 regents meeting at the UCLA Faculty Center. State Assembly Speaker Jesse Unruh argued that implementation of "tuition" would disproportionately affect the middle class. The regents voted down Reagan's proposal 14–7.

During lunch, the regents tried to smooth things over with the new governor, realizing they were dependent on him for next year's budget. They explained their concern over the word "tuition" and presented him with an alternate proposal drafted primarily by Murphy. When the meeting resumed, Reagan submitted a new plan proposing a "charge" to be paid

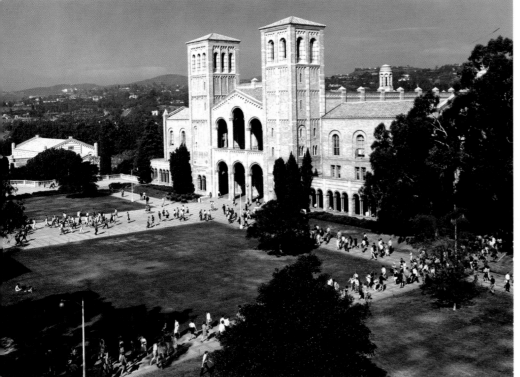

Commissioned by President Clark Kerr in March 1963, Ansel Adams photographed UCLA as part of the University of California's centennial commemoration, including a view southward of the sculpture garden and Bunche Hall from the top of Dickson Art Center (right) and the Royce quad (below).

be used to fund student services, not instruction costs, thereby keeping the university "tuition-free."

Meanwhile, the final state appropriation to the university for 1967–68 was $251.5 million, a reduction of 10 percent over the regents' initial budget request. Cuts to the university budget continued while Reagan was governor and had multiple ramifications in subsequent years. Among them: The university's extensive reorganization to convert its class schedule to a year-round quarter system of four 10-week sessions. While the university kept the quarter system it implemented in 1968, the fourth summer quarter was scrapped for budget reasons in 1970.

Battling a new governor reminded Murphy of his tumultuous past with Governor Docking, a foreboding thought. Student activism was also making Murphy increasingly disaffected. He disappeared from campus for extended periods of time—so much so, that the *Daily Bruin* noted his absence.

As the Vietnam War escalated between 1965 and 1967, students at UCLA were reacting more strongly in protest. On November 15, 1967, they staged a mass sit-in of the Administration Building while Murphy was in New York on business. Young and Dean of Student Activities Charles McClure defused the situation—sending the police away—and convinced the students to leave by promising them a meeting with the chancellor.

The next day, a *Daily Bruin* editorial asked: "Will Chancellor Franklin D. Murphy, now that he has returned to campus, continue the 'dialogue' which Young has initiated ... or will he withdraw into his office until the next crisis forces him out to try and soothe the angry masses?"

Just three months later, on February 16, 1968—a year after his scathing statement at the regents meeting and eight years after arriving on campus—Murphy announced his resignation, effective September 1, to become chairman and chief executive officer of the Times Mirror Company, owner of the *Los Angeles Times*.

Many were left stunned. Regents, fellow chancellors, and campus faculty and staff members expressed great regret over the news. "If it's true, I personally think it will be a calamity for UCLA and the University," Sherman M. Mellinkoff, dean of the medical school, told the *Daily Bruin*. "There couldn't be a worse blow at this time." A *Daily Bruin* headline, however, reported that an informal poll found that not all felt as strongly: "Student apathy meets Murphy's resignation."

The campus dynamic was changing and Murphy had grown weary. "I was getting short-tempered with the students," Murphy said in 1973. "Chuck Young and others would say, 'Franklin, you've never been like this before.' And I'd say, 'You know, you're right.' And I knew the time was ripe. ... I'd run out of gas."

by all resident students "to finance a program of student aid, faculty enrichment and/or other uses to be determined by the regents." After some discussion, he left the dollar amount up to the regents. The resolution was adopted by a majority voice vote. The regents delayed the issue until April 1968, when the board implemented a "registration fee" of $81—which would

"In the Middle of a Revolution"
1968–1975

Above: Anti-war activists make their views known during commencement, c.1970

Opposite: Charles E. Young's effectiveness in negotiating with students during the tumultuous 1960s played a key role in his selection as UCLA's chief executive.

*A*fter broad speculation, in July 1968, the Board of Regents announced the selection of Charles E. Young as UCLA's new chief executive. Young, the protégé of Franklin D. Murphy and his second in command, had run much of the university's day-to-day operations. At 36, he was the youngest chancellor ever chosen to head a University of California campus. Most significantly, he was the first alumnus to lead the almost 50-year-old institution.

From the start, Young's mettle was repeatedly tested—with challenges ranging from an issue at the core of academic freedom to campus unrest during the Vietnam War.

"The saying that to have the right man in the right place at the right time is invaluable certainly applies to Charles Young, UCLA and 1969," Dorothy Buffum Chandler, former regent and Los Angeles cultural benefactor, wrote to Young shortly after his inauguration. Young was invested as UCLA's seventh chancellor amid campus protests held in solidarity with Berkeley students after their fierce altercation with law enforcement over the use of People's Park.

A few months later, Young, with backing from recently appointed University of California President Charles J. Hitch, would stand up to Governor Ronald Reagan and the regents by staunchly defending the philosophy department's hiring of a young black Communist instructor— risking his job, but earning the faculty's long-term respect in the process. Two decades after the divisive loyalty oath controversy, the politicized issue thrust the university once again into a national debate over constitutional freedoms.

Amid the ongoing pressure, Young strived to continue the progress that Murphy had begun. "We who are associated with this institution

today intend to see to it that UCLA moves in the next 10 years from the position of one of the better universities in the United States to among the best," Young said.

In the wake of the Watts Riots, Young worked in tandem with students and administrators to increase diversity levels among the faculty and student body by instituting novel affirmative action programs—and funding them before federal dollars could be obtained. Although initially scarred by the shooting deaths of two students over control of the nascent Afro-American Studies Center, UCLA became a national model as the first university to establish four ethnic research studies centers that promoted a dialogue on the history and culture of underrepresented communities.

As the conflict in Vietnam escalated further, induction into the armed forces loomed over students' futures. By June 1969, 540,000 American soldiers were stationed in Vietnam, and almost 40,000 had died in combat. In November, President Richard M. Nixon signed an executive order establishing the first draft lottery since World War II, affecting all men aged 18–26. Screams could be heard across campus as UCLA's student radio station, KLA, aired draft announcements. Campus administrators, including a special assistant to the chancellor for Selective Service counseling, helped students file for deferment, and the Daily Bruin printed a special issue called "You and The Draft," which advised students of "every conceivable alternative from enlistment to leaving the country."

War protests that had drawn hundreds at UCLA just a few years prior began drawing thousands. Direct-action and defiance tactics adopted from the Free Speech Movement characterized the protests of the early 1970s as anti-war idealism turned into cynicism and distrust of the "establishment."

The advent of live news broadcasts brought the war into living rooms and dormitories across the country, and in May 1970, Americans watched news footage of an anti-war protest at Kent State University turning deadly as Ohio National Guardsmen fired upon a group of students. The incendiary event sparked hundreds of violent demonstrations on college campuses across the country, including UCLA, where administrators were forced to invoke the university's first-ever state of emergency, and subsequently shut down the campus for a week.

Even in this time of ferment, the campus was unified behind its championship-winning men's basketball team. The Bruins, led by Coach John R. Wooden, won their sixth NCAA championship in 1970 on their way to earning an unprecedented 10 titles in 12 years—helping make UCLA a household name in the process.

By 1972, draft resistance reached a historic high, and university and college campuses were the crucible for the anti-war movement, with its rebellious chant of "Hell no, we won't go!" Students at UCLA protested by ripping up draft cards at Meyerhoff Park, marching across campus and through Westwood, staging sit-ins of buildings and busy streets, and "striking" by walking out of classes. "Ending the war starts with you, not the next guy," a 1972 Daily Bruin editorial urged. "Keep marching, keep it shut down, until the war ends. It's the only way, people … the only way."

A year later, the military draft ended and while protests on campus diminished, they continued until the war's end in 1975 after the fall of Saigon.

As Young later described, it was a "dangerous" time that required "toughness and gentleness." The new chancellor proved an indefatigable arbiter who, by holding to his convictions, would guide UCLA skillfully through the most tumultuous era in its history.

THE YOUNGEST LEADER

Upon resigning, Murphy made no secret that he hoped his right-hand man and UCLA's No. 2 executive would succeed him.

"Chuck Young has been an extremely competent administrator—he's really done most of the work," Murphy said at a February 16, 1968, press conference after formally tendering his resignation to the regents to become chairman and chief executive officer of the Times Mirror Company. "And don't forget that he's been the restraining influence on me on a number of occasions."

Charles E. Young, UCLA's youngest chief executive, 1968.

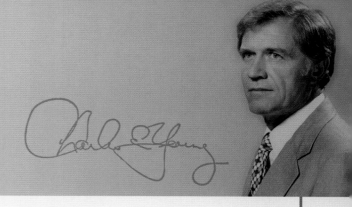

CHANCELLOR (1968–1997)

Charles Edward Young

Born on December 30, 1931, in San Bernardino, California, Charles E. Young would become the first alumnus to head UCLA, leading his alma mater for an unprecedented 29 years.

By the age of four, Young had taught himself to read using comics, and as a youth he worked in the local orange groves. While in high school, Young lied about his age and joined the Air National Guard. After graduating at the age of 16, he enrolled at San Bernardino Valley College. During his second year there, he met Sue Daugherty. Young dropped out of school and the couple married in June 1950. Two days later, the Korean War broke out and Young's unit was called to active duty. He was stationed at Misawa Air Base, 400 miles north of Tokyo, first working as a crew member on transport aircraft and then as the non-commissioned officer in charge of personnel services.

"I grew up during that period," Young recalled. "I came home convinced that I wanted to go back to school, that I wanted to get a degree, and that I wanted to do something with my life." He registered at the newly opened University of California at Riverside, where he was elected the first student body president

and earned his bachelor's degree in 1955. Subsequently, he got a rare first-year teaching assistantship in the political science department at UCLA, where he earned his master's in 1957, and his doctorate in 1960. During 1959–60, he worked on President Clark Kerr's staff as an administrative analyst, helping with California's Master Plan for Higher Education.

In August 1960, Young received a call from Chancellor Franklin D. Murphy, who—with Kerr's recommendation—hired him as his assistant. After serving in a series of executive positions, Young was chosen in July 1968 to succeed his mentor as chancellor. At 36, he was the youngest person at the helm of any major American university.

Young skillfully guided UCLA through times of great political unrest. Throughout his tenure, he was an ardent spokesman on behalf of educational opportunity, inclusiveness and the value of ethnic and cultural diversity to the university experience.

By 1997, Young had become the longest-serving chief executive among his fellow chancellors and presidents nationwide. He oversaw UCLA's transformation from a university with an operating budget of $170 million into a $2 billion enterprise. But after increasing tension between him and several regents and Governor Pete Wilson in the wake of Proposition 209, which banned the use of affirmative action in admissions, Young retired on June 30, 1997. "I've had the good fortune to work for … and be engaged in a love affair with UCLA," Young said.

In 1999, Young accepted a position as interim president of the University of Florida, where he stayed through 2003. In 2001, Sue died after a long battle with cancer, and Young married Judy Cornell a year later. From 2004–06, Young served as president of the Qatar Foundation in the Persian Gulf, and from 2008–10, he was chief executive officer of the Los Angeles Museum of Contemporary Art. He holds an appointment at UCLA's Luskin School of Public Affairs as a professor emeritus of political science, public policy and management.

In 1998, Circle Drive was renamed Charles E. Young Drive, and the research library was also dedicated in his honor.

"A different chancellor would have been satisfied to sit on UCLA's laurels and maintain the status quo," wrote alumnus and city councilman Zev Yaroslavsky in a 1994 tribute. "This leader of our university has tread where few sane men would dare tread, and the UCLA family is the better for it."

Right: An avid Bruins football fan, Young takes in a game from the sidelines, 1996.

Below: Young led UCLA for an unprecedented 29 years.

On April 14, 1969, the UCLA Band marches on stage for more than 20 million viewers in 37 countries at the 41st Academy Awards. Performing best song nominee "Chitty Chitty Bang Bang" with actress and dancer Paula Kelly, it marked the first time a college band appeared at the Oscars.

During Murphy's tenure, Young had attended most of the regents meetings, either with Murphy or in his stead. As vice chancellor for administration since 1963, Young developed a strong reputation for being the campus problem-solver and acted as the primary university mediator with student groups.

"Chancellor Murphy's recommendation would have substantial weight—but he in no way chooses his own successor," noted Theodore R. Meyer, chairman of the Board of Regents.

Some regents and faculty members questioned whether Young, who held an appointment as associate professor of political science and taught at least one course at UCLA annually, had enough experience in academic affairs and criticized him for lack of scholarship. Young, however, had established himself as an effective and energetic administrator who was popular with both professors and students.

The regents wanted to continue UCLA's academic momentum and fill what they considered a gigantic void left by Murphy, whose "dynamic leadership" they praised with a unanimously adopted resolution that expressed regret over his departure. Murphy-like "real star" quality was their litmus test.

Murphy's strong backing and grooming of Young counted a great deal, particularly to Regents Edward W. Carter and William E. Forbes. No one, Forbes said, was more aware of the significance of fostering UCLA's long-range academic development than Murphy, and Murphy would not recommend Young if he did not believe he could deliver.

Several candidates' names were floated in the press, including Riverside campus Chancellor Ivan Hinderaker and Santa Cruz campus Chancellor Dean E. McHenry—both former chairs of UCLA's political science department—and John W. Gardner, secretary of health, education and welfare under President Lyndon B. Johnson. Young, however, was most often mentioned as the frontrunner.

After the regents selected a new chancellor (William J. McGill) for the San Diego campus but did not announce a UCLA leader, the *Daily Bruin* ran an editorial criticizing the regents for delaying their decision and promoting Young as "the most obvious choice for the job."

"Young has been here eight years and knows from first-hand experience the problems that this campus presents and understands the structure as it exists," declared the June 25, 1968 editorial. "To bring in someone unacquainted with UCLA's intricate structure and problems at this time would be undesirable, both politically and academically."

After considering more than 100 names reflecting input from both students and the faculty, the regents on July 12 approved Young as UCLA's seventh chief executive.

At 36 and only eight years out of graduate school, he was the youngest executive ever appointed to lead a University of California campus, and reportedly the youngest chief executive at the helm of a major American university. A more significant milestone: Young, who received his master's and doctorate in political science from UCLA in 1957 and 1960, respectively, became the first UCLA graduate to hold the top job at the 28,000-student campus.

While the choice of a young alumnus promised an exciting new era for the campus, Young's appointment retained the reassuring vestige of Murphy's influence—something not easily relinquished.

"Dr. Murphy has had a major role in making the UCLA campus one of the most distinguished in the nation," President Hitch said in announcing Young's selection. "The University will miss him greatly, but it is fortunate that he will be succeeded by a very able young man who has worked with Dr. Murphy for the past eight years. Dr. Young's scholarly and civic activities will help keep UCLA at the forefront."

"Lo" … and Behold

At 10:30 p.m. on October 29, 1969, computer science Professor Leonard Kleinrock and his student assistant Charles S. Kline were working in their Boelter Hall laboratory. It had been a typical day, except for one thing—they were about to launch something that would revolutionize society.

Programmers at UCLA—officially the first node on the ARPANET, the precursor to the Internet—were attempting to log on to the Stanford Research Institute (SRI) host. The UCLA team was trying to send the word "login" over the system to SRI. All they had to do was type "log" and the computer would be smart enough to add the "in."

So Kline sent the "l," and SRI confirmed it was received. Then he sent the "o." Success again. Then, before the "g" arrived, the connection—50 kilobytes per second—crashed. But the pair had sent the first "host-to-host" message over ARPANET (Advanced Research Projects Agency Network), and as Kleinrock later described, the Internet uttered its first word: "lo."

That first message sent over the Internet was deceptively simple, yet as prophetic as "What hath God wrought?" Kleinrock said, referencing the phrase from the Old Testament's Book of Numbers sent by Samuel F.B. Morse to officially open the Baltimore-Washington, D.C. telegraph line in 1844. "Lo," as in "lo and behold," Kleinrock said, "was the shortest, most impressive message we could've sent, in that sense."

When the second attempt at logging in worked, "that was it," Kleinrock recalled. "Now we had two *bona fide* outside machines talking to each other that were connected with this magic network."

A third machine, at the University of California, Santa Barbara, was connected in November. A month later, another was added at the University of Utah. Under Kleinrock's supervision, UCLA was in charge of conducting a series of extensive tests to debug the network, serving for many years as the ARPANET Measurement Center. Kleinrock developed the mathematical theory of packet switching, the technology underpinning the Internet, between 1960–62 while enrolled as a graduate student at the Massachusetts Institute of Technology. The ARPANET was funded by the U.S. Department of Defense Advanced Research Projects Agency, which was created in February 1958—four months after the Soviets launched Sputnik—to aid the United States in regaining a scientific edge.

Although the team could not foresee the vast social and business implications its work would eventually have, members realized that something extraordinary was happening at UCLA. "As of now, computer networks are still in their infancy," Kleinrock said in July 1969. "But as they grow up and become more sophisticated, we will probably see the spread of 'computer utilities' which, like present electric and telephone utilities, will service individual homes and offices across the country."

But Kleinrock admits he did not envision just how comprehensively the Internet would change the way people lived and worked. "I indicated that the Internet would be ubiquitous, always accessible, always on, anyone would be able to connect any device to it from anywhere at any time, and it would be invisible," Kleinrock said. "But, I never anticipated that my 98-year-old mother would be on the Internet today … That is, I did not foresee, at that time, the way in which it would reach out to everyone everywhere and impact every aspect of our 21st century."

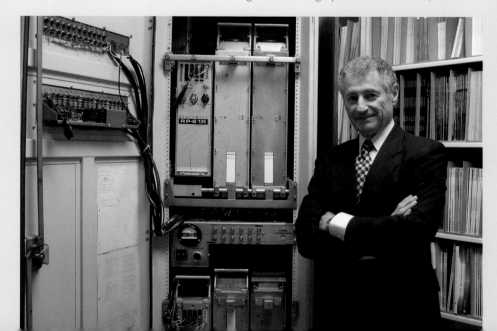

Professor Leonard Kleinrock with the Interface Message Processor in Boelter Hall, the first node on the ARPANET, the precursor to the Internet.

BLACK MOBILE

As president of the Black Student Union, Arthur Williams (right) created the Black Mobile, filled with history books and various artifacts, to go into the community and inform people about black history and culture, 1967.

EARLY VISION

Before becoming Murphy's assistant in fall 1960, Young had worked for University of California President Clark Kerr, assisting the academic team that drew up the Master Plan for Higher Education in California. He also worked on the university's growth plan and taught political science at the Davis campus in the spring of 1960.

Young, who took office on September 1, 1968, did not position himself as a scholar. Instead, he publicly acknowledged that he had chosen "a different route," while holding "the greatest respect for scholarship and an understanding of it."

His inaugural pledge was to advance UCLA "from the second level of good universities to the first rank of excellent universities." To assist him in this mission, he chose as his second in command David S. Saxon, dean of the Division of Physical Sciences, who two decades earlier had refused to sign the loyalty oath in the name of academic freedom. Saxon would eventually carry the newly introduced title of executive vice chancellor. Added consideration and support would be given to the professional schools, "to see to it that we are achieving as well in those areas as we are in the liberal arts," Young said.

Signaling a greater emphasis on external communications and community outreach, Young moved Paul O. Proehl, law professor and director of the African Studies Center, into the new position of vice chancellor for university relations and public programming. Young kept Murphy's top administrators. James W. Hobson, who had been vice chancellor for business and finance, assumed Young's old job of vice chancellor for administration; and Rosemary Park, who had been Murphy's vice chancellor of educational planning, became vice chancellor for student and curriculum affairs.

Immediately after his appointment, Young emphasized his commitment to minority student affairs and civic concerns. "Urban problems are the most serious ones we face," Young said, "and the university is the institution that can do most in this area." He added: "We need more student involvement in a substantive, meaningful way." UCLA's personnel newsletter called Young "one of a new breed" who understands that "university administration is a tough and demanding job in these days of social unrest."

Young's effectiveness in negotiating with students during times of turmoil was a key reason he was chosen. Unlike the conservative and impatient Murphy, who, if left to his choosing, would have called in the police more often than not, Young was able to relate to students, and he could just as easily reach a successful compromise as "wait them out" until things settled down. Young described himself as a "middle of the road liberal" who "can get along with people"—even those who did not share his views.

On the other hand, sometimes, an irascible Young would irritate students by simply walking away—although it was not unusual for him to follow through with the same individuals once dispositions cooled.

"Despite his rapport with students, Young is far from being a pliant tool of protesters," *Time* wrote in September 1968. "During one heated, profanity-filled meeting with some student rebels, he suddenly snapped: 'I don't have to listen to that kind of language' and walked out. Quick in temper, Young is also quick to clamp down on undergraduate activities that go too far."

Notwithstanding multiple protests throughout 1966 and 1967, Young permitted the Dow Chemical Company—the primary supplier of napalm to the U.S. military during the Vietnam War—to recruit on campus through the Student and Alumni Placement Center. "The University has an obligation," Young, who served in Japan during the Korean War, told the *Daily Bruin*, "to allow students who are interested in taking a job with the Dow Co. to get an interview." Young added that it would be "illogical" to "draw a line which only excluded the Dow Chemical Co."—a lightning rod for the anti-war movement.

Young also held firm in his support of civil rights and anti-discrimination policy on campus. After the Phi Kappa Psi fraternity blocked blacks and Hispanics from attending a party, the administration suspended the chapter for one year.

INAUGURAL CONCERNS

Young's inauguration was planned as a symbolic turning point in campus history. While Kerr's investiture had been highlighted over 16 days of ceremonies on seven campuses including UCLA, Murphy's celebration remained caught in the shadows of the president's office. It was a hastily planned event, which Kerr was unable to attend, accompanied by a poorly executed buffet luncheon at the Hotel Bel-Air. In contrast, Young's ceremony was to be a highly visible and momentous event installing UCLA's first alumnus chief executive 50 years to the day since Governor William D. Stephens signed the enabling legislation that created UCLA.

The inauguration was scheduled as the highlight of a weeklong celebration that included lectures, concerts and theater productions; the dedication of the social sciences

Right: Three former UCLA chancellors, (from left) Raymond B. Allen, Vern O. Knudsen and Franklin D. Murphy, with newly inaugurated Charles E. Young, May 23, 1969.

Below: Young held firm to open recruiting on campus, stating it would be "illogical" to exclude companies such as the Dow Chemical Company because of student anti-war protest.

Below right: Nobel laureate and former Bruin guard Ralph J. Bunche (center) and his wife, Ruth, bump into basketball player Lew Alcindor (Kareem Abdul-Jabbar) outside the Bunche Hall dedication ceremony, May 23, 1969.

building as Ralph Bunche Hall, honoring the distinguished alumnus and Nobel laureate; and a dinner gala hosted by the UCLA Alumni Association in commemoration of UCLA's golden anniversary at the Century Plaza Hotel. (The 50th anniversary jubilee continued throughout the year, culminating with a final event at the Dorothy Chandler Pavilion in November attended by 3,500 alumni and friends. It featured crooner Andy Williams as master of ceremonies with entertainment by alumna Carol Burnett, Bob Newhart and Frank Sinatra, who was awarded honorary alumnus status.)

An unforeseen and tragic event in Berkeley, however, would dampen the festivities. A week before the inauguration, on May 15, 1969, a major altercation occurred between students and police and National Guardsmen over occupation of People's Park—a free speech area three blocks off campus that had been adopted by Berkeley students and community members a month prior. The clash resulted in the shooting of a non-Berkeley student, who would die from his wounds several days later. Governor Ronald Reagan, who opposed the creation of People's Park and had been openly critical of the university administration for allowing student demonstrations, had overruled Chancellor Roger W. Heyns and sent in the forces.

The following day, UCLA students interrupted a Board of Regents meeting with Reagan in attendance at the UCLA Faculty Center. The students later told the *Los Angeles Times* they were planning to demand removal of ROTC from all university campuses and the banning of off-campus police in suppressing student demonstrations.

Young asked the students to settle down and suggested they might be heard at the end of the meeting, but their interruptions and intermittent shouts of profanities continued. Young then ordered everyone but regents, university officers and members of the press to clear the room. Outside, students began climbing on cars and the Faculty Center roof, breaking windows and overturning patio furniture. Campus and city police were called to disperse the approximately 550 students so that the regents could leave after the meeting ended. Two arrests were made.

The protest was followed by a sit-in at Murphy Hall (the administration building, renamed in honor of the former chancellor in October 1968, one month after his departure), where students talked openly of disrupting the inauguration

Above: A *Daily Bruin* editorial cartoon by Tony Auth illustrates the sentiment of People's Park protesters.

Left: As police approach, Bruins demonstrate in solidarity with Berkeley students after the People's Park incident, May 1969.

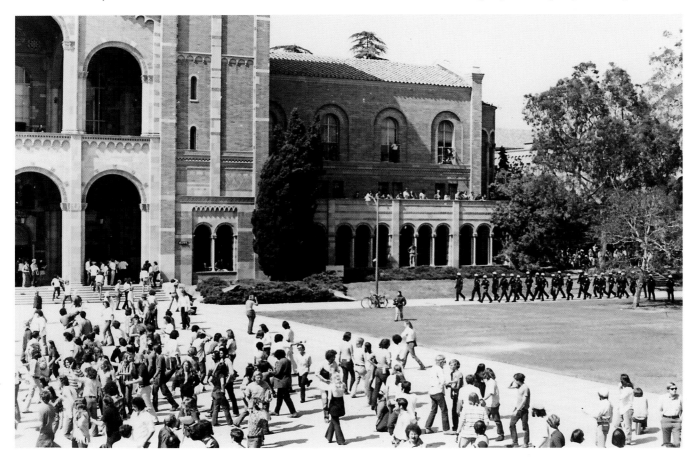

Top right: President Charles J. Hitch (left) and Rabbi Edgar F. Magnin (right) wait in the wings with Charles E. Young (center) prior to his investiture.

Top: A few demonstrators outside of Pauley Pavilion during Young's inauguration show support for the new chancellor.

Above: Young's inauguration, scaled down in acknowledgment of the political unrest at Berkeley, was held May 23, 1969, the 50th anniversary of UCLA's founding.

ceremony. University officials and attorneys for the Board of Regents began preparing legal documents seeking a temporary restraining order against the students and an injunction barring trespassing in campus buildings.

In a nod to the ongoing turmoil at Berkeley over People's Park, and concerned about safety, Young decided to scale down his inauguration ceremony. "This is a time of great travail for the University of California," Young wrote in a May 22, 1969 statement read by Saxon to more than 2,000 faculty members and students who packed Royce Hall and a crowd of 1,000 who spilled out onto the quad to hear the details over loudspeakers. "After consultation with President Hitch, I have decided to make my inauguration an act of solemn dedication to the deep issues which confront us."

All music, including the national anthem, was eliminated, as was the keynote address by U.S. Secretary of Health, Education and Welfare Robert H. Finch, a former university regent. Only four people would be seated on the platform: Young, Hitch, University Marshal Waldo

W. Phelps—the campus ceremonial officer—and Rabbi Edgar F. Magnin, who would lead the invocation. The customary honorary degrees would instead be awarded at a post-ceremony luncheon in Ackerman Grand Ballroom to Finch; former regent Dorothy Chandler; California Institute of Technology President Harold Brown; pianist Arthur Rubinstein; and Daniel P. Moynihan, counselor for urban affairs to President Nixon.

A measured student reaction followed the announcement, and sit-in protesters later voluntarily exited Murphy Hall and "liberated" Kerckhoff Hall, where students had occupied the second and third floors. Student leaders promised that any demonstration would be peaceful and acknowledged that Young was not the target of protest.

Young dropped the legal action and decided not to call in off-campus police, although about 130 police officers and two Los Angeles Police Department communications vans were stationed at the heliport near the Recreation Center off Sunset Boulevard. Hobson told the campus newspaper that the police "came of their own accord and were not requested by the Administration."

On the day of the inauguration, a rare front-page *Daily Bruin* editorial praised Young for his actions. "Chancellor Charles E. Young has taken a big step: yesterday afternoon he responded to campus pressure, eschewed outside pressure and changed the format of his inauguration." The paper continued, "Young put his job on the line Wednesday night by not calling police onto the campus—despite outside pressure to do so."

Student body President Tom Normington issued a statement endorsing a two-day student class strike and asked students not to obscure the issue of solidarity with Berkeley by introducing other causes with less support. "Further our strike must be completely voluntary; forcibly preventing attendance would deform the dignity of our protest."

Only Hitch and Young made speeches during the ceremony held in Pauley Pavilion. Hitch addressed the People's

Park situation and Young called for the UCLA campus to come together for the benefit of the university and society.

"We must find ways of working together as members of a community—academic, social, and political," Young said. "We must be able to accept good ideas for what they are rather than from whom they come. We must make our major concern substance rather than procedure. ... We must be committed to our institutions and communities rather than to our own status. Let each of us make this day—the 50th anniversary of UCLA and the day of my official inauguration—a day of dedication and commitment to this institution."

With the exception of some booing during Hitch's remarks, the ceremony went unmarred. *ABC News* reported: "At the University of California at Los Angeles, a new chancellor, Charles E. Young, was installed today and though there were advance warnings of demonstrations and possible violence, nothing happened—and that, in these times, is news."

"When strikers took over the main administration building, instead of calling police, officials bid them welcome.

The sit-in fizzled," the nationally televised news broadcast continued. "Why the relative stability at UCLA? A few reasons stand out. It's a middle-class commuter college, unlike the live-in Berkeley campus. But unlike other streetcar colleges, such as NYU, Columbia, or San Francisco State, UCLA is not a bastion of the radical. It attracts moderates like Notre Dame attracts football players. And across town, the city's other major school, Southern Cal, has also been quiet. So, the city which spawned the warfare of Watts, ironically is keeping it cool on the campus."

A vehicle implemented by the administration in fall 1968 was in part credited for the comparative calm of UCLA's campus: the University Policies Commission, which included students, faculty members and administrators, and advised on major policy decisions before they were instituted. The commission's first recommendation was to create the position of a campus ombudsman—or grievance officer—to act as an "impartial and independent official" and investigate complaints or suggestions from students, professors and staff members. Additionally, an expanded student role was established in association with various Academic Senate committees.

"We are in the middle of a revolution," Young stated shortly after his appointment. "The question is whether it can be peaceful rather than violent, constructive rather than destructive, and cumulative rather than displacing what went before."

A POLITICAL TEST

No sooner had Young been formally invested as chancellor than a crisis tried his commitment to the principles of academic freedom and pitted the new leader against regents and governor in a stand-off watched closely across the country. It was "California's most bitter fight over academic freedom since the loyalty oath tests in the late 1940s," according to *Newsweek*.

In May 1968, almost three years after the Watts Riots left 34 dead, more than 1,000 injured and almost 4,000 arrested, President Hitch rolled out a plan to broadly attack racial and social inequities in metropolitan areas. The Urban Crisis Program called for the university to increase minority employment and student enrollment, while simultaneously placing a greater emphasis on ameliorating urban problems through research and public service.

In November, Young unveiled a four-part plan for increasing minority faculty hiring. There would be an intensive effort to locate qualified professors of color, as well as individuals who had completed their degree work but whose research had not yet reached the necessary threshold for faculty appointment; UCLA departments would be encouraged to hire minority graduates of their own doctoral programs;

Left: Donald Hartsock, UCLA's first ombudsman, 1969–1991.

Below: Bruins picket arm in arm against the National Guard's actions at the Berkeley campus, May 27, 1969.

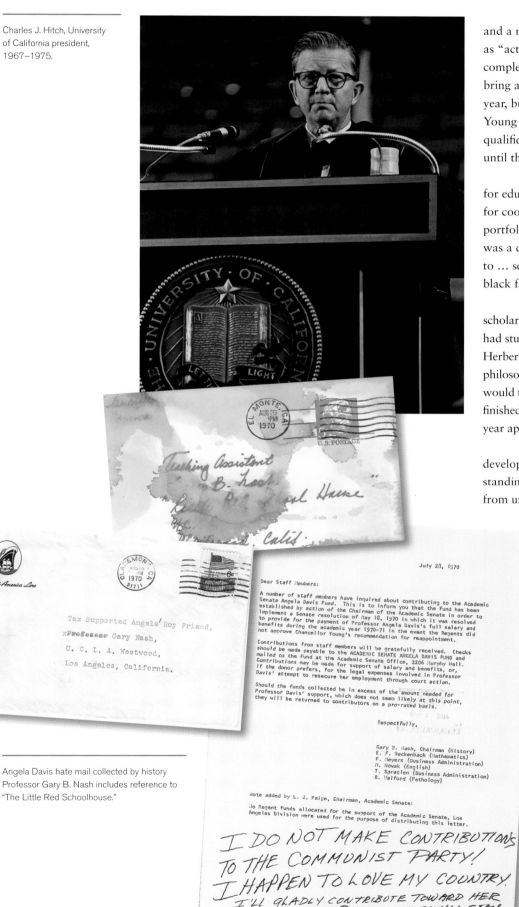

Charles J. Hitch, University of California president, 1967–1975.

Angela Davis hate mail collected by history Professor Gary B. Nash includes reference to "The Little Red Schoolhouse."

Tax Supported Angela' Boy Friend,
~~Professor~~ Gary Nash,
U. C. L. A. Westwood,
Los Angeles, California.

July 28, 1970

Dear Staff Members:

A number of staff members have inquired about contributing to the Academic Senate Angela Davis Fund. This is to inform you that the Fund has been established by action of the Chairman of the Academic Senate in order to implement a Senate resolution of May 18, 1970 in which it was resolved to provide for the payment of Professor Angela Davis's full salary and benefits during the academic year 1970-71 in the event the Regents did not approve Chancellor Young's recommendation for reappointment.

Contributions from staff members will be gratefully received. Checks should be made payable to the ACADEMIC SENATE ANGELA DAVIS FUND and mailed to the Fund at the Academic Senate Office, 2206 Murphy Hall. Contributions may be made for support of salary and benefits, or, if the donor prefers, for the legal expenses involved in Professor Davis' attempt to resecure her employment through court action.

Should the funds collected be in excess of the amount needed for Professor Davis' support, which does not seem likely at this point, they will be returned to contributors on a pro-rated basis.

Respectfully,

Gary B. Nash, Chairman (History)
E. F. Beckenbach (Mathematics)
F. Meyers (Business Administration)
H. Novak (English)
T. Spratlen (Business Administration)
R. Walford (Pathology)

Note added by L. J. Paige, Chairman, Academic Senate:

No Regent funds allocated for the support of the Academic Senate, Los Angeles Division were used for the purpose of distributing this letter.

I DO NOT MAKE CONTRIBUTIONS TO THE COMMUNIST PARTY! I HAPPEN TO LOVE MY COUNTRY. I'LL GLADLY CONTRIBUTE TOWARD HER FARE TO RUSSIA - IF SHE'LL STAY THERE!

and a new program would enable qualified candidates to serve as "acting instructors" or "acting assistant professors" while completing their doctoral degree. The plan was expected to bring approximately 50 minority professors to campus each year, but would not "dilute the quality of UCLA's faculty," Young told the *Los Angeles Times*. "Those who are not qualified faculty members will augment the qualified faculty until their skills are sufficient to enter its ranks."

C.Z. Wilson was hired as assistant vice chancellor for educational planning and programs with responsibility for coordinating UCLA's Urban Crisis agenda. As part of his portfolio, he oversaw the Faculty Development Program. "It was a discretionary program driven by the Chancellor's Office to … serve institutional needs," Wilson said. "We need more black faculty—that's an institutional need."

One of the program's recruits was a 25-year-old black scholar from the University of California, San Diego, who had studied under controversial Frankfurt School philosopher Herbert Marcuse. Angela Y. Davis was hired by UCLA's philosophy department as an acting assistant professor. She would teach an introductory course in philosophy while she finished her dissertation. In April 1969, Davis was offered a one-year appointment with the possibility of a second-year renewal.

On April 18, the Board of Regents, faced with legal developments affecting the constitutionality of their long-standing policy prohibiting members of the Communist Party from university employment, voted that their 1940 and 1949 resolutions adopted during the loyalty oath controversy were not valid and that "no political test shall ever be considered in the appointment and promotion of any faculty member or employee."

In July, on Davis' first day at UCLA, the *Daily Bruin* ran a commentary by recent graduate—and reputed FBI informant—William Tulio Divale, which stated that the philosophy department had made a two-year appointment to a member of the Communist Party. A week later, the *San Francisco Examiner* named Davis as the appointee.

Davis confirmed her Communist Party membership, but citing constitutional freedom and academic policy, told administrators that it wasn't their business and requested that she be paid her stipend, which had been delayed and was causing her hardship. The faculty took up a collection to pay Davis.

On September 19, the regents met for more than three hours in executive session, and the next day the *Los Angeles Times* reported that confidential sources said Davis had been dismissed. Although "most lawyers on the Board of Regents agree that this policy is not likely to stand up legally," the *Times* continued, "the regents apparently have chosen to fire Miss Davis and force her to test the policy in court." However, according to regents policy, before she could be officially dismissed, a hearing was required.

Davis responded four days later with a public statement. "The regents seem intent on meting out punishments which concur with the fascist tendencies of the times," Davis said. "The sole reason they give for their intention to fire me is my membership in the Communist Party. They have not questioned my qualifications, my academic training, or my ability to teach."

Said David B. Kaplan, associate professor and vice chairman of the philosophy department: "The attempt to dismiss her on the sole basis of her political affiliations is a direct violation of her academic freedom and that of her colleagues and potential students."

On October 3, at a special meeting of the regents, the board adopted a resolution that Davis would "be assigned no teaching duties," although she would continue to be paid through her appeals. Young interpreted the regents' action as barring Davis from teaching "regular courses," but not preventing her from teaching a non-credit course.

One year earlier, another issue concerning course credit and academic freedom had arisen. Eldridge Cleaver, a leader of the Black Panther Party—a militant activist group central in the black power movement—was scheduled to give 10 lectures on racism as part of an experimental course at Berkeley. Reagan objected. After vigorous discussion, on September 20, 1968, the Board of Regents voted 10–8 to limit Cleaver—or any guest speaker—to one appearance per quarter per credit course. The "Cleaver Rule," as it became known, had been introduced by Hitch as a compromise. Some faculty groups were not pleased by the ruling as they believed it weakened their authority over curriculum and hiring. In November, the regents barred credit for the course, while amending their previous ruling to allow each chancellor to make "exceptions." Reagan made a motion to forbid all guest speakers unless approved by Hitch, who promptly said he would transfer that authority to the campus chancellors. The motion failed 10–8. After the meeting, Hitch told news reporters that the controversy "had damaged the university."

While Davis was not a guest speaker, the "Cleaver Rule" actions lingered vividly. On October 6, 1969, the first day of fall classes at UCLA, some students wore Cleaver buttons sent from Berkeley that stated "on campus, for credit, as planned." Because of increased interest and security concerns, Davis' philosophy course, "Recurring Philosophical Themes in Black Literature," had been moved from the Dickson Art Center to Royce Hall. A request for television cameras to broadcast the lecture was denied, but the controversy still made the national evening news.

"It was a very important symbolic moment—for UCLA, but also for academia and the country in general to have somebody like that," said Scott L. Waugh, who attended Davis' first lecture when he was a student and would go on to be appointed UCLA's executive vice chancellor and provost in 2008. "It was a statement about what universities were about. … Open engagement. Free access to information. Ideas. And not closing things off for whatever reason there was. We all championed those kinds of things."

Far left: "Before I proceeded to lecture today, I asked the students whether or not they wanted me to teach," said Angela Davis after holding her first class. "They indicated that they did, and therefore, I lectured." Philosophy Chairman Donald Kalish, who hired Davis, stands behind her during the press conference, October 7, 1969.

Left: Black militant Eldridge Cleaver speaks in Pauley Pavilion, October 4, 1968, at one of the most well-attended events of the Associated Students Speakers Program.

Protesters march against Communism outside Royce Hall, while Angela Davis lectures to a filled auditorium, October 7, 1969.

The Academic Senate held an emergency meeting on October 9 and passed a resolution pushed by the Student Legislative Council that asked all UCLA professors to withhold grades for their students until Davis "is assured of her right to teach for credit." A suit against the regents was filed on Davis' behalf by a group of UCLA professors, and Superior Court Judge (and UCLA alumnus) Jerry Pacht ruled on October 20 that the regents had acted unconstitutionally. Pacht said it would be "unlawful and dangerous" for the regents to enforce a political "litmus paper test" as such power would make them "a kind of political elite entitled to decide whose views are acceptable." Course credit was restored, but the regents—led in their opposition by Reagan—appealed.

The contentious issue went on for more than six months, with Young holding steadfast to his position, realizing

his job could be in jeopardy. Sitting on the floor during one of Young's interviews with the *Los Angeles Times*, his nine-year-old daughter Lisa shared her view: "My daddy might get fired. If he does, I hope he runs for President."

In May 1970, Young told the regents that he intended to approve Davis' reappointment. The regents responded by stripping Young and Hitch of their authority to act in the matter, and the following month they fired Davis. The issue was headed to the courts, but became moot before it was ever resolved.

In August 1970, Davis was wanted in connection with an abduction and killing of Superior Court Judge Harold J. Haley. Davis was charged with conspiracy, kidnapping and homicide. After fleeing, she appeared on the FBI's Ten Most Wanted Fugitives list. Two months later, she was captured in New York. In 1972, she was found not guilty. (In 1991, Davis joined the faculty at the University of California, Santa Cruz, where she taught for 17 years before retiring.)

Decades later, Young described the Angela Davis issue as "a seminal moment" that would define his administration. "It allowed me to stake out my position with regard to academic freedom, several of the Bill of Rights issues—especially free speech—and the necessity to handle those issues within the context of responsibility," Young said. "It tested me, in terms of my ability to do this with reasonableness, and brought me into strong and direct contact—some confrontational, some supportive—with the Board of Regents, the other chancellors,

Charles E. Young takes a stand on academic freedom in the Angela Davis matter at a regents meeting.

the president of the university, the governor; and it brought me into a prominent position nationally in higher education."

He added: "It led to very strong, thoughtful interaction between the faculty at UCLA and me, which laid the groundwork for the next 28 years."

ADDRESSING STUDENT DIVERSITY

Beyond hiring more minority professors, Young sought to diversify the student population. "I was finally convinced by students, by faculty and other administrators, that affirmative action was never really going to work unless the chancellor came out very solidly for it, pushed for it and led the way," Young explained. "And I decided that was what I was going to do."

During one heated demonstration in 1968, students demanded that UCLA enroll more African-American and Hispanic students. While ethnic group student leaders were meeting with Young, others had occupied the area outside the Chancellor's Office and began chanting, "We want more!" Young turned to the students in his office: "How many more do you want?" The student leaders went outside to discuss the question with their constituents. The answer came back: "We want 50 each." Young's response: "You got it."

Out of this developed the High Potential Program, designed to admit students who did not meet the normal criteria, but had the potential to do so with remedial courses, counseling and other assistance. The program was under the umbrella of UCLA's Special Educational Programs, which also included the Educational Opportunities Program, a project that sought to increase the numbers of low-income, minority students on campus through the standard admissions process. The High Potential Program was started so quickly that for the first quarter, students went into the local community and did the recruiting themselves.

"The goal was to identify students who had high potential, but who may not have all of the requisite grades and test scores to have gotten into UCLA and to essentially give them an opportunity to get prepared for UCLA and be successful," said Winston C. Doby, a program evaluator for High Potential in 1969 who would later become vice chancellor for student affairs. While the program was unique within the University of California, High Potential students were admitted under the four percent "special procedures" exceptions—with two percent specifically reserved for disadvantaged students—identified under the Master Plan.

In September 1968, 52 African-American and 50 Mexican-American students enrolled in the program. The following year, Asian-American and Native American components were added. Each group had control over entrance requirements, and student and instructor selection. High Potential students took courses in subjects such as

Above: *The Black Experience*, a mural painted by seven art students (depicted in the image) in the aftermath of the Kent State shootings, is also a collage of photographs (inset) infusing important figures and events in African-American history. The artwork was covered in 1992, but remains preserved behind the walls of the restaurant Panda Express in Ackerman Union.

Left: The tumultuous 1960s gave rise to student media newsmagazines, which have since provided a voice to an increasingly diverse student population.

mathematics, English, chemistry and history that served as a bridge to UCLA admission. After the first quarter, almost 80 percent of the students enrolled in UCLA classes, and many moved into the Educational Opportunities Program to take advantage of financial aid and other services. Within its first three years, 17 students earned their bachelor's degree, three of whom went on to pursue graduate education. However, many more withdrew—either in good standing or in academic difficulty—and more than 20 percent were dismissed.

The program encountered other problems beyond attrition. Virgil Roberts, a leader in the Black Student Union who helped push for what became the High Potential Program, said that the students believed "the university process of selecting students was unfair in that it excluded a lot of minority kids who had high potential." But, he said, the program changed after it was created. "It became a much more political program than it was designed to be," Roberts said. "It became sort of 'Let's get in some Black Panthers, let's get in some political groups. ... So the program lost a lot of its legitimacy, I think even with students."

When Doby became acting director of Special Educational Programs in 1970, he found that sustaining two separate, parallel programs—one doing its own admissions—was expensive and inefficient. This led to a reorganization as recommended by a campuswide task force. "Responsibility for things like admissions

Right: The American Indian Studies Center, the Asian American Studies Center, the Chicano Studies Research Center and the Ralph J. Bunche Center for African American Studies, all created in the late 1960s, have earned worldwide recognition for their scholarly work and documentation of the ethnic experience in America.

Right: Police investigate the scene in Campbell Hall, where two High Potential students were killed in a shootout, January 17, 1969.

Below right: H. Rap Brown (left), chairman of the national Student Nonviolent Coordinating Committee, and Us organization founder and alumnus Maulana Karenga (right), in South Central Los Angeles, August 14, 1967.

went to the admissions office, financial aid went to the financial aid office, and so on," Doby said. "In essence, we mainstreamed the nonacademic support services into where they should normally reside. That was quite controversial."

The Educational Opportunities and High Potential programs were eliminated, replaced by the new Academic Advancement Program, which served minority and disadvantaged students at all levels of achievement. The program provided student academic support like peer tutoring and counseling to help students excel academically, while not concerning itself with the students' financial needs. Doby became its founding director.

"The issue is not whether UCLA is turning its back on minority youths, for the successor program holds out the promise of actually increasing the number on campus," stated a 1971 article in the *Los Angeles Times*. "It is instead an issue of what kind of students should be served by such a program and how it should operate—as separate ethnic units pretty much on their own, or as one unit under a centralized administration?"

The Academic Advancement Program evolved into the nation's largest university-based student diversity program, serving more than 6,500 students annually from underrepresented populations, low-income families and those who are first-generation college students.

Some time afterward, Doby asked Young: "Why did you give in to these students who were in your face demanding that you give them 50 each?" Young responded, "Winston, it is extremely important to do what is right even when others are demanding it."

In subsequent years, Young continued to champion affirmative action programs, and by the 1990s, UCLA would have one of the most diverse student populations in the nation. "I made a particular case for diversity and education because universities are the gateway to the world," Young said. "Improvements in our society must start with expanded access to high quality college education. Society is better off when historically excluded groups can attend our institution."

CAMPBELL HALL SHOOTINGS

On January 17, 1969, in a first-floor room of Campbell Hall, two black High Potential students—John Huggins, 23, and Alprentice "Bunchy" Carter, 26—were killed in a shooting that shocked the campus.

Huggins was described as an "area captain" of the Black Panthers—which created armed citizen patrols to guard against police brutality—while Carter was referred to as its "deputy minister of defense." The Black Panther Party was one of two external organizations competing to be the primary influence on the Community Advisory Council for the Black Student Union organization and the newly created Afro-American Studies Center. The Us organization, a cultural black nationalist group founded after the Watts Riots by UCLA alumnus Ronald M. Everett—who had changed his name to Maulana Karenga—was the second.

Huggins and Carter were shot and killed in an exchange of gunfire that reportedly left at least seven bullet holes in the walls. The slayings occurred after a meeting attended by about 150 individuals, predominantly members from both organizations, to discuss the director position for the Afro-

Vietnam War Protests

With an escalation of the Vietnam War, and the shooting deaths of four students at Kent State University by National Guardsmen, anti-war sentiment on campus hit its pinnacle in the early 1970s.

Right: Students mock "non-violent resistance" in wake of the Kent State tragedy, c.1970.

Left: On May 11, 1972, the second day of a multiday student strike, tensions erupt in a confrontation between protesters and police near Murphy Hall. Police carry away one demonstrator (below), as dozens of arrests are made.

Above: Protesters form a human chain and march down Wilshire Boulevard, May 10, 1972.

Below: As the campus reacts to the Kent State shootings, news crews and police survey the mêlée from the roof of Royce Hall (left), as police begin their sweeps of the quad (center) and demonstrators are arrested near Murphy Hall (right), May 5, 1970.

quick defense from supporters of the High Potential program, feelings of uneasiness and sorrow from white students and guarded silence from black leaders," wrote the *Daily Bruin* on January 21. But no further incidents followed, and campus officials credited African-American student leaders for how they handled the situation.

In February 1969, five individuals were indicted by a Los Angeles County grand jury on charges of conspiracy and murder. While some stated that the shootings had been a spontaneous reaction to an unrelated quarrel, the district attorney's office asserted that the shooting had been the result of a deliberate assassination conspiracy by members of the Us organization directed against Huggins and Carter as a result of continuing disagreements between Us and the Black Panthers. Still others believed that the event was incited by the FBI in an effort to destabilize both groups.

Campbell Hall, named for Shakespearean scholar Lily Bess Campbell and already home to the High Potential Program, became the quarters for the new UCLA American Cultures Project, announced a week after the shootings. The Cultures Project served as an umbrella over four autonomous ethnic studies programs: African-American, Chicano, Asian-American and Native American. Campus officials emphasized that the project had been under development for some time and was not in response to the killings.

Several months later, Young wrote a piece for *UCLA Alumni Magazine* that explained the philosophy behind the myriad diversity efforts.

"We have not developed our programs at UCLA out of response to pressure or violence or the threat of violence, but by working together because we thought they had to be

American Studies Center. The center had been developed through a joint effort between the administration and representatives of the UCLA Black Student Union. The Black Panthers and Us had been involved in a factional dispute over potential candidates for the director position and control of the organization.

In advance of its first meeting after the shootings, the Black Student Union issued an open letter to the black student body. "It appears that the historical irony of crises moulding together factions to create harmonious forces among men is once again the case," read the statement printed in the *Daily Bruin* on January 31, 1969. "In the face of the most tragic events ever to befall this campus or any other, we issue an appeal to every black student at UCLA, not only to mourn the awesome loss, but to bend his energies now toward building our institutions, such as the Afro-American Studies Center, in the image that John Huggins and Alprentice Carter died for."

The tragedy helped galvanize support for the center. "People felt even more then that we should go on and have the center, that we should, in fact, still build a black presence and a black power on campus, and that we should still have the department," Karenga said. "People were determined more than ever now to keep on and that that should not stop them."

Tensions on campus remained high for several weeks. While some students stayed away, others came to campus armed. "Friday's double murder of Black Panthers John Huggins and Bunchy Carter brought

Above: Student protests get out of hand when demonstrators begin lighting small fires and subsequently try to break in to the ROTC offices in the Men's Gymnasium, prompting the administration to call in police reinforcement, May 5, 1971.

Below: Violence erupts at UCLA the day after the Kent State shootings, forcing the first full-closure of the campus, which lasted a week.

Left: "On strike, shut it down!" is the rallying cry during the campus closure.

Above: Graffiti, broken windows and other vandalism embody demonstrators' discontent in Murphy Hall.

[the] opportunity for questioning [or] challenging and order; seeing to it that the former didn't become license and that the latter didn't become something akin to a police state."

Nationally, the anti-war movement continued to gain momentum. "It did linger with you," said 1971 student body President Keith Schiller, "the aspect of the unfairness of the war. And it did have a radicalizing effect on people, and that was the main source of protest throughout the period."

Protesters increasingly targeted campus military and intelligence recruiters, as well as the ROTC. In 1962, the Board of Regents had made the initial two years of the ROTC program voluntary, and opposition to ROTC at UCLA grew intense. During the early morning hours of June 5, 1970, a time-bomb exploded in the midshipman wardroom in the Men's Gymnasium, causing thousands of dollars in damage but no injuries. Public support for the battalion followed two days later when more than 3,000 showed up for the Sunset Review Dress Parade in UCLA's track-and-field stadium, with actor John Wayne in attendance and Reagan as the reviewing officer. As Wayne introduced Reagan, a skirmish broke out when 25 demonstrators were reportedly jumped in the aisles by pro-ROTC audience members. Later that month, a resolution to abolish ROTC was defeated in the Academic Senate by a vote of 826 to 398.

By 1972, draft resistance had reached its pinnacle, and there were more conscientious objectors than draftees. On May 9, 1972, Bruins gathered for a midday rally in front of Meyerhoff

Park organized by the Students for a Democratic Society. Activists spoke out against President Nixon's announcement the night before that North Vietnamese ports would be mined and that air strikes would continue, and demanded ROTC and military recruiters be removed from campus.

A crowd that started out as 500 students grew to more than 2,000, as protesters made their way to Royce quad and serpentined through several buildings, opening classroom doors and asking students to join the protest. At Murphy Hall, 200 of the protesters went to the Chancellor's Office, where they were addressed by Young. From there, the demonstrators descended Janss Steps and gathered in front of the Men's Gymnasium, protesting the ROTC. Ultimately, they linked arms and marched into Westwood, where a group sat down at the intersection of Wilshire Boulevard and Veteran Avenue near the Federal Building, shutting down traffic until police asked them to disperse. No protesters were arrested. The rally's effects, however, would spill over into the next several days.

"Today is not the day for 'business as usual,'" urged an editorial in the *Daily Bruin* the following day. "Today is not the day to go to class. Today is the day to rally, to march, to close down the University. Because today is the day to end the war."

Top left: Damage caused by a time bomb, which exploded in the ROTC offices in the Men's Gymnasium, June 5, 1970.

Above: Governor Ronald Reagan (left) and actor John Wayne (right) salute the ROTC color guard, during the Sunset Review Dress Parade, June 7, 1970.

quick defense from supporters of the High Potential program, feelings of uneasiness and sorrow from white students and guarded silence from black leaders," wrote the *Daily Bruin* on January 21. But no further incidents followed, and campus officials credited African-American student leaders for how they handled the situation.

In February 1969, five individuals were indicted by a Los Angeles County grand jury on charges of conspiracy and murder. While some stated that the shootings had been a spontaneous reaction to an unrelated quarrel, the district attorney's office asserted that the shooting had been the result of a deliberate assassination conspiracy by members of the Us organization directed against Huggins and Carter as a result of continuing disagreements between Us and the Black Panthers. Still others believed that the event was incited by the FBI in an effort to destabilize both groups.

Campbell Hall, named for Shakespearean scholar Lily Bess Campbell and already home to the High Potential Program, became the quarters for the new UCLA American Cultures Project, announced a week after the shootings. The Cultures Project served as an umbrella over four autonomous ethnic studies programs: African-American, Chicano, Asian-American and Native American. Campus officials emphasized that the project had been under development for some time and was not in response to the killings.

Several months later, Young wrote a piece for *UCLA Alumni Magazine* that explained the philosophy behind the myriad diversity efforts.

"We have not developed our programs at UCLA out of response to pressure or violence or the threat of violence, but by working together because we thought they had to be

American Studies Center. The center had been developed through a joint effort between the administration and representatives of the UCLA Black Student Union. The Black Panthers and Us had been involved in a factional dispute over potential candidates for the director position and control of the organization.

In advance of its first meeting after the shootings, the Black Student Union issued an open letter to the black student body. "It appears that the historical irony of crises moulding together factions to create harmonious forces among men is once again the case," read the statement printed in the *Daily Bruin* on January 31, 1969. "In the face of the most tragic events ever to befall this campus or any other, we issue an appeal to every black student at UCLA, not only to mourn the awesome loss, but to bend his energies now toward building our institutions, such as the Afro-American Studies Center, in the image that John Huggins and Alprentice Carter died for."

The tragedy helped galvanize support for the center. "People felt even more then that we should go on and have the center, that we should, in fact, still build a black presence and a black power on campus, and that we should still have the department," Karenga said. "People were determined more than ever now to keep on and that that should not stop them."

Tensions on campus remained high for several weeks. While some students stayed away, others came to campus armed. "Friday's double murder of Black Panthers John Huggins and Bunchy Carter brought

Wallace Clings to Small Lead

Los Angeles Times

UCLA EMERGENCY

War Protest Erupts in Violence

Lament of U.S. Wives: 'Mama and Mistress'

Permanent Halting of Red Infiltration Apparent U.S. Goal

Wallace Holds Thin Alabama Lead

Left: "On strike, shut it down!" is the rallying cry during the campus closure.

Above: Graffiti, broken windows and other vandalism embody demonstrators' discontent in Murphy Hall.

accomplished," Young stated. "Intellectually they were correct, morally they were right, conscientiously they were needed. Somehow we've got to reach people, to tell them what we're doing and why, and what would be the consequences of our actions or failure to act for the society. We haven't done that job of telling very well."

"SHUT IT DOWN"

On December 1, 1969, the first draft lottery since 1942 was held, affecting all men born in the years 1944 through 1950—approximately 850,000. The familiar placards proclaiming "Make love, not war" were joined by a rallying cry of "On strike, shut it down!" as the Vietnam War became personal.

"Every male on the campus had skin in this game," recalled Zev Yaroslavsky, who earned his bachelor's degree in 1971 and master's in 1972, before being elected in 1975 to the Los Angeles City Council, and subsequently, to the Los Angeles County Board of Supervisors in 1994. "Every one of us was on a student deferment, and the minute we got our bachelor's degrees, but for any other consideration, we were going to be draft eligible. And so the war wasn't an intellectual debate."

He continued: "When there was a demonstration on campus, it was a real demonstration. It was shut the class down. It was shut the campus down."

In May 1970, more than 100 student strikes were organized across the country in protest of the U.S. invasion of Cambodia. On May 4, the nation was aghast to see televised images of National Guardsmen firing upon anti-war protesters at Kent State University, killing four students and wounding nine others. The next day, violent protests erupted across the country at hundreds of college campuses, including UCLA.

Young was in Berkeley, and Saxon and Hobson, who had declined an earlier offer of police intervention, had Young's and Hitch's authorization for action if needed. With small fires breaking out and campus police concerned about protecting the Men's Gymnasium, which housed the ROTC offices, Saxon declared UCLA's first-ever state of emergency and called in the Los Angeles Police Department. Approximately 200 officers in riot gear arrived on motorcycles and lined up between the gyms, as well as on the hillside behind the residence halls. A police helicopter, or "whirlypig," as students labeled it, circled overhead providing tactical support for the ensuing sweeps. A loudspeaker truck blared, "In the name of the People of the State of California ..." but it was drowned out by thousands chanting "We are the people" and "Pigs off campus."

Individuals broke into Murphy Hall, shattering windows and plate glass doors, smashing walls and display cases, and spraying graffiti in corridors. In a violent clash with demonstrators, police made 81 arrests, but also injured students and professors, including linguistics Professor

Peter N. Ladefoged. "His face was bruised and bloody and his eyes appeared in very bad condition," reported history department Chairman Stanley A. Wolpert on Ladefoged's injuries to the Chancellor's Commission on the Events of May 5, 1970. "I could hardly recognize him at first." The report alleged that the police went beyond using reasonable force and moved into sections of campus far away from the disturbance, "physically attacking many innocent persons." The frenzied altercation led the administration to call for an unprecedented shutdown of the campus.

On May 7, Reagan followed suit by shutting down the state's 27 publicly supported college and university campuses for four days. "On Strike" was scrawled across chalkboards in some North Campus classrooms. For the rest of the quarter, sympathetic professors were lenient and many classes did not meet. Some professors asked students to simply turn in their notes to date for a grade. Of those courses that continued, many changed their content to reflect the current events.

Political science Professor Thomas W. Robinson allowed his students to either finish their papers on the Chinese Cultural Revolution, or write about their experiences following the Kent State shootings. The collected essays were published anonymously

Left: Mandatory fingerprinting for registration with the U.S. Selective Service, 1966.

Below: Men at UCLA take the Selective Service Draft Deferment Test, which partly determined the outcome of their induction status, 1966.

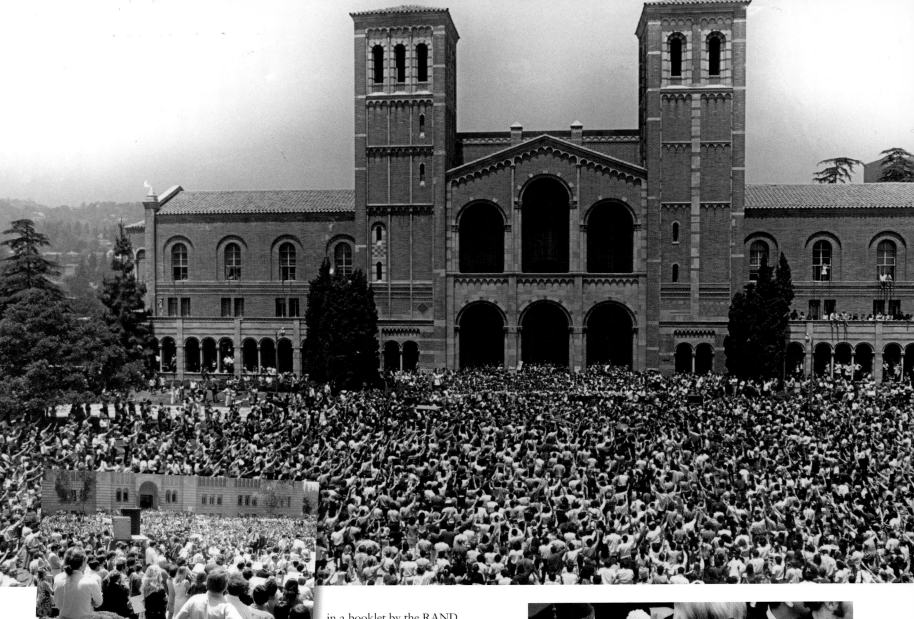

Above: More than 5,000 fill Royce quad to hear members of the UCLA Symphony and the Los Angeles Philharmonic conducted by Zubin Mehta (inset), perform Handel's "The Messiah" in a concert promoting peace, May 18, 1970.

Right: Flower power and peace at the 1970 graduation ceremony.

in a booklet by the RAND Corporation in April 1971. (Two months later the "Pentagon Papers," leaked by RAND's Daniel Ellsberg, were published in *The New York Times*.)

"Nothing the police did that day endeared them to the students, even the moderates and pacifists who came out the next day, organizing for a strike," one student wrote. "Once the LAPD arrived, everyone was a participant. Property damage ended, but in actuality it was over before the LAPD arrived. The immediate legacy was a strike which was far more effective over a longer period of time than any movement at UCLA had ever been."

Two weeks later, on May 18, 1970, more than 5,000 gathered in Royce quad to hear renowned conductor Zubin Mehta lead members of the UCLA Symphony and the Los Angeles Philharmonic in Handel's "The Messiah." The concert was organized by music department students and faculty members in an effort to foster a sense of collectiveness amid the instability on campus following the Kent State shootings.

"That was a period of such ferment," Young recalled. "We'd stay up all night … trying to provide a balance between

[the] opportunity for questioning [or] challenging and order; seeing to it that the former didn't become license and that the latter didn't become something akin to a police state."

Nationally, the anti-war movement continued to gain momentum. "It did linger with you," said 1971 student body President Keith Schiller, "the aspect of the unfairness of the war. And it did have a radicalizing effect on people, and that was the main source of protest throughout the period."

Protesters increasingly targeted campus military and intelligence recruiters, as well as the ROTC. In 1962, the Board of Regents had made the initial two years of the ROTC program voluntary, and opposition to ROTC at UCLA grew intense. During the early morning hours of June 5, 1970, a time-bomb exploded in the midshipman wardroom in the Men's Gymnasium, causing thousands of dollars in damage but no injuries. Public support for the battalion followed two days later when more than 3,000 showed up for the Sunset Review Dress Parade in UCLA's track-and-field stadium, with actor John Wayne in attendance and Reagan as the reviewing officer. As Wayne introduced Reagan, a skirmish broke out when 25 demonstrators were reportedly jumped in the aisles by pro-ROTC audience members. Later that month, a resolution to abolish ROTC was defeated in the Academic Senate by a vote of 826 to 398.

By 1972, draft resistance had reached its pinnacle, and there were more conscientious objectors than draftees. On May 9, 1972, Bruins gathered for a midday rally in front of Meyerhoff

Park organized by the Students for a Democratic Society. Activists spoke out against President Nixon's announcement the night before that North Vietnamese ports would be mined and that air strikes would continue, and demanded ROTC and military recruiters be removed from campus.

A crowd that started out as 500 students grew to more than 2,000, as protesters made their way to Royce quad and serpentined through several buildings, opening classroom doors and asking students to join the protest. At Murphy Hall, 200 of the protesters went to the Chancellor's Office, where they were addressed by Young. From there, the demonstrators descended Janss Steps and gathered in front of the Men's Gymnasium, protesting the ROTC. Ultimately, they linked arms and marched into Westwood, where a group sat down at the intersection of Wilshire Boulevard and Veteran Avenue near the Federal Building, shutting down traffic until police asked them to disperse. No protesters were arrested. The rally's effects, however, would spill over into the next several days.

"Today is not the day for 'business as usual," urged an editorial in the *Daily Bruin* the following day. "Today is not the day to go to class. Today is the day to rally, to march, to close down the University. Because today is the day to end the war."

Top left: Damage caused by a time bomb, which exploded in the ROTC offices in the Men's Gymnasium, June 5, 1970.

Above: Governor Ronald Reagan (left) and actor John Wayne (right) salute the ROTC color guard, during the Sunset Review Dress Parade, June 7, 1970.

Above: Walton is arrested after participating in a protest barricading Murphy Hall, May 11, 1972.

Right: Walton takes a jump shot during the NCAA Semifinals against Indiana University in St. Louis, March 24, 1973. The Bruins won 70–59 on the way to their seventh consecutive national title.

Right: Sophomore Bill Walton protests the Vietnam War by taking part in a sit-in on Wilshire Boulevard, May 9, 1972.

On May 11, on the second day of the multiday strike, 1,000 protesters barricaded the entrances to Murphy Hall. Dozens of students were arrested, including UCLA basketball center Bill Walton, an avid anti-war protester off the court.

Walton, an All-American, was just finishing his sophomore year after the Bruins won their eighth national championship in 1972. Chants of "Stop the war! Stop the war! Stop the war!" filled the air outside Murphy Hall. As the situation escalated, protesters lifted a parking service vehicle to put against the door. Police officers chased down the protesters, including Walton, and the students instinctively switched their chant to "Watch his knees! Watch his knees! Watch his knees!" because Walton was known to have bad knees.

"If one vignette describes the incongruity of the times, it was thousands of students shutting down the university," said Yaroslavsky, "but all the while being mindful of next year's basketball team."

"A Landmark Time for Us"

1975–1989

Above: *The Bruin* statue gussied up for UCLA's trip to the 1986 Rose Bowl. The Bruins were victorious, pounding the University of Iowa, 45-28.

Opposite: The Flags of Nations stretch along the intramural field as UCLA played host to the 1984 Summer Olympics.

*F*or 15 years after Governor Ronald Reagan's first state budget, UCLA experienced continuous financial pressures. Like many public universities nationwide, the campus was affected by the sagging economy and high inflation, changing governmental budgeting priorities, and a decline in federal dollars for university research.

UCLA had been elected in 1974 to membership in the Association of American Universities—joining Berkeley and marking the first time that a university system had more than one campus as a member of the group of leading North American research universities. A year later, UCLA's Executive Vice Chancellor David S. Saxon was selected as the 14th president of the University of California. Both actions acknowledged the emerging importance of UCLA.

Throughout his eight-year tenure, Saxon continually battled with Governor Edmund G. "Jerry" Brown Jr. to preserve state funding, which provided the core resources for the basic educational operation of the university's campuses. In 1978, California voters overwhelmingly approved Proposition 13, which significantly restricted property tax assessments, and resulted in the state providing "bailout" funds to cities, counties, schools and special districts, wiping out its $3.9 billion surplus.

Chancellor Charles E. Young's administration implemented careful allocations and controls of resources. Under his leadership, UCLA not only managed to bolster itself against the financial difficulties, but it did so while being named in 1983 as the second best public university in the nation by the Conference Board of Associated Research Councils. Enrollment reached unprecedented levels in the 1980s. So many prospective students wanted to attend UCLA that changes were

implemented that made admission to UCLA more selective, and eligible students were redirected to other University of California campuses.

"When I became chancellor in 1968, much of society was in turmoil," Young reflected in UCLA's first campuswide annual report, which covered the 1982–83 fiscal year. "Many young people had lost confidence in symbols of authority, particularly in large institutions. Traditional social values were called into question and there was a spirit of political rebellion. UCLA was part of this picture. It was a time in history when the strength of the institution was tested and its role in society challenged.

"What is remarkable," Young continued, "is that while there was so much turmoil in society, UCLA as an institution of higher learning—as a community of scholars—was actually getting stronger rather than weaker."

In 1982–83, the campus reached a milestone: UCLA was a billion-dollar enterprise with total assets exceeding $1.1 billion; in comparison, in 1968–69, UCLA's assets were approximately one-third of that, or $403 million. But UCLA needed to create a cushion from unpredictable state budget swings and, in 1983, the administration launched the university's first broad-scale fundraising campaign. Undertaken as the nation's most ambitious effort by a public university, the campaign succeeded in tripling annual private giving to UCLA, and in 1983–84 raised about 10 percent of the campus's operating budget.

Tired of clashing over state funding, Saxon stepped down in 1983, and was succeeded by David Pierpont Gardner, just seven months after the inauguration of new Governor George Deukmejian. The two formed a professional bond that would lead to a restoration of state funding to the level before Reagan's administration, and helped UCLA embark on its second long-range development plan, which included expansions to several professional school buildings and additional medical research space.

The 1980s brought a national upsurge of consumerism, and UCLA's name became popularized the world over through the launch of "Bearwear." People across the globe with no immediate connection to the campus were wearing Bruins gear in a phenomenon that store leaders found difficult to explain, but were quick to embrace. UCLA became the first university to license its name to clothing companies, and the trademark became the world's top-selling collegiate emblem.

"The initials 'UCLA' seem to convey the idea of youth, sunshine, health, sports—everything people like to identify with," store director Tim Bayley told the Los Angeles Times. Students also adopted the look, with the 1980 yearbook listing it among campus fads and fashions, "For virtually all [occasions]: anything with 'UCLA' printing—visors, t-shirts, dresses, beach towels, brandy snifters, night shirts …"

Tourism to UCLA, particularly from Japan, reached new heights. In 1984, the campus served as an Olympic village and hosted the gymnastics and tennis events of the 1984 Summer Games watched by billions. International media attention descended on UCLA again a year later, as Hollywood leading man Rock Hudson was admitted to the UCLA Medical Center. The actor was being treated for AIDS, a revelation that shocked the world and destigmatized a disease—first identified at UCLA in 1981—that would become a pandemic.

A decade after the turbulent protests that swept campus during the Vietnam War, students settled back into an academic rhythm and revived campus traditions that had waned over the years. They took seriously their expanded roles in campus affairs, achieved as a result of the prior activism, and developed a sense of corporate social responsibility. Their most significant achievement: a decade-long effort that ultimately prompted the University of California to divest from South Africa in protest of apartheid. Their model of activism left a legacy that would influence generations of students in the years ahead.

"NEW STANDING IN ACADEMIA"

Enrollment, which had remained relatively stable in the early to mid-1970s, unexpectedly began to swell. The escalation, particular to California's public and private universities, perplexed higher education leaders and admissions officers because the number of 18- to 24-year-olds nationwide was decreasing. In fact, UCLA academic leaders had been discussing plans to prepare for decreasing enrollment, and potentially having to actively recruit undergraduates. Some believed that, as in the Great Depression, a bad economy was compelling students to seek education rather than jobs. Others speculated that students were applying earlier in anticipation of further reductions in federal financial aid by the Reagan administration.

In 1978, so many qualified applicants selected UCLA as their No. 1 choice on University of California applications that for the first time the UCLA admissions office was forced to redirect prospective applicants—1,850—to other system campuses. In 1982, UCLA had to redirect 3,000 applicants. The following year, UCLA enrolled 34,754 students—the largest number of any campus systemwide. By 1984, of the 10,000 applications received, the admissions office had to redirect half, confusing and upsetting students, parents and high school counselors.

In a systemwide response to the popularity of both UCLA and Berkeley—which had been redirecting applicants for years, although was not experiencing as large a jump as UCLA—applicants to the University of California could apply to more than one campus for simultaneous consideration beginning fall 1985.

Admission would become more and more selective in succeeding years as demand continued to grow. In 1980, UCLA's admission rate was 75.4 percent compared with 53.9 percent in 1984. The new multiple filing policy increased UCLA's pool of freshman applicants from 16,000 to 27,000—for about 4,000 spots.

"So many people want to get in, that we are in the position to take those who have the strongest preparation and not anybody who meets minimum requirements," Rae Lee Siporin, director of UCLA admissions, told the *Daily Bruin* in 1985. Starting in fall 1987, in addition to GPA and test scores, all eligible applications were reviewed for factors including the rigorousness of high school course loads, honors-level courses,

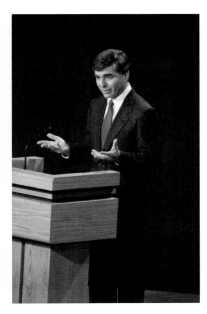

With only six days until the second debate of the 1988 presidential campaign, organizers called upon UCLA to host the event. Workers scrambled to transform Pauley Pavilion into a television studio where presidential hopefuls Vice President George Bush (above left) and Massachusetts Governor Michael Dukakis (above right) faced off. Dukakis became a visiting professor in the School of Public Policy and Social Research (later the Luskin School of Public Affairs) in the 1995–1996 academic year.

an essay and extracurricular activities. Previously, borderline cases were reviewed in this manner.

Amid all this growth, news broke in January 1983 that caught Young and other campus leaders by surprise. The results of the first major survey of faculty and graduate programs conducted in more than a decade were released by the Conference Board of Associated Research Councils. The assessment ranked UCLA second nationally among public universities—behind Berkeley—and No. 4 overall, behind Berkeley, Stanford and Harvard.

"The news so astonished UCLA administrators that they quickly set to work to verify the results," recounted a *Los Angeles Times* article published the following year. "They knew that UCLA's graduate programs had become good in the last two decades, but *that* good? Was it possible that a Southern California university, perhaps best known for basketball and beach boys, had beaten out revered private establishments in the East?"

Indeed, it turned out there had been an error in tabulations. UCLA was not fourth after all; Yale was. UCLA was actually tied at No. 5 with Princeton.

The article, titled "UCLA: New Standing in Academia," suggested that the administration's reaction was "indicative as anything of UCLA's disbelief at its new standing in the scholarly world" and "a pretty remarkable feat" for a university founded in the 20th century.

"There is always a kind of a funny transition period when you move from second-best to best, when you move from the best of the minor leagues to the real major leagues," William D. Schaefer, UCLA's executive vice chancellor from 1978–87, told the *Times*. "You're playing in different competition. You're competing with institutions that had really been beyond your grasp. What you're really doing now is playing hardball, major-league ball with the Ivy League schools and the major public universities of the country."

Although the study measured graduate programs, UCLA's rating also reflected on undergraduate programs, Young explained, because they shared the same faculty.

"It is gratifying to see UCLA's faculty receive this national recognition of their superior research and teaching," Young said. "When this survey is combined with the traditional strengths of our professional schools and colleges, we emerge as one of a very select number of distinguished American universities."

Of the 32 departments in the survey, 30 of UCLA's were in the top 16—and 17 were in the Top 10. They were: linguistics, second in the nation; geosciences, third; electrical engineering, philosophy, physiology and zoology, all ranked fifth; computer science and geography, each ranked sixth; anthropology, chemistry, psychology and Spanish, all ranked

Above: A 1980s class in the Graduate School of Management, which was founded as the College of Commerce in 1935.

Left: Computers become a part of academic life.

seventh; mechanical engineering, microbiology and sociology, all ranked ninth; and botany and economics, each ranked 10th.

Young had succeeded in fulfilling his inaugural promise to move UCLA "from the second level of good universities" into the upper echelons. "But we cannot rest on our laurels," he said. "There is much to be done as we continue our efforts to reach our full potential."

CAMPAIGNING FOR UCLA

One of the "most frustrating" problems UCLA needed to overcome to reach its potential, according to Young, was dealing with the year-to-year uncertainty of the state's funding level. Budgetary fluctuations made planning for and running such a large institution difficult. Moreover, parts of the campus were suffering, and added revenue was needed.

UCLA came out of the 1970s "a better institution than it went into it relative to other universities in the country," Young said. But faculty salaries still lagged behind those of peer institutions and there was concern that professors would accept more generous offers elsewhere. UCLA also lost ground in both the construction of new buildings, and the maintenance and operation of the physical plant. State funding had been available for a few projects, including nursing facilities in the Louis Factor Building; and there was a special state appropriation for the Jerry Lewis Neuromuscular Research Center obtained by the comedian himself. But from 1970 to 1981, there were no major state-funded facilities built on campus.

Neil H. Jacoby, dean of the business school, 1948–1973.

"To achieve its destiny, UCLA and the university as a whole will need additional financial support from both the Legislature and private sources," Young had outlined in his inaugural year. "This means UCLA is going to have to tell more people what we are doing and why we are doing it. We are going to have to rededicate ourselves to the task of making the public aware that UCLA's vision of its future is a vital part of the future envisioned for our state and nation."

Cultivating private dollars to make up the differential in state funding seemed an obvious course. But efforts had been hampered by ingrained philosophies and territorial lines dating back to the presidency of Robert Gordon Sproul. A gentlemen's agreement existed between the University of California and the state's premier private colleges and universities, including Stanford, USC and the California Institute of Technology. Since the University of California was a publicly supported state institution, its leadership conceded that soliciting private dollars from businesses or individuals other than alumni was off-limits.

In November 1958, Neil H. Jacoby, dean of the business school, came up against the agreement after he launched the UCLA Business Research Associates, quickly raising $1,000 apiece from 40 donors. Learning of Jacoby's success, Robert R. Dockson, dean of USC's business school, went to President Norman H. Topping, who in turn went to Asa V. Call, chairman of USC's Board of Trustees, who then called University of California Regent Edwin W. Pauley, and, according to Jacoby, complained: "What are you people doing here, trying to poach on our preserves? Your university is supported by the taxpayer. We have to look to business. Now you're becoming greedy and going to business as well."

Under directive from University of California President Clark Kerr, Chancellor Raymond B. Allen put restrictions on further fundraising and the Business Research Associates "lost their forward spirit," Jacoby said, noting he was also constrained from making public statements, or engaging in mass solicitations.

"I suggested to Chancellor Allen to meet with President Topping and try to persuade him that there was plenty of money in the community to support business research at both universities," Jacoby explained. "Our efforts to raise this money would not frustrate but would fortify USC's efforts. You know that Woolworth likes to be located next to Newberry because it draws customers to both. So if we were beating the drums for support of management research, it would help 'SC in their efforts." Jacoby found Allen sympathetic, but the chancellor would not pursue it.

Two years later, the Office of the President drew the private university leaders' ire directly, when it appeared that a staff member was exploring a statewide fundraising effort. Caltech President Lee Alvin DuBridge, Stanford President J.E. Wallace Sterling, Topping, Kerr, Chancellor Franklin D. Murphy and Young met at the California Club to discuss the gentlemen's agreement. The result: The agreement remained intact—although Murphy saw an opening to more actively solicit alumni and friends, including those who had already donated to UCLA.

Still, by 1980, UCLA did not have a strong development program and was bringing in less than $40 million, a mere fraction of what private universities were raising.

Alumnus and former campus counsel, Alan F. Charles, was appointed to the newly created position of vice chancellor for external affairs, overseeing both alumni relations and development efforts, including the UCLA Foundation. (Originally formed by the UCLA Alumni Association in 1943 as the Progress Fund, the non-profit entity—a vehicle to spur alumni giving on an annual or special basis—was renamed by Murphy in 1966.)

Richard D. Chamberlain, UCLA's assistant vice chancellor of development and executive director of the UCLA Foundation, persuaded Young and Charles to go forward with a large-scale fundraising campaign. In 1982, just as UCLA was preparing to announce the campaign, President Saxon called to express concern based on the long-standing agreement, and it was decided that the private institutions should be consulted before continuing. A dinner was held at the Chancellor's Residence, with at least a dozen leaders of the private institutions in attendance.

"The discussion went forward in a cordial atmosphere, and there was some trepidation expressed as to how this might affect each of them," Charles said. "Then to the rescue rode Neal Pings, the provost of USC, who declared the gentlemen's agreement dead and said we had much more in common as universities than differences as public or private. He said we competed for academic vigor and not for money, and that the efforts we might make would only increase the size of the pie for everyone." According to Charles, no one dissented—at least not out loud. UCLA encountered no further obstacles to fundraising from the President's Office or from the private institutions.

The UCLA Campaign launched in 1983 under the day-to-day management of James W. Osterholt, newly appointed assistant vice chancellor for development (who succeeded Chamberlain). Announced as the most ambitious effort undertaken by an American public university, its aim was to raise $200 million by summer 1987. It did so well, the goal was increased to $300 million. By 1988, the UCLA Campaign had surpassed the revised goal, raising $373 million and tripling annual giving to the campus. UCLA was raising more money each year than any other University of California campus, and ranked among the top five public universities in fundraising nationwide.

Among the most significant gifts was $15 million in 1987 from alumnus John E. Anderson and his wife, Marion, for the Graduate School of Management, which was renamed for the entrepreneur. It was the largest gift from an individual to the University of California.

"A campaign was very important at that point in time to establish UCLA as a major player in the private sector," Young said. "We needed to be able to raise money to help us move into a period in which it was very clear to me, at least, that the relative amounts of funds that had been coming from the public sector were going to be reduced."

UCLA NEEDS YOUR SUPPORT GIVE TO THE UCLA FOUNDATION

UCLA Needs Your Support GIVE to The UCLA FOUNDATION

THE RESTORATION

Even as the UCLA Campaign got underway, state cuts were looming. Relations between Saxon and the state's leadership had become increasingly adversarial, and in July 1983 the president officially stepped down from his post, acknowledging that he had grown "tired and tense" and was finding it more difficult to disagree with people.

New Governor George Deukmejian had taken office on January 3, 1983. In an executive action just minutes after being sworn in, Deukmejian implemented, among other measures, a state hiring freeze and a two percent spending cut that immediately affected the university's 1982–83 budget. Later that month, the Board of Regents, in an almost unanimous vote that included the governor, approved an emergency educational "surcharge" of $100 for Spring Quarter. Unlike board meetings shortly after Reagan entered office, the regents did not berate the governor for the cuts, and several expressed sympathy over the $1.5 billion state deficit.

Amid the financial crisis and the strain between the university and Sacramento, the regents moved rapidly to fill Saxon's post and, in August 1983, David Pierpont Gardner took office as the 15th president of the University of California. Gardner, formerly president of the University of Utah, was a Berkeley native and possessed both a background in fundraising and a history of successful interactions with the Utah Legislature.

Within months, Gardner and Deukmejian forged a close working partnership. Gardner succeeded in negotiating an unprecedented one-year, 30 percent increase in the university's budget, intended to restore operations to levels

prior to the 16 years of Reagan and Brown. On his own, Deukmejian even included a request to reduce student fees by $70 to be made up through an appropriation to the university.

"In addition now to the fact that UCLA won the Rose Bowl game again this year [UCLA 45–Illinois 9], I think we can be very proud of our achievements in higher education," Deukmejian said in his 1984 State of the State address. "But today, these achievements are threatened by problems, such as lagging faculty salaries, obsolete equipment, delays in building improvements and insufficient emphasis on the needs of high-technology and other growth industries. To address these problems, I am proposing a 30 percent increase in general fund support for the University of California."

For the next six years, state funding to the university rose by an annual average of five percent, inducing significant growth and achievement at all the campuses.

"The period of David Gardner's presidency was a great period for UCLA," Young said. "The economy had recovered. There were substantial funds available."

"Deukmejian's first priority was the University of California," Young continued. "We were supported at every turn on almost every issue. And David [Gardner] brought people to the Office of the President who understood what a president's office ought to do and what the campuses ought to

… and really moved the *de facto* decision-making process to the campuses."

Shortly after his appointment, Gardner initiated a symbolic gesture that helped foster a strong rapport between the president and Young. Gardner sought Young out as the senior chancellor—and in a similar manner to his initial meeting with

Above: Chancellor Charles E. Young embraces Coach Terry Donahue after his first game, and win, as head coach against Arizona State University, September 9, 1976.

Left: UCLA held the inauguration for President David Pierpont Gardner (left), 17th president of the University of California, April 12, 1984.

Deukmejian—traveled to UCLA without entourage, rather than asking Young to visit Berkeley. Impressed, Young offered to host Gardner's inauguration in the recently renovated Royce Hall. Gardner, who in his memoir wrote that he had not been received well or made feel welcome by Berkeley, accepted.

"The great majority of the state's population lived in southern California, five of the university's nine campuses were in the south, the state's major newspapers and main media outlets were in Los Angeles, the governor was from there," Gardner said, "and I knew that UCLA would do it right."

OLYMPIC GLORY

The additional funding from the state helped UCLA make immediate improvements to the campus and jumpstart its second long-range development plan in 1983.

"The building program, which had deteriorated into nothingness, became a strong program," Young said. There were so many projects ongoing during the 1980s that students dubbed the campus, "University of Construction, Like Always." Increased state resources prompted the formation in 1986 of Capital Programs, headed by Vice Chancellor (and alumnus) Peter W. Blackman, to manage the myriad building projects that would continue throughout the decade.

"As a vital and developing organization, UCLA has a high-powered cadre of academics and forward-looking goals," Blackman said. "The situation has created both an opportunity and an obligation for us to develop a rather aggressive capital program."

Above: Long wanting to create a summer family education camp similar to those at Berkeley and Stanford universities, UCLA took over management of the Lake Arrowhead Conference Center in 1982. Situated on 40 acres in the San Bernardino Mountains, the property was previously managed by the University of California as an Extension center. UCLA enlarged and remodeled the facility and, in 1985, the UCLA Alumni Association began hosting Bruin Woods, a fun-filled summer camp of 10 one-week sessions for 750 Bruin families a year.

Above right: Vice Chancellor Peter W. Blackman, appointed in 1986 as the first director of Capital Programs, kept the campus's aesthetic trust for more than 20 years.

Right: Alumni Association President James N. Thayer (left) and Chancellor Charles E. Young (right) admire *The Bruin*, a gift to the campus commemorating the Association's 50th anniversary.

One change to the campus landscape would shape future tradition. The UCLA Alumni Association, celebrating its 50th anniversary in 1984, commissioned *The Bruin* statue for a refurbished Westwood Plaza—later renamed Bruin Plaza. Alumni had long been frustrated that unlike crosstown rival USC, which installed *Tommy Trojan* in 1930, the UCLA campus still lacked an iconic symbol. *The Bruin* instantly changed all that, becoming a prominent campus landmark and gathering spot.

Unveiled on September 30, 1984, the teeth-baring bronze statue by artist Bill Fitzgerald measured 10 feet long, six feet tall, and three feet across, and weighed more than two tons. The ferocious grizzly was a departure from UCLA's familiar, friendly Joe Bruin mascot of the 1970s and early '80s. *The Bruin*, walking on all fours, was intended to demonstrate a fluid forward movement symbolizing the ongoing strength and progress of UCLA.

"You'll notice that it's formidable," Alexander "Jake" Hamilton, president of the Pioneer Bruins, told the *Los Angeles Times*. "It's the antithesis of fragility."

The 1983–84 annual report was titled "A Landmark Time for Us," a play on the new campus attraction, and a reflection of one of the most significant events ever held on the UCLA campus: the XXIIIrd Olympiad.

In 1932, UCLA had provided its newly rising Westwood campus as the site for field hockey training for the Summer Games. Half a century later, the university would play a far more integral role and simultaneously showcase its dynamic campus to an international television audience of billions.

Plans for UCLA's involvement in the 1984 Summer Olympics began as early as 1977, when civic organizers putting together Los Angeles' bid asked if UCLA would be willing to make Pauley Pavilion available for athletic events and allow use of the residence halls to house athletes. After Los Angeles was announced as the host for the 1984 Summer Games, Young was invited to be a member of the Los Angeles Olympic Organizing Committee's Board of Directors. In 1981, an agreement was reached for Pauley Pavilion to be the venue hosting the popular gymnastics competitions.

"Our participation in the Olympics will enable us to show the world what UCLA is like and to tell the world about UCLA's academic program," said Norman P. Miller, who, coinciding with his retirement as vice chancellor for student and campus affairs in 1979, was appointed director of UCLA's 1984 Olympic Games Office.

John Sandbrook, assistant to the chancellor for special projects, was appointed by Young as liaison with the Olympic Organizing Committee and along with Administrative Vice Chancellor James W. Hobson oversaw much of the campus planning.

Welcome to UCLA.

UCLA looks forward this summer to receiving visitors from throughout the world. This brochure is designed to make visits to UCLA pleasant and informative. In it you will find a map showing locations of Olympic venues and parking lots, as well as information about UCLA and special Olympic-related programs.

Left: Some 160,000 guides were distributed to orient Olympics visitors who flocked to UCLA to watch the gymnastics events in Pauley Pavilion and the tennis "demonstration" tournament in the newly built Los Angeles Tennis Center (below).

Below left: Norman P. Miller, who spearheaded the drive for the Sunset Canyon Recreation Center in the 1960s, was director of UCLA's 1984 Olympic Games Office.

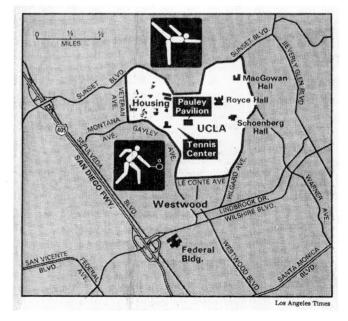

In total, 120 acres on campus were utilized for the Olympics. Athletes used the two gymnasiums, the John Wooden Recreation and Sports Center (completed in 1983), the Sunset Canyon Recreation Center, and Drake Stadium for training and practice. Spaulding Field provided a home for televising network ABC's trucks and equipment, while the top two floors of Ackerman Union, including the Grand Ballroom, bustled with the press corps. The Olympic Organizing Committee commanded the ground floor of the James West Alumni Center, and the building served as the exclusive entryway into the Olympic village. Alumnus and Olympic commissioner for archery Jim Easton greeted each arriving team as the village's mayor. Ceremonies welcoming the national delegations and other events occurred daily on a large stage in the newly renovated plaza at the foot of Bruin Walk, just outside of Ackerman Union.

UCLA benefited from campus physical improvements, including $1 million toward residence hall renovations, and the construction of a major facility. The $3.3 million Los Angeles Olympic Organizing Committee headquarters building was constructed on a UCLA parking lot on the corner of Le Conte and Broxton avenues with the understanding that it would be transferred to UCLA in January 1985. The building was criticized in the press for its "bunkerlike" qualities, with the Los Angeles Times architecture critic calling it "three slices of glass between four slices of concrete" and "the saddest of missed opportunities." But UCLA's 62,000-square-foot souvenir (later renamed the Peter V. Ueberroth building in honor of the Olympic Organizing Committee president), provided the campus with much-needed office space after the Olympics.

The Los Angeles Tennis Center, just west of Pauley Pavilion, was constructed in time to host the games' tennis "demonstration" tournament, where sold-out matches attracted more than 45,000. (Tennis was added as an official Olympic sport in 1988.) The $7 million tennis venue was jointly financed by the Southern California Tennis Association and UCLA—$2 million coming from Olympic village rental payments.

The games themselves started with one of UCLA's most renowned athletic heroes: Rafer Johnson, 1959 student body president and 1960 decathlon Olympic gold medalist, lit the Olympic flame during the Opening Ceremony at the Los Angeles Memorial Coliseum. For the next 15 days, the UCLA campus, normally more tranquil in the summer months, bustled in the glow of international attention and contributed to one of Los Angeles' finest moments.

An estimated 2.5 billion people across the globe watched the television broadcasts. More than 160,000 spectators came to Pauley Pavilion to witness firsthand the men's and women's gymnastics competitions, and rhythmic gymnastics made its Olympic debut in the UCLA arena.

As an Olympic village, UCLA housed more than 4,000 athletes, coaches and trainers from 62 countries in campus residence halls. A "main street" of shops lined the upper concourse of Drake Stadium overlooking the 142 Flags of Nations on the playing field below. In Bruin Plaza, the popular amateur "sport" of Olympic pin-trading reigned as the students store sold 8,000 pins in just two days. Hundreds of UCLA students worked as interpreters, ushers, info kiosk attendants, or in food service positions through the Associated Students, which handled all food and beverage sales.

Forty-eight UCLA students and alumni representing the United States and 10 other countries competed valiantly during the Summer Games. These Bruin Olympians—the largest number affiliated with any university—won 37 medals: 17 gold, 14 silver and six bronze.

The U.S. men's gymnastics team captured the all-around gold medal. Half of the six-member team—whose surprising victory over the People's Republic of China was called "the Miracle of L.A." by the *Los Angeles Times*—was composed of UCLA athletes: Peter Vidmar, Mitch Gaylord and Tim Daggett. It was the first gold ever for U.S. men's gymnastics. Daggett scored a perfect 10 on the high bar to help clinch the medal. Vidmar also won gold on the pommel horse and silver in the men's all-around competition, missing the gold by just 0.025 of a point. Gaylord earned four medals, including the team gold, which he helped the squad win with his risky signature release move on the horizontal bar, the Gaylord II.

Three members of the U.S. volleyball team that crushed Brazil to capture the gold medal were Bruins: Steven Salmons, Dave Saunders and Karch Kiraly. Under UCLA Coach Al Scates, the trio had led the Bruins to NCAA men's volleyball titles in 1979 and 1981; Saunders and Kiraly repeated the feat

Far left: Alumnus and 1960 decathlon gold medalist Rafer Johnson carries the Olympic flame in the Los Angeles Memorial Coliseum (left), before climbing 99 steps to light a fuse that burned through the Olympic rings and ignited the Olympic Torch.

Below: Pauley Pavilion not only hosted the men's and women's gymnastics events, but was the home for the debut of rhythmic gymnastics as an Olympic sport.

THE TORCH WILL BE LIT BY
RAFER JOHNSON
OLYMPIC GOLD MEDALIST
DECATHLON

Los Angeles 1984 Olympics

Right: Three of the six members of the U.S. men's gymnastics gold-medal winning team line up in Pauley Pavilion, including alumni Peter Vidmar (left) and Mitch Gaylord (center).

Below: Karch Kiraly digs the volleyball in a match against Brazil. The U.S. upended the South American country for the gold medal.

Below right: Sprinter Evelyn Ashford takes gold in the 100 meters.

Far right: Pharmacology chief Don H. Catlin (left), founding director of the UCLA Olympic Analytical Laboratory. The lab was the first in the United States to be accredited by the International Olympic Committee.

in 1982. Female Bruins excelled in track and field, with Evelyn Ashford as a double-gold medal champion, first in the 100 meters—setting an Olympic record of 10.97 seconds—and then as anchor of the 4x100-meter relay team. Jackie Joyner and Florence Griffith won silver in the heptathlon and the 200 meters, respectively.

During the games, the UCLA Medical Center, designated an official Olympic hospital, was visited more than 3,000 times by athletes and team officials. The Los Angeles Olympic Organizing Committee also selected the medical center to create the first Olympic drug testing facility in the United States.

The School of Medicine's Department of Pharmacology received $600,000 in new equipment and $900,000 in support funds to help establish the facility, which after the 1984 Olympics continued doping control analysis for international and Olympic-level sporting events.

"We are confident that drug-testing of athletes in 1984 will be swift and accurate," Ueberroth told the *Los Angeles*

Times. "The laboratory will be a source for research and development in sports medicine for years to come."

The lab, under the direction of UCLA's pharmacology chief Don H. Catlin, was accredited in November 1983 by the International Olympic Committee (IOC) after it received a perfect score on test samples designed to detect banned substances. Located in the Louis Factor Health Sciences Building, the facility screened more than 1,500 urine samples during the games; 12 athletes failed the drug tests and were proclaimed ineligible from competition.

The IOC expected the lab to set the standards for future competition. In subsequent years, the UCLA Olympic Analytical Laboratory, which moved two miles south of campus, worked with the NCAA, the National Football League and minor league baseball. It became the world's largest accredited anti-doping agency and was responsible for revolutionary scientific breakthroughs including identifying the first "designer steroid," norbolethone, as well as THG, short for tetrahyrogestrinone, which made worldwide headlines during several steroid controversies involving athletes such as Barry Bonds of the San Francisco Giants and U.S. sprinter Marion Jones, whose Olympic medals from 2000 were revoked.

"For years I had suspected that there were designer steroids," said Catlin, who would lead the lab for more than 25 years before retiring in 2007. "But you don't know their structure, you can't draw them, you can't tell what they are, you can't buy them, so how are you going to find them? Well, we finally figured out how to do it, and when we did, we made major noise. We'd found the first designer steroid."

"PATIENT ZERO"

Earlier in the decade, UCLA physicians made a grim discovery that would mark the official beginning of a worldwide health crisis.

Michael S. Gottlieb, an assistant professor and immunologist who had been at UCLA for six months, noticed

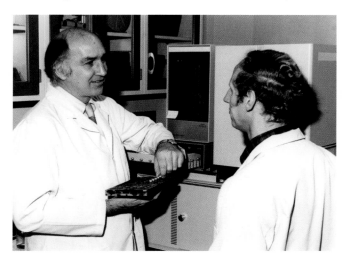

an unusual pattern among several patients he was treating in the summer of 1981.

"I met Michael, the man who became my Patient Zero, in early 1981," Gottlieb wrote in the *Los Angeles Times* 25 years later. "I was 33 years old; he was 31. He was rail thin with short, bleached-blond hair and high cheekbones. I remember him in more detail than patients I saw yesterday."

Michael had been admitted a few days earlier through the emergency room, and tests showed a rare type of lung infection called pneumocystis. The condition had been observed only in patients with severe immune deficiencies, but Michael was previously healthy. Using new medical technology available at UCLA, doctors tested his blood and found an absence of "T cells," critical white blood cells that activate a body's defenses.

In the weeks that followed, two more men with almost identical symptoms were referred by Joel Weisman, a physician in nearby Sherman Oaks. "Like Michael, each told me that he was gay," Gottlieb explained. "In those days, our subcultures—white-coated medics and gay men—were worlds apart. But that was about to change." Then, two more cases came in, and Gottlieb and his colleagues decided the information needed to be given to health authorities and made public.

"I knew I was witnessing medical history, but I had no comprehension of what this illness would become," Gottlieb told *Time* in 1985.

On June 5, 1981, the Centers for Disease Control and Prevention's "Morbidity and Mortality Weekly Report" published Gottlieb's findings on the very first cases of what was described as "newly acquired immunodeficiency"—the disease that became known as AIDS. That date would later be declared as the official onset of the AIDS epidemic. As soon as the report was released, the CDC and UCLA began hearing from doctors in San Francisco and New York.

"The report that came from Dr. Gottlieb and his colleagues had a profound impact on life as we know it," said Vice Chancellor Gerald S. Levey, who oversaw the medical sciences from 1994 to 2010, at the 25th commemoration of the disease's discovery. "The subsequent identification of the

human immunodeficiency virus as well as the further definition of the syndrome of AIDS reverberated not only through the medical profession, it reverberated through the public health community, through our society in general, and globally revealed a scope of disease and prevalence in many areas of the world that even now are beyond comprehension."

Gottlieb said that the technology and collaboration at UCLA made the identification possible. "The discovery of AIDS illustrates the value of academic medical centers—this didn't happen at a community hospital," Gottlieb said. "There was a certain core of expertise at the university. There was the ability to do T-cell subsets in Dr. [John L.] Fahey's laboratory. It was one of the first labs to be using those new monoclonal anti-bodies to detect T-cell subsets. We were able, using that test, to pinpoint the immunologic defect in people with AIDS."

Gottlieb added: "There is a certain critical mass that existed at UCLA. It's no accident that the discovery was made there."

Left: Actor Rock Hudson and alumna Carol Burnett at the Carol Burnett Musical Theater Awards, Schoenberg Hall, February 20, 1982.

Below left: Hudson is transported via gurney to an awaiting UCLA MedStar helicopter at Los Angeles International Airport, July 30, 1985.

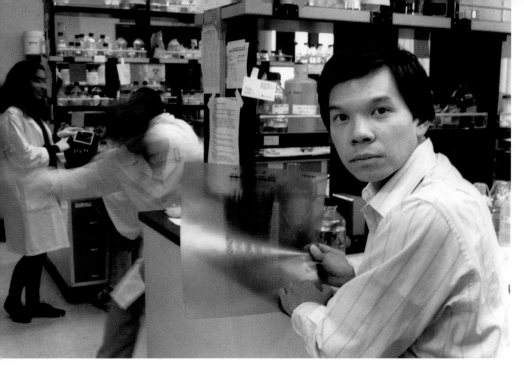

Above: Irvin S.Y. Chen, founding director of the UCLA AIDS Institute.

Below right: Tennis legend Arthur Ashe in 1984, a decade before he was named Alumnus of the Year. He received the award posthumously after having succumbed from complications of AIDS just a few months before the ceremony.

For several years after the illness was discovered, it remained a mysterious and marginalized disease. Misinformation abounded. Patients, once diagnosed, faced likely discrimination and, without a cure or treatment, almost certain death. Then, in 1985, a high-profile celebrity increased awareness among Americans and citizens of the world.

"It was the shocking news two weeks ago of Actor Rock Hudson's illness that finally catapulted AIDS out of the closet, transforming it overnight from someone else's problem, a 'gay plague,' to a cause of international alarm," *Time* stated

in April 1985. "AIDS was suddenly a front-page disease, the lead item on the evening news and a frequent topic on TV talk shows. There seemed no end to the reports."

Hudson had collapsed in a Paris hotel and was later flown to Los Angeles, where he was admitted to the UCLA Medical Center on July 30, 1985. Gottlieb, Hudson's physician, confirmed the actor's condition in a press conference, noting "the word cure is not yet in the vocabulary." Hudson, who had been undergoing experimental treatment, died two months later.

The following year, in 1986, UCLA was among the first 14 research centers to receive funding from the National Institutes of Health as part of the AIDS Clinical Trials Group. Multiple nonprofit organizations were created to raise funds and awareness. The Names Project, which created a massive quilt with panels bearing the names of those who died from AIDS, launched a 20-city, 12,000-mile tour in April 1988 at Pauley Pavilion.

In 1992, the UCLA AIDS Institute was established under the direction of internationally respected virologist Irvin S.Y. Chen. The institute bridges research in multiple disciplines drawing on the expertise of more than 160 researchers in the fight against HIV and AIDS. UCLA physicians have made significant contributions to HIV/AIDS research in the areas of prevention, treatment and education. Over the years, there have been numerous medical discoveries, including that by Yvonne J. Bryson and her pediatrics colleagues, whose research significantly reduced the transmission of HIV from mother to baby and led the way for global advances in prevention of mother-to-child transmission.

The institute's Clinical AIDS Research and Education (CARE) Center, which has seen patients since 1981, concentrates on evaluation, treatment and drug trials for men, women and children with HIV. Led by Ronald A. Mitsuyasu, a major investigator of gene therapy and potential vaccine treatments for HIV, the center opened an off-campus clinic in 2007 through the support of Arnold Klein, American Foundation for AIDS Research co-founder, and actress and AIDS activist Elizabeth Taylor, who lent her name to its endowment. "The patients at the CARE Center receive the best treatment available anywhere," said Taylor at the dedication, "which is why the CARE Center has one of the best survival rates of any HIV clinic in the country."

In 1993, tennis champion Arthur Ashe was selected to receive UCLA's highest alumni honor, the Edward A. Dickson Alumnus of the Year Award, presented by the UCLA Alumni Association. Ashe had contracted HIV through a blood transfusion during heart surgery in the 1980s, and had kept quiet about his illness until 1992, when he became an outspoken activist.

"When this virus is finally defeated—and it will be—we want to be able to look back and say to all concerned that we did what we had to do, when we had to do it, and with all the resources required," Ashe said in a video played during his tribute. The award was given posthumously—he died four months before the ceremony. (In 1997, the campus honored his memory in naming the Arthur Ashe Student Health and Wellness Center.)

As UCLA marked a quarter century after the identification of the first AIDS patients, Levey said: "We have gone from utter despair and fear to an era of hope, to an era of prevention, to an era in which there have been new medications that have been developed that in many instances turned AIDS from a fatal disease into a chronic disease.

"Now we enter an era where although it's going to be an amazing challenge as we've found out already, we do have hope ultimately for a vaccine, for prevention and/or treatment of this dreadful disease."

"CORPORATE CITIZENS"

Throughout the 1980s, UCLA's national and international reputation continued to grow, and "UCLA" took on global name-brand recognition.

In August 1979, the Bruins baseball team—defending Pacific 10 champions—made their international debut in Japan, playing eight games in 10 days starting with Chuo University, the national collegiate champion. A year later, the UCLA football team trounced Oregon State (34–3) in Tokyo's 1980 Mirage Bowl, creating a long-lasting local sensation. Young pop star Teppei Shibuya performed his recently recorded hit song "UCLA Feeling" with the UCLA Spirit Squad at a bowl-related event sponsored by the Japanese Alumni Association, which had been established in 1975.

Tourism to campus, especially from Japan, was at its peak, and UCLA initiated scholar exchange programs with several universities in Japan, China and Mexico. "No other American university has, as yet, made an effort to facilitate and coordinate as broadly-based an interaction with Japan as has UCLA," Professor Hans H. Baerwald, director of the UCLA-Japan Exchange Program, told the *Daily Bruin* in 1981. The program credited the development of Japanese business interests in Los Angeles and UCLA's win in the 1976 Rose Bowl (UCLA 23–Ohio State 10) in helping raise UCLA's visibility. Japan Airlines' magazine published a 15-article series on the university with topics ranging from women's liberation to a guide for prospective students. "There are currently some 200 students from Japan studying at UCLA," one article promoted. "Would you like to go to UCLA to study too?"

Ackerman Union had gone through a major expansion under the direction of Donald E. Findley, executive director of the Associated Students from 1970–81. He reinvented a struggling operation—and renovated a building that had been badly damaged during the Vietnam protest years—into a profit-making venture. Findley guided the development of UCLA's emblematic apparel program with precedent-setting licensing programs in Japan and other countries.

As the result of a campuswide contest held by the store in 1972, a student coined the term "Bearwear," launching a merchandising giant. In 1973, a Bearwear section selling everything from sweatshirts to key chains opened in Ackerman Union. Demand for items with the UCLA insignia or the Bruins moniker soared in the label-conscious "go-go '80s."

The new Associated Students Trademarks and Licensing Department brokered domestic and international licensing agreements promoting the brand, while monitoring the use of UCLA's trademark to protect the university's reputation and deter black market sales of the world's best-selling collegiate emblem. A mail-order catalog, featuring students or family members of UCLA faculty and staff members modeling the Bruin clothing, was sent to 170,000 addresses, bringing in more sales.

"It's called 'Bearwear' " and "it's nothing short of an international craze," the *Los Angeles Times* pronounced in October 1979. "Princess Caroline and husband Phillipe

Japanese teen idol Teppei Shibuya performs his hit song, "UCLA Feeling" (above), with backup from Spirit Squad members at an alumni event in Tokyo during the Mirage Bowl weekend. UCLA defeated Oregon State University, 34–3.

Junot are seen jogging in UCLA T-shirts in Paris' Bois de Boulogne, matinee idol Claude Brasseur is shown leaping out of bed in a Bruin shirt in the French film 'Les [Seins] de Glace,' and joggers from Stockholm to Tokyo to Toronto to Teheran sprint out in their blue-and-gold UCLA sports attire."

In its inaugural year Bearwear sold $420,000 in merchandise, compared with $3.2 million in 1981 through catalog and in-store sales. In 1982, $17 million was sold in Japan alone.

It was reputed that in Japan, UCLA's insignia was more popular than the Nike "swoosh" as a fashion statement, and in 1981, a UCLA tennis shoe manufactured by a UCLA licensee was reported as the best-selling Bearwear item there. Capitalizing on this, in 1987 the UCLA Alumni Association branded a pair of "Bruins" athletic shoes trimmed in blue and gold and featuring the UCLA script on the heel support. "The first reaction from most people is surprise—they can't believe there's actually a UCLA shoe," said John E. Kobara, the association's executive director. Within a month 2,000 pairs were sold.

As campus business boomed, student life, too, changed. Gone were bell-bottom jeans and other counterculture styles. Students proudly wore Bearwear to class and, after a tumultuous decade of activism, focused on their own academic advancement. They wanted to have fun and embraced campus traditions, which had waned during the Vietnam War. Greek life was once again popular. The football team was winning and the Rally Committee not only had the new *Bruin* statue to protect from rival USC

Launched in 1973 as a small section of the Associated Students store in Ackerman Union (above right), UCLA's Bearwear apparel (above) became "nothing short of an international craze" in the late 1970s. Heather Locklear (right) is just one of many Bruins who appeared in Bearwear catalogs. The brand continues to expand overseas, particularly in China, where the Beijing outlet (far right) is one of 80 in the country.

Bearwear Fall Stars '79

"Remember the Seniors"

"Look—everybody—notice that elegant gold University seal on our curtain in the Assembly. Is it not a clever, artistic piece of work?" asked the *Cub Californian* in December 1919, recording the first senior class gift ever presented to UCLA. "Look it over carefully—then remember the Seniors."

A source of pride for the students of the new university, the seal on the stage of Millspaugh Hall auditorium on the Vermont Avenue campus marked the beginning of a long-standing—albeit intermittent—tradition at UCLA. Although no comprehensive records were kept, UCLA seniors have been raising money to benefit the campus and memorialize their collective legacy ever since that first graduating class.

During the 1920s, some UCLA students experienced financial difficulty, but were ineligible for loan funds from the University of California because they were reserved exclusively for Berkeley students. Seniors from the classes of 1923 and 1924 raised money to create a loan fund specifically for Southern Branch students.

The Class of 1925, which included the first students to earn Bachelor of Arts degrees and was among the first group

Plaques commemorating senior class gifts since 1988 line Bruin Walk.

known as Grizzlies, presented the university with a large statue of a grizzly bear, in honor of their new totem.

The following year, the seniors, led by 1926 class President Frank S. Balthis, raised $300 to plant a grove of trees on the newly selected Westwood campus to line a "Senior Walk." At the time, such gifts required approval by the University of California Board of Regents, which recommended the gift be accepted and dedicated as requested. In early 1931, about 100 three-foot-high oak saplings were planted along the two walks that approached the Arroyo Bridge. A bronze plaque memorialized, "Senior Walk: the Trees Given by the Class of 1926." The trees and the plaque were removed, however, when the northern end of the arroyo was filled in 1947. A stone bench on the east side of Royce Hall pays tribute to them with the inscription "Trees of 1931."

Raising money for the library has been a popular choice. In 1922, the seniors collected enough money to buy an Oxford English Dictionary for the library at the Vermont Avenue campus. The Class of 1927 raised $300 for "books for the browsing room in the new library" at Westwood. In 1991, seniors donated funds to create the Powell Library 24-Hour Reading Room, and in 1995 the senior class contributed toward technological upgrades for the room.

There have been a couple of gifts for projects that never materialized. During commencement exercises in June 1943, senior Tom Papich gave President Robert Gordon Sproul a check for $250 raised by the graduating class "with the hope that it may be used as part of a fund that would create an International House" similar to those at Berkeley and the University of Chicago. A gift from the Class of 1996 was intended to go toward a bell tower on the new Arthur Ashe Student Health & Wellness Center. Although the bell tower was not constructed, the new building on Bruin Plaza was much-welcomed by a student body that had been accustomed to getting lost on the way to student health in the long, winding corridors of the Center for the Health Sciences. The Ashe Center, which opened in 1997, was the beneficiary of another senior gift: $150,000 for its registration area from the Class of 1994.

In 1963, seniors donated $1,000 for two kiosks to replace old bulletin boards, one on Election Walk and the other in front of the student union. The Class of 1967 decided to buy the Isamu Noguchi piece, *Garden Elements*, to add to the newly built sculpture garden.

Like many other campus traditions, class gifts lapsed during the 1970s. In the early 1980s, the Undergraduate Students Association Council made gifts on behalf of the student body averaging between $2,000 and $4,000, and on occasion donated unspent annual funds to causes like scholarships

or UniCamp. Then, in 1987, the Student Alumni Association (SAA) formally revived the tradition by organizing a fundraising campaign among seniors that brought in more than $17,000, enough to finance a speaker's podium for Meyerhoff Park.

SAA's Class Gift Campaign grew robust in subsequent years, giving seniors a chance to participate more directly and select a symbolic gift, rather than through default student fees managed by student government.

"Soon we'll be leaving UCLA," wrote Jennifer T. Poulakidas, executive director of SAA's 1989 Senior Class Cabinet, in the senior handbook. "We'll leave behind a lot of memories of good times and good friends—memories that will not fade. But it is up to us to see that the memory of our time together on campus doesn't fade either."

In commemoration of Royce Hall's 60th anniversary, the Class of 1989 raised more than $170,000 toward the creation of a fountain to anchor the west side of Royce quad at the top of Janss Steps. An inscription pays tribute to the class and quotes Chinese philosopher Lao-Tzu (604–531 B.C.): "A journey of a thousand miles must begin with a single step." (In 2004, the fountain was named for Ralph and Shirley Shapiro, in recognition of the couple's philanthropy to UCLA.)

SAA continued managing the senior gift campaign until 2002, when it was transferred to the UCLA Fund. Subsequent senior classes have contributed thousands of dollars for gifts such as lifetime email forwarding (Class of 2003) and undergraduate research (Class of 2006). Senior class gifts from 1988 onward have been memorialized with a bronze plaque on Bruin Walk.

The Shapiro Fountain anchoring Royce quad was a gift of the Class of 1989, which raised more than $170,000 toward its construction.

vandals, but it also had a Victory Bell to polish. The Student Alumni Association—created in 1984 in part to rekindle student traditions—was taking the long-standing musical competition Spring Sing, which had fallen dormant from 1968–78, to greater heights in its new home at the Los Angeles Tennis Center.

Still, student activism did not disappear. It simply took on a new form. The direct action protests of the 1970s were held against the backdrop of a highly publicized war and drew thousands. By the late 1970s, activists were beginning to create change from within the system.

"Chancellor Young was a genius in terms of developing the whole role of students in university governance," said Bobby Grace, 1983 student body president. "Students who were there in the late '70s and '80s had reached a point of sophistication."

Students were increasingly sitting on academic committees, and becoming more active even on the Associated Students Board of Control. The largest and most successful student activism of the 1980s stemmed from the anti-apartheid movement pressing the University of California to divest its investments from companies that did business in South Africa.

Student protests against apartheid in South Africa were visible on campus as early as the mid-1960s. In 1965, a dozen students picketed outside Kerckhoff Hall, preventing a photo shoot for an advertisement in a South African magazine. Anti-apartheid speakers occasionally took to the podium in Hyde Park, and the Collegiate Council on the United Nations presented a panel discussion in Franz Hall. In 1969, the African Studies

Center learned that its journal, which featured the work of five exiled South African writers, had been banned in South Africa.

By the 1970s, universities including Harvard, Princeton and Cornell, had started challenging businesses with operations in South Africa. At the University of California, the Student Body Presidents' Council urged the Board of Regents in 1973 to join an investor research service that examined the social responsibility of corporations, while President Charles J. Hitch recommended opening the regents

investment committee meetings. The regents rejected both ideas and, according to the *Daily Bruin*, "Hitch, whose proposals are hardly ever defeated, downplayed the issue after the meeting, calling it 'no big deal.'" A *Daily Bruin* editorial the following week questioned: "What kind of example do the Regents set for [University of California] students?" The Student Legislative Council sponsored what *The Bruin* called the campus's "first teach-in on racism," and events drawing attention to apartheid followed over the next several years.

In September 1977, the Student Legislative Council unanimously adopted a resolution—drafted by Community Services Commissioner (and future Alumni Association Executive Director) John Kobara—requesting that the University of California divest itself from South Africa and Rhodesia. Key to the resolution was the university's investment of its University of California Retirement System fund "in light of the recent enrollment of Associated Students employees." The resolution was submitted to the regents by Lieutenant Governor Mervyn Dymally in support of his proposal to divest. However, the regents voted against the proposal 11–6, with two abstentions.

Students continued pressing the issue with the board. "There were several discussions on it, and at one of them one of the regents had said: 'Well, your own Associated Students have money and investments in banks and other corporations that do business with South Africa. You should go divest your own stuff first,'" recalled 1981 undergraduate President Fred

Gaines. "So when I became student body president, I said, 'Well, we're gonna do that.'"

Under strong opposition from Findley, a motion to divest the Associated Students Board of Control failed in May 1980 before a volatile crowd of 150. Students with raised fists voiced their anger and took over the meeting table, prompting a recess and consequent meeting behind closed doors. In July 1980, the students led by President-elect and Board of Control Chairman Gaines, were successful in prompting the Associated Students board to divest. All six student members voted to divest, while the four non-students, including Findley and Associated Students Finance Director (and subsequent Executive Director) Jason Reed, voted against doing so.

In March 1981, after an eight-month search for an acceptable banking institution, the Board of Control broke

Berky Nelson, director of the Center for Student Programming (above), talks with students barricading Murphy Hall with a plywood shanty, before they were cleared away by police (left).

50-year-old ties with Security Pacific National Bank and its 12-year-relationship with Bank of America, and moved its accounts to Imperial Bank. "The only effective leverage on South Africa—if you're not going to be violent—is through economics," said graduate student Bob Hess, who wrote the divestment motion. UCLA's student association, the largest in the University of California's nine-campus system, was the last to transfer its funds. The move would "no longer give the Regents an opportunity for finger-pointing," said Board of Control Chairman Rod Gloss.

"Universities, as respected institutions in American society, should continue to lead the fight for ethical investments," wrote *Daily Bruin* News Editor Mary Astadourian in February 1981, introducing a four-part series on ethics and university investments. "Although change is slow, it remains steady nevertheless. The word divestment today carries a meaning that it never had before and university students, presumably future corporate leaders, can't help but become more aware."

A long line of student body presidents—Sam Law (1982), Grace (1983), Gwyn Lurie (1985) and Ron Taylor (1986)—continued driving students in applying pressure. While in 1979 the Board of Regents had used its votes as a shareholder

of General Motors to oppose the company's dealings in South Africa, the board still had not divested its broad holdings.

On campus, the Associated Students Board of Control considered banning Coca-Cola—UCLA students' drink of choice, making up almost 10 percent of campus food sales with 1.5 million cups and 200,000 cans consumed annually—for its business ties to South Africa. But a compromise was reached to serve Dr Pepper as an alternative beverage choice. Ironically, it was soon discovered that Coca-Cola bottled Dr Pepper. While Executive Director Reed said that the Associated Students would only sell the beverage in its fountain form, four months after the Associated Students began serving the soda,

Coca-Cola announced plans to acquire Dr Pepper. The vending contract with the soft-drink giant was not renewed, and Coca-Cola conducted business with the Associated Students on a day-to-day basis under the previous agreement terms. (While the merger did not go through, in September 1986, Coca-Cola announced it would sell its holdings in South Africa.)

Amid growing national concern, former UCLA student body President Gaines, serving as student regent during 1984–85 while attending Berkeley's law school, presented a divestment proposal to the Board of Regents in January 1985. Gaines had suggested to the *Daily Bruin* that the University of California "can divest now because we are a leader, or we can do it later because we are embarrassed." The regents voted unanimously to review their investment policies, and in June, created a committee chaired by Chancellor Young to review investments with companies that operate in South Africa on a case-by-case basis.

Within a year, demonstrations took hold on university campuses nationwide. At UCLA, several thousand gathered at Murphy Hall on April 23, 1985, in a peaceful protest believed to be the largest demonstration since the mid-70s Vietnam War-era.

"We don't stand alone here today," student body President Lurie told the crowd. "We stand together with

Mayor Tom Bradley and Senator Alan Cranston speak to 100 students gathered at Bruin Plaza, eliciting cheers after the politicians expressed their support for divestment.

students from all over the country. ... Today we even stand together with our sisters and brothers from USC." Lurie stated that the media had misrepresented the students' activism. "We are not the Free Speech Movement of the '80s," she said, alluding to the direct action tactics adopted by Berkeley students in the 1960s. Some students told the *Los Angeles Times* that they joined the demonstration not only because of their anti-apartheid beliefs, but because they resented, in the words of one student, being called "do-nothing, care-nothing, out-for-ourselves yuppies."

The protest included a staged sleep-in at Murphy Hall that had been prearranged with the administration but ended with 20 students being cleared out by campus police on April 25 after they refused to leave; 18 students were cited for trespassing and two were arrested. Lurie said she respected the protesters for their commitment but expressed disappointment in their actions. "Up to this point we had good relations with the administration," she told the *Daily Bruin*, noting that arrests were not part of the plan. "Loud statements can be made without breaking the law."

UCLA activists kept up the momentum. They pitched tents on Schoenberg quad, calling the area "Freedom City," and lived in them for several weeks. In spring 1986, students built a shanty at the foot of Bruin Walk, moving it around campus during protests. The efforts garnered major media attention and attracted politicians, including Mayor (and alumnus) Tom Bradley and U.S. Senator Alan Cranston, who came to meet with the demonstrators.

The issue faced firm opposition from University of California President Gardner, when Governor Deukmejian, citing increased bloodshed in South Africa, shifted his stance and called for full divestiture of state government and the University of California. On July 18, 1986, the Board of Regents voted 13–9 to approve a plan drafted by the governor to divest its $3.1 billion portfolio over four years. The action was "by far the single largest divesture move by any single public or private university in the United States, exceeding even the combined amount divested by all other U.S. colleges and universities to date," according to the *Los Angeles Times*.

UCLA law school graduate and member of UCLA Alumni for Divestment, Carolyn Ferstman, told the *Times*, "I don't think that Deukmejian would have come up with his own divestment plan without student protest."

Leslie Gilbert-Lurie, who served as student regent in 1980–81 while a UCLA undergraduate, said the 1980s provided a conducive environment for students to organize around divestment. "It was a sign of the times," Gilbert-Lurie reflected. "We had the luxury to think of things like divestment. ... Things were relatively conservative but calm, we could think of being corporate citizens."

CHAPTER 1

"So Far, So Fast"

1989–1997

Above: The decade was awash with protests against both regents policy and California Proposition 209, which ended the consideration of race, ethnicity and gender in admissions by public institutions.

Opposite: "Seventy-five years ago, this was just a tiny two-year … college on a dirt road in Hollywood," President Bill Clinton tells a packed Pauley Pavilion on the occasion of UCLA's 75th anniversary in 1994. "Now, it is one of the leading research institutions in the world, and a bridge to the future for tens of thousand of Americans and people who come from all around the world."

*P*ropelled by the prosperity of the 1980s and the high-reaching vision of Chancellor Charles E. Young and campus leaders, UCLA entered the 1990s a far more renowned and sophisticated institution than it had been a mere decade prior.

"In society and at UCLA, change is occurring at a phenomenal rate," Young said during an October 1991 "State of the Campus" address in Royce Hall, the first such presentation of his 23-year tenure. "This places new pressures and demands on the university, but it also presents us with exciting and unprecedented opportunities."

"The theme we have adopted is one of accelerated change," Young proclaimed. "But even more significant than the growth in our size has been the growth in our complexity as an institution."

By historical measures, UCLA was still a young university. Approaching the 75th anniversary of its founding, it had already realized a level of formidable growth and academic accomplishment unparalleled by any other university established in the 20th century.

Since 1968, UCLA had added more than 7,000 students and 10,000 faculty and staff members, for a total campus population of 55,000 in 1990. In fact, UCLA possessed the largest population on the smallest land area of any University of California general campus. The number of facilities had doubled, and an ambitious plan was underway that would add another 4.5 million square feet of assignable space—more than was contained by the entire Riverside campus.

By 1992, UCLA's operating budget topped $1.5 billion. Research funding exceeded the $300 million mark for the first time, while private giving rose to $113 million—the largest amount raised by any University of California campus.

An analysis by consulting firm KPMG reported UCLA as a top employer in Los Angeles County, with an annual impact on the national economy of $4 billion. By mid-decade, the U.S. Postal Service assigned UCLA its own ZIP code (90095), and the telecommunications switch serving the campus was larger than that of most midsize American cities.

Reflecting rapid demographic changes in California, the composition of the freshman class changed from 67 percent Caucasian in 1980 to 64 percent ethnic minority in 1991. Not only had UCLA attracted the most diverse entering class of any major research university in the country, it had done so while the high school grade-point average and SAT scores of its admitted freshmen reached a 20-year high.

"Our mission is to provide the finest and most challenging education to this growing mosaic of young people and help them learn to build the coalitions of common purpose that must be a counterpressure to the potential separation which flows from diversity," Young told the Legislative Assembly of the Academic Senate in November 1990. "The rapid pace of change in the world today occasionally outstrips the ability of tradition-bound institutions such as ours to respond. But it is imperative that we not only get out in front on this issue, but lead."

The end of the Cold War sent California's economy—buffered for years by federal defense spending and the aerospace industry—into a downturn that lasted longer than the national recession. Although the preceding restoration of state funding by Governor George Deukmejian helped the University of California weather the early 1990s, state support dropped almost 25 percent in the first three years of the decade. Young and other UCLA leaders, anticipating a permanent shift in the state's funding ability, implemented cost-saving measures and a priority-setting framework, including a restructuring of the professional schools, intended to preserve the university's overall academic quality.

A string of natural disasters and the Los Angeles riots of spring 1992 also adversely affected the economy. During the riots, UCLA was closed for several days—only the second time in its history—as a citywide curfew was imposed and the National Guard was dispatched to quell the widespread violence. Although looters raided Westwood Village, the campus and UCLA's William Andrews Clark Memorial Library in the West Adams District of South Central Los Angeles were untouched. Two years later, however, UCLA would not be spared from the devastating Northridge earthquake, which damaged some of the campus's iconic landmarks and accelerated comprehensive seismic retrofit plans.

In May 1994, UCLA formally celebrated a jubilant diamond anniversary with President Bill Clinton, who addressed a packed Pauley Pavilion, noting that Angelenos had "experienced earthquakes of all kinds, not just the real

earthquake of January, but social and economic upheavals." He added: "The trends that are shaking and remaking our entire society have hit California first and hardest."

Through all this, UCLA continued to beckon. "I call this the year of the thrill seeker," Rae Lee Siporin, director of admissions, told the faculty and staff newspaper UCLA Today in September 1994. "We've had the earthquake, the fires, floods and everything else, and they've decided to come to Los Angeles anyway." More students than had been anticipated—between four and five percent—enrolled. An increasing number of new students were interested in living on campus, and UCLA responded by implementing a bold plan that aimed to more than double student housing over the next decade.

Students consult course textbook lists outside the UCLA Store, October 7, 1994.

By 1995, Young had become an elder statesman of academe, with the longest tenure of any American university chief executive. As political forces converged to ban the use of affirmative action, first from University of California admissions and later from all of the state's public institutions, the chancellor made a firm public stand, as he had so many times before. This time, he would not succeed.

As chancellor for nearly 29 years, Young had signed two-thirds of all the diplomas ever issued by UCLA while overseeing the student body's transformation into the most diverse in the nation. When Young unexpectedly announced his resignation in February 1996, it signaled the end of a remarkable era.

A "STATE-ASSISTED" INSTITUTION

While the 1980s presented the University of California with a boon in state funding, the 1990s brought unprecedented cuts to the university's state budget allocation. Declining tax revenues in the wake of 1978's Proposition 13 were compounded by the 1988 passage of Proposition 98, which committed the state to spend a minimum 40 percent of its general fund plus an annual increase toward K–12 schools and community colleges.

From the mid-1970s until 1990, California's economy often outperformed the nation's by large margins, as seen through personal income and employment growth. However, the national recession of 1990 hit California surprisingly harder than other parts of the country, and the state struggled years longer to recover. The decline of aerospace and other military-related industries at the end of the Cold War, coupled with a slump in real estate, contributed to significant job losses and an unemployment rate higher than the nation's. Weak consumer spending and reduced tax revenues led the state into a projected $10 billion deficit and newly elected Governor Pete Wilson proposed a slate of tax increases and spending cuts.

To offset state reductions to the University of California's 1991–92 budget, Wilson recommended a 20 percent student fee hike. Facing a budget shortfall of $296 million, the Board of Regents went further, boosting undergraduate fees by 40 percent to $2,274 per year—the largest single increase in the history of the system.

"A Tough Blow, but UC Had to Raise Fees," headlined a February 1991 *Los Angeles Times* editorial that stated, "By their actions, the regents acknowledged that given the anticipated $10 billion deficit faced by the state—and in the absence of new and higher levels of taxation—those who depend on the government to pay the bills must decide their priorities and prepare to make sacrifices."

The URSA Lady

Any UCLA student who has called to enroll in classes by phone will remember URSA—the automated computer system officially titled University Records System Access. But the familiar, vaguely comforting monotone at the other end of the line that talked anxious students through the registration process was no computer-generated voice. There was a real person behind URSA: 1965 alumna Anita Cotter.

Cotter, who started work in the Registrar's Office after graduation and served as university registrar from 2004 until retiring in 2011, was the recorded voice for URSA from the system's inception in 1989. She had no idea at the time that she would achieve an almost cult-like following. "I didn't think it would be that big a deal," Cotter said.

Students have asked for her autograph, and during Spring Sing she performed a skit in which she pretended to date the Moviefone guy. On occasion when she was overheard by a student behind the windows of the Registrar's Office, she would get an immediate sign of recognition, "Oh! You're the URSA Lady!" While Cotter acknowledged she was sometimes hesitant to talk in a public setting, she found the recognition endearing.

She kept a scrapbook full of mementos collected over time. A note she found on her car read: "Sometimes when we are sad, we call you to make us feel better. You are what is good about UCLA. Thank you—you give us classes." It was signed, with love, from "the student body of UCLA, represented by fellow Lot 32 parkers."

Her favorite, however, was a 1996 *Daily Bruin* column that gave the reasons why the URSA Lady would be the ultimate girlfriend. Among them: "She's always home when you call. ... She knows everything about you. ... Even if she gets mad and hangs up on you, you can always call her right back and she'll act like nothing happened."

In 2002, when the phone system was replaced by online registration, an audio clip of Cotter's voice with her signature tag line was added to the website for loyal fans. Gooooo Bruins!

Dear URSA Lady,
We ♥ you!
(Heart stands for
L-O-V-E!)
Sometimes when
we are sad, we call
you to make us feel
better. You are
what is good about
UCLA. Thank you—
you give us classes.
Love,
The student body
of UCLA, represented
by fellow Lot 32
parkers.

A note left on the car of Associate Registrar Anita Cotter, a.k.a. the URSA Lady, in the 1990s.

Amid some student protest, there was also understanding. "If we intend to preserve UCLA's high academic quality, a 40 percent student fee increase, although unfortunate, seems inevitable," declared a *Daily Bruin* editorial, adding "students won't be the only ones to suffer."

The hikes generated $40.5 million, and the university implemented salary freezes, staff reductions, enrollment cuts and deferred maintenance to help make up the rest. Still, UCLA and the other system campuses needed to cut an additional $20 million from their 1991–92 budgets. By 1993–94, UCLA had sustained a five-year reduction of $111 million, roughly 25 percent of its state funding.

Students saw their annual fees more than double. A freshman entering in fall 1990 paid $1,820, compared with $3,727 three years later. Higher "differential" fees were implemented for professional school students—$3,000 per year for those in medicine, dentistry and veterinary services, and $4,000 for law and business programs.

With an overfunded University of California Retirement Plan, the university system implemented a Voluntary Early Retirement Incentive Program that reduced salary expenditures while allowing professors to be recalled to teach. More than 400 faculty members participated in the program at UCLA. "It was a way of ... unloading costs off the operating budget and putting them on a retirement system," Young said. "It was a way of dealing with those cuts without losing faculty or losing the ability to hire new faculty."

Young streamlined the administration to achieve an additional $1 million in salary savings. He created an executive committee and appointed Andrea L. Rich as executive vice chancellor and chief operating officer. (The appointment made Rich, who served as acting chancellor in Young's absence, UCLA's highest-ranking female executive ever.)

Further cuts would be made with a more selective focus—or the campus could risk mediocrity, the chancellor held.

"If we thought the cuts in state support were temporary and likely to be restored soon—as indeed we had optimistically thought in previous years—we might continue to spread the cuts fairly uniformly across our campus," Young said. "Indeed, I believe that the overall fiscal structure of the University of California has shifted permanently from that of a state-supported institution to a state-assisted institution. It's highly unlikely that state support, as a percentage of the university's resources, will ever return to the levels we have enjoyed historically."

According to Young, in 1992, faculty and student leaders implored him "to make hard choices, to set academic priorities and to distribute cuts selectively based upon those priorities." To that end, Young, Rich and Michael E. Granfield, vice chancellor for academic planning and budget, devised a plan that would

become known as the Professional Schools Restructuring Initiative, or PSRI. It reduced the number of UCLA's professional schools from 13 to 10 in an effort to save $8 million.

Under the initiative, the College of Letters and Science was classified as the highest priority, along with the schools of medicine, law and engineering; the UCLA Library; the ethnic studies programs; and International Studies and Overseas Programs. These were identified as essential "if we are to affirm the Master Plan [for Higher Education] and provide exemplary training and research to our increasingly multicultural and international society," Young said. While not exempt from cuts, they could expect smaller reductions than other units.

A second group of professional schools—theater, film and television; education; management; arts; and dentistry—were expected to absorb larger cuts because they were viewed as being more able to generate outside funding to support their activities, or had recently benefited from an infusion of resources.

The five remaining schools—architecture and urban planning; social welfare; public health; nursing; and library and information science—would be reorganized or consolidated into other areas. Urban planning, social welfare and the health policy components of public health would be part of a new School of Public Policy—achieving one of Young's long-standing goals. The remaining components of public health were transferred to the School of Medicine. Architecture was merged with the arts to create the School of the Arts and Architecture. The library school faculty would be transferred to the Graduate School of Education, and master's degree and doctoral programs in library studies would be eliminated. Nursing would concentrate on graduate training while the small undergraduate nursing program would be phased out.

The restructuring plan was met with sharp opposition from affected faculty members and students, and by an unforeseen public outcry. "It takes years to build a tradition of excellence and only hours to destroy it," said Professor John Friedmann, head of the urban planning program in the Graduate School of Architecture and Urban Planning. Friedmann was one of 250 faculty members who gathered in Rolfe Hall in October 1993 to hear Young outline the initiative while students protested outside. The cuts were painful, Young acknowledged, but he was confident the changes would make UCLA better in the long term.

"Chuck Young built this place, and, believe me, he loves all his children," Rich said in the spring 1994 issue of *UCLA Magazine*. "For him to have to say that he is going to invest in some of his children more than others was excruciating."

Young and Rich convened numerous meetings with deans and other academic leaders, as well as students. Young also presented the plan to the Board of Regents. "They kept saying, 'This is the only place within the University of

California, as far as we know, that anybody's ever sat down and seriously tried to develop priorities and then act on those priorities in the implementation of a budget process,'" Young later recalled. "I think UCLA's standing went up in that regard."

After months of careful deliberation, a few alterations were made. Instead of eliminating its graduate programs, the Graduate School of Library and Information Science was merged with the Graduate School of Education to form the Graduate School of Education and Information Studies.

The undergraduate nursing program considered harsh options. "There was a time when it was very, very dark after that PSRI, and [the School of Nursing] said, 'Why don't we just go up to UCSF and merge with that school of nursing?'" recalled Donna L. Vredevoe, acting dean of nursing from 1995–96. "That would've been the end of this program."

Instead, the baccalaureate nursing program suspended admissions in 1996, but it was not eliminated. "Immediately after they said they were going to close the baccalaureate, we sat around and thought, 'Well, what are our strategies?'" said Vredevoe, who was later appointed vice chancellor for academic personnel in 2001. "The strategy that we chose was a good one, and that was to put it in a dormant state where it could be reactivated." In 2006, when California experienced a statewide nursing shortage, a Bachelor of Science in nursing was re-established—the only one within the University of California.

Ultimately, the changes strengthened the schools, Young said, by forcing them to eliminate peripheral activities and focus on what needed to be done. He added: "The actions we were taking were in the best interests of the university and ... whether they recognized it or not, the units that were involved."

Bicycles near Bruin Walk, outside the Men's Gymnasium, c.1992.

PLANNING FOR THE 21ST CENTURY

Despite budget cuts, UCLA continued to plan for the future and in 1990 embarked on its third long-range development plan, laying the groundwork for a variety of new projects, including several designed as income-generating operations.

In an effort to appease community activists who expressed objections about large-scale construction projects and associated traffic congestion, the 15-year plan's overall density was scaled back by 750,000 square feet. An academic conference center that had been envisioned for the southwest campus on Lot 32—UCLA's vast parking lot fronting Wilshire Boulevard between Veteran and Gayley avenues—was eliminated from the plan. UCLA leaders also pledged to limit campus traffic.

Over protests from Westwood homeowners, the regents in September 1990 approved plans to build a 100-room guest house on the corner of Tiverton and Le Conte avenues to accommodate the families of UCLA Medical Center patients. "This is a sensibly, tastefully designed facility [that will] render public service," University of California President David Pierpont Gardner told the regents. "[It has] a pretty compelling purpose ... not for aggrandizing UCLA, but UCLA rendering a service for those who need it." Tiverton House, a self-supporting enterprise, opened in 1993, providing patients' families with an alternative to sleeping in hospital waiting rooms or their cars, as had often been the case.

Construction was completed in 1990 on the UCLA Medical Plaza, a trio of medical outpatient facilities on Westwood Plaza commonly known as the 100, 200 and 300 buildings. "This project was developed to meet the needs of a changing health care system, which has shifted its focus from the inpatient to the outpatient setting," Raymond Schultze, director of the UCLA Medical Center and administrative vice chancellor, said in *UCLA Today*. The medical center was treating more than 300,000 outpatients per year.

First to open was the 300 building, a four-story structure on the south end of the plaza, which housed outpatient and training programs for the Neuropsychiatric Institute (and later physical rehabilitation programs). It was followed by the 200 building (renamed the Peter Morton Medical Building in 2003 after a significant gift by the Hard Rock Cafe co-founder). A six-story facility in the center of the plaza, it contained an ambulatory surgery center with 12 operating rooms, as well as radiology, pharmacy and laboratory services.

The 100 building, a seven-story L-shaped structure, was owned and operated under a long-term lease by a developer specializing in private medical facilities. The building was designed to appeal to UCLA-affiliated physicians who had been working in private practice elsewhere in the region, in an

effort to bring them—and their patients—to campus. It also increased the business of faculty practices that previously had low profiles. The faculty dental group, for example, flourished after moving from a basement in the dental school. "Providing greater opportunities for the faculty to produce income through practice we could not only [eliminate] a deficit there but make that a profit center," Young said. (By 1998, about 25 percent of acute medical care being provided in the hospital was referred by physicians from the 100 building. The regents bought the edifice and ownership was transferred in 2009.)

Mindful of rapid expansion, UCLA leaders implemented conservation and recycling efforts to minimize environmental impacts. The campus had started a water conservation program in the mid-1980s that by 1990 reduced water consumption by 18 percent. In 1990, UCLA began a program that diverted approximately 70 percent of its solid waste—previously sent to landfills—into recyclable energy or reusable products.

"UCLA cares very deeply about the quality of life in this region," Young told the Chancellor's Associates in September 1990. "We will continue to search for ways to improve the environment and conserve our scarce natural resources."

The UCLA Energy Systems Facility, known as the "chiller" or "cogeneration" plant, opened in 1993. Capable of generating 85 percent of campus energy needs, the plant could produce chilled water, steam and electricity—in the process, reducing air pollution while saving money and energy.

In addition to infrastructure improvements, planners— under the direction of Vice Chancellor for Capital Programs

Peter W. Blackman—had to re-envision how to work with less open space, and simultaneously keep a coherent aesthetic throughout the campus's physical evolution.

"In the mid-80s the perception on campus was that UCLA's land area was nearly built-out," said Campus Architect Charles "Duke" Warner Oakley. "However, when the campus was really analyzed it became clear that there was plenty of room for new development—we just had to change our thinking about how to shape space." UCLA architects and engineers realized they could create a denser campus using "infill" techniques that took advantage of intricate spaces, while revitalizing the campus's Romanesque theme to provide greater architectural continuity. "The people who had gone before had built on the easy pieces of land," Oakley explained. "Now we would have to build on hillsides or on the periphery where new infrastructure would be needed."

Importance was given to achieving greater sensitivity to open spaces, landscaping, walkways and courtyards, "in order to preserve what we have created, a campus in a garden," Young said. "We are in a different mode of development and we must, therefore, plan quite differently than we have in the past." A parking structure was hidden under the Intramural Field, preserving the wide-open green space. The hasty 1958 addition to the back of Powell Library for book stacks—an earthquake and fire hazard—was demolished. A massive shear wall, clad in brick and stylistically referencing the Romanesque of the original building, fortified the building's south side, while opening into an inviting courtyard. Other buildings would be "laminated"—added to with new façades more compatible with the Romanesque tradition while creating additional program space—including three serial additions to the John Wooden Center and the expanded Hugh and Hazel Darling Law Library.

Preserving the campus's pristine appearance was an important aspect of the chancellor's long-term vision for UCLA. Young was notorious for jogging on campus in the early morning and observing maintenance details that he would report back to his staff for immediate attention, whether it be scattered litter, uncollected food trays or grass that needed mowing.

"The No. 3 sprinkler on the Royce quad, you know the one I'm talking about, that's facing Royce," Young might say as he walked into an 8 a.m. staff meeting. "It's spraying water all over the place. I want that fixed right now."

The 1990s brought about a dramatic change in student housing through the implementation of a formal plan that began to shift the university from a predominantly commuter campus to a residential one.

Provost Clarence A. Dykstra had championed a vibrant on-campus residential community in the mid-1940s, but those plans were pre-empted by post-World War II budget

The John Wooden Center (top) was transformed through a series of additions that "laminated" it to blend in with the campus's Romanesque theme (above).

Above: Two students in Sproul Hall, c.1984, and another pair (left) in the mid-2000s.

Far left: University of California President Emeritus David S. Saxon (second from right) and his wife, Shirley, dedicate the Saxon Residential Suite Complex, 1987.

concerns. In the early 1950s, after Dykstra's sudden death, other postwar building needs took priority. After a steady influx of veterans sought higher education at the University of California under the GI Bill, the regents established a guideline in 1955 recommending that the larger campuses—UCLA and Berkeley—accommodate 25 percent of their students in residence halls, and that the smaller ones house 50 percent. But the student unrest of the 1960s and 1970s made it difficult to pursue new housing for undergraduates. There was also a decline in demand, evident by the lack of a waiting list in 1970. After the Vietnam War ended, students once again sought creature comforts on campus.

By 1976, at least 3,000 students could not be accommodated. From the mid-1970s through the 1980s, the on-campus housing program operated at full capacity. To address demand, many of the dorm rooms, originally designed for two occupants, were converted into so-called triples by adding bunk beds and a loft berth over a third desk and closet.

Two residential suite complexes—later named after former University of California Presidents Charles J. Hitch

and David S. Saxon—opened in 1981, the first new housing built in decades. The 1983 Long Range Development Plan incorporated a goal to house 25 percent of enrolled students through a combination of university residence halls and privately owned apartments within one mile of campus.

Despite a 33 percent increase in housing, demand grew steadily each year with more than 4,000 wait-listed in fall 1986. About 17 percent of enrolled students lived in university residences that year; another 16 percent lived within a mile of campus in private housing. A committee representing student, administrative and academic interests developed a master plan to address the situation. Led by Sam J. Morabito, business enterprises administrator (and future vice chancellor for administration), the committee made recommendations that formed the basis for the 1986 UCLA Student Housing Master Plan, which called for 50 percent of UCLA's 33,000 students to be housed on campus or in nearby private accommodations by 2000.

In the fall of 1991, Sunset Village, a $90 million student residential complex, opened on the northwest campus, ushering in the first wave of what would be numerous housing additions in the years ahead. Unlike the high-rise dormitories, the new units resembled miniature apartments and boasted individual heating and cooling units, as well as highly coveted private bathrooms.

Not only did Sunset Village create housing for some 1,500 students, but the construction of Covel Commons—named for UCLA physician and donor Mitchel D. Covel and his wife, Susan, after they made a gift to fulfill a pledge that had fallen through because of the housing recession—offered a computer lab, study lounge, meeting space, dining hall and other amenities. Students could now mingle with resident professors, get tutoring and counseling, do homework, or just relax in an academic community setting. Even freshman seminars were held in the building. Across the way, an arcade and after-hours fast-food hangout named Puzzles provided additional escape. Hilltop, a mini-student union, sold items ranging from school supplies to popular music CDs. Sunset Village created a vibrant residential center that had been sorely missing—permanently changing life on "the hill."

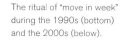

The ritual of "move in week" during the 1990s (bottom) and the 2000s (below).

Life on "the hill" changed in the early 1990s, after the opening of Covel Commons (top), which provides a study lounge, computer lab (center) and premier dining facility (above) among other amenities.

NORTHRIDGE QUAKE ROCKS CAMPUS

At 4:31 a.m. on January 17, 1994, Southern California was hit by a violent earthquake, centered approximately 17 miles north of Westwood in the San Fernando Valley. The 6.7 Northridge earthquake, which left 72 dead and almost 12,000 injured, caused $20 billion in damage and destroyed parts of the region's vast highway system, including a nearby section of the Santa Monica Freeway. The quake, which struck on Martin Luther King Jr. Day, lasted about 30 seconds, knocking out power and igniting several fires throughout the Southland.

At UCLA, windows shattered, doorways buckled, a million books tumbled off library shelves, and some buildings experienced internal flooding and chemical spills. The most serious damage was yet to be assessed. Classes were canceled the following day as inspectors cleared buildings for occupancy, and debris and spills were cleaned up.

Only hours after the temblor, Young, Blackman and Oakley stood on the lawn in front of Royce Hall, watching nervously as structural engineers surveyed ominous cracks visible in the building's trademark towers. When John A. "Trailer" Martin descended from one tower and Thomas A. Sabol from the other, they cautioned, "Back up guys—don't stand so close."

During the earthquake, the towers rocked more than the solid base below. As a result, the four concrete columns of each tower cracked all the way through, with only the steel reinforcing rods in the center keeping them together. "Another five seconds of rocking and either one—or both—of the towers would have come down and could have gone right through [the roof], depending on whether it fell forward or back," Oakley said.

The building was closed until later in the month, following construction of a "mine tunnel" to safely shield individuals who passed under the towers as they walked to and from classrooms. Royce Hall's auditorium, the centerpiece venue of UCLA's performing arts programs, was shuttered for the next four years while Royce was repaired and restored.

Kerckhoff Hall also sustained major damage as the earthquake rotated the four 30-ton spires atop the building by six inches. Oakley and his team began the process of figuring out how to remove them without damaging the architectural integrity and historic value of the Gothic-style ornaments. The solution was to cut each spire into three 10-ton pieces and remove them with a crane during a one-week period that required 12 complete evacuations of the building.

The UCLA Medical Center, operating with minimal holiday staffing, remained open in the quake's aftermath and called in emergency staff to handle an influx of patients. A patient and surgical team were rushed by ambulance from St. John's Hospital and Health Center in Santa Monica, which had lost power in the middle of an operation. "The

The 6.7 Northridge Earthquake on January 17, 1994, caused extensive damage on campus, including massive fissures in the iconic towers of Royce Hall (below) and South Campus classrooms (left).

Above: Some students were temporarily trapped in their dorm rooms after toppled furniture blocked doorways, as it did in this room in Sunset Village.

Far right: After the earthquake, a general feeling of uneasiness lingered amid frequent aftershocks and students spent time in the safety of hallways.

Right: Workers restore tiles in Powell Library's 10,000-square-foot Main Reading Room, which suffered damage in the quake, May 1994.

hospital had damage but it continued to function, and thank God, because it served others well," Oakley said. In post-earthquake inspections, it was learned that the UCLA Medical Center suffered extensive structural damage, and the Federal Emergency Management Agency (FEMA) would ultimately give approximately $432 million toward the construction of a new replacement hospital. (The Ronald Reagan UCLA Medical Center opened in 2008.)

Fortunately, at the time of the Northridge earthquake, seismic retrofitting had been completed on the residence halls, and two-thirds of the work on Powell had also been finished—although the library suffered fissures in its ornate tiled ceiling. The 1994 quake caused UCLA to accelerate that program, and many structures remained closed for months—or even years—for reinforcement and repairs, while a labyrinth of chain-link fences and plywood steered pedestrians around the construction.

The seismic plan had its roots in another major Southern California temblor, the 6.6 Sylmar earthquake of 1971. Although UCLA sustained no major damage during that

quake (or from the 6.4 Long Beach quake of 1933), the goal of making all campus buildings earthquake-resistant acquired new urgency. But a plan that would have shored up Royce Hall during renovations in time for the 1984 Olympics, potentially preventing the damage caused by the Northridge quake, met with resistance by President Saxon due to budgetary concerns and was not undertaken.

In September 1985, a joint administration and faculty earthquake safety committee warned that "UCLA's vulnerability is greater than that of any other campus of the University of California." They noted that the campus was in proximity to at least three earthquake fault lines that posed peril: the Santa Monica (Hollywood) fault just south of campus; the Newport-Inglewood fault, whose north end terminates a few miles north of campus; and the well-known San Andreas fault, about 40 miles to the northeast. Ten UCLA buildings were constructed before the 1933 Long Beach temblor (which occurred on the Newport-Inglewood fault), when no seismic standards were required by Southern California building codes. Others, including the high-rise

residence halls, were constructed in the 1950s and 1960s, before additional seismic fortifications were compelled. The report, titled "A Campus at Risk," estimated that 1,500 to 2,000 people would be killed and 4,000 injured on campus if a significant quake struck during an average midweek day.

A *Los Angeles Times* article on the committee's findings quoted Young as saying: "We've made forcible efforts. ... I can't manufacture money." By 1992, however, Young was determined to move forward. "We said: 'Look, we're going to have to do this on our own. If we sit around and wait for the money to do it, it will never get done,'" Young recalled.

A campuswide seismic safety program to address 30 top-priority buildings was implemented, starting with structures identified as "high-risk" and those that had the most potential for loss of life. Accordingly, seismic work began first on the high-rise residence halls as well as Powell Library (the No. 1 priority in the entire University of California system), Moore and Bunche halls and the math sciences building.

Some of the retrofitting necessitated innovative thinking. Before beginning renovations on Powell, campus planners had to figure out how to keep the undergraduate library functioning during construction. They went through the usual litany: Rent

space off-campus? Wouldn't be convenient for students. Bring in trailers? How many would be needed and where would they go? There was no obvious solution—until Oakley took a fortuitous drive along Pacific Coast Highway.

On his way to a Capital Affairs Council meeting to discuss the Powell project, Oakley saw the Cirque du Soleil troupe setting up their performance tent at the foot of the Santa Monica Pier.

"As I drove by I thought, if you can put a theater in a tent, why can't you put a library in a tent?" Oakley recalled, drawing on his knowledge of tensile structures. "So then at Capital Affairs Council, I brought it up. I said, 'How about a tent?' And people actually laughed. They thought I was trying to be funny."

UCLA brought in husband-and-wife team Craig Hodgetts, a UCLA associate professor, and alumna Hsinming Fung of Hodgetts + Fung to design a unique and functional structure. Nestled between the Men's Gymnasium and the Dance Building, "Towell" was a two-story, 36,000-square-foot structure made of shiny aluminum, yellow-and-white canvas, and exposed cables and fasteners. The $3 million facility featured two reading rooms, 500 study carrels and a 40-station

Towell Library, which opened at the foot of Janss Steps on September 21, 1992, was a colorful alternative to Powell Library, which had been shut down for renovation prior to the earthquake.

computer lab. Approximately 150,000 of Powell's volumes and journals were made available in Towell, while the rest were sent to storage.

Towell opened in September 1992 to mixed response from students but rave reviews in the press—even a cover feature in *Architectural Record*.

The New York Times architecture critic Herbert Muschamp wrote, "With its playful air of spontaneity bolted down by innate rigor, the Temporary Powell revives informality as an architectural ideal."

After Powell Library reopened four years later, Towell was briefly used as classroom space, and by the Associated Students as retail space during seismic retrofitting and expansion of the UCLA Store. When it was no longer needed at UCLA, it was given to California State Polytechnic University, Pomona.

A CULTURAL RENAISSANCE

After being out of commission for four years, a refurbished Royce Hall auditorium, complete with improved acoustics, celebrated its grand reopening with a star-studded gala in April 1998. The Center for the Performing Arts marked its return with the world premiere of "Monsters of Grace," an opera by composer Philip Glass. The $68.3 million renovation to the 1,828-seat theater was funded with a combination of FEMA, state and private dollars.

Since the 1930s, programming in Royce had made UCLA a cultural center of Los Angeles. That continued through the 1960s, when the Dorothy Chandler Pavilion, the Mark Taper Forum (home to the former UCLA Theatre Group) and the Ahmanson Theatre emerged in downtown, providing a counterbalance to the Westside arts scene.

Below: Students could access more than 150,000 volumes that had been transferred from Powell Library into the tent-like structure.

Above: Musicians Paul Simon, Stevie Wonder and Don Henley at the gala event marking the grand reopening of Royce Hall, four years after it was shut down for earthquake and seismic renovation, April 4, 1998.

Above: Theater student Nancy Olsen and alumnus David Norton star in a 1948 production of *Suspect*, directed by Professor William W. Melnitz.

Left: Since the 1930s, the checkerboard lobby of Royce Hall has greeted thousands to the performing arts venue.

"Historically, that aspect of UCLA was important and contributed to UCLA's development as a great university ahead of its time," Young said.

But there was one area that UCLA had long wanted to enhance: the visual arts. UCLA sponsored art exhibits on the Westwood campus as early as 1931. The art shows featured works by students, local artists, national exhibitors and on occasion the old masters. In 1953, Frederick S. Wight—from the Institute of Contemporary Art in Boston—joined the faculty on a special appointment that included overseeing UCLA's art galleries. "Through its treasures on display, the university serves the community, and the community in turn supports the university," Wight wrote as a guest columnist in the *Los Angeles Times* in December 1953. "The galleries wish to support the artists and designers of the region in every way possible. They feel a three-fold obligation—to the student, the community, and the practicing artist." By and large, that commitment was carried out, said Charles Speroni, dean of the College of Fine Arts from 1968–79.

Beginning with Franklin D. Murphy's administration, UCLA leaders had hoped to expand further and build an art museum nearby, but off-campus, where it could be more easily reached and not interfere with educational programming or add parking problems.

In the 1980s, industrialist and art collector Norton W. Simon made overtures to UCLA about constructing a museum in Westwood on Lot 32 along Wilshire Boulevard. (The property had been deeded to UCLA by the federal government for medical purposes in 1948 when UCLA was looking for a place to build its hospital; in 1986, Congress lifted the restriction on its use.) The building would have been a western

home for the Norton Simon Museum in Pasadena. There also were plans to build a motion picture theater and house the UCLA Film and Television Archive on the property. Young and Alan F. Charles, vice chancellor for external affairs, spent months talking with Simon to negotiate the arrangement, but Simon backed out. UCLA leaders, however, did not give up on the idea of an art museum.

In 1994, after two years of negotiations, UCLA announced it would be taking over management of the Armand Hammer Museum of Art and Cultural Center, built next to the Occidental Petroleum Corporation headquarters at Wilshire and Westwood boulevards. Longtime Occidental

Left: Noted cellist Yo-Yo Ma instructs music major Elizabeth Wright in a master class in Schoenberg Hall, March 24, 1994.

Below left: Frederick S. Wight (left), director from 1953–1973 of the UCLA Art Galleries, later renamed in his honor.

Below: Art students in Perloff Hall, 1950s.

Chairman Armand Hammer, a noted art collector, had opened the museum in November 1990, just two weeks before his death. Under the arrangement, UCLA's art department, headed by Wight Art Gallery Director Henry T. Hopkins, was responsible for running the museum.

"By developing the Museum as a genuine cultural center," Young said after the announcement, "we will strengthen arts offerings to our students and faculty, assist in revitalizing Westwood Village and provide an exciting cultural program for the community." (More than a decade later, in 2007, the Billy Wilder Theater opened in the Hammer, fulfilling the original vision of creating a public theater for UCLA Film and Television Archive screenings.)

UCLA ultimately did build a museum on campus. For years, 100,000 pieces of ethnic art lay hidden in a cramped basement of one of UCLA's original four buildings. The Museum of Cultural History, located in Haines Hall, was home to one of the largest collections of African and South Pacific art in the United States. Unfortunately, few people were familiar with the distinguished collection due to its obscure location. That changed on September 30, 1992, when the Fowler Museum of Cultural History officially opened its doors in a more prominent and permanent space near the base of Janss Steps.

Established by Chancellor Murphy in 1963 as the Museum and Laboratories of Ethnic Arts and Technology, the museum began as an independent research unit, acquiring artifacts over the years from donations and archaeological digs. It became the Museum of Cultural History in 1971. By 1975, when anthropology Professor Christopher B. Donnan was appointed director, the size and quality of its collections ranked it among the top four university museums in the country. Donnan later recalled the explicit mandate Chancellor Young gave him in their first meeting: "There's been a lot of talk about [a museum building] for many years, but I really want this to happen."

Detailed plans were drawn that included excavating the Arroyo Bridge to create an underground museum, with the south side of the bridge opening into an amphitheater. But those plans were abandoned with the realization that it was unwise to store perishable artifacts underground in a former ravine with a seasonal stream. Finally, Donnan, Young and Vice Chancellor for Institutional Relations Elwin V. Svenson unveiled the vision for a new building that would fully accommodate the immense collection, and be home to the Cotsen Institute of Archaeology. The $22 million structure was funded with private gifts and state resources. It was named in honor of the late Francis E. Fowler Jr., an inventor and avid silver collector, and his sons, Francis III and Philip, the facility's principal benefactors.

The new museum housed 160,000 pieces from the contemporary, historic and prehistoric cultures of Africa, Asia, Oceania and the Americas. Its collections represented

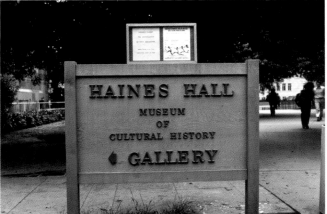

PRESIDENT CELEBRATES UCLA'S 75TH

For the second time in UCLA's history, a sitting U.S. president would address the campus community. Unlike Lyndon B. Johnson's 1964 visit in honor of the University of California's Charter Day, this was a celebration of UCLA's own special day, marking three-quarters of a century since Governor William D. Stephens signed the enabling legislation establishing UCLA.

Nine days before the event, the *Daily Bruin* finally confirmed the wishful speculation that had been circulating for months: President Bill Clinton had accepted UCLA's invitation to speak at its 75th anniversary convocation on May 20, 1994. Blue and gold banners proclaimed the diamond anniversary throughout Westwood, and a commemorative poster designed by American graphic designer Paul Rand adorned the campus.

"Challenging the Future" was selected as the anniversary's theme. "It's ongoing, action-oriented, forward-thinking," John E. Kobara, associate vice chancellor of alumni relations and chair of the anniversary executive committee, told the *Daily Bruin*. "We wanted to say that UCLA has reached a place, but we didn't want to be self-congratulatory."

Students, faculty and staff quickly claimed the 9,000 available tickets for the momentous occasion, held in Pauley Pavilion. For those without a ticket, the event was shown on closed-circuit television at the Los Angeles Tennis Center, Ackerman Grand Ballroom and the Northwest Campus Auditorium near Sproul Hall. Afternoon classes were canceled for security reasons, which also meant there was no need to skip school.

Cheers and whistles drowned out the ceremonial music as Young and Clinton, shaking hands with students along the way, led the procession of dignitaries and academics in full regalia to the stage.

Top left: Established in 1971, the Museum of Cultural History was hidden for years in the basement of Haines Hall, until it opened in the new Fowler Museum building in 1992 (center left).

Below left: One of the Fowler Museum's debut exhibits in 1992 was "Threads of Identity: Maya Costume of the 1960s in Highland Guatemala." The new showrooms were a stark contrast to the museum's once cramped and limited space.

Above: From left, museum Director Christopher B. Donnan details some of the items on display from the permanent Fowler collection to Charles E. Young, Philip Fowler and Franklin D. Murphy.

Below: UCLA's 75th anniversary logo, designed by graphic designer Paul Rand.

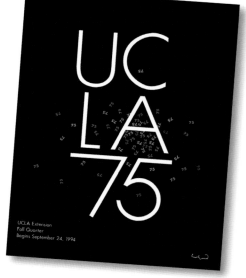

artistic traditions from around the world, and the Fowler was hailed for its rare focus on non-Western artifacts and cultures. Inaugural exhibitions included items on the elephant in African culture, Mayan dress of the 1960s, ancient Peruvian ceramics, and showcased the permanently featured Fowler collection of English, European and American silver.

"We desperately needed a place to exhibit our amazing collection," Donnan told the *Daily Bruin* the day before the museum's opening. "We have one of the world's finest African art collections and we just couldn't abide to students merely passing it in the basement of Haines."

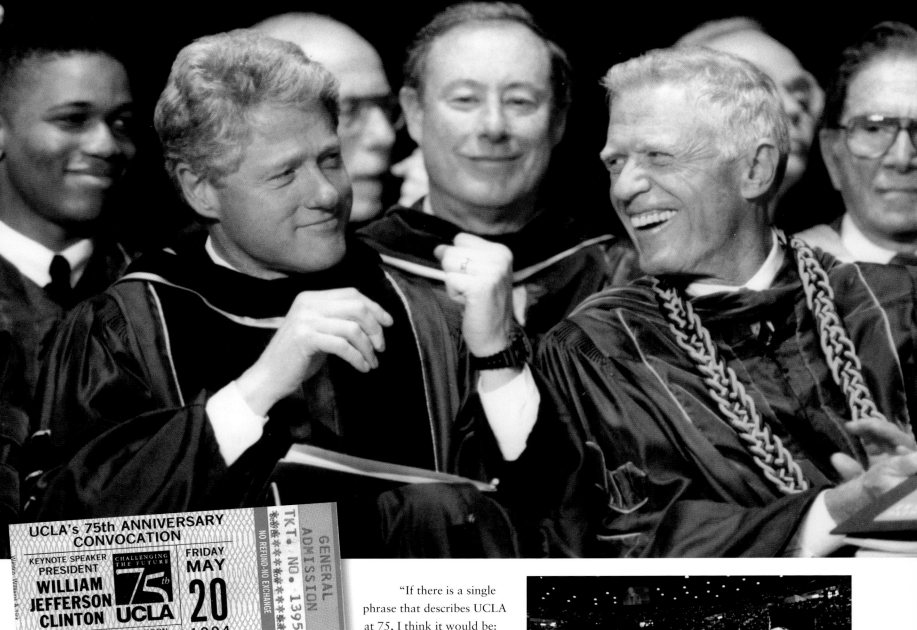

Above: President Bill Clinton (left) and Charles E. Young (right) enjoy a moment during UCLA's 75th anniversary convocation in Pauley Pavilion, which also honored Young's 25 years of service as chancellor.

Right: More than 9,000 tickets were quickly distributed to students, faculty and staff, who heard Clinton describe UCLA as a snapshot of society: "If you look around you at this incredible campus where minorities make up the majority ... you see the future."

"If there is a single phrase that describes UCLA at 75, I think it would be: 'So far, so fast,' " Young said in his welcoming remarks. "In the span of a single human lifetime, UCLA has risen from humble beginnings ... into the ranks of the nation's premier research and liberal arts universities. That distinction owes itself to the devotion and support of all of you—the students, faculty, alumni and friends of UCLA."

The 90-minute ceremony, which also honored Young's 25 years as chancellor, included speeches by 1994 student body President Kate Anderson and Graduate Student Association External Vice President Khosrow Khosravani. Young presented Clinton with the UCLA Medal, the university's highest honor.

In his keynote remarks, Clinton acknowledged UCLA's distinguished history and its culture of achievement and service, then turned his attention directly to the students.

"Americans of my generation have been bombarded by images ... about the so-called Generation X filled with cynics and slackers," he said. "Well, what I have seen today is not a generation of slackers, but a generation of seekers. And I am much encouraged."

The president singled out two UCLA students, Saru Jayaraman and Desiree DeSurra, founders of Women in Support of Each Other, a support group for at-risk teenage girls, as examples of UCLA's best. "Thousands of young people just here on this campus alone have made a decision to make a difference," Clinton said, noting that 4,000 UCLA students were involved in service programs.

The president also described UCLA as a barometer for the 21st century. "If you look around you at this incredible campus where minorities make up a majority, something that will be true for whole states in the not-too-distant future, you see the future."

"A Phoenix Department"

More than 400 students, faculty and community supporters stood outside Murphy Hall on June 7, 1993, to celebrate the end of a 14-day hunger strike and the creation of the César E. Chávez Center for Interdisciplinary Instruction in Chicana and Chicano Studies, culminating a movement that began more than 20 years earlier.

In 1967, the newly created United Mexican-American Students began pushing for increased representation of minority groups on campus, and worked with administrators in efforts that led to the creation of a Mexican-American research center under the umbrella of the UCLA American Cultures Project in February 1969. The research center helped establish an interdisciplinary Chicano studies program in 1973, drawing on faculty and courses from different departments to constitute an undergraduate major in the field.

But the retrenchment in California's social and budget policies during the 1980s, and the recession of the early 1990s, took a toll on the program, reflected in lowered enrollments and graduates. By 1989, funding had dwindled significantly and UCLA suspended new admissions to the program the following year.

Two months later, in April 1990, the Movimiento Estudiantil Chicano de Aztlán (MEChA) organized UCLA students, along with faculty and community members, staging a demonstration calling for the program's elevation to departmental status. An interdisciplinary program, they argued, posed conflicts for faculty members who had a primary obligation to the department in which they were hired, and where tenure was granted.

Negotiations continued for several years and an official proposal gained support in the Academic Senate. After more than three years of discussion, however, having considered the proposal in context of the serious budget cuts UCLA faced, Chancellor Charles E. Young announced on April 28, 1993, that it would not be implemented. The statement came on the eve of labor organizer César Chávez's funeral, timing that fueled emotions.

On May 11, 1993, what started as a peaceful rally challenging Young's decision turned violent when protesters—some from UCLA, others from the community—occupied the UCLA Faculty Center, breaking windows and causing total damage estimated at $27,000. The students locked themselves in a room and refused to come out. Young was in Japan on business and Executive Vice Chancellor Andrea Rich called in the Los Angeles Police Department, which sent more than 200 officers, some in riot gear, to bolster university police and clear out the students.

Almost 100 individuals were arrested; 83 charged with suspicion of felony vandalism and held in jail on a $10,000 bond until UCLA officials requested they be released and that most charges be reduced to trespassing, a misdemeanor. Senior Pablo Palacios said he participated in the peaceful portion of the march

Below: Hunger strikers, including Cindy Montañez, begin camping in tents outside Murphy Hall on May 25, 1993. One of nine individuals who began the 14-day water-only fast, Montañez was the first to require medical attention after collapsing on the fourth day.

Below: United Farm Workers co-founder Dolores Huerta speaks at a spring 1993 rally calling for the creation of a Chicano studies department. More than a decade later, a department was authorized and named for civil rights leader and United Farm Workers co-founder César E. Chávez.

because he believed that Young's decision and its timing were "a slap in the face." Although Palacios emphasized that he did not approve of the vandalism, he said he understood the anger behind it: "This is a way to make the students visible because often the university makes us invisible."

UCLA allowed some students who had been arrested to work off their debt by performing community service at a local nonprofit where they were credited $10 an hour. A year after the protest, UCLA dropped criminal misdemeanor charges against one student and agreed not to prosecute six others in connection with the Faculty Center protest damage, after an arrangement was made between the university and community leaders whereby UCLA accepted *The Mug*, a painting by Chicano artist Gronk, estimated to be worth between $15,000 and $18,000. The university also accepted a second piece of art from a different artist, valued at $7,000. Gronk's work was subsequently installed in the Faculty Center.

The movement for a full-fledged department continued with peaceful demonstrations, picking up momentum and support from state legislators including Tom Hayden and Art Torres, and also U.S. congressman Xavier Becerra. On May 25, five students, one professor and three community members began a hunger strike to protest Young's decision and the recent disciplinary action against student protesters. A village of tents sprang up outside Murphy Hall. The debate raged on campus and in the media, drawing national attention and numerous visitors ranging from actor Edward James Olmos to Mexican-American teamsters who circled past Murphy Hall in their trucks.

After lengthy negotiations, the strike ended when Young and the activists reached an agreement and signed a proposal for the renaming and creation of the new center. The chancellor told the *Daily Bruin* that political pressure had not changed his mind, only accelerated a process that was already in motion. "We have merged elements of our departments and programs into a new Center for Interdisciplinary Instruction which can provide increased stability and autonomy for our interdisciplinary programs—most immediately for Chicana and Chicano Studies," Young announced June 7.

The center would function as a quasi-department— without formal departmental status—and administrators would watch to see if it could flourish as an independent entity.

More than a decade later, in 2005, Chancellor Albert Carnesale approved the departmentalization of the program. In 2007, both the center for interdisciplinary studies and department were merged and officially recognized as the César E. Chávez Department of Chicana and Chicano Studies at UCLA.

"It's a phoenix department because it rose from the ashes of its previous incarnation," said Alicia Gaspar de Alba, department chair, to the *Daily Bruin* in 2008. "Once you have an undergraduate major and graduate program, you can say the department has now fully arrived."

Below: A sit-in outside the Faculty Center in support of Chicano studies, May 11, 1993, after which activists shattered windows and occupied the Faculty Center, causing $27,000 in damages.

Below right: More than 600 protesters outside Royce Hall call on Chancellor Young to reverse his decision not to create an independent department, May 12, 1993.

END OF AN ERA

In the mid-1990s, UCLA enrolled almost 36,000 students annually and educated more individuals than any other university in the Golden State. With more than 280,000 living alumni, it was estimated that one in every 170 Californians had a UCLA degree.

In 1994–95, for the third consecutive year, UCLA awarded more bachelor's and doctoral degrees to minority students than any other college or university, and ranked sixth in the number of master's degrees. "I don't think any educational institution in the United States did as much to bring about that change for the country as UCLA," Young said. "The leadership came from here."

Even as President Clinton held UCLA as a model of diversity for the nation, forces in California would soon change the nature of affirmative action in the university's admissions process, a move that would carry over into other states in the years ahead.

While the state's top 12.5 percent of high school graduates were University of California eligible under the

Students congregate at a noon rally on Bruin Plaza one day after rioting broke out following the acquittal of four Los Angeles police officers accused of attacking motorist Rodney King, April 30, 1992.

Right: Gary Trudeau's "Doonesbury" comic strip blasts fallen junk bond king Michael R. Milken's stint as a visiting professor at the Anderson School in the fall of 1993.

state's Master Plan for Higher Education, UCLA had become much more selective. The grade-point averages and test scores of those admitted reached record highs. The increased demand for a freshman spot resulted in more and more academically qualified students being turned away, leading many to appeal the decisions. Their visits, letters and phone calls at times inundated the admissions office at a rate of 400 per day.

"If you don't have enough places for everybody, you're going to have people unhappy to get turned down," said Rae Lee Siporin, admissions director from 1979 to 2001. "And there are people who got turned down who were very unhappy."

Such emotion-wrought appeals and scrutiny were not new to the University of California. In 1974, Allan Bakke, a white male applicant who had twice been rejected from the medical school at Davis, sued the university citing racial discrimination. In the 1978 landmark case *Regents of the University of California v. Bakke*, a divided U.S. Supreme Court struck down the school's quota-based affirmative action policy in a 5–4 ruling, while continuing to allow race as a "plus" factor in admissions.

UCLA did not use a quota system to admit students and was unaffected by the *Bakke* decision. Still, in 1988, allegations were made that UCLA discriminated against Asian-Americans by using illegal quotas in its admissions practices, triggering a federal inquiry. A multiyear investigation of UCLA admissions by the U.S. Department of Education's Office for Civil Rights found that UCLA did not use discriminatory practices in its undergraduate or graduate admissions.

UCLA's admissions evaluation process in the early 1990s assigned each applicant two scores: an academic score and a supplemental score, which considered factors such as whether the applicant was first-generation college-bound, from a low-income background or from an underrepresented minority. Of the successful applicants, 40–60 percent were admitted solely on the basis of their academic score. The remaining applicants were admitted by considering both the academic and supplemental scores.

Two decades after *Bakke*, the use of affirmative action in admissions again rose to the forefront of national discourse. This time, the Board of Regents—led by Regent Ward Connerly and Governor Wilson, advocating for "a colorblind society"—voted on July 20, 1995, to end "preferential treatment" on the basis of race, ethnicity, sex and national origin in admissions, employment and contracting in two resolutions known as SP-1 and SP-2.

"They chanted. They marched. They cried and were arrested," began an article in the *Daily Bruin*, describing two days of vigorous demonstrations by a thousand students and numerous political leaders, including the Reverend Jesse Jackson and former Assembly Speaker Willie Brown. "But in the end, the sudden flare of student and community activism was not enough to reverse the decision of the governor-appointed UC Regents, who chose to end the university's 30-year-old affirmative action policies."

During a 12-hour meeting, interrupted by civil disobedience and a bomb threat, the regents heard passionate pleas and rebuke from University of California faculty members and students, including 1996 UCLA student body President York Chang, as well as politicians and community leaders such as Dolores Huerta of the United Farm Workers.

University of California President Jack W. Peltason (who succeeded Gardner in 1992) stated that he "respectfully disagreed" with Connerly's recommendations, and noted that after a six-month review several changes were being put into place that included UCLA and Berkeley instituting a more comprehensive review of undergraduate applicants' background and qualifications, and that Davis and Irvine had discontinued the practice of granting admissions to all eligible underrepresented students who apply. He added that there was no evidence suggesting that efforts to increase diversity had compromised quality, and that entering students had the highest academic qualifications in the university's history, with the highest graduation rates.

Governor Wilson, who had issued an executive order on June 1, 1995, bringing an end to affirmative

action advisory committees under his control, argued that "California's diversity must be achieved naturally." The vote was characterized as a political victory for the Republican presidential contender, and it followed one day after President Clinton's declaration that affirmative action was "good for America" in an appeal for the nation to "mend it, not end it."

Well before the vote, Chancellor Young had taken a prominent stand against ending the university's use of affirmative action in admissions. He issued a campuswide education campaign and spoke impassionedly to the press. In the process he caught the ire of Connerly and several other influential regents.

"People keep saying UCLA must have sacrificed quality in order to do this, but the very period in time in which UCLA moved most dramatically to become a diverse campus was the same time in which it made its grandest move toward an increase in quality," Young reflected years later. "People never understood that and they still don't believe that, but it's true."

In the months that followed, thousands of students and community members took to the streets in protest. In October 1995, some 3,000 students marched across the UCLA campus and through Westwood Village, closing down Wilshire Boulevard, where 31 protesters, including Chang, were arrested. "It was absolutely essential and imperative that we demonstrate as a reaction to what occurred," said Chang, who added that he believed it was his duty as UCLA's student body president to take such a visible stance. "There was real clear outrage and public support for affirmative action."

Large-scale protests broke out on campus leading up to the November 1996 general election, which included Proposition 209.

Demonstrations swept University of California campuses. In addition to SP-1 and SP-2, Proposition 209—based on the university's policy and moved forward by Connerly's nonprofit American Civil Rights Institute—was set to go on the ballot in November 1996.

The measure, which incorporated similar prohibitions into the California constitution, passed with 54 percent of the vote. (The university would continue to comply with federal affirmative action rules governing staff and academic employment under an exception related to federal funding. The constitutionality of the Proposition 209 ban was challenged through multiple lawsuits in federal and state courts, and the California Supreme Court found the ban to be constitutional in August 2010 by a 6–1 majority.)

Young began working with his administration and other academic leaders to figure out ways to preserve diversity while complying with the new law.

"He was a real leader among the chancellors," said University of California President Richard C. Atkinson, who succeeded Peltason in November 1995. "I never thought of Chuck as a chancellor who just wanted things for UCLA. He was always dedicated to strengthening higher education throughout the University of California."

In December 1995, however, Young received an unexpected phone call from Atkinson. Less than two months later, after almost three decades at the helm of UCLA, Young shocked the campus by announcing his retirement in February 1996, to be effective on June 30, 1997.

Young, 64, had weathered the shifting priorities of four governors and five university presidents. In fall 1991, when Gardner announced his resignation, Young had been a top contender for the position. As *UCLA Magazine* later described: "It was believed that he had the right credentials, the experience, the ability to lead UC through its terrible budget crunch. It was also believed that he deserved it." The regents instead selected Peltason for a contract period of three years. But Young stayed firm in his commitment to the university and did not waver in tackling issues head-on, even when it could have cost him.

"Chuck was really the one who opposed SP-1 and SP-2 in a public way, and he became the lighting rod for a core of regents—very powerful at the time with the backing of the governor—who thought it was time for Chuck to leave," Atkinson said. "He would have stayed on with tremendous opposition."

Young had planned on staying on a few more years. There were still things he wanted to do, including working out new admissions practices and launching another fundraising campaign. But he decided it was time to move on.

"I've had the unusual privilege through most of my career of being able to do what I thought was right, damn the consequences, and make it work," Young reflected in September 2010. "It finally didn't work. It finally came to, well, Dick Atkinson saying, 'Now Chuck, you ought to retire.' I finally decided I couldn't win. And it would have been of no value to lose."

In his official farewell remarks to the UCLA family, Young emphasized that the university's foremost mission was to educate future leaders, and that he was proud of its continued tradition of innovation. "As the youngest of the nation's best universities, UCLA has never been slowed by old thinking," Young wrote in the spring 1997 *UCLA Magazine*. "We continue boldly pushing the bounds of discovery."

His address to students as he presided over his last commencement exercises that June was more emotional. The staunch leader—known as chancellor to three-fourths of UCLA's living alumni—told graduates they had something in common: "You see, today is a commencement of sorts for me, too."

Below: More than 800 students stage a rally against Proposition 209, marching through campus before heading toward the Federal Building in Westwood, October 23, 1996. After holding a sit-in, which forced the closure of Wilshire Boulevard for more than two hours, 34 demonstrators were arrested (below right) for refusing to leave the thoroughfare.

Below far right: Charles E. Young stepped down after 29 years at the helm of UCLA, having signed two-thirds of all diplomas ever issued by the university.

The New Millennium
1997–2007

Above: Students enter Haines Hall, a general classroom building and one of the original four structures on Royce quad.

Opposite: The Ronald Reagan UCLA Medical Center (left) takes shape across from the Center for the Health Sciences, November 2005.

With the retirement of Chancellor Charles E. Young, UCLA entered the 21st century with a new leader at the helm, embarking on an era that would be defined by scientific breakthroughs, but also marked by tragedy.

After a broad search, the Board of Regents looked outside the University of California system for a new chancellor, selecting Harvard Provost Albert Carnesale as UCLA's eighth chief executive. "UCLA educates more students than any other university in the state of California," Carnesale wrote in UCLA's annual report, published shortly after his arrival on July 1, 1997. "We have a special responsibility to bring forward future leaders who will reflect and serve every quarter of our society."

Interest in attending UCLA reached a milestone. In 1998, the campus received a record 32,600 freshman applications—more than any university in the nation. Its admittance rate of less than 33 percent made UCLA one of the most competitive universities in the country. Throughout the following decade, UCLA would remain the most popular institution among first-year applicants.

With the emergence of the World Wide Web, learning took on new forms. Through the Instructional Enhancement Initiative, UCLA became the first university in the nation to offer a website for each undergraduate course and a home page for every undergraduate student.

However, in the wake of Proposition 209, which banned race, ethnicity and gender from being considered as criteria in admissions to California state-supported schools, UCLA's much-hailed diversity suffered. As the number of African-American and Hispanic students dropped, both UCLA and University of California administrators sought new outreach models and other alternatives. The Board of Regents repealed its own ban in a symbolic gesture, but state law remained in effect. Efforts to reverse the declining

enrollment of underrepresented minorities would continue throughout the decade, while some vocal advocates beseeched Carnesale to do more, even violate the law.

After September 11, 2001, Carnesale would guide UCLA through the difficult times that followed the terrorist attacks that killed thousands, spearheading the creation of a seminar series designed to foster meaningful discussions and help undergraduates both grapple with and learn from the world-altering events.

The chancellor's background would also serve UCLA well at a time of significant scientific discovery. He championed advancements in genetics and information technology. Reflecting UCLA's prominence as a research university, two of UCLA's faculty received Nobel Prizes in back-to-back years: In 1997, Paul D. Boyer was awarded the Nobel in chemistry for his pioneering work in investigating how ATP (adenosine triphosphate)—the carrier for cellular energy—is formed; and in 1998, Louis J. Ignarro received the prize in medicine for his work showing that nitric oxide is an important factor in helping the body regulate key functions such as blood pressure and in preventing blood clots that can cause strokes—research that established the scientific foundation for the development of Viagra. Between 1997 and 2000, UCLA moved from twelfth to third in the nation in federal research funding, surpassing Stanford and Harvard universities, and the Massachusetts Institute of Technology.

By 1997, the university had launched a billion-dollar fundraising campaign, which would over a decade raise an unprecedented $3.05 billion, including a $200 million gift from entertainment magnate David Geffen to endow the medical school.

With the campaign's end, Carnesale surprised the campus by announcing that he would be stepping down earlier than anticipated to take a sabbatical focusing on his fields of expertise in national security.

He would be succeeded by longtime law Professor Norman Abrams, who was appointed acting chancellor after a search to find a permanent successor failed. Abrams, immediately faced with several crises, including a historic low in the number of African-American admittees and targeted violence against researchers by animal-rights extremists, directed UCLA with a steadfast and firm hand. The number of black students would double within a year, and recommendations from an animal testing task force became a national model for the protection of researchers.

THE NUCLEAR ENGINEER

With Chancellor Young stepping down from his post on June 30, 1997, the president and regents embarked upon a nationwide search in fall 1996 for a chief executive to lead UCLA into the 21st century.

Richard C. Atkinson, University of California president, 1995–2003.

University of California President Richard C. Atkinson described the ideal candidate as a leader who not only had experience managing a large, complex institution, but was also a distinguished academic. "A Nobel laureate who could not read a ledger would not be someone we would want," Atkinson told the *Los Angeles Times*. "And someone who came out of Peat Marwick and was a top administrator but had no academic background would not fly either."

The search was complicated by the unexpected resignation in July 1996 of Berkeley's popular chancellor, Chang-Lin Tien. Like Young, Tien had been an outspoken defender of equal opportunity in higher education. Not only did the regents need to fill the top jobs at the university's two largest campuses, but reports surfaced that some candidates had been "scared off" by the political tumult surrounding the regents' 1995 decision to ban affirmative action in admissions and hiring. (Another vocal chancellor on the issue, Karl S. Pister of Santa Cruz, had retired the previous month.)

The nine-campus University of California was undergoing a sweeping leadership transformation during a period of budgetary difficulties lingering from the recession of the early 1990s, an enrollment boom and the public battering over the divisive ban on affirmative action. Atkinson, in his job less than a year, had already named two chancellors: Robert C. Dynes, who succeeded him at San Diego, and M.R.C. Greenwood at Santa Cruz. The longest-serving campus chief was Riverside's Raymond L. Orbach, who had been appointed just four years prior.

Orbach, former provost of UCLA's College of Letters and Science, was considered a candidate for the UCLA position and received support from several regents, including

Albert Carnesale

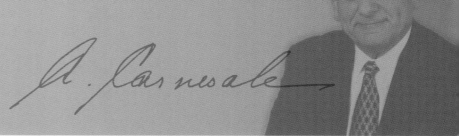

The son of a New York taxi driver and an office clerk, Albert Carnesale was born on July 2, 1936, and grew up in a Bronx tenement. His ambition as a child was to "find a job where you wear a white shirt and tie and earn at least $100 a week." The first person in his family to go to college, Carnesale said "there was never a question" that he would pursue higher learning.

Excelling in mathematics and the sciences, Carnesale was accepted to the Cooper Union for the Advancement of Science and Art in Manhattan. He graduated with a bachelor's degree in mechanical engineering in 1957. Carnesale then worked as a senior engineer in the nuclear division at Martin Marietta Corporation in Baltimore during the day, while pursuing his master's degree in mechanical engineering from Drexel University at night.

After receiving his master's in 1961, Carnesale began teaching at North Carolina State University, where he also earned his doctorate in nuclear engineering in 1966. He was a member of the faculty at North Carolina State until 1969, when he left to join the U.S. Arms Control and Disarmament Agency. As chief of the Defensive Weapons Systems Division, Carnesale was responsible for the formulation and evaluation of arms control policies and measures. From 1970–72, he was a member of the U.S. delegation to the Strategic Arms Limitation Talks (SALT I), which led to the Treaty on the Limitation of Anti-Ballistic Missile Systems and an interim arms control agreement between the United States and the Soviet Union during the Cold War.

Carnesale then returned to North Carolina State and stayed on the faculty until October 1974, when he joined Harvard University as a chaired professor and academic dean in the John F. Kennedy School of Government. In November 1991, he was appointed dean of the Kennedy school, and in July 1994, he became provost of Harvard, serving as deputy to the president. After 23 years at Harvard, Carnesale was selected as UCLA's eighth chief executive in July 1997.

At UCLA, Carnesale championed interdisciplinary endeavors, including the creation of the Center for Society and Genetics. He launched the UCLA in LA initiative, an umbrella program designed to strengthen UCLA's engagement with the broader community. During his tenure, UCLA doubled its research dollars from contracts and grants to more than $821 million. "So much of what Al did was invisible to the user," Executive Vice Chancellor and Provost Daniel M. Neuman told *UCLA Magazine* in 2006. "He's like a brilliant piece of software: You see the effects but not the inner workings."

In 2001, Carnesale met Robin Gerber through mutual acquaintances, and they married on the patio of the Chancellor's Residence in April 2002.

Highly regarded for his expertise in foreign and defense policy matters, including nuclear nonproliferation, Carnesale has acted as a consultant to U.S. government agencies including the departments of energy, state and defense; the Executive Office of the President; and the CIA.

In 2006, Carnesale stepped down from the chancellorship, taking a one-year sabbatical, before returning to research and teaching. He holds dual faculty appointments in the Luskin School of Public Affairs and the Henry Samueli School of Engineering and Applied Science.

Albert Carnesale, UCLA's second chief executive hailing from Harvard University. (Ernest Carroll Moore was the first.)

Lieutenant Governor Gray Davis. But Atkinson and other regents were wary of pulling leaders away from system campuses. Only once before had a chancellor moved from one campus to another: when Theodore L. Hullar left Riverside for Davis in 1987. Atkinson thought that such transitions sent the wrong message by appearing to create "a hierarchy that one campus was more important than another."

Atkinson and the search committee focused on other candidates. They had a strong interest in recruiting Stanford Provost Condoleezza Rice. "I said to her that I'm sure she would be the first choice of the regents and of me, if she were willing to take the job," Atkinson said. However, Rice (the White House specialist on the Soviet Union from 1989–91 and future national security adviser and secretary of state under President George W. Bush) declined consideration, stating "at this stage in my life I don't want to be a university president."

In February 1997, a year after Young announced his resignation, and after considering more than 200 candidates, the names of four finalists emerged. Two were well-regarded internal candidates: Susan Westerberg Prager, dean of UCLA's law school for 15 years; and Gerald S. Levey, dean of the UCLA medical school and provost for health sciences since 1994, and a former senior vice president at Merck & Co. The other two finalists were from the East: University of Pennsylvania Provost Stanley Chodorow, a history professor who had spent 26 years at the San Diego campus, including a period as associate vice chancellor for academic planning under Atkinson; and Albert Carnesale, Harvard provost since 1994 and former dean of the John F. Kennedy School of Government.

On March 6, on Atkinson's recommendation, the Board of Regents unanimously approved Carnesale, 60, as UCLA's new chief executive.

"Carnesale had a very strong image at the national level as an academic leader," Atkinson said years later. "I was extremely impressed by his stature in the academic side of the university and thought that would be to the long-term benefit of UCLA."

The regents also announced that University of Texas President Robert Berdahl would succeed Tien at Berkeley. "That the University of California, historically tight-knit and even ingrown at the top, would look outside the borders of the system for new campus leaders was taken as an indicator of how concerned its governing regents have become about the need for fresh education faces, views and ideas as the century ends," wrote *The New York Times*.

Carnesale, a nuclear engineer who worked for the U.S. Arms Control and Disarmament Agency in the early 1970s, had been deputy to Harvard President Neil L. Rudenstine and a key force in the Ivy League institution's $2.1 billion fundraising campaign. UCLA was preparing to launch the

most ambitious capital campaign ever undertaken by a public university—with a goal of $1.2 billion—and Atkinson thought Carnesale's experience would be beneficial.

"He is a dynamic leader and a man of principle who adheres to the highest standards," Atkinson said in the announcement of Carnesale's selection. "He is a good match for UCLA—a recognized authority in his academic field, a superb administrator, and a personable individual who will lead the campus as it continues its ascent begun under Chancellor Young's leadership as one of the world's premier academic centers."

CARNESALE TAKES COMMAND

From the start of his chancellorship, Carnesale faced tensions arising from the controversial affirmative action ban. Having been tied up in the appeals process for a year, the ban went into effect within months of his arrival at UCLA on July 1, 1997. As they did with Young, student activists and political leaders urged Carnesale to take action, some advocating that the chancellor defy the law outright.

Above: More than 1,800 witness the first chancellorial inauguration in almost 30 years, as Albert Carnesale is invested as UCLA's eighth chief executive, May 15, 1998.

"The disquieting part about it—that I hadn't really anticipated—was I arrived the same time it goes into effect, and so therefore, I'm associated with it," Carnesale reflected a decade later. "It was not rare for people to say I should resign—no, I should not implement it; I should violate it."

He added: "I just tried to push the envelope as far as you could push it. But I said, 'Look, if I violate the law, you've got a new chancellor the next day—you *should* have a new chancellor the next day.'"

Protests against the affirmative action ban continued on campus and across the state, even as the U.S. Supreme Court declined to hear the case. In October 1997, at a student-organized rally in Meyerhoff Park attended by more than 500 demonstrators, the Reverend Jesse Jackson called upon President Bill Clinton to supersede state laws by drawing upon federal civil rights legislation. "We must build bridges in California, not walls," Jackson said, as he encouraged students to march with him in Sacramento later that month.

Kandea Mosley, UCLA's 1998 undergraduate student body president, demanded that Carnesale draft a public statement taking a stand against the ban. "At a student government council meeting, Carnesale responded to a concerned student's question by saying, 'Some unjust laws must be adhered to,'" Mosley wrote in the *Daily Bruin*. "What we are witnessing today, virtually on the eve of the chancellor's inauguration, is a university caught in the grips of an ethical crisis—and a soon-to-be inaugurated chancellor who is shying away from taking an ethical stand."

Carnesale's inauguration in Royce Hall on May 15, 1998, heralded UCLA's first investiture in three decades. Outside Royce, more than 300 protesters demonstrated amid a heavy police presence. Inside, 1,800 dignitaries, faculty,

alumni and students were gathered—but the ceremony was not without its own drama. Student speakers Mosley and Graduate Student Association President Andrew Westall both criticized the new chancellor from the podium. After completing her remarks, Mosley sat down near center stage and raised her fist in the air. She remained there for 10 minutes until a member of the Black Alumni Association approached her and she subsequently left. While a few protesters were arrested outside, the ceremony continued largely uninterrupted.

In his inaugural address, Carnesale acknowledged the challenges of "the continuing explosion of knowledge" amid "a growing need for resources." He outlined his vision for moving UCLA forward, including increasing interdisciplinary instruction and research, and advocating for a greater emphasis on technology to advance the institution's mission in the Information Age.

"What excites me about UCLA is not primarily its current level of achievement, high as it is, rather, it is our potential to rise to even greater heights," he said. "My goal—indeed, our goal—is to place UCLA squarely among the ranks of the world's great universities. When informed people around the world are asked to name the very best institutions of higher learning, UCLA should be at or near the top of their lists."

Invoking a phrase used by UCLA's first chief executive, Ernest Carroll Moore, Carnesale also pledged his support to ensure a diverse campus while abiding by the new state law. "Diversity of the student body has long been a hallmark of this campus," Carnesale said. "Because I believe so strongly that a diverse student body will, indeed, 'lift the level of civilization of all of us,' I will do all that I can, within the law, to nourish that diversity and make it grow."

Right: President Richard C. Atkinson (left) bestows the chancellor's medal, the insignia of office, upon Carnesale.

Far right: Kandea Mosley, 1998 student body president, sits on stage during the inauguration ceremony in protest of the California ban on the use of affirmative action in admissions and hiring.

COUNTERING A DROP IN DIVERSITY

As many predicted, admissions of underrepresented students, specifically African-Americans and Hispanics, plunged in the wake of Proposition 209. UCLA's admitted class for fall 1998—the first freshman group affected by the ban—included 313 black students, down 39 percent from the previous year; and 994 Hispanic students, a drop of 34 percent. (At Berkeley, the numbers were even lower: 248 black students, a drop of 56 percent; and 649 Hispanic students, down 49 percent.)

Seeking to encourage admitted applicants to choose UCLA over other colleges and universities, and make them feel welcomed despite the negative publicity surrounding Proposition 209, black and Hispanic alumni groups hosted receptions and Bruin state legislators wrote letters to prospective students. The chancellor also reached out with a broad and explicit public appeal. "To all of those young scholars who are admitted to our freshman class—and especially students from underrepresented minorities—our message is simple and unequivocal: Come to UCLA," Carnesale wrote in an opinion piece in the *Los Angeles Times* in March 1998. "You will receive an outstanding education here and will help us to make this a great university. UCLA wants and needs you."

To increase the number of qualified underrepresented applicants, Carnesale and other campus leaders, including Vice Chancellor for Student Affairs Winston Doby, redoubled efforts to reach out to minority students. When state funding was reduced for the University of California's Early Academic Outreach Program, Carnesale provided funding so that the program—which helped students at 90 Los Angeles middle schools and high schools become university eligible—was not eliminated.

Overcoming initial resistance from student leaders who wanted to maintain autonomy, Carnesale focused the student government and administration outreach programs into a better coordinated effort. He established the Chancellor's Blue and Gold Scholarship Program to recognize the academic achievements of recently admitted freshmen who had attended Los Angeles County high schools that historically have sent few students to UCLA. The Student Affairs Office began raising funds to supplement the number of scholarships available, and in fall 2000 the program expanded to include two-year scholarships for transfer students attending community colleges in the Los Angeles region.

In March 1999, the Board of Regents approved a new admissions program, Eligibility in the Local Context, through which California students in the top four percent of their high school graduating class would be admitted to a system campus. Admission to a specific campus was determined through a subsequent, separate process.

The policy was adopted as a means to "ensure that high-performing students from all areas of the state, including students in rural and urban schools," would have access to the University of California "regardless of the level of course offerings or other educational opportunities at their schools." (From 2001–09, UCLA received the most applications and enrolled the second-highest number of students through the program, behind Berkeley.)

Despite these efforts, the number of underrepresented students was slow to increase in the years immediately following passage of Proposition 209. In April 2001, 1,673 underrepresented students were admitted to UCLA, about 15 percent of all those accepted. Activists continued pressing for change.

On March 14, 2001, while the Board of Regents met in UCLA's James West Alumni Center, more than 1,000 protesters—including students from several University of California campuses and high schools from across the state—rallied outside, pressing the regents to repeal their ban.

Emblematic of a new generation of activism, the students relied on cell phones and walkie-talkies with headsets. They retained a lawyer, in case it was necessary to negotiate terms of arrest. They trained their own security team, identifiable by red armbands, to keep safe perimeters and order. Rather than disrupting the meetings, as had been common in past decades, students signed up to make passionate pleas during the official public comment period.

"You have the opportunity today to take down the 'not-wanted' sign that students of color see at the UC and prove to the state and the nation that the UC values diversity," UCLA student Cynthia Mosqueda told the regents, while the chanting outside remained constant throughout the meeting.

The day culminated in more than 200 protesters occupying Royce Hall's auditorium, forcing cancellation of a scheduled televised debate among Los Angeles mayoral candidates, including UCLA alumnus (and future mayor) Antonio Villaraigosa. Carnesale and Berky Nelson, director of the Center for Student Programming, asked the protesters to leave before the debate. When they refused, Carnesale canceled the event rather than calling in the police to have the protesters forcibly removed—in contrast to a 1998 protest a few days after his inauguration when police in full riot gear were summoned and 85 students were arrested. Carnesale promised to write a statement supporting a repeal of the regents' affirmative action ban, and gave protesters an 8 p.m. deadline to leave the building—which they did, peacefully. The students then surprised administrators by coming back with trash bags to clean up.

"Chancellor Carnesale did an outstanding job of managing, coordinating and negotiating all aspects of the incident," said UCLA Police Chief Clarence Chapman, who noted that police presence was purposely kept low-key. "The outcome was absolutely successful in that there was no property damage, no arrests, and the students felt they had some political or moral victory."

Two months later, under pressure from a coalition of legislators led by Lieutenant Governor Cruz Bustamante and Assembly Speaker Robert Hertzberg, the regents rescinded their affirmative action ban by a unanimous vote of 22–0 (including Regent Ward Connerly, who had championed the ban) and resolved that "the University shall seek out and enroll, on each of its campuses, a student body that demonstrates high academic achievement or exceptional personal talent, and that encompasses the broad diversity of backgrounds characteristic of California." While the action was mostly symbolic since state law remained unchanged, university leaders hoped it would help end political infighting, repair the university's tarnished reputation, and revitalize interest among minority students.

The regents also recommitted to outreach efforts and charged the Academic Senate with devising new admissions recommendations that would no longer be restricted by the requirement that 50 percent to 75 percent of applicants be evaluated on academic criteria alone. In November 2001, the regents approved new guidelines that implemented a "comprehensive review" of applicants' academic and personal achievements. Each campus was provided flexibility in applying the guidelines.

"Living up to their reputation as 'the public ivies,' " the *Los Angeles Times* wrote, UCLA and Berkeley "have moved a step closer to emulating Ivy League admissions policies by putting a new emphasis on personal achievement."

In May 2002, the University of California announced that the number of underrepresented blacks, Hispanics and Native Americans throughout the system had risen to 19.1 percent of freshman enrollment, slightly higher than in 1997, the last year before the implementation of the affirmative action ban. Gains at the most competitive campuses, however, were more modest. UCLA increased the number of Hispanics enrolled to 15.6 percent, up from 14 percent in 2001; African-Americans enrolled rose slightly to 3.7 percent, up from 3 percent.

"We still haven't really fully recovered," Carnesale said in 2008, looking back on his tenure. Affirmative action was "the overwhelming and overriding issue at UCLA, especially since this was a campus where diversity was so highly valued and had been so relatively successful at it for so fine a university."

He added: "It was just the dominant issue, and for me personally, the most frustrating issue throughout the entire chancellorship."

"AN ATTACK ON ALL HUMANITY"
On September 11, 2001, members of the UCLA community, along with fellow Americans and people around the world, learned in horror that four American passenger airplanes had been hijacked by terrorists in a series of coordinated suicide attacks on the United States. With nearly 3,000 people killed,

it was the worst foreign assault on domestic soil in the nation's history.

The brutal events of that day—in which two planes crashed into the Twin Towers of the World Trade Center in New York causing them to collapse, another into the Pentagon in Virginia, and a fourth in a Pennsylvania field after being retaken by courageous passengers—forever altered the world. "A New State of Terror," cried the *Daily Bruin* banner headline.

Although the campus did not shut down, the UCLA Medical Center went on heightened alert in case of a local emergency while the nation reeled from the surprise attacks. University police stepped up campus patrols. Some departments decided on their own to close, including several in the College of Letters and Science, as well as the School of Public Policy. "Despite heightened senses, the campus seemed gravely empty," the *Daily Bruin* reported. "Most were home, watching television or calling friends and family."

Campus counseling centers offered help to those in need, while several hundred individuals gave blood to the UCLA Blood and Platelet Center—quadrupling its typical daily donations, making it the busiest day in the center's 26 years.

The Pacific-10 Conference canceled all games for the week, including UCLA's football home opener against Arizona State University at the Rose Bowl. UCLA athletic officials followed suit by postponing all matches and practices throughout the weekend due to safety concerns and out of respect for the victims.

On September 13, more than 5,000 students, faculty, staff and community members came together for a memorial on Royce quad to share in their grief and honor those who died—among them several alumni and members of the UCLA family. Together, they held out hope for those who might still be found in the rubble, while beginning the difficult steps toward emotional healing.

"The events of September 11 have left an indelible imprint on all of our lives," said Carnesale, as many in attendance bowed their heads, others cried openly. "What happened on Tuesday, September 11 was an attack on all humanity. … The loss is too great to be defined or measured."

"The time has come for us to direct our energies toward healing ... to come together to speak to one another, to hear one another, to teach one another, and to learn from one another," Carnesale continued, calling upon individuals to eschew fear and embrace tolerance and respect, inherent values in civil society.

"We will never forget this tragedy," said Donald Hartsock, former UCLA ombudsman. "Let us hope we will never forget the gathering of these people, in this place, to

The UCLA Blood and Platelet Center, which opened in 1975 specifically for patients undergoing orthopedic surgery, has grown to maintain a blood supply sufficient for patients at both the Ronald Reagan UCLA Medical Center and the Santa Monica UCLA Medical Center and Orthopaedic Hospital.

celebrate not the sounds and sights of terror, but the sounds and sights of those who responded to the terror and made us all proud to be linked with them. Let us remember, we can live in the present if we draw on the past, but we can't live in September the 11th, 2001."

The impending arrival of students for the beginning of fall classes spurred Carnesale and College of Letters and Science Provost Brian Copenhaver to create a purposeful response. Meeting at 10 a.m. on September 11, UCLA's top academic administrators determined they had a responsibility to do something. By week's end an "Urgent Call to Action" was made to the faculty, and within two weeks a series of 50 one-unit seminars had been organized. The seminars offered undergraduates what Carnesale described as a way to "better understand what happened, the global framework within which such tragic events can take place, the pros and cons of alternative responses to the terrorist attacks and the overarching need for tolerance and respect within our diverse community."

Drawing on his background in foreign policy and defense, Carnesale himself taught one of the seminars, "National Security in the 21st Century."

"It was important for me to meet with our university's youngest students—freshmen and sophomores—and engage them in meaningful dialogue on this difficult topic," explained Carnesale, who held a dual appointment in the public policy and engineering schools. "Teaching this fall reinforced my confidence in the character and intellect of today's young people."

Two days after the September 11, 2011, terrorist attacks, Chancellor Albert Carnesale comforts a bereaved campus during a memorial in Royce quad.

Three of the first seminars created were: "War, Terror and Violence: Reflecting on Machiavelli" taught by Copenhaver; "America as Hyperpower" led by Geoffrey Garrett, vice provost of International Studies and Overseas Programs; and "Understanding, Respecting and Honoring the First Amendment in a Terrorist Environment" by Joseph D. Mandel, vice chancellor for legal affairs.

Many of the students in the seminars were freshmen away from home for the first time. "They were not only adjusting to college life, but they were adjusting as well to their world having been turned upside down immediately before their arrival in Westwood," Mandel said. "Impacts included an awakening to the reality that life is complex and that not all questions can be answered in the black and white, and that the discomfort that results from this awakening is not to be feared but rather welcomed."

More than 550 students signed up for the "Perspectives on September 11" seminars. They were so popular, among both faculty and students, that additional courses were created for the following quarter. The seminars gave rise to the *Fiat Lux* Undergraduate Seminars, launched in fall 2002 to foster critical thinking about key issues of the day in a small-group setting. Named for the University of California's motto, "Let There Be Light," *Fiat Lux*, as popular as its precursor, was emulated by other University of California campuses.

Beyond the seminars, many professors incorporated issues related to September 11 into their course curricula or discussion sections. Others made a statement by deliberately carrying on without acknowledging the terrorist attacks in their classes. In February 2002, Carnesale delivered a public lecture titled "Rethinking National Security," offering 800 individuals gathered in Royce Hall a direct glimpse into the state of U.S. defense policy after 9/11.

His remarks were based, in part, on discussions that the chancellor had had with students taking his seminars. "They are the ones who always ask, 'Why does it have to be that way?'" Carnesale said. "This does force you to think about these subjects more critically, and to challenge your assumptions."

In the weeks that followed the attacks, Carnesale set three important goals for the campus: enforcing security to ensure the safety of students, employees and campus visitors; making the university a beacon of tolerance and respect; and providing a rational discourse regarding the attacks and their aftermath. One year later, Carnesale declared: "We will never forget the people who were lost on September 11. But we can take comfort in what we have learned since that day, and in what UCLA will continue to contribute to the broader community."

Reflected Vice Chancellor Levey: "Al's response to 9/11 defined him and his leadership."

"FRONTIER OF KNOWLEDGE"

In December 2000, recently elected Governor Gray Davis earmarked $300 million in state support for three California Institutes for Science and Innovation to be established at the University of California. The institutes would focus on scientific and engineering research in sectors key to boosting the California economy, bringing together faculty, undergraduate and graduate students, and industrial partners to work in cross-disciplinary teams aimed at developing the next generation of knowledge in the field.

"These centers of science innovation will not just be portals of the new economy, they will be the pilots of the new economy," said Davis as he announced the winning proposals via satellite from Sacramento. "No one knows for sure what breakthroughs will occur. But, believe me, those breakthroughs will occur in California."

A buoyant audience watching in Ackerman Grand Ballroom cheered Davis' selection of the California NanoSystems Institute (CNSI)—a joint venture of UCLA and the University of California, Santa Barbara—as one of the three winning proposals. (The other two centers selected were the California Institute for Telecommunications and Information Technology at San Diego in collaboration with Irvine; and the California Institute for Bioengineering, Biotechnology and Quantitative Biomedicine at San Francisco in collaboration with Berkeley and Santa Cruz.)

CNSI was established to explore the potential of manipulating structures, atom by atom, to engineer new materials, devices and systems that can bring about transformative technological change in fields ranging from health care to the environment. The goal was to bring UCLA inventions into the marketplace while fostering a new generation of researchers.

"Its establishment puts us on track to become the world's preeminent center for nanoscience research—science and engineering done at the scale of the nanometer, a billionth of a meter, the scale of individual atoms," Carnesale said. "This is an exciting day for us, for our campuses and for the people of California."

Governor Davis required the institutes to obtain a 2–1 match of the state-funded $100 million with non-state funds. Interest from the private sector, however, was so strong that the match quickly grew closer to 3–1. By 2007, CNSI was one of only three nanotechnology centers recognized by the U.S. government, and its researchers had already been awarded $350 million in federal grants.

When the institute's seven-story building, designed by Uruguayan architect Rafael Viñoly, opened in the Court of Sciences in December 2007, it was the most technologically complex building ever constructed at UCLA. Inside, high-tech

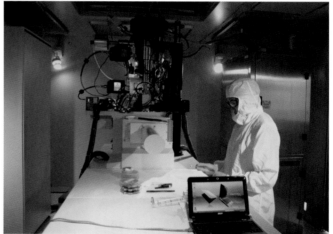

Above: The California NanoSystems Institute (CNSI), the most technologically complex structure ever built on campus, opens December 2007 on the Court of Sciences.

Left: A researcher in CNSI's Integrated Systems Nanofabrication Clean Room.

laboratories were carefully secured for both personal safety and intellectual property concerns. In the Integrated Systems Nanofabrication Clean Room, the number of particles in the air is tightly restricted, so that researchers can interact with DNA, single molecules, proteins and other small entities.

With the addition of the building, the institute was able to pursue interdisciplinary collaborations with private industry to advance economic development, while also training future generations of scientists. In March 2009, the institute opened an on-campus technology incubator, providing space for approximately 10 spinoff companies to develop their "proof of concept," and access to high-tech laboratories to help them succeed in launching UCLA inventions—from across campus departments—into the marketplace.

In 2007, NanoH20 became the first company to "incubate" at CNSI, and the first private company to lease space at a University of California campus. Founded on research by Eric Hoek, assistant professor of civil and environmental engineering, the company developed a promising desalination

Above: UCLA's intellectual property portfolio includes more than 1,800 inventions and 1,000 patents.

Right: The Gonda (Goldschmied) Neuroscience and Genetics Research Center on Westwood Plaza opened December 15, 1998, as home to UCLA's new Department of Human Genetics.

technology that could increase the world's freshwater supply. The venture has received several accolades, including being named a 2010 Global Cleantech 100 Company. Other top research initiatives undertaken by CNSI researchers include a polymer that could be used for portable electronic devices as well as building materials to convert sunlight into electricity; new blood tests to detect the possibility of lung cancer; a gasoline to fuel cars made of a natural gas derivation; and a lens-free cell phone microscope for medical purposes.

"It's not enough for us to change the world; our job is to shape it and make it a better place," said chemistry Professor and CNSI Director Paul S. Weiss, a decade after the institute's founding. "Our faculty and students are coming up with new materials and new, safer ways to manufacture materials. We're developing new ways to do biology in the study of the brain. New methods to develop drugs and to diagnose disease. We're developing stable, economic materials to turn sunlight into useable energy and make water safe to drink."

UCLA faculty research has led to an intellectual-property portfolio that as of the end of the 2010 fiscal year included 1,837 inventions; 590 U.S. patents and 604 foreign patents; 244 active licenses; and has delivered more than 90 new companies to market. Two of UCLA's most lucrative patents have been the nicotine patch (co-invented by Murray E. Jarvik, UCLA professor of pharmacology and psychiatry, postdoctoral fellow Jed Rose and his brother, Daniel) and the Guglielmi Detachable Coil—named after UCLA physician Guido Guglielmi—which seals the opening of a cerebral aneurysm, reducing blood flow and the risk of hemorrhage.

Some of the period's greatest scientific advancements in the life sciences were reflected in new initiatives at UCLA. Uniting the fast-evolving areas of molecular neuroscience and human genetics, the Gonda (Goldschmied) Neuroscience and Genetics Research Center was dedicated on December 15, 1998. The six-story building, on the corner of Westwood Plaza and Charles E. Young Drive (renamed from Circle Drive in 1998), became home to UCLA's new Department of Human Genetics—established just prior to the sequencing of the human genome. The center houses research groups focused on isolating genetic errors that lead to neurological and other diseases, and developing gene-based interventions to treat and prevent them. The structure was made possible by a $45 million gift from philanthropists Leslie and Susan Gonda. (Leslie Gonda, a Hungarian Holocaust survivor who had changed his name from Laszlo Goldschmied, honored his family members who died in the Holocaust by placing the Goldschmied name on the building.)

UCLA also created the Center for Society and Genetics—a major initiative advanced by Carnesale and Vice Chancellor Levey—to bring together experts in considering the broad social, ethical, cultural, legal, political and scientific implications of the new biology.

"The genetics revolution brings extraordinary promise and unprecedented challenges," Carnesale wrote in a 2001 advertorial in the *Los Angeles Times*. "UCLA will continue to be a leader at this crucial frontier of knowledge—using the code of human life to unravel the mysteries of complex diseases, to develop cures, and to prepare our society for a new scientific future."

The Little Marias

All their young lives, conjoined twins Maria Teresa and Maria de Jesús were only able to see each other with mirrors. But after more than 22 hours of unprecedented surgery at UCLA, that would change.

As the world kept vigil via the throng of international media camped outside UCLA's Mattel Children's Hospital, the largest medical team assembled in the university's history performed a marathon separation surgery so that the one-year-old Guatemalan girls, born fused at the head, could lead individual lives.

The 50-member surgical team was led by Jorge Lazareff, director of pediatric neurosurgery, and Henry Kawamoto Jr., surgical director of the UCLA Craniofacial Clinic. In all, hundreds of doctors, nurses and medical staff of the UCLA Medical Center—many who donated their services—were involved in the twins' care.

More than 11 hours after the first incision was made, a doctor announced, "They are separated." A moment later, Lazareff added: "You are looking at two children, two little girls. There will be two passports, two boyfriends, two weddings."

But there was no time for celebration. The meticulously planned and complex surgery was far from over. The painstaking process of reconstruction began. Finally, at 5:40 a.m. on August 6, 2002, the girls were wheeled into the pediatric intensive care unit, where after waking from a week-long sedation, they saw each other directly for the first time.

"The future looks very bright," said the girls' father, Wenceslao Quiej López, 21, at a press conference after the surgery. The twins and their mother, Alba Leticia Álvarez, 23, had been flown from Guatemala to UCLA after the charity, Healing the Children, approached Lazareff, who volunteered to take on the procedure. Michael Karpf, director of the UCLA Medical Center, approved the surgery, which was estimated to cost the hospital about $1.5 million.

"After seeing those kids, it was an easy decision," Karpf said. "They're very much distinct human beings who need every opportunity to be distinct human beings. This is UCLA doing the right thing."

Doctors said that both girls came out of the surgery with the same chance at life. However, when they went back to their native Guatemala, Maria Teresa contracted E. coli meningitis and suffered developmental delays. Years later, the twins attend school, while continuing to require medical care and physical therapy. They live in Southern California.

Below: Jorge Lazareff, director of pediatric neurosurgery (center) and Henry Kawamoto Jr., surgical director of the UCLA Craniofacial Clinic (behind him) led the marathon surgery to separate conjoined twins Maria de Jesús and Maria Teresa (bottom).

Bottom left: The medical team assembled was the largest in UCLA's history.

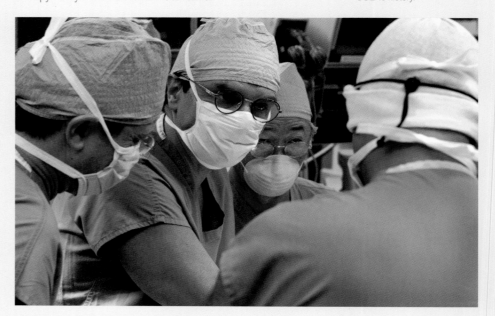

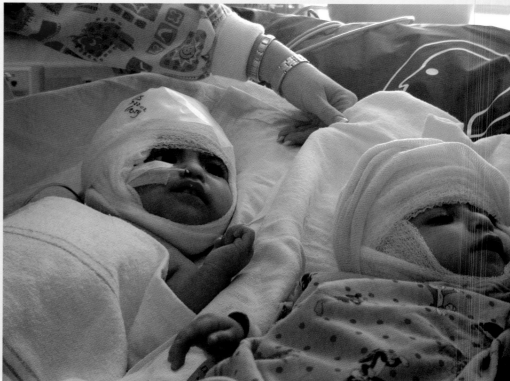

HOSPITAL FOR THE 21ST CENTURY

As the campus pressed onward with its ambitious seismic retrofit plan put in place after the 1994 Northridge earthquake, UCLA unveiled plans for a new $1.3 billion hospital and research complex to replace the 1950s-era structure that was significantly weakened by the 6.7 temblor. Engineers and hospital leaders had determined that it would be more prudent to build a new hospital than to retrofit the old one, as it would need to continue providing 24-hour trauma, surgical and emergency service during construction.

The new facility was designed by a team headed by renowned architects I.M. Pei and his son C.C. "DiDi" Pei. Made with 26,000 tons of steel, it was one of the first hospitals constructed to meet strict new California seismic standards that when adhered to should enable buildings to withstand the Big One, a "great quake" of 8.0 magnitude. The 18,000 panels of Ambralight travertine marble that cover its exterior are designed to cling securely to the building while moving as much as three feet in a quake, helping to keep the structure

intact. The marble—from the same quarry in Tivoli, Italy, used for the Getty Center in the Santa Monica Mountains a few miles northwest of campus—was presented to UCLA at $1 million below market rate by Carlo Mariotti, a former cancer patient who wished to express his gratitude after 12 years of treatment.

Capital funding included $432 million from the Federal Emergency Management Agency, $44 million from the State of California, $300 million from private donors, with the remainder from hospital financing and bonds. Accessibility was a key factor in determining the hospital's placement, accounting for its location on the main thoroughfare of Westwood Plaza between the cogeneration plant to the north and the UCLA Medical Plaza to the south. The hospital's four entrances facilitate efficiency by serving distinct patient populations: pediatric patients enter the children's hospital through a less intimidating entrance off Gayley Avenue; trauma patients arrive via the emergency entrance on Charles E. Young Drive South (or the roof helipad); psychiatric patients enter through a south entrance linked to UCLA Medical Plaza; and all other patients enter through the main entrance off Westwood Plaza.

The first time I.M. Pei visited the future hospital's site, he sat for four hours with Vice Chancellor Levey atop the parking structure located directly on it, observing the area, and then sketching what he thought the hospital should physically look like. Later Levey, Vice Chancellor for Administration Peter W. Blackman and several others, including physicians and campus architects, traveled to New York to tell Pei what they wanted in a hospital.

"We talked about the concept of light, and not making it overwhelming in size because we wanted it compartmentalized," recalled Levey. "[The] old hospital's like a bowling alley, it goes about a hundred yards from beginning to end. ... We didn't want a high-tech, modern hospital to be frightening."

The result was a combination of natural-light-filled form with open spaces, fountains and gardens that also incorporated high-tech functionality in a more compact design that could be upgraded as warranted to keep up with advances in medicine. "What is the true impact of space, light and nature on wellness?" asked Pei. "I believe the design ... will affect the people who work, visit, and receive care here. The principal objective is to create an environment of healing."

A group of donors led by A. Jerrold Perenchio, chief executive of Spanish-language television network Univision, raised $150 million to name the medical facility—initially dubbed the Westwood Replacement Hospital—after President Ronald Reagan, Perenchio's neighbor in nearby Bel-Air.

"Although Ronnie couldn't be here today, I hope everyone knows how grateful we are to have this fabulous new medical center named after him," said former First Lady Nancy

Reagan at the April 2000 announcement, speaking on behalf of her husband who was afflicted with Alzheimer's disease. "Perhaps one day the Ronald Reagan UCLA Medical Center will help cure diseases that are now hopeless for people."

Some, however, bristled at the choice of name. "Renaming UCLA's hospital after Ronald Reagan constitutes a new low in administrative pandering," said a *Daily Bruin* editorial, which described Reagan's cuts in federal funding to medical care for the poor, his political campaign against the University of California, and his role in the firing of Clark Kerr. "Renaming a UC hospital after an individual who did little to further either healthcare or higher education is questionable. Attaching the name of an enemy to both of these institutions, though, is ridiculous."

Students, professors, alumni, medical professionals and friends of the university wrote Chancellor Carnesale to voice similar opinions. Carnesale's response to the naysayers was that disagreement with some of Reagan's policies was "not adequate reason" to refuse the same honor that would be given to another individual in whose name a generous gift might have been made.

"There were a lot of people who didn't like Ronald Reagan—they were offended by this," said Michael C. Eicher, vice chancellor for external affairs from 1998 to 2006. "But donors promise you a big chunk of money, and on what grounds are you going to say, 'We will not name it for a president of the United States?'"

Said Levey: "Without the Reagan name, and the people who loved him and respected him and donated to this, we may not have been able to finish this hospital. So, whatever the president did or didn't do in the area of health care or the University of California, in his death, he'll have helped make possible one of the great medical institutions in the world. There'll be a lot of lives saved there."

Shortly after Reagan's death in June 2004, banners bearing the formal name, Ronald Reagan UCLA Medical Center, were installed on fences along the site facing the future entrances on Westwood Plaza and Gayley Avenue.

The 1-million-square-foot, 10-floor medical center (eight above ground) was the single largest project in the history of the University of California, taking six years to plan and eight years to construct. Its four acres encompass not only the Reagan hospital, but the Stewart and Lynda Resnick Neuropsychiatric Hospital and the Mattel Children's Hospital.

Finally, on June 29, 2008, the Ronald Reagan UCLA Medical Center was ready to open its doors and 520 beds to patients. First, however, 342 current patients had to be transferred from the old medical center across the street—some with respiratory equipment, monitors and intravenous drips. Hospital administrators had been planning the move for eight years—each step meticulously timed.

Left: The 1-million-square-foot, 10-floor medical center, resting on four acres, includes the Stewart and Lynda Resnick Neuropsychiatric Hospital and the Mattel Children's Hospital.

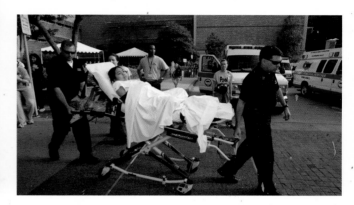

Left: "This building will bring healing, new cures and hope to the people of the world," said Nancy Reagan, on behalf of her husband, President Ronald Reagan, the hospital's namesake, during the hospital's dedication on June 4, 2007. With her, from left, Governor Arnold Schwarzenegger, Acting Chancellor Norman Abrams, Vice Chancellor for Medical Sciences Gerald S. Levey and Mayor Antonio Villaraigosa.

Below: In a meticulously orchestrated move, patients are transferred from the old hospital to the new one, June 29, 2008.

Below left: Hospital patients and staff leave behind their personal recollections and thanks to the Center for Health Sciences building, which housed the UCLA Medical Center for more than 50 years.

Ambulances transport the first patients (above) and the hospital is open for business (right).

A specially trained cadre of 2,100 nurses, doctors, administrators, porters, lift teams, ambulance drivers and respiratory therapists were at the ready. From 3 a.m. to 3 p.m., trauma ambulances were diverted to other area hospitals, although walk-in patients were still treated. At exactly 5 a.m., the old emergency room closed and the new one officially opened across the way. Thirty minutes later, the neuropsychiatric patients were the first to be moved. At 7 a.m., two teams designated "blue" and "gold" traversed separate routes along the hospital perimeters—closed to general traffic—transporting general patients for their 15-minute bed-to-bed journey. A "red" team moved neonatal and critical patients, who required more time and careful observation.

Overseeing this intricately orchestrated endeavor was Richard F. Azar, the medical center's director of transition planning. Azar was aided by university and Los Angeles police, transportation service officials, campus events staff and an outside company specializing in hospital moves. Administrators from other U.S. hospitals with impending moves observed the process.

The entire move went smoothly. At 12:40 p.m., almost three hours ahead of schedule, an announcement over the new PA system was met with cheers and applause: "The last patient has been moved in. Ronald Reagan UCLA Medical Center is officially open. Welcome."

Said David T. Feinberg, chief executive officer of the UCLA Hospital System, at a press conference just after the move was completed: "We're now functioning as a hospital. We have a couple mothers in labor. We have a liver transplant and a heart transplant that will probably take place sometime

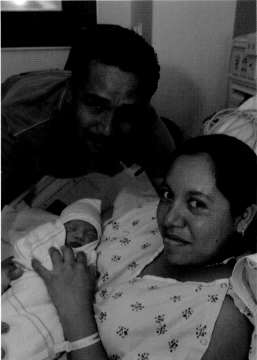

later today. There's somebody with an appendectomy in the ER. We're open and we're absolutely thrilled."

The first baby born at the Reagan hospital was delivered that day at 2:28 p.m. and mother and child were showered with toys, balloons and gifts by hospital staff. In honor of the former president and hospital's namesake, the proud parents named their firstborn, Antonio Ronald Morales.

"WHERE GREAT FUTURES BEGIN"

Six years prior to the opening of UCLA's new hospital, the School of Medicine was about to benefit from an extraordinary act of philanthropy.

In 2002, the medical school received only 13 percent of its funding from the state, forcing the school to seek out additional dollars from research grants, patient care revenue and charitable giving to fulfill its three-part mission of research, education and patient care. The school experienced its most expansive growth under the direction of its second dean, Sherman Mellinkoff, who presided for 24 years. "[He] took it from a small school out west to a national powerhouse," said Levey, the school's fourth dean.

When Levey arrived in 1994, the medical school was entering another growth phase. Yet the school had long suffered from a lack of high-quality research space, and the Northridge earthquake had damaged existing facilities. Levey determined early on that it was critical that the school raise a significant amount of additional funding in the form of several sizable donations from private donors. "State support was not what we would call either sufficient, or especially bountiful,"

Levey recalled. With support from the campus administration, he began putting together a development team. In summer 1995, UCLA secured $45 million from the Gonda family for a building in part to help house a new genetics department. It was a good start. The gift was the largest made by an individual to the University of California. At the back of his mind, however, Levey kept the notion of securing a nine-figure gift to endow the School of Medicine.

At the same time, Chancellor Young and the university administration were quietly putting together the underpinnings of UCLA's second full-scale fundraising campaign. After a two-year quiet phase, the campaign was publicly announced on May 17, 1997—with Chancellor-elect Carnesale in attendance—and sought to raise $1.2 billion over seven years. That amount was considered lofty by some of UCLA's academic leaders and administrators, and there was trepidation that the amount was unattainable.

Many Californians believed that most of UCLA's operating budget came from their tax dollars. In actuality, less than 23 percent of UCLA's expenditures were offset by the state when Campaign UCLA, with its theme "Where Great Futures Begin," was launched. Despite a downturn in the economy amid the dot-com bust of 2000, the campaign was exceedingly successful. In fact, the goal was raised upward twice, to $2.4 billion, and the drive extended by three years to the end of 2005.

The health sciences target for the campaign was $600 million, and Levey continued trying to find a donor to endow the School of Medicine. In the latter half of 2000, Levey met

Above left: David T. Feinberg was appointed chief executive officer of the UCLA Hospital System in June 2007.

Above: Antonio Ronald Morales, the first baby born in the Ronald Reagan UCLA Medical Center, June 29, 2008.

Top: The David Geffen School of Medicine was endowed with an unprecedented $200 million gift from the music magnate in 2002.

Above: The decade-long Campaign UCLA, which ended in 2005, raised $3.05 billion, a record for a public university.

in the country, one for $110 million and another for $100 million. Both schools and affiliated university hospitals were smaller and lower ranked than UCLA, Levey explained. "The hospital is always ranked in the top five in the country, and since it's staffed by our doctors, it's a reflection of the school," Levey said. Geffen asked what had been the largest gift ever made to a medical school. Levey responded that Vanderbilt University had received a gift of stock worth roughly $350 million to endow their cancer center, but it wound up being valued closer to $175 million after the stock lost value. The lunch ended with Geffen offering a $100 million naming gift to endow the school.

Within two days, Levey had met with Carnesale and Vice Chancellor Eicher, and lawyers had drafted and reviewed the proposal. Then Geffen wanted to meet with Levey once more.

"I'm not accepting this," Geffen said, according to Levey. "We're going to forget about this first gift." He ripped up the proposal, noting that Levey had been correct in the dollar amount he quoted and that he had decided to make a statement by giving $200 million. "With that mind-boggling endowment," Levey said, "he ensured the future of the School of Medicine."

As intended, the gift—remarkable in that it was made with no strings attached—was the most ever given to a medical school in the United States, as well as the most sizable made to the University of California. It would help the medical school retain physicians and scientists, launch new programs and initiatives, and recruit the brightest medical students to the renamed David Geffen School of Medicine at UCLA.

Geffen said he had two intentions in making the gift: "to support one of the most innovative medical schools in the world" and "to inspire others to do the same."

He added: "I believe each of us has a responsibility to give back in some way. Los Angeles is my home and I want to do my part in contributing to its future. I have great respect and affection for UCLA and my hope is that with this gift, UCLA's doctors and researchers will be better equipped to unravel medicine's mysteries—and deliver the cures for tomorrow."

While Geffen's gift was the largest made during Campaign UCLA, there were several other significant donations, including $23.2 million for the Eli and Edythe Broad Art Center from the Broads, and $18 million from Glorya Kaufman for the dance building, also renamed for its benefactor.

Campaign UCLA surpassed its fundraising goal by bringing in $3.05 billion—a record for a public university— from more than 225,000 donors in the 10-year period ending December 31, 2005.

A capstone of the campaign was the creation of a donor wall on the east end of Wilson Plaza at the bottom of Janss Steps honoring UCLA's alumni and friends

with Andy Spahn, who was head of corporate affairs and communications and handled charitable giving for DreamWorks SKG, the entertainment conglomerate created by director Steven Spielberg, film producer Jeffrey Katzenberg and music executive David Geffen.

Geffen served as a University of California regent from 1980–87, and in 1995 had made a $5 million donation to UCLA's Westwood Playhouse, which was subsequently renamed for the entertainment mogul. Levey pitched him several ideas, including endowing the School of Medicine. About 18 months passed before Levey received a call that Geffen wanted to talk with him. In April 2002, Levey was invited to lunch at Geffen's home. Geffen informed Levey that he had been asked to endow a medical school on the East Coast. "And he said to Andy, 'Why should I do that because I live here on the West Coast?'" Levey recounted. "And so he said, if I remember correctly, the expression was, 'Why don't we dust off the Levey proposal?'"

At the time, UCLA's request was for $150 million, but Geffen made clear he would only give $100 million. Still, he asked Levey how the $150 million figure had been derived. Levey explained that there had been two recent school namings

whose lifetime giving totaled at least $1 million. With the Court of Philanthropy, the university wanted to create an enduring monument honoring the vision and leadership of UCLA's most generous benefactors while reminding future generations of the vital role that private support has played in UCLA's rise to prominence.

As the campaign neared its end, and with the United States involved in wars in Afghanistan and Iraq, Carnesale decided he wanted to turn his focus back to matters of national security. He announced on September 6, 2005, that he would take a yearlong sabbatical beginning July 1, 2006—stepping down a year earlier than expected and two days before his 70th birthday. "Engineers solve problems and create opportunities," Carnesale told *UCLA Magazine* in July 2006. "I hope I've done that here."

A DEFT TRANSITION

In late April 2006, the *Los Angeles Times* broke the news with an article headlined "Field for UCLA Chief is Down to One." Deborah A. Freund, Syracuse University's second-in-command, was the frontrunner for UCLA's top job. Although she had strong supporters and was praised for her expertise in healthcare financing, critics charged that Freund lacked experience because she had never been a university president before, and that she came from a less prestigious institution. *The Times* noted that UCLA ranked 25th among top national universities, as rated by *U.S. News & World Report*, while Syracuse was 50th.

A few days later, Freund withdrew her candidacy, citing "family conflicts." Negotiations had reportedly ceased because her husband, chair of Syracuse's economics department, had not been offered a faculty position at UCLA. (Freund was selected as president of Claremont Graduate University in July 2010.)

With no candidates left, the Board of Regents decided to start the search anew. In the interim, University of California President Robert Dynes (who had succeeded Atkinson in 2003) turned to a familiar—and reassuring—UCLA figure. On July 1, 2006, Norman Abrams, a member of the law school faculty since 1959, vice chancellor for academic personnel from 1991–2001, and interim dean of the law school during 2003-04, took the helm of UCLA as a second search got underway. Abrams wanted to be appointed "chancellor" for the transition period—as Vern O. Knudsen had been—but he learned the process was complicated. Unlike the position of chancellor, which needs to be approved by the Board of Regents, an interim chancellor can be appointed by the president. Abrams asked Dynes for the title of acting chancellor, as opposed to interim chancellor.

"I don't want to be a caretaker,'" Abrams recalled telling Dynes, who responded, "I don't want you to be a caretaker." Abrams reinforced the point: "So I'm going to be chancellor and I'm going to do things." Dynes replied: "Yeah, that's what I want." Said Abrams: "So from that perspective, I wasn't acting, I was the chancellor, and he agreed with it."

From the start, Abrams was confronted with the first of what would become a yearlong series of crises necessitating firm action. During his first week in office he faced public uproar over the number of UCLA's African-American admittees, which had dropped to a 30-year low in California's post-Proposition 209 climate. Only two percent of students who declared their intent to enroll at UCLA for 2006 fall classes were African-American.

"That just cried out for action, and it was a real problem because there was a question about what one could do about it given Proposition 209," Abrams said. "I decided to focus my attention and take responsibility for certain things. This was a crisis that required the chancellor. ... In normal course, the chancellor doesn't spend a lot of time on admissions."

Abrams believed it was critical that the public view this as something he was taking seriously. He formed and chaired an internal working group that met weekly for the duration of the year to address the issue. He worked with the Academic Senate, which voted to change the admissions application review process to follow a more "holistic" approach—similar to that used by Berkeley and some private universities. A prospective student's entire application would be read by the same readers, instead of parsing portions out to different readers as was previously done.

Norman Abrams, acting chancellor, 2006–2007.

The Chancellor's Office covered the additional costs associated with administering the new application review process.

To address the issue from a broad-range perspective, Abrams established the African American Enrollment Task Force, which included students, alumni and community leaders, and was led by Peter Taylor, former regent and past president of the UCLA Alumni Association. One idea, which sought to circumvent restrictions of Proposition 209 while operating within the law, was to set up a scholarship fund entirely administered by an external group.

To attract admitted African-American students—who were often recruited by private institutions offering substantial scholarships—and entice them to enroll at UCLA, a legacy scholarship fund was created at the California Community Foundation, headed by alumna Antonia Hernández. The scholarship fund was entirely administered by the Los Angeles-based nonprofit, and championed by UCLA leaders and alumni groups, including the Black Alumni Association, which led fundraising efforts. In one year, $1.75 million was raised for scholarships, which ranged from one-time $1,000 grants to four-year awards of up to $9,000 per year.

"We can and will preserve the great heritage of young African-American leaders at UCLA—leaders who are equipped with a first-class education and who go on to accomplish great things for our communities," Taylor said when the scholarship fund was announced. "I am proud the UCLA family is stepping up to the plate, and that we're seeing decisive action that will make a difference."

Student and campus groups also took a lead role in an effort to counter reports that black students on campus felt uncomfortable and that some prospective students were reluctant to enroll. The Black Alumni Association and the African Student Union, in conjunction with the Academic Advancement Program and Student Affairs, organized a three-day admit weekend in the spring. "Black by Popular Demand," the African Student Union's program, hosted students for two nights in the residence halls, provided tours and offered informational meetings.

Within a year, African-American freshman enrollment nearly doubled to 204, or four percent of those who said they intended to enroll.

"UCLA's new admissions process is much fairer," said Darnell M. Hunt, director of the Ralph J. Bunche Center for African American Studies, in 2007. "It holistically considers not only what each applicant brings to the campus learning environment, but also his or her likely contributions to society. ... These are the defining elements of 'merit' that resonate with the mission of a public, land grant institution like UCLA."

Hunt noted that colleagues from other states where affirmative action had been eliminated or was under attack had contacted the Bunche Center about UCLA's revised admissions process. "It is imperative that we continue to strategize with others about how to build on this victory, particularly given the challenges that undoubtedly lie ahead."

Abrams became immersed in another pressing issue just two months into his tenure—one dealing with matters of life and death. UCLA researchers were increasingly being targeted by animal rights activists, both on campus and at their homes.

The names, addresses and phone numbers of several faculty members and administrators who conducted or supported scientific experiments on primates or other animals were posted online. More than half a dozen researchers were subjected to a violent campaign of intimidation and harassment designed to pressure them to abandon their scientific work. The researchers received hundreds of threatening emails, phone calls and home visits, and the activists asserted that they would not cease until researchers stopped using animals in their work.

A package including razor blades and animal fur was sent to the wife of one researcher with a message telling her to persuade her husband to stop his animal research, or "what he does to the animals we will do to you." The threats escalated into violent actions. Several cars were firebombed, one family was terrorized by firecrackers repeatedly being thrown onto their balcony at night, and in June 2006 an incendiary device meant for a UCLA professor was mistakenly left on a neighbor's doorstep. Although it failed to ignite, investigators said the device had enough explosives to kill the occupants. Animal extremists took credit for the incident and the FBI became involved.

A month after Abrams assumed his post, he learned that a researcher had decided to give up his research citing the safety of his family, and that the faculty was complaining that the administration was not providing enough support. It was then, Abrams said, that he had been apprised of the extensive harassment that the faculty had been enduring. Abrams, an expert in anti-terrorism law, was shocked. He called the acts "domestic terrorism" and, upset that he had not been aware of the situation sooner, took immediate steps to protect the faculty. "It was very clear that this was unacceptable—to have our faculty being harassed without us doing enough," Abrams said later.

The acting chancellor enlisted campus counsel and other legal experts to explore litigation against the "ringleaders" who allegedly incited the illegal activity, as well as against those who claimed to be responsible for the acts themselves. He imposed tightened security measures and extended the immediate response services of campus police to support faculty who had experienced harassment at their homes. UCLA contributed to the FBI's reward, doubling it to $60,000 in exchange for information leading to the arrest

The Rolfe Courtyard is overrun with giant octopi, bananas and students dressed as colorful characters from Thomas Pynchon's postmodern novel *Gravity's Rainbow* for the English department's fifth annual "marathon reading," May 2000. The much-beloved tradition, which lasted a decade, began in 1996 with the reading of Herman Melville's *Moby Dick*. About 1,000 attended and more than 300 readers, ranging from students to celebrities, took turns reading passages during a non-stop 24-hour period, with actor Charlton Heston delivering the gripping last lines. In 1998, more than 4,000 attended a 20-hour reading of Ralph Ellison's *Invisible Man*, with actor John Lithgow reading the first passage and civil rights activist Rosa Parks making a special guest appearance.

and conviction of persons responsible. In conjunction with the University of California—other campuses had experienced similar acts of harassment and violence—Abrams lobbied for the Animal Enterprise Terrorism Act, which strengthened criminal penalties and made such acts a federal crime. It passed in November 2006. Abrams turned to the media to make sure the extended UCLA community knew where the university stood and that he was taking things seriously.

"As an academic institution, UCLA is open to differing opinions and encourages free speech," Abrams wrote in a message published in the *Daily Bruin* in August 2006. "I condemn in the strongest possible terms, however, the use of violence and deplore the harassment that some of our faculty members have been subjected to." Abrams, who would also become subject to demonstrations outside his home, added that UCLA would renew its commitment to support humane and tightly regulated animal research, but would not halt biomedical research. Such an action, he said, would risk taking "away the hope from millions of people" afflicted with diseases that could be cured. "Without animal research many of the advances that could lead to the next breakthroughs in medical knowledge would not be possible," he continued. "We will not be deterred by the actions of a few fanatic and misguided extremists."

The Royce Hall portico illuminated at night, c. 2007.

Abrams appointed the Task Force on the Protection of Faculty Research and Researchers, led by Jonathan D. Varat, former law school dean. Three months later, the group issued a report, which, among other steps, recommended creating a "one-stop service" for the affected UCLA employees and their families, as well as the department chairs, deans and students associated with them. The group's recommendations put in place ongoing measures that would help with future incidents, while also becoming a national model. The Committee for the Use of Animals in Research at the Society for Neuroscience, for example, created a "Best Practices for Protecting Researchers and Research" based upon UCLA's report. (In 2008, the situation further escalated when a UCLA vanpool vehicle was set on fire in Irvine, California, and an incendiary device exploded on a professor's porch, causing extensive damage. UCLA obtained a temporary restraining order prohibiting the activists from posting UCLA researchers' contact information online and restricting them from coming within 150 feet of their homes.)

"We had a system, but it wasn't consistent, there wasn't follow-through," Abrams said. "Again, like the African-American admissions, having the chancellor pay attention to it makes a difference. And things get done more quickly when you put the weight of your office and your authority behind something, and just more gets accomplished. It'd be nice if you could do that on everything—you can't, you have to be selective."

Abrams earned the respect of the faculty and others on campus for his swift actions and confident manner in running the university. Some urged him to consider applying to become chancellor permanently. Abrams, who was approaching the age of 75, gave it some thought. He had enjoyed the experience and believed that "it was the right thing to do," but ultimately decided against pursuing the post. After 13 months, a successor had been named, and Abrams ended his service on July 31, 2007. His tenure, albeit brief, was widely noted. And his desire of being an "acting" chancellor had been achieved.

"Interim college chiefs may sit in the president's chair, but they usually don't act like presidents," declared the *Chronicle of Higher Education* in June 2007. "Norman Abrams, acting chancellor of the University of California at Los Angeles, has bucked that trend."

Toward a Centennial
2007 and Beyond

Above: Students perform the Eight-clap on the roof of the Union Rescue Mission in downtown Los Angeles after spending the day washing down walls and windows and serving hundreds of meals to the homeless on Volunteer Day, September 21, 2010.

Opposite: During the College of Letters and Science commencement ceremony on June 10, 2011, graduating seniors bear flags representing the 139 countries the Peace Corps has served since its creation in 1961. UCLA is the alma mater to more than 1,800 Peace Corps volunteers.

*O**n December 21, 2006, the University of California Board of Regents appointed UCLA's ninth chief executive: Gene D. Block, provost of the University of Virginia. The campus Block took charge of in 2007 had evolved into a $3.8 billion enterprise, with 37,000 students as well as 27,000 faculty and staff members. By this time, UCLA was generating an estimated $9.3 billion impact on the local economy.*

In the fourth quarter of 2008, however, the United States entered a financial downturn that economists labeled the Great Recession. Not since the Great Depression of the 1930s had the economy experienced such a severe decline. "The recession we had previously hoped to avoid is now with us in full gale force," wrote David Shulman, senior economist with the UCLA Anderson Forecast, the business school's economic forecasting group founded in 1952 and one of the nation's most widely watched and often-cited economic outlooks. In 2009, the personal income of California residents dropped for the first time since World War II.

As in other times of economic uncertainty, pursuing higher education was a refuge for America's youth. UCLA remained the nation's most popular university, with an unprecedented 57,000 high school students applying for about 4,700 spots in the fall 2010 entering class—making the university, with a 23 percent admittance rate, among the most competitive in the nation. UCLA was also the most economically diverse institution among its peers in the Association of American Universities. Based on financial need, 36 percent of UCLA undergraduates were awarded Federal Pell Grants in 2010–11. UCLA reached another milestone that year, topping $1 billion in competitively awarded research grants and contracts, an increase of 15 percent since 2007. The David Geffen School of Medicine received the largest amount, $405 million, while the College of Letters and Science brought in $143 million.

The strength of UCLA's teaching and research training was showcased when two alumni, both of whom earned multiple degrees at UCLA, won Nobel Prizes. Elinor Ostrom, a triple degree holder in economics, was awarded the Nobel in 2009. The following year, Richard F. Heck, who had obtained his bachelor's and doctorate at UCLA, received the Nobel in chemistry. Also in 2010, the National Research Council released its most recent ratings of doctoral graduate programs, and 40 of UCLA's 59 programs received scores that placed them in the top 10. Only two institutions, Berkeley and Harvard University, had more programs in the top 10. In comparison, of the 36 UCLA doctoral programs examined in 1995, 24 ranked in the top quartile.

But the state's staggering economic crisis—with an estimated $25 billion budget deficit—was taking its toll on UCLA. "As I look ahead, I see a magnificent institution that is slowly starving," Block wrote in the January 2010 issue of UCLA Magazine. "UCLA, as it was envisioned and as it has always fulfilled that vision, is an endangered species. Right now, while California lawmakers try to repair the state's fiscal health, other elite universities are circling, ready to poach our talent." In response, Block has begun working with UCLA administrators to implement a strategy for "safeguarding UCLA's financial future," which includes cost-cutting measures and revenue generating vehicles such as increased licensing of intellectual property.

In November 2010, in light of continued fee increases, the Board of Regents approved a historic measure that changed the terminology for the "educational fee" to "tuition"—a word the regents had avoided for decades in light of the 1960 Master Plan for Higher Education's promise that every Californian could attend the state's university systems "tuition-free." Said University of California President Mark G. Yudof: "I wish UC were free. But that's not the world we live in."

In July 2011, the state further reduced its contribution to the University of California to an all-time low of 11 percent of the university's operating budget. Consequently, revenue from tuition surpassed state support for the first time.

While UCLA officials sought ways to absorb a projected $125 million in cuts for the 2011–12 academic year, they also began planning for the Centennial Campaign—the campus's third broad-based fundraising drive—leading up to UCLA's 100th anniversary in 2019. Block also asked UCLA alumni and friends to step up as ambassadors and do what they could as advocates for the university. Several alumni and faculty members gave back to their alma mater with transformative gifts.

"The people of California, who have long depended on UCLA, are now looking to us to steer the state through this difficult period to a better tomorrow," Block said. "They are expecting us to continue providing world-class education, top-ranked medical care, cutting-edge discoveries and so much more."

Gene D. Block (left) and Robert C. Dynes (right) at a press conference in the James West Alumni Center after the announcement of Block's selection as UCLA's ninth chancellor, December 21, 2006.

THE BIOLOGIST

Gene D. Block, 58, who had been the University of Virginia's provost for almost six years, was selected as UCLA's chancellor from a nationwide pool of nearly 100 candidates. At Virginia, Block was credited with helping to increase racial and gender diversity among the student body and faculty—a high-profile issue at UCLA, which was recovering from a decline in underrepresented student admissions in a post-Proposition 209 climate.

"Both the University of Virginia and its provost, Gene D. Block, exude stability," wrote the Los Angeles Times. "But now the alarm clock is ringing for change in Block's life." Although UCLA is a century younger than Virginia, with about twice as many students, the Times noted that Block would find notable similarities between the two universities. "Both are state institutions with high admissions standards, fiercely proud alumni, vaunted athletic programs and important hospitals and law schools." However, UCLA's stronger emphasis on engineering and related sciences appealed to Block.

Block, a renowned expert in circadian rhythms, and the sixth UCLA chief executive to posses a background in the sciences, began his career at Virginia in 1978 as an assistant professor of biology. Before being appointed Virginia's provost, he was the institution's vice president for research and public service. Although Block spent almost three decades in Charlottesville, Virginia, he carried West Coast credentials, having earned his bachelor's degree in psychology from Stanford University and both his master's and doctorate in psychology from the University of Oregon.

On May 13, 2008, Block was formally invested as UCLA's ninth chief executive. The inauguration was unique in its focus on diverse cultural performances. UCLA's Music of African-Americans Ensemble sang the national anthem. Other performances included a jazz group led by legendary guitarist and UCLA Professor Kenny Burrell, UCLA Chinese and Brazilian music ensembles, Mariachi de Uclatlán, and a Balinese welcoming

Gene David Block

UCLA's ninth chief executive Gene D. Block was born in 1948, in Monticello, New York. The son of a Catskills dairy distributor, Block—who would become a circadian biologist of international renown—was captivated as a child with the inner workings of objects such as transistor and vacuum-tube radios.

Although interested in science from an early age, Block followed a winding course through his early college career. On the advice of his older brother, a graduate student at Stanford University, Block moved to California. He enrolled at Foothill College, a community college near Palo Alto. He then transferred to Berkeley, but left after a quarter. During the winter of his second year in college, Block switched to Stanford, where he earned his bachelor's degree in psychology in 1970, and found his calling in academia. After graduation, he married his hometown sweetheart, Carol. Subsequently, Block earned both his master's and doctorate in psychology, with specializations in neurobiology, from the University of Oregon in 1972 and 1975 respectively.

Right: Chancellor Gene D. Block at his inauguration in Royce Hall, May 8, 2008.

Below: UCLA Volunteer Day, 2010.

After returning to Stanford for postdoctoral work in 1975, he studied with "the father of biological timing," Colin S. Pittendrigh, and with Donald Kennedy, who headed the university's program in human biology and later served as president of Stanford.

In 1978, Block was appointed as an assistant professor of biology at the University of Virginia. After working his way through the professorial ranks, he moved into Virginia's administration in 1993 as vice provost for research. Five years later, he became vice president for research and public service, before being appointed in 2001 as vice president and provost—the No. 2 position—at Virginia. Block was in the post for six years when, in December 2006, he was selected as UCLA's new chancellor, effective August 2007.

Throughout his administrative career, Block continued to pursue scientific research. An expert in circadian rhythms—the cellular and neural mechanisms of sleep-and-wake cycles—Block has investigated the effects of aging on the cells in the brain that form the biological clock. In 1991, he became founding director of the National Science Foundation Center for Biological Timing at the University of Virginia, which he oversaw for more than a decade. The inventor of numerous devices, Block co-invented a patented non-contact respiratory monitor for the prevention of Sudden Infant Death Syndrome.

At UCLA, he maintains a laboratory and holds faculty appointments in psychiatry and biobehavioral sciences in the David Geffen School of Medicine, and in physiological science in the College of Letters and Science.

As chancellor, Block has focused on building an affinity with students in both academic and informal settings. He has taught *Fiat Lux* seminars, held regular breakfasts with undergraduates and attended move in week at the residence halls. Students have even found him staffing the "Ask Me" booth in Bruin Plaza during Welcome Week. Block also has maintained a commitment to community outreach, frequently visiting local schools and—recalling his experience as a transfer student—community colleges, where he emphasizes that going straight from high school to a four-year university is not always a direct route and that "anything is possible."

Pledging that UCLA would become more involved in societal engagement, at his inauguration on May 13, 2008, Block said: "I believe we have before us a remarkable opportunity to define for California and the nation what it means to be a public research university in contemporary urban America."

dance with a ceremonial scattering of flowers. The program reflected UCLA's diversity and represented the broad range of music taught at the new UCLA Herb Alpert School of Music, established with a $30 million endowment in November 2007 from A&M Records co-founder Herb Alpert and his wife, Lani. A vibrant ceremonial Staff of Office, made of glass beads, wood, iron and cloth of the Yoruba Peoples in Nigeria, was borrowed from the Fowler Museum for the momentous occasion.

"We biologists like to talk about DNA, the genetic material in the cells of living organisms," Block said in his inaugural address. "It is sometimes compared to a set of blueprints that contain instructions. What's in UCLA's DNA? What has been handed down to us from those who came before?"

Block outlined several UCLA hallmarks, including a "spirit of discovery and collaboration—an eagerness to create knowledge together." He referenced Nobel laureate Paul D. Boyer as having remarked that "at UCLA cooperation trumps competition," and that UCLA's "unique, deliberate research culture" capitalizes on the depth and breadth of disciplines and the exchange of ideas among scholars.

He also noted UCLA's decades-long commitment to diversity and to educational opportunity for individuals from all backgrounds. "UCLA serves more students from low-income families than any other major research university in the nation," Block said. "More than one-third of UCLA undergraduates are on Federal Pell Grants. One in four is—as I was—part of their family's first generation to attend college."

As part of his vision for the university, Block said he would continue the university's commitment to academic excellence, increase and strengthen the diversity of the campus community, and ensure financial security by creating larger endowments through private support—all while deepening UCLA's societal engagement.

"As we move this agenda forward, I will call upon every member of the Bruin family and all the people of Los Angeles and California, the owners of UCLA, to participate," Block said. "We each have a role to play."

SPIRIT OF SERVICE

Since his arrival, Block—a vocal champion of public higher education—had also promoted deepening UCLA's civic engagement, part of the university's tripartite mission of teaching, research and service. "I think we're going to see that UCLA is going to have a much greater presence in Los Angeles in the future," Block said during a service announcement that aired on local public television station KCET in fall 2010. "At least that's my dream."

A year earlier, the Chancellor's Office created the UCLA Volunteer Center, an organization, financed by the UCLA

Foundation, which is intended to heighten UCLA's commitment to public service by linking students, alumni, faculty and staff with the broader community through thousands of volunteer engagement efforts. "Civic engagement and community involvement are core values of our institution," Block wrote to the campus community in May 2009. "At a time when volunteer participation is viewed increasingly as a national priority, it is critical for UCLA to be a catalyst for social change and to serve as a leader, inspiring other institutions as well."

On September 22, 2009, two days before the start of fall classes, 4,300 UCLA students—an army of blue and gold T-shirt-clad undergraduates, primarily freshmen—fanned out across Los Angeles. They were participating in UCLA Volunteer Day, the biggest single-day public service event ever held by the university.

The students were transported by 100 buses and led by more than 300 alumni, professors, staff members and returning undergraduates. During the five-hour event, approximately 1,000 new students worked in Griffith Park repairing hiking trails and clearing brush, 1,000 more cleaned up Point Dume in Malibu, 500 helped with gardening and maintaining graves at the Veterans Affairs hospital and cemetery in West Los Angeles, and 500 students went to each of five Los Angeles Unified School District (LAUSD) schools for painting and other beautification projects.

At Samuel Gompers Middle School in South Los Angeles, Mayor Antonio Villaraigosa, a UCLA alumnus, joined Chancellor Block as the pair grabbed brushes to help

Above: Royce quad, May 23, 2011.

Below right: Renee (left) and Meyer (right) Luskin, 2011.

paint the school. "We wanted to give the young people of UCLA here a sense of connectedness to their community and give the young people at Gompers an opportunity to see what the future could look like, that they too could go to UCLA," Villaraigosa told the *Los Angeles Times*. Student volunteer Shuchita Vandra, a junior, told the *Times*, that a university education should not be taken for granted. "With such a tremendous privilege, we should definitely use our education and resources for good," Vandra said. "Why not benefit the community around us?"

Following President Barack Obama's call on Americans to engage in acts of service, students are more interested than ever in participating in community service, according to UCLA's annual survey of entering freshman students at four-year universities nationwide administered by the Higher Education Research Institute at the Graduate School of Education and Information Studies (GSEIS). In fall 2010, approximately one-third of the more than 200,000 entering freshmen surveyed stated that there was a "very good chance" they would participate in volunteer or community service work, a record high since the question was first asked in 1990.

Said Block: "Service is key to UCLA's mission as a public university, but I want our students' commitment to it to last a lifetime."

Also in September 2009, UCLA entered into a partnership with the LAUSD, launching a pilot-program school in the Robert F. Kennedy Community Schools Complex, located on the site of the former Ambassador Hotel in the nearby Pico-Union neighborhood. The UCLA Community School was the first of five small, autonomous public schools united by a social justice philosophy that honors the legacy of Senator Robert F. Kennedy, who was assassinated at the Ambassador in 1968. The school, which originally opened to students in kindergarten through fifth grade, has since expanded to include all of K-12. Unlike charter schools that recruit students from across the city, the UCLA Community School exclusively teaches neighborhood students, providing high-quality education in an underserved area.

UCLA's Center X, the GSEIS arm for school reform, brought in faculty members, student teachers and other experts as volunteers to help support the school's mission. Where Pioneer Bruins once danced at the Cocoanut Grove nightclub, students now perform theater skits, sing or recite original poetry using sign language. "What makes our school so unique is the fact that we have so many opportunities to work directly with the faculty and staff from UCLA," said Principal Georgia Ann Lazo, an alumna of UCLA's Principal Leadership Institute. "It's not only comforting to know that the university is there for us, but it's very rewarding to see how many professors and instructors are willing to commit so much time to our students."

BUILDING A FUTURE

As campus leaders began discussions for launching the university's third fundraising campaign, culminating with UCLA's centennial in 2019, several individuals made significant gifts that helped advance the university.

In January 2011, Southern California business leader Meyer Luskin and his wife, Renee—both alumni—donated $100 million, the second largest gift ever made to UCLA.

Half of the Luskin donation was directed to the School of Public Affairs, which was renamed for the couple. The money went toward endowments supporting fellowships, as well as emerging research areas, including new programs in urban studies and social justice.

"Renee and I have been asked, why the School of Public Affairs?" Luskin said during the naming ceremony. "We believe that our society's most important problem is: How do we do a better job of living together? ... If we don't learn to live and let live, if we do not create a community and a world where an equal opportunity, justice and an active regard for the environment is the rule, then no act of technological genius will matter because the likelihood is that some of us, or most of us, will be denied the enjoyment of the wonders of this planet and the gifts of science. It is imperative that we develop the plans, techniques and laws for a peaceful and productive society."

Another 40 percent of the gift was designated for a new conference center, which would also be named for the couple. "Hosting scholars from around the world and engaging with the community to address leading problems require modern facilities and overnight accommodations for participants," said Executive Vice Chancellor and Provost Scott L. Waugh. The final 10 percent helped fund the College of Letters and Science's Luskin Endowment for Thought Leadership, providing support for academic conferences and an annual lecture. The endowment is intended to help fund conferences that otherwise may have difficulty securing funding. For example, academic

departments in the humanities frequently have fewer resources at their disposal than those in the sciences or medicine.

Luskin, president and chairman of Scope Industries, which recycles bakery waste to make an animal-feed ingredient, said that a $30 scholarship allowed him to continue his UCLA career, which had been interrupted by military service during World War II.

The graduate student fellowships could benefit future students for the next 50 to 70 years, said Frank Gilliam Jr., dean of the public affairs school. As state support for graduate fellowships has diminished in the last few years, Gilliam explained, there has been a trend of graduate students turning down UCLA for other schools that can offer them more money. The fellowship funding will help continue to keep UCLA competitive in attracting top talent in both the faculty and student body, while expanding UCLA's role in developing a contemporary learning environment for the next generation of public leaders, he added.

"The Luskins' generosity will enable us to expand a regional and national debate on some of the most challenging questions of our time," Gilliam said." How do we design modern cities that are livable and sustainable? How do we assimilate immigrants while securing our borders? How do we move toward a more just and equitable society?" Previously, Luskin had donated $5 million to the university to create the Luskin Center for Innovation in 2008, a problem-solving center devoted to applied research and policy development

relevant to the needs of Los Angeles, including addressing environmental issues such as pollution. The center moved to the School of Public Affairs in January 2010.

The Luskins' donation followed another transformational gift. Professor Paul Ichiro Terasaki, who had enrolled in UCLA as a transfer student in 1948, earned his bachelor's, master's and doctorate degrees, all in zoology, before becoming a renowned faculty member and pioneer in organ transplant medicine. In 1964, he developed a test that became the international standard for tissue typing—a procedure for determining the compatibility of organ donors and recipients. Since then, all kidney, and select heart, liver, pancreas, lung and bone marrow donors were matched to recipients using the test he developed.

In May 2010, Terasaki donated $50 million to the Division of Life Sciences in the College of Letters and Science—the largest gift ever made to the college. In recognition of his achievements and generosity, UCLA's new life sciences building was named in Terasaki's honor when it opened in October 2010. The building houses 33 laboratories, where scientists conduct interdisciplinary research in fields such as cell biology, neuroscience, genomics and stem cell research.

"I owe my whole career to UCLA," he said. "UCLA gave me the opportunity to do the research that led to the development of tissue typing. At many other universities, I would not have had that kind of freedom in the lab."

Terasaki, who along with his family, spent three years in an internment camp during World War II, said he never considered attending any university but UCLA. Fees, he added, were $39 a semester.

"In the long run, I think philanthropy is going to be the major determinant in how we can continue to be excellent with reduced state support," Block told the *National Journal* in March 2010.

In January 2011, after recently elected Governor Edmund G. "Jerry" Brown Jr. (who also served from 1975–83) presented his state budget proposal, President Yudof (who succeeded Robert C. Dynes in 2008) asked Block to prepare UCLA for cuts of nearly $100 million—the campus's share of a $500 million reduction for the university system.

"That leaves me, along with the chancellors of other UC campuses, staring at a possibility that was unthinkable only a few years ago: the slow dismantling of the greatest university system in the world, one that champions the American dream of a college education," Block wrote in an April 2011 opinion piece in the *Los Angeles Times*. Generations of post-World War II students were products of the state's university systems, Block continued, fueling California's growth as they went on to become entrepreneurs, scientists, doctors or other innovators. "For those who think this is yet another example of a public

Below left: Professor Paul Ichiro Terasaki, in front of the Terasaki Life Sciences Building, 2010.

Below: Looking east over the heart of campus toward downtown Los Angeles, August 5, 2009.

official crying wolf, let me assure you that the opportunity for California's less affluent and even middle-class students to attend the University of California is diminishing with each budget cut, and California's present and future are sinking with it."

In fall 2000, undergraduate students paid $3,700 annually to attend UCLA. By 2011–12, they would pay $13,908—almost a four-fold increase. In April 2011, Brown warned that without relief in the budget situation, annual tuition could rise to as much as $25,000 in the future.

Meanwhile, the university has sought to recruit a greater number of out-of-state students, who pay higher fees, thereby bringing in more revenue. Nonresidents made up about 12 percent of the incoming freshman class for fall 2011, up from eight percent the year before. UCLA's nonresident population, including international students, is slightly higher, at 18 percent.

More than 3,000 international students, almost two-thirds being graduate students, attended UCLA in 2010–11.

"A moderate increase in the proportion of non-residents would generate millions of dollars in new revenue to protect instructional programs for all UCLA students," Block wrote to UCLA faculty and staff in a June 2009 budget update. "There are strong intellectual arguments for geographical diversity; non-resident students can enrich the educational experience for all."

Located on the Pacific Rim, UCLA has long extended outreach efforts to Asian colleges and universities, and Block has sought to raise UCLA's international profile even further. UCLA has signed 39 agreements with educational institutions in China, and in fall 2011, an estimated 1,200 students from China enrolled in undergraduate and graduate degree programs at UCLA—the most from any foreign nation. Since debuting in the late 1970s, UCLA's emblematic apparel remained popular in China, with more than 80 UCLA merchandise outlets throughout the country. Other nations, including South Korea, Taiwan, India and Japan have sent numerous students to study at UCLA as well. In June 2009, UCLA and Peking University in Beijing opened a joint research institute in science and engineering, encouraging extensive research collaborations between more than 100 faculty members from both institutions, making it one of the largest collaborative research efforts between any University of California campus and an overseas university.

"The quality of our academic programs and reputation, as well as our location on the Pacific Rim, gives UCLA a competitive edge in bringing the best and brightest students from overseas," said Bob Ericksen, director of the Dashew Center for International Students and Scholars in Tom Bradley International Hall, named for the five-term mayor who attended UCLA from 1937–40.

Although a growing number of students may be coming from outside of California, more than three-fourths of UCLA's alumni remain in the region after graduation. Many of them have become leaders in business and society. It was no coincidence that the aerospace industry and Silicon Valley emerged in California, Block wrote in his *Times* opinion piece. While the California state university systems are not in danger of disappearing, he added, students will have difficulty pursuing the same paths to innovation if they graduate with a tuition debt of $50,000 or more. "It is our generation's responsibility to prove that the California dream need not die with the baby boomers," Block implored.

"As difficult as the current fiscal challenges are," Block said. "I have every confidence that we will emerge from this time strong and thriving. Excellence is in UCLA's DNA. The institution has great forward momentum energized by a history of accomplishment."

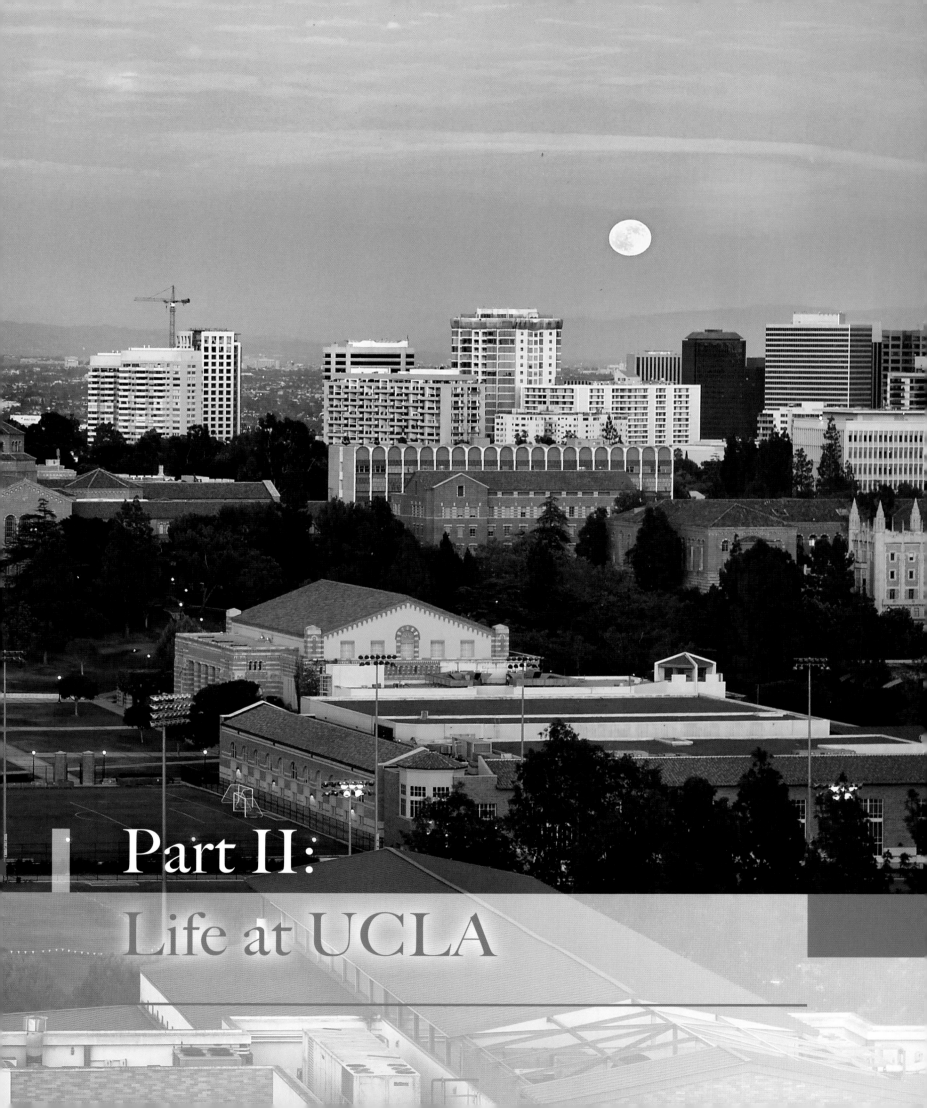

Part II:
Life at UCLA

On Rolling Hills

Above: A view northward of the land that would become UCLA, with the arroyo that divided east and west campus (center) and Wilshire Boulevard (running horizontally at bottom), c. 1925.

Opposite: Looking west at UCLA, August 2007. Hilgard Avenue borders the campus near the bottom of the page, with the 405 Freeway at top.

*I*t is difficult to picture the urban UCLA campus, with its densely constructed 419 acres, as tranquil pastoral fields. Yet as recently as the mid-1920s, the land upon which UCLA lies was part of the largest undeveloped property tract remaining in western Los Angeles.

"It was pretty much as nature had created it," University of California Regent Edward A. Dickson wrote in his memoir, recounting the day in spring 1923 when he and friend Irwin J. Muma discovered the area "rather by accident."

Out for a leisurely walk over the rolling hills of what was then known as the Wolfskill Ranch, the pair decided to crawl through the crossbars of a dilapidated wooden fence and hike up to the crest. From this vantage, they could see clear out to the Pacific Ocean, and behind them, the rising slopes of the Santa Monica Mountains. The scene evoked memories of Berkeley, their alma mater, with its hilly topography and view of the Golden Gate. Instinctively, Dickson knew it would be the ideal site for a permanent campus of the Southern Branch of the University of California, as UCLA was first called.

While land in neighboring Beverly Hills and Santa Monica was rapidly being developed, this tract was kept fairly intact despite having been sold multiple times since the region was first colonized in the early 19th century.

During Spanish rule of Alta California, Don José Máximo Alanis settled on the bucolic landscape, raising horses and cattle. Alanis, who had been an officer in the Spanish army, named his property Rancho San José de Buenos Ayres. Twenty years later, under Mexican rule and surrounded by powerful landowners, Alanis became wary of the intentions of neighbor Francisco Sepúlveda of the Rancho San Vicente y Santa Mónica and petitioned the Mexican government to secure his ownership of the land. In 1843, Alanis was granted the 4,438 acres, which extended from what would become Sawtelle

Boulevard, east to Beverly Hills, south to Pico Boulevard and north to the foothills of the Santa Monica Mountains.

Alanis died three years after the end of the Mexican-American War and the resulting Mexican Cession of 1848. In 1851, his heirs sold the land and subsequently it exchanged hands several times, including purchase by Benjamin "Don Benito" Wilson, a Tennessee fur trapper who became the second elected mayor of Los Angeles under California statehood and the namesake of Mount Wilson in the nearby San Gabriel Mountains. In 1884, Wilson sold the land for $40,000 to California pioneer John W. Wolfskill. A '49er turned politician and rancher, Wolfskill raised thoroughbreds and farmed a small portion of the land, dubbed the Wolfskill Ranch. His house was located on the southern flatlands of the tract, where the Mormon temple on Santa Monica Boulevard was later built.

In 1887, Wolfskill sold the majority of his ranch to the Los Angeles and Santa Monica Land and Water Company for a planned residential subdivision called Sunset. He also donated 300 acres in 1888 to the federal government to help build the Old Soldiers' Home on Sawtelle Boulevard. The Sunset town site, however, failed to materialize and Wolfskill, who had not been paid in full, was given back his land through foreclosure proceedings. In 1902, he sold 300 acres to the Los Angeles Country Club, but otherwise kept his land whole.

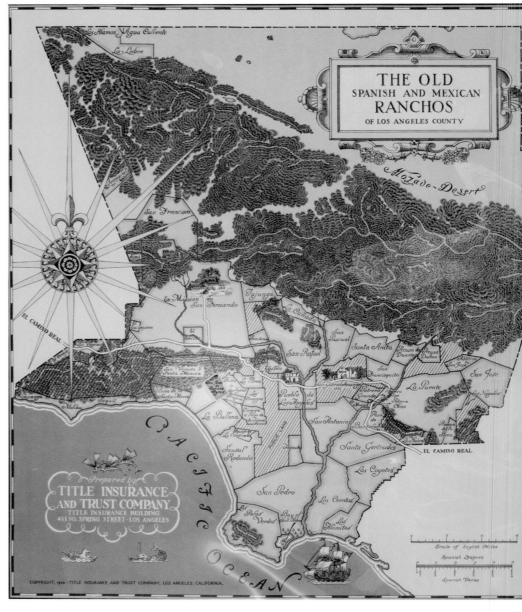

Left: The home of John W. Wolfskill, 1910s.

Above: A 1930 map of the historic Spanish and Mexican Ranchos of Los Angeles County, including San José de Buenos Ayres (outlined in yellow), future site of UCLA.

Left: A northeast view of the Wolfskill Ranch, 1925. Tree-lined Wilshire Boulevard is at lower right, and the heart of the campus would rise between the dirt road, later Westwood Boulevard (center) and the arroyo (to its right).

After Wolfskill's death in 1913, his children held on
to the property, unwilling to sell, until Arthur Letts, founder
of the Broadway department store chain, offered $2 million
in April 1919. Letts intended to develop the land into a
residential community.

In 1923, amid reports that part of the land was to be
subdivided, Dickson paid Letts a visit to discuss his idea. "My
thought was that if enough acreage could be secured for our
future campus needs, we would locate our new University in
the very center of this virgin area," Dickson said. "The owner
could then build up about it an ideal college town—complete
with a business section, student housing, and restricted
residential area."

Letts was enthusiastic about Dickson's idea, but died of
pneumonia shortly after their meeting. His daughter, Gladys,
had married real-estate developer Harold Janss in 1911, and
Letts had been passing more and more of his land on to his son-
in-law and his brother, Edwin Janss. The Janss brothers—the
second generation to run the family-owned Janss Investment

Corporation, one of the largest residential subdividers in
Los Angeles—were left in charge of the vast estate.

The brothers began developing residential tracts north
of Wilshire Boulevard in an area they named Westwood Hills.
They also promoted the district south of Wilshire as "The
Second Hollywood," drawing in William Fox, who established
his movie studio (later 20th Century Fox) on Pico Boulevard,
as well as silent screen star Harold Lloyd, who built a
production studio on Santa Monica Boulevard (sold in 1937
for the Mormon temple site). About 400 northeast acres were
developed by the brothers into the lavish estates of Holmby
Hills, named after Letts' birthplace of Holdenby, England.

In 1924, when the Board of Regents agreed that a new
campus was needed to accommodate the growing university,
Dickson met with the Janss brothers and presented his idea
once again. The brothers agreed to sell 383 acres. Alfonzo
Bell Sr., developer of the nearby Bel-Air estates, added eight
acres to the northern edge of the site. Seeing an opportunity
to develop a residential area and college town around the
campus, the Janss brothers offered the land at $1.1 million,
well below the market value estimated as high as $10 million.

"It was evident that Fate had kept this vast tract
unoccupied … in spite of the attempted encroachment of
progress, for Rancho San Jose de Buenos Ayres offered a
perfect setting upon which to create in great unimpeded glory
the physical design of the University," said the 1930 *Southern
Campus*.

A CAMPUS RISES

On May 3, 1927, construction began on the first structure built on campus: a bridge crossing the deep chaparral-covered ravine that divided the east and west parts of the site.

University of California Supervising Architect George W. Kelham created a Beaux-Arts master plan in 1926 for the campus along an east-west axis, with the Roman-aqueduct inspired Arroyo Bridge as the formal gateway to campus from the east off Hilgard Avenue. Given Southern California's history, a Spanish motif—early Californian and Spanish colonial— had been weighed. However, considered too commonplace, it was abandoned for the Romanesque style in the Lombard tradition—which had also been the signature of UCLA's Vermont Avenue campus, designed by architectural firm Allison & Allison. Noting that Westwood's gentle hills and sunny climate evoked the landscape of Northern Italy, administrators and planners found the architectural scheme fitting. "The style lends itself beautifully to texture and color in brick and terracotta, colorful tile roofs, and the richness of ornamental detail," Kelham wrote to Director Ernest Carroll Moore. Kelham along with David C. Allison, who was retained from the Vermont Avenue campus, worked together to create the original harmonious grouping of campus buildings.

Moore turned the first shovelful of earth during a simple groundbreaking ceremony on September 21, 1927, marking the beginning of construction on the main classroom building (Royce Hall) and the Library (Powell). Steam shovels promptly picked up where he left off.

Engineers found that the land was covered with two to three feet of adobe soil, and a sub-soil below that varied from clean sand to clay-shale that was so hard in some areas that

Above: Royce Hall nears completion, July 1928.

Far right: A four-color red brick blend (right) and buff-colored terra cotta (left) make up the campus palette.

air drills and blasting were needed for excavations. Rains also slowed early work, as no roads had been built to the bridge, making it difficult for supply trucks to move about the site. Mules were used to transport some construction supplies to the area of the main quad, where workers had begun constructing the steel-framed buildings with reinforced concrete, red brick and terra cotta. A concrete mixing plant was centrally located near the buildings, and a frame bucket tower was installed high enough to drop the concrete alternatively in hoppers from one

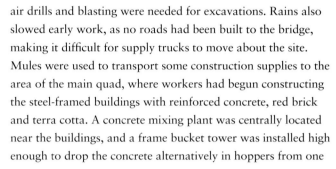

California motifs, such as stained glass windows of a '49er, the brown bear, and the squirrel are incorporated throughout Kerckhoff Hall. The former cafeteria and store were adorned with representations of medieval attendants serving tobacco (right) and food (far right).

building to another. Underground, an elaborate network of tunnels more than six feet high and four feet wide was constructed to connect the buildings' basements and provide a distribution system for steam pipes used for heating and hot water, as well as gas and electric conduits.

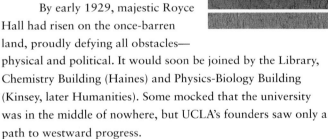

By early 1929, majestic Royce Hall had risen on the once-barren land, proudly defying all obstacles—physical and political. It would soon be joined by the Library, Chemistry Building (Haines) and Physics-Biology Building (Kinsey, later Humanities). Some mocked that the university was in the middle of nowhere, but UCLA's founders saw only a path to westward progress.

"When those huge piles of brick somehow became Royce Hall and the Library, looming there on the brow of the bare and beany barleyed hills, we Oxy students would race by on our way down Sunset Boulevard to the beach, with a cocked snook at what we called the Southern Branch of San Quentin," recalled University Librarian Lawrence Clark Powell in 1954, commemorating the 25th anniversary of the Westwood campus's opening. "What has happened at Westwood in a quarter-century—the flowering of buildings where once the beanflower bloomed—is typically Southern Californian. Everything we have here came the hard way—hard, that is, on those who sought to stand in the way."

In 1931, UCLA's first student union opened its doors. Kerckhoff Hall was "designed in a style of its own for it has a purpose of its own," declared Allison, although he and Moore initially received criticism for its architecture. Kerckhoff's turrets, doors of wrought-iron scrollwork and stained glass with depictions of medieval life gave it a distinction that set it apart on campus. California motifs were also incorporated, including stained glass images of the orange, brown bear and squirrel, as well as a '49er panning for gold.

Both Royce and Kerckhoff are muted examples of the churches that inspired them. Kerckhoff is a constrained version of the ornate Tudor gothic style modeled after Henry VII's chapel at Westminster Abbey, while Royce Hall is a toned down version of its prototype, Milan's Basilica di Sant'Ambrogio. Royce's iconic towers mirror the basilica's asymmetry, with one tower containing two arches and the other having three. But in the Milanese original, the two towers differ more dramatically. Both of Royce's towers are of equal height, while in Milan the older tower, built in the ninth century by monks, is shorter and simpler than the newer one, completed in the 12th century and commissioned by nobles in the Lombard style.

Directly across from Royce, Powell Library is designed in the Italian Romanesque style, with its octagonal dome

Left: Ornate detail of Royce Hall terra cotta archway.

Below: George W. Kelham's rendering of a section of Powell Library, on linen, August 25, 1927.

modeled on that of the Basilica del Sepolcro in Bologna. The main doorway is reminiscent of the Basilica di San Zeno in Verona. The figure of the owl of wisdom, flanked by the kneeling gods of light and learning, watches over the entrance.

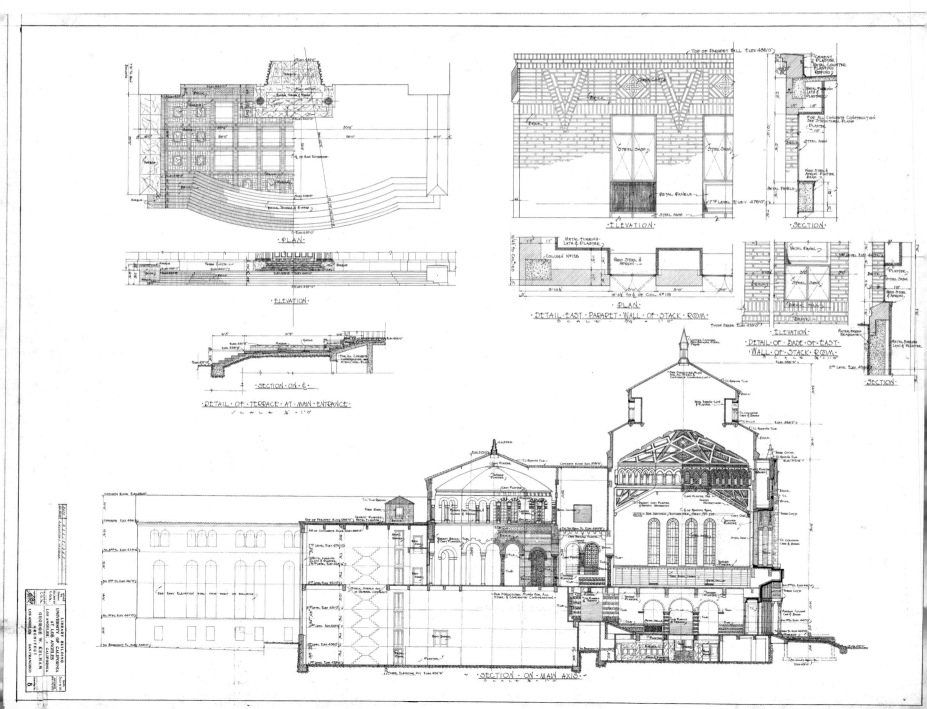

feature of the dome, emblematic of the mission of libraries, is the representation of the 40 colophons from 15th- and 16th-century printers, including William Caxton, Aldus Pius Manutius, and Fust and Schöeffer.

Praising the architects and designers of the new buildings for taking inspiration from the past, the 1930 *Southern Campus* wrote: "they have at the same time created something genuinely new, not merely presented a reincarnation of a past age. Such has resulted in a symbol of the true spirit of the university, a recognition of the worth and beauty of things of the past, and a realization of the value of the living present."

By the end of 1932, a total of 11 buildings had been completed. Two years later, Bay Area architect Kelham retired from his responsibilities in Los Angeles, and the regents selected Allison as supervising architect for the continued expansion of the campus.

"The real strength of the campus architecturally is not in individual buildings—which are, nevertheless, often quite good—but in the way the buildings work together to make a memorable place," said Charles "Duke" Warner Oakley, campus architect from 1986 to 2000. "Allison's restrained architecture allows this concert of buildings to sing together rather better than a series of quirky, self-important monuments might have."

Above: Main Reading Room, Powell Library, late 1940s.

Above right: The Associated Students Cafe, 1930s.

Inside, the dome of the main reading room reflects Moorish style with a vibrant color scheme including gold, teal and vermilion. The ceiling tiles made of antique wood are decorated with star shapes inspired by the medieval Spanish churches of Granada and Toledo. The long panels between the deep beams of the rotunda are filled with intricate ornamentation. Symbols include the Words of Wisdom, and the Four Elements: earth depicted by the lion, air by birds, fire by salamanders and water by sea horses. The primary

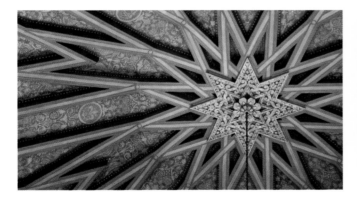

Top: The Moorish-influenced domed ceiling of Powell Library.

Above: "Novices shall love poverty and strive after the right intention," inscription by St. Ignatius of Loyola, Royce Hall third floor loggia ceiling.

Right: East view of the campus, early 1950s.

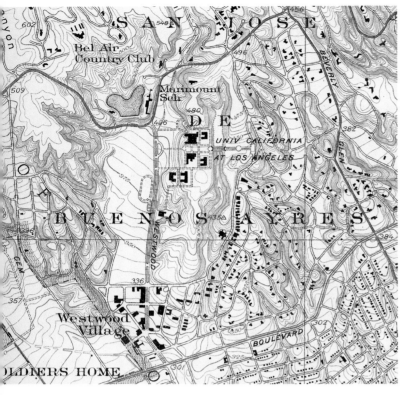

In 1935, Allison and landscape architect Ralph D. Cornell created a development plan that continued the use of Romanesque design. Among other features, it included a campanile—similar to that at Berkeley—and a grand-scale outdoor amphitheater. But the plan would not be implemented. Financial constraints imposed by World War II and the postwar building boom placed efficiency and affordability above form and design.

Anticipating an enrollment influx of GI Bill veterans, Allison drafted another plan in 1944 that would create more land to build upon. His newest vision unified the campus into one articulated unit by filling in the arroyo, an intrinsic barrier, which not only divided east from west, Allison said, but also strangled campus growth. Despite objections from those who wanted to save the natural landscape, the Board of Regents approved the plan. As a compromise, however, the bridge was not leveled. Instead, in 1947, reinforced concrete retaining walls were added to the sides of the Arroyo Bridge and the northern part of the ravine was filled in with more than 400,000 cubic yards of earth, creating approximately 24 additional acres of useable land. Although hidden underground, the bridge was preserved and continued to function as the daily entrance to the campus. "Poets wept when the lovely brick span across the arroyo was shored up to take the weight of the earth which would soon hide the bridge forever," *UCLA Alumni Magazine* lamented.

Also disappearing with the ravine were many indigenous flora and fauna. The arroyo had been covered with fragrant coastal sage scrub and chaparral, interspersed with native grasses. The loss of wildlife on campus mirrored that of other areas in Los Angeles transformed by urbanization. Biology professor and ornithologist Loye Holmes Miller kept a detailed record of the "wild folk."

A Bridge Still Standing

Hailed as "the avenue to the future" when it opened in 1929, the Arroyo Bridge—the first structure built on the Westwood campus—has been a storied part of UCLA's history ever since.

For almost 20 years, the bridge, with its Romanesque-inspired design and intricate rosette and diamond patterns of carved limestone and inlaid brick, served as the main entrance to campus for pedestrians and automobiles off Hilgard Avenue. During the Great Depression, the bridge—which stood approximately 300 feet long, 75 feet wide and 50 feet above the chaparral-covered arroyo—provided shelter for impoverished students. In wartime, when the Japanese were targeting the California coast via submarine, enough food was reportedly stored beneath it to feed 50,000 people—in case of attack.

In the postwar years, anticipating burgeoning enrollments as veterans sought higher learning through the GI Bill, administrators planned new buildings to accommodate them. They needed additional acres, but the arroyo was a natural impediment. "The arroyo can never be a logical part of the campus," wrote Supervising Architect David C. Allison in 1944. "It is out of key with the formality of massive buildings and ground, pattern to which the campus [already] is committed and from which it cannot retreat. The arroyo strangles campus use and normal growth."

By March 1947, concrete slabs had been built as retaining walls along the edges of the bridge and the northern part of the ravine was filled in with more than 400,000 cubic yards of soil, creating about 24 additional acres of usable property on the campus—including where the Franklin D. Murphy Sculpture Garden and Schoenberg Hall were later situated.

Not everyone had been keen on filling in the arroyo. Some faculty petitioned against it, mourning the loss of the bridge's beauty and the picturesque setting of the arroyo. Provost Clarence A. Dykstra, anticipating the need for additional parking spaces, thought the area should be converted into an underground parking garage. "The day will arrive, and sooner than most of us realize," Dykstra predicted, "when tens of thousands of cars will come to campus and need such space in which to park." (An underground parking structure would be built in 2002 under the Intramural Field.)

Other ideas for the space arose over the years, but never materialized. In 1937, administrators considered creating a men's dormitory under the bridge. In the 1990s, detailed plans were drawn to excavate the Arroyo Bridge and create a museum underground to house what would become the Fowler Museum, but the idea was abandoned when planners realized that it would be unwise to store cultural artifacts subterraneously in a former ravine. To coincide with UCLA's 75th anniversary in 1994, administrators considered excavating the south side to create an amphitheater—but the plan was dropped because of financial considerations.

The arches of the Arroyo Bridge remain hidden underground at Dickson Court, often ignored by those crossing it. A sign cautions a weight restriction, and it continues to be inspected to meet safety and earthquake standards. It is, after all, still a functioning bridge.

Retaining Walls U.C.L.A. Campus
Architect - D. C. Allison
Contractor - Johnson Western Co.
Date - 2/25/47
Operation - Placing Slabs
Direction - Looking Northwest.

Above: A view from beneath the bridge, May 6, 2011.

Left: Concrete retaining walls are set in place to protect the structure of the Arroyo Bridge before the ravine is filled in, February 25, 1947.

Miller documented that the first to be displaced were species that required wide-open spaces, such as the horned lark and the prairie falcon—which had flown over the campus's founding ceremonies in 1926, but was only seen once more, in 1931.

The perennial Stone Canyon Creek that ran along the campus's west side was routed underground beginning in the 1930s to make way for the construction of the men's and women's gyms on the creek bed near the foot of Janss Steps. By the 1940s, the naturally banked stream, running west of the university elementary school (and later behind the Anderson School of Management complex built in 1995), was funneled into a storm drain that runs underneath the campus and into Westwood along Gayley Avenue, merging with the Sepulveda Channel before running through the Ballona Creek watershed and finally emptying into the Santa Monica Bay. As a result, deer, several species of birds, frogs and salamanders reliant on the creek also disappeared. One bird that Miller had annually reported hearing from his office was the California thrasher. When the arroyo was filled, Miller noted, "Thrashers no more." Some of the animals, such as roadrunners, moved to the western terrace of the campus. As student housing was developed there, most vanished.

The California quail was seen until the construction of the nine-acre Sunset Canyon Recreation Center, which opened in February 1966 in the northwest corner of campus. The property was deeded to the university by the Bel-Air Association, with restrictions that precluded its use for the construction of

15

large buildings such as residence halls, classrooms or parking structures. Associate Dean of Students Norman P. Miller, who as campus recreation coordinator championed the project, noted that the area was intended to enhance "educational objectives through creative uses of leisure time on campus and to reduce the anonymity and impersonal atmosphere of a large urban university." Shortly after the center's opening, the *Los Angeles Times* highlighted the unique nature of the space on a university campus. The designers focused on creating a space that would be "non-rectangular, defying modules, minus the defined spaces" of a student union. "The emphasis was on nonemphasis, to make something people could shape to their own needs."

Seven acres near the arroyo on the east side of campus were preserved as botanical gardens. Started shortly after the campus opened in 1929, George C. Groenewegen, the garden's first manager, obtained horticultural donations from the United States Department of Agriculture, the Huntington Botanical Gardens and other sources. By 1947, the garden—a research unit

Top: UCLA Lab School students clear away vines and weeds (right) to revive the natural state of the above-ground portion of Stone Canyon Creek, which then disappears underground into a storm drain (left), November 2010.

Above: The California quail, as documented on campus by ornithologist Loye Holmes Miller.

Left: Leisurely days at the Sunset Canyon Recreation Center, late 1960s.

Far left: The Mildred E. Matthias Botanical Gardens.

for the life and medical sciences—contained about 1,500 species and varieties of plants. The campus flourished as an arboretum under Cornell's direction and, in the 1960s, with the support of Chancellor Franklin D. Murphy, garden director Mildred E. Mathias helped develop it into "the university garden," while also opening it for public tours. Renamed in 1979 for Mathias, who oversaw the garden from 1956–74, the garden grew to be one of the most important living botanical collections in the United States, with more than 5,000 species of plants from all over the world.

In 1947, the regents asked Los Angeles architect Welton Becket to serve as UCLA's consulting architect. Charged with developing a contemporary style, he would become UCLA's most prolific builder. "We had to get away from Romanesque because the ornamental façades were too expensive and the towers and cupolas of that style are very inefficient and space-wasting,"

Becket told *UCLA Alumni Magazine* in 1964. "Though we are continuing with the same basic building materials, they are being used in a completely modern way—except, in the older central portion, where harmony is being preserved by the use of tile roofs and more traditional architectural statements."

In 1948, as administrators were looking for a site to build a hospital, UCLA was deeded 35 acres of land from the federal government that stretched from Veteran to Gayley avenues, north of Wilshire Boulevard and south of Strathmore Drive. In the 1950s, university officials decided that the hospital should not be built on the deeded land but instead on the south end of the campus near Le Conte Avenue, anchoring the newly conceived Court of Sciences. The Administration of Veterans Affairs lifted the restriction on the deeded land's use in 1986. Several plans for the property—including constructing an art museum to house industrialist Norton Simon's collection—did not come to fruition. However, in 2004, residents moved into Palm Court, the first of several Mediterranean-style building units to open as part of Weyburn Terrace, a graduate student housing complex. UCLA has also been in conversations with city officials about the potential to build a subway portal on the southwest campus property near Wilshire Boulevard. Combined, Westwood and UCLA have the second-highest employment density in the city, behind downtown Los Angeles. Any further developments on the site, according to campus planners, would undoubtedly take into consideration the long-term future of the campus and likely be "high-density" development projects.

Growth of UCLA seen through subsequent campus maps:
Top row: 1958, 1967.
Bottom row: 1987, 1992, 2011.

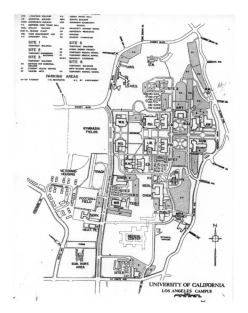

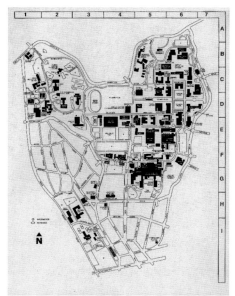

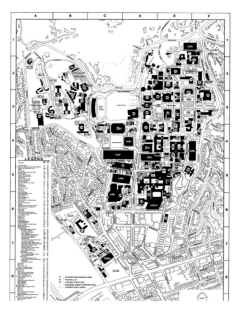

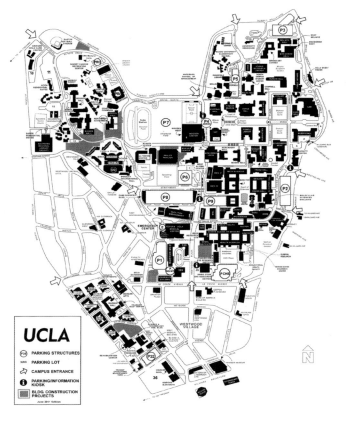

A MODERN CAMPUS

When Chancellor Murphy arrived in 1960, one of his first actions was to obtain permission to close Westwood Boulevard, which ran north through the heart of campus to Sunset Boulevard, to through traffic. With the opening of Ackerman Union and four high-rise residence halls, there were concerns that the several thousand students who regularly crossed Westwood Boulevard would be in harm's way.

In 1963, UCLA adopted its first long-range development plan, which called for building expansion and the incorporation of infrastructure, such as parking lots and an internal campus road that looped them all together. UCLA campus planner George Vajna, who along with Becket was responsible for

implementing it, emphasized attention to minute detail: "The aesthetic and functional must travel hand in hand; planning must embrace not only the skyline, but also the trash bin."

Voters passed three successive state bond measures in the 1960s—the first such measures since the 1920s—providing UCLA with $95 million for campus expansion. With matching funds and self-amortizing projects, UCLA embarked on the ambitious long-range development plan. More than 50 building projects were completed during this period, including Pauley Pavilion.

One building caused a stir even before it was completed. Students puzzled over the design of the Social Sciences Building, which opened in 1964. "Patchwork Campus: Who Is to

Wading into the Inverted Fountain

UCLA's most unconventional fountain could have started off in a most ordinary way: shooting water skyward. But Chancellor Franklin D. Murphy had other ideas. He challenged UCLA's architectural landscape team, which included Jere Hazlett, to do something other than "squirt water into the air," recalled Howard Troller, who conceived the Inverted Fountain's theme.

In fact, the team realized Murphy's challenge was a necessity. A wind tunnel in Franz Hall court would have sprayed the fountain's water in all directions, potentially catching unsuspecting passers-by.

For inspiration, Troller turned to a childhood memory: Yellowstone's bubbling hot springs. He had long been wanting to portray that natural landscape in a modern representation.

On March 18, 1968, Troller's vision became reality. Unlike traditional fountains, the water of the Inverted Fountain flows inward across a bed of multi-colored rocks, handpicked by Troller in the foothills of the San Gabriel Mountains just north of Claremont, California. The current then meets at an off-center well, creating a miniature waterfall plunging into a 12-foot wide, 5-foot deep center that recirculates the water at 10,000 gallons per minute. The water's movement adds a natural, yet distinct, sound to the east end of campus—that of a flowing mountain stream.

Since its unveiling, the Inverted Fountain has become steeped in student tradition and lore. In its early years, students would cannonball into the fountain, so administrators worried about injuries took steps to cut the depth of the pool. These days, during orientation, freshmen are commonly initiated by being told to wade in or touch the water, and then warned that doing so again before graduation will tack on an extra quarter to their academic career. That's why one just might see graduating seniors wading into the fountain to celebrate their last final exam, water guns in tow to blast nearby underclassmen. At least, that's how the story goes.

The Inverted Fountain, inspired by Yellowstone's hot springs, lies on the campus's Grand Axis, which stretches from the Broad Art Center southward to Franz Hall.

Blame?" asked a *Daily Bruin* headline in October 1963. The "radical" style spurred controversy and students soon dubbed it "Uncle Welton's Waffle," alluding to the consulting architect. Actually designed by Maynard Lyndon, the 11-story building housed faculty offices, and its height allowed for a maximum usage of space. Constructed with as little window area as possible, the building's square windows were coated with "solar bronze," a breakthrough film intended to reduce heat and glare. A separation of several inches between the windows and the outside building wall allowed for the upward flow of air, lending an additional cooling effect.

A feature added to the building—not in the original plan—was to raise it on pillars so as not to restrict access to the sculpture garden or impede the north-south axis of the campus, which extended from the garden to Franz Hall.

However, one notable alumnus decidedly appreciated the building. "I could wish also that the name given me by my father would be as vividly descriptive and could convey as much meaning as the informal appellation heretofore attached to this impressive edifice—'The Waffle,'" said Ralph J. Bunche at the dedication of the hall renamed in 1968 for the Nobel Peace Prize winner. "It could come to pass, of course, that in those compromises in usage which time often effects, this fine hall may come to be known as 'Bunche's Waffle.' Any way I look at it, Bunche Hall is beautiful—may I be permitted to add—even though it isn't black."

Subsequent architects and planners determined that the construction of the period failed to give justice to the architectural heritage of the campus. "One gets the sense that in the late '50s and the '60s, this explosion of activity resulted in

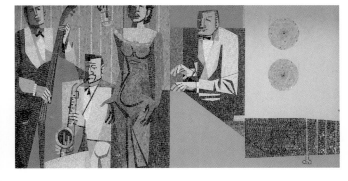

desperate space need and construction … regardless of any kind of reasonable land planning model," said Peter W. Blackman, former vice chancellor of administration, who oversaw Capital Programs from 1986 to 2007. "It was contemporary need. It was practical to the task. It wasn't the right thing in the long run."

In the 1970s, a lack of state funding and other budgetary constraints led to little capital development on campus. By 1983, however, additional funding from the state

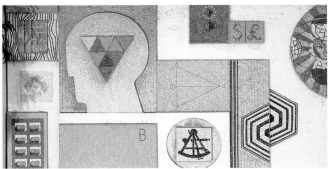

Right: Bunche Hall was raised on pillars so as not to close off access to the sculpture garden.

Below: Schoenberg Hall, which opened in 1955, features a colorful 164-foot mosaic by Richard Haines, depicting the history of music through the ages, including jazz (below right). More than 2,000 colors were used.

Bottom right: The Mathematical Sciences Building showcases "The History of Mathematics," a mosaic by Joseph Young, completed in 1968.

helped UCLA undertake its second long-range development program. UCLA began a decades-long process of building for growth and modernizing structures, while at the same time returning the campus to its aesthetic roots.

"The physical manifestation of the place is very important," Blackman said. "People remember walking through the Royce-Powell quad. It's an essential part of what it meant to be an undergraduate here. It's in your bones."

Using the base iconography of the campus—the Romanesque style of Royce quad—an in-depth plan and set of ground rules were adopted. Constant attention to detail has been given to maintaining the campus's architectural identity. The Shapiro Fountain that anchors the west end of Royce quad, for example, was built in 1995 from bricks dug from the same quarry used in the 1929 construction of the four original buildings. There is some room for variation for modern buildings, but from a consistent set of architectural ground rules.

"New buildings may relate to the historic core without being Italian Romanesque," said Jeffrey Averill, appointed campus architect in 2003. "They may be much more modern in their expression, but use a consistent palette of brick and buff color, and an appropriate scale and richness, so that they have a resonance and connection to reinforce the campus as an integrated whole."

The Molecular Sciences Building, which opened in November 1993, is an example of a modern facility designed to provide high-tech research labs and offices and where, according to Nobel laureate and chemistry Professor Donald J. Cram, "molecules just discovered meet instruments just invented to dance to the tune of orchestrated science."

After the 1994 Northridge earthquake, the university accelerated a plan to seismically reinforce all campus buildings. During the process, improvements were also made to buildings in terms of function and design. The acoustics in Royce Hall were enhanced by tearing out concrete walls that blocked sound. Buildings were wired for technological improvements, and some, including the John Wooden Center, were brought into closer alignment with the campus's Romanesque iconography through "lamination" techniques that apply a new façade over an existing building. "It put a face on what was a large concrete box in the middle of campus," Averill said. "We created new façades that were integrated into the aesthetic of the campus."

Some changes may only be visible after multiple steps. The renovation of Bruin Walk, which was modernized from its once dirt and asphalt-paved roads—some carved out as "desire lines" by pedestrian traffic—was carried out as a series of projects over two decades, culminating in 2004. Every walkway on campus contributes to the ground plane, and

Above: Campus planners keep a close eye on everything from student media kiosks to trash receptacles and acorn lamps, painted a dark brown color known as "Charles E. Young Brown," to make sure every detail blends into the campus's overall landscape.

Far left: A southeast view of Royce Hall at dusk, December 11, 2010

Left: Three floors of the California NanoSystems Institute, with its zigzagging walkways, rest over a parking structure.

maximized available space. Three of its floors are situated over a parking facility, and the central courtyard features a network of suspended stairs and bridges that zigzag the complex for easy mobility and increased interactivity.

Being steadfast to a long-range vision is key. "You have to stick with it over 20 years, and then you have to have single, consolidated leadership that is literally obsessive about this or else it won't happen, because every time you turn around somebody will change the trash cans or stop replacing every light with an acorn light," Blackman said. "And you have to have a control point that says, 'That's not permitted. There's nothing wrong with what you're doing, it's just not what we are doing here on this campus.' "

Approaching its centennial in 2019, UCLA is essentially in "second-generation planning," said Averill. In the future, buildings that have outlived functionality or do not make the best use of space may be replaced.

Within the context of UCLA's long-range development plan, the campus's capital financial plan, covering 2009–19, has three major goals. The first is to complete the comprehensive seismic program that began in the 1980s. Between 1994

Top: The concave glass and red brick of the Neuroscience Research Building, completed in 2005, blends the architectural attributes of North and South Campus.

Above: An elevator in the Physics and Astronomy Building depicts scientists Albert Einstein, Galileo Galilei and Marie Curie on its steel doors.

paths are often redone as part of changing traffic patterns from new development.

"The interesting thing about a college campus is that it is itself alive," Oakley said. "It's not a painting that when you hang it on the wall, that's the way Mr. Van Gogh wanted it. It's always changing." With limited open space, planners needed to think differently by building on unusual spaces or by utilizing space in more efficient ways with so-called infill projects. The Anderson School complex, completed in 1995, is an example of construction in "leftover space," Oakley explained, that also makes the campus function better. "The Anderson School itself allows you to go up and get to the back of Royce; go up further and get up to North Campus facility," Oakley said. "So it connected the up and the down which, except for Janss Steps, there was no other connection. The seven-story California NanoSystems Institute building in the Court of Sciences was not only the most technologically complex building ever constructed at UCLA when it opened in December 2007, but it also

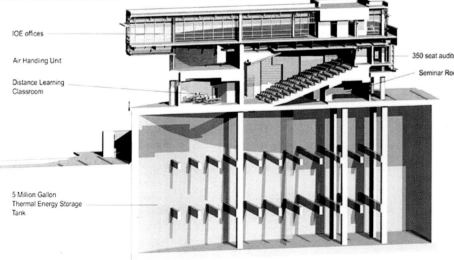

IOE offices

Air Handling Unit

Distance Learning Classroom

350 seat auditori

Seminar Room

5 Million Gallon Thermal Energy Storage Tank

La Kretz Hall (above), which opened in 2005, is the first LEED certified building at UCLA. Constructed from recyclable materials, it sits over a five-million-gallon thermal energy storage tank (left).

and 2009, UCLA allocated 92 percent of its funding from the state general fund to seismic and life safety upgrades. By 2009, the campus had completed work on more than 74 percent of seismically deficient areas, with upgrades still pending or in progress on the Center for Health Sciences facilities (11 structures and more than 1.6 million square feet) and the Extension Building.

Second, the plan seeks to continue transforming UCLA into a residential academic community. By 2009, approximately 11,000 students lived on campus, while another 2,700 resided in university owned off-campus housing. In 2011, construction was underway to add another 2,000 beds for undergraduates and graduates, continuing a three-decade-long process that changed UCLA from a commuter school to a primarily residential one.

The third major initiative is to advance campus sustainability practices. UCLA leaders have committed the university to achieving environmental certification for all new construction and major refurbishment projects. Under University of California climate protection goals, system campuses are expected to return to 1990 greenhouse gas emission levels by 2020. UCLA plans to reduce its carbon footprint and meet that goal several years ahead of schedule.

La Kretz Hall, which opened in 2005 and provides space for undergraduate classrooms and academic conferences, is home to UCLA's Institute of the Environment and Sustainability. The structure was the first on campus to be certified "green" by the Leadership in Energy and Environmental Design (LEED) Green Building Rating System, which recognizes buildings that meet strict environmental criteria. It was constructed above a five-million-gallon thermal energy storage tank that provides chilled water reserves for the campus. The hall was also built with renewable woods, highly recyclable materials and solar shading devices.

Beyond building in an environmentally conscious manner, planners have committed to keeping open spaces to preserve the campus's beauty.

"Open space is an essential component of the aesthetic and social life of campus," Averill said. About 142 acres, or 34 percent of UCLA's campus, consisted of green spaces such as gardens, courtyards or recreational areas in 2011. Several of these areas—including Royce quad, the sculpture and botanical gardens and Meyerhoff Park—hold a cherished place in the campus's history, and have been designated as "preserves" in the long-range development plan.

Overall, architects intend to maintain the integrity of the campus's historic core, Averill said, including, "respect for the architectural and landscape traditions that give the campus its unique character."

Top Left: Completed by 2006, Rieber Plaza in Northwest Campus is bordered by residential dormitories Rieber Hall, Rieber Vista and Rieber Terrace.

Above: Wisdom, one of six academic-themed stained glass windows in Royce Hall.

An Artful Haven

In the lifetime of a garden, they are but brief moments of respite or play, meditation or seriousness: A toddler coos "pretty horsey" while petting Deborah Butterfield's *Pensive* under the approving gaze of his mother. A group of students plays Frisbee in a shallow dell beneath the shade of feathery jacarandas and California sycamores. A young woman retreats to the lawn in an intense cell phone discussion with her boyfriend—assured her audience of steel and bronze statues will never reveal the details. And by George Tsutakawa's *Obos 69*, the garden's only fountain sculpture, four men practice Tai Chi, their measured precision nearly camouflaging them among the artwork.

It's a typical afternoon in the Franklin D. Murphy Sculpture Garden, five acres of paradise on north campus that is whatever you want it to be: museum, sanctuary, study hall or social hub. The moments—both the ordinary and the precious—fulfill a larger vision conceived by Murphy, UCLA's chancellor from 1960 to 1968. He pictured the garden as part of everyday campus life. He dreamed of a place where young adults could gain an appreciation of art in an unobtrusive setting, taking in sculptures spontaneously over a span of years, yet being infinitely influenced by them.

"Young people need to grow up in the presence of the arts," Murphy said. "My own view has always been that you cannot expect to develop beauty of character without beauty of environment."

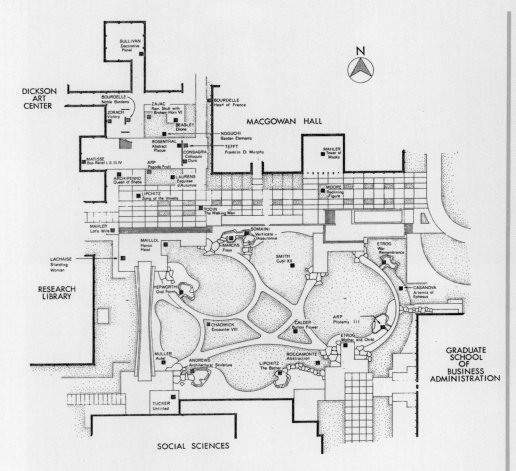

First-time visitors often are surprised by the garden's lushness and notable collection of 19th- and 20th-century figurative and abstract sculpture by such seminal artists as Alexander Calder, Henri Matisse, Joan Miró, Auguste Rodin and David Smith.

When shaping his idea for the sculpture garden, Murphy drew on his studies and travels in Europe, where he witnessed the continent's great civic and urban-planning movement. He was especially taken with Italy's great plazas, which provided public spaces in an artful environment.

Above: Map of the Franklin D. Murphy Sculpture Garden in North Campus, 1960s.

Left: Franklin D. Murphy studies Rodin's *The Walking Man* in the garden he created, 1980s.

Below: A bust of Murphy, sculpted by Edlen Tefft in 1960, welcomes visitors to the garden.

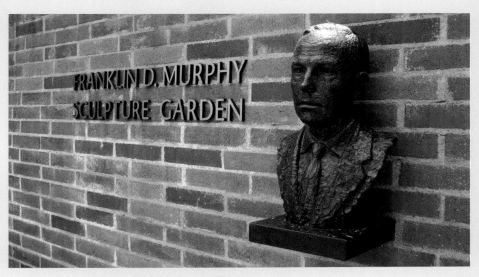

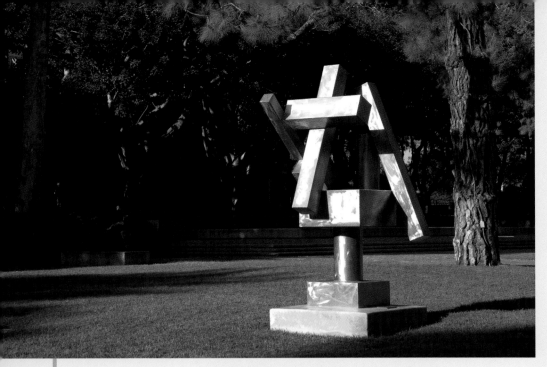

"He wanted to create a sculpture garden as a transition zone on campus, as a place for reflection of the unforced, unmediated kind," said Cynthia Burlingham, director of UCLA's Grunwald Center for the Graphic Arts and the garden's curator.

Murphy and UCLA landscape architect Ralph D. Cornell transformed what was originally the "fair-weather parking lot"—so-called because the dusty lot became a quagmire when it rained—into one of the nation's most renowned outdoor sculpture gardens. Curators from museums and universities around the country regularly visit UCLA to glean ideas when developing or modifying their own gardens.

"With its broad range of bronze, steel, and marble works by European and American artists who have defined some of the most important directions in 20th-century sculpture, it not only clarifies modern sculpture but also champions sculpture in general," wrote art critic Michael Brenson. "It makes the objects in it as important as buildings and trees, as essential as architecture and nature. Sculpture here seems part of all creative life, including nature."

The garden is tripartite in design. It consists of a formal red brick plaza in front of the Eli and Edythe Broad Art Center; the gothic allée—as Murphy dubbed it—a triple row of South African coral trees creating a promenade with a cathedral-like canopy that divides the plaza from the third section, an informal sweep of rolling hills set with meandering pebbled pathways and six free-form seating areas.

There is no main entrance, so one can encounter the garden in many different ways. This was deemed such an important element that during the expansion of Bunche Hall, part of the building was raised on piers so it would not obstruct the walkway from the garden to the central campus.

The sculpture garden has continually evolved since it was dedicated in 1967 with an initial installation of 31 works, including 11 from the estate of David E. Bright. Painstaking consideration of sculpture placement dates back to the garden's planning, when Murphy and Cornell went around the site with papier-mâché stand-ins of the artworks. Throughout the years, each addition has been carefully placed. George Rickey's kinetic sculpture *Two Lines Oblique Down (Variation III)* is positioned strategically to catch the wind. Rodin's *The Walking Man* is located so that it can be seen from several vantage points, and when entering from the north side at night, it is the only sculpture visible at the end of the long walkway.

With more than 70 pieces, the garden is essentially considered complete by curators. However, UCLA has accepted new pieces that are in "the spirit of the garden."

"The garden isn't necessarily frozen in time, but it does have a certain integrity to it," Burlingham said. "If you destroy that integrity, it's just sculpture and landscape as separate things. It's the relationship of the sculpture to the landscape, and of the sculptures to each other, that form integral pieces, and that's something you have to preserve. But it doesn't mean it can't allow for change."

One of the garden's more recent additions, *T.E.U.C.L.A.*, a 42.5-ton torqued ellipse by Richard Serra, was installed in September 2006 on the plaza of the Broad Art Center, coinciding with the building's opening. With thought to the center's design and surrounding landscape, several sculptures were moved. Jacques Lipchitz's *The Song of the Vowels* and Isamu Noguchi's *Garden Elements* were placed to greet visitors at the southeast entrance to the garden near the School of Public Affairs Building. Additional works by Jean Arp, Émile-Antoine Bourdelle, Pietro Consagra, Henri Laurens and Bernard Rosenthal were also relocated. Anna Mahler's limestone *Tower of Masks* went on view for the first time since it was restored after being damaged in the 1994 Northridge earthquake.

Throughout the garden, sculptures are set so that they can be approached easily from all angles. In this sense, "few sculpture installations are as instructive about the nature of sculpture," Brenson wrote. "It makes clear that sculpture must be walked around, seen from near and far, and, perhaps most important, touched. In museums, sculptures are as untouchable as the paintings to which they are therefore almost inevitably subservient, but here, your approach can be hands-on."

Many visitors from outside the university marvel at the garden's openness. Others worry about the safety of the pieces. Murphy never had such concerns.

"Security-minded people said we would have to build a fence around the garden to protect it," Murphy told *ArtNews* in 1985. "It was feared vandals might spray obscenities on the nudes. At the height of the Vietnam difficulties, graffiti were scrawled elsewhere on campus and windows were broken. But the sculpture was not touched. The garden has an almost spiritual quality, you know. And the students understand that this is their garden. They protect it. I believe they always will."

Left: Visitors to the garden often find a moment's refuge, July 7, 2011.

Below: Sculptures by such seminal artists as Gerhard Marcks (*Maja*, 1941, foreground) and Barbara Hepworth (*Elegy III*, 1966, far right) are integrated with a lush landscape of jacarandas and rolling pathways designed by Ralph D. Cornell.

First to 100

*F*ounded in the 20th century, UCLA entered the intercollegiate sports tradition decades after most venerable American institutions of higher learning. Yet in the span of less than a century, UCLA rose to the top of the athletic elite, becoming the first university to earn 100 team championships in NCAA competition.

That record is even more remarkable when considering UCLA's humble athletic beginnings.

In 1919, the University of California Southern Branch's athletic program was under the direction of Frederick W. "Doc" Cozens, a Berkeley alumnus who had coached the Golden Bears' freshman football, baseball and soccer teams. Cozens, who was hired as both a professor and the director of the men's physical education department, put together a nascent athletic program with the full support of chief executive Ernest Carroll Moore. The budget was so small, however, that Cozens constituted the entire staff—from athletic director to coach and trainer for each sport instituted that first year. Undeterred, Cozens moved forward immediately, and with great determination.

"There is no question of our making a very favorable showing in Southern California sports if we make conscientious efforts in that direction," Cozens said. "I believe the school spirit of S.B.U.C. is right and I am sure the men will reassure me by their turnout for the various activities."

On the first day of classes, Cozens put a call out to football players "who have had any experience at all" and held tryouts the next day. A high-spirited pep rally encouraged the male students to venture forth onto the gridiron. Nearly 100 men—more than half the entire male population in a student body where women outnumbered men six to one—showed up on the sawdust-covered back lot of the Vermont Avenue campus. Known as Moore Field, it

OCT. 24.

CUBS

FIRST FOOTBALL VICTORY CUBS – 7 OXY FROSH – 2

SWIMMING

All Set!

was little more than a dirt plot that had been used as an old World War I soldier training ground and turned into a quagmire when it rained. On that field assembled a motley-attired crew. There were soldiers in olive drab and sailors in blue. Some men wore work overalls while others came in old sweaters and pants. "From such clay was moulded a fighting football team," wrote the 1920 *Southern Campus*.

The *Los Angeles Times* covered the practice, noting that "football life" was visible at the Southern Branch. "It is said that the men are heavy, averaging a fair beef," the *Times* wrote. "As early as it is now to tell anything, it would seem from a casual glance that the bunch would out produce a team that would at least show its competitors plenty of scrappy fight. Go ahead and show 'em what's what, Little YouSee."

Despite the big turnout, Cozens was faced with a student body population that only consisted of first- and second-year students, and wound up with 19 players—not enough to conduct a full scrimmage. Most of the men were freshmen. Nevertheless, Cozens put together an eight-game schedule against local high schools, Los Angeles Junior College, a team from the USS Idaho, and the Occidental College frosh team. Although considered practice matches, the high school games were logged into the season's official record.

The first game came barely two weeks into the academic year. On October 3, 1919, the Cubs—the moniker chosen by students to represent their fledgling status and provide a connection to Berkeley's Golden Bears—faced the Artisans of Los Angeles Manual Arts High School. Despite a valiant effort, the Cubs lost by an inglorious 74–0.

"The best that can be said for Coach Cozens' team is that the men fought hard, but it was like a light-weight pugilist against a heavy-weight," wrote the *Los Angeles Times*. "Coach Cozens has had his team on the field for less than two weeks, and they have not even had a scrimmage, there being no 'scrub'

team against which to play owing to a dearth of candidates."

A week later the Cubs lost again, this time to Hollywood High School, by a score of 19–6. But the score reflected an achievement, as Captain Wayne Banning intercepted a pass with only three minutes left in the game and ran it 65 yards to score UCLA's first-ever recorded touchdown. The Cubs lost a third game in as many weeks when the team was defeated at Bakersfield High School, 27–12.

Finally on October 24, the Cubs won what was promoted as "the first official game of the season"—7–2 against the Oxy frosh—on their own slippery home field. About 250 fans paid 11 cents each to witness an unexpected win against a college team. The Cubs won again the following week, against Los Angeles Junior College. But that would be the last victory of the season, and the Cubs finished with a 2–6 record.

Still, they had made enough of a showing that the Southern Branch was invited to join the Southern California Intercollegiate Athletic Conference, which consisted of Pomona, Occidental and Whittier colleges, Redlands University and the California Institute of Technology. UCLA filled the spot vacated by the University of Southern California, which had left to become independent and would join the Pacific Coast Conference in December 1921.

Baseball, basketball, tennis and track were also instituted as men's sports during UCLA's first year. The Cubs fared best in basketball, finishing second in the Southern Conference with a 12–2 record. "Basketball was our first entry in intercollegiate athletics," wrote the 1920 *Southern Campus*. "Therefore our 'casaba throwers' were watched with particular interest by the various institutions in the south." Except in basketball, victories were scarce among the Cubs' athletic teams.

Above left: The 1920 *Southern Campus* celebrates the Cubs' first football victory, against the Occidental Tigers, October 24, 1919.

Above center: With no pool, the men's swim team trekked every afternoon to the Bimini Baths near Third Street and Vermont Avenue for practice under Coach Albert W. Dowden. "It is rumored that if the student is graced with a long enough life, he may some day find a swimming pool on the Campus," said the 1923–1924 student handbook. Fortunately, students only had to wait one year.

Above right: The men's gymnastics team on the Vermont Avenue campus, coached by alumnus Cecil Hollingsworth, shows off its acrobatic skill for the camera, mid-1920s. Hollingsworth, who became the Bruins coach in 1927–1928, was later hired by the City of Santa Monica to coach gymnastics at Muscle Beach, where many UCLA gymnasts in the 1930s honed their talent.

Basketball was the first sport instituted by the Women's Athletic Association, which was created in 1919 to "raise the standard of athletic efficiency and sportsmanship" among the women of the Southern Branch. Ten teams were formed, each representing a different campus department. The physical education team took first place and automatically represented the Southern Branch in the Women's Intercollegiate Association of Southern California. Baseball, tennis and track were also added as women's sports in the first year.

Wrote the 1920 *Southern Campus*: "Whatever great victories and fame the future may hold, those who have aided in overcoming the difficulties of the past year may always say with pride that they were the first."

Right: Women's field hockey, 1927.

Below: William C. Ackerman, men's tennis coach, 1925–1950.

Above: Women's baseball, 1926. "For many years only the male representative of our civilization knew the supreme thrills of a homerun struck, a high fly caught, or a speedy grounder stopped," wrote the *Southern Campus*.

Right: In 1927, the undefeated men's ice hockey team, led by Captain Harvey Tafe (standing, third from left), was the two-time champion of the Southern Intercollegiate Hockey League.

ENTERING THE PACIFIC COAST CONFERENCE

Before the second season, Cozens turned over responsibility for the football team to Coach Harry Trotter, who also served as head track coach from 1921–46. Due to a conference rule, freshmen were not allowed to play on the varsity squad. "With only a single class, the sophomore, from which to draw for material, Trotter faces the hardest task of any college coach in the south," the *Los Angeles Times* wrote.

While the football team was winless over the next two years, and had losing seasons through 1924, basketball—under the continued guidance of Coach Cozens—excelled. The Cubs won Southern Conference championships in 1921 and 1922, and tied for first in 1923. Coach Pierce H. "Caddy" Works took over as head coach in 1925, and the basketball team (captained by future athletic director Wilbur Johns) won the championship that year as well. Baseball won the conference in 1924. And, in tennis, William C. Ackerman coached the Cubs to titles each year from 1921–25. The women's tennis team participated for the first time in the Ojai Valley Tennis Tournament, a tradition that continued in subsequent decades. With multiple championships earned, the students grew tired of being called Cubs—an appellation that would often be translated in the press as the baby blue and gold or Berkeley's younger sibling—and the executive council voted to adopt the more mature "Grizzly."

Under University of California policy, intercollegiate athletics was run by the Associated Students. The Men's Athletic Board developed an internal, individual award system during the 1923–24 academic year. A blue "C" (for California) outlined with a thin line of gold was adopted as the official varsity letter. All athletes who earned a letter in a major sport were invited for membership in the Blue C Society, and those who lettered in the minor sports—such as boxing, wrestling, handball and ice hockey—were similarly included in the Circle C Society. The managers organization was dubbed Ball and Chain, and freshmen in major sports were given blue numerals. Among the first to receive basketball "1" honors was Ralph J. Bunche, who would join the varsity team as a guard and helped capture the conference championship in 1925.

The 1923–24 year also marked the founding of UCLA's intramural athletics program, headed by Ackerman. Students responded enthusiastically. Track, swimming, tennis and indoor baseball were among the favorite activities, particularly with fraternity and other student groups. The women's intramural program was extremely popular, and participants were rewarded with cups, trophies and letters. Almost nine decades later, renamed UCLA Recreation, the intramural program grew to include 30 leagues, dozens of clubs sports—ranging from badminton to the Harry Potter-influenced Quidditch—and numerous tournaments, with more than 8,000 participants each year.

In 1924, the separate positions of athletic manager and business manager were consolidated into the new Associated Students general manager position. After serving as the assistant manager since 1930, Ackerman took on the graduate manager job in 1933, becoming responsible for UCLA athletics. He was head of the Associated Students for almost 35 years.

With the addition of the third and fourth years of instruction in 1923 and 1924, respectively, Moore and Cozens had hopes for a more successful and higher profile football program. After lackluster results under three separate coaches—the 1923 team won only two games and the 1924 Grizzlies tied three times but never won a game—Moore sought out Coach William H. "Bunker Bill" Spaulding of the University of Minnesota. Spaulding—known nationally as the coach who stopped legendary University of Illinois running back Harold "Red" Grange—was named the Southern Branch's head football coach in 1925.

"Bill Spaulding, who will play the part of Moses in leading the Grizzlies out of the wilderness of football defeat, arrived in Los Angeles yesterday from the Midwest," wrote the *Los Angeles Times* in August 1925. "Bill's job is to put the Branch on the map in an athletic way—which means from a football standpoint. The Grizzlies have been the weak sister of the Southern California Conference in football, but with Spaulding here the cry on Vermont avenue is 'Them days is gone forever.' "

Under Spaulding, the Grizzlies lived up to their more ferocious moniker, winning four of their first five games during his first season. Other colleges were taking notice and tried to schedule matches. The Grizzlies finished second in the conference in 1925 and 1926, and in 1927 the Southern Branch and Pomona shared the conference crown. With their newfound success, Southern Branch athletic teams sought entrance to the Pacific Coast Conference. Since the conference already had a team with the Grizzly moniker, in 1926 students adopted a third—and final—appellation: Bruins.

In February 1927, the Board of Regents officially changed the name of the university from the Southern Branch to the University of California at Los Angeles, and UCLA entered the Pacific Coast Conference, eligible for league play in January 1928. Later, the Board of Regents would speculate that admissions had risen at UCLA because of the visibility that Spaulding had brought to the campus. Soon after UCLA

moved to Westwood in 1929, the football training field was named in his honor.

On September 28, 1929, the Bruins played crosstown rival USC for the first time, during the season opener. There was much excitement going into the game, but the result was a disastrous trouncing of 76–0. "Not until the declining sun cast cold shadows over the Los Angeles Memorial Coliseum was a truce called, and some forty weary Bruins stumbled to the training quarters, as 35,000 shivering, bewildered fans dwindled from the scene of a massacre," chronicled the 1930 *Southern Campus*. "But be it forever remembered that the Bruins were courageous, praiseworthy martyrs."

After that, UCLA athletic officials wanted to schedule the USC game later in the season, so that the Bruins could play a few conference opponents before taking on the Trojans. But USC refused. UCLA also stood firm, and the series was discontinued. A rematch would be delayed until 1936, when USC agreed to a year-end contest—the start of a decades-long tradition. More than 85,000 spectators gathered at the Coliseum—home field for both UCLA and USC—on Thanksgiving Day to watch the game, which ended in a 7–7 tie. In 1933, UCLA faced Berkeley for the first time, at the Coliseum, with the game ending in a scoreless tie. The Bruins would have to wait until 1936 to beat the Golden Bears.

WAR CHANGES THE GAME

Coached by Ackerman, men's tennis won UCLA's first PCC championship in any sport in 1932, and Jack Tidball was the National Intercollegiate Singles Champion of 1933. Basketball teams during the 1930s did not fare as well as the tennis teams, struggling to maintain their success of the previous decade. Baseball and track continued on what would later be referred to as their building years. One significant addition was the introduction in 1932 of men's crew, which recorded its first intercollegiate victory three years later.

In 1938, Spaulding was appointed UCLA's athletic director, and retired from coaching football (although he continued to coach men's golf into the 1940s). As athletic

Far right: Basketball is one of the most popular sports among women in the 1938 season.

Center: The Bruins, led by Coach William H. Spaulding, pounded Pomona College 21–0 on October 11, 1930.

Below: The Bruin mascot plays football on the pages of the *Southern Campus*, 1929.

Right: On Thanksgiving Day in 1936, after a five-year hiatus from playing crosstown rival USC, the Bruins make their best showing so far with a 7–7 tie. "Civil war will break out on the Coliseum front a week from today," the *Los Angeles Times* wrote. "The U.C.L.A. and the U.S.C. Trojans will shoot the works in the greatest civil combat the city of the Angeles has seen to date."

Far right: Jack Tidball, National Intercollegiate Singles Champion of 1933.

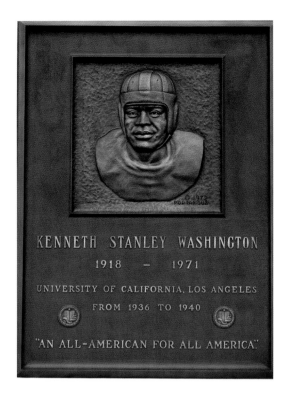

KENNETH STANLEY WASHINGTON

1918 — 1971

UNIVERSITY OF CALIFORNIA, LOS ANGELES

FROM 1936 TO 1940

"AN ALL-AMERICAN FOR ALL AMERICA."

director, however, Spaulding was mainly concerned with scheduling, public relations and other matters not related to the direct management of the athletics program, which remained in the hands of Ackerman, the Associated Students general manager.

Edwin C. "Babe" Horrell took over head coaching duties for football. Three of UCLA's greatest halfbacks of the period, Kenny Washington (UCLA's first All-American), Woody Strode and Jackie Robinson—who would go on to make history by breaking the color barrier in Major League Baseball—led the Bruins to victory on numerous occasions. Along with Ray Bartlett, there were four black players on UCLA's team at a time when only a few dozen played on all other college teams combined. Robinson was UCLA's first

four-star letterman, in football (1939 and 1940), basketball (1940 and 1941), baseball (1940), and track and field (1940). Ironically, his weakest sport while at UCLA was baseball—he batted just .097 in 1940. Washington and Strode were two of the first African-Americans to play in the modern National Football League—for the Los Angeles Rams in 1946 (no blacks had played in the league from 1933–45).

On December 6, 1941, UCLA and USC played to a 7–7 tie in front of a raucous Coliseum crowd of 60,000. The next day, Japan attacked Pearl Harbor and the United States entered World War II. War altered the athletics program as it did all aspects of campus life. Student enrollment dropped, and coaches did not know from one game to the next which players would be available. The resulting shortage of team

Above left: Kenny Washington, single-wing tailback from 1937–1939, and UCLA's first All-American, 1939.

Above: Jackie Robinson, a member of UCLA's first undefeated football team, 1939. The Bruins' tally for the season was 6–0–4.

Below: Robinson was UCLA's first four-sport letterman, in basketball, track and field, football and baseball.

members prompted the lifting of a restriction against allowing freshmen to play on varsity teams.

Before the full effects of the war were felt on campus, UCLA's football team—led by quarterback Bob Waterfield—surprised fans by winning all but one game in 1942 and earning an invitation to its first Rose Bowl. The berth was clinched after a 14–7 victory over USC at the Coliseum, UCLA's first triumph over its crosstown rival. On New Year's Day 1943, the Bruins met the No. 2 ranked University of Georgia, which scored all of its points in the fourth quarter to win 9–0. About $50,000 of the gate receipts were donated to the American Red Cross as a combined donation from both universities, the PCC and the Tournament of Roses Association.

In 1939, alumnus Wilbur Johns was appointed head basketball coach. Robinson provided highlights as the top-scoring basketball player in the PCC's Southern Division during 1940 and 1941, despite the Bruins' lackluster seasons. Tennis wins were scarce, although future tennis Coach J.D. Morgan served as captain in 1941. The football team struggled as well. "We were the best morale builders for service teams on the West Coast last year," said Coach Horrell of the 1943 season. "We lost to all of them."

After the war, as veterans enrolled at UCLA in record numbers, athletics were strengthened considerably. With Spaulding's retirement in 1947, Johns was appointed director of athletics. Johns took on an increased management role within the department, until he finally headed the full program, while Ackerman devoted himself completely to other Associated Students business. Johns made several new hires, including Bert

LaBrucherie as head football coach—the first alumnus to hold the position—and 1926 Bruin track captain Elvin C. "Ducky" Drake, as head track coach. Drake would coach both 1959 student body President Rafer Johnson and teammate C.K. Yang, who won gold and silver in the decathlon, respectively, in the 1960 Summer Olympics in Rome. The duel is known as one of the most dramatic in Olympic history.

More than 200 lettermen, freshmen and former servicemen showed up for football practice at the beginning of the 1946 season. That year's squad was the first undefeated, un-tied team in UCLA's history, sweeping a 10-game schedule, and producing UCLA's first consensus All-American choice in Burr Baldwin. Attendance at football games climbed to 426,196, a one-season record until 1988. Some 93,714 fans were on hand November 23 to see the Bruins beat the Trojans 13–6 to clinch the PCC crown and another Rose Bowl bid. The threat of rain, which had fallen the night before the rivalry game, kept away 8,000 more who had tickets. Sawdust was

A Gridiron Home

Notwithstanding the decades-old rivalry between the Bruins and Trojans, Charles E. Young and USC President James H. Zumberge found themselves allied over football in the summer of 1982.

The issue of mutual concern: negotiations between the Los Angeles Memorial Coliseum Commission and the Oakland Raiders in the professional football team's impending move to Los Angeles.

Both USC and UCLA had called the Coliseum their home since the 1920s. With the exception of a bitter dispute in 1932 over USC's sudden demand for a preferential 10-year lease that would essentially have given USC a monopoly over the stadium's use—a request that was denied after UCLA alumni petitioned both the Los Angeles City Council and the Los Angeles County Board of Supervisors—the two universities coexisted amicably for decades. The teams also shared the facility without incident with the National Football League's Los Angeles Rams from 1946 until 1979, when the Rams moved to Anaheim.

Under a longstanding agreement based on seniority, USC had first choice of dates, UCLA second and the Rams third. UCLA logistically worked out alternate Saturdays around the USC schedule, and the Rams had never presented a problem.

But the Raiders were not satisfied with the arrangement. Jim Hardy, Coliseum general manager, visited campus to inform Young and other senior administrators about the status of negotiations. Hardy explained that the Raiders insisted on having scheduling priority, control of locker rooms and all the revenue from proposed luxury boxes, among other preferences, and that the Coliseum Commission intended to comply. Although UCLA leaders found the revenue issue troubling, they were most irked by what they viewed as being demoted to third place after a half-century standing agreement.

Young and Zumberge were invited to the final Coliseum Commission meeting in July 1982, just weeks before the start of football season. Despite their vociferous objections, the deal with the Raiders was approved. "They just turned a deaf ear on us," Young recalled. Immediately after that heated meeting, Young decided to open negotiations with the City of Pasadena to relocate UCLA's home football games to the venerable Rose Bowl, beginning with the upcoming season.

Pasadena had made overtures in the past about getting UCLA, or even USC, to play at the Rose Bowl. Although some Pasadena residents were not pleased at the prospect of game-day traffic another half-dozen times a year, the revenue from a UCLA football schedule was appealing, especially as it had the potential to offset the Rose Bowl's drain on the city's existing financial resources.

Moreover, UCLA alumni had long been unhappy with the Coliseum's location in rival USC's backyard. For some, it raised regret that UCLA did not build its own stadium in the 1930s, when surrounding land was more available.

The last realistic opportunity for an on-campus stadium died in the 1960s. A 44,000-seat multipurpose outdoor venue was among the proposals outlined in UCLA's 1963 Long Range Development Plan. But strong opposition enveloped the project. It ranged from Governor Edmund G. "Pat" Brown considering it "ill advised" to proceed with a stadium before meeting more pressing educational needs to professors and students who, in separate referenda, voted against the construction of a stadium. Student activists staged a "play-in," a football game in the hall outside of Chancellor Murphy's office, in protest.

Ultimately, the Board of Regents approved a scaled-down 10,000-seat on-campus track and field facility, completed in 1969. (In 1973, the venue was named Drake Stadium, in honor of Elvin C. "Ducky" Drake, who spent more than 60 years at UCLA as a student-athlete, track coach and athletic trainer.)

Subsequent student and alumni initiatives in the 1970s died quietly. But in the early 1980s, an activist group of leading alumni and donors formed their own committee, commissioned designs and offered to help raise money to place a full football venue on the site of Drake Stadium.

"The political turmoil that would have resulted from an attempt to do that in our affluent Westside neighborhood in the 1980s was unimaginable," said alumnus Alan F. Charles, former campus counsel and vice chancellor for external affairs from 1979–93.

So amid a backdrop of clamoring alumni, an alienating Coliseum Commission, and football season just a couple months away, negotiations with Pasadena began quickly. When a mutually satisfactory agreement was on the table, Young called an evening meeting at the Chancellor's Residence with UCLA administrators

In 1983, a total of 104,991 fans watch the Bruins' 24–14 victory over the University of Michigan at UCLA's new home field, the Rose Bowl.

Top: The City of Pasadena welcomes UCLA to the Rose Bowl on August 18, 1982.

Above: Joe Bruin rides a Clydesdale mocking Tommy Trojan's Traveler during the first crosstown rivalry game on UCLA's new home field, November 20, 1982. Led by Coach Terry Donahue, UCLA won 20–19 in a cliffhanger ending where the Bruins stopped the Trojans on a two-point conversion with no time left.

representing athletics and alumni relations.

"We were all angry about the treatment we had received from the Coliseum," Charles said. "My anger was compounded by my fear that our influential alumni with their new stadium plan would push us into a battle with our neighbors and local officials. We decided that night to move to the Rose Bowl, and to announce it right away."

Word of the move to the Rose Bowl caused another kind of political turmoil that was not anticipated. Los Angeles Mayor Tom Bradley, a former Bruin track star who attended UCLA from 1937–40, called Young to complain that UCLA would be deserting the central city, taking jobs away from lower-income families and sticking another dagger into the heart of the Coliseum, which had already lost one tenant (the Rams).

There was also internal pressure—ranging from University of California President David S. Saxon to student body President Bobby Grace—not to leave Los Angeles, flout tradition or risk alienating fans by the resultant change in seating assignments. Young stood firm. "David, I can't change my mind, and if Tom wanted to help, he should have gotten in and helped earlier," said Young, responding to Saxon's inquiry. Bradley appeared before the Board of Regents, requesting that they overturn Young's decision. But the regents, on July 16, supported Young, leaving the authority for the decision with him.

On July 23, a press conference formally announcing the move was held in the James West Alumni Center, featuring Pasadena Mayor Loretta Thompson-Glickman, whom university leaders credited with helping deflect criticism that UCLA was guilty of elitism and white flight. The mayor, herself African-American, made the case to television cameras that there were low-income families in Pasadena, too, who could benefit from the jobs UCLA's presence would generate.

On August 18, 1982, the City of Pasadena, the Pasadena Chamber of Commerce and the Pasadena Tournament of Roses Association officially welcomed the Bruins to their new home field.

Head football Coach Terry Donahue introduced his players to more than 1,000 cheering fans who came to inspect both players and field. "We begin our season here on Sept. 11," Donahue said, "and there's no doubt in my mind that if everything goes well, we'll end it here on Jan. 1, 1983."

The Bruins did just that, with a 24-14 victory over Michigan on New Year's Day, and the move to the Rose Bowl ushered in a new era in UCLA football. The Bruins were the Pac-10 representative in the Rose Bowl Game on New Year's Day in three of the first four years after the move, each ending with a Bruin victory over the Big Ten champion (1983 vs. Michigan; 1984 vs. Illinois; 1986 vs. Iowa) on what was then and continues to be the Bruins' home field. (UCLA has committed to the site for home football games until at least 2042.)

"We had chafed under the Coliseum situation for a long time," Young said. "Within six months everybody totally changed their mind and decided that this was the best thing we ever could have done."

A postscript to the Rose Bowl move occurred a few years later. The Raiders livened up their halftime shows in the Coliseum by bringing in outside bands, including UCLA's, which were paid for their services. The UCLA Marching Band made what would be its final appearance at a Raiders game on October 29, 1989. A few days later, Charles received a report from the Los Angeles Police Department, which read in part:

"[Officer] responded to a vandalism investigation at the L.A. Memorial Coliseum. Upon arrival…was advised by Witnesses of possible field tampering conducted by numerous UCLA band members during the half time show of the L.A. Raiders football game. [Witness] stated he was standing on the 40 yard line on the L.A. Raiders side of the field during the half time show. He observed the suspects, approximately 250 UCLA marching band members performing, spelling the letters 'UCLA' during marching band formation on the middle portion of the football field. At which time he observed all band members drop to one knee & pull out a clear plastic baggie from various locations. Witness then observed the band members sprinkle an unknown substance which was located inside the baggies onto the field. At which time the band members rubbed the substance into the grass lawn with their shoes. After the band exited the field Witness recovered a plastic zip lock baggie containing a white powdered substance, which was located on the playing field. [The Police lab] stated the substance was possibly a powdered lye, but would conduct further testing."

Even though the Coliseum grounds crew tried their best to cover up the burned grass, the UCLA script was still visible on the field during the television broadcast of the UCLA-USC game on November 18, 1989.

The day after receiving the police report, Charles sent a note to UCLA Marching Band Director Gordon Henderson. "It is my duty to admonish you that this act was the product of evil minds, and was very naughty," Charles wrote. "Grass is our friend. Moreover, the Raiders are our friends. If it weren't for the Raiders, we would still be playing football at the Coliseum." The letter was posted in the band's office as a badge of honor for many years.

THE GOAL POST

SAINT MARY'S vs. U. C. L. A.

spread on the worst places, but the Bruins were able to use a "mud strategy" to defeat USC. On January 1, 1947, UCLA met the University of Illinois in the Rose Bowl, losing 45–14.

NATIONAL CHAMPIONS

Johns made two additional hires that would profoundly change the course of UCLA athletics. In 1948, he hired John R. Wooden, former Purdue University All-American, to succeed him as basketball coach. Wooden, who would attain legendary status and be hailed as the greatest collegiate men's basketball coach ever, led the Bruins for 27 seasons before retiring in 1975 with multiple records, an unparalleled streak of 88 consecutive victories and 10 NCAA championships in 12 years. Winning was not as important to Wooden as teaching, and during his tenure he mentored dozens of Bruin greats, including Lew Alcindor (later Kareem Abdul-Jabbar) and Bill Walton, inspiring a legacy that went well beyond athletics.

Later in 1948, after an unexpected 3–7 record on the gridiron, LaBrucherie and three of his assistant coaches abruptly quit. "Bruin students forced Bert LaBrucherie to resign," wrote

1947
EAST·INTERCOLLEGIATE FOOTBALL·WEST
PASADENA
NEW YEARS DAY
Established Price $1.50
Tax Paid 30
ROSE BOWL
JANUARY FIRST 2 P.M.
Total · $1.80
SUBJECT TO CONDITIONS ON REVERSE SIDE
This ticket must be presented with Associated Student Membership Card, and admits bona fide holder to Student Rooting Section.
U. C. L. A. ROOTERS
ENTER TUNNEL · 3 or 4 ·
3415

Left: The Bruins regularly matched up with the dominating St. Mary's Gaels during the 1930s and 1940s, but managed two shutouts, 6–0 on November 12, 1934, and 39–0 on October 14, 1944.

Bottom left: Coach Bert LaBrucherie (center) led the Bruins to their first undefeated, un-tied regular season (10–0–0) in UCLA history, and a 1947 Rose Bowl berth, where the Bruins lost 45–14 against the University of Illinois.

Below: Wilbur Johns (center) changed the course of UCLA athletics by hiring John R. Wooden (right) as head basketball coach in 1948 and Henry R. "Red" Sanders (left) as head football coach in 1949.

the *Los Angeles Times.* "Part of LaBrucherie's troubles, so they said at Westwood, was his lack of public relations savvy."

After unprecedented success, LaBrucherie was unable to meet heightened expectations. "Any institution which shoots up as swiftly as UCLA has," said the *Times,* "is bound to experience growing pains."

Johns and Provost Clarence A. Dykstra recruited Henry R. "Red" Sanders from Vanderbilt University. Sanders, who earned his nickname because of a crimson sweater he wore as a youth, established UCLA as a national football power during his nine seasons as head football coach. When he introduced the single-wing formation at UCLA, critics called it outmoded, to which Sanders responded: "I suppose it is, like a horse and buggy system, but with a television in the dashboard." Sanders coined the expression, often inaccurately attributed to others, "Winning isn't everything—it's the only thing."

UCLA football dominated in the 1950s. Under Sanders' guidance, the Bruins finished first in the PCC three times,

second three times, tied for second once, and were third twice. His win-loss record was 66–19–1.

On November 20, 1954, UCLA's undefeated football team battled it out with USC in front of 102,548 fans at a sold-out Coliseum. The Bruins had gained a sense of invincibility during the season by shutting out four of the eight teams they played and holding all but one team to a single touchdown.

But in a closer-than-expected contest, UCLA held only a 7–0 lead entering the fourth quarter. In the final 15 minutes, however, the Westwood 11 exploded with four touchdowns to rout the Trojans 34–0, capping a perfect pigskin season (9–0) and earning a second consecutive Pacific Coast Conference crown.

In post-game defeat, Trojan Coach Jess Hill told the *Daily Bruin,* "They're the best team we've played, but they're not that good. I don't know the statistics. ... I'll never admit that they're 34 points better than we." But when the final statistics were released, they revealed that the Trojans had gained only a net of five yards from running plays and 103 from passing—completing only nine passes while throwing five interceptions. When later asked by reporters if the Bruins deserved their No. 1 ranking, Hill replied, "Yes sir I do!" The

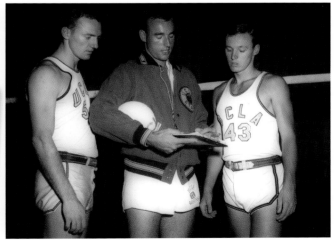

UCLA BRUINS
National and PCC Champions
1954

AERIAL VIEW OF CAPACITY CROWD AT LOS ANGELES MEMORIAL COLISEUM • USC VS. UCLA • NOV. 20, 1954
ATTENDANCE: 102,548 • SCORE: USC - 0, UCLA - 34

Above: The 1954 National Champs.

Opposite: Top row: Women's polo, 1930s; Courtney Matthewson, 2008; Jimmy Connors, 1971; Football at the Coliseum, late 1970s; Men's crew at Ballona Creek, 1964; **Second row:** Tom Bradley, late 1930s; Coaches Sharron Backus and Sue Enquist with Kelly Inouye-Perez, early 1990s; Sam Balter, 1929; Rooters salute 1947 footballers; Intramural Field, 2007; **Third row:** Don Barksdale, 1947; Mohini Bhardwaj, 2001; *Goal Post*, 1964; *The Hoop*, 1969; Coach Walt Hazzard and Reggie Miller, 1987; Troy Aikman, 1988; **Fourth row:** Florence Griffith, early 1980s; J.D. Morgan (center) and 1969–1970 NCAA championship-winning coaches from left: Bob Horn (men's water polo), John R. Wooden (basketball); Glenn Bassett (men's tennis) and Al Scates (men's volleyball); Women's rifle team, 1930s; Coach Tommy Prothro, 1965; **Fifth row:** Women's lacrosse, 2008; 1937 intercollegiate ski team; Chris Woo, late 1970s; Natalie Williams, early 1990s; Karch Kiraly, early 1980s; Gail Goodrich and Walt Hazzard, 1964; **Bottom row:** No. 1 Bruin rooter "Ma" Crandall with Wooden; 1947 football squad; Quarterback Mark Harmon with Coach Pepper Rogers, early 1970s; Coaches Mark Gottfried (left), Jim Harrick (center), Steve Lavin (right) and Lorenzo Romar (above), 1995.

1954 team was voted national champions by United Press International and No. 2 by the Associated Press. However, the best team in UCLA's history was denied a bid to the Rose Bowl because of the "no-repeat" rule, which stated that a PCC team could not go to the bowl in successive years. The Trojans went instead, losing to Ohio State University.

In the spring of 1956, a five-year conference investigation of alleged booster improprieties surfaced publicly, and on May 19, the PCC fined UCLA and imposed sanctions that made the entire Bruin squad ineligible for play. UCLA alumni and administrators believed that UCLA was being unfairly singled out for a practice that was widespread. The University of Washington was also fined, although to a lesser degree, and sanctions would later be imposed on Berkeley and USC. After a bitter three-year ordeal, the Pacific Coast Conference dissolved and was replaced in July 1959 by the newly formed Athletic Association of Western Universities. UCLA was a charter member. The conference was renamed Pacific-8 in 1968, then Pacific-10 in 1978, after two Arizona universities were added as members. In 2011, it became the Pacific-12, after the conference expanded yet again to include the University of Colorado and the University of Utah.

A lasting result of the PCC scandal was the removal of athletics from the control of the Associated Students, both at UCLA and at Berkeley. In 1960, University of California President Clark Kerr put the athletics departments under chancellorial oversight.

BUILDING THE BRUIN DYNASTY

In the early 1960s, with the UCLA athletics budget running in the red, Chancellor Franklin D. Murphy turned to alumnus and former tennis Coach J.D. Morgan to oversee and stabilize the troubled program.

On February 8, 1963, when Murphy announced his selection of Morgan to succeed the retiring Johns, restoring financial stability to the program was at the forefront of his mind. Murphy's two other priorities were to bring sports back onto the UCLA campus by building new venues and to encourage greater student participation. "We needed a competent business person who also knew something about athletics and [had an] abiding interest in sports," Murphy said later.

As UCLA's new director of intercollegiate athletics, Morgan—the championship-winning men's tennis coach and previously the associate university business manager—would revitalize the sports program, catapult Bruin teams into the national spotlight, and ultimately redefine UCLA athletics as a model respected by universities across the country.

He did this in part by liberating his coaches from their administrative responsibilities. During Morgan's first year, Wooden's team won the Athletic Association of Western Universities conference and qualified for the NCAA tournament. One evening, Morgan stopped by Wooden's office before the tournament. Morgan asked Wooden what he was working on. "I'm getting your budget ready," Wooden responded. "Mr. Johns wanted it always by the first of April." Morgan walked over to the desk, picked up the budget documents and threw them in the wastebasket. "I'll take care of the budget, you take care of your team," Morgan said. "You're getting ready for the tournament." Wooden, who had coached 15 previous Bruin teams, was freed from all non-coaching responsibilities, including budgeting, equipment management and scheduling. His undefeated 1963–64 squad—led by senior point guard, All-American and National Player of the Year Walt Hazzard—won UCLA's first NCAA basketball championship, beginning a dynasty.

As associate business manager, Morgan had played a key role in obtaining the financing for several major building projects, including Ackerman Student Union and the four high-rise residence halls. At the time of his appointment, plans for an on-campus indoor sports arena were moving forward. Morgan would not only oversee the completion of Pauley Pavilion, but also of Drake Stadium and a boathouse for crew in Marina del Rey.

Morgan was instrumental in arranging lucrative television contracts, and pushed Wooden to play in the Astrodome on January 20, 1968, where a record crowd of 52,693, plus a nationwide television audience, watched the No. 2 ranked University of Houston Cougars snap the No. 1 ranked Bruins'

47-game win streak in a 71–69 upset. "The Game of the Century" was the first NCAA regular season basketball game broadcast nationally, and established the sport as a television commodity. The Bruins would have their revenge when the teams faced off again that season in the 1968 NCAA tournament. A healthy Alcindor, not plagued by the eye injury that had slowed him down to shooting a rare less-than-50 percent from the field (he shot over 60 percent during his UCLA career), led the No. 2 ranked Bruins over the top ranked Cougars in the semifinals, 101–69. The Bruins advanced to defeat the University of North Carolina Tar Heels for the national title.

During Morgan's 16-year tenure, UCLA won an unprecedented 30 NCAA championships—10 in basketball, seven in volleyball, six in tennis, four in track and field, and three in water polo—more than any other university over the same period. His main objectives for the program included rekindling Bruin "family" support, providing greater assistance for the coaching staff, and fostering a strong and balanced recruiting program. He earned the nickname "J.D. Midas" because everything he touched turned to gold.

But some found Morgan difficult, even arrogant. He was known to engage in battles with alumni, the press and

referees, often vilifying the officials as he sat on the Bruin bench during basketball road games. These outbursts were so frequent that, in an effort to limit his public displays, rival Pac-8 basketball coaches came together and voted to ban athletic directors from the team bench.

Morgan's success was fueled by his intensely competitive nature and fierce Bruin loyalty. On his desk, he kept a small sign that read: "Winning Solves All Problems." But victory at any cost was not his creed. "Sports is a co-curricular activity of the institution, and excellence on the playing field should complement classroom excellence," he said.

A career Bruin, Morgan came to UCLA in the late 1930s and was a four-year letterman on the men's tennis team. Following graduation from the UCLA College of Business Administration, he commanded a Navy torpedo boat in the

Above: The 1956 UCLA-USC game in the Men's Gymnasium.

Above left: John R. Wooden and J.D. Morgan watch from the sidelines during the NCAA Championship Semifinals in 1975.

Far left: The starting five of the 1964 NCAA championship men's basketball team, from left, Gail Goodrich, Keith Erickson, Fred Slaughter, Jack Hirsch, Walt Hazzard. The title was the first of 10 under Coach Wooden.

Left: Wooden (right) and Assistant Coach Gary Cunningham (left) huddle with Bill Walton (back to camera), early 1970s.

Coach

Coach John Robert Wooden, or simply Coach, as he preferred to be called, built what has been called an "incomparable dynasty" at UCLA—one "against which all others are compared, and usually pale." Winning an unprecedented 10 NCAA men's basketball team championships in 12 seasons and holding an unmatched 88 consecutive game win streak, Wooden's teams dominated the sport from 1964–75.

Wooden, however, contributed more to UCLA than a supreme sports legacy. Just ask those who played for him, worked with him or were inspired by him.

"It would be safe to say that John Wooden has contributed more to the actual and perceived quality of UCLA than any other individual, including Nobel laureates," said Chancellor Charles E. Young. "When you think of UCLA you think of basketball/Wooden. You think of quality, you think of character, you think of building people."

The understated coach, who could catch an individual off-guard with his dry sense of humor, often attributed his philosophy toward life, including his well-known "Pyramid of Success," to his father, Joshua Hugh, and his religious upbringing.

Wooden was born October 14, 1910, in Hall, Indiana. The third of six children, he grew up on a farm in the small rural town of Centerton, eight miles outside of Martinsville, Indiana. His home had no running water or electricity, and Wooden's introduction to basketball was rudimentary: His mother made him and his three brothers (his sisters died in childhood) their first basketball by sewing together old rags stuffed in black cotton stockings. After chores—such as milking the cows—were done, Wooden and his older brother would shoot baskets in the barn's hayloft, where his father had mounted an old tomato basket with the bottom knocked out. "It's hard to imagine now, but I still think we were able to dribble that thing," Wooden wrote in his memoir, *They Call Me Coach*.

Wooden had proved athletically gifted in elementary school and played baseball and basketball—but he liked baseball best. In 1924, hard times forced Wooden's family to move into town. At Martinsville High School, however, there was no football team or baseball team, so he focused on basketball and his talents emerged. (Subsequent injuries would prevent his continued pursuit of baseball and football.) An intense and fiery competitor, Wooden led his team to the state championship finals in three consecutive years, from 1926–28, winning the title in his junior year. Wooden received All-State honors each year.

In 1928, he enrolled at Purdue University in West Lafayette, Indiana, where he lettered in baseball and basketball his freshman year. Wooden played basketball under the guidance of Coach Ward Lewis "Piggy" Lambert, who Wooden credited as being the greatest influence on his playing and coaching careers because of his "fetish for details." Although Wooden was a sought-after player, there were no athletic scholarships. He paid his way through school by working odd jobs—from scrubbing out fraternity kitchens to purchasing all the rights to sell concessions during the train ride from Lafayette to Chicago for the annual Purdue-University of Chicago football game at Soldier Field.

Soon, the 178-pound, five-foot-ten-and-a-half Wooden became a nationally acclaimed basketball player, known for his hustle and sharp eye. He set a Big Ten scoring record, leading the Boilermakers to the national championship in 1932. He also helped Purdue capture the Big Ten conference titles in 1930 and 1932. The first player ever named a three-time consensus All-American, he was team captain in his junior and senior years, and earned the nickname the "India Rubber Man" for getting right back up after his hard dives onto the court. Regarded as one of the best Big Ten players ever, Wooden was in the second class elected to the Naismith Memorial Basketball Hall of Fame in Springfield, Massachusetts, in 1960. An English major, Wooden earned the Big Ten's Medal for Outstanding Merit and Proficiency in Scholarship and Athletics during his senior year—an accomplishment of which he was equally proud.

After graduating with his bachelor's degree in 1932, Wooden married his high school sweetheart, Nell Riley, whom he had met at a carnival when he was 15. They had two children, Nancy (1934) and James (1936), and eventually many grandchildren and great-grandchildren. Family, Wooden always said, was what mattered most in life.

In September 1932, Wooden began his first coaching job, accepting the athletic director position at Dayton High School

Above: Coach John R. Wooden, 1949.

Right: Wooden, a three-time consensus All-American at Purdue University, 1932.

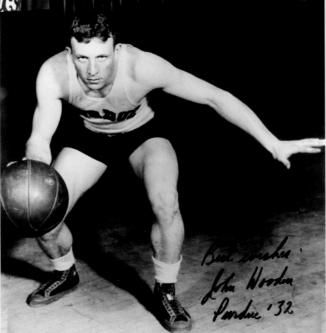

Best wishes
John Wooden
Purdue '32

in Dayton, Kentucky. He taught English and coached the Green Devils basketball team, ending the season with a 6–11 record—the only losing season of his career. The next year his team made the playoffs. In 1934, Wooden moved back to Indiana, accepting a teaching and coaching position (for basketball and baseball) at South Bend Central High School. His 11-year high school basketball coaching record was 218 wins, 42 losses.

For six years while he was teaching—before the National Basketball Association was developed—Wooden played professional basketball for three teams in three different leagues, including the Indianapolis Kautskys (later the Indianapolis Jets). He earned $50 a game for the Kautskys, but earned a special $100 bonus when he scored his 100th consecutive free throw—a record he stretched to 134 without a miss.

World War II interrupted his coaching career, as Wooden enlisted and was called up to active duty a year later, serving as Navy lieutenant from 1943–46 providing fitness training to combat flyers. After the war, Wooden accepted a position coaching at Indiana State Teachers College (later Indiana State University), in Terre Haute, where his record was 44–15. During his two years there, he also obtained a master's degree in education, and completed his doctoral thesis, but did not have the time to complete the rest of the requirements toward the degree.

At Indiana State, Wooden led the Sycamores to a 17–8 record to finish his first season, winning the conference and earning an invitation to the 1947 National Association for Intercollegiate Basketball (NAIB) postseason tournament. Held in Kansas City, Missouri, it posed an "unexpected crisis" for him: Wooden was asked to leave Clarence Walker, his sole black player, at home. Wooden declined the invitation. The next year, the Sycamores finished 27–7 and were invited to the tournament once again. This time, the Sycamores were on the national radar because of Wooden's fast-break style of play, and the NAIB presented a different scenario: Walker could play, but he could not stay with the team or be seen publicly with the other players. Wooden declined once again. However, the National Association

for the Advancement of Colored People (NAACP) asked Wooden to reconsider because Walker would be the first black player ever permitted to play in a national college basketball tournament. Wooden posed the situation to Walker and his family, who decided to do it. The team found itself introduced to Jim Crow laws, and the Sycamores ended up losing in the finals to Louisville 92–70. But Wooden said the experience had been profoundly rewarding for him and the players. "Years later an all-black team won the event, and I would guess a few coaches never forgave me for fielding the first team that included a black student-athlete," Wooden wrote in *My Personal Best*. Years later, at UCLA, Wooden would find himself faced with issues of racism again while traveling to Houston and other parts of the South with his teams.

After two successful seasons in Terre Haute, Wooden began receiving other coaching offers. The ones that interested him most were from his alma mater, from Minnesota and from UCLA. Wooden and Nell had no desire to leave the Midwest, and Wooden hoped to coach in the Big Ten. Purdue, he said, was "the one I loved more than any of them, but I felt they were treating the man I was replacing miserably." Instead, Wooden was poised to accept the offer from Minnesota, on condition that he could hire his own assistant. However, an act of nature interceded. Wooden had arranged it so that Minnesota officials would call him at 6 p.m. with an answer; the UCLA call was scheduled next, for 7 p.m. But a snowstorm kept the Minnesota athletic director from getting through on the phone. Fifteen minutes after he accepted the UCLA position, Minnesota called with the offer, but it was too late. Wooden would not go back on his word. He was destined for UCLA.

Wooden, 37, was hired by Athletic Director Wilbur Johns in April 1948. The coach had requested a three-year contract, which would have the unintended effect of keeping him at UCLA when Purdue came calling two years later. Wooden, excited about the Purdue offer, tried to break his contract, but Johns and Associated Students Manager William C. Ackerman reminded him that he was the one who had insisted on the third year. Although irritated, Wooden honored the contract. After the third year, he didn't want to leave.

Affectionately called Johnny Wooden in those early years, and even "Jovial John" in the yearbook, the students quickly embraced their new head men's basketball coach. When Wooden arrived, UCLA was slated by the press to finish last in the conference. The team had a 12–13 season the year before. Wooden had his work cut out for him, but he resolved to work hard and "recruit like mad" the following year.

"'Let's hit 'em from this angle,' instructed Johnny Wooden, UCLA's first season basketball miracle man, as he prepared the Bruin team for the Oregon State tussle," wrote

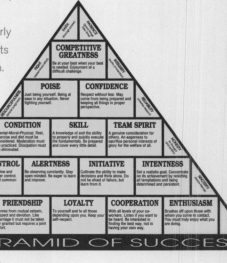

THE PYRAMID OF SUCCESS

the 1949 *Southern Campus*. "The pre-season rated 'cellar chumps' turned out to be the 'Southern champs' and a gang that made the Beavers work for the PCC crown. They'll pack 'em into the crackerbox gym next season … television here we come."

The Bruins won the Southern Division with a 22–7 record in 1949, the most wins in a season ever, until the following year, when the Bruins achieved a 24–7 season and UCLA's first-ever Pacific Coast Conference title and NCAA Tournament bid. In his first four UCLA seasons, Wooden's Bruins won four PCC Southern Division championships—UCLA had only won two in the 30 years prior—along with two outright PCC Championships and participated in two NCAA Tournaments.

Still, that was just the beginning, and playing conditions were difficult. Wooden wished that UCLA had a major arena, and did not have to hold practice and play in the Men's Gymnasium, nicknamed the B.O. Barn. Mopping the floor of the men's gym, where he coached teams for 17 years, was a daily ritual, as dirt accumulated quickly—something Wooden attributed to Westwood Boulevard running through campus all the way to Sunset Boulevard.

Gymnastics and wrestling all shared the floor, and other than cramped quarters, sometimes there also were distractions. "On the other side of the floor were two trampolines, and I say occasionally our coeds would be up there up in leotards, jumping up and down on the those trampolines while we were having practice," Wooden recalled. "At least that's what my players told me. I said, of course, I never noticed them at all."

Wooden was also responsible for preparing the budget, renting equipment and uniforms, and virtually every detail of the team's management. But after 15 seasons at UCLA, things changed when J.D. Morgan was hired as athletic director. Morgan freed Wooden from all of his administrative responsibilities, and the following year he won the first of his string of NCAA championships.

Wooden, however, noted that his own personal views helped move his coaching to the next level. For years, Wooden acknowledged that he was resentful that recruiting had to go through the admissions director at Berkeley, or that top players would pick other schools, including USC or Oregon, over UCLA.

"I was upset many times where [we had] the same academic requirements as Berkeley, and yet they were getting some players in that we couldn't get," Wooden said. "It bothered me to the point, in my opinion, honestly, I think it hurt me. I don't think I was doing the job I was capable of doing, because I did something against [what] father tried to [instill]: Don't compare and never complain about what you *don't* have, make the best of what you *do* have.

"In retrospect, I think I'm trying to analyze myself, and that's difficult, but I think, probably, I was letting things bother me over which I had no control, and when I finally overcame that, which I did, is when we won our first two national championships."

Then, Wooden said, "We began to attract more nationwide attention." And in June 1965, Pauley Pavilion opened. "The best thing that ever happened to me when I came to UCLA was getting Pauley Pavilion," Wooden said. "And yet, we'd won our first national championships prior to that."

Wooden prided himself on never leaving Southern California to recruit. "I don't think anywhere in the country there's the wealth and talent in certain areas as in Southern California," he said, "and in almost any sport you can name."

During John Wooden's 27 years as UCLA's head coach, he produced 17 All-Americans, beginning with George Stanich in 1950. In 10 UCLA NCAA championship seasons, 10 All-Americans played for Coach Wooden: Walt Hazzard, Gail Goodrich, Lew Alcindor (later Kareem Abdul-Jabbar), Lucius Allen, Michael Warren, Sidney Wicks, Henry Bibby, Bill Walton, Keith Wilkes (Jamaal Wilkes) and David Meyers.

A rolled-up program became Wooden's trademark, and as he often quipped, possibly a security blanket as well. In moments of anguish, he would exclaim, "Goodness gracious, sakes alive!" But never anything stronger, a moral value instilled by his father at a young age. However, sometimes, he was found shouting at officials or opposing players, something he later regretted.

"In a towering of rage, he may coldly inform an official: 'Your eyesight isn't as good tonight as it was last week,'" said Vic Kelley, UCLA Sports Information director from 1945–81.

Wooden believed in long practices that were often in the evening, coinciding with game times, for conditioning and drills to perfect fundamental skills. He began each season by teaching players how to put on their shoes and socks the right way, something he said was key to preventing blisters and maintaining high performance.

"I didn't have many rules, but when I had a rule, I stuck to it," Wooden said. One of those rules barred facial hair, which, he said, he developed out of personal experience from his playing days.

"I didn't want hair or sweat getting in a player's eyes and obstructing his vision," Wooden wrote in *UCLA Magazine* in summer of 2000, recounting a well-known story. "One day Bill Walton came to practice wearing a beard. I said, 'Bill, have you forgotten something?' He said, 'Coach, I think I should be allowed to wear it. It's my right.' So I asked him, 'Do you believe in it that strongly?' He said, 'Yes, I do, coach.' I said to him, 'Bill, I have great respect for individuals who stand up for those things in which they believe. And the team is going to miss you.' Bill shaved and returned to practice. There were no hard feelings."

During the Vietnam War-era, protests enveloped the campus, and several players, notably center Bill Walton, were avid activists off the court. Wooden, who respected his players' beliefs, did not allow them to interfere with practice or the atmosphere of being on the court. He told his players to leave their activism at the door, and not to miss practice. "There's always problems—in every era," Wooden said, reflecting years later. "Problems change, but you're not going to get away from them."

There was a time when Wooden admonished Walton for his activism. "I remember once Bill Walton laying down on Wilshire Boulevard and stopping traffic during a demonstration," Wooden wrote in *UCLA Magazine*. "I said to him, 'Suppose there's an ambulance rushing somebody to the hospital and it can't get there.' He said, 'I didn't think about that.' I said, 'Those are the things to think about. You have a right to your beliefs and your actions as long as they don't interfere with the rights of others.'"

Said Wooden: "I always considered myself a teacher, and a teacher must set an example."

Another part of Wooden's coaching philosophy, he said, was to make "every player feel important," using an analogy to depict how a team works together. "Your role may be entirely different," Wooden recalled saying. "You're like a powerful automobile. Now, here's an Alcindor: he's the engine, ooh, powerful, and very difficult to replace. And you are just a wheel. And you're just a nut that holds that wheel on. Now which is more important for us to have success?"

Said Kareem Abdul-Jabbar: "He set quite an example. He was more like a parent than a coach. He really was a very selfless and giving human being, but he was a disciplinarian."

Walton said it was only years later that some of the players came to that realization.

"We did not understand the full extent of his approach while we were living our dreams at UCLA," wrote Walton in *UCLA Magazine* in 2000. "We thought he was nuts, a walking antique and more than a bit crazy. It wasn't until after I'd graduated and encountered the adversity he told us would be there that it started to dawn on me just how special it had been at UCLA. When I left UCLA in 1974 and became the highest-paid player in the history of team sports at that time, the quality of my life went down. That's how special it was to have played for John Wooden and UCLA."

At the 1975 NCAA Semifinals in San Diego, following an exciting 75–74 overtime win over Louisville, Wooden stunned his team—and fans alike—by announcing that win or lose, he would retire immediately after the championship final.

Far left: Coach John R. Wooden with his trademark rolled-up program, in one of his favorite photos.

Below left: From right, Wooden with Assistant Coaches Gary Cunningham and Frank Arnold, and sophomore forward Marques Johnson, on the bench during Wooden's final game in the 1975 NCAA Championship at the San Diego Sports Arena.

Below: A ticket for the national championship game, when UCLA beat Kentucky 92–85, on March 31, 1975.

Bottom: Coach Wooden reluctantly agreed to pose in a publicity photo surrounded by his career UCLA trophies.

"I didn't know myself [until] a few seconds before," Wooden said. "It just came on me this is the time, and my wife didn't know—if anyone was going to know early it'd have been Nellie, but nobody … people have a hard trouble believing that."

Morgan, Wooden said, was furious and spent much of the night trying to talk Wooden out of his decision, even offering more money.

Two days later, the Bruins rose to the occasion, and UCLA won its 10th national championship by defeating Kentucky—it also marked Wooden's first win ever over the Wildcats. Wooden said that game was his favorite that he had ever coached, followed by the semifinal game.

"In many ways, going out with a championship being unexpected, and having a team that caused me no problem on or off the floor the entire season—that's very pleasant," he said. In the locker room, Wooden stood on a chair that had been pulled out for him and told the team: "I want you to know that I never had a group that has given me more pleasure and more satisfaction, and that's a rather nice thing to say about the last team you'll ever teach." The players, Wooden recalled, were silent. He went over to the pressroom and made the same announcement—they were a bit more boisterous.

Wooden said he never regretted retiring, and that he did not miss games or the tournament—just practices. "I always loved practice," he said. If a coach asked him to talk to the team or attend practice, he was happy to do so—but only if asked, he emphasized.

Wooden was the first person inducted into the Naismith Memorial Basketball Hall of Fame as both a player, in 1960, and a coach, in 1973. In 2003, thanks in part to the efforts of Bruin Andre McCarter, he was awarded the Presidential Medal of Freedom, the highest honor given to a civilian. The press, and many others, dubbed him, "The Wizard of Westwood." But it was an appellation he did not care for. "I'm no wizard, and I don't like being thought of in that light at all," Wooden explained. "I think of a wizard as being some sort of magician or something, doing something on the sly or something, and I don't want to be thought of in that way." But, he added, "Coach, is fine."

For decades, Wooden attended Bruins games in Pauley Pavilion, sitting in his reserved seat behind the Bruin bench. It was something he did as often as he could, interrupted only by ill health in later years. On June 4, 2010, Wooden died at the Ronald Reagan UCLA Medical Center just a few months shy of his 100th birthday. His Pauley seat was permanently retired. "That was an absolute," Athletic Director Dan Guerrero said, adding that any time Bruins come to games "they will remember where he sat and what he meant to the program." Wooden, however, "did, perhaps, more for the university after he stopped coaching, because of the continued legacy that he built over the years," Guerrero said. Certainly UCLA evolved a great deal since 1948, when Wooden first arrived.

"As far as UCLA is concerned, it's exactly what Dutch Fehring said that: 'UCLA is a young university, but in my opinion, it's going to be a great university in all aspects, but it isn't now, and you'll find it quite different in basketball than you're accustomed to back in Indiana,'" Wooden recalled of his conversation with his longtime friend from Purdue, who served one-year as an assistant UCLA football coach and had recommended Wooden for the coaching job. "He was absolutely right.

"It was a young university then; still is, in comparison to some of the others," Wooden said in 2006. "But it was very young then. … I've seen it [transform] from a fairly good university to a great university."

Coach certainly had a hand in that.

Right: The legendary court in Pauley Pavilion was named for Nell and John Wooden on December 20, 2003.

Far right: Coach Wooden's cherished seat (Section 103b, Row 2, Seat 1) behind the Bruin bench in Pauley Pavilion is highlighted during his memorial on June 26, 2010. It will forever remain unoccupied, in honor of his memory.

South Pacific during World War II before returning to his alma mater in 1946 to accept a position in UCLA's accounting office and simultaneously serve as assistant tennis coach under Ackerman. In 1951, Morgan was appointed head coach of the men's tennis team, succeeding Ackerman, and went on to mentor Bruin tennis legends Arthur Ashe and Charlie Pasarell, among others. He guided his teams to seven NCAA championships, and continued coaching even after taking on the directorship. He stepped down from coaching in 1966 to focus full-time on athletic director duties, passing the mantle of UCLA tennis head coach to Glenn Bassett. A co-captain of the 1950 men's tennis team, which won UCLA's first NCAA team championship in any sport, Bassett would coach the Bruins for 27 seasons, compiling a 592-92-2 record with seven NCAA team championships, and training three NCAA singles champions, including Jimmy Connors in 1971.

During the Morgan era, UCLA's athletic teams brought new meaning to the phrase "gutty little Bruins," coined in the 1940s by Dean Cromwell, USC's track coach. Cromwell's track teams never lost to UCLA, and he reportedly said "Oh, we're going to meet Ducky Drake's gutty little Bruins." In the mid-1960s, under football Coach Tommy Prothro, the expression gained a more positive connotation. With the Bruins trailing 6–16 with four minutes to play against rival USC on November 20, 1965, sophomore Gary Beban unloaded two aerial touchdown "bombs," one for 34 yards and the other for 52, for a 20–16 victory that gave UCLA the conference title and Rose Bowl bid. "The thing he did best for us," Prothro told the *Los Angeles Times*, "was give the rest of our kids a tremendous amount of confidence."

In the New Year's Day game, Beban, nicknamed "The Great One," scored two touchdowns to give UCLA a 14–0 lead over the No. 1 ranked Michigan State Spartans. After closing to within eight points, the final moments of the game were tense, as Michigan State scored a touchdown to pull within two with 31 seconds left. Although UCLA was "outweighed and out-manned," according to *Sports Illustrated*, "a gutty UCLA defense

stunned the Spartans and provided the biggest sensation." The Bruins foiled the Spartans' two-point conversion attempt, and UCLA won 14–12, earning its first Rose Bowl victory.

Beban threw for 301 yards and scored two touchdowns in a heartbreaking one-point loss to USC on November 18, 1967. Two weeks after the game, Beban won a controversial vote over USC running back O.J. Simpson, to receive the Heisman Trophy, awarded annually to the nation's top college football player. Beban went 23-5-2 as starting quarterback in his three seasons as a Bruin.

One year after Morgan was hired as athletics director, he approached Ducky Drake with an ultimatum. Drake had been serving as head athletic trainer since 1942, as well as head track coach since 1947. "When Mr. Morgan came in, he said: 'You have to choose. It's too much. You can't do a good job in both of them,'" recalled Wooden. "He chose to be the head trainer, because he could have an association with all the athletes."

Jim Bush, who in his three years as head track coach at Occidental College never lost to UCLA, succeeded Drake in 1964. Two years later, he led the Bruins to their first win over USC and the 1966 NCAA championship. The Bruins also earned three consecutive NCAA championships from 1971–73, and another in 1978.

Top left: Arthur Ashe (left) and Charlie Pasarell (right), January 1963.

Left: Coach Jim Bush is carried off the field of the Los Angeles Memorial Coliseum by members of the 1966 men's track-and-field team after UCLA's first win over USC in the sport. The Bruins were on their way to winning the national championship, where their 48-point margin of victory was an NCAA record.

Below left: Nicknamed "The Great One," quarterback Gary Beban was awarded the Heisman Trophy in 1967.

Above: Media guide for the 1978–1979 women's basketball season.

Above center: Coach Billie Moore and Ann Meyers (with net) celebrate winning the 1978 AIAW basketball championship.

Above right: Gail Devers (left) and Jackie Joyner run the 4x100-meter relay at the UCLA–USC track-and-field meet, May 29, 1985.

In 1979, after 33 years at UCLA, Morgan was forced to announce his retirement due to rapidly deteriorating health. He continued to serve as a consultant to the athletics department until his death in December 1980. At the time of his retirement, when asked by the *Herald Examiner* what UCLA would miss most about him, he replied: "They're going to miss my style." The J.D. Morgan Center, home to UCLA's Department of Intercollegiate Athletics, was formally dedicated in his honor in 1984.

Judith Holland, director of the Department of Women's Intercollegiate Sports, greets former President Gerald Ford during his visit to UCLA in 1978, acknowledging UCLA's leadership role in elevating women's athletics.

WOMEN IN SPORT

In 1974, anticipating the enforcement of landmark federal regulations originally enacted in 1972—popularly known as Title IX—which would prohibit gender discrimination in university athletics, Chancellor Charles E. Young announced the establishment of the Department of Women's Intercollegiate Sports. The department introduced 10 varsity women's teams and one coed squad (badminton) in its initial year.

With the move, UCLA became one of a few universities to elevate women's programs to full status. Caspar Weinberger, secretary of the U.S. Department of Health, Education and Welfare—the government agency responsible for Title IX compliance—cited UCLA's efforts as a model for the country to follow. In May 1975, President Gerald Ford signed Title IX regulations, which included a provision prohibiting sex discrimination in athletics and established a three-year window for educational institutions to comply.

A year earlier, Ann Meyers (later Ann Meyers Drysdale) became the first female to receive a full athletic scholarship from UCLA. Meyers, under the direction of women's basketball Coach Billie Moore, and along with forwards Denise Curry and Anita Ortega, led the Bruins to the 1978 Association for Intercollegiate Athletics for Women (AIAW) national championship game, where they defeated the University of Maryland, 90–74. The game, held in Pauley Pavilion, drew a record AIAW crowd of 9,351. Meyers, a four-time All-American in basketball, was also a member of the 1975 AIAW track-and-field national championship team. In 1988, she was the first woman inducted into UCLA's Athletics Hall of Fame.

Judith Holland, appointed the department's first full-time athletics director in April 1975, was busy establishing a foundation for the women's program. Working out of a green trailer camped on the lawn in front of the Women's Gymnasium, she began with a meager $283,000 budget. Holland devoted the majority of those funds to scholarships, which meant she could only hire a part-time coaching staff.

"I still recruited the best coaches but sold them on the 'blue and gold' and what would happen over time," she said.

During Holland's first year, UCLA hired 188 women, with Holland doing much of the recruiting herself. With an eye to the department's future, she implemented a five-year plan to bolster the program's available funding, allow for full-time coaches, provide more aid for student-athletes, and increase travel funds.

In addition to Moore, Holland made several other key hires who quickly helped strengthen the women's program. Originally hired as a part-time coach in 1975, Sharron Backus led the Bruins softball team, featuring slugger Sue Enquist, to the AIAW championship in 1978. The Bruins did not allow a single run throughout the entire tournament. Enquist joined the coaching staff in 1980 as an assistant under Backus, before being promoted to co-head coach in 1989. After softball became an NCAA sport in 1982, UCLA won six of the first nine championships. From 1988–90, the Bruins won three consecutive NCAA titles with a record of 163–19. Backus, who retired in 1997, coached many standout players, including Dot Richardson and Lisa Fernandez, who was the first softball player to win the Honda-Broderick Cup as the nation's top female collegiate athlete. Enquist succeeded Backus as head coach in 1997, and steered the Bruins to another three national titles (1999, 2003 and 2004) before retiring in 2006.

Alumnus Andy Banachowski, a two-time volleyball All-American who had been coaching the Bruin women on and off since graduating in 1968, was rehired by Holland in 1970. Banachowski led the women's volleyball team to the national championship in 1972, and repeated the feat in 1974 and 1975. After women's volleyball became an NCAA sport, he led the Bruins to a national title in 1984. Spikers Natalie Williams and Elaine Youngs helped the Bruins earn additional titles in 1990 and 1991. The following year, Williams was voted the NCAA's National Player of the Year. In addition, she was a four-year starter for the women's basketball team and held All-American honors in that sport.

Holland would also hire track-and-field coaches Pat Connolly—who had initiated women's cross-country at UCLA in 1973—and Bob Kersee, who gained international acclaim by training female competitors for UCLA and for the Olympics. Among his most notable athletes were: sprinters and Olympic gold medalists Florence Griffith (later Florence Griffith Joyner) and Gail Devers, as well as heptathlete and long jumper Jackie Joyner (later Jackie Joyner-Kersee). Joyner, who became recognized as one of the greatest athletes of all time, was also a basketball starter at UCLA from 1980–83 and 1984–85. (She red-shirted during 1983–84 to concentrate on training for the heptathlon for the 1984 Summer Olympics.) Under Coach Kersee's guidance, the Bruins won back-to-back NCAA championships in 1982–83 in outdoor track and field.

As Title IX initiated the modern era of women's sports, some criticized Morgan for starting the department as an independent unit, suggesting that in doing so, he had tried to hold back women's athletics. Holland strongly refuted that notion. "When I first came, everyone was very quick to tell me to watch out for J.D.—that he was not really behind women's sports," Holland said. "That was not the truth at all. He was very much for women's sports, and he really felt they should develop on their own, that they shouldn't be a tagalong for men's sports."

But once they had been allowed to strengthen and mature for a few years, the ultimate intention was always to integrate women's athletics with the Department of Intercollegiate Athletics. In 1980, that finally happened. The following year, the NCAA began to award championships for Division I women's athletics, and Holland pushed to switch UCLA's teams from the AIAW to the NCAA. The move was controversial at the time and Holland, a former AIAW president, was labeled a traitor. "Having done as much for the organization of women's athletics as any, Holland is amazed and saddened to find herself branded a turncoat," wrote the *Los Angeles Times* in March 1981. One of Holland's primary concerns was money: In order to maintain financial independence, the AIAW was seeking to tax the revenues of the larger programs to support the smaller ones. Another issue was the AIAW's separatist viewpoint, according to Holland. Although the NCAA had a history of dismissing women's athletics, Holland believed that the organization had the ability to provide equality with men's athletics, produce greater visibility and ultimately do

Left: Sprinter Evelyn Ashford in Drake Stadium, mid-1970s. Ashford was the 1977 AIAW national champion in the 100-meter and 200-meter races, and helped lead the Bruins to the national title that year.

Above: Pitcher Lisa Fernandez, a four-time All-American, early 1990s.

Under the direction of Al Scates—who was hired in 1963 by Johns—the men's volleyball team won its first NCAA title in 1970, and dominated the sport over the next three decades. Over 36 years, Scates guided the Bruins to 19 championships—becoming the winningest coach of any sport in UCLA history and the most successful collegiate volleyball coach of all time. He coached 52 NCAA All-Americans, and mentored stars such as Karch Kiraly, Steve Salmons, David Saunders and Sinjin Smith. In May 2011, Scates announced that he would retire after the end of the 2012 season, having coached for 50 years. His three undefeated seasons—1979, 1982 and 1984—remained the only undefeated seasons in the history of the sport.

In addition to the powerhouse volleyball team, the early 1980s featured a football team that was on the cusp of a resurgence under Coach Terry Donahue. What's more, they would soon have a home to call their own. Just before the 1982 season, the university ended its longtime agreement with the Coliseum and moved home football games to the Rose Bowl. UCLA ended that season with a successful 9–1–1 record and the Pacific-10 crown. The Bruins went on to play in the 1983 Rose Bowl game, where they triumphed over the University of Michigan Wolverines, 24–14, beginning a new era of UCLA football.

In June 1983, Chancellor Young stunned the UCLA community by announcing that he had selected alumnus Peter T. Dalis, head of UCLA's Office of Cultural and Recreational Affairs (UCLA Recreation) as UCLA's new athletic director.

more for the evolution of women's athletics.

"The first and foremost goal was to be the best women's collegiate program in the nation," Holland recalled. "I believe that we did accomplish this goal."

She added: "UCLA set the benchmark for other people. In other words, they didn't wait to be dragged kicking and screaming into the 20th century for women's sports, they took the leadership on this, and said, 'Well, let's do this the right way.'"

100 AND COUNTING

After Morgan's sudden retirement due to health reasons in 1979, Robert A. Fischer was appointed interim director of athletics. Fischer, an alumnus of the Class of 1945, had joined the Department of Intercollegiate Athletics in 1964 and served as Morgan's top assistant for 15 years. In 1980, after a nationwide search, and with Morgan's recommendation, he was given the job permanently. He held the post for three years before retiring.

"I don't think there's a coach here J.D. didn't hire," Fischer told the *Los Angeles Times* shortly after his appointment in July 1980. "He assembled the team. I'm inheriting a department I feel certain is among the top five in the nation. My goal is to keep us up there."

During his stint as athletic director, UCLA won eight NCAA team championships, including two in women's outdoor track and field, and one each in softball, men's swimming and diving, and men's tennis. Men's volleyball won the other three.

The question on the minds of many was: "How can the intramural director be qualified to run UCLA Athletics?" But insiders knew that Dalis had long held Young's ear, as well as that of Vice Chancellor Elwin V. Svenson, whom Young had appointed to provide additional oversight of the department. Before becoming athletic director, Dalis had also managed all of UCLA's sports facilities, including the Sunset Canyon Recreation Center, and was the driving force behind the $10 million John Wooden Center from the planning stages in the mid-1970s to its opening in 1983. Earlier in his UCLA career, Dalis had directed women's athletics. It was Dalis who had recommended to Young that women's athletics become a separate entity and who had also participated in the selection of Holland.

During Dalis' first year on the job, a change in television contract revenue presented the department with a $900,000 budget deficit. Increased expenses related to the expansion of women's sports also contributed to the deficit, which grew to $3 million. A task force was convened to determine how to address the financial constraints while meeting Title IX obligations. In 1991, the group recommended cutting men's water polo and crew. A subsequent task force suggested in 1993 that men's swimming and gymnastics be eliminated.

"After a long, rancorous and laborious discussion, it was decided we were going to cut some sports, which we did, and no one was happy about that, but in our opinion, financially, it was inevitable," Dalis said. Many were outraged, particularly with regard to cutting the men's gymnastics program, members of which had propelled the United States to its first ever all-around team gold medal, in the 1984 Summer Olympics. Three of the six American gymnasts on the team—Peter Vidmar, Mitch Gaylord and Tim Daggett—were Bruins. An agreement was made that if the programs could become self-sustaining they would be spared. In the end, men's gymnastics and swimming were eliminated, while men's crew became a club sport. But after securing outside funding, men's water polo was able to continue as an intercollegiate sport. The team won five NCAA titles in the 15 years after it had been slated for possible elimination.

The task force also recommended cutting women's gymnastics in 1993, but that idea was immediately rescinded after vocal opposition. In fact, strong support fueled the addition of women's sports instead, in an effort to increase opportunities for women in accordance with Title IX. In fall 1993, women's soccer started play, and subsequently, in winter 1995, women's water polo began competition. Seven years later, in winter 2002, women's crew was also added as an intercollegiate sport, giving UCLA a total of 21 sports—11 women's teams and 10 men's teams. Women's crew joined the roster after the Department of Education Office of Civil Rights found that while the women's rate of participation had increased by nine percentage points over the previous three years, it still had concern that the ratio of

female participation rates at UCLA was not in proportion to the number of females enrolled in the university.

UCLA won more NCAA team championships during Dalis' tenure than that of any other university athletic director: 39 total, including 22 men's titles and 17 women's titles. Football, under Donahue, who coached the Bruins from 1976–95, experienced its longest bowl game winning streak: from 1983–94, the Bruins won eight consecutive bowl games. Additionally, from 1991 until Donahue's retirement, the Bruins beat crosstown rival USC every year. That five-game streak was continued for three more years by his successor, head football Coach Bob Toledo, until finally ending in 1999.

In 1995, UCLA won its first men's basketball championship in 20 years. The team was coached by Jim Harrick, who was fired a year later after the university found alleged financial improprieties. On March 19, 1995, during the second round of the NCAA tournament, senior point guard Tyus Edney made one of the most memorable shots in Bruin

Top: The Bruins play Michigan State after the dedication ceremony of the Nell and John Wooden Court in Pauley Pavilion, December 20, 2003.

Above left: Ben Howland, coaching the Bruins to their third consecutive NCAA Final Four appearance on April 5, 2008, in San Antonio, Texas.

Above: *Bruins*, February 2007 game program.

history. Down by one point with 4.8 seconds left in the game, Edney dribbled 85 feet and made a running bank shot as time expired to beat the University of Missouri, 75–74. After the game, sophomore guard Cameron Dollar told the *Los Angeles Times*: "I gave him the ball and it was like, 'Go, Tyus, go.'" The buzzer-beating win propelled UCLA all the way to the championship game against the University of Arkansas, where the Bruins, led by team captain Ed O'Bannon, earned an 11th NCAA title with an 89–78 victory. Assistant Coach Steve Lavin, who would succeed Harrick, called it a "storybook finish," and reportedly promised to name his future son after Tyus.

When Dalis became athletic director in 1983, there were no endowed athletic scholarships. By 2002, there were 174, totaling $24 million. He also oversaw a $13 million remodeling of the Morgan Center completed in 2000, the expansion of the UCLA Athletics Hall of Fame in 2001, and the beginning of the Acosta Center, which houses weight rooms, locker rooms and a training facility.

Dalis retired in 2002, and was succeeded by alumnus Dan Guerrero in July of that year. Guerrero, who had played second base on the Bruin baseball team in the 1970s, spent the previous decade as athletic director at the University of California, Irvine. In his first year at UCLA, he fired football Coach Bob Toledo and hired alumnus Karl Dorrell, who played wide receiver at UCLA from 1982–86.

On December 2, 2006, Dorrell led the Bruins to a stunning upset over USC, ruining the Trojans' bid for a berth in the national title game. After taking a 7–0 lead in the first quarter, UCLA trailed at halftime by two points, 9–7. Place kicker Justin Medlock gave the team a 13–9 lead midway through the fourth quarter, and the Bruins' defense held the Trojans scoreless in the second half. The victory, the first over USC since 1998, kept the Bruins' record of eight consecutive wins in the rivalry intact.

Following the 2007 season, Guerrero fired Dorrell and brought back alumnus Rick Neuheisel as head football coach. Neuheisel had played with Dorrell in the 1984 Rose Bowl game, where they combined for two touchdowns to help the Bruins pummel the Fighting Illini, 45–9. Guerrero had also fired basketball Coach Lavin in 2003, whom he replaced with Ben Howland. Under Howland, the Bruins made three consecutive NCAA Final Four appearances from 2006–08—the longest such streak since the Wooden era.

During Guerrero's tenure the athletics budget increased from $42 million to $64 million in 2010–11, helping to support approximately 650 athletes in 24 men's and women's sports. Because of increases in tuition and the cost of room and board, the scholarship budget alone rose from $5.2 million to more than $11 million in 2011 for the same number of student athletes. Guerrero made it a top priority to ensure that the department remained on solid financial ground. Under his leadership, the department increased revenues through private fundraising, corporate sponsorship programs, improved television and media deals, as well as shoe and apparel contracts. "I've practiced the wisdom of Coach Wooden who said, 'Build a shelter for a rainy day,' and that's exactly what we did," Guerrero said. "We've been able to build a reserve that is allowing us to get through the tough times, and we anticipate a new Pac-12 television contract to go into effect in 2012–2013, which allows us some breathing room as we move forward in the future."

Far right: The Bruins and the Trojans at the line of scrimmage on December 2, 2006, when UCLA upset USC's chance to play for a national championship by beating them 13–9.

Below: Cobi Jones, who started his career at UCLA in 1988 as a walk-on, is one of the university's all-time greats, finishing his collegiate career with 23 goals and 37 assists. In 1990, he was a catalyst for UCLA's NCAA championship run, where the Bruins beat Rutgers University 4–0 in penalty kicks to earn the national title.

Right: As a player, assistant coach and coach of men's and women's water polo, Adam Krikorian has won 14 national championships.

Far left: The women's golf team on the Intramural Field, 1932.

Left: The 2011 NCAA women's golf champions after earning UCLA's 107th NCAA team title.

"To be the first school to win 100 NCAA team championships is a great tribute to all of the outstanding student-athletes, coaches and support staff who call UCLA home," Guerrero said at the time of the victory. "UCLA has a rich athletic history and it is important to remember and celebrate those who built the foundation and earned the early championships, as well as those who have contributed to the recent successes."

The "First to 100" slogan became emblematic of UCLA's athletic prowess. However, Guerrero said that far above winning, integrity always will remain first and foremost the hallmark of UCLA's program.

"We are tremendously proud of the success that we've been able to achieve and even more proud to have done it with integrity and ethics—great sportsmanship and 'doing it right' are at the core of everything we do," Guerrero said. "We don't win at all costs. We strive to create a balance in our program for our coaches and our student athletes that reflects the philosophy that athletic success goes hand in hand with academic achievement."

During the first nine years of his tenure, UCLA won 21 national championships in 11 different sports. Three of those championships—2003, 2004 and 2010—were won by the women's gymnastics team, coached by Valorie Kondos Field. Since taking the head coaching job in 1995, Kondos Field has led the Bruins to six NCAA titles.

In 2007, the women's water polo team, coached by alumnus Adam Krikorian, captured UCLA's 100th NCAA national title by defeating Stanford, 5–4. It was the third consecutive championship for the team. "It's pretty special and it's great to be No. 100," said Courtney Matthewson, who scored three goals, to the *Los Angeles Times*. "But there's going to be 100 more." In 2008 and 2009, the women earned their fourth and fifth consecutive titles. Krikorian, who had been recruited to UCLA by his predecessor Guy Baker, captained the men's water polo team in 1995 to its first NCAA title since 1972. In 1996, Krikorian became an assistant coach, and in 1999, co-head coach. He was appointed head coach in 2001, when Baker joined USA Water Polo. In 2009, Krikorian once again succeeded Baker, this time as the USA women's coach. Between Baker and Krikorian, the pair have helped bring home 12 national titles in UCLA men's and women's water polo. Seven of those titles were earned by the women's team.

In fact, during the first decade of the 21st century, the number of women's championships won by Bruins exceeded the men's for the first time, 18–7.

"UCLA was at the forefront of creating excellence in its women's program," Guerrero said. "Women's water polo, winning the 100th, was a win for everyone in this program. One might say it was appropriate that it was a women's program that won it because they had carried the flag for so many years."

The milestone was celebrated with a yearlong series of events, including bringing back members of championship teams during halftime at football and basketball games. A gold "C," the Roman numeral for 100, was added to athletic uniforms for the duration of the year.

Left: Coached by Valorie Kondos Field (left), six women's gymnastics teams have won NCAA championships between 1994–2010, including the 2004 squad.

Below: In 2007, women's water polo brought home UCLA's 100th NCAA team championship.

UCLA's First 100 NCAA Team Championships

#	Sport	Coach	Date	#	Sport	Coach	Date
1.	M. Tennis	Bill Ackerman	6/23/1950	51.	Softball	Sharron Backus	5/29/1984
2.	M. Tennis	J.D. Morgan	6/28/1952	52.	W. Volleyball	Andy Banachowski	12/16/1984
3.	M. Tennis	J.D. Morgan	6/26/1953	53.	Softball	Sharron Backus	5/26/1985
4.	M. Tennis	J.D. Morgan	6/27/1954	54.	M. Soccer	Sigi Schmid	12/14/1985
5.	M. Track/Field	Elvin Drake	6/23/1956	55.	M. Gymnastics	Art Shurlock	4/25/1987
6.	M. Tennis	J.D. Morgan	6/30/1956	56.	M. Volleyball	Al Scates	5/2/1987
7.	M. Tennis	J.D. Morgan	6/25/1960	57.	M. Track/Field	Bob Larsen	6/6/1987
8.	M. Tennis	J.D. Morgan	6/25/1961	58.	M. Golf	Eddie Merrins	5/24/1988
9.	M. Basketball	John Wooden	3/21/1964	59.	Softball	Sharron Backus	5/29/1988
10.	M. Basketball	John Wooden	3/20/1965	60.	M. Track/Field	Bob Larsen	6/9/1988
11.	M. Tennis	J.D. Morgan	6/19/1965	61.	M. Volleyball	Al Scates	5/6/1989
12.	M. Track/Field	Jim Bush	5/22/1966	62.	Softball	Sharron Backus, Sue Enquist	5/28/1989
13.	M. Basketball	John Wooden	3/25/1967	63.	Softball	Sharron Backus, Sue Enquist	5/28/1990
14.	M. Basketball	John Wooden	3/23/1968	64.	M. Soccer	Sigi Schmid	12/2/1990
15.	M. Basketball	John Wooden	3/21/1969	65.	W. Volleyball	Andy Banachowski	12/15/1990
16.	M. Water Polo	Bob Horn	11/29/1969	66.	W. Golf	Jackie Tobian-Steinmann	5/26/1991
17.	M. Basketball	John Wooden	3/21/1970	67.	W. Volleyball	Andy Banachowski	12/21/1991
18.	M. Volleyball	Al Scates	4/25/1970	68.	Softball	Sharron Backus, Sue Enquist	5/25/1992
19.	M. Tennis	Glenn Bassett	6/20/1970	69.	M. Volleyball	Al Scates	5/8/1993
20.	M. Basketball	John Wooden	3/27/1971	70.	M. Basketball	Jim Harrick	4/3/1995
21.	M. Volleyball	Al Scates	4/24/1971	71.	M. Volleyball	Al Scates	5/6/1995
22.	M. Tennis	Glenn Bassett	6/19/1971	72.	M. Water Polo	Guy Baker	12/3/1995
23.	M. Track/Field	Jim Bush	6/19/1971	73.	M. Volleyball	Al Scates	5/4/1996
24.	M. Water Polo	Bob Horn	11/27/1971	74.	M. Water Polo	Guy Baker	12/8/1996
25.	M. Basketball	John Wooden	3/25/1972	75.	W. Gymnastics	Valorie Kondos	4/18/1997
26.	M. Volleyball	Al Scates	4/29/1972	76.	M. Soccer	Sigi Schmid	12/14/1997
27.	M. Track/Field	Jim Bush	6/3/1972	77.	M. Volleyball	Al Scates	5/2/1998
28.	M. Water Polo	Bob Horn	12/2/1972	78.	Softball	Sue Enquist	5/31/1999
29.	M. Basketball	John Wooden	3/26/1973	79.	M. Water Polo	Guy Baker, Adam Krikorian	12/5/1999
30.	M. Track/Field	Jim Bush	6/9/1973	80.	W. Track/Field (Indoor)	Jeanette Bolden	3/11/2000
31.	M. Volleyball	Al Scates	5/11/1974	81.	W. Gymnastics	Valorie Kondos	4/14/2000
32.	M. Basketball	John Wooden	3/31/1975	82.	M. Volleyball	Al Scates	5/6/2000
33.	M. Volleyball	Al Scates	5/10/1975	83.	M. Water Polo	Guy Baker, Adam Krikorian	12/3/2000
34.	M. Tennis	Glenn Bassett	6/21/1975	84.	W. Track/Field (Indoor)	Jeanette Bolden	3/10/2001
35.	M. Volleyball	Al Scates	5/1/1976	85.	W. Gymnastics	Valorie Kondos Field	4/20/2001
36.	M. Tennis	Glenn Bassett	6/7/1976	86.	W. Water Polo	Adam Krikorian	5/13/2001
37.	M. Track/Field	Jim Bush	6/3/1978	87.	M. Soccer	Tom Fitzgerald	12/15/2002
38.	M. Volleyball	Al Scates	5/5/1979	88.	W. Gymnastics	Valorie Kondos Field	4/25/2003
39.	M. Tennis	Glenn Bassett	5/29/1979	89.	W. Water Polo	Adam Krikorian	5/12/2003
40.	M. Volleyball	Al Scates	5/9/1981	90.	Softball	Sue Enquist	5/26/2003
41.	M. Swim/Dive	Ron Ballatore	3/27/1982	91.	W. Gymnastics	Valorie Kondos Field	4/16/2004
42.	M. Volleyball	Al Scates	5/8/1982	92.	W. Golf	Carrie Leary	5/21/2004
43.	M. Tennis	Glenn Bassett	5/23/1982	93.	Softball	Sue Enquist	5/31/2004
44.	Softball	Sharron Backus	5/31/1982	94.	W. Track/Field (Outdoor)	Jeanette Bolden	6/12/2004
45.	W. Track/Field (Outdoor)	Scott Chisam	6/4/1982	95.	M. Water Polo	Adam Krikorian	12/5/2004
46.	M. Volleyball	Al Scates	5/7/1983	96.	W. Water Polo	Adam Krikorian	5/15/2005
47.	W. Track/Field (Outdoor)	Scott Chisam	6/5/1983	97.	M. Tennis	Billy Martin	5/24/2005
48.	M. Gymnastics	Art Shurlock	4/14/1984	98.	M. Volleyball	Al Scates	5/6/2006
49.	M. Volleyball	Al Scates	5/5/1984	99.	W. Water Polo	Adam Krikorian	5/14/2006
50.	M. Tennis	Glenn Bassett	5/20/1984	100.	W. Water Polo	Adam Krikorian	5/13/2007

CHAPTER 15

Bruin Rites of Passage

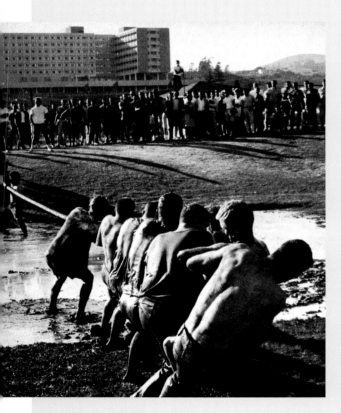

Above: The 1962 tug of war, a highlight of the Frosh-Soph Brawl, a decades-long tradition that began when UCLA was a two-year college.

Opposite: Song girl Elaine Nakagiri, c.1965.

*F*rom the moment that UCLA was founded as the Southern Branch of the University of California, students took up the mantle of self-government and began fostering tradition with a determined energy.

On September 15, 1919, the students who flooded the halls of the Vermont Avenue campus knew it had been a years-long battle to create a public university in the Southland. These pioneers welcomed their shared responsibility to promote the university's growth and develop a new identity, not only for themselves but for future generations.

"The Regents of the University of California predict a brilliant future for the new intellectual Mecca of Los Angeles," wrote the Cub Californian in its debut edition on September 29, 1919. "We shall have difficulty in persuading folks to quit talking about the normal school and to speak instead of the Southern Branch of the University of California, but everyone who wants his words to be the correct names of the things he is talking about will do that."

One issue facing the students in creating organized student life: the lack of a senior class. As junior college students, they were expected to transfer to Berkeley or elsewhere for their third and fourth years of instruction, so there were no upperclassmen. This would form the foundation of a robust, albeit friendly, division of rank between the freshmen and sophomores that lasted decades and included the annual Frosh-Soph Brawl with its trademark muddy tug of war.

No student government officers retained their posts from the Los Angeles State Normal School, which was enthusiastically declared "dead" by the student newspaper. Few clubs, groups or societies survived the transition from the Normal School, as they were deemed "unsuited to larger university needs and problems."

Ernest Carroll Moore, UCLA's founding chief executive, formed a committee of 12 students "to inaugurate a new system of student self-government for a totally new institution." The committee would oversee all student activities until an executive council was elected. They proceeded with great resolve.

"Now what is needed more than anything else is that rather overworked term college 'spirit,'" proclaimed the *Cub Californian* in Vol. 1, No. 1. "Usually a fine school spirit is the result of years of cooperation and mutual interest. But we are not going to wait for our college 'spirit' to develop with the years. We are going to create it now!"

Within two weeks, students organized the weekly newspaper, put together a football team, selected yell leaders, and planned several dances and socials. A month after classes began, they had already held general assemblies and large-scale pep rallies to cheer on the team.

Initially, UCLA students felt a need to prove their loyalty to Berkeley and demonstrate that they measured up to the northern school's standards. They adopted the University of California's colors and its alma mater, "All Hail Blue and Gold." They chose Cubs as their moniker, in acknowledgment of their university's emerging status, while providing a link to Berkeley's Golden Bears. (Students noticed a month later that Cubs was also S.B.U.C.—the common abbreviation for the Southern Branch of the University of California—spelled backward.) One of the earliest rally yells, introduced in October 1919, cried:

Cubs we are,
Bears we'll be,
Californians all,
Branch U.C.!

"Our friends in Berkeley need not hesitate to admit that we are connected with them when we can show them a record like that," the *Cub Californian* wrote in October 1919. "And we ourselves need not attempt to make excuses because we are members of 'the old Normal School,' as some call it, but rather announce boldly and proudly that we are active members of the University of California Southern Branch."

The Committee of Twelve drafted a student government constitution based on Berkeley's. It was ratified, article by article, in a student assembly on November 17.

The constitution would be amended multiple times over the years with regard to limiting or expanding scope of authority, modifying election procedures, and reorganizing financial control, among other changes. "One of the favorite sports of any newly elected council has been that of trying to rewrite the ASUCLA constitution," said alumnus William C. Ackerman, who began working for the Associated Students

Top left: Dean of Men Earl J. Miller (third from right) and Graduate Manager Stephen Cunningham (second from right) with members of the Associated Students executive council, c.1930.

Above: Fraternity Sigma Pi, organized at UCLA in 1923, Vermont Avenue campus.

Below: William C. Ackerman headed the Associated Students from 1933–1967.

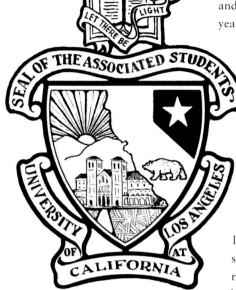

in 1932 as an assistant to the general manager and would later head the organization for 34 years, until retiring in 1967. "The first thing that council members do is to arrange a parking space for themselves, second is to find some furniture for their offices, and third to tear the constitution apart. The pattern varies little from year to year."

In late November 1919, elections were inaugurated as stipulated in the constitution. John McManus was chosen as the first student body president, and Helen Easton as vice president. With their installation on December 5, 1919, "the life of the Associated Students began." The student council implemented an honor code requiring each individual to be responsible for their personal conduct in the library, on campus, in examinations and at social gatherings, and also asked them to report any issues that demanded attention. Students affirmed: "I pledge myself to self-government and will do everything in my power to make it succeed in our school."

Financing was another obstacle. "Every student in school" was expected to pay a 50-cent fee during the first session, which by January 1920 had been raised to a $5 annual

fee "after considerable discussion and mature deliberation." Under the "California" plan, modeled after Berkeley, students needed to buy "student body cards"—or membership—to the Associated Students to be eligible to participate in general activities, such as voting in class elections or attending social functions and sporting events. "You, as students of the Branch University, have been called on during the past few months for both material and moral support for numerous activities," the *Cub Californian* said of the fee announcement. "But this occasion may well be considered as the first real test of your spirit and loyalty."

Under University of California policy, the student body was responsible for finding the resources needed to support athletics, as well as securing the use of non-academic facilities in which students were to work. Without a student union, Moore allocated space in Millspaugh Hall, the Vermont Avenue campus's administration building. As was the case at Berkeley, the Associated Students were responsible for running the athletics department (which would be removed from Associated Students control on July 1, 1960) and commercial

Above: The seal of the Associated Students, designed by student body President William B. Keene in 1948.

Below: Associated Students membership cards, 1935–1937.

Far right: Millspaugh Hall, both the administration building and the hub for student organizations, Vermont Avenue campus, 1919.

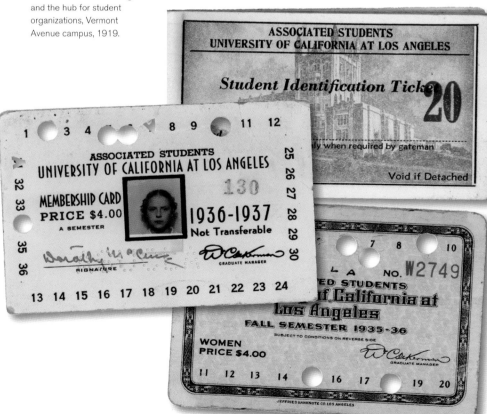

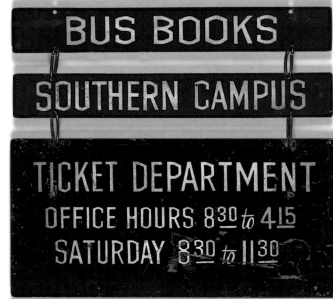

WE PAY CASH FOR YOUR CURRENT USED TEXTS

BUS BOOKS
SOUTHERN CAMPUS

TICKET DEPARTMENT
OFFICE HOURS 8:30 to 4:15
SATURDAY 8:30 to 11:30

THE CO-OP.
FOR STUDENTS' SUPPLIES

OUR BUSINESS

TEXT BOOKS
STATIONERY
FOUNTAIN PENS
LEATHER NOTE BOOKS
CHEMISTRY APRONS
DISSECTING INSTRUMENTS
DRAWING INSTRUMENTS
PAINTS, INKS
SMALL JOB PRINTING

OUR SPECIALTIES

UNIVERSITY JEWELRY
PENNANTS, PILLOWS
BANNERS
PHOTOGRAPHS
POSTALS
GYM SUITS
TENNIS SUPPLIES
ATHLETIC GOODS

Students' Co-Operative Store

A. W. KNOX, Jr., *Manager*

184

enterprises on campus, such as food services and book sales. The Students' Co-Operative Store opened for business on September 18, three days after classes started. One benefit of bearing this financial responsibility was that student publications and other enterprises were given a great degree of independence from the administration.

"Organization" was the watchword among students during UCLA's inaugural year. The old traditions of the Normal School were soon forgotten and myriad departmental, social, business, fraternal and honor groups were formed. There were successes and failures, all part of a normal evolution. (By the 2010s, the number of student organizations would number almost 900.) "There is still much to be desired—still precedents to be set, details to be looked after," McManus noted at year's end. "The activities of the Associated

Above: Original sign for the Students' Co-Operative Store, on the Vermont Avenue campus, which sold all the school supplies a student could need (far left).

Above left: Alumni Ralph Stilwell and Mary Boynton staff Alumni Membership Headquarters in Kerckhoff Hall, 1939.

Below left: Stocking up on pencils at the Associated Students store, with the Bruin Pipe Shop in the far back, Kerckhoff Hall, 1946.

Below center: Vending machines on the second floor of Kerckhoff Hall sell everything from milk to Eskimo Pies, 1950s.

Below: The Treehouse, Ackerman Student Union, 1970s.

Students, the drafting of the Constitution, the building of traditions—in a word, the operation of a co-ordinated student government has become a reality that promises much for the new Southland University."

VERMONT AVENUE RITUALS

With the introduction of a senior year of curriculum, student leaders announced on March 21, 1924, that the Associated Students had been Cubs long enough and that they had decided to drop the dependent nomenclature, adopting the fiercer Grizzlies. The newspaper changed its name to the *California Grizzly* (becoming the *Daily Grizzly* on September 13, 1925, when it began publishing five days a week). "The bears grew up and became Grizzlies," commemorated the student handbook. To celebrate the occasion, students called their University of California Charter Day celebration Grizzly Day instead, "and established it as a tradition peculiarly our own," featuring a barbecue, daytime and evening rallies, and a "monster bonfire."

However, as the Southern Branch sought membership in the Pacific Coast Conference in 1926, the University of Montana, whose teams were already known as the Grizzlies, forced

students to come up with yet another name. UCLA student leaders received a show of support from their Berkeley brethren, who decided to relinquish Bruins—which they had been using in addition to Golden Bears—and offered the name to UCLA.

"Bruins, not Grizzlies, will swing into action against the Pomona Sagehens in the Coliseum tomorrow afternoon," announced the newly named *Daily Bruin* in October 1926. "Bringing to a close the three-weeks investigation concerning a totem to replace Grizzly, the Associated Students Council Wednesday night unanimously passed the recommendation of the committee in charge and consequently Grizzly is replaced by Bruin as the official totem of the University. The change is officially made with the publication of today's paper." Four months later, on February 1, 1927, having taken into account growing resentment toward the name Southern Branch, the Board of Regents officially renamed the campus the University of California at Los Angeles, a name that UCLA students, and some professors and administrators, already had been using unofficially.

By this time, UCLA students had developed several cherished traditions. The Rally Committee, formally organized

Right: The *Daily Bruin* staff, c.1950s.

Below: Greek drama, Vermont Avenue campus, 1920s.

Far right: Pajamarino serpentine on Moore Field, Vermont Avenue campus, 1923.

Below right: Constructing the bonfire pile for the pajamarino rally, the foremost event of the football season, the night before the big game against Occidental College, 1925.

A Mascot for the Ages

"The S.B.U.C. is a fine place," wrote the *Cub Californian* in October 1919. "We have a winning grid team, a real honest-to-goodness constitution and everything. But there's something lacking. You've guessed it—a mascot."

Students at the month-old Southern Branch of the University of California inherited an unofficial mascot named Rags—a lovable stray mutt found by the gardener that the Los Angeles State Normal School students had adopted. Rags wandered freely about the Vermont Avenue campus, occasionally attending chemistry and other classes, and was well-cared for by the students and faculty. Still, students wanted a symbol reflective of their newly coined "Cubs" moniker, chosen by the student body as "truly representative" of the fledgling school's association with the older Berkeley campus and its "Golden Bear" totem.

"Since we are the offspring of the 'Bears,' it follows naturally and is wholly in accordance with the laws of nature, that we must be the 'Cubs,' stated an editorial in the first issue of the *Cub Californian*. "Every bear cub is endowed with all the natural ability and power of its parent." The name was intended to be temporary, however, until the campus grew "broader and greater" and "capable of standing on its own two feet" while developing its own individuality and traditions.

Amid pleas for an official mascot, students brought a teddy bear with a big blue-and-gold bow "for a luck charm" to

games, rallies and dances. In 1922, after the Cubs won their second straight Southern California basketball championship, the celebration included the introduction of Prunes, the first live bear cub to set foot on the campus. Unfortunately, the bear—brought just for the day—bit one of the basketball players during the festivities.

By 1924, when the regents authorized UCLA to provide a fourth year of instruction and the campus became a baccalaureate-granting institution, students had grown tired of being Cubs and shed the diminutive bear cognomen, embracing the more mature "Grizzly" instead. "From this time forward for evermore we denounce the adolescent short-comings of the 'Cub' as a totem, and as an expression of our status in university life," the newly named *California Grizzly* declared in March 1924.

In 1926, however, as UCLA sought to enter the Pacific Coast Conference, the University of Montana—already a member—pressed its case for sole Grizzly ownership. Once again, students were in search of a moniker. After considering everything from Buccaneers to Gorillas, they remained in a quandary. At the time, Berkeley was using both Bears and Bruins. Berkeley's student leaders voted to give up the Bruin name and finally, in October 1926, UCLA had its permanent totem.

During the 1930s, spirited student demand for a mascot prompted the Associated Students to rent live bears and their trainers from Hollywood studios for appearances at home football games. While the bears greatly entertained the crowds at the Los Angeles Memorial Coliseum, the wild animals proved difficult to handle, and the Coliseum banned their appearance in the early 1940s.

UCLA was without a mascot again until 1950, when students and alumni united to bring Little Joe Bruin, a female black Himalayan bear cub, to games. The Student Executive Council voted to make Little Joe the official mascot for the 1950 football season. The bear, which was kept in a secret location known only

Above left: Rags, UCLA's unofficial mascot, *c.*1919.

Above: The live bears, which would run out onto the field and entertain the Coliseum crowd, were much beloved, but difficult to keep.

Left: In 1950, UCLA's mascot was a live bear known as Little Joe Bruin.

Depictions of Joe Bruin have evolved over the years. **Top row:** 1919, the Southern Branch's cub; 1920s, a more mature grizzly; 1930s, a mousy bear. **Second row:** 1940s, Joe goes off to war; 1950s, "Grrrrrrl" says the national champ; 1960s, "He shoots, he scores!"; **Third row:** 1970s Smiley Joe; 1980s, introducing *The Bruin*; 1996, a reinvented Joe.

to her keeper and the head yell leader, would race out in front of the rooting section during games sporting a yellow sweater with a large "Bruins" spelled out in blue on the front. Expectations were that Little Joe would remain a mascot for three years, until she grew too large to handle. However, in a year, the furry one-time runt reached 200 pounds and could stand eye-to-eye with a six-foot-tall man. After Little Joe escaped her pen once, her keeper sold her to the circus in early 1951. The following year, the Associated Students bought a new bear from the Griffith Park Zoo.

For the 1961 season, alumni boosters presented the campus with the first Josephine Bruin, a four-month-old, 18-pound Malayan sun bear from India. Josephine, also known as Jo, lived in Rally Committee Chairman Russ Serber's backyard, but she grew very quickly, and was given to the San Diego Zoo in January 1962. "I began by handling the bear, but now it handles me," Serber said.

Although much beloved, the live bears proved difficult, and were not always available. The difficulty in obtaining and

caring for live bears eventually led to the appearance in the mid-1950s of costumed student mascots, and by the mid-1960s, they took over the sole role as official mascot. Several students were chosen to take turns playing Joe, who was joined in 1967 by a costumed Josephine—or Josie, as she became known in later years. UCLA was one of a select few universities that had both male and female mascots.

Depictions of Joe Bruin have evolved over time, from a Mickey Mouse-like image in the 1930s to a tougher, snarling Joe in a leather-flap football helmet during the 1950s (including the 1954 championship season) to a pleasant, smiling Joe (later called Retro Joe) in the 1970s and '80s, and a more buff Joe in later years. The mascot costumes also varied, not always matching the illustrations. One unusual costume made its debut in 1979. UCLA band director F. Kelly James wanted a mascot that would work closely with the band and stand out in a crowd. Walt E. Disney Productions designed and donated a $7,000 costume

meeting his specifications. The new mascot costume stood seven feet tall with features reminiscent of the animals in Disneyland's Country Bear Jamboree attraction. The ungainly bear outfit was difficult for students to wear and perform in, however, and was short-lived. By the summer of 1980, smiling Joe and Josephine were front and center again, although Big Bruin Bear remained in the mix for a few more years.

In 1984, the UCLA Alumni Association donated *The Bruin* statue to campus, showcasing a massive and powerful bear, with a forward moving motion. Then, in the 1990s, alumni and athletics boosters increasingly wanted a more self-assured mascot to match. To some, Smiling Joe looked like a teddy bear. In other words, he was a wimp compared to other university's mascots. Bearwear sales and license agreements with companies for UCLA merchandise were suffering, and the athletics department had stopped using the mascot altogether.

"The cuddly, totally mellow, have-a-nice-day ursine character was beginning to look as dated as lava lamps and bell-bottoms … much better suited to a disco floor than the playing fields of the leaner, meaner '90s," wrote *UCLA Magazine* in winter 1996, after Joe Bruin underwent a 13-month makeover.

The updated version of Joe Bruin was not a hit with all fans. His costumed body included bulging muscles and his face seemed in a perpetual freeze-frame with a smile and simultaneously raised eyebrows, earning him the nicknames "Steroid Joe" or "Psycho Joe." Alumni and fans wrote numerous letters of complaint. More troubling, the students could not maneuver in the costumes. The musculature and foot design did not allow for running or for raising one's hands over the head—making it impossible to do an Eight-clap, UCLA's signature yell. Joe underwent a few additional modifications and emerged with a

toned-down look—still powerful, but retaining his good nature. Josephine subsequently underwent a similar transformation.

Jennifer Pickett, who was Josie from 1996–98, said she enjoyed entertaining once and future Bruins. "One of the great things I loved about it was having these little kids run up to you in their dresses and their blue and gold and their faces painted and sit there on your lap and stroke your big nose and say 'Oh, I love you Josie,' " Pickett said. "It was really sweet, and I remember doing that when I was a little kid."

While the latest design has become familiar to generations of Bruins, others remain fond of Retro Joe, who in the 2000s made a strong comeback gracing Bearwear in the UCLA Store. Each mascot incarnation has had its loyal followers, but there's no doubt Joe and Josie will continue to delight fans of all ages as the universal figures representing UCLA.

the frosh bible

Welcome to UCLA!

FROSH + FEET = SHOE RUSH

YE LOWLY FROSH—HOW MEEK

BARBER SHOP "A la SOPH"

Thirty-five

Freshmen: "You are a university student now."

Above: Two illustrations from the student handbook, 1947–1948.

Above right: The Frosh Bible, 1952.

Far right: Freshman initiation rituals, 1923.

Below: First-year women were required to wear a green "Freshie" button on their left shoulder, or else, 1922. The Vigilante Committee's warning posted to frosh men, fall 1925.

in 1922, was responsible for the high-spirited annual pajamarino and bonfire football rally. "A thousand men in weird styles of night clothes strung a serpentine around a blazing bonfire that could be seen miles away," chronicled the 1924 *Southern Campus*. "The field was crowded outside of the range of the scorching heat by the rest of the students and those interested in college activities."

The labor of building bonfires—and finding the necessary wood—was often reserved for freshmen. It was just one of a series of class traditions that had emerged, and was monitored by "vigilantes" known to dunk freshmen, or "peagreeners," into the fish pond in front of Millspaugh Hall, or perform other hazing rituals, to enforce the rules.

Student handbooks, or "frosh bibles," clearly spelled out the rules for all incoming students. "The Scribes, whom you shall know as your upperclassmen, through their benevolence and kindliness, pass this following

knowledge to the in-coming freshmen," outlined the first such handbook, published in September 1920. "Never shall a freshman forget that at all times he is subject to extreme punishment if he violates these sacred words of advice."

Freshmen were not to wear high school jewelry or other insignia—"you are a university student now." Smoking on campus was a privilege for upper-classmen only, "unless you have lost your desire to live." Among other rules, freshmen were admonished not to cheat, procrastinate or skip class. "Don't knock the university," it stated. "If you don't like it get out." And perhaps the best advice, "Don't tell anyone you are a Freshman unless asked."

In subsequent years, however, certain fashion rules were implemented and the classes wore distinguishing paraphernalia. Male freshmen were required to don blue and gold "dinks," or beanies, while females had to wear a green "Freshie" button. The smoking rule was changed so that freshmen could smoke—but only a corncob pipe. And in respect of tradition, smoking was not allowed by anyone on the main quad. Sophomores were accorded the right to wear blue jeans, while juniors and seniors wore corduroys. Only seniors "had the sole right to wear the sombrero"—ranger-like hats.

Once a year, freshmen were liberated from their obligations in a celebration called Green Day. Still, not all

Freshie Button

QUARANTINE
WARNING
CAMPUS INFECTED WITH INCIPIENT DISEASE
FRESHMANITIS
ISOLATION NECESSARY FOR GANG-GREENS

ENTIRE SITUATION TO BE HANDLED BY THE EFFICIENT AND CAPABLE
DR. '26
Drastic Measures Will Be Taken if Conditions Become Acute–High School Stars Will be Smeared Into Complete Oblivion with Gobs of Red

Germs Surviving will take the Following Antiseptic Measures:
1. Frosh Hat Poultice Applied to Pimple on Shoulders in Hope of Bringing it to a Head.
2. Tobacco Smoke Strained Thru Antiseptic Corncobs Permitted to Puny Physiques, Pipes and Pills are for Men.
3. Get Vaccinated with the Serum of Campus Knowledge.

A FEW REMEDIES PRESCRIBED BY DOCTOR '26

1. Wear Your Frosh Hat Always
2. No Queening!
3. Smoke only Corncobs–Don't Smoke on the Front Quad
4. Forget Your Prep School and Your Prep Record
5. Get the "Cal" Spirit–do Something for Your University

Bruinisms

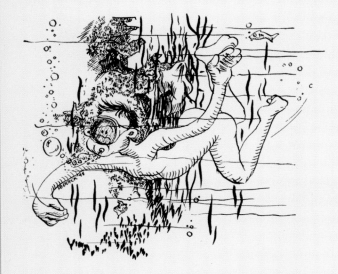

Goofs: Reserve football squad in the 1920s.

Smokers: Boxing matches in the 1920s.
"Local Greeks assembled at the Men's Gym ... to watch their representatives maul and tug at one another in the annual Interfraternity Smoker. ... In the fast-gathering nicotine fog, the thinly clads stepped into the arena and inaugurated the slaughter." —1924

Uclans: Term for Bruins in use from the 1930s through the mid-1960s.

Berkeleyites: Term for Berkeley athletes in the 1930s through 1950s.

Hersheyites: Hershey Hall residents in the 1930s through 1950s.
"It is rumored by houseboys in Hershey Hall kitchens that Hersheyites eat well. However, campus males are more interested in halls where the girls do their own cooking." —1938

Yell kings: Yell leaders during the 1930s through the 1950s.

Song leaders: Cheerleaders during the 1930s through the 1950s.

Mermen: Men's swimming and water polo players from the 1930s through the 1950s.

Brubabes: Freshman athletes from the late 1930s through the early 1970s.

The Libe: The library from the 1920s through the 1940s.
"The library is a place where books are kept, or so they say. It's also a good place in which to get cool on hot days, or to sit when the Co-op is full and you have an hour before your next class. But most of all the library is a good place to get a date for next Saturday night, or to see the cute Navy man in your Econ class. They have some good magazines in the library, and the ceiling is very pretty, so are the pictures on the wall. Some people go to the libe to study ... they are eager." —1945

Racketeers: Tennis players in the 1920s through the 1950s.
"Bill Ackerman's Grizzly racketeers last season captured the Southern Conference championship for the fifth consecutive time, disproving the predictions of the dopesters that the Grizzly tennis reign was about to be ended." —1926

Uni-Prep: Orientation in the 1960s through 1970.
"The UCLA con artists were out in full force at Uni-Prep. They were selling new activities to the new students. If only they knew!" —1965

Spikers: Track athletes in the 1950s and 1960s; volleyballers from the 1970s through the early 1990s.

Dormie: Resident of the campus dormitories from the 1960s through the early 1980s.
"If not always a positive force, the 'dormie' at least does not feed off and parasitically drain university vitality." —1963

Mick: An easy class in the 1970s and 1980s.
"What our parents termed 'Mickey Mouse' classes, students of the eighties have shortened to the present slang: a 'Mick.' It translates to a class in which it is possible to attain the highest grade with the least amount of effort." —1986

North vs. South: Stereotypical distinction for liberal arts and humanities students who are said to hail from North Campus, and those from the science-dominated South Campus, from the 1980s to present.
"The battle rages on: North Campus majors are airheads, South Campus majors are pinheads. Bagels cost less on South Campus but then again North Campus has the cookies." —1986

Above left: Mermen, 1947.

Below: A street in Burbank, California, hails the Uclan.

Bottom: Smokes and uppercuts, 1921.

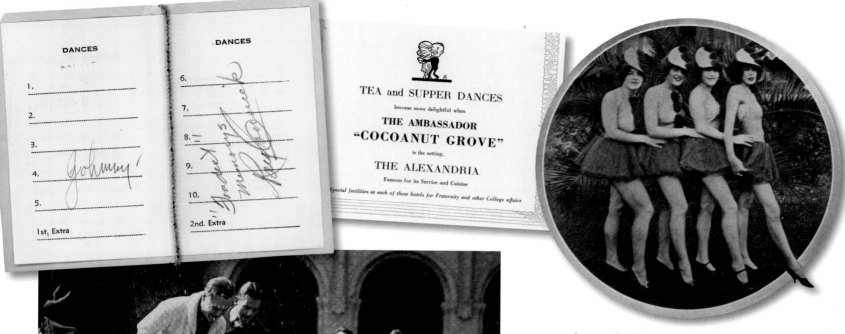

DANCES

1. _____
2. _____
3. _____
4. _Johnny!_
5. _____

1st. Extra

DANCES

6. _____
7. _____
8. _____
9. _____
10. _____

2nd. Extra

TEA and SUPPER DANCES

become more delightful when

THE AMBASSADOR
"COCOANUT GROVE"

is the setting.

THE ALEXANDRIA

Famous for its Service and Cuisine

Special facilities at each of these hotels for Fraternity and other College affairs

Top: A dance card from the Roaring '20s, where students danced the night away at the Cocoanut Grove (center).

Top right: A dance routine from the Press Club Vode, c.1926.

Above: Sophomores dunk a rule-breaking "peagreener" into the fish pond, a common hazing practice, 1922.

freshmen followed the rules. Harry Zide, who took pre-med classes at UCLA from 1926–29, defiantly refused to buy the required beanie to avoid being hazed. Zide said he wore his ROTC uniform to campus instead. "That was the only smart thing I did," he quipped.

At times, when the Vigilante Committee decided to act, some felt most for the fish. "The innocent pastimes which the sophomores provided for the freshmen are to be commended in that they were highly amusing for all concerned, but the dilapidated condition in which the pond was left is one of serious concern," the *Daily Grizzly* reported in September 1926. "Keeping the marine vegetation alive in the pond has been a great problem for the University gardener. As soon as the water lilies are in a state of flourishing growth and the gold fish are good and fat, along comes some sophomores and a poor innocent freshman and the paradise of water lilies and sleek gold fish is rudely and brutally interrupted."

In 1927, Dean of Men Earl J. Miller attended a convention for Western state deans and learned that hazing was

more prevalent on the West Coast than in the East. But overall, deans were inclined to reduce or eliminate such rituals. Six months later, the student council voted to end hazing, although some of the traditions that inspired it were still observed. "Hazing is out of style and in its place you will find that all students, including your traditional rivals, the sophomores, are stressing helpfulness," said the 1930–31 student handbook. "An icy dip into the nearby reservoir would be welcome compared to the disgust and disapproval of your [fellow] Californians in the event of non-compliance with California Traditions."

UCLA's first decade coincided with the good times of the Roaring '20s. Students often frequented the Cocoanut Grove, a premier nightspot, at the Los Angeles Ambassador Hotel. Each Tuesday evening was "celebrity night," and such headliners as Paul Whiteman and His Orchestra—he was the bandleader who commissioned George Gershwin to write "Rhapsody in Blue"—and the Rhythm Boys, which included Bing Crosby and Harry Barris, graced the stage with songs from the Jazz Age like "It Had to Be You."

The campus threw dances for almost every occasion, starting with the Halloween Prom, held on October 31, 1919. The ladies carried dance cards, which hung from their wrists with tassels and noted the names of men who had been given the privilege of reserving a dance. UCLA held proms well into the 1950s. In December 1944, famed bandleader Xavier Cugat headlined the Yankee Yuletide Prom in Kerckhoff Hall with his "maraca-accented rhythms" as Bruins danced the evening away and competed in rumba and jitterbug contests. One of the most successful dances was the Junior Prom in fall 1949, attended by 3,500 students, at Paramount Studios. Comedian Bob Hope served as master of ceremonies and one fortunate student won the prize of the evening: a prom date with 17-year-old actress Elizabeth Taylor. Another Hollywood icon, Marilyn Monroe,

who had enrolled in a literature course through Extension, attended the Junior Prom in the fall of 1951.

During Prohibition, women drank punch (mostly), while men secretly sipped liquor from silver flasks. Even the characteristically stern Moore turned a blind eye now and then. On one occasion, students managed to procure a couple of barrels of wine and hid them at a campus party. Moore summoned the student responsible to his office and asked him if he was aware that alcohol was prohibited and that anyone who was caught would be expelled. When the nervous student acknowledged that he knew the regulation, a satisfied Moore dismissed him from his office without further reprimand.

But Moore was not always so lenient. Students had started an annual vaudeville show in 1919 called the Press Club Vode, which included more than two dozen acts ranging from skits to song and dance numbers featuring elaborate sets and costumes. It was a popular tradition, but one that Moore said showcased "vulgarity and exhibitionism." The 1927 show resulted in the Student Affairs Committee suspending six students and reprimanding 11 others for excessive drinking. It was the last of the Vode.

"INSTANT TRADITION"

After the move to the Westwood campus, students had both the opportunity—and to a certain extent the obligation—to adopt traditions inspired by their new surroundings.

"Steps are being taken by one of the campus organizations to make the stepping upon the Seal of the University, in the foyer of the Library, a breach of campus tradition," wrote the *Daily Bruin* in October 1929. "The idea is a good one, and although it is not original, it will tend towards the accomplishment of having traditions upon the campus which are distinctive from those now used at the University of California at Berkeley. Some day in the far future, UCLA will have traditions which will apply to the campus itself, rather than having those transplanted from some great rival institution."

Springtime Revelry

Mardi Gras, for decades UCLA's largest student-run activity, had roots in a "Carnival" held on May 13, 1943, in the women's gym. It featured jigs and reels, a swing dance in Elizabethan costumes, and athletic competition.

Some accounts describe Mardi Gras festivities beginning as a masquerade ball in 1941, or earlier as an annual event presented by a Masonic affiliate club. However, as little record exists recounting the ball, the details of the true origins of the extravaganza remain unclear. What is known is that an event called "Mardi Gras" was held on campus in 1945, furthering the festival spirit of the 1943 social. Sponsored by the University Recreation Association, the evening included dancing and 40 decorated concessions operated by university organizations and ended with the coronation of the king, a favorite professor elected by the students.

As the event evolved, UCLA's annual spring tradition moved outdoors, and eventually settled onto the Intramural Field. Months of student preparation culminated in the annual carnival and proceeds benefited UniCamp, a summer camp for underprivileged children and UCLA's official student charity.

In the 1960s, a go-go show thrilled spectators, and students elected Mardi Gras kings by casting penny votes. In 1962, actress Jayne Mansfield crowned basketball Coach John R. Wooden as Mardi Gras king.

The entertainment grew in size and scope. In a typical year, more than 130 student organizations competed for awards in best entertainment, food or games. In 1975, Mayor Tom Bradley explored the Fun House. In 1980, the popular Laserama show was introduced, and in 1985, actor Bob Newhart was the grand marshal. Mimes and clowns made their way through myriad themed booths. Some of the perennial favorites included the Ferris wheel and House of Horrors.

At its height, Mardi Gras was a featured local attraction that drew more than 80,000 visitors and generated $200,000 in proceeds for UniCamp. "UCLA's Mardi Gras is a high-spirited carnival for the whole family," described the *Los Angeles Times* in 1987. "From roaming Smurfs to daredevil rides … the weekend festival at UCLA's Athletic Field is packed with old-fashioned sideshow atmosphere."

The celebration continued for more than half a century, until financial difficulties and security concerns brought the tradition to an end. UCLA held its final Mardi Gras in 1995.

Above: A Student Alumni Association booth at Mardi Gras, 1987.

Right: Round Up, a favorite Mardi Gras ride.

Far right: Hollywood actress Jayne Mansfield crowns John R. Wooden as king of the 1962 Mardi Gras, while a bashful Wooden points to his wife, Nell.

Hail to the Hills of Westwood

Alma Mater

UCLA and Berkeley shared an alma mater until 1925, when UCLA student Bert Price wrote "Hail Blue and Gold." The song remained UCLA's official alma mater until students formally objected to the reference of UCLA as the "California of the South" in 1960. "Hail to the Hills of Westwood," written by Jeane M. Emerson in 1929, replaced the earlier song. Traditionally, outstretched fingers in the form of a "V"—representing victory—is held high over the head while singing the alma mater after sporting events.

> Hail to the hills of Westwood,
> To the mighty sea below;
> Hail to our Alma Mater,
> She will conquer every foe.
> For we're loyal to the Southland,
> Her honor we'll uphold;
> We'll gladly give our hearts to thee,
> To the Blue and to the Gold.

"Strike Up the Band for UCLA"

The UCLA song written by George and Ira Gershwin was adapted from their show tune, "Strike Up the Band." It was presented to UCLA at an All-University Sing in September 1936 and was hailed as "the official song of the University of California at Los Angeles" for many years. The brothers received UCLA identification cards and were made honorary members of the student body.

> "Strike Up the Band for UCLA"
> Let the drums roll out!
> Let the trumpets call,
> Let the whole world shout UCLA.
> With our battle cry Bruin! Conquer all!
> We will do or die!
> There's a game to be won, to be won!
> Put the foe on the run, on the run!
> And it's got to be done,
> To be done here today!
> With our flag unfurled, we can lick the world!
> You see, we're UCLA!

"Rover"

In the late 1960s, a band student wrote lyrics to a popular tune being played during football games, "I'm Looking Over a Four Leaf Clover." The UCLA version was named "Rover." At the height of the legendary John Wooden era, "Rover" was played only after lopsided basketball victories—virtually every game. Later, the UCLA Varsity Band began playing "Rover" after all UCLA victories, immediately following the alma mater.

> We're looking over our dead dog, Rover,
> That we overran tonight (all right!)
> One leg is broken, the other is bent,
> And in his head, there's a great big dent.
> No need explaining the parts remaining
> Are scattered all over the court (next page).
> We're looking over our dead dog, Rover,
> That we overran tonight!

"Sons of Westwood" and the "Eight-clap"

During the early 1960s, the UCLA Marching Band adopted new Bruin-oriented lyrics to Berkeley's "Big C" and composed "Sons of Westwood." The "Eight-clap" yell introduced by a UCLA student in 1948, accompanies the song. In the 1990s, a UCLA band member began extending the "L" in the Eight-clap, and the innovation caught on with some fans—although others still prefer the short "L," leading to simultaneous variation.

Inset: Jeane M. Emerson, Class of 1929, author of UCLA's alma mater.

Below: George Gershwin plays "Strike Up the Band for UCLA" accompanied by undergraduate singers, 1936.

We are Sons of Westwood,
And we hail the Blue and Gold;
True to thee our hearts will be,
Our love will not grow old. (Fight! Fight! Fight!)
Bruins roam the hills of Westwood,
By the blue Pacific shore;
And when they chance to see a man from USC,
Ev'ry Bruin starts to roar.

U! (3 claps)
C! (3 claps)
L! (3 claps)
A! (3 claps)
U-C-L-A! (Fight! Fight! Fight!)

"Mighty Bruins"

To commemorate its 50th anniversary, the UCLA Alumni
Association commissioned a new fight song. After a contest
soliciting lyrics from students and alumni, Academy Award-
winning composer Bill Conti chose the winning lyrics (from
alumni Barbara Lamb and Don Holley) and wrote the music to
"Mighty Bruins." The song made its gridiron debut in October
1984 at the Stanford football game, with Conti conducting the
UCLA Marching Band.

We are the Mighty Bruins,
The best team in the West.
We're marching on to victory,
To conquer all the rest.
We are the Mighty Bruins,
Triumphant evermore.
You can hear from far and near,
The Mighty Bruin roar!

Directed by composer Bill
Conti, the UCLA Marching
Band plays the university's
new fight song "Mighty Bruins"
for the first time, Bruin Plaza,
September 30, 1984.

Postcards from the 1930s of the Men's Club Room (above)
and the Women's Lounge (below) in Kerckhoff Hall.

One of UCLA's founders tried to cultivate rituals by
helping the students adapt other Berkeley traditions. Regent
Edward A. Dickson—who as a junior at Berkeley was part of
the group that stole the Stanford Axe in 1899, instigating a
long-standing tradition—wanted UCLA's earliest students to
experience a rich cultural heritage.

At Dickson's behest, a 75-ton boulder was brought
from the hills of Perris Valley to mark the place where he
and friend Irwin J. Muma first stood surveying the land for
the future Westwood campus. Founders' Rock starred in the
Westwood campus's first dedication ceremony on October
25, 1926, held on what was otherwise a largely barren field.
Dickson hoped that Founders' Rock would emulate the
similar landmark at his alma mater, on which Berkeley's senior
class had placed a memorial tablet during the University of
California's Charter Day ceremonies in 1896. At UCLA,
Founders' Rock was intended to be a major gathering spot
for campus activities and the site for an annual Founders' Day
ceremony. Students were meant to include it in celebratory
processions, but the tradition never really caught on.

"What Mr. Dickson wanted was instant tradition
because he remembered Berkeley, and he wanted to establish

certain things on the southern campus that would grow up or in time would become traditions," recalled 1926 alumna Ann Sumner, who had been "adopted" by Dickson and his wife, Wilhelmina. "I do smile at it because he really desperately wanted tradition ... and tradition takes years to build."

The first classes at Westwood were held just weeks before the stock market crash of 1929 that catapulted the nation into the Great Depression. Although students felt the sting of the bad economic times, the opening of Kerckhoff Hall in January 1931 finally provided them with a home to run their activities. The new student union included offices for executive council members and a boardroom initially used by the regents, until they tired of climbing the three flights of stairs and moved their meetings to the administration building. The room became the domain of the student council thereafter. The student union also contained men's and women's lounges, a bookstore, a cafeteria, and the Associated Students administrative offices. (Kerckhoff Hall served as the student union until Ackerman Student Union opened in 1961.)

Although the building and its furnishings were donated, the $1,000 monthly maintenance costs, coupled with a reduced revenue stream from football ticket sales and from membership dues—82 percent of students purchased memberships in 1925–26, compared with 60 percent in 1929–30—almost bankrupted the organization until the regents supplied an emergency $50,000 loan. The Associated Students relinquished financial control to the regents during this time, and UCLA Assistant Comptroller Deming G. Maclise was put in charge of a receivership to manage the finances on behalf of the regents. Since all students benefited from Kerckhoff Hall, one remedy for the solvency troubles was to suggest compulsory membership in the Associated Students. On November 1, 1933, with more than 70 percent of the student body voting, the proposition passed

Above left: The victory flag flies on Royce quad after a Bruin win, 1932. Students (above) toss coins on the worn-out flag to raise funds for a new one, c. 1950.

Left: Rafer Johnson, 1959 student body president, leads an executive council meeting.

with an overwhelming majority. With the increased revenue and deep budget reductions in administrative and athletic expenses, the Associated Students paid off the loan by August 1940, becoming solvent and regaining financial control.

During the 1930s, interest in social clubs waned as students became more interested in the issues of the times and in promoting peace through the strong youth anti-war movement. The Associated Students abandoned the enforcement of the honor code and transferred judicial matters to the administration, including the dean of men and the dean of women.

Some traditions held firm, however, including the revered Wednesday Sing, which had started in the 1920s—and, surprisingly, continued well into the 1950s. The idea emanated from Charles Henry Rieber, dean of the College of Letters and Science, who suggested it to the Traditions Committee members who approached him in 1924. The ritual was one that Rieber recalled from his days at Berkeley. Each Wednesday morning students would open classes by spending several minutes singing songs such as the alma mater, "By the Old Pacific's Rolling Waters" or "Strike Up the Band for UCLA"—a new rendition of the show tune that had been given to UCLA by the Gershwin brothers in 1936. The *Daily Bruin* promoted the tradition by printing lyrics to the selections in its Wednesday edition, and one year it printed the names of the professors who discouraged the tradition in their classes. The Minute Men were responsible for furnishing classes with song leaders, but there were not always enough to go around, and students were left on their own to continue the practice. "Professors will give you the time for singing—but they will not force you to sing," the *Daily Bruin* wrote in September 1937. "You can lead or not, and sing or not, just as you please. But it would be nice if you would sing."

WAVING THE BLUE AND GOLD

As UCLA's athletic teams grew stronger and became increasingly victorious, loyal Bruin fans searched for a new way to celebrate. *Daily Bruin* Editor Carl Schaefer had waged a campaign on the pages of the newspaper during fall 1930 to procure a flag that could be flown in all its glory from the Gimbel Flagpole after wins.

On February 25, 1931, West Los Angeles Rotary Club President Edward Coe formally presented the gift of UCLA's first victory flag to student body President Earle Swingle at a noontime ceremony on Royce quad. The 12-by-31-foot flag with "UCLA" spelled out in blue and gold across a massive white field was hoisted just below the American flag after each UCLA victory. Later it would also be flown to mark other student achievements. In May 1934, for example, it was raised to honor students who won oratorical and literary competitions.

The victory flag flew for 18 years, until the weathered banner was retired. Missing the tradition, students started raising funds for a new flag. Coinciding with the death of A.

J. "Sturzy" Sturzenegger, Associated Students assistant graduate manager, former baseball head coach and assistant football coach, students dedicated the effort in his memory. Each day they spread out the torn banner on Royce quad, and individuals made their contributions by tossing coins onto it. The money was collected daily until there was enough to purchase a new flag. This victory flag, which included a dedication to Sturzenegger on the bottom, flew proudly until the student unrest of the 1970s brought the tradition to a halt.

From the start, Bruins have followed their teams near and far to cheer for them. Strict dress codes of white shirts or blouses, and rooters caps for the men, were required of students for decades to present a more uniform appearance. Those who did not conform were not allowed to sit in the students' section.

In 1931, the Bruin football team played at Stanford University for the first time in three years. "Every loyal Bruin who could beg, borrow, or steal a ride to Palo Alto migrated from Los Angeles on the occasion," wrote the 1932 *Southern Campus*. More than 300 rooters—including students, alumni, band members and spirit leaders—boarded the H.F. Alexander steamship at Long Beach Harbor on October 30 at 4 p.m. "The spirit of the occasion was festive, not to say hilarious; dancing and other amusements whiled away the time until the boat docked at nine-thirty Saturday morning," the yearbook said. After witnessing a nerve-wracking game (UCLA 6, Stanford 12), the rooters returned wearily to the ship, which departed at 1 a.m. "There was little time to be tired, however, for celebration of the near victory was essential, and the merry-making started long before sailing time; the participants had a better time, if possible, on the return trip than on the voyage up," added the *Southern Campus*.

Below: An advertisement for a steamship voyage to Palo Alto for the 1931 UCLA–Stanford football game.

Right: The Rally Committee's innovative card and light stunts, including their trademark UCLA signature, were featured in the national press.

Make Reservations Now for the Bruin-Indian Game at Palo Alto, Oct. 31st

Sails Friday · 4:00 p. m.
on the Super Ship
"H. F. Alexander"

SPECIAL RATES

Direct Sailing to San Francisco

PACIFIC STEAMSHIP CO.

501 W. 5th St.
6615 Hollywood Blvd.

111 W. Broadway, Long Beach
372 E. Colorado, Pasadena

UCLA RALLY COMMITTEE
SECTION SEATING PASS
UCLA vs. USC
November 22, 1952 5
ROW 4 SEAT 5
NOT GOOD FOR ADMISSION
Enter General Admission or Rooters Gate
After Admittance
Enter Tunnel 23 ONLY
Void After 1:30 p.m.

In 1923, the Rally Committee introduced spectacular card stunts in the student section at home games in the Los Angeles Memorial Coliseum. Animated stunts, spell-outs and three-dimensional effects produced by having certain students stand with their card were added in the 1940s. One Bruin invention showcased an American flag that magically unfurled, and UCLA set a record when 3,600 students, using 12 different colors, participated in the biggest card stunt ever attempted. The UCLA script spell-out, appearing as though an invisible hand were writing it out, quickly became a UCLA trademark. "The mechanics of the stunt presented a serious problem, but the committee went into a huddle, and the artists came up with a plan," wrote *UCLA Magazine* in November 1945. "They decided to number the cards forming the script in the order they should come up, so that the gold cards flip up in the correct order as the rally chairman calls off the successive numbers, and there it is—a gold UCLA, in script, another Bruin first. As a matter of fact, the script stunt has proven so successful that it is to be adopted as our signature stunt."

UCLA was known for its continuous innovation of the stunts, even as they were emulated by other universities across the country. In 1935, light stunts were introduced when the football team played the University of Hawaii at night. The rooting section was wired and students were given four light bulbs, each a different color. While the daytime card stunts continued, the night tradition ended when mandatory blackouts were imposed during World War II. In 1953, at the urging of Ackerman, the Rally Committee revived the tradition. However, because the light bulbs and wiring were not only difficult to handle but expensive as well, the students developed a card similar to the type used in ordinary card

stunts with eight different light filters placed in a circular pattern. Each student was given a flashlight to shine through the filters. The method debuted at the home opener against Oregon State on September 20, 1953, and the stunts were featured in *Life* and *Time* magazines.

THE RIVALRY

There is perhaps no more beloved tradition than the taunting and teasing of crosstown USC, in what has become one of the fiercest collegiate rivalries in the nation. The only such rivalry between two major universities in the same city—a mere dozen miles apart—it extends to all sports and student activities.

The rivalry hearkens back to the university's fledgling days, when University of Southern California students would mock Southern Branch students by calling them "twigs." It only escalated from there.

Since 1929, when the Bruins and Trojans first faced one another in football, favorite harassments have included humorous mock campus newspapers that lampooned each university, and an endless number of practical jokes and sarcastic slogans directed at the opposing school. In 1931, a dispute over scheduling brought a halt to the gridiron matchup, which was reintroduced in 1936.

In 1941, one incident greatly contributed to the crosstown grudge match. After a UCLA game against Washington State at the Coliseum, some USC students dressed as Bruins stole the keys to the truck used to transport UCLA's Victory Bell and drove off. The bell—originally belonging to a Southern Pacific Railroad locomotive—had been presented

During the 1950s, Victory Bell rallies often spilled into the streets of Westwood.

Below right: The Bruin in hibernation before the big game until USC vandals pierced the protective tarp, splashing UCLA's iconic statue with red and yellow paint (far right), November 25, 2009.

Bottom center: Students enjoy the glow of the bonfire during Beat 'SC week, 2005.

Bottom right: On December 5, 2006, during a basketball halftime celebration, Coach Karl Dorrell (in gray vest), football players and Rally Committee members show off the Victory Bell, which returned home after the Bruins beat the Trojans 13–9 at the Rose Bowl.

Below: Bruins from all over show their UCLA spirit, especially in California where UCLA is the only university to have its own specialty license plate.

to UCLA by the Alumni Association in 1939. For two years, the 295-pound bell, mounted on an undercarriage with wheels, was toted to rallies and football games and proudly rang out once for each Bruin point scored.

After the Victory Bell was stolen, students began a rash of vandalism at USC and UCLA. Tommy Trojan was defaced several times, while "USC" was burned into UCLA's green lawns and painted in red on Founders' Rock. In December 1941, UCLA swiped USC's banner; USC returned the favor in the middle of the 1942 season. Bruins tried to keep the bell's memory alive by ringing cowbells after each point. Then a

photograph of the Victory Bell appeared in an issue of USC's humor magazine, and a plot unfolded to kidnap USC's student body president if the bell was not returned.

After extensive negotiations led by UCLA's 1943 student body President William C. Farrer and USC student body President Bob McKay, the Trojan students finally agreed to return the bell on the condition that it become a permanent game trophy. UCLA requested that USC purchase a half-interest in the bell—$150—which was put into a maintenance fund. During the bell's absence, it had been divided into three components that were hidden separately: the carriage, which had been kept near the USC campus; the bell itself, stored in Santa Barbara; and the clapper, which was never returned.

A "Peace Pact" was signed and the bell returned in time for the fall 1942 matchup "where it tolled a history-making victory," as UCLA won 14–7. The bell has remained a victor's trophy ever since. During the 1950s, Victory Bell rallies often spilled into the streets of Westwood.

The rival schools' mascot statues have been a favorite target of pranksters, and students began camping out to watch over them. During the week before the big game, *The Bruin*—a fixture in Bruin Plaza since 1984—was covered in a heavy tarp with a sign reading, "The Bruin Bear is hibernating" and

guarded by Rally Committee members. In November 2009, however, the Rally Committee failed to protect *The Bruin* from USC hoodlums who ripped into the tarp and doused the bear with non-water-soluble red and yellow paint, causing thousands of dollars in damage. Starting in fall 2010, *The Bruin* has been enclosed in a wooden structure before the big game, and security cameras installed nearby. Across town, the Tommy Trojan statue has also been kept under wraps, having been the object of many Bruin pranks, including being splashed from head-to-toe in blue and gold paint and having its sword stolen so many times that it was replaced with a less-expensive wooden replica. During one notorious prank in 1958, UCLA students set out to drop manure on the statue from a helicopter—although they missed.

CHANGING CAMPUS LIFESTYLES

World War II thoroughly altered campus life. As men went off to war, freshmen were allowed to play football. Women filled many of the student government posts and other leadership roles in student organizations. Student activities were also modified in light of the scarcity of material.

"Bruin students have found the 1942 football season very different from any in U.C.L.A.'s history," reported the *Daily Bruin* that October. "Shortages of materials have made the rooter's cap and megaphone things of the past. For the same reason, the wearing of white shirts is no longer required of rooters. Cards from the half-time stunts must not be torn up if there are to be any more stunts."

The students continued to hold dances, but they were kept nearby. In 1943, popular band leader Freddy Martin played for a packed alumni dance in the Kerckhoff Men's Lounge. Commencement ceremonies, previously held at the Hollywood Bowl, were moved to campus for the first time after the opening of the recently excavated outdoor amphitheater. In 1943, the homecoming parade—which had traditionally wound its way through Westwood since debuting in 1933—featured miniature floats that paraded across the Royce Hall stage instead.

After the war, the homecoming parade returned to Westwood with its many floats and student group entries. But a couple of dangerous incidents portended the end of one long-lived tradition that had become associated with homecoming weekend: the bonfire.

In 1945, a prankster added dynamite into the bonfire and it exploded. While no one was hurt, Ackerman reported the

Above left: The 1958 Homecoming Committee. Kneeling: Dean Ambrose (left) and Kent Lewis (right); First row, from left: Alan Charles, Marilyn Florida and Kim Strutt; Second row, from left: Bretta Dietrich, Judy Hellyer, Corky Gilbert; Top Row, from left: Denny Henderson, Joel Wachs, Mike Edelen, Steve Lomas and Keith Gamet.

Above: Robert Gordon Sproul crowns Phyllis McMeen as the 1958 homecoming queen on Janss Steps.

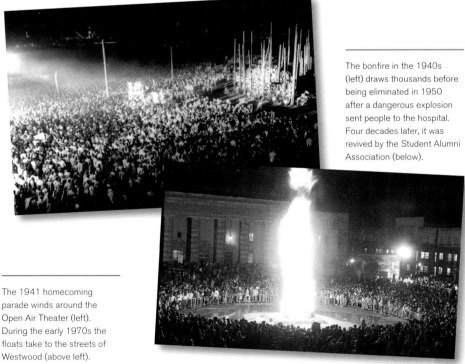

The bonfire in the 1940s (left) draws thousands before being eliminated in 1950 after a dangerous explosion sent people to the hospital. Four decades later, it was revived by the Student Alumni Association (below).

The 1941 homecoming parade winds around the Open Air Theater (left). During the early 1970s the floats take to the streets of Westwood (above left).

Top: The Delta Zeta quartet tests its vocals for Master of Ceremonies Ronald Reagan in a warm-up to the May 3, 1957, Spring Sing.

Above: 1964 Spring Sing program.

Above right: Spring Sing talent directors Sara Jayne Daquioag and LaRita Williams with Stevie Wonder, the 2002 George and Ira Gershwin Award recipient. The Gershwin Award, for lifetime musical achievement, has been presented by the Student Alumni Association since 1988.

Far right: Members of the UCLA Dance Team, from left, Rebecca Steinberg, Kyrra Richards and Melissa Fong, 2003.

funded GI Bill. In many instances, the veterans were married, and had families of their own, which shifted campus demographics to a more mature student body focused on vocational aspirations.

By the 1950s, the military men who had been stationed in fraternity houses during the war were long gone, and Greek life again flourished. Many of the student body presidents and vice presidents elected during these years were fraternity men and sorority women.

One of UCLA's oldest traditions, Spring Sing began in the 1940s as fraternities competed for the title of "Champion Serenaders of Sorority Row." As its popularity grew, Ackerman arranged for the student musical competition to be held in Royce Hall in 1945. At its height in the late 1950s and early 1960s, after Spring Sing had moved to the Hollywood Bowl, more than 10,000 people regularly attended the event. Celebrities—such as actor Ronald Reagan—served as master of ceremonies and judges.

Interest in Spring Sing waned during the Vietnam War era, and the event entered a decade-long hiatus in 1968, before students and alumni revived the tradition, moving it back indoors to Royce Hall. In 1986, the Student Alumni Association became the official organizer of the event in an attempt to restore Spring Sing to its former grandeur. Since then, the event has enjoyed sell-out crowds in Pauley Pavilion, and under the stars in the Los Angeles Tennis Center.

In the 1960s, UCLA's status as a commuter college changed significantly as four high-rise residence halls opened on campus—previously only Hershey Hall had provided living quarters to some female students. In September 1959, the 10-story Dykstra Hall opened to 800 male residents. Although UCLA officials had hoped to make the dormitory coed, members of the Board of Regents were against the notion, and the administration dropped the request. Things were different a year later when Sproul Hall opened in 1960, and 400 men and 400 women moved into the dormitory.

UCLA "promised parents that it would aim for 'maximum security,'" wrote *Time* in August 1960, comparing

blast was so powerful that he was thrown about 15 feet. Five years later, a fireworks company provided the powder to ignite the blaze. "Unfortunately, the company swept everything up from its factory floor and donated this to UCLA," Ackerman said. "In the powder was tetra ethyl, which is stronger than dynamite. The fire exploded when it was lighted." The professor who lit the bonfire suffered a serious arm burn, and altogether nine people had to be treated at the hospital.

"The 67-foot-high bonfire, erected by students of crates, boxes, scrap lumber and other inflammable debris, blew up in the middle of the home-coming celebration in view of thousands of spectators and celebrants," wrote the *Los Angeles Times* in October 1950, noting that windows had shattered on several blocks in the vicinity. "It tossed flame and debris hundreds of feet into the air." That was the last of the bonfires for four decades, until the tradition was revived in 1990 by the Student Alumni Association.

In the postwar years, UCLA witnessed a boom in the student population as veterans enrolled through the federally

dorm security to San Quentin prison. "We are not planning to set up flamethrowers or machine guns at strategic passes," Dean of Students Byron H. "Barney" Atkinson told *Time*. "All we can do is try not to make it easy to break the rules." *In loco parentis* regulations, such as curfews, were instituted, and female students in those earliest years recall their particular warning system: the "man on floor" shout-out.

"Many looked upon this, the University's first major venture into planned co-educational living, as rashly experimental and doomed to failure," wrote Atkinson in the *UCLA Alumni Magazine* in spring 1964. "In retrospect, our trepidations were groundless. The co-educational hall became socially acceptable almost overnight." Dykstra Hall was converted into a coed dormitory in fall 1960 and both Rieber (1963) and Hedrick (1964) halls opened in the same manner.

Curfews and a dorm lockout were enforced until fall 1967. "A long time ago the purpose of lockout was to protect the virtue of women," said Dean of Student Housing Services William Locklear to the *Daily Bruin*. However, Locklear added that "because of lockout many women were staying out until the last minute just to stay out."

During the 1970s, traditions on campus fell to a near-dormant state. Anti-war and other anti-establishment activism dominated campus life. More UCLA students were interested in pursuing classes in the Experimental College—a non-credit course program run by the student government and taught by volunteer instructors on topics that students selected themselves—than organizing traditional extracurricular activities.

Even after the end of the Vietnam War, student government stayed focused on more serious matters. For example, several UCLA student body presidents worked with their counterparts from other University of California campuses, lobbying successfully to create a voting student regent position on the university's governing board.

Some students, however, sought to fill the void in campus traditions that had been left by student government. In 1984, the volunteer-driven Student Alumni Association (SAA) was created in part to help rekindle interest in activities such as Spring Sing,

homecoming, the bonfire and related "Beat 'SC" activities.

"Student government had changed to policy and issues of the day, and was not concerned with the fun side of student life," said Keith E. Brant, who oversaw SAA for 11 years as its first staff adviser, before being appointed executive director of the Alumni Association in 1995. "SAA's niche was making student life fun again while helping make students feel good about being Bruins."

The UCLA Alumni Association founded SAA on a broader mission of developing students' lifelong loyalty to UCLA while building connections between students and alumni through such new programs as career networking. Dinner for 12 Strangers—which brings together a dozen students, alumni and professors who share a meal at a volunteer host's home—became a model replicated by universities nationwide. (Originally created in 1968, by the support group Gold Shield Alumnae of UCLA, SAA took over responsibility for the dinners in 1986.)

"The Alumni Association is reinvesting in tradition," Brant said in 2002 as SAA revived the homecoming parade again for the first time in seven years. "We feel that today's students don't have an appreciation for what happened in the past. Part of that is our own fault for not investing more resources in telling students about the history of the campus."

Above: The Beat 'SC Car Smash is a popular annual tradition held in Bruin Plaza.

Below: Bruin Walk, 2011

Below left: Student Alumni Association, inaugural year, 1984. Kneeling: Keith E. Brant, adviser. First row, from left: Parvoneh Poorkaj, Kari Miner, Becky Takeda, Dale Nishimura and Ryan Crenshaw. Second row, from left: Anne-Marie Flynn, Richard Ness and Annalee Ryan.

Living Legends

Illustration from the 1947–1948 student handbook.

Ever hear Royce's shrieking ghost? Or see the potato trees near Moore Hall resulting from the radioactive experiment gone wrong? Did you accidentally tread onto the sixth Janss step and have to stay at UCLA an extra year?

Since UCLA's earliest days, students have been immersed in rituals and legends handed down from generation to generation. It's often difficult to pinpoint their origin—and renditions change with successive classes. However, with most of these stories based on a grain of truth, it's easy for unsuspecting freshmen to get caught up in the embellishment.

In the 1940s, upperclassmen initiated a fable to compel freshmen to avoid walking over the university seal in the library—a tradition dating back to the Westwood campus's opening in 1929. The library foyer, they revealed, had once been home to Bosco, a trained circus seal. Unhappy with his confined surroundings, he would snap at anyone who came near him. Eventually, Bosco was returned to the Ringling Brothers, and his pool was filled in with a mosaic of the university's emblem. Still, students would not step on the seal out of fear of old Bosco. "There are even a few old-timers who say that if you listen closely as some luckless student is taken away by the 'Library Seal Vigilantes Committee,' you can hear a laughing sound, not unlike that of the bark of a seal," wrote the *Daily Bruin* in July 1946.

In the 1960s, a new eatery was constructed in the Court of Sciences, near the nuclear reactor (decommissioned in 1984) in Boelter Hall. Students, who had grown up during the Cold War and recalled regular morning air raid drills from elementary school, thought the mostly below-ground-level structure, with its bunker-thick concrete walls, looked like a bomb shelter. The nickname stuck, and over the years, students came to believe that the Bombshelter was built to provide protection from nuclear attack. In actuality, UCLA's real Civil Defense fallout shelter lay underground in the eerie catacombs that run the length of UCLA. Well, they are not actually catacombs—although William G. Kerckhoff is said to lie beneath the original student union he donated to campus. The "catacombs" are basements connected by miles of six-foot-wide tunnels originally built as a conduit for pipes channeling hot water and steam throughout campus (later housing electrical, telecommunications and other utility systems).

Although strictly off-limits to explorers, the tunnels have developed a cult following. In recent years, some students have managed to sneak in, commemorating their accomplishment by posting digital snapshots online. (Word is that one is eligible for immediate expulsion if caught down there.) During rainstorms in the 1930s and 1940s, the tunnels were used for more practical purposes, including accommodating long lines of students waiting to register for classes. Students would fill out registration cards and have their pictures taken in the Women's Gymnasium before traveling via tunnel to the Men's Gymnasium to pay their fees. On occasion, the tunnels were used as escape routes for high-profile speakers. In 1967, American Nazi Party leader George Lincoln Rockwell was escorted through the tunnels to avoid an angry crowd that had gathered after he delivered a controversial speech in Royce Hall.

Orientation Program staff took the art of Bruin storytelling to a whole new level during the 1980s. Student counselors guided incoming freshmen on the infamous "midnight tour," telling them everything they needed to know—and more—about their new campus.

For example, the Inverted Fountain was designed by a USC student who thumbed his nose at UCLA by making it look like a toilet bowl from a certain angle. With the help of NASA, Bunche Hall was lifted by helicopters and rotated 90 degrees so that the reflection from its windows wouldn't blind drivers on the San Diego Freeway. "When I entered UCLA in 1989, my orientation counselor, Steve Callaghan, managed to convince us that there was a swimming pool on the roof of the Anderson Graduate School of Management building [later Public Affairs]," recalled Julie Brotherton Gehr. "We totally bought it. I don't know how much later I figured out that he had pulled one over on us, but let's just say I was no longer a freshman."

The tours, no longer held at midnight, continue with counselors imparting valuable new tidbits such as: If you are ever lost on campus, just raise your BruinCard and someone will stop to help you. Students still avoid stepping on the university seal in Powell, and follow new traditions such as rubbing *The Bruin* statue's back paw for good luck before finals.

There was a scare in the early 1990s when the orientation initiation tour was almost discontinued after a group of duped students threatened to sue the university. But the tradition was saved. As a compromise, orientation participants are eventually told that the legends are tall tales. And that's the absolute truth … right?

During the 1990s through the 2010s, UCLA continued its transformation in becoming a residential academic community with multiple residence halls opening on campus. As more and more students lived on campus, the very essence of student life changed—sometimes, even before students attended their first UCLA class.

Summer orientation programs, for example, became more effective when students could stay in the dorms for several days at a time, immersing themselves in campus life from the start. Orientation counselors became notorious for imbuing freshmen with Bruin lore, such as the infamous tidbit of one of the Janss brothers being buried beneath the steps that bear their name. They also "Bruintized" freshmen by having them wade into the Inverted Fountain during orientation, warning them not do so again until graduation, or risk having an extra year tacked on to their undergraduate career.

Some student traditions stemmed directly from life in the dorms. In the 1980s, a group of students took a break from studying during finals week and tried to relieve some of the stress by yelling at the top of their lungs at midnight. The action caught on, and soon—whether everyone liked it or not—a tradition known as Midnight Yell was born. Various accompaniments were added, ranging from blasting stereo music to the occasional electric guitar rendition of the national anthem. However, in 1999, students gathered off-campus took the concept too far, reportedly becoming rowdy while in a drunken state and setting several couches and tree branches on fire. Police made 20 arrests over two days. Chancellor Albert Carnesale and other administrators clamped down on the tradition, as did campus police.

But as rituals at UCLA often do, it evolved. Out of Midnight Yell developed a new tradition in spring 2002, when founder Eric Whitehead and 12 other male students in their skivvies ran out onto Glenrock Avenue. "Undie Run, as it inevitably became known, was our sophomoric act of defiance against UCPD for deploying scores of officers to prevent another Midnight Yell from again digressing into a melee of broken windows and burning couches," wrote one of its progenitors, 2004 alumnus Brad Greenberg, in the October 2006 *UCLA Magazine*. "Four years later, Undie Run has become a bona fide Bruin tradition. … I was dumbfounded by our little run—and myth it has become." After some students raced atop parked cars and caused other damage off campus, administrators instituted a designated path through campus. By 2006, the Undie Run attracted more than 5,000 participants. In 2009, however, administrators deemed the tradition—which was drawing non-UCLA students—hazardous and canceled it, pushing the event underground.

Indeed, Bruin traditions have changed over the years in ways one could not predict. Being waded into the Inverted Fountain by an orientation counselor might not be the direct descendant of getting sopped into a fishpond. Nor does the Undie Run have its roots in the pajamarinos. But they all share a place in UCLA's storied rites of passage.

Acknowledgments

Practically every individual with a UCLA connection with whom I have interacted these past eight years has contributed knowingly, or even unknowingly, to this effort. It is impossible to list everyone, but I appreciate every official historical document or anecdotal tidbit ever shared with me. They have all blended to give me an understanding of this institution that would simply not have been otherwise possible.

I am grateful to the UCLA Alumni Association and Gold Shield Alumnae of UCLA for coming together in sponsorship of this project, recognizing that a history of UCLA was long overdue. Moreover, a project of this magnitude would not have been possible without the firm support of the Ahmanson Foundation, which generously provided additional research funding.

I am indebted to the Board of Regents, the Office of the President and the Chancellor's Office for providing access to minutes, both open and closed, and other university records, which allowed me to delve into certain issues with much-needed context and detail. I am particularly grateful to Anne Shaw, associate secretary of the regents, and Linda Thomas, director of the UCLA Chancellor's Communications Service, for their incomparable command of historical records and for providing me with a home-away-from-home during my long weeks of research in their respective offices.

My thanks to University Librarian Gary Strong and the UCLA Library, as well as Executive Director Bob Williams and the Associated Students, both steadfast supporters of this project since its inception.

The keepers of UCLA's institutional memory have my deep admiration and gratitude. UCLA Archivist Charlotte Brown and her staff, including Dennis Bitterlich and Monique Leahey Sugimoto, along with Julie Jenkins, spent countless hours providing their expertise and hospitality in the University Archives. Vicki Steele, Kevin Mulroy, Tom Hyry and the entire UCLA Department of Special Collections shared their vast knowledge of UCLA holdings, and provided special assistance with archives and photographic collections. Teresa Barnett, director of the Oral History Department, provided in-depth expertise and access to UCLA's treasure trove of skillfully conducted oral histories.

The history book steering committee kept the project moving forward in its critical first stages, and I am obliged to its members, many of whom served on various subcommittees: Anne Berkovitz, Charlotte Brown, Sheila Cameron, April Dammann, Steven Halpern, Barbara Kahn, Harlan Lebo, Ann Rieber Plauzoles and John Sandbrook; as well as those members who, in addition, were editorial advisers: Keith Brant, Alan Charles, Karen Mack and Pat Hardwick, who chaired the steering committee. Pat, Sheila, Steve and Keith also spent numerous hours in the archives, reviewing several record series and bringing critical documents to my attention.

All told, we have reviewed tens of thousands of documents, and many student assistants and interns helped me cast a wide research net in the early years as well as plug holes and fact check in the later ones, and it was a delight to work with them all: Tram Nguyen (2003–04), Khang Nguyen (2003–04), Vanessa Nguyen (2004), Tam Tran (2004), Shawn Iwaoka (2004–05), Kristin Glasgow (2005–06), Patricia Glavan (2005–06) Kim Anderson (2005–07), Janelle Sharer (2007), Derek Lipkin (2007), Camille Ray (2007–08), Katerina Belova (2008–09), Genie Moon (2008–09), Katie Boeck (2008–10), Cailin Crockett (2009–10) and Michael Mocciaro (2009–11).

Three students, Diana Hernandez (2004–07), Shanon Levine (2008–09) and Rachel Mundstock (2008–11), stayed on as invaluable editorial and photo research assistants for a year after graduation.

Journalists Anita Chabria and Veronique de Turenne assisted in conducting dozens of key interviews, as did Talleah Bridges McMahon, who also translated her tremendous expertise as a film documentarian into photo research.

I am obliged to Beth Bloom, who began with the project as an interviewer and then transitioned into the role of fact checker and associate director for four years, keeping the day-to-day functions of the UCLA History Project running smoothly, while I focused on manuscript development.

Special thanks also to Berkeley Archivist David Farrell, and Susan Snyder and the staff of the Bancroft Library, who not only made my weeks of researching UCLA's early history there productive, but also gave me access to unprocessed papers including those of Clark Kerr.

Many individuals and UCLA campus departments have contributed materials or insight over the years. My thanks to:

John Sandbrook for his encyclopedic memory and support.

Marc Dellins and the UCLA Sports Information staff, who shared their knowledge of UCLA Athletics, and provided access to their biographical files and photographs, and Bill Bennett, for his research assistance in going through those files with a sharp eye for interesting details.

Pete Blackman, particularly for his 7 a.m. walking tour of the campus, and architects Jeff Averill, Duke Oakley and everyone from the Capital Programs department, for their in-depth knowledge of the campus's physical evolution. Harriet Hutton, of Capital Programs, who walks around campus during her lunch break capturing the university and everyday life through images, and who contributed several of the photographs on these pages, including the First to 100 photo that opens chapter 14.

Joe Mandel, Kevin Reed and Amy Blum for their considered legal expertise.

Cindy Holmes, of UCLA Trademarks & Licensing, who lent her stamp of approval from the beginning, along with her enthusiasm for the project.

Arvli Ward, director of UCLA Student Media, for providing access to *Daily Bruin* back issues and photographic archives, as well as for his keen observations on student life.

Anne Pautler, creative director of University Communications, for sharing wonderful stories and photographs over the years, as well as access to historical images.

Todd Cheney and Don Liebig of the Associated Students photo department, for searching and providing access to many of their archival images, as well as shooting new photographs specifically for the book. Todd also went back through his *Daily Bruin* negatives and provided a great many historical images, which, in particular, illustrate the 1980s divestment protests.

Dan Chavkin for his beautiful photos, including those of the Royce Hall and Kerckhoff Hall stained glass, and to Gina Oken, art director of the Alumni Association, and Leroy Sisneros and his Facilities Management team for the elaborate scaffolding and logistical coordination it took to help make them a reality.

Don Browne for his eager assistance and determined sleuthing in photo identification of founding faculty members and others.

The superlative executives and editorial staff of Third Millennium Publishing, including Julian Platt, Joel Burden, Chris Fagg, Bonnie Murray, Michael Jackson and, in particular, Matt Wilson, for his masterful design work and good humor while burning the midnight oil across international time zones. The book would not be the same without Connie Binder's comprehensive indexing and Marie Loggia-Kee's eagle-eye proofreading.

Karolynne Gee, Val Maisner and Tanis Harris, and all the Gold Shield presidents and members who gave their unyielding backing and promotion of the project, as well as to all my colleagues at the UCLA Alumni Association, and to JC Schnabl, Mark Davis, Ralph Amos and Rhea Turteltaub for supporting this publication.

Burke Anderson, Jennifer Carvajal, Lance Olson and Lee Stickler for their up-to-the-last moment help with compilation of end matter, and a special thanks to Camille Ray, Kelly O'Donnell and Judy Ismaili for going above and beyond in the final days before press.

My profound thanks to Ann Rieber Plauzoles who shared not only the stories of her Bruin legacy, but offered these words of advice at the start: "Write it how you believe you should write it;" to Alan Charles for his continuous sage counsel and encouragement; and to Keith Brant, who had the vision to found this project and house it at the Alumni Association against all practical purpose, and who gave me the opportunity to chronicle UCLA's history full-time, providing immeasurable guidance along the way.

Finally, I want to thank my family and friends, for their love, unwavering support and patience, particularly with my frequent utterings of "on deadline."

Marina Dundjerski
Los Angeles
September 2011

Credits

Reproduction Credits

© 2011 Artists Rights Society (ARS), New York / VG Bild-Kunst, Bonn 289
© Bowness, Hepworth Estate 289
© 2011 Calder Foundation, New York / Artists Rights Society (ARS), New York 289
© Estate of Gerhard Marcks 289
    Photographed by Joshua White/©*Joshua White*
© Estate of David Smith / Licensed by VAGA, New York, NY 288
    Photographed by Joshua White/©*Joshua White*

The above images were originally published in *The Franklin D. Murphy Sculpture Garden at UCLA* by Cynthia Burlingham. Hammer Museum, (Los Angeles: The Regents of the University of California, 2007).

© 2011 Artists Rights Society (ARS), New York / ADAGP, Paris 152
    Courtesy UCLA University Archives
© Bowness, Hepworth Estate 152
    Courtesy UCLA University Archives

Los Angeles Times

Copyright © 1935 Los Angeles Times. Reprinted with permission 58
Copyright © 1938 Los Angeles Times. Reprinted with permission 71
Copyright © 1935 Los Angeles Times. Reprinted with permission 75
Copyright © 1934 Los Angeles Times. Reprinted with permission 76
Copyright © 1951 Los Angeles Times. Reprinted with permission 112
Copyright © 1970 Los Angeles Times. Reprinted with permission 185
Copyright © 1984 Los Angeles Times. Reprinted with permission 200
Barbara Davidson/Copyright © 2009 Los Angeles Times. Reprinted with permission 267

Songs

"Tokyo Rose"
*L (Special) 99–12, Abe Burrows Collection of Sound Recordings, Rodgers and Hammerstein Archives of Recorded Sound, The New York Public Library for the Performing Arts 86

"Sons of Westwood"
Written by Jerry Livingston, Kelly James and Bill Hansen 332

Images identified by page reference here are either copyright to or the property of the persons or institutions listed. All images, apart from those listed below, are reproduced with the permission of, and are copyright to, the Regents of the University of California. The following images appear in alphabetical order and are copyrighted as follows:

The Academy of Motion Picture Arts and Sciences 172x4; Ansel Adams/UCLA University Archives 167x2; Courtesy of the Arnold Schönberg Center Foundation 97; Associated Press 313; ASUCLA 6, 32, 50, 73, 82, 83, 88, 100, 102, 103, 122, 132, 133, 149, 159, 160, 161, 171, 180, 182, 190, 193x3, 197, 198, 223, 242, 243x2, 259, 263, 272, 277, 301, 302, 307, 311, 324, 327, 338; Courtesy of Darlene Bailey 71; ©Ballantine Books, a subsidiary of Random House, image courtesy of Captain Ahab's Rare Books 110; The Bancroft Library/University of California, Berkeley 26, 37, 86x2, 99, 121x2, 163; Leslie Barton 266; The Benjamin and Gladys Thomas Air Photo Archives, Spence Air Photos Inc. 61, 270; Courtesy of Stan Benson 153; Betty Jane Blakely 86; Beth Bloom/ UCLA History Project 65; Courtesy of Adelcarol Booth and Robert. G. Brownstein 321; Eloisa Gomez Borah/UCLA History Project 38; Gus Bronstrup/*San Francisco Chronicle*/The Hearst Corporation 28; Courtesy of Janet Conser Bowen 337; Courtesy of Keith E. Brant 337; Courtesy of Jack Brown 302; *Bruin Life* 25, 27, 31, 40, 59, 70, 82, 87, 88, 89x2, 114, 128, 144, 145, 277, 290, 292x2, 293x2, 295x2, 301, 302, 318, 322, 323, 324, 327x2, 328x4, 329, 330, 331, 335, 342, 343x2; California NanoSystems Institute 248x2; Dan Chavkin/UCLA History Project 49x3, 63x3, 264, 275, 276, 277, 283, 285, 286; Todd Cheney 211, 212x2, 213x2; Todd Cheney/ASUCLA 86, 197, 208, 209, 246, 256x2, 279, 284, 316, 340, 343; *Chicago Herald-American*/The Hearst Corporation 77; Used with the permission of the Conrad Estate 166; Corbis 305; Courtesy of Anita Cotter 217; *Daily Bruin* 22, 27, 31, 45, 53, 74, 76, 77, 81x2, 87, 89x2, 150, 160, 162, 176, 183, 189, 214, 225x2, 232, 234, 236x2, 237x2, 338; *The Daily Californian* 121; Peter DaSilva Photography 240; Stephanie Diani 222, 223, 238, 302; Stephanie Diani/UCLA Communications 244, 245; Brad Feinknopf 284; Fowler Museum 230x3; Getty Images 86, 136, 138, 204; *Goal Post* 295, 300, 302x3; Courtesy of Steven J. Halpern 201, 202x2; Henry J. Bruman Map Collection in the Charles E. Young Research Library 13, 23, 37; Henry Samueli UCLA School of Engineering and Applied Science 94x2; *Herald Examiner* Photograph Collection/Los Angeles Public Library 12, 36, 54, 162, 186, 311; Courtesy of Hodgetts + Fung 226; Courtesy of Lucille Hodges 321; Beatrice Hohenegger 191; Reed Hutchinson 263, 265; Reed Hutchinson/UCLA Alumni Association 239; Reed Hutchinson/UCLA Communications 267, 268; Reed Hutchinson/UCLA Health Sciences Media Relations 251, 252x2, 253x3, 254; Harriet Hutton 209, 280, 291, 302; I.K. Curtis Services/ UCLA Capital Programs 271; Ira and Leonore Gershwin Trusts 332; Francine Kellerman 335; Courtesy of Leonard Kleinrock 173; Don Liebig/ASUCLA 47, 309; Don Liebig/UCLA College of Letters and Science 261; *Life* Magazine 335x2; Los Angeles *Evening Express*/The Hearst Corporation 40; Los Angeles Public Library 12x2, 13, 165, 184, 186, 188, 189, 272, 302x2; *The Los Angeles Daily News* Negatives/UCLA Library Department of Special Collections 126, 130x2; *Los Angeles Times* Photographic Archive/UCLA Library Department of Special Collections 51, 52, 75, 77, 105x2, 110, 113, 151, 152, 153, 157, 162, 164x2, 166x2, 178, 180, 183, 184x2, 189, 204, 210, 222, 267, 339; Courtesy of *Los Angeles Times*/UCLA Sports Information 309; Courtesy of Jerry and Susanne McClain 339; Courtesy of Dorothy Marie McCune 321; Courtesy of Steve McNichols 160; Medical Science Development 113; Courtesy of Larry Miles 161; Mississippi Department of Archives and History 160; Courtesy of Kelsey Mitchell 343; Michael Mocciaro/ UCLA History Project 280; Michael Moran 286; Sandra Morgan 313; Courtesy of Gary Nash 179; Tram Nguyen/UCLA History Project 328; ©Nobel Foundation 137; © 2003 by Alan Nyiri, courtesy of the Atkinson Photographic Archive 249; Courtesy of the Pasadena Tournament of Roses 67; Courtesy of Sirena Pellarolo 232; Scott Quintard/ASUCLA 309, 314, 339; Scott Quintard/ UCLA Health Sciences Media Relations 250x2; Sharif Rahman 221x2, 256, 275x2, 284; Robert G. and Ida B. Sproul Collection/The Bancroft Library 54; Courtesy of The Rockefeller University 138; Alain Ronay 164; Norm Schindler/ASUCLA 313; Courtesy of Craig Schwartz and Teri Bond 342; Steve Solis/UCLA Volunteer Center 260; *Southern Alumnus* 80; Courtesy of Stanford Graduate School of Business 139; Steinkamp/Ballogg Photography 285; Courtesy of Ann Sumner 10; Courtesy Ginny Supple 342; Courtesy of Lynn Yoakum Taylor 332; Thelner and Louise Hoover Collection/ UCLA University Archives 18, 33, 34, 42, 43, 46, 48x2, 52, 53x2, 60, 63, 64, 66, 68, 69, 80, 157, 159, 273, 274x4, 294, 334, 342; Stan Troutman/ASUCLA 320, 322; ©1993 G.B. Trudeau. Reprinted with permission of Universal UClick 235; UCLA Alumni Association 50, 83, 137, 197, 199x2, 205, 258, 330, 337, 339; UCLA Athletics Hall of Fame 307; UCLA Bruins Marching Band 206, 332, 342x2; UCLA Capital Programs 273, 278; UCLA Chicano Studies Research Center 232; UCLA Communications 24x3, 30, 45, 46x2, 47, 52, 53, 55x3, 58x2, 65, 66, 70, 89, 90, 92, 110, 120, 137, 138, 141, 142, 148, 150, 154, 156, 158x2, 163, 169, 175, 184, 187x2, 188, 192, 194x2, 196x2, 199, 207, 210, 216, 220, 222, 223, 228, 237, 251, 257, 262, 278, 280, 293, 297, 301, 302, 311, 316, 320, 322x2, 323, 326, 329, 330, 334, 335, 337x2, 302x7, 342x3; UCLA Ethnomusicology Archive 154; UCLA Extension 15, 230; UCLA Film & Television Archive 229x2; UCLA Health Sciences Media Relations 250, 253, 254, 255; UCLA History Project 8–9, 30, 32, 39, 41, 61, 71, 90, 112x2, 113x2, 114, 143, 148x2, 150x3, 151, 153, 160, 162, 174, 182, 183, 185, 195, 196, 198, 200, 203, 206, 211, 219, 220x3, 221, 222, 224x2, 225, 227x2, 231, 241, 244, 247, 255, 256, 278, 281, 285x2, 295, 296, 297, 299, 301, 308, 311, 312, 322, 324, 327x2, 329, 330, 332, 335, 337x2, 338, 340, 341, 342x6; UCLA Jules Stein Eye Institute 147; UCLA Library Department of Special Collections 62x4, 148, 272; UCLA Live 227; UCLA Louise M. Darling Biomedical Library 108; *UCLA Magazine* 29, 71, 81, 82, 85, 88, 89, 90, 92x2, 93x2, 95, 98, 99, 101, 229, 322, 326; UCLA Office of Cultural and Recreational Affairs 200, 280; UCLA Office of Intellectual Property 249; UCLA Sports Information 127x2, 129, 202, 294, 296x2, 287, 297, 298, 301, 302x7, 303, 304x2, 305, 308x2, 310, 312, 314x2, 315x3, 316x2, 326x2, 337; UCLA Student Alumni Association 331, 340; UCLA Trademarks & Licensing 325; UCLA University Archives 11, 14, 15, 17, 18, 19x2, 21, 23, 25, 28, 29x2, 32x2, 33, 35, 36, 38, 41, 42x2, 44, 45, 48, 50, 52, 53, 57, 59, 60, 61, 62, 64, 66x2, 67, 68, 72, 73, 74, 75, 76, 78, 79, 84, 85, 90, 91x2, 93x2, 95x2, 96, 97x2, 98x2, 104, 105, 106x2, 107, 109, 111, 112, 114x2, 115x3, 116, 117, 118, 119, 123, 124, 125x2, 131x2, 134, 135, 136x2, 140, 142, 143, 144x2, 145, 146, 147, 148, 151, 152x2, 154x3, 155, 156, 157, 161, 168, 170, 171, 175, 176, 178, 179, 181x2, 185, 192, 195, 201, 203x3, 207, 227, 228x2, 230, 232, 233, 273, 274, 275, 276, 277, 278x2, 279, 282, 283, 287, 292, 293, 295, 299, 301, 304x2, 306, 308, 310x2, 319, 320, 321x2, 323x2, 330, 331, 332, 333x2, 334, 337, 338x3, 302x6, 342x5; UniCamp 60x2; Courtesy of University of Delaware 139x2; Courtesy of University of Indiana 139; Courtesy of Bob Vogel 184, 185, 187; William Andrews Clark Memorial Library 64, 65x3; Matthew Wilson/UCLA History Project 2, 36, 49, 56, 256, 277, 282, 283, 287, 288, 289; *Yesterday LA* 38; Courtesy of Charles E. Young 175, 177x3, 201x2, 205, 215, 231x2

Source Notes

Each note begins with the page number, followed by the abridged quotation and source information.

PART I: A CHRONOLOGICAL HISTORY

CHAPTER 01 / Origins: 1913–1919

10 "What do you want:" Ann Sumner, interview by Winston Wutkee, 1971, UCLA Oral History Program, 187. • "The only appointment:" Andrew Hamilton and John B. Jackson, *UCLA on the Move*, (Los Angeles: Ward Ritchie Press, 1969), 20.

13 "Whoever brings water:" In a telephone conversation with Cindy Ventuleth, director of development for the Cal State Northridge Oviatt Library, Catherine Mulholland, granddaughter of William Mulholland, confirmed that her grandfather did say, "Whoever brings water brings people," 2009.

14 "The rapid growth:" Edward A. Dickson, *University of California at Los Angeles: Its Origin and Formative Years* (Los Angeles: Friends of the UCLA Library, 1955), 4. • "Public trust:" California Constitution of 1915, art. 9, sec. 9. • "Entirely independent of:" Ibid. • "Full powers of:" California Constitution of 1918, art. 9, sec. 9.

15 "The danger could:" Dickson, *Origin and Formative Years*, 7. • "The University of California:" Ibid. • "A step at a time:" Ibid.

16 "This was a very:" Ibid., 8. • "Municipal University Plan:" *Los Angeles Times*, "Municipal University Greatest Achievement in History of the City," May 30, 1915. • "While this bill:" Dickson, *Origin and Formative Years*, 10. • "We need such:" Hamilton and Jackson, *On the Move*, 4. • "Experiment for one year:" Benjamin I. Wheeler to Edward A. Dickson, Feb. 16, 1916, Edward A. Dickson Papers, Department of Special Collections, UCLA (hereafter cited as Dickson Papers). • "We are not anxious:" Ibid. • "I was very much disappointed:" Dickson, *Origin and Formative Years*, 11. • "It is a distinct duty:" Ibid. • "Quiet campaigning:" Walter Morris Hart to Edward A. Dickson, May 15, 1916, Dickson Papers. • "We would come into distinct:" Benjamin I. Wheeler to Edward A. Dickson, Sept. 15, 1916, Dickson Papers. • "Step two:" Dickson, *Origin and Formative Years*, 16.

17 "The fact that I:" Ibid., 26. • "Men of vision:" Ibid., viii.

18 "They kept repeating:" *Biographical Notes on Ernest Carroll Moore* (Montrose, Calif.: The Ledger, 1959), 1. • "I should preach:" Hamilton and Jackson, *On the Move*, 14. • "An incurable disease:" Ernest Carroll Moore, *I Helped Make a University* (Los Angeles: Dawson's Book Shop, 1952). • "Stressed time and time:" "Ernest Carroll Moore: 'Pillar of a Man,'" UCLA Biographical/Subject Files and Publications compiled by John B. Jackson, UCLA University Archives (hereafter cited as Jackson Collection). • "He was a pillar:" Ibid.

20 "I was not greatly:" Dickson, *Origin and Formative Years*, 18. • "My ultimate objective:" Ibid., 19. • "Developed what seemed:" Ibid. • "It was not easy:" Ibid. • "The training of elementary:" Ibid., 20. • "It is not said:" Moore, *I Helped Make a University*, 46. • "I found Dr. Moore:" Dickson, *Origin and Formative Years*, 21. • "The new Census:" Minutes of the Executive Committee, University of California Board of Regents, March 10, 1919, Records of the President of the University of California, Special Problems Folders, 1899–1958, University Archives, Bancroft Library, University of California, Berkeley (hereafter cited as Special Problems Folders).

21 "Los Angeles should contain:" Otherman Stevens, "University Here, Plan of Shiels," *Los Angeles Examiner*, Nov. 6, 1918. • "Teachers colleges:" Will C. Wood, "Items of Public Interest from Proceedings of the State Board of Education, January 1919," *California Blue Bulletin*, March 1919. • "I saw our prized:" Moore, *I Helped Make a University*, 43. • "The regents will:" Ibid., 47. • "The *Evening Express* says:" Microfilm of Ernest Carroll Moore's Diary, Ernest Carroll Moore Papers, Department of Special Collections, UCLA (hereafter cited as Moore Papers). • "A few students were:" Ibid. • "Old-fashioned horse trading:" Hamilton and Jackson, *On the Move*, 1.

CHAPTER 02 / A "Twig" Grows: 1919–1925

22 "The Normal School:" Editorial, "The Normal School Is Dead–Long Live the Branch University," *Cub Californian*, Sept. 29, 1919. • "We are all starting:" Ibid.

24 "The expressed object:" *Cub Californian*, "Assembly Today. R.O.T.C. a Reality," Dec. 17, 1920. • "Jazzy first-class dance:" *Cub Californian*, "Radio Club Plans Music by Wireless," Nov. 10, 1921. • "The cards, the queens:" Associated Students, "Student's Handbook of the University of California, Southern Branch," 1926–27, UCLA History Project Collection.

25 "A sentiment sympathetic with:" Henry F. Withey to State Normal School Board of Trustees, July 5, 1918, Subject Files (Vermont), UCLA University Archives, UCLA. • "The beautiful buildings:" Associated Students, Southern Branch of the University of California, *Southern Campus* (1920), 18.

26 "They were enhanced:" Ibid. • "We were off:" Moore, *I Helped Make a University*, 51. • "We were embarked:" Ibid., 59. • "In a normal school:" Ibid., 60. • "Our kind of work:" Ibid., 61. • "Mr. Sproul quite took:" Ibid.

27 "Will never be anything:" Ibid., 51. • "Six years was:" Dickson, *Origin and Formative Years*, 31. • "We must not only:" Editorial, "The Normal School Is Dead–Long Live the Branch University," *Cub Californian*, Sept. 29, 1919. • "The normal school that:" Moore, *I Helped Make a University*, 63. • "Oski wow-wow!:" Verne A. Stadtman, ed., *The Centennial Record of the University of California* (Berkeley, Calif.: University of California Print Department, 1967), 115.

28 "It is an absolute:" Editorial, "U.C. at L.A.," *Cub Californian*, Nov. 17, 1922. • "Just the thing:" Ibid. • "As a rule editorially:" Dickson, *Origin and Formative Years*, 34. • "Keep the University Intact!:" Editorial, "Keep University Intact," *San Francisco Chronicle*, Jan. 13, 1923. • "If something in the nature:" Dickson, *Origin and Formative Years*, 34.

29 "The 'third year issue':" Ibid., 28. • "We are trying to:" Moore, *I Helped Make a University*, 67.

31 "The welcome news:" *Cub Californian*, "Regents Vote Complete Four-Year Courses for Liberal Arts College," Dec. 12, 1923. • "The regents have established:" Marjorie Butler, "Cubs Joyous Over Branch Expansion," *Los Angeles Record*, Dec. 13, 1923. • "I'm drunk:" Author's Note: Derived from accounts in 1924 *Southern Campus*, p. 49, and "25 Years Ago–December, 1923" by Mimi Koumrian, *UCLA Magazine*, Dec. 1948. • "There was intoxication:" Southern Branch of the University of California, *Southern Campus* (1924), 49.

32 "What is research?:" Loye H. Miller, *The Fossil Birds of California* (Los Angeles: University of California at Los Angeles, 1929), 2. • "The instructor needs:" Ibid., 3. • "No less does:" Ibid. • "Research should be:" Ibid., 4.

33 "A symbol of a long:" Southern Branch of the University of California, *Southern Campus* (1924), 49.

CHAPTER 03 / Westwood Bound: 1925–1929

34 "Eager Rush:" Mildred Adams, "Eager Rush of Students Swamps Colleges," *The New York Times*, Sept. 26, 1926. • "California Colleges:" *The New York Times*, "California Colleges Unequal to Demands," Nov. 14, 1920.

36 "The campus is so:" Unidentified local newspaper, author's collection. • "The institution must:" Robert G. Sproul to Edward A. Dickson, March 26, 1923, Dickson Papers. • "To secure a satisfactory:" James R. Martin, *The University of California (in Los Angeles); A Resume of the Selection and Acquisition of the Westwood Site* (Los Angeles, 1925), 72. • "A university location:" William W. Campbell to James R. Martin, Dec. 2, 1924, Committee on Sites for the Southern Branch of the University Administrative Files, UCLA University Archives (hereafter cited as Committee on Sites).

37 "We had a splendid:" Dickson, *Origin and Formative Years*, 41. • "To possess superior advantages:" William W. Campbell to James R. Martin, Dec. 2, 1924, Committee on Sites. • "None of us:" Dickson, *Origin and Formative Years*, 47.

38 "In every way:" Hamilton and Jackson, *On the move*, 60. • "In a few days:" Janss Investment Corporation advertisement, UCLA History Project Collection. • "Drive into Westwood:" Ibid. • "The corner store:" *Los Angeles Times*, "First Westwood Business Unit," Aug. 26, 1928. • "The Village:" *Los Angeles Times*, "Westwood Shopping Area Springs from Bean Field," Nov. 28, 1976.

39 "I took my hydraulic:" Herbert B. Foster, interview by Amelia Roberts Fry, Regional Oral History Project, Bancroft Library, University of California, Berkeley, 121. • "The coming Park Avenue:" Janss Investment Corporation advertisement, UCLA History Project Collection. • "As UCLA and Westwood:" "UCLA and Westwood Grew Up Together," a speech by Charles E. Young, Aug. 7, 1980, Administrative Files of Nancy Naylor, UCLA University Archives.

40 "Being an established institution:" Martin, *Resume of the Selection and Acquisition*, 83. • "We, the City Council:" Ibid., 195. • "Is protected on three:" Ibid., 84. • "Ralph, I think:" Ralph P. Merritt, interview by Corrine S. Gilb, 1956, UCLA Oral History Program, 63.

41 "Parents! Keep the University:" "Parents! Keep the University for Our Children," Subject Files (Campus [Westwood] Site Selection), UCLA University Archives. • "The amount asked from:" Transcript of Fred Jordan's speech on KNX May 2, 1925, Committee on Sites. • "There should not be:" Ibid. • "For I am certain:" William Fox to James R. Martin, April 22, 1925, Committee on Sites.

42 "Greatest bonfire:" *Los Angeles Times*, "Huge 'Bond Fire' Tonight at New Westwood Site," May 4, 1925. • "During the last two:" Ibid.

43 "The rock was:" Marina Dundjerski, "For Six Bruin Pioneers, Returning to Campus Awakens Vivid Memories of When Both They and UCLA Were Very Young," *UCLA Magazine*, Fall 2002. • "There was dirt:" Ibid. • "Glowing hopes:" Loye H. Miller, *Birds of the Campus* (Berkeley, Calif.: University of California Press, 1947), 2.

45 "Each person there tried:" Moore, *I Helped Make a University*, 106. • "It is to be:" *Hollywood Citizen*, "Founders' Rock Comes 85 Miles to Start a New Tradition at U.C.," Feb. 20, 1926. • "Around which student body:" "UCLA Founder's Rock: Chronology," University Archives Reference Collection. • "We were extremely pleased:" William E. Forbes, interview by David P. Gist, 1989, UCLA Oral History Program, 47.

46 "Just as our parent:" Dickson, *Origin and Formative Years*, 59.

47 "Avenue to the future:" Unidentified local newspaper, "University Celebrates Work Done," Oct. 23, 1927, Subject Files (Arroyo Bridge), UCLA University Archives. • "In opening this bridge:" Ibid. • "The traditions of:" Hamilton and Jackson, *On the Move*, 55.

48 "Royce knows everything:" Moore, *I Helped Make a University*, 99. • "His name will not:" Ibid. • "Why not paint:" Ibid., 102.

49 "Education is learning:" Ibid., 100.

50 "It states the only:" Ibid., 101. • "Here is an anomalous:" William Wallace Campbell to Garret W. McEnerney, March 9, 1925, Records of the President of the University of California.

51 "Resolved, if and when:" Moore, *I Helped Make a University*, 68. • "I lived in a:" Ibid., 70. • "What I object to:" Ibid., 49. • "We win:" Ibid., 50. • "'Cal Hall':" *Southern Alumnus*, "'Cal' Hall Burns to the Ground in Spectacular Campus Fire," January 1929. • "Everyone said that:" Ibid. • "That old barracks:" Hamilton and Jackson, *On the Move*, 62.

52 "Taking possession:" Microfilm of Ernest Carroll Moore's Diary, May 31, 1929, Moore Papers. • "It was a thrilling:" Ibid.

53 "Thus do long dreams:" Illustration, "Director E.C. Moore," *Daily Bruin*, Sept. 20, 1929. • "Your University welcomes you:" Ibid. • "U.C.L.A. looks forward:" *Daily Bruin*, "Assembly Occupies Royce Hall for First Time Yesterday," Sept. 24, 1929.

54 "The Relation of Physical: *Addresses Delivered at the Dedication of the New Campus and New Buildings of the University of California at Los Angeles*, March 27 and 28, 1930, UCLA History Project Collection, 3. • "It is well:" Ibid., 55. • "When shall we realize:" Ibid., 56. • "California is more willing:" *Los Angeles Times*, "Western Schools Praised," March 28, 1930. • "Closer to the people:" Ibid.

55 "We conceive of it:" *Addresses Delivered at the Dedication of the New Campus*. • "It is in this spirit:" Ibid., 83. • "This University:" Ibid.

CHAPTER 04 / "Boastfulness in California:" 1926–1936

56 "One university:" Author's Note: Robert Gordon Sproul first used the term and idea of "One Great University" in a speech to UCLA students, Sept. 27, 1932, which subsequently became referred to as "One University." • "Los Angeles rises:" Chapin Hall, "Los Angeles Rises Above Depression," *The New York Times*, Aug. 7, 1932.

59 "While it does not:" *California Daily Bruin*, "Financial and Scholastic," Dec. 8, 1930. • "The girl under the bridge:" Hamilton and Jackson, *On the Move*, 73. • "Some other girl:" Ibid. • "This was really:" Bernice Woodson Park, interview by Mary Lee Greenblatt and Betty Lou Young, UCLA Oral History Program, 584. • "Most of us:" Dean E. McHenry, interview by Dale E. Treleven, 1991, UCLA Oral History Program, 109. • "Depression Dance:" *California Daily Bruin*, "Dance Interprets Depression," Oct. 8, 1931.

60 "Suitable:" Ibid. • "Before we'd even:" Adaline C. Guenther, interview by Bernard Galm, 1975, UCLA Oral History Program, 398. • "With financial conditions:" Editorial, "Increased Registration," *California Daily Bruin*, Sept. 14, 1930.

61 "The air riveters:" Ernest C. Moore to John Graham Brooks, Jan. 9, 1932, Moore Papers.

62 "Inadequate to meet:" "History of the UCLA Library," 1962, Subject Files (Library 1950–69), UCLA University Archives. • "The quality of the library:" Franklin D. Murphy, interview by James V. Mink, Dec. 6, 1973, UCLA Oral History Program, 240. • "Mr. Librarian:" Lawrence Clark Powell, "Beanfields, Builders, and Books," Oct. 19, 1954, Jackson Collection.

66 "Unlike his predecessor:" *Time*, "California's Investment," June 2, 1930.

67 "If he leaned out:" Bernice Woodson Park, interview by Mary Lee Greenblatt and Betty Lou Young, UCLA Oral History Program, 586. • "My interest in U.C.L.A.:" John B. Jackson, "Sproul of California," *The U.C.L.A. Magazine*, Oct. 1939, 13. • "Bob Sproul was more:" John Mosqueda, "Dr. Robert Gordon Sproul, Ex-President of UC, Dies," *Los Angeles Times*, Sept. 11, 1975.

68 "I realize I come to this office:" Wallace Sterling, "Robert Gordon Sproul Oral History Project," vol. 2, interview by Suzanne B. Riess, Regional Oral History Office, University of California, Berkeley, 617. • "The greater the scholar:" Cyril C. Nigg, interview by Dale E. Treleven, March 24, 1993, UCLA Oral History Program, 91. • "I am no carpet-bagger:" *Los Angeles Times*, "U.C.L.A. Cheers Sproul's Talk," Sept. 17, 1930. • "We doubt if:" *California Daily Bruin*, Sept. 17, 1930. • "Whizzzz-sock:" *California Daily Bruin*, "Students Welcome First Snow On Local Campus With Miniature War," Jan. 18, 1932.

69 "Only the brave:" Ibid.

70 "Probably no more important:" "Struggle for Graduate Work," Dickson Papers. • "Pork:" Minutes of the Executive Committee, University of California Board of Regents, Aug. 8, 1933, Special Problems Folders. • "Why do we abdicate:" Ibid. • "If, when and as the financial condition:" *Los Angeles Times*, "Fight Won by U.C.L.A.," Aug. 9, 1933. • "We thought we ought to have:" James E. LuValle, interview by Ranford B. Hopkins, Aug. 19, 1986, UCLA Oral History Program, 52. • "It was just trying to be:" Ibid. • "Jimmy LuValle made it possible:" TeriAnne Carpenter, "Building Dedicated to Alumnus for His Contributions to UCLA," *Daily Bruin*, March 4, 1985. • "He was my idol:" Ibid.

71 "Bruin, Brain, Brawn:" *Los Angeles Examiner*, "Ex-Grid Player Wins Ph.D.," June 12, 1938.

72 "Our committees up to this time:" Waldemar Westergaard, interview by Doyce B. Nunis Jr., 1963, UCLA Oral History Program, 104. • "The most important step:" Gustave O. Arlt, interview by Bernard Galm, 1970–71, Oral History Program, 122. • "There has been a growing demand:" *Los Angeles Times*, "Unit Added by U.C.L.A.," Nov. 20, 1935. • "In its new College:" Frederick W. Cozens, "The College of Applied Arts," *Southern Alumnus*, June 1939. • "I am not prepared:" Ibid. • "We have something which:" Ibid. • "We'll all be graduating soon:" Hamilton and Jackson, *On the Move*, 188.

73 "The [Berkeley] Alumni Association:" Author's Note: Derived from multiple quotes by Jackson regarding the formation of the UCLA Alumni Association. John B. Jackson," interview by James V. Mink, 1984, UCLA Oral History Program, 78. • "Absolutely not:" Ibid., 79. • "Independent control of finances:" George Elmendorf, "A New Alumni Association," *Southern Alumnus*, April 1934. • "The Cal people:" John B. Jackson, interview by James V. Mink, 1984, UCLA Oral History Program, 80. • "Sproul tried to get:" Author's Note: Derived from multiple quotes by Jackson regarding the formation of the UCLA Alumni Association. Ibid., 81. • "When it was a lower division:" Verne A. Stadtman, *The University of California, 1868–1968* (New York: McGraw-Hill, 1970), 269. • "May I count upon you to raise:" *Daily Bruin*, Oct. 30, 1936.

74 "A single University of California:" Minutes of the Committee on Educational Policy, University of California Board of Regents, Feb. 11, 1937, Regents of the University of California, Office of the Secretary and Chief of Staff. • "Hypersensitivity against Red:" Author's Note: Derived from "Provost Ernest Carroll Moore of U.C.L.A. is distinguished for his hypersensitiveness to Red." *Time*, "Provost's Purge," Nov. 19, 1934.

75 "Did I hear someone mention:" Waldemar Westergaard, interview by Doyce B.

Nunis Jr., 1963, UCLA Oral History Program, 114. • "Communist psychosis:" Ibid., 111. • "By force if necessary:" *Time*, "Provost's Purge," Nov. 19, 1934. • "Where they would be visible:" *Los Angeles Times*, "Symbols Blaze at U.C.L.A.; Handbills Distributed; Strike Awaited," April 11, 1935. • "Eerie figures swarmed:" Ibid. "Peace Hill:" handbill, Student Activism Collection, UCLA University Archives.

76 "University of the Black Hand:" Upton Sinclair, *The Goose-Step: A Study of American Education*, (Pasadena, Calif.: The author, 1923). • "Using their offices to assist:" Ernest Carroll Moore, Memorandum, Oct. 29, 1934, Chancellor's Office Administrative Files of Provost Ernest Carroll Moore, UCLA University Archives (hereafter cited as Moore Administrative Files). • "100 per cent in any action:" Handwritten petition, Moore Administrative Files.

77 "I disapprove of Communists:" *Los Angeles Times*, "Sproul's Plea Blocks Student Class Strike," Nov. 6, 1934. • "The University must tell its students:" *Southern Alumnus*, "The University Faces the Problem of Radicalism," June 1934. • "Happens to be a man:" Editorial, *Los Angeles Evening Post*, Nov. 15, 1934. • "It is 19 years since:" Microfilm of Ernest Carroll Moore's Diary, March 25, 1936, Moore Papers.

CHAPTER 05 / "We Are at War:" 1936–1945

78 "The Yanks are not coming:" *Los Angeles Times*, "Students Oppose War Preparations," May 25, 1940. • "Joe Bruin votes for a warless world:" Handbill, Student Activism Collection, UCLA University Archives.

80 "War instead of peace:" *California Daily Bruin*, "War Instead of Peace," February 1942.

81 "Los Angeles area:" *California Daily Bruin*, "Bombers Near Coast," Dec. 9, 1941.

82 "We are at War:" Editorial, "Verse from the Campus," *California Daily Bruin*, Dec. 9, 1941. • "The present emergency:" *California Daily Bruin*, "Students, Faculty Warned by Hedrick in Emergency," Dec. 12, 1941. • "To look for enemy planes:" *California Daily Bruin*, "Southland Darkened for First Complete Blackout," Dec. 11, 1941. • "We went up:" Earl J. Miller, interview by John B. Jackson, 1975, UCLA Oral History Program.

83 "Normalcy in as many:" *Daily Bruin*, "Local Social Events Held Despite War," Jan. 6, 1942. • "A new University:" *California Daily Bruin*, "War Council Proposes Three Year Curriculum," Jan. 5, 1942.

84 "With all the changes:" *UCLA Alumni Monthly*, "A Message From the President," September 1942. • "Prepare ourselves:" *California Daily Bruin*, "Our Part of the Job," Dec. 9, 1941. • "There are approximately 200:" *California Daily Bruin*, "Nisei Tell War Role," Dec. 10, 1941. • "Since the Pearl Harbor:" Jimmie Arima, "From a Japanese Student," *California Daily Bruin*, Jan. 8, 1942.

85 "Professor Hedrick stumbled:" A.L. Buckman to Alexander Hamilton, July 5, 1966, Pioneer Alumni Association Correspondence and Memorabilia, UCLA University Archive. • "America will be responsible:" *The U.C.L.A. Magazine*, "Dr. Hedrick Retires," September 1942. • "Through his research:" William M. Whyburn, Bennet M. Allen and Waldemar Westergaard, "Earle Raymond Hedrick, 1876–1943," *University of California: In Memoriam* (University of California, Academic Senate).

87 "I really don't know:" Toshiko Nakamura Wilkerson, interview by Talleah Bridges McMahon (UCLA History Project), May 11, 2007. • "You felt like:" Meriko Hoshiyama, interview by Talleah Bridges McMahon (UCLA History Project), May 11, 2007. • "To the general population:" Naoyuki Takasugi, interview by Talleah Bridges McMahon (UCLA History Project), May 11, 2007. • "Prescribe military areas:" Executive Order no. 9066, *Resulting in the Relocation of* Japanese, (1942). • "Military necessity:" *Los Angeles Times*, "Alien Barred Zones Fixed," March 3, 1942. • "Instructions to All Persons:" Western Defense Command and Fourth Army Wartime Civil Control Administration, Poster "Instructions to All Persons of Japanese Ancestry," UCLA History Project Collection. • "All students who leave:" *California Daily Bruin*, "University Grants Full Refunds for Students Hit by Evacuation Order," March 5, 1942. • "Surprise!:" Hitoshi Yonemura to Betty Jane Lissner, Nov. 24, 1943, UCLA History Project Collection.

88 "Well, the government's:" Frank Mankiewicz, interview with Talleah Bridges McMahon (UCLA History Project), Jan. 19, 2007. • "And of course:" Ibid. • "Be our guests:" Editorial, "Letter from Babe," *Daily Bruin*, Dec. 8, 1942. • "Message:" Associated Students UCLA, *Southern Campus* (1943), 240.

89 "Stay behind the team:" *Daily Bruin*, "And Here's What You Can Do To Help Them," Dec. 11, 1942. • "Blew their horns:" *Daily Bruin*, "War Bond Drive Nets Huge Total," Dec. 14, 1942. • "Bury Hitler:" Associated Students UCLA, *Southern Campus* (1943), 240.

91 "Meatless Tuesday:" *The U.C.L.A. Magazine*, "The Campus and the War," December 1942. • "If a single car:" *California Daily Bruin*, "Gas Pains," Nov. 4, 1942. • "The immediate duty:" Robert G. Sproul, "A Message from the President," *The U.C.L.A. Magazine*, September 1942. • "We were plucked up:" E. Russell Hardwick, interview by Veronique de Turenne (UCLA History Project), Oct. 31, 2006. • "We have given you:" Ibid.

92 "The university could:" Ibid. • "There was a constant:" Robert Alshuler, interview by Talleah Bridges McMahon (UCLA History Project), Oct. 28, 2006.

93 "The day will surely come:" Flora Lewis, "A Man's World?," *Daily Bruin*, Aug. 5, 1941. • "Nowadays practically every one:" *Los Angeles Times*, "War Has Blacked Out Life for 'Joe College'" July 21, 1943. • "It goes to prove:" Lucy Guild Quirk, "Our Campus Goes to War," *The U.C.L.A. Magazine*, Feb. 1943.

94 "What part:" John B. Jackson, "A School of Aeronautical Engineering for U.C.L.A." *The U.C.L.A. Magazine*, March 1943. • "An Act to provide:" "Assembly Bill 1140," *The U.C.L.A. Magazine*, March 1943.

95 "It is particularly appropriate:" *The U.C.L.A. Magazine*, "U.C.L.A. Engineering School Assured as Governor Warren Signs Bill," June 1943. • "Southern California is now:" Ibid. • "Fronts:" *The National Academies*, "El Niño and La Niña: A Meteorologist Looks at the Sea," Oct. 6, 2010.

96 "He arrived here:" Gustave O. Arlt, interview by Bernard Galm, 1975, UCLA Oral History Program, 59. • "He told me:" Ibid. Full quote reads "He told me who he was and said he would like to get a Ph.D. in Germanic languages. Well, he was about forty, forty-two years old at the time, and after looking over his record I told him he would have to complete an undergraduate major before he could get into graduate school." • "I came to this country:" William W. Melnitz, interview by Bernard Galm, 1976, UCLA Oral History Program, 30. • "Luckily enough:" Ibid., 40. • "He was a spectacular:" Gustave O. Arlt, interview by Bernard Galm, 1975, UCLA Oral History Program, 60. • "The greatest empiricist:" *Stanford Encyclopedia of Philosophy*, "Hans Reichenbach," Aug. 24, 2008. • "UCLA presented:" Jan Popper, interview by Leslie K. Greer, 1979, UCLA Oral History Program, 93.

97 "I like the young:" *The U.C.L.A. Magazine*, "Arnold Schoenberg," May 1940. • "While every one:" *Journal of the Arnold Schoenberg Institute*, "A History of the First Complete Recording of the Schoenberg String Quartets," Feb. 1978. • "Certainly that is not:" *California Bruin*, July 28, 1943. • "Gain a wide background:" "UCLA Course Will Teach Americanism," Administrative Files of the Chancellor's Office, UCLA University Archives. • "Students usually know more:" Ibid.

98 "I know that:" Hamilton and Jackson, *On the Move*, 100. • "I am engaged:" *UCLA Magazine*, "UCLA Prof. Contributed to Bomb Development," Sept. 1945.

99 "The trouble here:" Robert M. Underhill, interview by Verne A. Stadtman, 1967, Regional Oral History Office, University of California, Berkeley, 254.

100 "Now I knew:" Ibid., 249. • "But I couldn't tell:" Ibid. • "Our fighting forces':" Program from the presentation of the Army-Navy "E" Production Award, Oct. 16, 1945, Robert Gordon Sproul Personal Papers as President and President Emeritus of the University of California, University of California, Berkeley University Archives (hereafter cited as Sproul Personal Papers) • "The peoples:" *The UCLA Magazine*, "Recognition Given University's Role in Bomb Development," November 1945.

101 "Late campus [habitués]:" Anne Stern, "Siren Wail Jolts Bruins into V-J Demonstration," *California Bruin*, Aug. 17, 1943. • "Many tears:" Ibid.

CHAPTER 06 / A Maturing Campus: 1945–1959

102 "Manpower will still:" *California Daily Bruin*, "Campus Population Rises," Oct. 26, 1945. • "The largest single:" *Los Angeles Times*, "Large New Campus Building to Greet UCLA Students," Sept. 5, 1948.

104 "L.A.'s invisible builder:" Christopher Reynolds, "Long Overlooked, Welton Becket is Getting His Due," *Los Angeles Times*, March 6, 2003. • "Foe of Reds:" *Los Angeles Times*, "Dr. Allen Slated for Chancellor of UCLA," Dec. 14, 1951. • "The University realizes:" *UCLA Magazine*, "Office of Veteran Affairs Established on Westwood Campus," March 1945.

105 "They knew better:" Paul A. Dodd, "Patient Persuader," interview by Thomas Bertonneau, 1981, UCLA Oral History Program, 173. • "Wheelchair scholars:" *Daily Bruin*, "UCLA Registers Greatest Number of Student Paraplegics in US," Sept. 13, 1948. • "Finest of its kind:" Mimi Koumrian, "What's Doing On the Quad," *The U.C.L.A. Magazine*, December 1947.

106 "Earlier in the year:" Clarence A. Dykstra to George I. Haight, Nov. 2, 1944, Clarence A. Dykstra Papers, Department of Special Collections, UCLA (hereafter cited as Dykstra Papers). • "In a sense:" Ibid. • "We hope to get:" Letter, "Dykstra Invites Campus Public to Open House," *Daily Bruin*, April 27, 1945.

107 "Out into the world:" Hamilton and Jackson, *On the Move*, 109. • "We can do great:" Ibid., 110. • "Many of our larger:" Clarence A. Dykstra, "Tomorrow's Colleges Will Be Crowded Too," Andrew Hamilton Papers, Department of Special Collections, UCLA (hereafter cited as Hamilton Papers). • "For he's a jolly good fellow:" Associated Students UCLA, *Southern Campus*, (1949), 24. • "Which was the only:" *UCLA Alumni Magazine*, "Clarence Addison Dykstra, 1883–1950," May 1950. • "Provost Dykstra will:" University of California Office of Public Information, Sherrill Luke Remarks at Clarence A. Dykstra Memorial Service, news release, May 10, 1950, Administrative Files of the Chancellor's Office, UCLA University Archives.

108 "Being able to disagree:" Ibid. • "You've got to have:" Andrew Hamilton, "They Can't Say No to 'Dyke,'" Andrew Hamilton Papers. • "It's your department:" Ibid. • "Plane leaving for:" Ibid. • "This series of losses:" Harvie Branscomb to Clarence A. Dykstra, Jan. 24, 1949, Administrative Files of the Chancellor's Office, UCLA University Archives. • "Handmaidens of medicine:" Myrna Oliver, "Lulu Hassenplug: Founded UCLA School of Nursing," *Los Angeles Times*, Sept. 1, 1995.

109 "Purposeful as an:" *California Bruin*, "Introducing a Provost," Feb. 9, 1945. • "Much to be said:" Associated Students UCLA, *Southern Campus* (1950). • "We are training:" Harry Nelson, "Woman of the Year: She Broadens Nurses' Horizons," *Los Angeles Times*, Feb. 15, 1959. • "I don't know what:" Lulu Wolf Hassenplug, interview by Judi Goodfriend, 1987, UCLA Oral History Program, 223. • "So we said:" Ibid., 224. • "You can get your:" Ibid., 225.

110 "I had no money:" Ray Bradbury, "Fahrenheit 451 Revisited," *UCLA Magazine*, Summer 2002. • "The wonderful thing:" Ibid.

111 "It is vital that:" Stafford L. Warren to James H. Corley, June 3, 1947, Administrative Files of Stafford L. Warren, UCLA University Archives. • "There is no area:" *UCLA Magazine*, "The University at Sacramento," March 1946, 4.

113 "Everyone expected:" *UCLA Medicine*, "The UCLA School of Medicine Celebrates 40 Years of Excellence," Fall 1991. • "This means that you:" Ibid.

114 "What really gave:" Ibid.

115 "Because this is:" William S. Barton, "UCLA Atomic Age Center to Get Start," *Los Angeles Times*, Aug. 5, 1951.

116 "Ever since the establishment:" *UCLA Magazine*, "Regent Edward A. Dickson Establishes Alumnus Award," June 1946. • "UCLA was where:" *Los Angeles Times*, "UCLA Notables," Oct. 21, 1979. • "It was during:" Ibid. • "Irrelevant to the:" Keith E. Brant, interview by Bill O'Reilly, "The O'Reilly Factor" (Fox News Network), May 12, 2003. • "The forerunner of a long line:" *UCLA Magazine*, "Regent Edward A. Dickson Establishes Alumnus Award," June 1946.

117 "A law school:" Robert Gordon Sproul to William H. Waste, March 15, 1933, excerpted in W.C. Pomeroy, "Excerpts from Report on Legal Education," March 1934, UCLA University Archives. • "In terms of numbers:" Ibid. • "I felt the need:" William Rosenthal, interview by Bernard Galm, 1986, UCLA Oral History Program, 3. • "Too provincial:" Ibid., 6. • "Being a novice:" Ibid., 3.

118 "As soon as my bill:" Ibid., 20. • "Unasked and unsponsored:" *California Bruin*, "Legislature Puts OK on Law School Bill," June 26, 1947.

119 "His view concerning:" Victor R. Hansen to Robert G. Sproul, Dec. 23, 1948, Special Problems Folders. • "There are no Communists:" "UCLA Law Dean Tells Affiliates: No Communists on Law Faculty," unidentified local newspaper, Feb. 9, 1950, Biographical Files (L. Dale Coffman), UCLA University Archives. • "Harvard was always:" Dan Gordon, "History of UCLA School of Law: A History of Innovation," *UCLA Law*, Fall 2004. • "Our first several:" Ibid.

120 "The greatest contaminant:" Kerr, *The Gold and the Blue*, vol. 2, Political Turmoil, 28. • "Isolate, expose and remove:" Minutes of the Regents of the University of California, Regular Session, March 25, 1949.

121 "Providing that all facilities of the University:" Minutes of the Regents of the University of California, Executive Session, Feb. 25, 1949. • "I have never:" *California Daily Bruin*, "Dykstra Upholds Student Rights," Nov. 16, 1945. • "I do not believe:" excerpted from Board of Regents minutes, March 25, 1949. Regents of the University of California, Office of the Secretary and Chief of Staff. • "I am not a member:" Transcript of Regents Meeting, June 24, 1949, Regents of the University of California, Office of the Secretary and Chief of Staff.

122 "The University of California:" Editorial, "U.C. Loyalty Oath," *San Francisco Chronicle*, Feb. 28, 1950. • "Singled out:" *San Francisco Chronicle*, "Warren Lambastes UC Loyalty Oath," Feb. 28, 1950.

123 "Do I understand:" John Caughey, "A University in Jeopardy," *Harper's Magazine*, November 1950. • "University personnel cannot:" *Tolman v. Underhill*, 39 Cal. 2d 708 (1952). • "Civil defense workers:" John W. Caughey, "Farewell to California's 'Loyalty' Oath," *Pacific Historical Review*, May 1969, 125. • "The cost was:" David S. Saxon, interview by James V. Mink and Dale E. Treleven, 1994, UCLA Oral History Program, 135.

124 "Evils of centralized administrative authority:" "Report of Sub-committee on Appointment of a Provost at U.C.L.A.," Oct. 13, 1950, to the Committee on Southern California Schools, Colleges and Institutions. Administrative Files of the Chancellor's Office, UCLA University Archives. • "Single head not on paper, but in fact:" Report of the Committee on Southern California Schools, Colleges and Institutions," Oct. 26, 1950. Administrative Files of the Chancellor's Office, UCLA University Archives. • "Chancellor and president:" Memo, Edward A. Dickson, "Reorganization Plans," Dickson Papers.

125 "He has threaded:" *Time*, "Diplomat's Progress," Dec. 24, 1951. • "A Communist is incompetent:" John T. McQuiston, "Raymond B. Allen, Ex-Chief of University of Washington," *The New York Times*, March 24, 1986. • "His appointment at UCLA:" *Los Angeles Times*, "Raymond B. Allen, First Chancellor at UCLA, Dies at 83," March 22, 1986. • "I feel that I have adequate:" John B. Jackson, "Chancellor States Views and Policies For His New Administration at UCLA," *UCLA Alumni Magazine*, December 1952. • "I feel that I have completed my job:" Dick Turpin, "UCLA Chancellor Dr. Allen Resigns," *Los Angeles Times*, June 13, 1959.

126 "Designed to do:" News release, University of California Office of Public Information, March 30, 1951. • "The position was totally:" Kerr, *The Gold and the Blue*, vol. 1, Academic Triumphs, 24. • "Sproul's opposition:" Ibid., 46. • "There is, then, nothing:" George Pope Shannon, "Academic Freedom and Tenure: Report of Committee A for 1947," *Bulletin of the American Association of University Professors*, Spring 1948, 127. • "Allen formula:" *Los Angeles Times*, "Dr. Allen Slated for Chancellor of UCLA," Dec. 14, 1951. • "Academic freedom consists:" Ibid. • "His fight to oust:" Ibid. • "We have looked:" Ibid.

127 "Contact man:" Rue Corey, "New Chancellor Given Local Contact Man Job," *Daily Bruin*, Nov. 17, 1952. • "Committed itself to setting up:" Jack Weber, "Sproul Hits Charge of UC 'Spy System'," *Daily Bruin*, March 31, 1952. • "It involved no espionage:" Ibid. • "It's hard for anyone:" Byron H. Atkinson, interview by Tine Brouwer Spencer, 1974, 88, UCLA Oral History Program. • "The Oregon schools:" Cyril C. Nigg, interview by Dale E. Treleven, March 24, 1993, UCLA Oral History Program, 128.

128 "Secret deals with athletes:" *Los Angeles Times*, "UCLA Probe Under Way on Charges of Grid Pay," March 4, 1956. • "No surprise:" *Los Angeles Times*, "No Surprise, Says UCLA's Chancellor," May 20, 1956. • "If out of the investigations:" Ibid. • "Injustice:" *Los Angeles Times*, "Gov. Knight Asks Regents for Action," May 24, 1956. • "The reaction has been:" Editorial by Harry Longway, "The PCC Controversy," *UCLA Alumni Magazine*, July 15, 1956. • "I'll get it done the next time:" Robert and Blanche Campbell, interview by John B. Jackson and Joel Gardner, UCLA Oral History Program, 73. • "It is regrettable:" University of California Office of Public Information, "Statement by Dr. Raymond B. Allen, Chancellor at U.C.L.A.," news release, May 22, 1956. Records of the President of the University of California, Numerical Bound Folders, 1929–1958, Berkeley University Archives (hereafter cited as Numerical Bound Folders).

129 "I shall fight:" Raymond B. Allen speech to the Commonwealth Club, June 8, 1956, Numerical Bound Folders. • "What it all boils:" Andrew Hamilton to Robert Gordon Sproul, July 13, 1956, Numerical Bound Folders. • "Their thought processes:" Ibid. • "His coach, Chuck Taylor:" Paul Zimmerman, "Proposal by Knight Ignites Controversy," *Los Angeles Times*, July 14, 1956. • "Immediate steps:" Minutes of the UCLA Alumni Association Executive Council, June 18, 1957, UCLA Board of Directors Minutes 1955–1957, UCLA Alumni Association. • "Telephone switchboards at Southern Cal:" Frank Finch, "SC, UCLA Withdrawal Threats Die Out," *Los Angeles Times*, Dec. 4, 1956.

130 "In the end:" Kerr, *The Gold and the Blue*, vol. 1, Academic Triumphs, 108. • "Long-simmering differences:" Dick Turpin, "UCLA Chancellor Dr. Allen Resigns," *Los Angeles Times*, June 13, 1959. • "Perhaps I was wrong:" Raymond B. Allen to Robert G. Sproul and Ida Sproul, 1967. Sproul Personal Papers. • "These are interesting and challenging times:" Turpin, "Dr. Allen Resigns." *Los Angeles Times*, June 13, 1959. • "Factional fighting:" Kerr, *The Gold and the Blue*, vol. 1, Academic Triumphs, 337. • "In particular, their wishes:" Ibid.

131 "May or may not:" Leo P. Delsasso, Gold Medal Award –1967, *Journal of the Acoustical Society of America*, Vol. 42, 1967. • "Keep on thinking and:" Chancellor's Farewell Address to the Graduates, June 10, 1960, UCLA University Archives. • "Over the past 30 years:" Editorial, "The Achievements of Vern Knudsen," *Los Angeles Times*, July 7, 1960. • "Most men would be content:" Ibid.

CHAPTER 07 / Fighting for Identity: 1959–1968

132 "Tidal wave:" Marian L. Gade and George Strauss, "Clark Kerr," *University of California: In Memoriam* (University of California, Academic Senate). • "Tuition free:" Liason Committee of the Regents of the University of California and the California State Board of Education, *Master Plan for Higher Education in California, 1960–1975* (Assembly of the State of California, 1960).

134 "'Independence' seems to be:" Al Rothstein, "UCLA Asserts Its Independence," *Daily Bruin*, March 20, 1961. • "Multiversity:" Clark Kerr, *The Gold and the Blue: A Personal Memoir of the University of California, 1949–1967*, vol. 1, *Academic Triumphs*, (Berkeley: UC Press, 2001), 268. • "We must be in:" Franklin D. Murphy, "The Relevance of the University (Farewell to Graduates)," June 9, 1966. Administrative Subject Files of Franklin D. Murphy, UCLA University Archives. • "Filthy speech:" *Los Angeles Times*, "Top State Nominees–Ronald Reagan–Republican for Governor," Sept. 13, 1966.

135 "An impossible job:" Franklin D. Murphy, interview by James V. Mink, Oct. 18, 1973, UCLA Oral History Program, 18. • "Could enter a room:" Ursula Vils, "Secretary With the Answers," *Los Angeles Times*, July 10, 1968. Full quote reads "He's the only man I know who can go out two doors at once." • "Murphyisms:" Hamilton and Jackson, *On the Move*, 134. • "Free marketplace:" Robert Vosper, "Introduction" in Franklin D. Murphy, interview by James V. Mink, Oct. 18, 1973, UCLA Oral History Program. • "Intellectual ferment:" Hamilton and Jackson, *On the Move*, 134. • "Often such a designation:" Robert Vosper, "Introduction" in Franklin D. Murphy, interview by James V. Mink, Oct. 18, 1973, UCLA Oral History Program.

136 "The future:" Willard F. Libby, "Banquet Speech," Nobelprize.org, http://www.nobelprize.org/nobel_prizes/chemistry/laureates/1960/libby-speech.html. • "The theoretical achievements:" Robert Finkelstein, Margaret Kivelson and David Saxon, "Julian Seymour Schwinger, Physics: Los Angeles," *University of California: In Memoriam* (University of California, Academic Senate). • "for their development:" "The Nobel Prize in Chemistry 1987," Nobelprize.org, http://www.nobelprize.org/nobel_prizes/chemistry/laureates/1987/. • "Cages:" Ron Bell, "UCLA Professor Wins Nobel Prize," *Daily Bruin*, Oct. 15, 1987. • "I have always felt:" Ibid.

137 "Currency of cells:" UCLA Media Relations, "UCLA Biochemist Paul Boyer Wins 1997 Nobel Prize in Chemistry," news release, Oct. 15, 1997. • "The

Nobel Prize:" Cynthia Lee, "A Hero Comes Home," *UCLA Today*, Oct. 28, 1998.

138 "May there be:" Ralph Bunche "Acceptance Speech," Nobelprize.org, http://www.nobelprize.org/nobel_prizes/peace/laureates/1950/bunche-acceptance.html. • "For their discoveries "The Nobel Prize in Chemistry 1951," Nobelprize.org, http://www.nobelprize.org/nobel_prizes/chemistry/laureates/1951/. • "UCLA was my only:" Glenn T. Seaborg, *Adventures in the Atomic Age* (New York: Farrar, Straus and Grioux), 17. • "After that course:" "UCLA Alumni Honored as Nobel Laureates," UCLA Gateway, http://www.ucla.edu/alumnistudenthonors/nobel-alumni.html. • "Simple and ingenious:" The Royal Swedish Academy of Sciences, "The 1984 Nobel Prize in Chemistry," news release, October 17, 1984. • "Merrifield Breakthrough:" "1997 Alumnus of the Year Program," Award Files, UCLA Alumni Association. • "I received all:" Ibid.

139 "Both had a major:" William F. Sharpe, "Autobiography," Nobelprize.org, http://www.nobelprize.org/nobel_prizes/economics/laureates/1990/sharpe.html. • "Analysis of economic:" "The Sveriges Riksbank Prize in Economic Sciences in Memory of Alfred Nobel 2009," Nobelprize.org, http://www.nobelprize.org/nobel_prizes/economics/laureates/2009/. • "I was assigned:" Ibid. • "For palladium-catalyzed:" "The Nobel Prize in Chemistry 2010," Nobelprize.org, http://www.nobelprize.org/nobel_prizes/chemistry/laureates/2010/.

140 "Must definitely not:" Kerr, *The Gold and the Blue*, vol. 1, *Academic Triumphs*, 336. • "Anti-UCLA:" Ibid., 337. • "Dominant regents:" Ibid., 337.

141 "'Brash' and 'pushy:'" Ibid., 338.CITE? • "Perfect for UCLA:" Ibid., 217. • "Charismatic and self-confident:" Ibid., 338. • "Fighting Irishman:" Mort Saltzman, "Murphy Tells Plans for UCLA Distinction," *Daily Bruin*, Sept. 19, 1960. • "Impossible job:" Franklin D. Murphy, interview by James V. Mink, Oct. 18, 1973, UCLA Oral History Program, 18. • "Would destroy a man:" Ibid., 277. • "Have the necessary:" Franklin D. Murphy to Edwin W. Pauley, March 21, 1960, Franklin D. Murphy Papers, Department of Special Collections, UCLA. • "The man from the Midwest:" Mort Salzman, "Kansan Murphy Gets UCLA Post," *Daily Bruin*, March 17, 1960. • "We must have the means:" Mort Salzman, "Murphy Tells Plans for UCLA Distinction," *Daily Bruin*, Sept. 19, 1960. • "You have no idea:" Franklin D. Murphy, interview by James V. Mink, Oct. 18, 1973, UCLA Oral History Program, 33. • "That was the best:" Ibid.

142 "A man of integrity:" Ibid. • "Didn't have any scars:" Ibid., 34. • "Troubleshooter:" Ibid. • "Most effective working:" Ibid., 36. • "After a little while:" Ibid. • "I like to preoccupy:" Ibid., 35. • "Bill is a very decisive:" Ibid., 36. • "So I had the team:" Ibid., 37. • "I conceived of myself:" Ibid., 37.

143 "Executive heads:" University of California Board of Regents, Standing Orders and Bylaws, chap.. IX, sec. 3, March 23, 1951. • "In charge of whatever:" Kerr, *The Gold and the Blue*, vol. 1, *Academic Triumphs*, 42. • "Equal opportunities:" Ibid., 331. • "He must have suffered:" Ibid., 197.

144 "Fully accepted:" Ibid., 203. • "End of the Corley Empire:" Ibid. • "An unspoken vote:" Kerr, *The Gold and the Blue*, vol. 1, *Academic Triumphs*, 198. • "I came in later:" William Trombley, "UCLA Autonomy Fight Believed Won," *Los Angeles Times*, July 25, 1966. • "One university:" Franklin D. Murphy, interview by James V. Mink, Oct. 18, 1973, UCLA Oral History Program, 83. • "University of California:" Ibid., 45.

145 "Harry, I authorized it:" Ibid., 46. • "Berkeley had preempted:" Ibid., 289. • "We will make:" Ibid. • "There were hundreds:" Ibid., 46.

146 "Any time you ask:" Kerr, *The Gold and the Blue*, vol. 1, *Academic Triumphs*, 338. • "Tearing down Clark Kerr's:" Charles E. Young, interview by the author (UCLA History Project), April 17, 2008. • "Whether it was:" Ibid. • "The Berkeley people:" Franklin D. Murphy, interview by James V. Mink, Oct. 18, 1973, UCLA Oral History Program, 50. • "I finally concluded:" Ibid., 59. • "Incidental fees:" Ibid., 285. • "Without Clark Kerr:" Adrian H. Harris, interview by Susan Douglass Yates, 1996–97, UCLA Oral History Program, 91.

148 "All my life:" Ibid, 222.

152 "In his way:" Charles E. Young, interview by the author (UCLA History Project), April 29, 2008. • "He had ties:" Ibid. • "He realized that one:" Charles E. Young, interview by the author (UCLA History Project), May 5, 2006.

153 "Dangers of today:" *Daily Bruin*, "Complete Johnson Text," Feb. 24, 1964. • "Let us:" Ibid. • "Knowledge and freedom:" *Daily Bruin*, "Text of López Mateos Speech," Feb. 24, 1964. • "From these classrooms:" Ibid.

154 "Frankin Murphy was:" William W. Melnitz, interview by Bernard Galm, 1976, UCLA Oral History Program, 74. • "He was interested:" Ibid., 75.

155 "Being on the third:" John R. Wooden, interview by the author (UCLA History Project), Feb. 1, 2006. • "We were down there:" Ibid.

156 "Sing for a Pavilion:" Rue Corey, "A Welding Force for Campus Unity," *Daily Bruin*, April 18, 1952.

157 "The house that Wooden built:" Richard Hoffer, "UCLA Basketball: Coach Is Secure, Team Is Young," *Los Angeles Times*, Oct. 17, 1980. • "Night and day:" Wooden, interview by the author (UCLA History Project), Feb. 1, 2006. • "We broke their:" Lynn Shackelford, interview by the author (UCLA History Project), March 7, 2008.

158 "Poor Gary:" Ibid. • "It may be true:" Audio of Martin Luther King Jr. speech, April 27, 1965, Associated Students Distinguished Speakers Series, UCLA University Archives.

159 "[Murphy] immediately:" Robert Singleton, interview by Elston L. Carr, Dec. 20, 2006, UCLA Oral History Program, 43–44. • "We would go to:" Ibid., 46. • "One of the things:"Robert Singleton, interview by Talleah Bridges McMahon (UCLA History Project), Dec. 20, 2006.

160 "A sham:" Editorial, "A Sham," *Daily Bruin*, March 9, 1962. • "Create a precedent:" Dave Lawton, "Riders Told to Apply For University Funds," *Daily Bruin*, March 19, 1962. • "Hyde Park:" *Daily Bruin*, "Cuba Debate Opens Forum," Oct. 25, 1962.

161 "We firmly believe:" Ronald Moskowitz, "Free Speech Stand by UCLA Official," *San Francisco Examiner*.

162 "Open forum:" Dini Seigel, "Kerr Limits Group Recognition," *Daily Bruin*, Sept. 18, 1961. • "*Bona fide* students:" Kerr, *The Gold and the Blue*, vol. 2, *Political Turmoil*, 127. • "Far from fostering:" Harry Shearer, Editorial, "The Speech & Reality," *Daily Bruin*, Nov. 6, 1961. • "It was like the world:" Andrea Rich, interview by the author (UCLA History Project), March 31, 2006. • "second greatest:" Kerr, *The Gold and the Blue*, vol. 2, *Political Turmoil*, 161.

163 "Your fellow students:" *Daily Bruin*, "Bruins Urged to Join FSM Drive," Dec. 1, 1964. • "Autocracy:" Transcript, "Mario Savio: Sproul Hall Steps," Dec. 2, 1964, Library, University of California, Berkley, http://www.lib.berkeley.edu/MRC/saviotranscript.html. • "There's a time:" Ibid. • "Me-too clause:" Rick Tuttle, interview by Talleah Bridges McMahon (UCLA History Project), Aug. 26, 2006. • "I didn't want:" Jeffrey Donfeld, interview with Talleah Bridges McMahon (UCLA History Project), Sept. 28, 2006.

164 "Individual rights:" Douglas Kinsey to UCLA alumnus, Jan. 13, 1965, Sproul Personal Papers. • "Even though Mario Savio:" Ibid. • "The Free Speech Movement:" Joel Siegel, "What Do They Say About FSM?" *Daily Bruin*, Dec. 3, 1964. • "Considering the fact:" *Time*, "The Man from U.C.L.A.," Oct. 21, 1966. • "Vacillating administration:" Author's Note: Derived from May 12, 1966 Gubernatorial Primary Campaign Address, "The Morality Gap at Berkeley."

165 "Twilight of a:" Editorial, "Twilight of a Great University," *New York Times*, Jan. 22, 1967. • "There was a lot:" Andrea Rich, interview by the author (UCLA History Project), March 31, 2006. • "If they want tuition:" Art Berman, "Teachers' Union Plans to March on Sacramento," *Los Angeles Times*, Jan. 24, 1967. • "Free and open:" Ibid. • "Fired with enthusiasm:" Kerr, *The Gold and the Blue*, vol. 2, *Political Turmoil*, 309.

166 "Engaged in sprawling:" Seth Rosenfeld, "Reagan, Hoover and the UC Red Scare," *San Francisco Chronicle*, June 9, 2002. • "Kerr is no good:" Memo from C.D. DeLoach to Mr. Mohr, March 20, 1961 (FBI/ Freedom of Information, Privacy Acts), Clark Kerr Personal and Professional Papers (unprocessed), Berkeley University Archives. • "I look on this:" Kerr, *The Gold and the Blue*, vol. 2, *Political Turmoil*, 69. • "Tragedy:" Franklin D. Murphy, interview by James V. Mink, Oct. 18, 1973, UCLA Oral History Program, 164. • "In spite of everything:" Ibid. • "I had no problem:" Ibid., 168. • "I do not intend:" William Trombley, "22,400 Turn-Away," *Los Angeles Times*, Jan. 10, 1967. • "Tuition:" Minutes of a special meeting of the University of California Board of Regents, August 30, 1967, Regents of the University of California, Office of the Secretary and Chief of Staff, 11. • "Tuition-free:" *Master Plan for Higher Education in California, 1960–1975*.

167 "Will Chancellor Franklin:" Editorial, "Ready to listen," *Daily Bruin*, Nov. 16, 1967. • "If it's true:" Chuck Benrubi, "Resignation Stuns University; Officials Praise Murphy," *Daily Bruin*, Feb. 16, 1968. • "Student apathy:" *Daily Bruin*, "Student Apathy Meets Murphy's Resignation," Feb. 19, 1968. • "I was getting:" Franklin D. Murphy, interview by James V. Mink, Oct. 18, 1973, UCLA Oral History Program, 167.

CHAPTER 08 / "In the Middle of a Revolution:" 1968–1975

168 "The saying that to have:" Dorothy Chandler to Charles Young, June 17, 1969, Murphy Administrative Files. • "We who are associated:" Charles E. Young, "From his Fiftieth Anniversary Address to the UCLA Affiliates," *UCLA Alumni Magazine*, Spring 1969.

170 "You and the Draft:" *Daily Bruin*, You and the Draft," Oct. 30, 1967. • "Every conceivable alternative:" *Daily Bruin*, "The Draft–It's Killing Us," Oct. 30, 1967. • "Ending the war starts with you: Editorial, "Strike," *Daily Bruin*, May 10, 1972. • "Dangerous:" Charles E. Young, interview by the author (UCLA History Project), Sept. 2, 2004. • "Chuck Young has been:" Jeff Perlman, "Murphy Officially Resigns; Young Likely Successor," *Daily Bruin*, " Feb. 19, 1968.

171 "I grew up:" Charles E. Young, interview by James V. Mink and Dale E. Treleven, Oct. 29, 1984, UCLA Oral History Program, 25–26. • "I've had the good fortune:" Program from the Public Launch of Campaign UCLA and a Tribute to Chancellor Charles E. Young, May 17, 1997, UCLA History Project Collection. • "A different chancellor:" Zev Yaroslavsky, "25 Years Young," *UCLA Magazine*, Spring 1994.

172 "Chancellor Murphy's recommendation:" Jeff Perlman, "Murphy Officially Resigns; Young Likely Successor," *Daily Bruin*, Feb. 19, 1968. • "Dynamic leadership:" Ibid. • "The most obvious choice:" Editorial, "Indecision," *Daily Bruin*, June 25, 1968.

173 "Dr. Murphy has had a major role:" *University Bulletin*, "Dr. Charles E. Young, 36, Appointed by U.C. Regents to Succeed Dr. Franklin D. Murphy as UCLA Chancellor," July 12, 1968, Biographical Files (Charles E. Young), UCLA University Archives. • "What hath God wrought?:" Leonard Kleinrock, interview by the author (UCLA History Project), Aug. 4, 2005. • "Lo and behold:" Ibid. • "That was it:" Ibid. • "As of now, computer networks:" UCLA Office of Public Information, "UCLA To Be First Station in Nationwide Computer Network," news release, July 3, 1969. • "I indicated that the Internet:" Leonard Kleinrock, email message to Mark Davis and Marina Dundjerski, Sept. 28, 2005.

174 "A different route:" John Dreyfuss, "Regents Appoint Charles E. Young Head of UCLA, *Los Angeles Times*, July 13. 1968. • "From the second level:" "Charles E. Young, 1968–1997," UCLA, http://www.pastleaders.ucla.edu/young.html. • "To see to it:" Charles E. Young, "A Blueprint for the Future," *UCLA Magazine*, Summer 1969, 65. • "Urban problems:" John Dreyfuss, "Regents Appoint Charles E. Young Head of UCLA," *Los Angeles Times*, July 13, 1968. • "One of a new breed:" *UCLA Personnel News*, "Chancellor Charles E. Young To Be Inaugurated May 23," May 1969.

175 "Middle of the road liberal:" Pam Gentry, "New Chancellor Outlines Opinions, Plans," *Daily Bruin*, July 16, 1968. • "Despite his rapport with students:" *Time*, "Young in Heart," Sept. 20, 1968. • "University has an obligation:" John Parker, "Dow Chemical Co. Interviews Picketed," *Daily Bruin*, Feb. 28, 1967. • "Illogical:" *Daily Bruin*, "Young Clarifies Administration's Position," Nov. 15, 1967.

177 "This is a time:" Statement by Charles E. Young, May 22, 1969, Murphy Administrative Files. • "Liberated:" Dial Torgerson, "Radical Coalition's Strike Call at UCLA Gets Slight Support," *Los Angeles Times*, May 23, 1969. • "Came of their own accord:" *Daily Bruin*, "Portable Police," May 23, 1969. • "Chancellor Charles E. Young:" Editorial, "Young's Inauguration–A Big Step," *Daily Bruin*, May 23, 1969. • "Young put his job:" Ibid. • "Further our strike:" *Daily Bruin*, "Norminton Offers Support for UC Sympathy Strike," May 23, 1969.

178 "We must find ways:" *UCLA Magazine*, "Chancellor Charles E. Young Inaugural Address," May 23, 1969. • "At the University of California:" John Davenport, *ABC News*, television broadcast, May 23, 1969, New York: American Broadcasting Companies, Inc. • "Impartial and independent official:" *Daily Bruin*, "UPC Open Meeting Will Discuss Ombudsman," Feb. 25, 1969. • "We are in the middle of a revolution:" *UCLA Personnel News*, "Chancellor Charles E. Young to Be Inaugurated May 23," May 1969. • "California's most bitter fight:" *UCLA Alumni Magazine*, "The Case of Angela Davis," Fall 1969.

179 "Acting instructors:" John Dreyfuss, "UCLA Chancellor to Press Minority Faculty Recruitment," *Los Angeles Times*, Nov. 25, 1968. • "Dilute the quality of UCLA's faculty:" Ibid. • "It was a discretionary program:" C.Z. Wilson, interview by Talleah Bridges McMahon (UCLA History Project), Jan. 23, 2007. • "No political test:" *AAUP Bulletin*, "Academic Freedom and Tenure: The University of California at Los Angeles," Autumn 1971.

180 "Most lawyers on the Board:" William Trombley, "Admitted Red Fired From UCLA Faculty," *Los Angeles Times*, Sept. 20, 1969. • "The regents seem intent:" Angela Davis, Public Statement, Chancellor's Communication Service, Sept. 23, 1969. • "The attempt to dismiss her:" David Kaplan's Press Statement, Sept. 23, 1969, Donald Kalish Papers, UCLA Department of Special Collections. • "Be assigned no teaching duties:" "Resolution Adopted by the Regents," October 1969, Student Activism Collection, UCLA University Archives. • "Regular courses:" Ron Moskowitz, "Regents Bar Red Teacher—UCLA Fears Trouble," *San Francisco Chronicle*, Oct. 4, 1969. • "Cleaver Rule:" John Dreyfuss, "Student Body at UC Demands Regents Rescind Cleaver Ruling," *Los Angeles Times*, Sept. 24, 1968. • "Had damaged the university:" John Dreyfuss, "Limit on Cleaver," *Los Angeles Times*, Sept. 21, 1968. • "On campus, for credit:" Debbie Ashin, "Students pack Davis class," *Daily Bruin*, Oct. 7, 1969. • "It was a very important:" Scott Waugh, interview by the author (UCLA History Project), Feb. 8, 2008 • "Before I proceeded to lecture:" Angela Y. Davis at press conference, *NBC News*, television broadcast, Oct. 7, 1969, New York: National Broadcasting Company.

181 "Is assured of her right:" Addendum of the call to the emergency meeting of the Los Angeles Division of the Academic Senate, Oct. 9, 1969, Chancellor's Communication Service. • "Unlawful and dangerous:" *Daily Bruin*, "Judge says no to UC," Oct. 21, 1969. • "My daddy might get fired:" William Trombley, "Angela Davis: A Time of Testing for Young," *Los Angeles Times*, May 17, 1970. • "Seminal moment:" Charles E. Young, interview by the author (UCLA History Project), Sept. 2, 2004. • "I was finally convinced:" Charles E. Young, interview by the author (UCLA History Project), April 17, 2008. • "We want more!:" Winston Doby, interview by the author (UCLA History Project), Jan. 25, 2008.

182 "The goal was to identify:" Ibid. • "Special procedures:" *A Master Plan for Higher Education in California 1960–1975*. • "The university process:" Virgil P. Roberts, interview by John Huggins, Sept. 17, 1996, UCLA Oral History Program, 62. • "Responsibility for things:" Winston C. Doby, interview by the author (UCLA History Project), Jan.25, 2008.

183 "The issue is not:" Noel Greenwood, "UCLA Phasing Out Program for High-Risk Minority Youth," *Los Angeles Times*, May 3, 1971. • "Why did you give in:" Winston C. Doby, interview by the author (UCLA History Project), Jan.25, 2008. • "I made a particular case:" Charles E. Young, speech to American Association of University Professors, Jan. 26, 1996. • "Area captain:" William J. Drummond and Kenneth Reich, "2 Black Panther Students Slain in UCLA Hall," *Los Angeles Times*, Jan. 18, 1969. 17.

185 "It appears that the historical:" *Daily Bruin*, "BSU Issues Statement to Black Student Body," Jan. 31, 1969. • "People felt even more:" Maulana Karenga, interview by Elston L. Carr, UCLA Oral History Program, 182. • "Friday's double murder:" Martin Rips, "Campus Reacts to Murders, Blacks Silent, Whites Uneasy," *Daily Bruin*, Jan. 21, 1969. • "We have not developed our programs:" Charles E. Young, "UCLA: A Response to the Future," *UCLA Magazine*, Winter 1970.

186 "Intellectually they were correct:" Ibid. • "Every male on the campus:" Zev Yaroslavsky, interview by the author (UCLA History Project), Feb. 22, 2008. • "Whirlypig:" Thomas W. Robinson, ed., *Student Views of American Society: Essays Occasioned by the May 5th, 1970 Incident at U.C.L.A.* (Department of Political Science, UCLA, and Social Science Department, Rand Corporation, 1971), 6. • "In the name of the people:" Ibid., 5. • "His faced was bruised:" "Violence at UCLA: May 5, 1970," A report by the Chancellor's Commission on the Events of May 5, 1970, UCLA University Archives. • "Physically attacking:" *UCLA Weekly*, "Chancellor's Commission Reports on May 5, 1970 Disturbance," Jan. 25, 1971.

187 "Nothing the police did:" Robinson, ed., *Student Views of American Society*, 7. • "That was a period:" Charles E. Young, interview by the author (UCLA History Project), April 29, 2008.

188 "It did linger with you:" Keith Schiller, interview by Talleah Bridges McMahon (UCLA History Project), Sept. 15, 2006. • "Today is not the day:" Editorial, *Daily Bruin*, May 10, 1972.

189 "Stop the war!:" Zev Yaroslavsky, interview by the author (UCLA History Project), Feb. 22, 2008. • "Watch his knees!" Ibid. • "If one vignette:" Ibid.

CHAPTER 09 / "A Landmark Time for Us:" 1975–1989

190 "Bailout:" *Los Angeles Times*, "Anger, Confusion Greet State's 'Bailout' of Southeast," July 2, 1978.

192 "When I became Chancellor:" UCLA Public Affairs Department, *UCLA Annual Report, 1982–83*, "A Message From the Chancellor," 2. • "The initials 'UCLA':" *Los Angeles Times*, "Bearwear is everywhere," Oct. 21, 1979. • "For virtually all [occasions]:" Associated Students UCLA, *Southern Campus*, (1980), 81.

193 "So many people want to get in:" Julie Ogasawara, "Application Increase Causes Stricter Entrance Requirements," *Daily Bruin*, May 31, 1985.

194 "The news so astonished UCLA:" Anne C. Roark, "UCLA: New Standing in Academia," *Los Angeles Times*, July 8, 1984. • "Indicative as anything:" Ibid. • "There is always a kind:" Ibid. • "It is gratifying:" UCLA Office of Media Relations, "UCLA Is Second in Nation Among Public Universities, in Top Five Overall," news release, Jan. 26, 1983. • "From the second level of good universities:" UCLA Office of Media Relations, "UCLA Chancellor Charles E. Young," biographical profile, May 17, 1994. • "But we cannot rest:" UCLA Public Affairs Department, *UCLA Annual Report, 1982–83*, "A Message From the Chancellor," 2. • "Most frustrating:" Ibid.

195 "A better institution:" Young, UCLA Oral History Program, 318–19. • "To achieve its destiny:" Charles E. Young, "A Blueprint for the Future," *UCLA Magazine*, Summer 1969. • "What are you people doing here:" Neil H. Jacoby, interview by James V. Mink, 1974, UCLA Oral History Program, 195. • "Lost their forward spirit:" Ibid. • "I suggested to Chancellor Allen:" Ibid, 196.

196 "The discussion went forward:" Alan Charles, email message to author, June 22, 2010. • "A campaign was very important:" Young, UCLA Oral History Program, 333.

197 "Tired and tense:" Gary Lee Seto,"Saxon To Quit Presidency July 1," *Daily Bruin*, Sept. 28, 1962. • "Surcharge:" Anne C. Roark, "Surcharge Urged for UC Students," *Los Angeles Times*, Jan. 13, 1983.

198 "In addition now to the fact:" *Los Angeles Times*, "Text of Deukmejian's State of the State Address to the Legislature," Jan. 11, 1984. • "The period of David Gardner's presidency:" Charles E. Young, interview by the author (UCLA History Project), May 9, 2006. • "Deukmejian's first priority:" Ibid.

199 "The state's population:" David Pierpont Gardner. *Earning My Degree: Memoirs of an American University President*. (Berkeley, Calif.: University of California Press, 2005), 195. • "The building program:" Young, UCLA Oral History Program, 447. • "As a vital and developing organization:" UCLA Public Affairs Department, *UCLA Annual Report, 1982–83*, "Construction at UCLA: A Campus Transformation," 22.

200 "You'll notice that it's formidable:" David Ferrell, "Move Over, SC, Bruins Are Baring Their Teeth," *Los Angeles Times*, Oct. 1, 1984. • "Our participation in the Olympics:" "Games to Pay for Campus Improvements," Young Administrative Files.

201 "Bunkerlike:" John Dreyfuss, "L.A.'s Olympic HQ Drops the Torch," *Los Angeles Times*, Dec. 3, 1982. • "Three slices of glass:" Ibid. • "saddest of missed opportunities:" Ibid.

202 "Main Street:" "Report of Activities of 1984 Olympics at the Los Angeles Campus," Oct. 10, 1984, Item for information to members of the Committee of Finance, University of California, Board of Regents, UCLA Chancellor's Communication Service. • "Miracle of L.A.:" Richard Hoffer, "U.S. Pulls Off Miracle of L.A." *Los Angeles Times*, Aug. 1, 1984.

203 "We are confident:" Kenneth Reich, "UCLA Will House Drugs Laboratory for 1984 Olympics," *Los Angeles Times*, Mar. 10, 1982. • "For years I had suspected:" *Daily Bruin*, "Professor Works for Integrity of Sport," March 17, 2009.

204 "I met Michael:" Opinion, Michael S. Gottlieb, "Patient Zero, and AIDS, Enter the History Books," *Los Angeles Times*, June 5, 2006. • "Like Michael:" Ibid. • "I knew I was witnessing:" Claudia Wallis, "AIDS: A Growing Threat," *Time*, April 18, 2005. • "Morbidity and Mortality:" Michael S. Gottlieb, H.M. Schanker, P.T. Fam, A. Saxon, J.D. Weisman, I. Pozalski, "Pneumocystis Pneumonia–Los Angeles:" *Morbidity and Mortality Weekly Report, Centers for Disease Control*, June 5, 1981. • "The report that came from:" Gerald S. Levey, "25 Years of Curing," remarks, UCLA AIDS Conference, June 5, 2006. Author attended event. • "The discovery of AIDS:" Michael Gottlieb, interview by Anita Chabria (UCLA History Project), Sept. 20, 2006. • "There is a certain critical mass:" Ibid.

205 "It was the shocking news two weeks ago:" Claudia Wallis, "AIDS: A Growing Threat," *Time*, April 18, 2005. • "The word 'cure' is not yet in the vocabulary:" Ibid. • "The patients at the CARE center:" *UCLA AIDS Institute Insider*, "New Endowment Honors Elizabeth Taylor's Legacy of AIDS Advocacy, Jan. 2006.

206 "When this virus:" Arthur Ashe's remarks from a video tribute shown posthumously at the presentation of his 1993 Edward A. Dixon Alumnus of the Year Award. • "We have gone from utter despair and fear:" Gerald S. Levey, 25 Years of Curing," remarks, UCLA AIDS Conference, June 5, 2006. Author attended event. • "No other American university:" Caren Parnes, "Japanese Are Bullish on Bruins' Culture and Curios," *Daily Bruin*, Oct. 19, 1961. • "There are currently 200:" Ibid. • "It's called 'Bearwear':" *Los Angeles Times*, "Bearwear Is Everywhere," Oct. 21, 1979.

207 "The first reaction:" UCLA Office of Media Relations, "Bruin Fans Now Sporting New UCLA Athletic Shoe," news release, Dec. 16, 1987.

208 "Look—everybody:" *Cub Californian*, "Senior Gift," Dec. 19, 1919. • "Senior Walk:" Letter from Officers of the Class of 1926 to Ernest Carroll Moore, June 10, 1926, Moore Administrative Files. • "Senior Walk: The Trees:" *Southern Alumnus*, "Trees By The Class of '26," March 1931. • "Books for the browsing room:" Advisory Administrative Board Agenda, June 9, 1927, Chancellor's Moore Administrative Files. • "With the hope that it may be used:" *The U.C.L.A. Magazine*, "The U.C.L.A. Year in Review," June 1943.

209 "Soon we'll be leaving UCLA:" *Senior Handbook*, 1989, UCLA History Project Collection.

210 "Chancellor Young was a genius:" Bobby Grace, interview by Talleah Bridges McMahon (UCLA History Project), Nov. 1, 2006.

211 "Hitch, whose proposals:" Editorial, "Regents Reject Hitch Proposal," *Daily Bruin*, Oct. 22, 1973. • "What kind of example:" Editorial, "UC Investments," *Daily Bruin*, Oct. 24, 1973. • "First teach-in on racism:" Dave McNary, "South African Professor Criticizes American Investments," *Daily Bruin*, Nov. 9, 1973. • "In light of the recent enrollment:" Resolution, "Divestment of South Africa," *Daily Bruin*, Nov. 26, 1977. • "There were several discussions:" Fred Gaines, interview by Talleah Bridges McMahon (UCLA History Project), Oct. 30, 2006.

212 "The only effective leverage:" Mary Anne Ostrom, *Daily Bruin*, "AS Switches to Imperial Bank," March 11, 1981. • "No longer give the Regents:" Ibid. • "Universities, as respected institutions:" Mary Astadourian, *Daily Bruin*, Feb. 10, 1981.

213 "Can divest now:" Allison Murad, "Financial Ties May Be Cut if Plan Is OK'd by Regents," *Daily Bruin*, Jan. 10, 1985. • "We don't stand alone:" Laurie Becklund, "Huge Rally at UCLA Attacks Ties to S. Africa," *Los Angeles Times*, April 24, 1985. • "We are not the Free Speech Movement:" Ibid. • "Do-nothing, care-nothing:" Ibid. • "Up to this point:" Russell Covey, "Murphy Arrests Not in Plan, Lurie Says," *Daily Bruin*, April 26, 1985. • "Single largest divestiture:" Anne C. Roark, "UC to Sell Investments With Links to S. Africa," *Los Angeles Times*, July 19, 1986. • "I don't think that Deukmejian:"Ibid. • "It was a sign of the times:" Leslie K. Gilbert-Lurie, interview by Talleah Bridges McMahon (UCLA History Project), Oct. 10, 2007. • "We had the luxury:" Ibid.

CHAPTER 10 / "So Far, So Fast:" 1989–1997

214 "In society and at UCLA:" "State of the Campus Address," Oct. 16, 1991, Young Administrative Files. • "The theme we have:" Ibid. • "Seventy-five years ago:" Office of the Press Secretary, The White House, "Remarks by the President to UCLA 75th Anniversary Convocation," May 20, 1994, Chancellor's Communication Service

216 "Our mission is to provide:" UCLA Academic Senate Legislative Assembly Minutes, Nov. 27, 1990, UCLA Academic Senate. • "Experienced earthquakes of all kinds:" Office of the Press Secretary, The White House, "Remarks by the President to UCLA 75th Anniversary Convocation," May 20, 1994, Chancellor's Communication Service. • "I call this the year:" Cynthia Lee, "Freshman Enrollment Reaches Seven-Year High," *UCLA Today*, Sept. 9, 1994.

217 "A Tough Blow:" Editorial, "A Tough Blow, but UC Had to Raise Fees," *Los Angeles Times*, Feb. 16, 1991. • "I didn't think:" Marina Dundjerski, "Voice Recognition," *UCLA Magazine*, Fall 2001.

218 "If we intend to preserve:" Editorial, "Fee Rise Needed, If Unpleasant," *Daily Bruin*, Feb. 19, 1991. • "Differential:" James Snyder, "Graduate Reg Fees May Skyrocket," *Daily Bruin*, Dec. 9, 1993. • "It was a way of … unloading:" Charles E. Young, vol. II, interview by James V. Mink and Dale E. Treleven, Nov. 3, 1998, UCLA Oral History Program, 555. • "It was a way of dealing:" Charles E. Young, interview by the author (UCLA History Project), Sept. 23, 2010. • "If we thought the cuts:" Charles E. Young, "State of the Campus" address to Chancellor's Associates, Oct. 7, 1993, Young Administrative Files. • "To make hard choices:" Ibid. • If we are to affirm:" Charles E. Young, "Annual Report: Grappling With Troubled Times," *UCLA Magazine*, Winter 1994. • "It takes years:" Ralph Frammolino and Marina Dundjerski, "Plan to Dismantle 4 UCLA Schools Protested," *Los Angeles Times*, Oct. 15, 1993. • "Chuck Young built:" Mona Gable, "25 Years Young," *UCLA Magazine*, Spring 1994. • "They kept saying:" Charles E. Young, vol. II, interview by James V. Mink and Dale E. Treleven, Nov. 3, 1998, UCLA Oral History Program, 559.

219 "There was a time:" Donna L. Vredevoe, interview by the author (UCLA History Project), Feb. 9, 2006. • "The actions we were:" Charles E. Young, vol. II, interview by James V. Mink and Dale E. Treleven, April 22, 1998, UCLA Oral History Program, 380. • "This is a sensibly:" Lelia Ansari, "Regents Approve Disputed Off-Campus Guest House," *Daily Bruin*, Sept. 24–27, 1990. • "This project was developed:" Thy Dinh, "New UCLA medical plaza opens across from Med Center," *Daily Bruin*, May 30, 1990.

220 "Providing greater:" Charles E. Young, vol. III, interview by James V. Mink and Dale E. Treleven, Nov. 17, 1998, UCLA Oral History Program, 581. • "UCLA cares very:" "State of the campus address to Chancellor's Associates, Sept. 7, 1990, Young Administrative Files.

221 "In the mid-80s:" Charles "Duke" Warner Oakley, email message to author, April 12, 2011. • "The people who:" Ibid. • "The No. 3 sprinkler:" John E. Kobara, interview by Beth Bloom (UCLA History Project), Nov. 29, 2006.

224 "Back up guys:" Charles "Duke" Warner Oakley, interview by Talleah Bridges McMahon (UCLA History Project), Sept. 13, 2007. • "Another five seconds:" Ibid.

225 "The hospital had damage:" Charles "Duke" Warner Oakley, interview by Talleah Bridges McMahon (UCLA History Project), Sept. 13, 2007. • "UCLA's vulnerability:" "A Campus at Risk," Report of the UCLA Ad Hoc Joint Senate-Administration Earthquake Safety Committee, September 1985, Young Administrative Files.

226 "We've made forcible:" Scott Harris and David Smollar, "2,000 at UCLA Could Perish in Quake, Study Shows," *Los Angeles Times*, Oct. 19, 1985. • "We said: 'Look:" Young, interview by the author (UCLA History Project), Sept. 23, 2010. • "As I drove by:" Charles "Duke" Warner Oakley, interview by Talleah Bridges McMahon (UCLA History Project), Sept. 13, 2007.

227 "With its playful:" Herbert Muschamp, "Architecture View; A Bright Balloon of a Building Soars at U.C.L.A.," *The New York Times*, Aug. 8, 1993.

228 "Historically that aspect:" Charles E. Young, vol. III, interview by James V. Mink and Dale E. Treleven, Dec. 15, 1998, UCLA Oral History Program, 622. • "Through its treasures:" Frederick S. Wight, "UCLA Art Building Promising, Exciting," *Los Angeles Times*, Dec. 20, 1953. • "The galleries wish:" Ibid.

229 "By developing the Museum:" UCLA Community and Governmental Relations, "UCLA Assumes Operation of Hammer Museum," *UCLA Community Update*, Spring 1994. • "There's been a lot:" Christopher B. Donnan, interview by Veronique de Turenne (UCLA History Project), Nov. 11, 2006.

230 "We desperately needed:" Cecilia de la Paz, "Fowler Museum Opens Soon," *Daily Bruin*, Sept. 29, 1992. • "It's ongoing, action-dash oriented:" Vicky Gomelsky, "UCLA gears up for its 75th Anniversary," *Daily Bruin*, May 17, 1994.

231 "If there is a single:" "Charles E. Young: Chancellor's 75th Anniversary Convocation Remarks," Chancellor's Communication Service. • "Americans of my generation:" Office of the Press Secretary, The White House, "Remarks by the President to UCLA 75th Anniversary Convocation," May 20, 1994, Chancellor's Communication Service. • "Thousands of young people:" Ibid. • "If you look around:" Ibid.

233 "A slap in the face:" Larry Gordon and Marina Dundjerski, "Protestors Attack UCLA Faculty Center," *Los Angeles Times*, May 12, 1993. • "We have merged:" Debbie Kong, "Chicana/o Studies Center Planned," *Daily Bruin*, June 10, 1993. • "It's a phoenix:" Neha Jaganathan, "Chicana, Chicano Studies Has Grown With UCLA," *Daily Bruin*, Nov. 25, 2008. • "Once you have an undergraduate:" Ibid.

234 "I don't think:" Young, interview by the author (UCLA History Project), Sept. 23, 2010.

235 "If you don't:" Rae Lee Siporin, interview by Beth Bloom (UCLA History Project), Nov. 7, 2006, UCLA History Project, 20. • "Plus:" *Regents of the University of California v. Bakke*, 438 U.S. 265 (1978). • "A colorblind society:" Bill Stall and Virginia Ellis, "Wilson Takes Swipe at Affirmative Action Politics," *Los Angeles Times*, June 2, 1995. • "They chanted:" Patrick Kerkstra, "Protests Explode in Wake of Decision," *Daily Bruin*, July 23, 1995. • "Respectfully disagreed:" Remarks of the President, Minutes of a meeting of the University of California Board of Regents, July 20, 1995, Regents of the University of California, Office of the Secretary and Chief of Staff.

236 "California's diversity:" Phillip Carter, "Regents End UC Affirmative Action Policies," *Daily Bruin*, July 23, 1995. • "Good for America:" Paul Richter, "Clinton Declares Affirmative Action Is 'Good for America,'" *Los Angeles Times*, July 20, 1995. • "Mend it:" Ibid. • "People keep saying:" Young, interview by the author (UCLA History Project), Sept. 23, 2010. • "It was absolutely:" York Chang, interview by Talleah Bridges McMahon (UCLA History Project), Dec. 19, 2007.

237 "He was a real:" Richard C. Atkinson, interview by the author (UCLA History Project), Oct. 13, 2010. • "Chuck was really:" Richard C. Atkinson, interview by the author (UCLA History Project), Oct. 28, 2010. • "I've had the unusual:" Young, interview by the author (UCLA History Project), Sept. 23, 2010. • "As the youngest:" Charles E. Young, "Letter from Chancellor Young," *UCLA Magazine*, Spring 1997. • "You see, today:" "Charles E. Young: Life Sciences Commencement," June 14, 1997, Regents of the University of California, Office of the Secretary and Chief of Staff.

CHAPTER 11 / The New Millennium: 1997–2007

238 "UCLA educates:" University Communications, *UCLA Annual Financial Report, 1996–97*, "Letter from the Chancellor," 3.

240 "A Nobel laureate:" Kenneth R. Weiss, "Finalists for Top UCLA Post Are Interviewed," *Los Angeles Times*, Feb. 26, 1997. • "Scared off:" Ibid.

241 "Find a job:" UCLA Sports Information Office, *UCLA Football Guide 1997*, "Dr. Albert Carnesale," 223. • "There was never:" Mary Daily, "The Carnesale Legacy," *UCLA Magazine*, July 2006. • "So much of:" Ibid.

242 "A hierarchy:" Richard C. Atkinson, interview by the author (UCLA History Project), Dec. 4, 2010. • "I said to her:" Ibid. • "At this stage:" Kenneth R. Weiss, "Finalists for Top UCLA Post Are Interviewed," *Los Angeles Times*, Feb. 26, 1997. • "Carnesale had a very strong:" Richard C. Atkinson, interview by the author (UCLA History Project), Dec. 4, 2010. • "That the University of California:" B. Drummond Ayres Jr., "University of California Goes Far Afield to Fill 2 Top Jobs," *The New York Times*, March 7, 1997. • "He is a dynamic:" University of California Office of the President, "Harvard Provost is New UCLA Chancellor," news release, March 6, 1997.

243 "The disquieting part:" Albert Carnesale, interview by the author (UCLA History Project), April 25, 2008. • "I just tried to push:" Ibid. • "We must build bridges:" *Los Angeles Times*, "Jesse Jackson at UCLA to Urge Prop. 209 Protest," Oct. 7, 1997. • "At a student government:" Opinion, Kandea Mosley, "Inauguration Brings Questions About Carnesale to Light," *Daily Bruin*, May 13, 1998. • "The continuing explosion" and "a growing need:" Albert Carnesale, UCLA Inaugural Address, May 15, 1998. • "What excites me:" Ibid. • "Diversity of the student body:" Ibid. • "Because I believe:" Ibid.

244 "To all of those young:" Commentary, Albert Carnesale, "A New Test for the New Freshman Class," *Los Angeles Times*, March 20, 1998. • "Ensure that high-performing:" University of California Office of the President, "UC Will Extend Eligibility to Applicants From 'Top 4 Percent' Whose Transcripts Were Not Submitted," news release, Dec. 22, 2000. • "Regardless of the level:" Ibid. • "You have the opportunity:" Marina Dundjerski, "Regents to Discuss Possible SP-1 Repeal," *UCLA Today*, March 28, 2001. "Chancellor Carnesale did an outstanding job:" Ibid.

246 "The University shall seek:" University of California Office of the President, "Guidelines for Implementation of University Policy on Undergraduate Admissions," 2002. • "Comprehensive review:" Ibid. • "Living up to:" Rebecca Trounson and Kenneth R. Weiss, "UC Admissions to Weigh 'Personal Achievement'," *Los Angeles Times*, Nov. 19, 2001. • "We still haven't really fully recovered:" Carnesale, interview by the author (UCLA History Project), April 25, 2008. • "The overwhelming:" Ibid. • "It was just the dominant:" Ibid. • "A New State of Terror:" Michael Falcone and Linh Tat, "A New State of Terror," *Daily Bruin*, Sept. 11, 2001. • "Despite heightened senses:" Daniel Wong, "University Continues on Through Day of Tragedy," *Daily Bruin*, Sept. 11, 2001. • "The events of September 11:" Albert Carnesale, Sept. 11, 2011, Memorial, Royce quad, public address, Sept. 13, 2011, Chancellor's Communications Service. • "The time has come:" Ibid. • "We will never forget:" Donald Hartsock, "Healing Begins With a Broken Heart," *UCLA Magazine*, Fall 2001.

247 "Urgent Call to Action:" Donna Foote, "Islam, Arabic and Afghanistan 101," *Newsweek*, Nov. 12, 2001. • "Better understand what happened:" Albert Carnesale, "From Murphy Hall," *UCLA Magazine*, Winter 2001. • "It was important:" Ibid. • "They were not only:" Joseph D. Mandel, email message to the author, April 22, 2011. • "They are the ones:" "Albert Carnesale: Rethinking National Security," public address, Royce Hall, Feb. 28, 2002. Author attended event. • "We will never forget:" Albert Carnesale, "From Murphy Hall," *UCLA Magazine*, Fall 2002. • "Al's response to 9/11:" Mary Daily, "The Carnesale Legacy," *UCLA Magazine*, July 2006.

248 "These centers of science:" Marina Dundjerski, "Nanosystems institute a 'go'," *UCLA Today*, Dec. 12, 2000. • "Its establishment puts us:" Ibid.

249 "It's not enough:" Wendy Soderburg, "CNSI: Celebrating a decade of discovery," *UCLA Today*, Dec. 16, 2010. • "The genetics revolution:" Advertorial, Albert Carnesale, "Genetics and Society: Unraveling the Mysteries of Life," *Los Angeles Times*, Nov. 20, 2001.

250 "They are separated:" Marina Dundjerski, "The Little Marias," *UCLA Magazine*, Fall 2002. • "After seeing those kids:" Ibid.

251 "Great quake:" Ronald Reagan UCLA Medical Center Dedication Program, June 4, 2007, UCLA History Project Collection. • "We talked about the concept:" Gerald S. Levey, interview by the author (UCLA History Project), July 18, 2006. • "What is the true impact:" Ronald Reagan UCLA Medical Center Dedication Program, June 4, 2007, UCLA History Project Collection. • "Although Ronnie couldn't be here:" Roxanne Moster, "New Hospital to Be Named For Reagan," *UCLA Today*, April 25, 2000.

252 "Renaming UCLA's hospital:" Editorial, "Medical Center Shouldn't Honor Reagan Legacy," *Daily Bruin*, April 26, 2000. • "Not adequate reason:" Albert Carnesale, email message to Joan C. Mills, April 25, 2000, Chancellor's Communications Office. • "There were a lot of people:" Michael C. Eicher, interview by the author (UCLA History Project), June 22, 2006. • "Without the Reagan name:" Gerald S. Levey, interview by the author (UCLA History Project), July 18, 2006.

253 "This building will bring:" Nancy Reagan, Ronald Reagan UCLA Medical Center dedication, public address, June 4, 2007. Author attended event. • "The last patient:" Public Announcement, Ronald Reagan UCLA Medical Center, June 29, 2008. Author attended event. • "We're now functioning:" Press conference, Westwood Plaza, June 29, 2008. Author attended event.

254 "[He] took it from a small:" Gerald S. Levey, interview by the author (UCLA History Project), July 18, 2006. • "State support was not:" Ibid.

255 "And he said to Andy:" Ibid. • "I'm not accepting this:" Ibid. • "To support one" and "to inspire others:" UCLA Office of Media Relations, "Geffen gift anchors future of medical school," news release, May 7, 2002. • "I believe each of us:" Ibid.

256 "Engineers solve problems:" Mary Daily, "The Carnesale Legacy," *UCLA Magazine*, July 2006. • "Field for UCLA Chief:" Rebecca Trounson and Stuart Silverstein, "Field for UCLA Chief is Down to One," *Los Angeles Times*, April 28, 2006. • "Family conflicts:" Saba Riazati, "Chancellor Search Persists," *Daily Bruin*, Oct. 16, 2006. • "I don't want to be a caretaker:" Norman Abrams, interview by the author (UCLA History Project), March 14, 2008.

257 "That just cried out:" Ibid. • "Holistic:" UCLA Office of Media Relations, "UCLA Adopts a Holistic Approach to Reviewing Freshman Applications," news release, Sept. 28, 2006. • "We can and will preserve:" California Community Foundation, "Local Foundation Announces $1.75 Million Scholarship Fund for African Americans Admitted to UCLA," news release, March 28, 2007. • "UCLA's new admissions process:" Darnell M. Hunt, "About the Bunche Center: A Message from the Director," Ralph J. Bunche Center for African American Studies at UCLA, 2007. http://www.bunchecenter. ucla.edu/about_caas_main.html.

258 "It is imperative that we:" Ibid. • "What he does to the animals:" Andrew Murr, "Targeting Researchers," *Newsweek*, Feb. 27, 2008. • "Domestic terrorism:" Rebecca Trounson and Joe Mozingo, "UCLA to Protect Animal Research," *Los Angeles Times*, Aug. 26, 2006. • "It was very clear:" Norman Abrams, interview by the author (UCLA History Project), March 14, 2008. • "Ringleaders:" Advertisement, "Letter to the Campus Community," *Daily Bruin*, advertisement, Aug. 28, 2006. • "As an academic institution:" Ibid. • "Away the hope:" Ibid.

259 "One-stop service:" "UCLA Report of the Task Force on the Protection of Faculty Research and Researchers," UCLA Chancellor's Communications Service, Dec. 19, 2006. • "Best Practices:" Society for Neuroscience,"The Society for Neuroscience Releases 'Best Practices for Protecting Researchers & Research,' " news release, Feb. 6, 2008. • "We had a system:" Norman Abrams, interview by the author (UCLA History Project), March 14, 2008. • "It was the right thing to do:" Ibid. • "Acting:" Paul Fain, "Acting Chancellor, Active Year," *The Chronicle of Higher Education*, June 22, 2007. • "Interim college chiefs:" Ibid.

CHAPTER 12 / Toward a Centennial: 2007 and Beyond

260 "The recession:" *UCLA Anderson Forecast*, " 'Nasty Recession' For U.S. To Include Four Quarters of Declining GDP," Dec. 11, 2008.

262 "As I look ahead:" Gene D. Block, "Measuring Up," *UCLA Magazine*, January 2010. • " 'Educational fee' to 'tuition':" Minutes of the Committee on Educational Policy and Committee on Finance, University of California Board of Regents, Nov. 18, 2010, Regents of the University of California, Office of the Secretary and Chief of Staff. • "I wish UCLA were free:" Nanette Asimov, "Tensions Flare Outside UC regents' Meeting," *San Francisco Chronicle*, Nov. 18, 2010. • "The people of California:" Gene D. Block email message to the Campus Community, Jan. 7, 2010, UCLA History Project Collection. • "Both the University:" Larry Gordon, "Yes, Virginia, He's Coming to Lead UCLA," *Los Angeles Times*, June 24, 2007.

263 "The father of biological timing:" Author's Note: Derived from a 1997 Stanford University memorial resolution stating that Colin S. Pittendrigh is "universally acknowledged as the founder of 'circadian' biology." "Anything is possible:" Felicia Brannon, executive director of UCLA Community and Local Government Relations, in a telephone conversation with the author, confirmed that Gene D. Block has used this phrase when speaking with community college students, Aug. 24, 2011. • "I believe:" Gene D. Block, UCLA Inaugural Address, May 13, 2008. Author attended event.

264 "We biologists:" Ibid. • "Spirit of discovery:" Ibid. • "UCLA serves more:" Ibid. • "As we move:" Ibid. • "I think we're going:" Gene D. Block, KCET public

service announcement, "A Greater Presence in L.A," 2010. http://chancellor.ucla.edu/updates/video-2013-a-greater-presence-in-l.a. • "Civic engagement:" Gene D. Block email message to the campus community, May 14, 2009, UCLA History Project Collection.

265 "We wanted to give:" Larry Gordon, "UCLA Volunteers Fan Out Across City," *Los Angeles Times*, Sept. 23, 2009. • "With such a tremendous:" Ibid. • "Very good chance:" "The American Freshman: National Norms Fall 2010," *Research Brief*, Higher Education Research Institute, UCLA, January 2011. • "Service is key:" Bethany Powers, "Well Served," *UCLA Magazine*, January 2010. • "What makes our school:" Cynthia Lee, "Community School Starts Year With Successes, Challenges," *UCLA Today*, Sept. 23, 2010. • "Renee and I:" Meyer Luskin, "Luskin School of Public Affairs Naming Ceremony," public address, March 18, 2011. http://www.youtube.com/watch?v=WMtv089BQSM&feature=relmfu "Hosting scholars:" UCLA Office of Media Relations, "Local Business Leader Donates $100 Million to Transform UCLA's Role in Civic Participation, Education of Future Public Leaders," news release, Jan. 26, 2011.

266 "The Luskins' generosity:" Franklin D. Gilliam Jr., "Luskin School of Public Affairs Naming Ceremony," public address, March 18, 2011. http://www.youtube.com/watch?v=WMtv089BQSM&feature=relmfu "I owe my whole career:" UCLA Office Media Relations, "Paul Terasaki Donates $50 Million to UCLA's Life Sciences," news release, May 13, 2010. • "In the long run:" Eliza Krigman, "Public Universities Struggle to Stay Afloat," *National Journal*, March 10, 2010. • "That leaves me:" Op-ed, Gene D. Block, "Cuts to Higher Education: The Master Plan Turncoats," *Los Angeles Times*, April 17, 2011. • "For those who think:" Ibid.

267 "A moderate increase:" Gene D. Block, email to UCLA Faculty and Staff, "Latest Budget Update," June 30, 2009, UCLA History Project Collection. • "The quality:" Kevin Matthews and Letisia Marquez, "UCLA a Mecca for International Students, Study Abroad," *UCLA Today*, Nov. 17, 2010. • "It is our generation's responsibility:" Op-ed, Gene D. Block, "Cuts to Higher Education: The Master Plan Turncoats," *Los Angeles Times*, April 17, 2011. • "As difficult as:" Gene D. Block, email to the UCLA community, Jan. 12, 2012, UCLA History Project Collection.

PART II: LIFE AT UCLA

CHAPTER 13 / On Rolling Hills

270 "It was pretty much:" Edward A. Dickson, *Origin and Formative Years*, 42. • "Rather by accident:" Ibid., 41.

273 "My thought was that if enough acreage:" Ibid. • "The Second Hollywood:" Display advertisement, Janss Investment Company, UCLA History Project Collection. "It was evident that Fate:" UCLA, *Southern Campus* (1930), 18.

274 "The style lends itself:" George W. Kelham, letter to Ernest Carroll Moore, Nov. 27, 1929. Moore Papers.

275 "When those huge piles of brick:" Lawrence Clark Powell, "Beanfields, Builders, and Books," 1954, Jackson Collection. • "Designed in a style:" Author's Note: Derived from Ernest Carroll Moore's address at the Jan. 20, 1931, dedication of Kerckhoff Hall, where he recounted a conversation he had with David C. Allison. • "They have at the same time:" UCLA, *Southern Campus* (1930), 18.

277 "The real strength of the campus architecturally:" Charles "Duke" Oakley, email to author, Nov. 24, 2010.

278 "Wild folk:" Loye Holmes Miller, *Birds of the Campus* (Berkeley: University of California Press, 1947), 1.

279 "Avenue to the future:" Unidentified local newspaper, "University Celebrates Work Done," Oct. 23, 1927, Subject Files (Arroyo Bridge), UCLA University Archives. • "The arroyo can never be:" David C. Allison, letter to Robert G. Sproul, Sept. 15, 1944. Administrative Files of the Chancellor's Office, UCLA University Archives. • "The day will arrive:" Hamilton and Jackson, *On the Move*, 112.

280 "Thrashers no more:" Author's Note: Derived from a reproduction of Loye Holmes Miller's notecard recording observations of California Thrashers 1930–1947 as included in "419 Acres: UCLA's Natural History," a conference presentation by Travis Longcore and Catherine Rich, California's Biodiversity Crisis: The Loss of Nature in an Urbanizing World, UCLA Institute of the Environment, Oct. 24–25, 1998. • "Educational objectives:" *Daily Bruin*, "Recreation Center 'To Contribute Basically to Our Educational Needs'," Jan. 29, 1963. "Non-rectangular, defying modules:" Art Seidenbaum, "Working On Answers to the New Leisure," *Los Angeles Times*, June 19, 1966. • "The emphasis was on non-emphasis:" Ibid.

281 "The university garden:" "History of this Garden," UCLA Mildred E. Mathias Botanical Garden, http://www.botgard.ucla.edu/history.html, "We had to get away:" *UCLA Alumni Magazine*, "Conversation with Welton Becket," November–December 1964.

282 "Squirt water:" Howard Troller, interview by Diana Hernandez (UCLA History Project), Jan. 27, 2006. • "The aesthetic and functional:" UCLA Long Range Development Plan, December 1963, UCLA History Project Collection. • "Patchwork Campus:" Sharon Moore, "Patchwork Campus: Who is to Blame?" *Daily Bruin*, Oct. 14, 1963.

283 "Uncle Welton's Waffle:" Ibid. • "I could wish:" Ralph J. Bunche, "Ralph J. Bunche Hall Dedication Address," May 23, 1969. Ralph J. Bunche Papers, Department of Special Collections, UCLA. • "One gets the sense:" Peter W. Blackman, interview by the author, Feb. 22, 2006.

284 "The physical manifestation:" Ibid. • "New buildings:" Jeffrey Averill, interview by the author (UCLA History Project), Feb. 1, 2005. • "Molecules just discovered:" Cynthia Lee, "New Molecular Sciences Building Opens for Research," *UCLA Today*, Sept. 9, 1993. • "It put a face:" Jeffrey Averill, interview by the author (UCLA History Project), Nov. 30, 2010.

285 "The interesting thing:" Charles Warner "Duke" Oakley, email to author, Nov. 24, 2010. • "Leftover space:" Charles Warner "Duke" Oakley, interview by Talleah Bridges McMahon (UCLA History Project), Sept. 13, 2007. • "You have to stick with it:" Peter Blackman, interview by the author (UCLA History Project), Feb. 22, 2006. • "Second-generation planning:" Jeffrey Averill, interview by the author (UCLA History Project), Feb. 1, 2005.

286 "Open space:" Ibid. • "Preserves:" *UCLA 2009–19 Capital Financial Plan*, July 2009, 5. http://www.ucop.edu/capitalprojects/documents/cfp09-10/la.pdf "Respect for:" Jeffrey Averill, interview by the author (UCLA History Project), Feb. 1, 2005.

287 "Young people need:" Marina Dundjerski, "A Walk in the Garden," *UCLA Magazine*, Spring 2002.

288 "He wanted to create:" Ibid. • "Fair-weather parking lot:" Cynthia Burlingham and Elizabeth Shepherd, eds., *In the Sculptor's Landscape*, (Los Angeles: Wight Art Gallery, Grunwald Center for the Graphic Arts, UCLA, 1993), 8. "With its broad range:" Ibid., 28. • "The garden isn't necessarily:" Marina Dundjerski, "A Walk in the Garden," *UCLA Magazine*.

289 "Few sculpture installations:" Cynthia Burlingham and Elizabeth Shepherd, eds., *In the Sculptor's Landscape*, 28. • "Security-minded people:" Paul Gardner, "Murphy's Secret Garden," *ArtNews*, January 1985, 14.

CHAPTER 14 / First to 100

290 "There is no question:" Chris Roberts and Bill Bennett, *UCLA Football Vault: The History of the Bruins*, (Atlanta: Whitman Publishing, LLC, 2008), 8.

292 "From such clay:" Associated Students, Southern Branch of the University of California, *Southern Campus* (1920), 162. • "It is said:" *Los Angeles Times*, "Football Life Shown at U. of C. Branch," Sept. 17, 1919. • "The best:" Paul Lowry, "Manual Arts Displays Class," *Los Angeles Times*, Oct. 4, 1919. • "Basketball was our first:" Associated Students, Southern Branch of the University of California, *Southern Campus* (1920), 165. • Above center: "It is rumored:" (YMCA/YWCA), *The University Handbook of the University of California, Los Angeles* (1923–1924), 83.

293 "raise the standard:" Ibid., 176. • "Whatever great victories:" Ibid., 161. • "With only a single:" Paul Lowry, "Trotter Lines Up Bear Cubs," *Los Angeles Times*, Sept. 15, 1920. • Above: "For many years:" Associated Students, Southern Branch of the University of California, *Southern Campus* (1926), 309.

294 "Bill Spaulding, who will:" *Los Angeles Times*, "Spaulding on the Job Early," Aug. 14, 1925. • Right: "Civil war will break:" *Los Angeles Times*, "Turkey Day Foes Drill," Nov. 19, 1936.

295 "Not until the declining:" Associated Students, UCLA, *Southern Campus* (1930), 246.

297 "We were the best:" *Illustrated Football Annual, 15th Year*, 1944.

298 "They just turned a deaf ear:" Charles E. Young, interview by the author (UCLA History Project), Aug. 8, 2008. • "Ill advised:" *Daily Bruin*, "Governor Hits $4.5 Million Stadium Plan," Dec. 2, 1964. • "Play-in:" Steve Weinberg, "Students stage play-in to protest use of incidental fees for stadium," *Daily Bruin*, Nov. 16, 1965. • "The political turmoil:" Alan Charles, email message to author, Oct. 27, 2005.

299 "We were all angry:" Ibid. • "David, I can't change:" Charles E. Young, interview by the author (UCLA History Project), Aug. 8, 2008. • "We begin our season:" Mayerene Barker, "Cheers Ring Out for Bruins at Bowl," *Los Angeles Times*, Aug. 22, 1982. • "We had chaffed:" Charles E. Young, interview by the author (UCLA History Project), Aug. 8, 2008. • "[Officer] responded:" Los Angeles Police Department, Property Report #89-0334862, Oct. 30, 1989. • "It is my duty to admonish you:" Alan Charles to Gordon Henderson, Nov. 3, 1989, UCLA History Project Collection.

300 "Bruin students forced:" Braven Dyer, "Sports Parade," *Los Angeles Times*, Dec. 18, 1948.

301 "Any institution which shoots up as swiftly:" Ibid. • "I suppose it is:" Hamilton and Jackson, *On the Move*, 178. • "Winning isn't everything:" Joel Sayre, "He Flies on One Wing," *Sports Illustrated*, Dec. 26, 1955. • "They're the best team:" Jim Harrigan, "Dejected Hill Dissatisfied Over Showing by Trojans," *Daily Bruin*, Nov. 22, 1954. • "Yes sir I do!:" Ibid.

303 "We needed a competent:" From Dr. Franklin D. Murphy, former UCLA chancellor, UCLA History Project Collection. • "I'm getting your budget ready:" John R. Wooden, interview by the author (UCLA History Project), Feb. 1, 2006.

304 "J.D. Midas:" UCLA Department of Intercollegiate Athletics, Gary Rausch, draft news release. • "Winning solves problems:" Ibid. • "Sports is a co-curricular:" Ibid.

305 "Incomparable dynasty:" Frank Litsky, "John Wooden, Who Built Incomparable Dynasty at U.C.L.A., Dies at 99," *New York Times*, June 6, 2010. • "Against which all others:" Ibid. • "It would be safe to say:" Charles E. Young, interview by the author (UCLA History Project), Aug. 8, 2008. • "It's hard to imagine now:" John Wooden with Jack Tobin, *They Call Me Coach* (New York: McGraw-Hill, 2004), 27. • "Fetish for details:" Steve Jamison "A Brief Professional and Personal History Timeline: August, 1928," The Official Site of Coach John Wooden, http://www.coachwooden.com.

306 "Unexpected crisis:" John Wooden with Steve Jamison, *My Personal Best* (New York: McGraw-Hill, 2004), 77. • "Years later an all-black:" Ibid., 80. • "The one I loved more:" John Wooden, interview by the author (UCLA History Project), Feb. 1, 2006. • "Recruit like mad:" John Wooden with Jack Tobin, *They Call Me Coach* (New York: McGraw-Hill, 2004), 76. • "Let's hit 'em from this angle:" UCLA *Southern Campus* (1949), 95.

307 "On the other side:" John Wooden, interview by the author (UCLA History Project), Feb. 1, 2006. • "I was upset many:" Ibid. • "In retrospect, I think:" Ibid. • "We began to attract:" Ibid. • "The best thing that ever:" Ibid. • "I don't think:" Ibid. • "Goodness gracious, sakes alive:" Bill Becker, "The Coach Who Arranges Chaos," *Sport Magazine*, March 1966. • "In a towering of rage:" Jim Murray, "Wooden the Intellect," unidentified local newspaper, 1963, Jackson Collection. • "I didn't have many rules:" John Wooden, interview by the author (UCLA History Project), Feb. 1, 2006. • "I didn't want hair or sweat:" Cal Fussman, "Coach!," *UCLA Magazine*, Summer 2000.

308 "There's always problems:" John Wooden, interview by the author (UCLA History Project), Feb. 1, 2006. • "I remember once:" Cal Fussman, "Coach!," *UCLA Magazine*, Summer 2000. • "I always considered:" John Wooden, interview by the author (UCLA History Project), Feb. 1, 2006. • "Every player feel:" Ibid. • "Your role may be:" Ibid. • "He set quite an example:" "Coach John Wooden, 1910–2010," UCLA Newsroom, http://newsroom.ucla.edu/portal/ucla/john-wooden-dies-84109.aspx, June 4, 2010. • "We did not understand:" Bill Walton, "John Wooden: Simply The Best," *UCLA Magazine*, 2000.

309 "I didn't know myself:" John Wooden, interview by the author (UCLA History Project), Feb. 1, 2006. • "In many ways, going out:" Ibid. • "I want you to know:" Ibid. • "I always loved practice:" Ibid. • "I'm no wizard:" Ibid. • "That was an absolute:" Dan Guerrero, interview by the author (UCLA History Project), Dec. 13, 2010. • "They will remember where he sat:" Ibid. • "Did, perhaps, more for the university:" Ibid. • "As far as UCLA is concerned:" John Wooden, interview by the author, Feb. 1, 2006. • "It was a young university then:" Ibid.

310 "Gutty little Bruins:" Thomas Bonk, "This Gets to the Guts of the Story," *Los Angeles Times*, May 20, 1995. • "The thing he did:" Jeff Prugh, "Gary Beban Wins Heisman Trophy," *Los Angeles Times*, Nov. 29, 1967. • "Outweighed and out-manned:" *Sports Illustrated*, "UCLA Fight Song," Jan. 10, 1966. • "When Mr. Morgan came:" John R. Wooden, interview by the author (UCLA History Project), Feb. 1, 2006. • "They're going to miss:" Doug Krikorian, "A Few Words With the Man Who Ran UCLA," *Herald Examiner*, Nov. 4, 1979. • "I still recruited:" Judith Holland, email message to Mark Davis, May 21, 2006.

312 "When I first came:" Judith Holland, interview by Beth Bloom (UCLA History Project), Oct. 26, 2006. • "Having done as much:" Richard Hoffer, "The Time Came to Make a Stand," *Los Angeles Times*, March 2, 1981.

313 "The first and foremost goal:" Judith Holland, email message to Mark Davis, May 21, 2006. • "UCLA set the benchmark:" Judith Holland, interview by Beth Bloom (UCLA History Project), Oct. 26, 2006. • "I don't think there:" Mark Heisler, "A Worthwhile Wait for Fischer," *Los Angeles Times*, July 24, 1980.

314 "After a long rancorous:" Peter Dalis, interview by the author (UCLA History Project), Dec. 1, 2010.

315 "I gave him the ball:" *Los Angeles Times*, "UCLA Beats Clock and Missouri West Regional," March 20, 1995. • "Storybook finish:" David Wharton, "He Went Great Length for Bruins," *Los Angeles Times*, March 21, 2002. • "I've practiced the wisdom:" Dan Guerrero, interview by the author (UCLA History Project), Dec. 13, 2010.

316 "It's pretty special:" Peter Yoon, "UCLA Is First to Win Its 100th NCAA Title," *Los Angeles Times*, May 14, 2007. • "UCLA was at the forefront:" Guerrero, interview by the author (UCLA History Project), Dec. 13, 2010. • "To be the first:" *UCLA Today*, "UCLA First to Win 100 NCAA Team Championships," May 14, 2007. • "We are tremendously proud:" Guerrero, interview by the author (UCLA History Project), Dec. 13, 2010.

CHAPTER 15 / Bruin Rites of Passage

318 "The Regents of the University of California:" *Cub Californian*, "Old State Normal School Becomes Branch of U.C.," Sept. 29, 1919. • "We shall have difficulty:" Ibid. • "Dead:" Editorial, "The Normal School is Dead—Long Live the Branch University," *Cub Californian*, Sept. 29, 1919. • "Unsuited to larger:" Associated Students, Southern Branch of the University of California, *Southern Campus* (1920), 41.

320 "To inaugurate:" William Coit Ackerman, *My Fifty Year Love-in at UCLA* (Los Angeles: Fashion Press, 1969), 2. • "Now what is needed:" Editorial, "The Normal School is Dead—Long Live the Branch University," Sept. 29, 1919. • "Our friends in Berkeley:" Editorial, " 'Cubs' Record Unexcelled—Keep Up the Good Work," *Cub Californian*, Oct. 24, 1919. • "One of the favorite sports:" Hamilton and Jackson, *On the Move*, 157.

321 "I pledge myself:" *Cub Californian*, "Honor Pledge," Oct. 17, 1919. • "After considerable discussion:" Editorial, "University Loyalty on Trial, Verdict Rests with Students," *Cub Californian*, Jan. 9, 1920. • "You, as students:" Ibid.

322 "Organization:" Associated Students, Southern Branch of the University of California, *Southern Campus* (1920), 41. • "There is still much:" Ibid., 42.

323 "The bears grew up:" Associated Students University of California, Southern Branch, *Student's Handbook of the University of California, Southern Branch*, 1926–27. • "Bruins, not Grizzlies:" *California Daily Bruin*, " 'Bruin' New Totem," Oct. 22, 1926.

324 "The S.B.U.C.:" *Cub Californian*, "Cubs Feel Need of a Mascot," Oct. 31, 1919. • "Since we are the offspring:" Editorial, "Name Cub Connects Us Closely with U.C. Proper," *Cub Californian*, Sept. 29, 1919. • "Broader and greater" and "capable of standing:" Ibid. • "For a luck charm:" *Cub Californian*, "Cubs Feel Need of a Mascot," Oct. 31, 1919. • "From this time:" Editorial, "Cub No Longer," *California Grizzly*, March 21, 1924.

325 "I began by:" *Daily Bruin*, "UCLA Mascot, Too Big, Donated to Zoo," Jan. 30, 1962.

326 "The cuddly:" Janine Sieja, "Hey Joe," *UCLA Magazine*, Winter 1996. • "Steroid Joe:" *Daily Bruin*, "Joe Bruin, Stanford Tree Walk the Mascot Walk," Oct. 31, 1997. • "Psycho Joe:" Letter, Michael J. McSunas, "New Bear on Campus," *UCLA Magazine*, June 1996. • "One of the great things:" Teresa Jue, "Retro Joe to Modern Bruin," *Prime/Daily Bruin*, Oct. 18, 2010.

327 "A thousand men:" Associated Students, Southern Branch of the University of California, *Southern Campus* (1924), 146. • "The field was:" Ibid., 147. • "The Scribes, who you:" Scimitar and Key Society, Southern Branch of the University of California, *Freshman Handbook of the University of California, Southern Branch*, 1920–21, 16, UCLA History Project Collection.

328 "Local Greeks:" Associated Students, Southern Branch of the University of California, *Southern Campus* (1924), 112. • "It is rumored:" Associated Students, UCLA, *Southern Campus* (1938), 401. • "The library is a place:" Associated Students, UCLA, *Southern Campus* (1945), 92. • "Bill Ackerman's Grizzly:" Associated Students, University of California, Southern Branch, UCLA, *Southern Campus* (1926), 235. • "The UCLA con artists:" Associated Students, UCLA, *Southern Campus* (1965), 18. • "If not always:" Associated Students, UCLA, *Southern Campus* (1963), 458. • "What our parents:" Associated Students, UCLA, *Bruin Life* (1986), 288. • "The battle rages on:" Ibid., 400.

329 "That was the only:" Marina Dundjerski, "Coming Home," *UCLA Magazine*, Fall 2002. • "The innocent pastimes:" *Daily* Grizzly, "Hard on the Fish," September 1926. • "Hazing is out:" Associated Students, UCLA, *Student's Handbook of the University of California at Los Angeles*, 1930–31, 128. • "Maraca-accented rhythms:" *California Bruin*, "Cugat Rhythms Spice Holiday Promenade," Dec. 15, 1944.

330 "Vulgarity and exhibitionism:" George Garrigues, *A History of the UCLA Daily Bruin, 1919–1955*: "The Daily Bruin is Born," (Internet Edition 2001). • "Steps are being taken:" *Daily* Bruin, "The Library Seal," October 1929.

331 " 'Carnival':" *California Daily Bruin*, "U.R.A. Recreational Previews Spectacle," May 13, 1943. • "Mardi Gras:" *California Bruin*, "U.R.A. Plans Carnival Scene," Jan. 31, 1945. • "UCLA's Mardi Gras:" Ellen Melinkoff, "Fun, Games at UCLA's Mardi Gras," *Los Angeles Times*, May 16, 1987.

333 "What Mr. Dickson wanted:" Ann Sumner, "Distinguished Alumna," interview by Winston Wutkee, 1970, UCLA Oral History Program, 63.

335 "Professors will give:" *California Daily Bruin*, "Just a Song at Class Time," Sept. 15, 1937. • "Every loyal Bruin:" Associated Students, UCLA, *Southern Campus* (1932), 176. • "There was little time:" Ibid., 177.

336 "The mechanics:" *The U.C.L.A. Magazine*, "Card Stunts," November 1945.

337 "Where it tolled:" Associated Students, UCLA, *Southern Campus* (1943), 163.

339 "Unfortunately, the company:" William Coit Ackerman, *My Fifty Year Love-in at UCLA* (Los Angeles: Fashion Press, 1969), 171. • "The 67-foot-high bonfire:" *Los Angeles Times*, "UCLA Orders Inquiry into Bonfire Blast," Oct. 22, 1950. • "Promised parents:" *Time*, "Boys & Girls Together," Aug. 15, 1960.

340 "Many looked upon:" Byron H. Atkinson, "Boys and Girls Together," *UCLA Alumni Magazine*, May–June 1964. • "A long time ago:" *Daily Bruin*, "Dorm Lockout Abolished," April 1967. • "Student government had changed:" Keith E. Brant, interview by the author (UCLA History Project), May 15, 2011. • "The Alumni Association is reinvesting:" Marina Dundjerski, "Coming Home," *UCLA Magazine*, Fall 2002.

341 "There are even:" Frank Mankiewicz, "Bosco, the Library Seal," *California Bruin*, July 2, 1946. • "When I entered UCLA:" Julie Brotherton Gehr email to the author, July 11, 2002.

343 "Undie Run:" Brad Greenberg, "The Naked City," *UCLA Magazine*, October 2006.

Selected Bibliography

UNPUBLISHED SOURCES

ARCHIVAL COLLECTIONS
UCLA University Archives
Administrative Files of Chandler Harris; Administrative Files of Charles E. Young; Administrative Files of Nancy Naylor; Administrative Files of the Chancellor's Office; Administrative Files of Robert A. Fischer and J.D. Morgan; Associated Students Distinguished Speakers Series; Administrative Subject Files of Franklin D. Murphy; Chancellor's Office Administrative Files of Provost Ernest Carroll Moore; Administrative Files of the Committee on Sites for the Southern Branch of the University; Pioneer Alumni Association Correspondence and Memorabilia; Records of the Loyalty Oath Controversy; Records Pertaining to Campus Unrest; Student Activism Collection; UCLA Biographical/Subject Files and Publications compiled by John B. Jackson; UCLA University Archives Reference Collection; War Training Program Records (unprocessed)

UCLA Department of Special Collections
American Civil Liberties Union of Southern California Records; Andrew Hamilton Papers; Charles E. Young Papers (unprocessed); Clarence A. Dykstra Papers; Donald Kalish Papers (unprocessed); Earle R. Hedrick Papers; Edward A. Dickson Papers; Ernest Carroll Moore Papers; Franklin D. Murphy Papers; Jakob Bjerknes Papers; John W. Caughey Papers; Loye Miller Papers; Manzanar War Relocation Center Records; Ralph D. Cornell Papers; Ralph J. Bunche Papers; Vern O. Knudsen Papers; Westwood Chamber of Commerce Records

University of California, Berkeley University Archives
Clark Kerr Personal and Professional Papers (unprocessed); Records of the President of the University of California; Robert Gordon Sproul Personal Papers as President and President Emeritus of the University of California

Other Archives
USC University Archives; California State Assembly Chief Clerk Legislative Document Archives; Los Angeles Department of Water & Power; Henry J. Bruman Map Collection, Charles E. Young Research Library, UCLA; Scripps Institution of Oceanography Archives; The Huntington Library, Art Collections, and Botanical Gardens

INTERVIEWS
More than 250 interviews were conducted by the author and UCLA History Project researchers. The list below does not account for them all, neither does it show the many follow-ups, shorter conversations or email exchanges with additional individuals that contributed to this book.

Conducted by the Author
Norman Abrams (Feb. 8, 29 and March 14, 2008); Richard C. Atkinson (Oct. 13, 28 and Dec. 14, 2010); Jeffrey Averill (Feb. 1, 2005 and Nov. 30, 2010); Peter W. Blackman (Feb. 22 and April 6, 2006); Gene D. Block (Jan. 3 and May 27, 2008); Donald G. Browne (March 29 and Sept. 8, 2006); Ad Brugger (April 26, 2006); Albert Carnesale (Jan. 23 and Feb. 3, 2006 and April 25, 2008); Alan F. Charles (March 20, June 23 and Nov. 21, 2005); Peter T. Dalis (Dec. 1, 2010); Winston C. Doby (Jan. 25, 2008 and Dec. 17, 2010); Michael C. Eicher (Jan. 3, March 26 and June 22, 2006); William Russell Ellis (July 11, 2006); Lawrence Grobel (May 24, 2004); Dan Guerrero (Dec. 13, 2010); Gordon Henderson (April 29, 2005); Ben Howland (Dec. 19, 2010); Bill Jepson (March 2, 2006); Herbert G. Kawahara (Jan. 14, 2008); Leonard Kleinrock (Aug. 4, 2005); Gerald S. Levey (July 18, 2006); Lawrence H. Lokman (March

10, 2006); David Lowenstein (April 7, 2006); Joseph D. Mandel (Feb. 13, 17 and March 3, 2006); Sherman M. Mellinkoff (Nov. 9, 2007 and Feb. 15, 2008); Antoinette G. Mongelli (March 27, 2006); Ann Rieber Plauzoles (June 22, 2005); Andrea L. Rich (March 31, 2006); John Sandbrook (Jan. 12 and Aug. 18, 2004); Lynn Shackelford (March 7, 2008); Ann Sumner (June 22, 2005); Elwin V. Svenson (Feb. 17, 2006); Rhea Turteltaub (Nov. 14, 2007 and Jan. 18, 2008); Rick Tuttle (June 14, 2006); Donna L. Vredevoe (Feb. 9, 2006); Scott L. Waugh (Feb. 8, 2008); Bruce Whiteman (Sept. 26, 2005); Robert Williams (Dec. 7, 2010); John R. Wooden (Feb. 1, 2006); Zev Yaroslavsky (Feb. 22, 2008); Charles E. Young (Sept. 2, 2004; May 9, 2006; April 17, 23, 29 and Aug. 8, 2008; and Sept. 9, 23 and Oct. 10, 2010)

Conducted by UCLA History Project Researchers Talleah Bridges McMahon, Veronique de Turenne, Anita Chabria, Beth Bloom and Diana Hernandez
William R. Allen (June 8, 2007); Robert E. Alshuler (Oct. 18, 2006); Kate Anderson (Nov. 15, 2006); Alexander Astin (Sept. 27, 2006); Tony Auth (Feb. 11, 2007); Bruce Barbee (Oct. 19, 2006); Albert Barber (Nov. 1, 2006); Anne Berkovitz (Nov. 1, 2006); Charles A. Berst (Sept. 13, 2006); B.J. Blakely (Dec. 9, 2006); Lewis F. Blumberg (April 23, 2007); Annette Franklin Blumner (Aug. 22, 2006); Paul D. Boyer (Oct. 17, 2006); Keith E. Brant (Oct. 30, 2006); Renee Turkell Brook (Jan. 22, 2008); Scot Brown (Jan. 26, 2007); Yvonne Brathwaite Burke (Jan. 28, 2008); Carol Burnett (Oct. 30, 2009); Richard P. Byrne (Dec. 28, 2007); Lindsay Conner (Nov. 8, 2007); Brian Copenhaver (Nov. 15, 2006); Craig Cunningham (Dec. 4, 2006); Gerald d'Amboise (Nov. 9, 2008); Jeff Donfeld (Sept. 28, 2006); Christopher B. Donnan (Nov. 11, 2006); Irv Drasnin (Nov. 28, 2008); Edmund D. Edelman (Jan. 22, 2008); Craig Ehrlich (Sept. 24, 2006); Zada Folz Evans (Sept. 21, 2006); Seymour Feshbach (Dec. 7, 2006); Donald E. Findley (Nov. 7, 2006); Sydney Finegold (Dec. 7, 2006); Greg Fischer (Jan. 23, 2008); Billy Fitzgerald (Nov. 3, 2006); Dean Florez (April 25, 2007); Tikako Yamamoto Fujimura (April 2, 2008); L. Alice Wilburn Gable (Sept. 5, 2006); Fred Gaines (Oct. 30, 2006); Jack Gibbons (Oct. 4, 2006); Leslie K. Gilbert-Lurie (Oct. 10, 2007); Dorothy Goldman (Aug. 22, 2006); Hy Goldman (Aug. 17, 2006); Michael S. Gottlieb (Sept. 20, 2006); Bobby Grace (Nov. 1, 2006); Sherman Grancell (Aug. 3, 2006); Steven J. Halpern (Nov. 6, 2006); Alan Hanson (Sept. 8, 2006); E. Russell Hardwick (Oct. 31, 2006); Adrian Harris (Oct. 6, 2006); Donald Hartsock (Oct. 31, 2006); Gordon Henderson (April 29, 2005); Irene Hetzel (Aug. 26, 2006); Richard H. Hill (Nov. 24, 2006); Judith Holland (Oct. 26, 2006); Meriko Hoshiyama (May 11, 2007); Darnell Hunt (Sept. 13 and 17, 2007); Louis Ignarro (March 27, 2007); Ikue Itami (April 25, 2007); Charles Jacobs (Aug. 23, 2006); J. Daniel Johnson (Oct. 10, 2006); Rafer Johnson (Jan. 9, 2007); Willard R. Johnson (Feb. 2, 2007); James Jordan (March 25, 2008); Maulana Karenga (Oct. 5, 2007); Kenneth L. Karst (Aug. 21, 2007); Charles F. Kennel (Nov. 17, 2006); James Klain (Sept. 7, 2006); Charlotte Klein (Dec. 13, 2006); Archie Kleingartner (Sept. 28, 2006); John E. Kobara (Nov. 29, 2006); William Kuehne (April 3, 2007); Hillel Laks (Nov. 15, 2006); Lewis Leeburg (Sept. 29, 2006); Jacqueline Leisure (Dec. 12, 2006); Sherrill Luke (Sept. 21, 2006); Dave Lund (July 3, 2008); Gwyn Lurie (Nov. 9, 2006); LaMar Lyons (Nov. 1, 2007); W. Brian Maillian (May 8, 2008); Frank Mankiewicz (Jan. 19, 2007); Richard C. Maxwell (April 20, 2007); Larry May (Jan. 8, 2008); Ann Meyers Drysdale (Nov. 10, 2006); Robert S. Michaels (Sept. 4, 2006); Larry W. Miles (Sept. 4, 2006); James V. Mink (Nov. 27, 2007); Herbert Morris (Oct. 21, 2007); Donald Morrison (Jan. 26, 2009); Goldie Jacobson Moss (Aug. 14, 2006); Rosalio Muñoz (Nov.

10, 2006); Gary Nash (Oct. 12, 2007); Berky Nelson (April 17, 2007); Helen Carey Nelson (Aug. 21, 2006); Tom Norminton (Nov. 18, 2006); Charles Warner Oakley (Sept. 13, 2007); Mary Oda (March 19, 2008); Russell R. O'Neill (Nov. 1, 2006); Raymond L. Orbach (Dec. 10, 2007); Elinor Ostrom (March 23, 2010); Bob Overpeck (Nov. 20, 2007); Lowell J. Paige (Feb. 2, 2007); John Parker (Jan. 7, 2008); Anne Pautler (Nov. 16, 2006); Gertrude Pepp (Aug. 21, 2006); Judy Postley (Oct. 18, 2006); Susan Westerberg Prager (Dec. 4, 2006); Harry Pregerson (Sept. 25, 2007); William L. Prensky (Jan. 9, 2007); Mark Pulido (Dec. 2, 2006); Neil Reichline (March 5, 2008); Virgil P. Roberts (May 19, 2008); Martin Rosen (Jan. 7, 2008); Suz Rosen Rubel (Sept. 23, 2006); James Sackett (Sept. 25, 2007); Al Scates (Nov. 2, 2006); Roz Scherer (May 2, 2007); Keith Schiller (Sept. 15, 2006); Murray Shapiro (March 24, 2007); William Sharpe (Nov. 8, 2006); Cedrick Shimo (Jan. 29, 2008); Paula Shuman (April 3, 2007); Clancy Sigal (Feb. 18, 2008); Laurence Simpson (Nov. 5, 2007); Robert Simpson (Nov. 5, 2007); John Singlaub (April 19, 2007); Robert Singleton (Dec. 20, 2006); Rae Lee Siporin (Nov. 7 and 8, 2006); Marty Sklar (Dec. 8, 2006); Robert Stevenson (June 10, 2007); Margaret Ann Kelley Tagge (Aug. 30, 2006); Naoyuki Takasugi (April 2, 2007); Vu Tran (Nov. 16, 2006); Howard Troller (Jan. 27, 2006); Rick Tuttle (Aug. 26 and 27, 2006); Chand Viswanathan (Oct. 9, 2006); Bill Walton (Sept. 24, 2007); Brian Weiss (Feb. 6, 2008); Gloria Werner (Feb. 19, 2008); Toshiko Nakamura Wilkerson (April 2, 2008); Arthur Lee Williams Jr. (Sept. 7, 2006); C.Z. Wilson (Jan. 23, 2007); Stanley Wolpert (March 26, 2007); Miwako Yamaguchi (April 17, 2007); Moore Ruble Yudell (Dec. 11, 2008); Harry Zide (Aug. 16, 2006)

ORAL HISTORIES
UCLA Oral History Program
Benjamin Aaron; Page Ackerman; Bennet M. Allen; George B. Allison; Robert E. Alshuler; Gustave O. Arlt; Byron H. Atkinson; Tom Bradley; John E. Canaday; James A. Collins; Donald J. Cram; Edward A. Dickson; Paul A. Dodd; Elvin C. Drake; George R. Ellis; Donald E. Findley; William E. Forbes; Hansena Frederickson; Leonard Freedman; Ralph Freud; John S. Galbraith; Pia Gilbert; Adaline C. Guenther; H.R. Haldeman; Andrew J. Hamilton; Adrian H. Harris; Donald E. Hartsock; Lulu Wolf Hassenplug; Alma Hawkins; Mary Jane C. Hewitt; DeWitt A. Higgs; Judith R. Holland; Thelner Hoover; Henry T. Hopkins; Harold W. Horowitz; John B. Jackson; Neil H. Jacoby; Maulana Karenga; Kenneth L. Karst; Margaret G. Kivelson; James Klain; Vern O. Knudsen; Willard F. Libby; William P. Longmire; James E. LuValle; Dean E. McHenry; Frances McQuade; Ella Mae Reidy Manwarring; Richard C. Maxwell; William W. Melnitz; Earl J. Miller; Norman P. Miller; Webster E. Moore; J.D. Morgan; Franklin D. Murphy; Judith Murphy; Gary B. Nash; Cyril C. Nigg; Rosemary Park; Mimi Perloff; Jan Popper; Lawrence Clark Powell; Project India: The Early Years; George W. Robbins; Virgil P. Roberts; Robert A. Rogers; Franklin P. Rolfe; William Rosenthal; John Sandbrook; David S. Saxon; Corrine A. Seeds; Russell Shank; Paul H. Sheats; Foster H. Sherwood; Robert Singleton; Louis B. Slichter; Reidar F. Sognnaes; Charles Speroni; Ann Sumner; Elwin V. Svenson; UCLA Institute of Ethnomusicology; UCLA Student Leaders Series; Harold E. Verrall; Robert Vosper; Stafford Leak Warren; Gloria Werner; Waldemar Westergaard; Westwood Pioneers; Frederick S. Wight; Charles E. Young; William G. Young

Regional Oral History Office
(University of California, Berkeley Library)
William B. Baker; James V. Corley; Herbert B. Foster; David Pierpont Gardner; John William Gregg; Joel Hildebrand; Norman Jacobson; V. Wayne Kennedy; John H. Lawrence;

Dean McHenry; Ralph Palmer Merritt; John Francis Neylan; Jack W. Peltason; Karl S. Pister; William French Smith; Ida Wittschen Sproul; Robert Gordon Sproul; Robert M. Underhill; The University of California Office of the President and its Constituencies, 1983–1995; Harry R. Wellman •

Other Oral History Collections
Amateur Athletic Association of Los Angeles; State Government Oral History Program, California State Archives; UCLA Engineering Oral History Collection; University of Wisconsin, University Archives Oral History Project

THESES
Garrigues, George Louis. "Loud Bark and Curious Eyes: A History of the UCLA *Daily Bruin*, 1919–1955." Master's thesis, UCLA, 1970.
Johnson, Clyde Sanfred. "Student Self-Government: A Preliminary Survey of the Background and Development of Extra-Class Activities at the University of California, Los Angeles." Master's thesis, UCLA, 1948.
Medeiros, Francine Marie. "Edward A. Dickson: A Study in Progressivism." Master's thesis, UCLA, 1968.
Nystrom, Richard Kent. "UCLA: An Interpretation Considering Architecture and Site." Ph.D. thesis, UCLA, 1968.
Sullivan, Meg. "The Return of Stone Canyon Creek." Senior thesis, UCLA Extension, 2007.

RECORDS AND MINUTES OF UNIVERSITY OFFICES
Associated Students UCLA; Office of UCLA Extension; Regents of the University of California, Office of the Secretary and Chief of Staff; UCLA Academic Planning and Budget; UCLA Academic Senate; UCLA Alumni Association; UCLA Capital Programs; UCLA Chancellor's Communication Service; UCLA Department of Atmospheric and Oceanic Sciences; UCLA Department of Intercollegiate Athletics; UCLA Library; UCLA Office of Residential Life; UCLA Registrar's Office; UCLA School of Medicine; University of California Academic Council; University of California Office of the President

WEB RESOURCES
berkeley.edu
ucla.edu
University of California History Digital Archives. sunsite. berkeley.edu/uchistory/index.html.
University of California Libraries. "Calisphere." calisphere. universityofcalifornia.edu/.

PUBLISHED SOURCES

BOOKS AND OTHER MEDIA
Ackerman, William Coit. *My Fifty Year Love-In at UCLA*. Los Angeles: Fashion Press, 1969.
Brant, Keith E. and Jocelyn S. Macaraeg, eds. *UCLA Traditions: A Collection of UCLA Stories, Customs and Rituals*. Los Angeles: UCLA Alumni Association, 1991.
Burlingham, Cynthia. *The Franklin D. Murphy Sculpture Garden at UCLA*. Los Angeles: Hammer Museum, 2007.
Burlingham, Cynthia and Elizabeth Shepherd, eds. *In the Sculpture's Landscape: Celebrating Twenty-Five Years of the Franklin D. Murphy Sculpture Garden*. Los Angeles: Wight Art Gallery, Grunwald Center for the Graphic Arts, UCLA, 1993.
Cannon, Lou. *Governor Reagan: His Rise to Power*. New York: PublicAffairs Books, 2003.
Davis, Margaret L. *The Culture Broker: Franklin D. Murphy and the Transformation of Los Angeles*. Berkeley, Calif.: University of California Press, 2007.
Dickson, Edward A. *The University of California at Los Angeles: Its Origin and Formative Years*. Los Angeles: Friends of the UCLA Library, 1955.
Ferrier, William Warren. *Origin and Development of the University of California*. Berkeley, Calif.: Sather Gate Book Shop, 1930.
Gardner, David Pierpont. *The California Oath Controversy*. Berkeley, Calif.: University of California Press, 1967.
Gardner, David Pierpont. *Earning My Degree: Memoirs of an American University President*. Berkeley, Calif.: University of California Press, 2005.
Hamilton, Andrew and John B. Jackson. *UCLA On the Move: During Fifty Golden Years, 1919–1969*. Los Angeles: Ward Ritchie Press, 1969.
Hawkins, David, Edith C. Truslow and Ralph Carlisle Smith.

Project Y: The Los Alamos Story. Los Angeles: Tomash Publishers, 1983.
Hewlett, Richard G. and Oscar E. Anderson, Jr. *A History of the United States Atomic Energy Commission*. University Park, Pa.: Pennsylvania State University Press, 1962.
Hoddeson, Lillian, Paul W. Henriksen, Roger A. Meade, and Catherine Westfall. *Critical Assembly: A Technical History of Los Alamos During the Oppenheimer Years, 1943–1945*. New York: Cambridge University Press, 1993.
Kerr, Clark. *The Gold and the Blue: A Personal Memoir of the University of California, 1949–1967*. Vol. 1, *Academic Triumphs*. Berkeley, Calif.: University of California Press, 2001.
Kerr, Clark. *The Gold and the Blue: A Personal Memoir of the University of California, 1949–1967*. Vol. 2, *Political Turmoil*. Berkeley, Calif.: University of California Press, 2003.
Kesaris, Paul, ed. *A Guide to Manhattan Project: Official History and Documents*. Washington, D.C.: University Publications of America, 1977.
Klain, James and Arnold J. Band. *Royce Hall*. Los Angeles: UCLA, 1985.
Lee, Eugene C. *The Origins of the Chancellorship: The Buried Report of 1948*. Berkeley, Calif.: Center for the Studies in Higher Education and Institute of Governmental Studies, University of California, Berkeley, 1995.
Martin, James R. *University of California (in Los Angeles): A Resume of the Selection and Acquisition of the Westwood Site*. Los Angeles: University of California, 1925.
Miller, Loye H. *Birds of the Campus: University of California, Los Angeles*. Los Angeles: University of California Press, 1947.
Moore, Ernest Carroll. *I Helped Make a University*. Los Angeles: Dawson's Book Shop, 1952.
Mowry, George E. *The California Progressives*. Berkeley, Calif.: University of California Press, 1951.
Muchnic, Suzanne. *Odd Man In: Norton Simon and the Pursuit of Culture*. Berkeley, Calif.: University of California Press, 1998.
Pelfrey, Patricia A. *A Brief History of the University of California*. 2nd ed. Berkeley, Calif.: University of California Press, 2004.
Pettitt, George A. *Twenty-Eight Years in the Life of a University President*. Berkeley, Calif.: University of California, 1966.
Roberts, Chris and Bill Bennet. *UCLA Football Vault: The History of the Bruins*. Atlanta: Whitman Publishing, 2008.
Robinson, Thomas W., ed. *Student Views of American Society: Essays Occasioned by the May 5th, 1970 Incident at U.C.L.A.* Department of Political Science, UCLA, and Social Science Department, Rand Corporation, 1971.
Roy, George, Erik Kesten and Liev Schreiber. *The UCLA Dynasty*. DVD. New York: HBO Home Video, 2008.
Sandbrook, John and Buddy Epstein, eds. *The 25 Wooden Years*. 2nd ed. Los Angeles: UCLA Communications Board in conjunction with the UCLA Department of Intercollegiate Athletics, 1973.
Seaborg, Glenn Theodore and Ray Colvig. *Roses From the Ashes: Breakup and Rebirth of the Pacific Coast Intercollegiate Athletics*. Berkeley, Calif.: Institute of Governmental Studies, UC Berkeley, 2000.
Stadtman, Verne A., ed. *The Centennial Record of the University of California*. Berkeley, Calif.: University of California Print Department, 1967.
Stadtman, Verne A. *The University of California, 1868–1968*. New York: McGraw-Hill, 1970.
Starr, Kevin. *Inventing the Dream: California Through the Progressive Era*. New York: Oxford University Press, 1985.
Starr, Kevin. *Endangered Dreams: The Great Depression in California*. New York: Oxford University Press, 1996.
Starr, Kevin. *The Dream Endures: California Enters the 1940s*. New York: Oxford University Press, 1997.
Starr, Kevin. *Embattled Dreams: California in War and Peace, 1940–1950*. New York: Oxford University Press, 2002.
UCLA. *Bruin Life Yearbook*. Vols. 64–89. Los Angeles: ASUCLA Communications Board, 1983–2011.
UCLA. *Addresses Delivered at the Dedication of the New*

Campus and New Buildings of the University of California at Los Angeles, March 27 and 28, 1930. Berkeley, Calif.: University of California Press, 1930.
UCLA. *Southern Campus Yearbook*. Vols. 1–63. Los Angeles: Associated Students UCLA, 1920–1982.
UCLA Alumni Association. *California of the Southland, A History of the University of California at Los Angeles*. Los Angeles: UCLA Alumni Association, 1937.
University of California, Berkeley. *Blue and Gold Yearbook*. Vols. 49–52. Berkeley, Calif.: Associated Students of the University of California, 1923–1926.
White, Lonnie. *UCLA vs. USC: 75 Years of the Greatest Rivalry in Sports*. Los Angeles: Los Angeles Times Books, 2004.
Wooden, John and Jack Tobin. *They Call Me Coach*. New York: McGraw-Hill, 2004.

Departmental Histories
Andrews, William J., ed. *UCLA School of Engineering and Applied Science: 50th Anniversary Historical Review 1945–1995*. Los Angeles: UCLA School of Engineering and Applied Science, 1995.
Arthur, Ransom. *By the Old Pacific's Rolling Water: Birth of the UCLA School of Medicine*. Los Angeles: School of Medicine, UCLA, 1992.
Blacet, Francis E. *A Half Century in Chemistry at UCLA, 1932–1982*. Los Angeles: Academic Publishing Services, ASUCLA, 1987.
History Committee of the UCLA School of Nursing Alumni Association. *History of the UCLA School of Nursing*. Los Angeles: Regents of the University of California, 1999.
Mack, Karen, ed. *A Celebration of the Doctor of Philosophy Degree at UCLA, 1938–1988*. Publications Office, UCLA Public Affairs Department, 1988.
Mellinkoff, Sherman M. *Life is Short, the Art is Long: Three Longmire Generations*. Los Angeles: UCLA Publications Services Department, 1991.
Richard, Virginia. *The Origin and Development of Graduate Education at UCLA, 1933–1964*. Los Angeles: UCLA Graduate Division, 1965.
Robertson, George Ross. *History of the Chemistry Department, UCLA*. Los Angeles, 1959.

GOVERNMENT DOCUMENTS
California State Library; Los Angeles City Controller; Los Angeles County Auditor-Controller; Supreme Court of the United States; U.S. Census Bureau; U.S. National Park Service

National Archives and Records Administration
U.S. Army Corps of Engineers, Manhattan Engineer District, 1945, Manhattan Engineer District History, Book VIII (Los Alamos Project [Y]), Volume 1 (General): Records of the Defense Threat Reduction Agency, Record Group 374, National Archives and Records Administration.
U.S. Army Corps of Engineers, Manhattan Engineer District, 1945, Manhattan Engineer District History, Book VIII (Los Alamos Project [Y]), Volume 3 (Auxiliary Activities), Chapter 1 (Los Angeles, California, Procurement Office): Records of the Defense Threat Reduction Agency, Record Group 374, National Archives and Records Administration.

MAGAZINES AND JOURNALS
The Bruin Pioneer; California Alumni Fortnightly; The California Monthly; California Quarterly; Chronicle of the University of California; Life; Los Angeles Magazine; The New Yorker; Newsweek; The Saturday Evening Post; Southern Alumnus; Sports Illustrated; Time; U.S. News & World Report; UCLA Alumni Association Occasional Paper; The U.C.L.A. Magazine; UCLA Magazine; UCLA Monthly; UCLA Today; University of California Faculty Bulletin; University of California Record

Newspapers
California Grizzly; Christian Science Monitor; Daily Bruin; Hollywood Daily Citizen; Los Angeles Evening Herald-Examiner; Los Angeles Sentinel; Los Angeles Times; Normal Outlook (Los Angeles State Normal School); Outlook (Santa Monica, Calif.); The Sacramento Bee; The Sacramento Union; San Francisco Chronicle; San Francisco Examiner; The New York Times; The Wall Street Journal; The Washington Post; Westwood Villager

Index